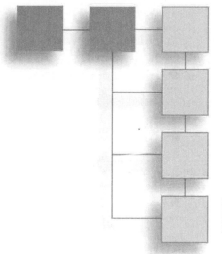

UDK™ GAME DEVELOPMENT

ALAN THORN

Cengage Learning PTR

CENGAGE
Learning·

Australia • Brazil • Japan • Korea • Mexico • Singapore • Spain • United Kingdom • United States

CENGAGE
Learning·

UDK™ Game Development
Alan Thorn

**Publisher and General Manager,
Cengage Learning PTR:** Stacy L.
Hiquet

Associate Director of Marketing:
Sarah Panella

Manager of Editorial Services:
Heather Talbot

Marketing Manager: Mark Hughes

Senior Acquisitions Editor: Emi Smith

Project Editor: Kate Shoup

Technical Reviewer: Robert Chin

Copy Editor: Kate Shoup

Interior Layout Tech: MPS Limited,
a Macmillan Company

Cover Designer: Mike Tanamachi

Indexer: Kelly Talbot Editing Services

Proofreader: Kelly Talbot Editing
Services

For product information and technology assistance, contact us at
Cengage Learning Customer & Sales Support, 1-800-354-9706

For permission to use material from this text or product,
submit all requests online at **www.cengage.com/permissions**

Further permissions questions can be emailed to
permissionrequest@cengage.com

Unreal is a registered trademark of Epic Games. Unreal Development Kit is trademarked by Epic Games. All other trademarks are
the property of their respective owners.

All images © Cengage Learning unless otherwise noted.

Library of Congress Control Number: 2011942331

ISBN-13: 978-1-4354-6018-8

ISBN-10: 1-4354-6018-9

Cengage Learning
20 Channel Center Street
Boston, MA 02210
USA

Cengage Learning is a leading provider of customized learning
solutions with office locations around the globe, including Singapore, the United Kingdom, Australia, Mexico, Brazil, and Japan.
Locate your local office at: **international.cengage.com/region**

Cengage Learning products are represented in Canada by Nelson
Education, Ltd.

For your lifelong learning solutions, visit **courseptr.com**

Visit our corporate website at **cengage.com**

Printed in the United States of America
2 3 4 5 6 7 13

Acknowledgments

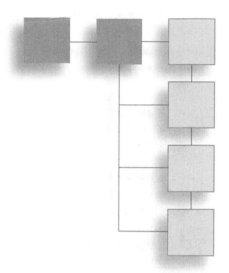

This book, and its quality, would not have been possible had it not been for a number of people whom I would like to thank. Specifically, Kate Shoup for her editorial skills and for keeping my prose both concise and clear. Robert Chin and his technical skills for ensuring that my oversights and slip-ups never made it to print. And Emi Smith for overseeing the project. I would also like to thank you, the reader, for choosing this book. I hope it proves helpful.

—Alan Thorn, 2011

About the Author

Alan Thorn is an author, mathematician, and independent video-game developer with more than 11 years of industry experience. He works for some of the world's largest entertainment companies and has lectured on game development at universities throughout Europe. He is the founder of Wax Lyrical Games, a game development studio, and is the author of several other popular books on video-game development.

Contents

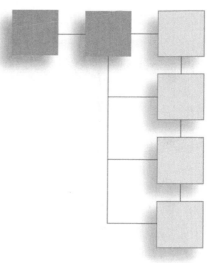

INTRODUCTION

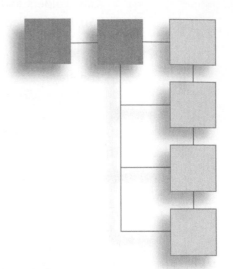

> Many drops make a bucket, many buckets make a pond, many ponds make a lake, and many lakes make an ocean.
>
> —Percy Ross (*Attributed*)

Taken as a whole, the games industry is a multi-billion-dollar industry. There has been a gradual increase in the number of universities and colleges worldwide offering courses focusing specifically on game development. There has also been an increase in both the number of platforms and systems on which games can be played and in the rate at which games for those platforms are released on a commercial basis. These increases coincide with a rise in the number of people entering the games industry annually for full-time work, either by finding employment at an established game-development studio or by founding their own independent teams.

Despite the increasing number of games and game developers, the attention span and the purse of the potential gamer remains finite—meaning more games must compete for the attention and money of gamers. In this competitive marketplace, developers often seek to gain a head start over the competition by using ready-made, third-party tools and engines that enable them to make high-powered games more quickly and more simply than if they had chosen to create the game from scratch themselves. In response to this growing demand among developers, there has not only been a rise in the number of tools and engines available, but also an overall reduction in the licensing fees a developer must pay to use these tools and engines, making them more accessible to a greater number of developers. This book is about one such engine: the UDK.

WHAT IS THIS BOOK ABOUT?

This book is about a set of software tools created by Epic Games for use by programmers and artists to make computer games. This set of tools is referred to as the *Unreal Development Kit, or* the UDK. The UDK is analogous to most other kinds of tools for getting things done. That is, it is intended to be used by game developers to assemble games in the same sort of way that hammers, cranes, bricks, and mortar are intended to be used by construction engineers to assemble buildings.

The UDK is one among a range of competitive tools that enables game developers to turn their raw materials of graphics, sounds, ideas, concepts, and plans into fully working and cohesive games. In isolation, the graphics and sounds and logic of a game can do little or nothing by themselves—at least, until they are brought into a structured and meaningful relationship to each other. For example, the graphic of a game character does not bring itself to life, does not animate itself, and does not move or rotate itself. Likewise, the recorded sound of a gunshot does not play of its own accord and it has no inherent knowledge of when and when not to play. Rather, something extra, over and above these raw materials, must be added to them into a game in which characters run and jump and in which gunshot sounds play at appropriate times. The digital tools necessary for bringing digital assets to life in this way are the kinds of tools provided by the UDK.

The UDK Is Not for Content Creation

The UDK was defined as a tool or a set of tools whose purpose is to bring digital assets, such as graphics, sounds, and others, to life in the form of a computer game. This definition highlights an important feature or quality of the UDK: The UDK *works on* assets, but is not used to *create* assets. The UDK is a compositional tool in that it assumes the game developer has already created his or her own game assets—models, graphics, sounds, and animations. It assumes the developer already has his or her assets to import into the UDK engine and to compose into a game. For this reason, the main focus of this book is not on the creation of game content, but rather on how existing game content can be assembled with the UDK into fully working and playable games. This is not a book for artists who want to learn how to model, texture or light; nor is it a book for sound engineers who want to learn how to compose tracks and sound effects for games. Rather, it is a book for level designers and programmers who want to learn how to use the high-level UDK tools to compose games from assets. The section titled "Who Is This Book For?" later in this introduction addresses the issue of the target audience for this book in more detail.

The Main Features and Benefits of the UDK

To summarize: The UDK is a set of graphical user interface (GUI) programs and easy-to-use tools for making computer games for a selection of different platforms, including Windows PC, Mac, consoles, and mobile devices. Some of the fundamental features and reasons for using the UDK follow:

- **UDK increases accessibility, speed, and power.** The UDK features a level-editor tool with a mouse-driven GUI and uses a drag-and-drop paradigm for building game levels. This editor tool offers developers three fundamental benefits. First, it increases the accessibility of game development by its intuitive interface. The term *accessibility* here refers to the ease with which any person can pick up the tool and use it effectively. A tool's accessibility increases when its ease-of-use factor increases, but there is no corresponding decrease in its power and flexibility. The UDK GUI and its related tools for graphically building levels, for defining materials and lights, and even for scripting behavior, help to empower people and to widen the range of people who can use these tools for making games. The second benefit is that the UDK can increase the speed with which games can be made. The simple-to-use drag-and-drop paradigm, and the ability to edit and tweak a game in combination with a real-time preview that shows the effects of those edits in the game, combine to reduce the time taken to get things done. Finally, the UDK increases the power of all developers by making readily available a whole slew of cutting-edge and competitive features, which they would otherwise have had to create manually. These include indirect illumination, shadow casting, mesh importing, material editors, particle system editors, mesh editors, scripting editors, viewports, real-time previews, and more.

- **UDK supports industry-standard file formats.** The UDK can be considered open—not in the sense that it is open source, but in the sense that it enables game assets, graphical and audible, to be imported from third-party applications in a range of industry-standard formats. These include PNG, TGA, DAE, FBX, WAV, and others. That means developers are not locked into using specific content-creation tools, such as specific 3D modeling software or specific sound-editing software. Instead, they are free to choose from any and all applications that support the same industry-standard formats.

- **Programmers can focus on game creation.** The UDK comes complete with a game engine called the *Unreal Engine*. As such, it offers a ready-made foundation or infrastructure on which a game can be built. This engine or foundation benefits the programmers of the team by saving them a lot of work and enabling them to better focus on coding the content of the game. Specifically, the engine relieves programmers of having to create or code the game foundations themselves, and permits them to invest their time in coding the content of the game—its behavior.

Non-UDK Subjects

It has been said already that the main subject matter of this book is the use of the UDK for the purpose of making games—hence the title of the book, *UDK Game Development*. The UDK is not the only subject covered in this book, however. That's because the subject of game development is far wider than the scope of the UDK, and so much of what is said or mentioned here can be abstracted from this context and applied in other contexts. In addition to the UDK, this book also considers some valuable theoretical concepts underpinning game development and software development more generally, including coding and design patterns, planning and design techniques, and core geometric concepts such as three-dimensional coordinate systems, vertices, planes, polygons, transformations, and other related subjects in linear algebra. It also considers other third-party software tools, including content-creation tools such as Autodesk 3DS Max and Autodesk Maya for exporting meshes and animation data into the UDK, and development tools such as Visual Studio and the nFringe plug-in for coding and customizing the UDK and UDK games through the UnrealScript language.

Who Is This Book For?

This book has been written with a selection of hypothetical readers in mind. To be more exact, the sentences, terms, subjects, and ideas included in this book are arranged and presented based on assumptions that I, the author, must make about you, the reader. Making assumptions is not something I like doing, primarily because they can be very much mistaken. In addition, mentioning these assumptions, as I do in this section, may discourage or turn away readers who feel as though they do not "make the grade," even when it is possible that they could read this book and feel very much improved by it. But making assumptions about the readership is necessary to ensure that my intended audience gets the book it expected—that the book contains everything that audience wanted to know about the subject and that the subject was explained in language they could understand. It is important for me to stress, however, that the assumptions made about the readership of this book should be taken with a pinch of salt—as only a rough guide to the kind of people I think will benefit most from this book and its contents. It should not be read as a precise criteria or a set of qualifications that the reader must have in order to understand this book. I do not wish to discourage or underestimate the abilities of anybody who is willing to learn and keen to succeed.

This book is probably for you if you match any of the four following character profiles:

■ Benjamin is studying game development at university and is working as a programmer intern at a local game-development company. He has tried his hand at some graphics applications like 3DS Max and Maya, and has about a year of experience in programming in C++ and JavaScript, but he has never used or heard of the UDK before.

■ Samantha is an experienced 3D artist with around five years of experience in 3DS Max, Maya, and Photoshop. She works freelance via the Internet on a regular basis for a variety of game-development companies. She has thought about starting her own game-development studio, making games using a 3D engine. She has tried with success some online tutorials that teach programming and is now interested in learning more about what the UDK can do for her.

■ Mohammed has recently started a new job at a game-development studio that uses the UDK to produce its games. He gained the position on the basis of his willingness to learn and on his background in software design, but he has no knowledge of the UDK. His employer would like him to learn.

■ Esmeralda is a game developer with 10 years of experience as a C++ programmer, game designer, and 3D artist. She has traditionally worked in Visual Studio, but has used XNA, SDL, OGRE 3D, and other game-development tools. She is thinking of switching to the UDK. She has downloaded the UDK, tested it, and experimented with it, but has found its documentation lacking. She would like a book that can detail the basics of its use and can help her to develop greater confidence with its tools.

This book is probably not for you if you match any of the two following character profiles:

■ Miguel enjoys playing computer games, especially first-person shooters and massively multiplayer online role-playing games (MMORPGs). He has developed ideas for his own smash-hit RPG and plans to implement it alone using the UDK. He has no experience in game development, has never tried programming, has never used any 3D modeling software, and loses interest in projects very quickly when he gets stuck or is unsure how to proceed.

■ Catherine is an experienced game developer with around five years of experience in both computer programming and 3D graphics. She is also the leader of a team of three, consisting of artists and musicians. Her studio has been involved in the development of free, online-based casual games that play in 2D perspective and in Web browsers via the Adobe Flash player. She is looking to learn the UDK as an alternative for developing *browser-embedded* games.

WHY IS THIS BOOK NECESSARY?

So why is a book on the UDK even necessary? How can it be justified? This question can be interpreted in at least two different senses in the context of the UDK; this section attempts to address both in turn.

The first sense in which one might question whether such a book is necessary runs as follows: The licensing costs of the UDK are so prohibitively high that the UDK must be the privilege of only an elite group of game developers working with multi-million-dollar budgets. The majority of independent developers are by necessity excluded from using it. Therefore, such a book can appeal only to a very limited readership; it cannot be justified to most readers.

This line of reasoning is flawed. In fact, at the time of writing, the UDK is free to download and use as a game-development tool. If the resulting game is released non-commercially, then no license fee is assessed. If the game is released commercially, then the developer must pay the required licensing fees—which have been adjusted by Epic Games in recent months to increase the affordability of the engine for development teams of most sizes and budgets. In the past two years, a whole range of smaller independent studios have released popular and successful commercial titles with the UDK, including *The Ball* by Teotl Studios, *Adam's Venture* by Vertigo Games, and *Warm Gun* by Emotional Robots Inc., to name but a few. The point is, the new licensing terms of the UDK mean that the UDK is now accessible to and used by a range of smaller development studios. The UDK can also be downloaded from the official site free of charge by anybody, at any time, without prior application or approval. The new licensing terms and the easy availability mean that the UDK is now more accessible than ever before to a greater number of game developers and game-development students across the world. For this reason, a tutorial book on the UDK for the purposes of game development gains greater import, significance, and value to the majority of game developers and students.

Note

The UDK licensing terms can be accessed from www.udk.com/licensing.

The second sense in which one might question whether such a book is necessary runs as follows: The UDK is now a well-established, high-profile, and popular game-development tool, and already has a plethora of documentation available. This documentation includes the official UDK documentation available via the Unreal Developer Network, 3D Buzz video tutorials, community forum support, YouTube video tutorials, and other tutorials scattered across the Internet. So extensive is the documentation, some might argue, a book on the subject such as this one must surely be redundant. Even a book that was twice as long could not hope to cover the amount of ground and detail that a reader could learn by consulting the tutorials online produced through the collective efforts of hundreds of people.

The key problem with this objection is that it forgets that a book is not less useful just because it does not contain everything there is to know about its subject. Indeed, this book does not claim to teach you everything there is to know about the UDK, and it is true that one could learn all the information contained within it by spending hours or even days consulting hundreds of different Internet articles and forum posts. But by sharing with you the benefit of my experience using the UDK—experience that has been gained over years of use—this book saves you from having to spend days and weeks scouring disparate sources of information about the UDK and consolidating together a whole that can be called a strong foundational knowledge. In addition, this book provides a structured introduction to the UDK newcomer. Those approaching the UDK with little or no experience in how it works might be at a loss for where to begin, for which subjects to consider and to what extent, and for the optimum order in which to consider them. This book is written and structured for such a newcomer, arranged so that each of the core foundational UDK components is considered in depth and one by one, and in the best order in which to tackle them. The result is that after having read the book from cover to cover, the reader should have a firm grasp of the UDK essentials and be ready to learn more on an independent basis through the Internet. For this reason, this book should be seen more as a complement and precursor to independent learning and less as a replacement for it.

HOW SHOULD THIS BOOK BE READ?

This book has been written so that it may be read as either a reference or a guide. Reading it as a reference, the reader can perform a directed search through either the table of contents or the index for the subject in mind and then jump to the relevant pages of the book. Reading it as a guide or tutorial, the reader can consider the book from cover to cover, reading the chapters in sequence. Although readers differ in their needs and experience, my personal view is that readers will get the most from this book by reading it *first* as a guide from cover to cover, and then use it *later* as a reference.

The chapters of the book are divided by subject matter, with each chapter focusing either on a specific feature or set of features, or on a specific practical application of the UDK. For example, feature-based chapters are explanatory and consider issues such as meshes, or materials, or lights. Application-based chapters, by contrast, consider how to do things with the UDK, such as how to make a level with destructible scenery, or how to make a level with dynamic lighting effects. In addition, application-based chapters will ask you to do things, such as click a menu item or drop an asset into a level. They are written with the assumption that you will be following along with the steps listed as the chapter progresses. It is recommended, therefore, that you follow along with me, completing each step as appropriate before proceeding with the next.

THE LIFETIME OF THIS BOOK: IS IT OUT OF DATE?

The lifetime of a book refers to the number of years in which the information in a book is accurate and relevant. There are some books whose subjects do not change at all, such as books describing the basics of arithmetic. In those cases, the lifetime of the book is potentially infinite. Most books, however—and computing books in particular—have finite lifetimes because their subject changes frequently and dramatically over time. The lifetime of books with finite lifetimes, like this one, is inversely proportional to both the frequency of change and the extent of change to the subject. That is, the more frequently and dramatically a subject changes, the shorter the lifetime of the book, and the less frequently and dramatically a subject changes, the longer the lifetime of the book. The question of the lifetime of a book is an important one because most readers will want to begin this book feeling comfortable that the information contained herein is not only relevant and accurate to the UDK at the time of reading, but also stands a chance of remaining accurate for some time to come.

So what can be said about the lifetime of this book? Estimating the lifetime of this book depends largely on assessing the rate and extent of change to the UDK that has occurred since its release in 2009. Looking at the rate of change, it is tempting to think that this book might already be out of date. That's because the UDK development team has released updates or service packs for the UDK either once or twice per month for each and every month since its release. But to say that this book is out of date because an update is released once or twice per month would be like saying that a book about Microsoft Windows was out of date simply because Microsoft released updates on a weekly basis.

It is important to draw a distinction between the rate of change, which refers to the frequency with which updates are released, and the extent of change, which refers to the amount of change made on each update. Each new update of the UDK typically includes bug fixes and repairs, performance enhancements to make the existing features work faster, and a few new features. That being said, changes and updates are typically made to the UDK in such a way as to not invalidate or dramatically alter the way existing tools work. For this reason, the documentation and tutorials for the UDK that were produced in 2009 are as relevant today as they were when they were written, and there is no reason to expect the lifetime of this book will be anything less than the lifetime of other UDK documentation when they were released.

It is of course highly likely that by the time you read this book and use the UDK, further releases will have been issued, and those releases will have repaired various bugs and will have added some new features that are not documented here. But, it is also highly likely that none of these amendments will have invalidated or changed the accuracy of the information contained here. So, the UDK's frequency of change need not be a major concern for readers because the nature of those changes is such that they are compatible or do not break the features and techniques that applied to previous versions.

CONVENTIONS USED IN THIS BOOK

This book uses a number of different conventions—formatting, styles, structures, headers, and so on. Specifically, the conventions used in this book are as follows:

- Keywords are jargon words that have industry-standard and accepted meanings. These include words such as vertex, local space, normals, mesh, materials, and so on. This book attempts to define keywords wherever possible. The first occurrence of a unique keyword in this book is styled in italics. Italics are also used in the conventional sense to emphasize significant or important words in a sentence, such as the man was *not* tall, or the height of the door was *less* than and not greater than that of the woman.

- Each chapter in the book begins with an itemized list of the main skills and knowledge that a reader should gain by reading the chapter. The skills and knowledge to be gained varies on a chapter-by-chapter basis, but each skill or unit of knowledge falls into one of two kinds: UDK specific and general. UDK-specific skills and units of knowledge pertain to the UDK specifically, and include such things as importing meshes, using the content browser, working with Unreal Matinee, and building Lightmass solutions, among others. The general set of skills and units of knowledge include transferrable items—that is, items that can be applied not only to the UDK, but to game development or even software development as a whole. These include things such as coordinate systems; editing meshes; understanding vertices, polygons, and transformations; and planning and designing levels, among others.

- Each chapter of the book ends with a conclusion section. It summarizes what has been covered throughout the chapter, and might go on to make suggestions about further reading or how to proceed on an independent basis where appropriate. It also orientates you in the book by encouraging you to think back over what you have learned so far, to reflect on how far you have come, to consider how to improve your skillset, and to think about what must be studied next.

- Some chapters of the book feature notes, sidebars, and tips. The formatting and arrangement for each differs to reflect their distinct purposes. Notes are small snippets of information that stand apart from the main text but are related to it. They are in many ways equivalent to an aside in speech; they might have begun with a phrase such as "Oh, by the way…" or "I should also mention…." Sidebars are larger, more substantial sections that stand apart from the main text of the chapter but are related to it. Unlike notes, they are comprehensive subjects in their right, but are not covered in depth in this book. Sidebars contain small and cursory digressions into subjects insofar as they relate to the UDK to provide you with a general overview of the subject so as to work effectively in the UDK. Finally, tips are small boxes of optional information or are reminders that are included alongside the main text and are intended to be useful in some way. Tips might include keyboard shortcuts, workflow tricks, handy techniques, reminders, or even questions that are intended to get you thinking about the subject from a different angle.

ASSETS USED IN THIS BOOK

Throughout this book, we will use the UDK tools to build a number of levels or mini-games. Those levels will, as will any game, depend upon a variety of assets. *Assets* refers to the externally referenced digital data—such as meshes, textures, sounds, and others—that the game uses to work as designed. The game might include music, animated characters, weapons, lighting effects, particle systems, and others, and all these elements will refer to some extent to assets that are stored in files external to the main game or level module. In short, without assets, the game will not and cannot run successfully. The levels constructed in this book will be no different from other levels in that they will reference external assets. Those assets, however, will not be custom assets made specifically for this book, nor will they be assets from commercial or third-party sources. Instead, the assets used throughout all levels constructed in this book will be those included free with the UDK tools. This will ensure that confusion does not arise in referencing the assets, that assets do not go missing, and that assets do not cease to become compatible. Once you have downloaded the UDK, you will already have access to all the assets needed for building the levels in the book.

COMPANION FILES

It was mentioned in the previous section that throughout this book, we will be building levels and mini-games using the UDK. These levels will be stored in UDK-compliant level files in the proprietary UDK file format, and they will be referenced in later chapters by filename. They will be made available to you for your inspection and use as companion files, which will be available to you from both the official book home at the Cengage Learning Web site www.courseptr.com/downloads and from my own personal Web page at www.alanthorn.net.

Note

In addition to the UDK levels constructed in this book, the book's companion files also contain source code for the UnrealScript language as well as other material and mesh files. These additional files will be discussed and detailed later in the relevant chapters.

Part I

UDK Getting Started

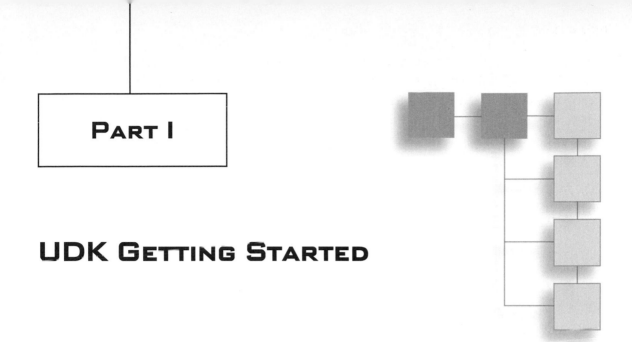

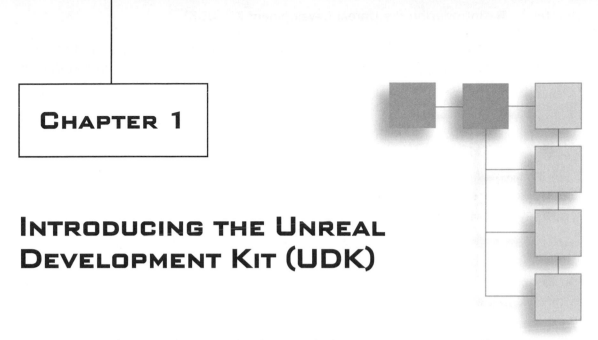

CHAPTER 1

INTRODUCING THE UNREAL DEVELOPMENT KIT (UDK)

> If you can't say it clearly, you don't understand it yourself.
>
> —John Searle

By the end of this chapter, you should:

- Understand what the UDK is.
- Appreciate the many ways in which the UDK can be used.
- Have a general idea about the UDK's wide variety of features.
- Be able to download and install the UDK.
- Be more familiar with the UDK's directory structure.

You may already have some idea about what the Unreal Development Kit (UDK) is and does, even if that idea is not fully formed or wholly accurate. This chapter is concerned primarily with developing that idea by summarizing the UDK clearly and by discussing some of its fundamental concepts and features.

It might be tempting to dismiss this chapter as mere promotional material. Or perhaps it might seem as though this chapter discusses subject matter that will become apparent as you start using the UDK to build real-world projects. In fact, however, failing to read this chapter may lead to confusion further along the line!

One might liken the scope and range of the UDK to a large and labyrinthine city. To navigate such a city with confidence and purpose, the traveler would require a map that charted the arrangement of streets and marked identifiable features and landmarks. The traveler would also require an understanding of the map to orientate

3

himself and to travel to his destination without the hassle of getting lost and wasting time. Just as this strategy for success applies to navigating a large city, so too does it apply to finding our way around the vastness of the UDK. Thus, this chapter concentrates on building our map.

WHAT IS THE UDK?

UDK stands for three words: Unreal Development Kit. In short, the UDK is game-making software. That is, it is a collection of development tools, such as editors, scripting systems, and compilers, for making real-time 3D video games.

The first word in its title, Unreal, is not a philosophical statement that the development kit does not exist. That is, it does not mean that the kit is not real. Instead, it is the name of the game engine used to power games created with the development tools in the kit. Just as a car engine is used to power an automobile, a *game engine* is used to power a game. Thus, at the highest level, the UDK consists of two fundamental and complementary pieces: the Unreal Engine and the development tools (see Figure 1.1).

Note

The UDK is typically updated by Epic on a monthly basis. The projects and files in this book were created using the May 2011 build of the UDK, but all the files have been tested in later releases to improve compatibility.

Unreal Engine

The Unreal Engine is the game engine used to power games made with the UDK (see Figure 1.2). However, to call the Unreal Engine a game engine raises the fundamental question of what a game engine actually is. To more fully understand the concept of a game engine, it is first necessary to distinguish it from game content. That is, in order to talk about what an engine *is*, it is first helpful to think about what it *is not*.

Game content refers to all the digital assets in a specific game, such as models, textures, sounds, and animations. A weapon sound that is emitted when the player fires

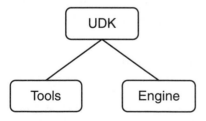

Figure 1.1
UDK structure.

Figure 1.2
The Unreal Engine at work. Sample level provided with the UDK: DM-Deck.

a rocket launcher is an example of a game asset, specifically an audio asset. The rocket launcher model itself is an example of another asset, specifically a mesh asset. These are but two assets among potentially thousands that, together, constitute the game content for a specific game. Other assets might include the player model, the menu screen buttons, the background music, the health bar, and explosion effects. Game content is thus varied in that any one asset can be very different in form from any other asset. For example, an explosion sound is unlike grass, yet each is an asset. That being said, all assets do have at least one common characteristic: They are specific to one game. A Sonic the Hedgehog model will be used for a *Sonic the Hedgehog* game, but not for a *Super Mario* game, because that game will have its own specific collection of assets.

There is another—and more telling—characteristic common to all game assets that hints at the developmental need for a game engine: All game assets are lifeless. That is, bitmap images do not move of their own accord and sound files do not play by themselves. Assets just *are*. Like most inanimate objects, they do not move and they do not act—at least, not on their own initiative. That's because they have no initiative. This presents a serious and thought-provoking problem for the game developer: Lifeless assets that do nothing do not make for fun games. Thus, there is a need to bring game assets to life, to give them motion and momentum, to bring them into relationship with one another and to make them behave in believable ways. This is part of the rationale for the game engine: Its main duty is to bring game assets to life.

The game engine, then, is the general and logical core or infrastructure supporting game assets to make them work together as intended by the developers. For example, the engine is responsible for pulling game objects to the ground under the effects of gravity, ensuring that exit buttons quit the game when clicked, and playing sounds to the speakers when appropriate, among other things. In these ways, the engine brings life to assets.

Of course, bringing life to assets is easier said than done. Assets differ greatly in their form, and games differ greatly in their requirements. But beneath this supposed diversity, a developer can identify a set of behaviors, relationships, and requirements common to all (or at least most) games. For example, almost every first-person shooter requires the following:

- A 3D environment in which game objects and actors exist, each with their own position, orientation, and scale in 3D space

- A world that is subject to Newtonian physical laws, such as gravity, inertia, and momentum

- A menu system that the player can use to start, load, and exit games on demand

These are not just the requirements of just one, specific first-person shooter game; they are the requirements for almost all games in the first-person shooter genre. That is to say, all first-person shooters need these features. Additionally, these or similar requirements will apply to many—perhaps most—other game genres.

Taking this idea to its logical extents, a programmer can identify *all* the fundamental behaviors and processes common to *all* games (including the aforementioned features), encode them into a single core, and then use and reuse that core as the base, template, or starting point for powering *all* their games. This core is the game engine. It makes a game developer's working life easier because its recyclable nature spares developers from having to re-invent the same code for each game they make.

The Unreal Engine, then, is a game engine that has been made for developers by Epic Games. The development tools that ship with the Unreal Engine enable developers to import their assets into the engine to create a game using a GUI editor, without having to concern themselves unduly with the underlying mechanics of the game, such as the calculation of shadows, gravity, trajectories, the resource management system, and the menu systems. All games developed with the UDK will be powered by the Unreal Engine. This engine saves developers a lot of work, enabling them to spend less time coding the fundamentals and more time creating game content.

Unreal Development Tools

The Unreal Development Tools ship with the Unreal Engine. Together, these form the Unreal Development Kit (UDK). The development tools serve at least three main purposes:

- To enable developers to create new assets for their games
- To help developers import existing assets from third-party applications to the unreal system
- To let developers design and arrange their assets into environments that work to create a game

The main, high-level development tools consist of the UDK Editor, the Unreal Front-end, and the SpeedTree application. The most notable of these tools is the UDK Editor; this is where most UDK users spend their time when creating UDK-based games. These tools are discussed in more detail later in this chapter.

The key point to note here for game developers is that the development tools are neither a part of the Unreal Engine, nor a part of the game content of UDK-made games. That is, the tools themselves do not feature in games made with UDK and are not distributed with the final game products. Developers do not ship their completed games with the UDK Editor, for example. Rather, the tools exist exclusively to help developers connect their assets with the Unreal Engine at design time. The aim is to compile and build workable games that run on a standalone basis.

WHAT CAN THE UDK BE USED FOR?

The UDK is defined both by what it is and by what it does. What it *is* is a software development kit. What it *does* is make real-time 3D applications powered by the Unreal Engine.

The terms *3D* and *real-time 3D* require a definition. In a sense, all graphical applications—like games—are 2D, not 3D. Ultimately, they all draw pixels onto the flat, two-dimensional surface of a computer monitor, where they are seen by the user.

Even so, the term 3D is used to describe a specific group of graphical applications. These are ones that allow both gamers and content creators to visualize and work in all three dimensions, mathematically speaking. Thus, a game that calculates the position and orientation of its objects in a three-dimensional space using x, y, and z axes would be classified as a 3D game, even though the view of that world as seen from a camera in 3D space is eventually presented on the two-dimensional surface of a monitor. By this definition, games such as *Unreal Tournament*, *Half-Life*, *Gears of War*, and *Bioshock* are 3D games because the gamer can move in all three dimensions: up and down, left and right, and forward and backward. Further, graphical modeling applications such as Maya 3DS Max, ZBrush, and MudBox are 3D applications because content creators can visualize and model their scenes in three dimensions—that is, along all the x, y, and z axes. In contrast, games such as *Diner Dash*, *Mystery Case Files*, *Braid*, and *Scott Pilgrim vs. the World* are not 3D games because they restrict the player character to moving in only two dimensions: left and right and up and down. By drawing this distinction, it is certainly not my intention to suggest that 2D games are inferior to 3D games in terms of fun. After all, one of my favorite games, *Toejam and Earl*, is 2D. Rather, it is to say that there is a technical and mathematical distinction to be made between the two types. Strictly speaking, all games created using the UDK are 3D, although, developers can configure the camera or design their levels to give a 2D appearance and feel to their game.

But UDK games are not just 3D; they are *real-time* 3D. Real-time 3D, which is a specific form of 3D graphics, is often compared to pre-rendered 3D. Although the distinction between real-time 3D and pre-rendered 3D is blurring, the distinction still exists. To help you understand the difference, let's first discuss pre-rendered 3D. The Maya and 3DS Max modeling applications produce pre-rendered 3D graphics. These are static, 2D images that depict a 3D scene from a fixed camera point, with their lighting and material information calculated by a renderer in advance. After the renderer produces the output image, the image is frozen, like a photograph. Nothing the viewer does can change the position or orientation of the camera. If you wanted to see the scene from a new vantage point, you would have to ask the artist to reopen the modeling software, adjust the camera to your requirements, and then produce a completely new and separate render of the scene.

The advantage of this method is that the renderer can harness vast amounts of computing power and take as long as it likes to calculate the effects of lighting and materials in a scene to produce a render that is almost photo-realistic. The disadvantage, as has been mentioned, is that the camera location in the scene is fixed when the render is made. The viewer cannot change that location to see the scene in other places. For this reason, although pre-rendered 3D graphics might be useful for movies, animations, and still images—indeed, almost all computer-generated movies, such as *Shrek* and *Toy Story*, are pre-rendered—it poses a problem for games due to its lack of interactivity. For games, real-time 3D is required.

Real-time 3D graphics are graphics produced by a real-time 3D renderer. Unlike the renderers in 3DS Max and Maya, which can consume almost all system resources for hours or even days, a real-time renderer uses as few resources as possible to create renders as quickly as possible—often at standard movie frame rates or even faster, generating perhaps a 100 images per second. Real-time 3D graphics work like a cartoon animation flipbook, in which each subsequent page in the book contains a sketch that represents the next frame in the animation. The reader plays back the complete animation by flipping through the pages of the book in sequence, from start to finish.

Speed of render is important for real-time rendering; fast renders help to create the effects of animation and motion and to provide a continuously updated view of a live 3D environment, as seen from a specific camera. The continuously updated view is what enables gamers to control the camera to view the scene from almost any angle and position and to see the results of their movement as it happens—that is, in real-time. It is also what enables gamers to understand the motion of objects and actors in the game as they move about the scene.

The primary disadvantage of the real-time rendering system is a direct result of its very specific need for speed—that is, its need to generate images many times per second. The high-powered renderers of 3DS Max and Maya have hours or even days to produce the high-quality details of an image, whereas their real-time counterparts have only fractions of a second. The result is that the real-time renderers cannot produce images of the same quality as the alternatives when those alternatives are configured to work at their best. To compensate for this, both the real-time renderers and the game developers who use them must resort to a series of optimizations—tricks and techniques to fake and simulate the effects produced by the higher-powered alternatives.

Fortunately, the Unreal Engine features a real-time renderer equipped with all sorts of strategies to help game developers produce impressive 3D scenes. That does not mean, however, that there is nothing for game developers to concern themselves with regarding this issue. Game developers must create their assets within a specific set of industry-accepted parameters to help the Unreal Engine's renderer work effectively. Some of the guidelines and techniques for optimizing assets and scenes will be illustrated throughout this book.

In short, then, the Unreal Engine is a real-time 3D engine because its renderer generates images of 3D environments in real time. This real-time aspect has implications for the kinds of uses for which the Unreal Engine is suited and is not suited. Specifically, these include the following:

■ **For creating real-time interactive applications.** The UDK is especially suitable and intended for creating real-time 3D applications—typically, applications that require user interaction. The most notable type of interactive real-time application is a computer game, but the UDK is not technically limited to games. It is a multi-purpose engine. It is possible to use the UDK for simulators, kiosk shows, product visualizations, 3D presentations, and more. The focus of this book, however, is on games exclusively, and it assumes the reader is a game developer.

■ **Not for pre-rendered movies.** The UDK is not and is not intended to be a substitute for 3DS Max, Maya, or other 3D animation applications. The UDK offers almost no features for creating complex and detailed 3D models from scratch, and almost no features for creating the UV mapping of those models. Furthermore, it offers comparatively little control over the rendering process; its real-time renderer is fine-tuned for performance, not for spending hours or even days rendering photo-realistic static images or pre-rendered computer-graphic (CG) movies. Typically, game-content creators produce their models in third-party applications and then import them from those applications into the UDK.

UDK Alternatives

The much-publicized release of the UDK in 2009 arguably marked an important milestone in game-development history. It was the first time an AAA-standard game engine and its associated tools became available to both hobbyist and independent game developers on affordable terms, enabling them to create commercial games.

Note

There are two main releases of the Unreal Engine and its development tools for game developers. One is used by engine licensees, which are development studios that pay a premium for use of the Unreal Engine, its development tools, *and* the engine's C++ source code. The other release is the UDK release, which features the Unreal Engine and its development tools but no engine source code. The main difference between the two, then—besides pricing and royalty terms—relates to the access to the engine source code. The UDK does *not* allow developers to access the engine source, although the engine can still be customized extensively through UnrealScript, as you shall see.

However, despite the recent euphoria among many developers surrounding the UDK's availability, it is important to recognize that the UDK is not the only 3D game-development tool on the market. In forum discussions across the Internet, game developers from all backgrounds argue as to which game development tool is the best, comparing feature sets and tools. It can sometimes be tempting to immediately come down in favor of the UDK due to its use in big-budget projects; after all, if the big budget studios are using it, then it must be the best. But even if this line of reasoning were valid, the conclusion would not follow because there remain large studios that do not use the UDK. And even though the UDK is much more accessible to smaller teams, many teams are using other game-development tools. The point is, there is no one best solution for all cases. Each development tool has its own advantages and disadvantages, and is more or less suited to specific purposes. This section considers briefly some alternatives to the UDK, which are discussed in no particular order.

Unity

Unity—sometimes known by its former name, Unity 3D—differs in many respects from the UDK, especially in its workflow. The UDK is spread across many different but related applications; the UDK Editor is designed for arranging and creating levels, the SpeedTree application is designed for building tree and foliage models that will later be imported into the editor, and the Unreal Frontend is used for compiling and packaging levels into a final game. In contrast, Unity features a completely integrated environment. That is, Unity is a single, standalone application. It is an all-in-one editor that enables developers to design levels, write script, build and import content, and then compile the game to target platforms without ever leaving the editor environment. At present, games developed with Unity can be deployed for various platforms, including PC, Mac, iPhone, Android, Xbox 360, PS3, and even the Web. Unity can be inspected and downloaded from www.unity3d.com.

Note

Licensing fees for this engine might vary depending on the target platform for the developed game.

ShiVa 3D and DX Studio

Both ShiVa3D and DX Studio take a similar approach to game development as Unity in that both feature their own integrated all-in-one editor. The editor is used for creating levels, creating scripts, and building and compiling games for target platforms. There are differences between them as to the scripting languages supported, the feature set of the editors, the abilities of the real-time render engine, and the target platforms supported, among other things. ShiVa 3D can be inspected and downloaded from www.stonetrip.com, and DX Studio can be inspected and downloaded from www.dxstudio.com.

Do-It-Yourself Engine

The term *DIY engine* refers here not to any specific engine available on the market, like the UDK or Unity, but to a developer's decision to make his or her own engine for his or her own games. There are two key reasons game developers might choose to avoid using a pre-made, third-party engine and to instead build their own. One is economical and the other is technical.

First, the economical reason: Most game engines (including the UDK) are not free to use for commercial projects, and some are not free to use even for non-commercial projects. Pricing models differ from engine to engine. Some engines, like the Unity engine, require developers to make a one-time payment that grants them royalty-free and non-exclusive right to use the engine on a limited number of development workstations, to make either a limited or an unlimited number of games. Here, developers pay once and can then start making games for sale. Another model is the royalty-based model, in which developers do not pay a one-time fee, but instead pay a royalty to the engine developers from the sales of games made using that engine. Whichever method is used, some developers find the cost of an engine to be prohibitive. This is especially true when other factors are considered, such as the size of their development team, the intended price of their product, the time required for the development of their product, and additional development expenses such as the cost of equipment, the rental of office space, the cost of advertising and promotion, and the cost of staff or freelancers.

The second reason is technical: The feature set of third-party engines—such as the UDK or Unity engines—are specifically tailored to meet the needs of most game developers. They are designed in many senses to be general purpose—useful for first-person shooters, for third-person RPGs, for racing and action games, etc. But some game developers fall outside that majority of developers by the specificity of their needs. For example, a developer might be creating an experimental game project, pushing boundaries and testing entirely new and innovative kinds of features, physics systems, and styles of gameplay. This experimental project poses a potential problem for the developer wanting to use an existing third-party engine. That's because the engine developers did not create their engine with this style of game in mind, but rather with the typical set of gaming genres. This engine might not prove wholly inadequate, however, because the game developer might be able to use the existing tools in new and creative ways to achieve his or her purpose. It must be admitted, however, that the engine was never designed with such usage in mind, and as a result it could prove awkward and time-consuming to use for such a specific game. Consequently, the game developer might instead reason that it would be quicker, simpler, and more cost-effective to create his or her own custom engine designed specifically for the style of game he or she has planned.

Table 1.1 Custom Engine Components

Component	Library	URL
Render system	OGRE 3D	www.ogre3d.org
Audio system	OpenAL	www.openal.org
Physics system	Bullet 3D	www.bulletphysics.org
Input system	OIS	www.sourceforge.net/projects/wgois
Scripting system	LUA	www.lua.org
Base framework	Boost	www.boost.org

Regardless of the motivations that a developer might have for creating his or her own custom engine, there are several options open for those who choose this route. Engine developers with the necessary knowledge and skill set can create their own game engine entirely from scratch if they wish. This would mean implementing custom physics systems, render pipelines, audio frameworks, and all the other appropriate components. Another solution, however, is to assemble a game engine using components from many different open-source and dedicated third-party libraries, the same way a seamstress completes patchwork quilt by stitching together many different patches. Taking this collage route, developers can build the foundations of their engine in many ways; one might be to integrate the libraries shown Table 1.1.

The UDK Feature Set In Depth

As mentioned, the UDK is software for making real-time 3D games and applications. The UDK ships with two main components: the Unreal Engine and the Unreal Development Tools, the main tool being the UDK Editor for creating and editing 3D environments. Like most game-development software, the UDK boasts a set of features. This section considers most of those features, providing both a general overview of the kinds of things the UDK can do and a rough roadmap of the work to be covered throughout the rest of this book.

Note

A *feature set* is a collection of features. A *feature* is a unique selling point, benefit, or reason for using the software. Hence, the UDK feature set is a list of reasons for using the UDK.

Game developers might want to ask at least two questions about the extent to which each feature is a benefit for them and their project. First, how much flexibility and power does the feature offer for realizing their plans? The kind of thing developers should keep in mind here is whether the software limits them in implementing their designs in any significant way. For example, a developer might be planning to create an MMORPG that will feature a city filled with hundreds of buildings. If the engine in question limits the number of meshes and actors allowed in a scene at any one time, this might have serious implications for developer's plans. In this case, the developer might need to consider a different engine or modify his or her plans. The ideal situation for most developers is to find an engine that supports their plans unmodified.

The second question to ask about a feature is, how easy is it to use? Or, how easy is it to get things done using this feature? This is an important question for a game developer because power and flexibility in software can often come at the price of complexity and awkwardness when the feature is not well designed—problems for game developers. Complexity and awkwardness can unnecessarily increase the time taken to use the feature, which can cause needless frustration and stress. Because both time and peace of mind are valuable assets to almost anybody working in a multi-disciplinary field such as game development, complex and awkward features are therefore costly and wasteful. Specifically, they waste time in an industry where time is already short enough, and they cause aggravation where it can be avoided. So when options are available, most game developers will seek to evade features that are not intuitive to use. Thankfully, the UDK—though by no means perfect—offers many features that are both powerful and simple to use.

Note

A distinction should be drawn between poorly designed and needlessly complex features, and features that just take a while to learn and understand. Features that do not have an immediate pick-up-and-use feel are not necessarily poorly designed or needlessly complex. There might be a rationale behind their design—a guiding principle as to why the feature is as it is. For example, some features in the UDK are accessed through interfaces that at first sight might appear complex and intimidating (such as the Matinee, Kismet, and Cascade interfaces). But this is not sufficient reason to dismiss the feature off hand or to avoid trying to understand how it works. Patience, familiarity, and understanding can help you see the reasoning behind the feature's design and understand the benefits that the design offers.

The UDK Editor

You can think of the UDK Editor, the primary editing tool in the UDK, as a level maker or world-creation tool. It is the primary tool in the sense that it has the widest and most varied feature set of all the UDK tools. It is also where game developers spend most of their development time. When developers want to build their game

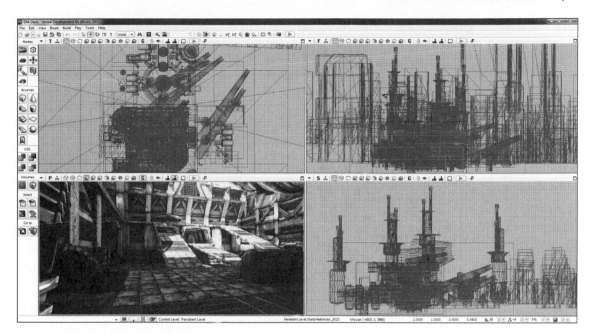

Figure 1.3
The main UDK Editor interface.

by dragging and dropping their 3D assets into the game world, the UDK Editor, shown in Figure 1.3, is where they go.

Although the official UDK documentation calls the editor a "*complete* editing environment," this is not entirely accurate. That's because the editor offers no native interface for editing UnrealScript files—the programming files that can customize the behavior of elements in the engine. Furthermore, the editor does not offer an interface for setting and changing the properties of the INI configuration files that you will need to edit later in the book to get the engine running as needed. Putting these gripes aside, however, the UDK Editor does offer a powerful, flexible, and simple-to-use GUI interface for making real-time 3D games.

You can control the editor using the keyboard, the mouse, or both. It consists of several parts, or sub-editors: the Level Editor, the Matinee Editor, the Kismet Editor, the Sound Editor, the Material Editor, and the Cascade Editor, as well as some other editors. Each of these editors has a dedicated function. For example, the Sound Editor is used to add special effects to sounds—looping effects, echo effects, positional effects, and mixing effects, among others.

The Level Editor

The Level Editor is the focus of the UDK Editor and is where game worlds are constructed. They are constructed using a GUI interface in which the designer drags and drops copies of game assets into the 3D environment. Each copy added to the environment is called an *actor* because it takes on a role in the game, however minor. Every item in a level is recognized by the UDK and the Unreal Engine as an actor. For example, a car is an actor, a character is an actor, a set of stairs is an actor, a table is an actor, and so are walls, floors, and doors. The designer then selects, positions, orientates, and scales actors in the level according to his or her designs to build the complete environment for the game.

To enable you to construct levels with ease, the UDK Level Editor offers a set of helpful tools. These include Copy, Paste, and Delete, as well as organizational tools for naming and finding actors in the level and for grouping related actors, such as all the trees in a forest, so they can be selected in the editor as one group as opposed to individually. Furthermore, the editor offers real-time previewing of levels. That means designers can construct their level and then play it immediately in the editor from the perspective of the gamer, complete with animations, sound, and physics, if any exist. The UDK Editor also offers a wide selection of keyboard shortcuts to speed up workflow and abbreviate tasks. All these features (and more) will be considered in detail later in this book.

The Matinee Editor

The UDK Level Editor enables designers to drag and drop assets into the world as actors to construct 3D environments. But working only with the Level Editor, making use of no other UDK tools, will result in a level that is static and motionless. The player character will be able to walk around according to user input, but nothing else will move. Cars will not travel along the road, helicopter propellers will not spin, elevators will not raise and lower, and doors will not swing on their hinges to open and close. In short, nothing will move—unless it is brought to life through the Matinee Editor (see Figure 1.4).

The Matinee Editor is the interface to part of the Unreal Animation System—the system that creates motion. The Matinee Editor enables animators to create and edit key-frame–based animation for actors in the level. *Animation* refers to motion; *key-frame–based animation* refers to a specific kind of computer-generated motion. A *key frame* is a frame in an animation in which the animated object is in a critical or defining state. To illustrate, consider a door-open animation—that is, an animation that begins with the door in a closed state and ends with the door in an open state. Each of these two states—the start and the end—is a key frame. Between these start and end frames, the door will be in some intermediary state, moving from fully closed to fully open. In key-frame animation, the animator creates the key frames for the object, and the computer uses a mathematical curve known as an

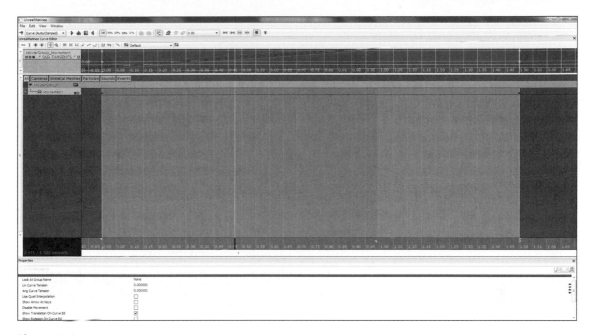

Figure 1.4
The Matinee Editor.

interpolation curve to automatically generate all the frames in between. This is, in essence, how key-frame animation works. The Matinee Editor, then, enables animators to create any number of key-frame animations for any number of actors in a level. The editor features an intuitive design and helpful tools for adding, removing, editing, and defining key frames, as well as tools for adjusting the interpolation curves generated between key frames.

Note

The Matinee Editor is discussed in detail alongside the Kismet Editor in Chapter 9, "Kismet and Matinee: Beginning with Visual Scripting and Animation."

The Kismet Editor

Levels populated with actors and animations might seem very lively and interesting, but they might not be immersive. Gamers typically expect the environment not only to move but also to be interactive. That is, they expect to be able to act or to have an effect on the environment, and for the environment to respond to their actions in meaningful and believable ways. If the gamer grabs the handle of a door to open it, then the door ought to open (provided it is a conventional door and is not locked). Similarly, if the gamer throws a grenade behind enemy lines, then he or she expects to see both an explosion shortly afterward, followed by the deleterious repercussions of that explosion on the environment and the enemies.

All these scenarios involve animation, motion, and change. However, these animations are not supposed to play at absolutely any time during the game, or in any place, or in all circumstances. They are not supposed to begin as the game begins and to continuously play on a loop until the game ends. Rather, these animations play under specific conditions, in specific circumstances, and in response to specific actions performed by the gamer or other characters. Thus, playback of these animations is conditional on specific events occurring.

The point of this example is to illustrate that each game level has its own underlying logic or structure defining how actors in the level behave and relate to each other. In most game engines, this level structure or logic is defined by programmers or level designers using a scripting language. The scripting language used differs from engine to engine. The UDK uses the UnrealScript language as its standard scripting language.

A lot of level behavior and logic can be defined using a mouse-driven GUI instead of a scripting language. The Kismet Editor, shown in Figure 1.5, is one such GUI—a visual scripting system that is part of the main UDK Editor. With this system, the designer uses a mouse to visually build a graph of nodes connected with wires. This

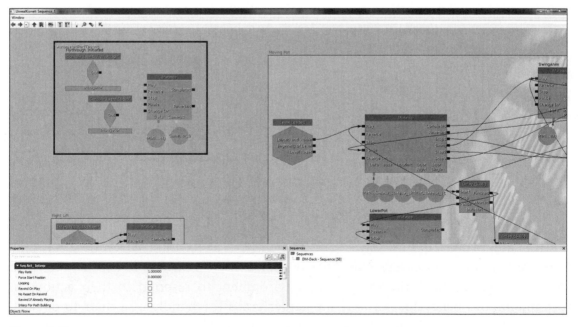

Figure 1.5
The Kismet Editor.

graph specifies the logic and flow of behavior in the level. It can be used to trigger animations or other behavior in response to game events, to reset the level, to play sounds and music, to keep track of scores and statistics, to change lighting, and much more. In short, the Kismet Editor is a GUI front-end to the UnrealScript language. That is, scripted behavior is generated behind the scenes by the UDK when the designer builds the graph in the Kismet Editor, just as HTML code is generated when a Web developer uses the GUI design tools of Web-development applications such as Adobe Dreamweaver. Furthermore, not only can designers use Kismet to visually script the logic of their levels, but programmers can customize Kismet through UnrealScript to extend its functionality, adding their own custom behavior as visual nodes that can be used in the Kismet graph.

Note

This book will delve more deeply into Kismet in later chapters, beginning with Chapter 9.

The Material Editor

A *material* defines how the surface of a 3D model appears when illuminated by a light source. For example, a cube object that is supposed to be made of brick will need a brick material—that is, an image of brickwork—applied to each of its faces. Similarly, a flat surface that is supposed to act as the ground plane in a forest will need a dirt or grass material—that is, an image of dirt or grass—pasted onto its surface, just as wallpaper is pasted onto a wall. In each case, a material is used to adjust the appearance of a 3D object to increase the realism of the scene. That is, the material is what makes the surface of 3D geometry appear to be constructed from real-world materials.

The UDK provides a Material Editor, shown in Figure 1.6, as part of the main editor. The purpose of the Material Editor is to offer designers a GUI and mouse-driven interface to import, create, and edit the materials being applied to actors in the level. Using the Material Editor, designers can control not only the kinds of images applied to 3D models—such as brick, grass, wood, etc.—but also the surface type of those models, such as whether they should appear shiny, reflective, chrome-like, rough, smooth, or soft, among others.

Note

There is much more to be said about materials and about the related concept of maps and mapping. Materials, textures, maps, and mapping coordinates in the UDK are discussed in more detail in Chapter 5, "Materials, Textures, and UV Mapping."

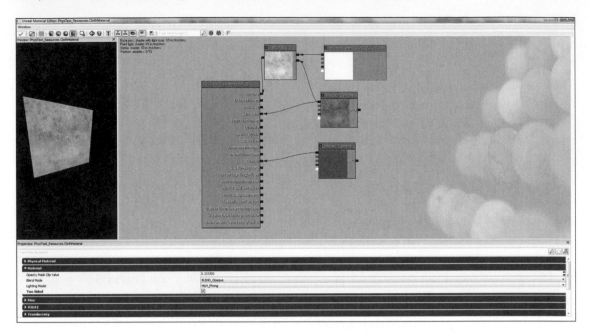

Figure 1.6
The Material Editor.

The Sound Editor

The UDK recognizes sound as any audible asset—that is, any asset that can be heard via the speakers. This includes music (such as a three-minute ambient score) and sound effects (such as a two-second gunshot sound). To aid with these assets, the UDK Editor includes the Sound Editor, shown in Figure 1.7. The Sound Editor has a GUI interface that offers features for importing WAV files into the engine and for applying effects and processes to those imported files, such as echo effects, mixing effects, loop instructions, and positional effects. The final sound—the one that results from the WAV file combined with the effects and processes—can be dropped into the level as an actor.

The UDK offers the same standard set of tools for positioning, scaling, and rotating sound actors in the level as it offers for mesh and light actors. The position of a sound in the level is significant because it influences how that sound is heard by the gamer during the game. If an enemy fires a weapon, players standing nearer to that enemy will hear the weapon more intensely than those standing farther away. That's because the volume of the sound falls off or diminishes over distance from the sound source, fading from full volume to silence. The falloff of any sound can be controlled by designers in the UDK using graphical tools. In short, each sound in the level is surrounded by an invisible sphere whose size describes how the volume of the sound falls off over distance, from full volume to silence. The position of the sound

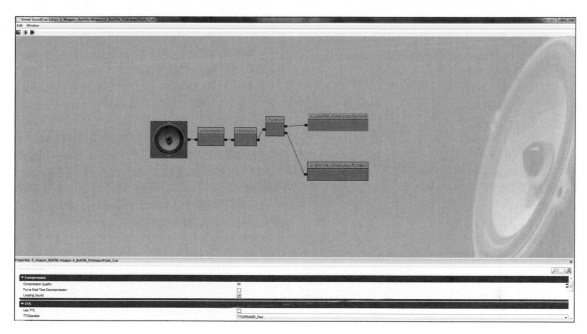

Figure 1.7
The Sound Editor.

in the level marks the central point of the sphere; the nearer to this central point the gamer stands, the louder the sound will be played for him or her. The volume falls off the farther from this point the gamer moves, until finally, the sound can no longer be heard.

Note

For more on sound in the UDK, see Chapter 7, "Music and Sound."

The Cascade Editor

Game developers use particle systems to create special effects in which many separate entities (particles) are governed by a common logic or behavioral pattern. For example, a particle system can be used to create the weather effect of rain. Here, many droplets of water (each droplet being a particle) follow a common behavior or logic by falling from the sky to the ground under the effect of gravity. The droplets and their behavior together form a particle system. Similarly, a flock of birds could be a particle system. The birds (the particles) share a common behavior in flying through the sky from a source point to a destination. There are endless uses for particle systems in games, but some other examples include fairy dust floating through the air, explosions casting debris in all directions, bees patrolling their hive, crowds of people flocking toward a landmark, and ants marching in search of food.

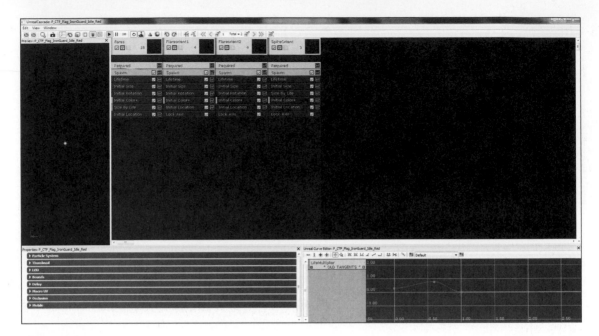

Figure 1.8
The Cascade Editor.

To create particle systems, the UDK offers the Cascade Editor, which is part of the main UDK Editor. This editor, shown in Figure 1.8, offers a visual paradigm to construct and test particle systems in real time. It breaks down particle systems into two conceptual pieces: the emitter and the particle. The *emitter* represents the logic of the particle system. It is responsible for spawning or emitting new particles into the level at a specific location and for defining how those particles will behave once emitted. The *particle* is a descriptive object (a single rain droplet, a single bird, a single bee, etc.) that the emitter uses as a template when generating new particles. Using the Cascade Editor, designers can build complex and varied particle systems that can be added to the level as actors.

Note

Later chapters consider particle systems further—specifically Chapter 11, "Particle Systems with Unreal Cascade."

Lightmass

Lighting serves many purposes: It can add color, drama, motion, suspense, detail, and realism. Indeed, the importance of lighting in a level for all these reasons should not be underestimated. Even more importantly, a level without a light source appears

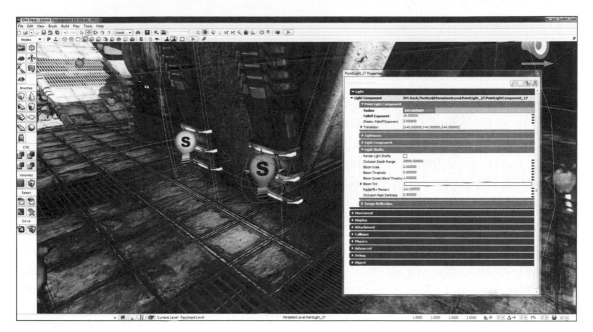

Figure 1.9
Lightmass.

completely black. No matter how beautiful and detailed the game assets might be, nobody will ever see them if the level in which they are contained has no light source. For this reason, a UDK level must have at least one light source—that is, one actor that casts illumination. Typically, however, a UDK level has more than one light.

The UDK features a complex and powerful lighting system, called Lightmass. Lightmass, shown in Figure 1.9, offers designers a range of lighting source types that vary in the way they cast light, including point lights, spotlights, and directional lights. Using the Level Editor, one can position and arrange each of these light types as actors, in the same way other game assets can be positioned. Likewise, their properties can be tweaked. This enables designers to define how light is cast and how it behaves in the level.

As you shall see, the Lightmass system supports a global illumination model for lighting. That means the lighting system can simulate the way in which light behaves in the world, bouncing from both reflective and non-reflective surfaces. The result is highly detailed and highly realistic images in real-time.

Note

The subject of lighting is addressed in several chapters of this book, beginning with Chapter 8, "Lighting."

Terrain Tools

As mentioned, the UDK is not a primary modeling tool. It offers little in the way of features for building 3D models from scratch. By *3D models*, I mean assets such as character models, vehicles, weapons, doors, and architecture, among others. All these models are composed from polygons, edges, and vertices. Typically, these kinds of assets are constructed and textured individually in third-party modeling programs such as 3DS Max, Maya, or Blender. When the model is completed, the artist then imports it alongside his or her other assets into the UDK. The UDK Level Editor is used not so much to build models as to position, orientate, and scale them into a single 3D real-time environment. There is, however, one possible exception to this rule—the rule that models are not built in the UDK—and it is terrain.

The term *terrain* is used in the UDK in a technical sense, not in a general sense. In the UDK, terrain refers to all meshes in a level that have been built using the UDK's terrain tools and that define the level's fundamental landscape—its terra-firma. When land surveyors examine the environment around them, they might take in the sights: the hills, canyons, forests, and fields. Although they might call all these things "terrain," the UDK will recognize them as such only if they are constructed in the UDK using the specific terrain tools—not if they are built in a third-party modeling package and imported as meshes.

The terrain of a level is fundamental not in the sense that it is essential to the level (because it is optional; there are levels with no terrain element) but because it is a base element in the same way that a painter begins his or her painting using base colors. Typically, a level designer does not rely entirely on the terrain tools for the layout of a level. Rather, the terrain tools are used to construct a rough landscape that is a foundation or base that defines the general extent and contours of the level landscape—the mountains, the forest floor, the rough rocky plains, etc. Onto that, more detail is added through standard meshes. The level designer might create a mountainous landscape, and then on top of that add models of bridges, roads, houses, statues, walkways, and fences.

As shown in Figure 1.10, the UDK offers designers a range of visual tools for constructing and editing landscape meshes from scratch. Specifically, it enables designers to begin with a flat plane of geometry—a plane composed of polygons, edges, and vertices. Then it provides a range of free-form tools that can deform or sculpt the terrain geometry into the desired arrangement. The UDK's terrain brush tools work similarly to the brush tools found in most photo-editing software. They enable the designer to control the shape, size, and softness or hardness of the brush. When the brush is applied to the terrain geometry, detail is added to it in the form of

Figure 1.10
Terrain tools.

displacement. The brush enables designers to push and pull the terrain up or down, and to sculpt and mold it like clay into the shape of mountains, hills, canyons, rivers, etc. Furthermore, the UDK enables designers to import grayscale height maps whose luminance levels can parametrically deform the terrain mesh (more on this later). In short, the terrain tools offer designers a way to quickly build vast terrains for their levels.

Note

This subject is discussed in more detail in Chapter 6, "Building Game Worlds with Static Mesh Actors."

Cinematic Tools

The events in an Unreal game are witnessed by the gamer from an eye-point, which equates to the lens of a camera positioned in the 3D environment. Typically, in a first-person game, the gamer witnesses events as seen from the eye of the player character. In a third-person game, the gamer witnesses events from some other vantage point outside of the player character.

Because games are noted for their interactivity—that is, their ability to let the gamer do things—the gamer therefore has control of what is seen in the game world most of the time. There are, however, times when this control must be taken from the gamer, putting him or her in the position of a passive observer—akin to someone watching the scenes of a movie. Such an occasion might be when players must watch the irreversible effects of their action, such as when they kill a central character in the story or when they complete a level. When the gamer is in this passive mode, most games seek to apply the principles of cinematography to present the scene to the gamer in an interesting and emotive way.

One of the things moviemakers do to add drama to a scene is to fiddle with the camera. They might move the camera to show the scene from a different angle, change the camera's focal length to zoom in on specific actors, or adjust the camera's depth of field—for example, sharpening the focus of foreground objects and blurring the focus of background objects—to draw the viewer's attention in a particular direction. All these effects and more can be achieved using the UDK cinematic tools (see Figure 1.11). These tools, which are spread across several parts of the editor interface, enable designers to animate almost all the properties of a camera, including its position, orientation, focal length, zoom, depth of field, and more.

Note

The subject of cinematics is considered in more depth in Chapter 9, during the discussion on the Kismet Editor and Matinee Editor. Cinematics are also touched on in subsequent chapters.

Figure 1.11
Cinematic tools.

Fractured Meshes

Most video games are said to be interactive—that is, supporting two-way communication. When the player does something, something happens in response. To feel that
a game is interactive is to feel that your actions as a gamer make a difference to the
game world and in what is happening in the game.

Game developers use many techniques to heighten interactivity in games. Interactivity can be heightened through scripting, animation, sound, and lighting. Another way
to heighten interactivity is through what the UDK calls *fractured meshes*. A fractured
mesh works like this: An artist creates a standard mesh—let us say a car, for example
—and then imports it into the UDK. The artist then uses a GUI editor to add mathematical information to the mesh. This information describes all the places in the
mesh where it should be sliced or broken (fractured). When this information is
added, the mesh will not look broken initially when placed in the game level. To
the gamer, it will initially appear completely intact, just as an apple sliced into segments can look complete when those segments are fitted together. The point of this is
to create a mesh actor in the level that can be blown to pieces when struck by ammunition, force, or explosions. In short, fractured meshes are what enable developers to
create destructible scenery in a game—scenery that is responsive. Destructible scenery
heightens the interactivity of a game because, by being blown to pieces, it is respond-
ing to the actions of gamers. The UDK features a detailed set of tools for creating
fractured meshes (see Figure 1.12).

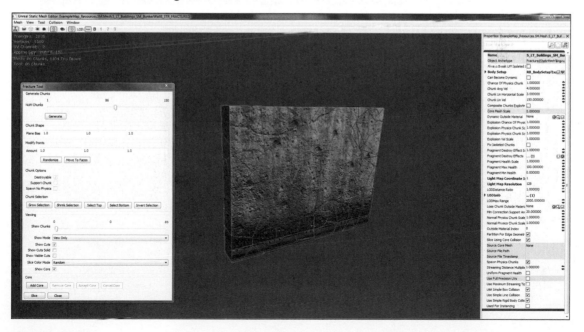

Figure 1.12
Fractured meshes.

Note

The UDK's tools for creating fractured meshes are discussed in Appendix, "Q&A: Taking It Further with the UDK."

SpeedTree

Most parts of the inhabited world feature trees and foliage—and lots of them. For this reason, video games featuring outdoor environments often need trees and foliage in order to look believable. But the creation of tree and foliage models poses something of a problem for the graphic artists and content creators who work in games. The first problem is that outdoor environments typically have a lot of trees and foliage—and they all look very different. This is a problem because tree and foliage models are organic and complex, and are thereby time consuming to model in traditional modeling software. The second problem is that trees and plants each have many branches, and each branch features many leaves. Although this complexity can be modeled with patience and perseverance, the modeling and repetitive positioning of all these elements is considered by many to be a laborious and dull process.

The UDK attempts to resolve these two issues for game developers by offering a separate, third-party application called SpeedTree. SpeedTree, shown in Figure 1.13, is a

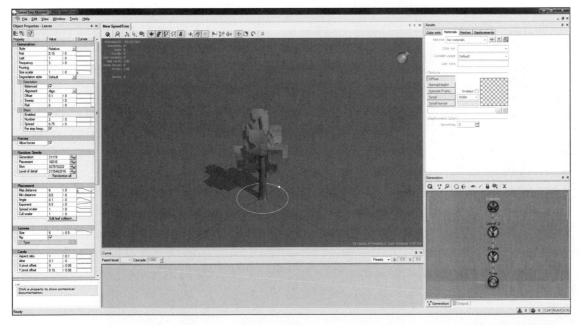

Figure 1.13
SpeedTree.

GUI tool that enables content creators to parametrically generate trees and foliage for UDK games very quickly. The term *parametric* is used here to mean that an artist can use the application to automatically calculate and generate a unique-looking tree or plant on the basis of several parameters and numbers. Parameters include values such as number of branches, number of leaves, radius of trunk, and more. Based on these, SpeedTree can create tree and foliage models that are mapped and optimized for games and can be imported into the UDK as standard mesh actors.

Note

SpeedTree is discussed later in this book, in Appendix.

FaceFX

Two features required by games with lots of characters and dialogue are the ability to lip-sync accurately and to control expressions on a character's face. *Lip-sync* refers to synchronizing the animation of a character's lips with the vocal track that is played for his or her voice when the character is talking. *Expression control* refers to the ability to manipulate the expressions on a character's face to convey emotion—raise eyebrows, smile, blink, wink, laugh, cry, etc. To achieve both of these, the UDK offers the third-party FaceFX tool, shown in Figure 1.14. This tool is integrated into the

Figure 1.14
FaceFX.

main editor and offers an impressive range of features for controlling the animation of character faces.

Note

This tool is mentioned here for completeness. A deeper discussion of this tool is beyond the scope of this book.

UnrealScript

Game designers who want to create levels in the UDK beyond those that are static and motionless will need to create animations and scripted behavior. The scripted behavior defines the underlying logic of a level; it specifies how actors behave and the nature of the relationships that exist between actors.

Much of this type of scripted behavior can be created visually in the UDK using the Kismet Editor (refer to the section titled "The Kismet Editor"). But despite its versatility, the Kismet Editor has its limitations. That is, there are some things that it cannot do or is not suited to do. Consequently, there will be times when a programmer must go beyond the Kismet Editor and use the scripting language used by the Unreal Engine, known as UnrealScript, to create custom behavior (see Figure 1.15).

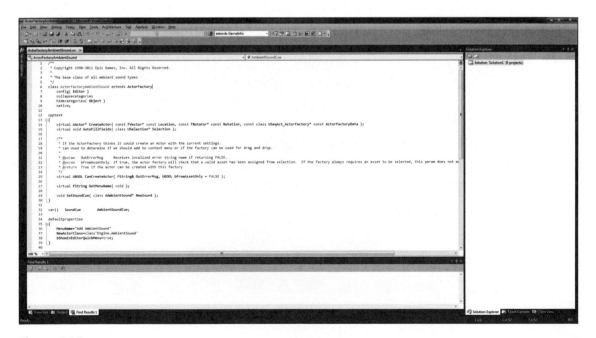

Figure 1.15
UnrealScript.

The syntax of UnrealScript is based on that of the older and widely established languages of Java and C++. UnrealScript is a class-based, object-oriented language. Programmers add new functionality to Unreal by deriving new classes from those that exist already. The UDK does not provide a native editor for creating and editing UnrealScript—at least not at present. Instead, programmers can either write script in standard text files or download the Microsoft Visual Studio editor in combination with the nFringe plug-in for both the IntelliSense and the code-completion features.

Note

Later chapters in this book demonstrate how to work with the UDK using UnrealScript, starting with Chapter 12, "Scripting with UnrealScript."

DOWNLOADING AND INSTALLING THE UDK

The UDK Editor tools and the Unreal Engine are resource intensive; they demand a lot of computing power. To run this software successfully and reliably, it is important to use a computer that can meet its demands. The minimum requirements refer to the lowest or least-powered hardware configuration capable of running the UDK in a way that's considered acceptable. In short, your system should at least equal the minimum requirements. That does not mean your system should be exactly the same as the minimum requirements, with the same model of graphics card and the same processor. Rather, it means that it should feature hardware working in unison to produce a system capable of equivalent performance. Ideally, however, your system will be capable of achieving better performance than that which could be achieved by the minimum. Thus, there is also a recommended system specification, detailing the lowest kind of hardware and performance needed to run the UDK at its best. The minimum and recommended system requirements vary over time with each release, as new features are added. This book assumes that the reader is using a system equivalent to or higher than the minimum requirements of the UDK. Those whose systems fail to meet the minimum may experience poor performance and unexpected behavior.

The minimum requirements, at the time of this writing, are as follows:

- Windows XP SP2 or Windows Vista
- 2.0+GHz processor
- 2GB system RAM
- SM3-compatible video card
- 3GB free hard-drive space

The recommended requirements, at the time of this writing, are as follows:

- Windows 7 64-bit
- 2.0+GHz multi-core processor
- 8GB system RAM
- NVIDIA 8000 series or higher graphics card
- Plenty of HDD space

The UDK is available to download free in both 32-bit and 64-bit editions for 32-bit and 64-bit operating systems, respectively. It can be downloaded from the official UDK home page at www.udk.com. Once downloaded, simply run the installer and follow the onscreen instructions to install the UDK to the computer.

Note

Though the UDK is available for download and use free of charge, this does not necessarily mean that the UDK remains free of charge for users who go on to sell the games they produce. To create commercial products using the UDK—that is, products you plan to sell—various charges may apply. More information about applicable costs for UDK developers can be found at the licensing page at the official UDK Web site: www.udk.com/licensing.

After installing the UDK, it is recommended that you restart your computer even if the installer does not explicitly request a restart. This is because some essential libraries required by the UDK Editor do not register correctly on every system until after a restart. Starting the UDK Editor for the first time after an installation without first restarting the system might cause the editor to fail on startup.

A GUIDED TOUR OF UDK DIRECTORIES AND FILES

The purpose of the UDK installer is to extract all the UDK files to a specified folder on the local computer. This folder will act as the permanent home of the UDK in the file system and is the root folder inside which all the UDK files will be contained. These files are further arranged and distributed across a set of sub-folders (folders inside the root folder). This arrangement is neither arbitrary nor unimportant. The directory structure of the UDK, shown in Figure 1.16, is the result of design and purpose. Specifically, each top-level folder in the UDK folder hierarchy is designed to contain a set of related files, and UDK users are expected to conform to this design when creating their own files.

Figure 1.16
The UDK directory structure.

The design governing the naming and arrangement of the UDK folders is as follows:

Note

Before examining the folder structure installed by the UDK as detailed here, be sure to run the UDK Editor at least once. Some of the UDK folders and files are created by the editor at startup, and not by the installer.

- **Binaries.** The Binaries folder is home to all the executable files of the UDK tools except the Unreal Engine, along with their related binary and pre-compiled data. This folder contains the executable files for the main UDK Editor, both the 32-bit and 64-bit versions, along with the SpeedTree application, the FaceFX plug-in, and other plug-ins. UDK users will typically have no need to edit the contents of this folder. In fact, editing the contents of this folder and its sub-folders could have application-breaking results. That is, it could have unintended consequences that will prevent the UDK from running as expected.

- **Development\Src.** The top-level Development folder contains a sub-folder named Src, short for "source," which is itself short for "source code." This folder contains all the UnrealScript source code used by the engine, editor, and sample levels provided with the UDK. This folder does not contain the C++ source code for the Unreal Engine core, but rather all the higher-level and game-specific code written in the UnrealScript language that is necessary to run the engine, editor, and sample levels. The code in this folder will be compiled by the UDK UnrealScript compiler at compile time. The UDK ships with plenty of source code already included in this folder. Typically, UDK users will not edit or remove any of the default code included here. Rather, users will either add their own code created from scratch or create derived classes from the existing ones to extend and override their behavior. At run-time, both the Unreal Engine and the UDK tools will ultimately reference not the source code from this folder, but the compiled versions of the source code, which are contained in a different folder.

■ **Engine.** Just as the Binaries folder contains all the executable, binary, and configuration data specific to the UDK tools and editors, the Engine folder contains all the data that is similarly specific to the Unreal Engine itself. Remember that the UDK Editor tools and the Unreal Engine are distinct entities. The tools are used to build games that will be powered by the engine. Typically, UDK users will never need to adjust the contents of this folder.

■ **UDKGame.** The UDKGame folder is a working folder for UDK users. This folder and its sub-folders contain content that is supposed to be viewed, edited, and modified by UDK users as they go about building their game. The UDKGame folder contains several notable sub-folders:

■ **Config.** The Config sub-folder contains a collection of text files, each with an .ini file extension, short for "initialization." It is appended to the name of any text file whose contents are read and processed by the Unreal Engine when the engine initializes—that is, when the engine starts. The purpose of an INI file is to contain a series of settings and values that describe how the engine is to behave when running. All INI files contain human-readable text. Furthermore, each line of text in the file follows an industry-standard convention. They are not just written in any way and in any style. Each line contains a key-value pairing. That is, it contains a key and a value, separated by an equal sign. For example, the line MaxPlayers=32 contains a key (MaxPlayers) and an integer value (32), and these two are separated by an equal sign. This particular line tells the engine at initialization that the maximum number of players allowed in any specific level is 32. With this setting applied, the engine will ensure that the number of players in any level will be less than or equal to 32, but not more than 32. In short, the Config folder contains many INI files, each INI file has many lines, and each line customizes the behavior of the Unreal Engine in some specific way. The result of these files and their settings is a particular set of rules that apply to the engine when run. This set of rules will ensure the engine behaves as expected throughout the duration of the game. This Config folder and its files will be considered in more detail later in this book.

- **Logs.** The Config sub-folder represents a collection of text files that are input into the engine when it starts. In contrast, the Logs folder contains none, one, or more text files that are *output* from the engine when it ends. The output text files are not INI files, but are instead log files (which use the .log filename extension). Log files contain-human readable text about some of the critical things that the engine actually did while it was running. The word *critical* is used here to emphasize that the engine reports on only a selection of things that it does or fails to do. (The engine potentially performs thousands of different operations per second; to record them all in a log would result in a file that was intimidating and unreadable.) Each time the engine executes, it produces a text log in the Logs folder that contains information about key events that occurred during the engine's execution. This includes the name of the graphics card on the system that was used to show graphics, the version of DirectX used to power the game, and the details of critical errors that prevented the engine from running successfully (if any), among other things. Because the Logs folder contains files output by the engine and nothing else, the UDK user will not have cause to edit the files in this folder. They are for viewing only.

- **Script.** The Script folder is related to the Development\Src sub-folder mentioned earlier. The purpose of the Development\Src sub-folder is to contain all game-related source code written in the UnrealScript language. At compile time, the UDK compiler will examine the source code and automatically generate a compiled version in the UDKGame\Script folder. Both the UDK Editor and the Unreal Engine will reference the compiled version of the script in the Script folder, and not the original source code in the Development\Src folder. Because the compiled version of the code is generated in this folder automatically on each compile, the UDK user will have little reason to add to or amend the contents of this folder.

- **Content.** The Content folder contains game-content—that is, all the external and game-specific assets referenced by the engine for the purposes of the game. This includes level maps, materials, sounds, meshes, animations, videos, and more. This folder does not contain the original assets in their native formats, such as textures as bitmap files or sounds as WAV files. Instead, it contains copies of those assets imported and packaged together into the Unreal proprietary asset formats, known as *packages*. So, a collection of bitmap textures is typically compiled into one package of textures, and a collection of sounds is typically compiled into one package of sounds, just as many files can be compressed into a single ZIP file. The Unreal Engine references not the original assets but the packages, and UDK users typically distribute the packages and not the original assets with their games. Assets are imported or converted into the engine as packages using the UDK Editor tools and plug-ins, as you shall see in later chapters.

■ **Splash.** The term splash is short for "splash screen." It follows, then, that the Splash folder contains one or more splash screens. A *splash screen* is a logo or branded image that is shown on the screen for a few seconds while the engine starts and the game is loading. Classic examples of splash screens are the images shown during the startup of applications such as Adobe Photoshop, Microsoft Word, and 3DS Max. The UDK Splash folder comes with at least one image that appears when any UDK game is started. UDK users can replace this default file with their own splash-screen images.

■ **Movies.** The Movies folder is home to all the Bink-encoded movies played by the Unreal Engine. A Bink-encoded movie is a movie file that has been converted using Bink technology from one of the standard movie formats, such as AVI or MPG. Movies encoded into Bink perform well when played in hardware-accelerated games, such as those games powered by the Unreal Engine. All UDK-powered games play at least one Bink movie automatically on startup, shown after the splash screen. This movie displays an animated version of the Unreal logo. This movie must be shown on startup as it is by default and it cannot lawfully be edited or removed by UDK developers. It is —at least at present—a condition of using the UDK for making games.

UDK Documentation, Help, and Information

This book is primarily an introduction to the UDK. Its purpose is to help readers build their confidence in using the UDK to create real-time 3D video games. As such, Part II of the book, "UDK Essentials," contains many chapters dedicated to exploring some of the most fundamental features of the UDK and the Unreal Engine. Chapters in Part III, "Building a Project (*The Nexus*)" are intended to help the reader apply that knowledge to complete some real-world and more advanced projects.

That said, this book is far from a comprehensive and complete guide. It does not contain everything there is to know about the UDK and its uses. The UDK is a vast and multi-faceted tool, and it is used in many creative and interesting ways that perhaps even the developers did not foresee. Hence, in a book of finite length about a tool with potentially infinite uses, there must necessarily be a lot left unsaid. For this reason, there might be times when you get stuck and are at a loss for how to proceed on more complex projects that demand skills and knowledge beyond the scope of this book. In these cases, it is useful to know where help and further information can be sought. In the case of the UDK, it can be found in at least two different places:

- **The Unreal Developer Network (UDN).** The UDN is an online, freely available and searchable knowledge base of articles, references, and tutorials on using the UDK. It contains tutorials on the basics as well as on more advanced topics. It also contains a selection of sample games that can be downloaded and examined in the UDK Editor. The UDN represents one of the first places a UDK developer might visit when seeking how-to information—that is, information about how to do some specific action or information about how to achieve some specific end. The UDN can be found at http://udn.epicgames.com.

- **The UDN forums.** This is a community area of the UDN Web site where users publicly discuss the use of the UDK and learn from each other. The forum is searchable, meaning that visitors can search for the text of all previous forum discussions for content related to their present query. It is possible that visitors before you have had the same questions as you, and that others were able to help answer those questions. In these cases, the forum already offers the answers you need, provided you know what to search for. If not, you can start your own thread on the forum to find the information you seek. The UDN forums can be found at http://forums.epicgames.com.

RELATED TOOLS: NFRINGE, VISUAL STUDIO, AND PLUG-INS

As earlier sections of this chapter have demonstrated, the UDK features the following tools:

- A Level Editor for creating and editing real-time 3D maps

- Kismet and Matinee Editors for customizing and defining the behavior, motion, and logic of elements in the level

- Sound-editing and creation tools for importing sound into the game world and controlling its properties in 3D space

Despite these features, the UDK poses two problems. First, it lacks a native, or built-in, GUI editor for creating and compiling UnrealScript files. It is true that users can create script files without a native GUI editor. They could instead code the script in a standard text application, such as Notepad, and then compile the text file using a command-line interface via tools that the UDK does provide. But this approach does not give the UDK a complete, GUI, all-in-one feel. To solve this issue, two third-party tools can be installed: Microsoft Visual Studio Express (www.microsoft.com/express)

and nFringe (www.pixelminegames.com/nfringe). Together, these tools, discussed in more detail later in the book, offer developers an integrated development environment (IDE) for UnrealScript, complete with the ability to debug and compile script, and with syntax highlighting and IntelliSense for script files.

The second problem is that UDK does not at first sight appear to offer developers any native way to import 3D meshes—character models or vehicles, etc.—from third-party modeling programs such as 3DS Max or Maya. As you shall see, the UDK does in fact provide such tools for selected modeling programs, but they are not accessible via the main editor interface. Instead, they are provided as separate plug-in files for those applications and are stored away in a folder in the UDK folder hierarchy. The process of installing these plug-ins for some 3D applications is discussed in later chapters. Here it is enough to mention that they are to be found in the Binaries\ActorX sub-folder.

CONCLUSION

The main point of this chapter has been to summarize the UDK as a game-development tool—to discuss what it is, what it is not, and what it can do. In short, the UDK can be used to make triple-A–standard, real-time 3D games. The number of UDK-based triple-A games on the market is testament to this. This alone is enough to excite most developers and to catch their interest. However, this chapter has gone on to also detail at some length a selection of the key features of the UDK. In so doing, it has outlined the ground that this book will cover. Furthermore, this chapter has considered some of the limitations of the UDK—specifically, why some third-party tools are desirable complements.

The next chapter dives in at the deep end, so to speak. There, you will not be starting with the conventional baby steps into the basics of the UDK. Instead, you will build a complete level, with scripting, animation, and sound. Only after that chapter is completed will you stop to look back at the level you created—what it was that you did and how exactly you did it. So let's get started.

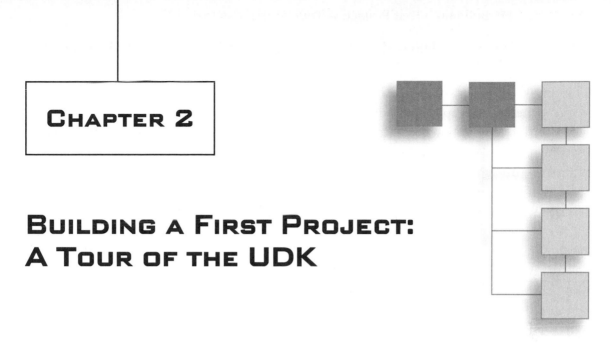

CHAPTER 2

BUILDING A FIRST PROJECT: A TOUR OF THE UDK

Focus is a matter of deciding what things you're not going to do.

—John Carmack

By the end of this chapter, you should:

- Have a basic grasp of the UDK Editor interface.

- Get a feel for the UDK workflow involved in creating a level.

- Appreciate the order in which development tasks are performed.

- Have a rough understanding of the Level Editor, Kismet Editor, Matinee Editor, and Content Browser.

- Appreciate the reasoning behind this book's roadmap for learning more about the UDK.

This book could have taken several approaches to getting started learning the UDK. One might have been to take a logical progression of baby steps. This approach would have involved describing all the individual features of the UDK in a linear sequence, beginning with the most basic and fundamental and ending with the most complex and hybrid. It might have begun by first considering the user interface, its buttons, and dialog boxes. It might then have proceeded with an explanation of how basic levels can be constructed using a set of brush tools. Finally, after many descriptions and explanations of different features, it would have ended by showing you how to apply your knowledge of the UDK and its features to construct a complete level or game.

This book, however, does not take this conventional, baby-step approach. Instead, it begins where that approach ends. Specifically, this chapter walks you through how to use the UDK and its tools to construct a playable level complete with meshes, materials, lights, animations, cameras, sounds, and scripted logic. This chapter does not offer much in the way of in-depth description or a complete explanation of the tools that are used. Instead, it offers brief summaries for the purposes of clarity and readability. For example, this chapter does not explain the intricacies of the Kismet Editor, even though that editor will be used. Nor does it discuss all the uses to which meshes can be put or the limitations of the BSP Brush tools. It does not feature many descriptive sentences that begin with phrases like, "This tool is…" or "The purpose of this feature is…" and so on. Descriptive and explanatory material is reserved for later chapters in the book. This chapter is more instructional and less descriptive. It reads like a guided tour, walkthrough, or tutorial in that it asks the reader to do things, such as, "Click this button," or "Open this dialog box," or "Scale this mesh," among other things. In short, this chapter expects you to follow along in building a level using the UDK, but it does not expect you to know how to use the UDK at all.

Note

As will be explained in more detail later in this book, the Builder Brush and BSP Brushes are distinct. The former is used to act as a template for creating instances of the latter, just as a single rubber stamp can print many marks in its own image.

So why does your learning begin here and not elsewhere? After all, is it not putting the cart before the horse to construct a level using tools that have not yet been explained? There are three main reasons behind the decision to avoid describing the UDK features before using them to build a project:

- Descriptions without examples can be dull to read—and dull reading is not conducive to learning. When a software feature is described in the abstract, without reference to a concrete example, it can sometimes be difficult to visualize the many different ways in which that feature is practically useful. For example, it might be valuable to know that the UDK BSP Brush is designed for creating solid geometry and has a set of options for customizing how that geometry is created. As valuable as this information might be, it is still difficult to visualize exactly how the brush is used, how it helps to build levels, and why its options are important. This book could spend many paragraphs elaborating on these details, of course, but a practical and hands-on example can often speak much better.

- There is much to learn about the UDK, and it can be difficult to know where to start. Creating a level can help you to orientate yourself amidst the intimidating sea of UDK information. Orientating yourself involves getting an overview of the UDK. It is about realizing that its many features and details can be organized into conceptual groups by kind—for example, scripting, lighting, sound, and others. It is about appreciating that those groups are the constituent pieces of the UDK, and that learning the UDK involves coming to understand those pieces. For example, when someone moves into a new neighborhood, there are various ways in which he or she can start to become familiar with the surroundings—the layout of the streets and the locations of local amenities. The new resident could consult a map or ask questions. But a friendly neighbor or other long-standing resident could also offer to accompany that newcomer to the nearest town or shopping mall. In accepting the neighbor's offer, the man or woman does not become an expert about the local area; and nor does he or she discover the location of all local landmarks. But that person does begin to get a general idea about distances and about his or her own orientation, however small. What it does is establish a rock, anchor, or starting point from which new learning can begin. The creation of such a starting point is what is achieved by creating a UDK level.

- I want to show you how quickly and easily a completely playable level can be constructed in the UDK.

PROJECT OVERVIEW

The point of this chapter is to detail how a complete and playable level can be created using the UDK. Before starting on this, it will be helpful to describe the level that is to be created from your work throughout this chapter. This level, shown in Figure 2.1, is small, but to create it you will need to call upon a wide variety of UDK tools—from BSP Brushes and static meshes to the Kismet Editor, the Matinee Editor, and the Content Browser.

It will not be necessary to create any UnrealScript, so neither Visual Studio nor the nFringe plug-in will be required. All the assets used for this project, such as the meshes, textures, sounds, and animations, are among the sample assets that are provided free with the UDK. You will not need to import any external assets or use any plug-ins or third-party modeling packages. Everything you need for this level is

Figure 2.1
The project to be created.

provided for you by the UDK Editor. This applies not only to this chapter, but to most chapters throughout the book (except where otherwise stated).

The level you will build in this chapter consists of a small, industrial/sci-fi–themed arena. When the level begins, the player will spawn into the arena with a weapon in his or her hand and will be standing in front of a spinning portal. The portal represents the means by which the player traveled to the arena and leads back to the player's place of origin (although the player will not actually be able to travel back there). The arena contains some machines, pipes, and devices among other things. In addition, on the floor and at the center of the arena are two sliding trap doors that are locked and sealed. The player can use the elevator in the corner of the arena to travel to a raised platform; at the end of this platform, there is a switch on the wall. When the switch is pressed, the sealed doors on the floor slide open, revealing a bottomless void beneath. If the player lowers himself or herself into this void, the player will surely perish. This constitutes the whole of the level to be created in this chapter, although some suggestions will also be made as to ways in which the level can be made more interesting. You are encouraged both to follow along with this chapter and to attempt the suggestions made. So let's get started.

CREATING A NEW LEVEL

Creating a new level represents the starting point for any project—the point from which work begins. If you have not done so already, start the UDK Editor. The editor shows a splash screen as it loads. After it loads, it presents you with a new and empty level, ready to be edited. Alternatively, if you already have the UDK Editor open, create a new level by opening the File menu and choosing New.

A newly created level is empty in the sense that it features no content—no meshes, no lights, no animations, no sound, nothing except an empty 3D space with the x, y, and z axes. At first sight, the level might not appear to be empty, but to contain a wireframe cube centered at the origin. As you shall see, however, that cube is for visualization purposes only. It does not in fact exist in the level as an actor.

THE FOUR-VIEWPORT VIEW

When you create a new project, the UDK Editor should look something like the screen in Figure 2.2. You'll see a toolbar and menu stretching horizontally across the top of the editor (1), a toolbox to the left of the editor (2), and four large viewports that, together, occupy most of the screen space (3). It is possible, however, that you will not see four viewports, but instead see only one large viewport, as shown in

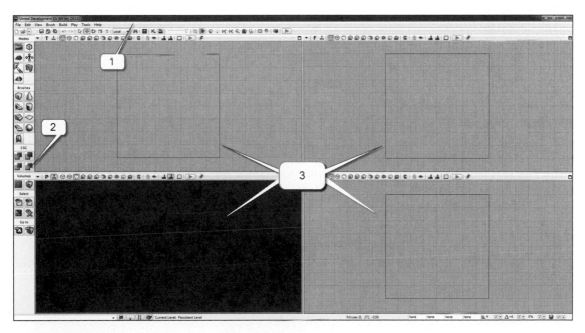

Figure 2.2
The UDK Editor, ready for a new project in four-viewport mode.

Figure 2.3
The UDK Editor, ready for a new project but with a single, maximized viewport.

Figure 2.3. In that case, click the Restore Viewport button in the top-right corner of the toolbar (1) to toggle between a four-viewport layout and a single-viewport layout.

Note

You can use your mouse to select a viewport. A yellow border surrounds the currently selected viewport.

Setting the Viewport Type

The UDK Level Editor consists mainly of four viewports, all offering a view into the same 3D level. When the editor is in four-viewport mode, you can see all four viewports simultaneously. There is much to be said about viewports, considered later in this book. In short, however, a viewport does two things:

- It offers the level designer a real-time preview of the level. That is, it offers a director's view of the level's contents or actors, such as its meshes and lights, and of the position of sounds and other special effects.

- It enables the level designer to move and navigate around his or her level.

Using the viewports together, designers can move forward, backward, left, and right in a level to see its actors from almost any angle or perspective.

There are two main kinds of viewports, each with its own purpose, advantages, and disadvantages:

- **Orthographic viewports.** Orthographic viewports, which are essentially two dimensional rather than three dimensional, look like wireframe blueprint views of the level. They offer the designer a technical and precise view of the level from a fixed perspective—namely the top, side, and front.

- **Perspective viewports.** Perspective viewports resemble much more closely what gamers will see when they play the level in a game. In a perspective viewport, the designer can freely navigate around the level, zooming in and out and rotating the view to take in the sights of the level from any chosen perspective.

Note

One key difference between viewports in the editor and the camera used for the player in the game is that viewports can show things that the game camera cannot. Specifically, viewports can show diagnostic and other level information that is useful to the designer, but not so for the gamer. This information includes the position of sounds and lights, the arrangement of barriers that mark the edges of a level, and the wireframe structure of meshes, among other things.

The standard configuration for viewports in the UDK Editor shows three orthographic viewports (Top, Side, and Front) and one perspective viewport (Perspective). To determine the view of any viewport—that is, whether it is a Front, Side, Top, or Perspective viewport—you can consult the Viewport Type button on the Viewport toolbar in the Editor. This button is labeled with a letter that indicates the type of the viewport: F (Front), S (Side), T (Top), and P (Perspective). Clicking this button enables you to cycle between the viewport types; right-clicking the button displays a menu from which you can select from any of the four types, as shown in Figure 2.4.

The arrangement that I recommend, and the one I use throughout this book, is to position the Top viewport in the top-left corner of the editor, the Front viewport in the top-right corner, the Perspective viewport in the bottom-left corner, and the Side viewport in the bottom-right corner, as shown in Figure 2.2. This arrangement is not essential, however. Readers can use whichever setup is most convenient for them.

Showing Viewport Information

Each viewport in the UDK Editor, whether perspective or orthographic, can be configured in its behavior. It can also be set to show or hide different kinds of actors in the scene, such as lights, meshes, and sounds. The latter feature—showing or hiding actors in the viewport—can be useful when a level designer wants to simplify the

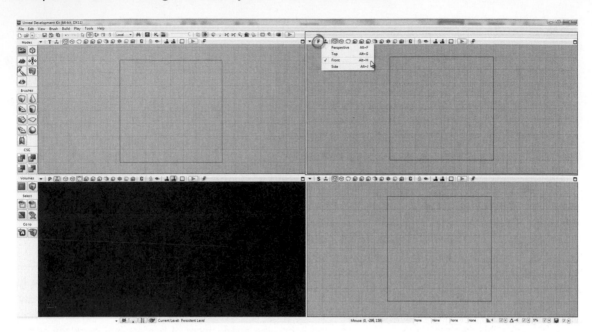

Figure 2.4
Right-click the Viewport Type button to select a viewport type.

view of a level while working. For example, a designer might be using the Perspective viewport to position and arrange static meshes such as characters, vehicles, walls, and floors in the level. While doing this, the designer will likely want to avoid clutter and unnecessary information in the viewport. Because the designer is positioning meshes, he or she will not want to see the mapping coordinates of polygons, the artificial intelligence (AI) information for paths, or any other non-mesh–related data. In addition, the designer will not want to accidentally select, move, or edit non-mesh actors in the level, such as lights and sounds. For these reasons, the designer might adjust the viewport options to restrict what he or she sees in the viewport to better focus on the work in hand. For example, the designer can hide all actors in the level belonging to various types such as all lights, all meshes, all brushes, etc.

Although being able to restrict what one sees in the viewports can be of great benefit to experienced level designers to speed up their workflow, it can also be a source of confusion and irritation to newcomers to the UDK. That's because newcomers often explore the UDK by playing around with its interface and settings. In doing this, however, they can inadvertently hide specific actors in the viewport. Then, when they add content to the level, they find that it does not appear in the viewport. This inevitably causes them to wonder whether they've made a mistake or encountered a bug, when in fact they have simply changed a setting in the viewport options. To avoid these kinds of problems, take a moment to configure the visibility settings for

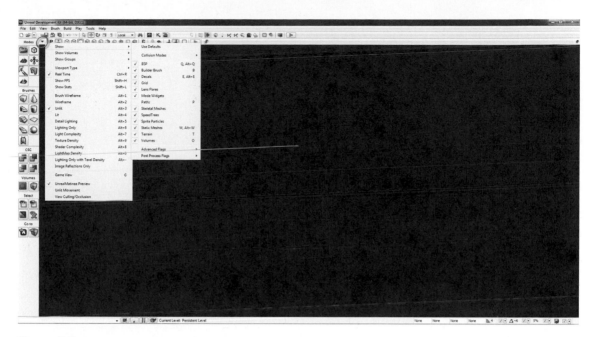

Figure 2.5
Perspective viewport options.

both the perspective and orthographic viewports to ensure your visibility settings match mine so that what you see in your viewports matches what's shown in the figures in this chapter. To access these options, click the Viewport Options button in the Viewport toolbar. Then, in the menu that appears, ensure that the checkmarks selected match mine, as shown in Figure 2.5 and Figure 2.6. (Figure 2.5 shows viewport options for perspective viewports; Figure 2.6 shows viewport options for Orthographic viewports.)

Note

Chapter 3, "UDK Fundamentals," discusses viewports and their options in further detail.

In addition to viewport options, also make sure that your general UDK Editor options match mine. This will ensure that all my instructions and comments will be relevant. To access the UDK options, shown in Figure 2.7, open the View menu and choose Preferences.

Note

At the time of this writing, the UDK supports both DirectX 9 and DirectX 11. Please be sure to select DirectX 9 instead of DirectX 11 from the main menu if your game is intended to support older graphics hardware.

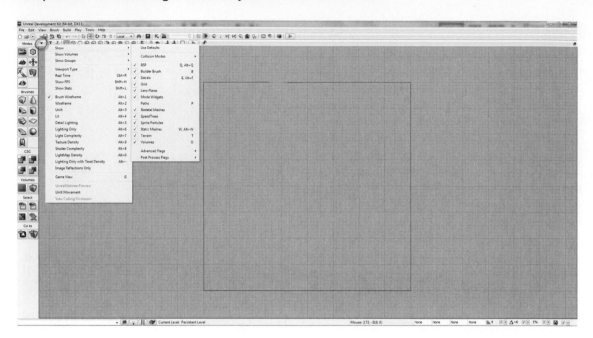

Figure 2.6
Orthographic viewport options.

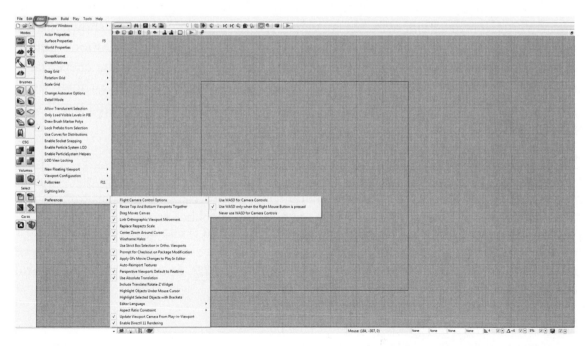

Figure 2.7
UDK options.

Configuring the Grid and Snapping

Each of the four viewports in the UDK Editor displays a grid by default. In short, the grid is a reference object that will appear in viewports at design time but will not be visible to the game camera when the level is played by the gamer.

Note

The details of the grid and its use are discussed in more detail in Chapter 3.

The grid serves at least three purposes:

- It can be used by the designer to measure distances and to understand size in the level in terms of Unreal world units, the UDK unit of measure.
- It can be used as a visual reference for precisely aligning, positioning, and scaling actors in a level, especially mesh actors.
- It can be used for *snapping*—that is, for locking or fixing actors in position exactly in line with the grid lines.

The grid and its snapping options are technically not essential for building a level in the sense that a level designer could make a level without ever once using the grid or snapping. However, both the grid and snapping options can make a level designer's work much easier and smoother in many different ways. For this reason, use will be made of these options, especially when scaling and positioning actors in a level. Before starting your level-creation work, you should set the grid and snapping options to starting values, although these values will be adjusted as your work proceeds.

To start, enable snapping for translation, rotation, and scaling operations. That means actors in the level can be moved, rotated, and scaled, respectively, in exact and specific increments in line with the viewport grid. To do this, check the Toggle Grid Snapping (to enable the snapping of translation operations), Toggle Rotation Snapping (to enable the snapping of rotation operations), and Toggle Scaling Snapping (to enable the snapping of scaling operations) checkboxes on the status bar in the bottom-right corner of the UDK Editor, as shown in Figure 2.8. Next, use the drop-down arrows to the right of each of checkbox to set its snapping increment. Set Toggle Grid Snapping to 4 units, Toggle Rotation Snapping to 6 degrees, and Toggle Scale Snapping to 5% (again, as shown in Figure 2.8).

CREATING AN ARENA WITH BSP AND CSG

At this stage, both the editor and viewports should be configured appropriately to begin the construction of the level. "Configured appropriately" in this case means that the three orthographic viewports show blueprint and wireframe style views of the level

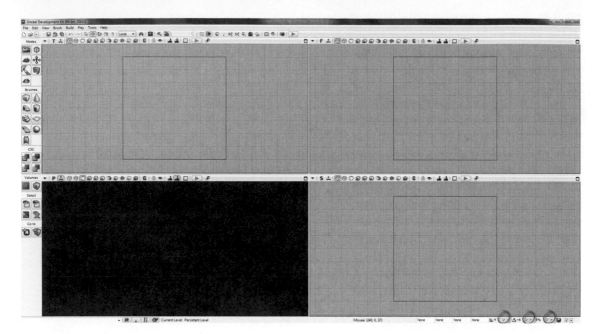

Figure 2.8
Grid and snapping settings.

from the top, side, and front perspectives, the Perspective viewport displays the level in a shaded mode and not a wireframe mode, and the grid is visible in all viewports. Furthermore, snapping should be enabled for translation, rotation, and scaling operations.

This section begins the construction of the level by detailing the creation of the walls, floor, and ceiling of the game environment. It is *not*, however, concerned with adding furnishings, such as doors, chairs, lights, machines, platforms, and other decorative and functional objects. Nor is it concerned with adding other kinds of actors, such as sounds, animations, and game logic. Important though these features are to the final level, they must come later.

First, the basics or the foundation must be put in place. The foundation in this case consists of the main architecture of the game environment. This environment will architecturally be a standard box room—that is, four walls, one floor, and one ceiling. This room will be created not in a third-party modeling program, such as Maya or 3DS Max, but in the UDK Editor itself, using BSP Brushes.

BSP stands for *binary space partition*. A BSP Brush is a tool for creating *constructive solid geometry* (*CSG*), which refers to any static 3D geometry—cubes, spheres, cylinders, planes, and other arrangements of polygons. The geometry created by the brush is said to be *static* because it can be neither moved nor animated. This has important implications. For example, if a level designer chooses to use a BSP Brush to create a wall in the level and later decides that the wall must be moved elsewhere, he or she will have to delete the original wall and replace it with a newly constructed wall in the new location. That's because the original wall—being static geometry—cannot be moved. Such a proviso need not trouble you unduly when using static geometry to create the game environment, as long as you plan your work in advance. Typically, walls, floors, and ceilings do not move once fixed in their correct places (although geologists, seismologists, and other authorities on the earth and the movement of continental plates could no doubt dispute this point). For the purposes of games, you can remain content with static geometry. Thus, the BSP Brush can and will help you create CSG for the walls, floor, and ceiling of the game environment.

Note

The BSP Brush and its details are the focus of Chapter 4, "BSP Brushes, the Builder Brush, and CSG."

Building the BSP Brush for the Arena

The polygonal geometry for the arena's walls, floor, and ceiling must be constructed from the BSP Brush tool. To do this, you must resort to the tools found in the Brush section of the UDK toolbox on the left of the editor interface (see Figure 2.9). Clicking any of the pre-defined shape options in the toolbox—such as the cube, cyl-

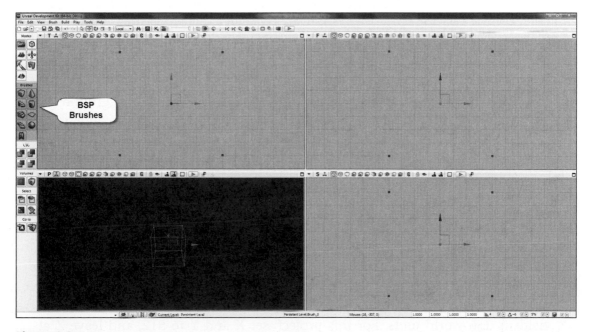

Figure 2.9
BSP Brush tools.

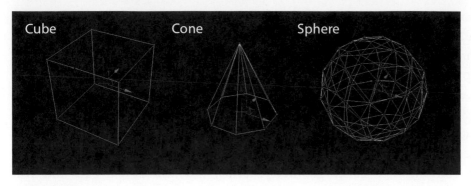

Figure 2.10
Common BSP Brush templates.

inder, or cone—will change the structure and shape of the BSP Brush accordingly in
the viewport. Figure 2.10 shows some of the common BSP templates.

Note

Changing the Builder Brush to any of the common primitive shapes does not automatically add geometry
to the level. It simply changes the shape and construction of the BSP Brush.

Note

The UDK usage of the term *cube* for the cube-shaped brush is not correct, mathematically speaking. The
mathematical definition of a cube states that a cube is a primitive with six sides, all of which are equal
in size. With the Cube BSP Brush, however, it is possible to size the brush differently in each dimension
and thus to produce a box shape that is not a cube. Nevertheless, this book will continue to use the UDK
term *cube* to refer to the Cube BSP Brush for reasons of clarity and consistency.

1. The arena to be created is a standard box shape: one floor as a ground plane,
   four walls surrounding the floor and perpendicular to it, and one ceiling plane
   on top of the walls and parallel to the floor. The room is therefore constructed
   from six adjacent planes or polygons. The most appropriate Builder Brush to
   approximate that shape is the Cube Brush. Right-click the Cube Brush button in
   the Brush section of the UDK toolbox. This opens a Brush Builder dialog box, in
   which both the shape and size of the brush can be customized (see Figure 2.11).

2. The Brush Builder dialog box enables users to customize the shape and size
   of the Cube Brush parametrically—that is, by typing in numerical values. The
   top-most values of X, Y, and Z correspond to width, length, and height, respectively, as measured in Unreal world units. The default value for all three of these
   fields is 256 world units. For this project, set X and Y to 512, and leave Z at
   256. This will maintain the height of the Builder Brush and thus the height of

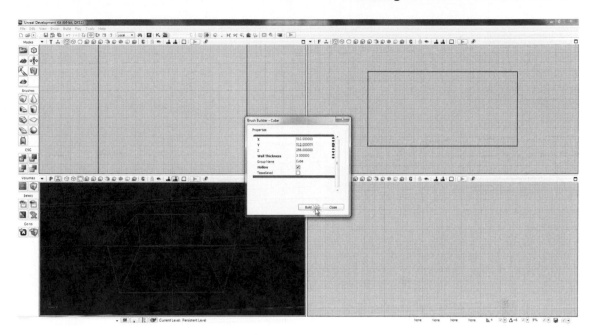

Figure 2.11
The Brush Builder dialog box.

the room, but change the width and length. In addition, check the Hollow checkbox to make the cube double-sided, and set the Wall Thickness to 3. The complete settings for this brush are shown in Figure 2.11. Finally, click the Build button to accept your changes to the brush settings. Note that this does not add any geometry to the level; it just accepts the settings for the brush.

3. Make sure the Builder Brush is selected in the Perspective viewport, if it is not already. To do this, click the brush wireframe in any viewport. Once selected, the brush changes color, and a multicolored transformation widget appears at the center of the brush. This widget looks like three perpendicular arrows of red, green, and blue. Press the Home key on your keyboard to center or focus all viewports on the selected object. The four-viewport layout of the editor should now look something like Figure 2.12.

4. Check the brush from all angles by rotating around it. To do this, hold down the L key on your keyboard as you press both the left and right buttons on your mouse. Then, slide the mouse left, right, up, or down to rotate around the brush in the Perspective viewport.

5. To create CSG from the brush, click the CSG Add button in the CSG section of the toolbox. When you do, polygonal geometry is added to the level in the shape of the Builder Brush. This geometry represents the room's floor, walls, and

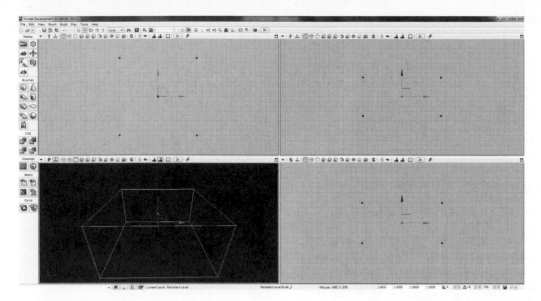

Figure 2.12
The BSP Brush, centered in the viewports.

ceiling. Notice that the newly generated geometry has a checkered appearance or material in the Perspective viewport, although it appears unshaded in the three orthographic viewports. The checker material is the default applied to the surface of all newly added CSG in the level. You can change it using the Content Browser, as you shall see. Notice also that the BSP Brush does not disappear from the viewport. It remains selected and can be used again. (See Figure 2.13.)

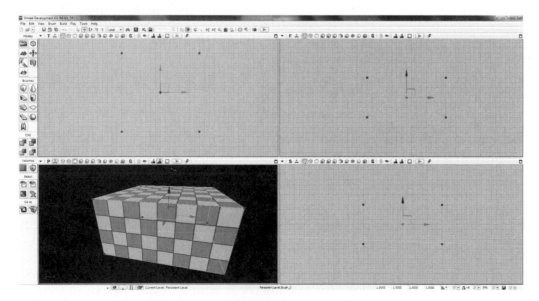

Figure 2.13
Newly created CSG for the arena.

Transformation and Navigating Viewports

Having the Builder Brush hang around in the viewport after generating CSG in the level can be useful for the designer, especially when the brush is intended as a template to be used more than once—for example, to create multiple rooms. In this case, however, you have created the one and only room you need. As it stands, the brush appears directly on top of the newly created CSG, making it difficult to distinguish one from the other in the viewport. To fix this, move the BSP Brush out of the way. Then jump into the Perspective viewport to take a first-person look around the level you have created so far.

1. Open the View menu and choose Preferences. From there, disable the Link Orthographic Viewport Movement option. (You'll learn more about this option later.)

2. Click inside the Top viewport. A yellow border should appear around its edges to indicate that it is activated.

3. Select the Builder Brush, if it is not selected already.

4. To move the brush in the level, use the transformation widget. (Remember, the transformation widget is indicated by the multicolored axes that appear at the brush's center when the brush is selected.) Ensure the widget is in Translation (move) mode by clicking the Translation button (the one with the crosshair icon) on the UDK toolbar, as shown in Figure 2.14.

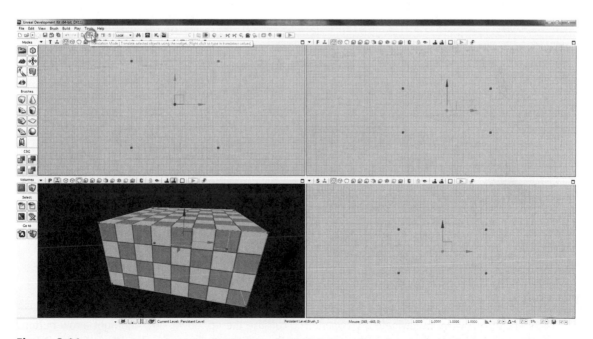

Figure 2.14
Switch the transformation widget to Translation mode.

5. While pressing the right mouse button, drag slowly inside the viewport to pan the view. As you pan, the cursor changes from the standard mouse pointer to a hand image. Pan the view to align the Builder Brush on the left side of the viewport, leaving empty space visible on the right. Panning the viewport in this way has the effect not of moving the brush in the level, but of moving the viewport or camera to bring other regions of the level into view.

6. The brush still appears directly on top of the CSG, making it difficult to distinguish between the two. To move the brush along the x axis into the empty space on the right side, move the mouse cursor over the right-pointing arrow of the transformation widget at the center of the Builder Brush in the Top viewport. The widget arrow changes color, and the cursor changes to a set of crosshairs like those in the icon for the Translation button. When this happens, click and drag the Builder Brush to the right edge of the viewport and away from the CSG, separating the two. (See Figure 2.15 and Figure 2.16.)

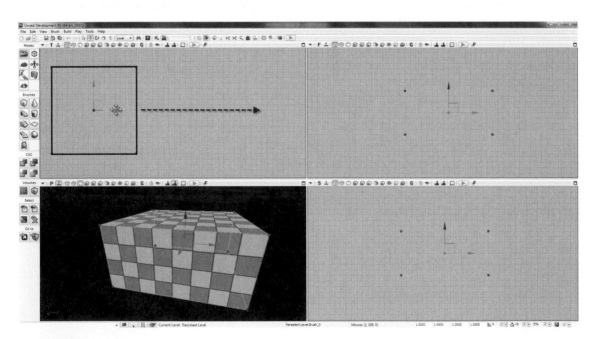

Figure 2.15
Moving the BSP Brush.

Viewport Navigation

There are several ways to navigate a viewport. You can use the up, down, left, and right arrow buttons on your keyboard to track and pan the viewport in the respective directions. (The W, A, S, and D keys perform the same panning and tracking functions as the arrow keys when the right mouse button is held down.) *Panning* and *tracking* are terms borrowed from cinematography. Both of them involve translation but not rotation. Stepping left and right are examples of panning, and sliding forward and backward are examples of tracking.

You can also hold down the right mouse button and then move the mouse to rotate the view to look in any direction. By combining these two techniques—using the arrow keys on the keyboard and the right mouse button on the mouse—you can simulate first-person controls in the Perspective viewport.

You can also navigate the viewport using mouse-only controls, if you prefer. Holding down the left mouse button and dragging will track and pan the viewport along the x and y axes. Holding down the left and right mouse buttons together while moving the mouse will raise and lower the camera along the z axis. (In the UDK, the vertical axis (up/down) is referred to as z, not y.)

The mouse scroll wheel can also be used to track forward or backward along the viewing direction. Try these viewport-navigation controls before proceeding with the rest of this chapter. It is recommended that you get to know these controls well. Table 2.1 summarizes the viewport-navigation controls.

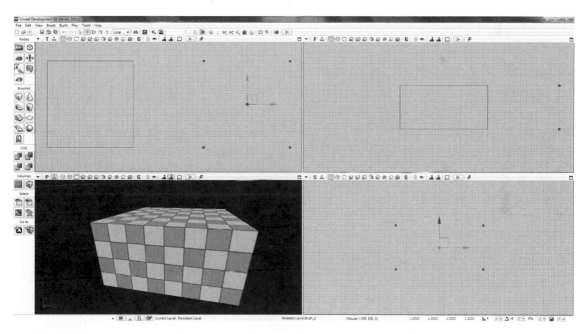

Figure 2.16
The BSP Brush is moved.

Note

The level created so far is in the companion files under Chapter2\DM-Void_Level_01_CSG.udk.

Table 2.1 Viewport-Navigation Controls	
Input	**Function**
↑ key, ↓ key, ← key, → key	Pan and track: Moves forward, backward, left, and right
W key, A key, S key, D key	Pan and track: Moves forward, backward, left, and right
Right mouse button	Rotates view on mouse move
Left mouse button	Pan and track: Moves forward, backward, left, and right
Left mouse button and right mouse button	Raises and lowers view along z axis
Scroll wheel	Tracks camera forward or backward

Creating a Hole in the Floor

The level created so far consists entirely of a hollowed 512 × 512 × 256 CSG box centered at the origin of the coordinate system. Together, the faces of this box represent the floor, walls, and ceiling of the main arena, inside which the game will take place. However, there is still something to be added to the architecture of the room. It was mentioned earlier in this chapter that there is to be a hole in the center of the floor that is initially covered by two sliding trap doors. When these doors are opened through the activation of a switch on the wall, the player and any enemies risk falling through the hole and into the void beyond and dying. The doors covering the hole will be added later as static mesh actors, but the hole itself can be created right here and now using BSP Brushes. This section explains how to do that.

1. Using the viewport-navigation techniques listed in Table 2.1, navigate the Perspective viewport inside the hollowed cube to get a clear view of the room within and its floor. See Figure 2.17 for an example.

2. The objective is to puncture a cylindrical hole in the center of the floor using BSP Brushes. To do this, click the Cylinder button in the BSP section of the toolbox; then use the mouse scroll wheel to zoom out in the Top viewport to get a better view of the cylinder-shaped Builder Brush in the level. Also examine the size of the cylinder brush from both the Side and Front viewports. It is likely to be too large for the hole in the floor. To reduce the size of the cylinder brush, right-click the Cylinder button in the BSP section of the toolbox to display the Brush Builder dialog box.

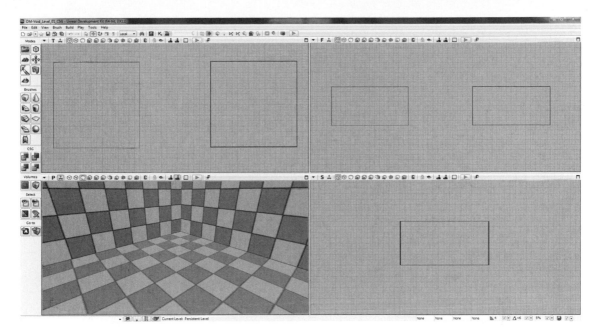

Figure 2.17
View of cube interior.

3. Change the settings for the cylinder to adjust its size. Change the Z (height) setting to 50, the Outer Radius and Inner Radius settings to 60, and the Sides setting to 8. Also ensure that the Hollow checkbox is not checked. Finally, click Build. The settings for the cylinder are shown in Figure 2.18.

4. The cylinder is now sized and configured to act like a cookie cutter for punching a hole through the floor of the level, but it is not currently positioned appropriately at the center of the floor. In the Top viewport, select the Cylinder Builder Brush if necessary; then switch the transformation widget into Translation mode by clicking the Translation button in the toolbar. Next, drag the cylinder to the center of the floor in the same way you earlier dragged the Cube Builder Brush away from the CSG in the preceding section. Notice that the transformation widget displays three axes as before: red, green, and blue. Experiment with dragging over each of these three axes to observe how the brush movement in the level is constrained along the selected axis.

Tip

If you are finding the transformation widget difficult to use, take a brief look ahead at the section "World Actors" in Chapter 3. It discusses the use of the transformation widget in more detail.

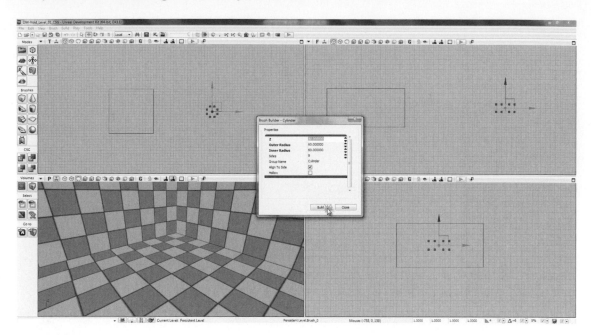

Figure 2.18
Configuring the cylinder size.

5. Use the transformation widget in either the Side or the Front viewport to move the Cylinder Builder Brush down into the floor of the level. The brush should intersect the floor so that the top of the brush is above the floor and the bottom of the brush is below the floor. See Figure 2.19 for the final arrangement of the Cylinder Builder Brush in preparation for cutting a hole in the floor. Do not forget to use the tracking and panning controls where appropriate to get a better view of what you are doing. Also, feel free to use the grid as a reference for center-aligning the cylinder to the floor in the Top and Side viewports, ensuring that there are an equal number of grid spaces on each side.

6. The Cylinder Builder Brush should now be positioned so that it intersects the center of the floor mesh. From here, the Builder Brush can be subtracted or cut away from the floor mesh, leaving a hole in its place. To do this, click the CSG Subtract button in the CSG section of the toolbox. The Cylinder BSP Brush is subtracted from the floor mesh, and the viewports update immediately to show the amended floor, complete with a hole. Move the BSP Brush away from the CSG to avoid confusion. (See the results of this operation in Figure 2.20.)

Note

The level created so far can be found in the companion files under Chapter2\DM-Void_Level_02_CSGHole.udk.

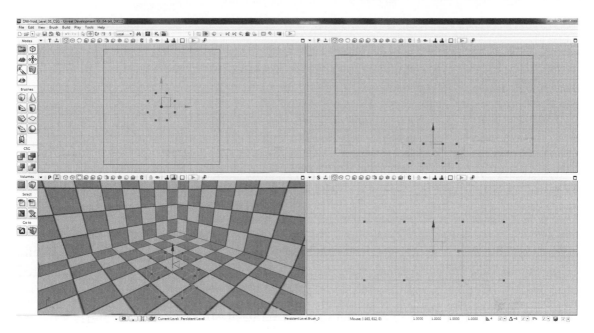

Figure 2.19
Positioning the cylinder in the floor. Note the use of the pan and track features in the viewports to get a clear view of the work in hand.

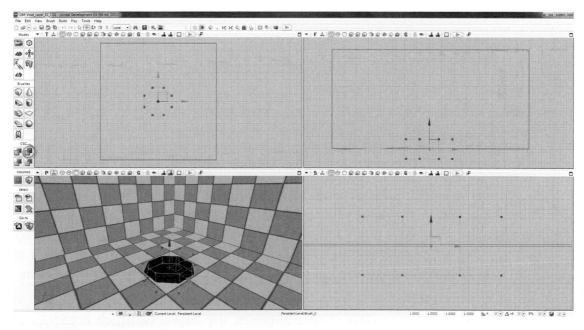

Figure 2.20
A floor with a hole. The Cylinder brush is subtracted from the floor mesh.

ADDING MATERIALS TO THE ARENA

The level now contains walls, a ceiling, and a floor, and the floor has a hole punched through its center. This stage of development marks the end of your BSP and CSG work. Nothing else in this level will require you to call upon the BSP Brush tools to model polygon geometry. The remaining geometry will be imported into the level as pre-constructed static meshes, as you shall see in the next section.

The focus of this section is to increase the realism of the level. At present, the surfaces of the arena's walls, floor, and ceiling have a default checker-patterned material applied to them. That is, they appear to be constructed from a synthetic set of checkered tiles. This material might be appropriate under some very specific circumstances—for example, if the designer intended to construct a Salvador Dali-esque environment. But in most cases, including this project, the checker pattern applied to the arena damages the realism of the level because the arena does not appear to be constructed from real-world architectural materials, such as brick, concrete, or wood.

You can address this issue by applying new materials to the arena. Materials define how the surfaces of meshes and other geometry appear under lighting conditions. They can be applied to actors in the level—such as the walls, floor, and ceiling of the arena—by a drag-and-drop method using the UDK Content Browser. The Content Browser is a specific kind of asset manager. That is, it offers designers a Windows Explorer–style interface for inspecting and selecting their game assets, including materials, meshes, sounds, particle systems, and more. Using the Content Browser, designers can view an ordered list of thumbnail previews for their assets and drag-and-drop those assets from the browser into the level. Let us now use the Content Browser to remove the checkered look of the arena by adding new materials.

Note

The Content Browser is discussed further in Chapter 3.

1. You can open the Content Browser in one of three ways. One is to open the View menu, choose Browser Windows, and select Content Browser (see Figure 2.21). Another is to click the Open the Content Browser button, marked with the Unreal Engine logo (a U shape) as shown in Figure 2.22. A third way is to press the Ctrl+Shift+F keyboard shortcut. (First make sure everything in the level is deselected by pressing the Shift+N keyboard shortcut.)

2. The Content Browser consists of several panes, the largest of which is the Asset pane. This pane contains thumbnail images of all available assets—that is, of all assets that have already been imported into the UDK toolset and are ready to

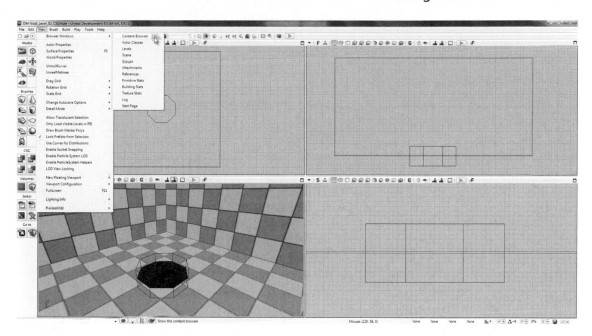

Figure 2.21
Accessing the Content Browser from the View menu.

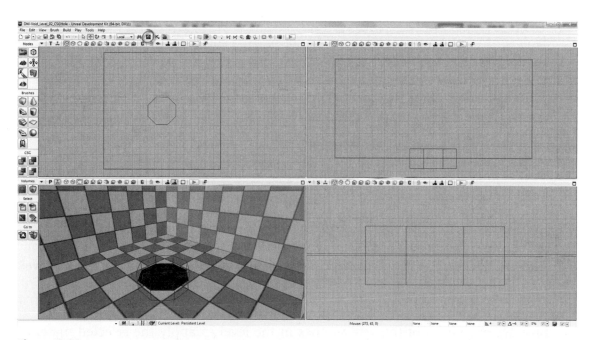

Figure 2.22
Accessing the Content Browser from the toolbar.

Figure 2.23
Filtering material assets.

drop immediately into the level. The top-most pane is the Search and Filter pane; it enables designers to filter or restrict the kind of assets shown in the Asset pane. To find a material for the walls of the level, click the All Assets button in the top-left corner of the Content Browser, beneath the Unreal logo. This ensures that all assets are visible in the Asset pane. Then check the Materials checkbox in the Search and Filter pane to filter the assets so that only material assets are shown. (See Figure 2.23.)

3. Type walls in the Search field in the Search and Filter pane to search available assets for those that are suitable for walls. Then select a wall material. I opted for the one named M_HU_Walls_SM_FlatWall, as shown in Figure 2.24. Feel free to select a different wall material from the Content Browser, should you prefer another style. There is no clear-cut right or wrong choice here. This is your level, after all.

4. Although you could simply drag and drop the material from the Content Browser onto each of the wall meshes in the level to apply the selected material to the walls, there is another option, described here. Close the Content Browser and click any of the walls in the level to select it. Then select all connected walls by right-clicking the selected wall and choosing Select Surfaces and then Adjacent Walls from the menu that appears (see Figure 2.25).

Figure 2.24
Finding a material.

Note

You can also select multiple actors in a level by holding down the Ctrl key on the keyboard while clicking them with the mouse.

5. Right-click any of the selected walls and choose Apply Material from the menu that appears. The material you selected in the Content Browser is applied with a default mapping to the selected polygons in the level. (See Figure 2.26.)

6. Mapping determines how the material is tiled across the surface of the mesh. In this case, the mapping is not suitable because the material is tiled for too many repetitions. This damages the believability of the level. To adjust the mapping of the walls, select all four walls in the editor (if they are not selected already). Then right-click any of the selected walls and choose Surface Properties from the menu that appears. The Surface Properties dialog box opens, in which the mapping for the material can be changed.

7. Use the Scaling options in the Surface Properties dialog box (see Figure 2.27) to adjust the tiling of the material. Click the Custom option button to select it, change the scaling in both the U and V fields to 2, and click the Apply button.

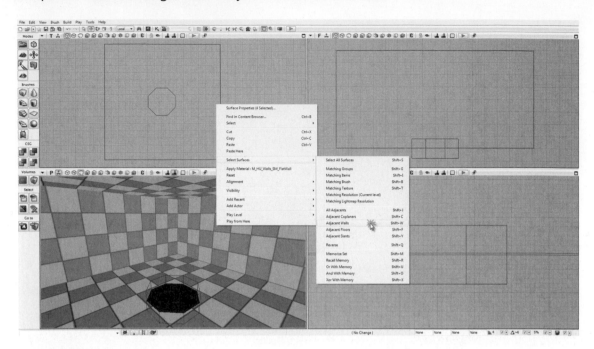

Figure 2.25
Quick-selecting all four walls.

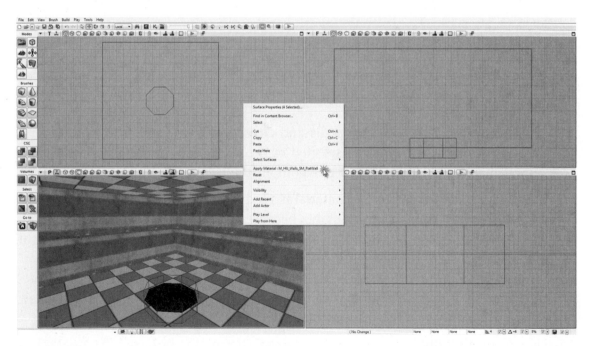

Figure 2.26
Applying materials to the walls.

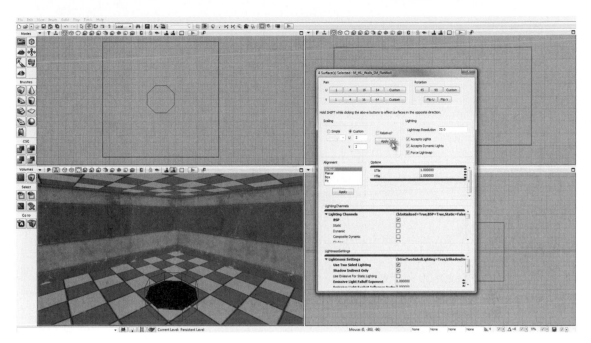

Figure 2.27
Controlling the mapping of the walls.

This scales the texture to twice its size horizontally and vertically, halving the tiling of the material.

8. It is now time to apply a material to the floor. Select the floor in the editor; then open the Content Browser. Next, type floor in the Search field in the Search and Filter pane. This restricts the Asset pane to show only those materials tagged as being suitable for flooring. Finally, select a suitable material from the list (I chose M_HU_Floors_BSP_Gray_Tiles) and drag and drop it onto the floor. The material selected in the Content Browser is applied to the floor, as shown in Figure 2.28.

9. Now for the ceiling. Navigate in the Perspective viewport to bring the ceiling of the room into view. Then select the ceiling in the editor and return to the Content Browser. This time, a floor material will be applied to the ceiling. Select a suitable material of your own or use my choice (M_LT_Floors_BSP_Reycle05). Drag and drop this material onto the ceiling in the level to apply it. Adjust the mapping if required using the Surface Properties dialog box. The essential architectural elements of the arena (its floor, walls, and ceiling) now sport new and more realistic looking materials. Take a look at Figure 2.29 and also take a tour around the Perspective viewport to see the results of your work so far.

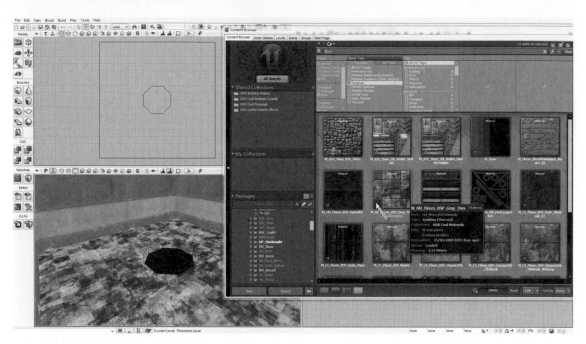

Figure 2.28
The floor material is applied.

Figure 2.29
The arena with materials applied.

Use the Restore and Maximize viewport buttons in the top-right corner of each viewport to get a larger and more immersive look at the contents of the level.

Note

The level created so far is in the companion files under Chapter2\DM-Void_Level_03_BasicMat.udk.

ADDING STATIC MESHES

You should now have a level constructed of CSG—specifically, walls, a ceiling, and a floor with a hole at its center. These components have also had materials applied to them to enhance the realism of the level—that is, to make them appear to be made from real-world building materials. The problem with the level at present is its emptiness. It has no props, furnishings, or objects to give it character and context.

The arena is meant to have a sci-fi/industrial theme. In such a setting, one might expect to see blinking computers, rusted machines, metallic fences and walkways, and electronic doors, among other similar mood setters. These sorts of objects must now be added to the level. They will be added as static mesh actors. The term *mesh* here refers to any 3D object or geometry that has been imported into the UDK from a third-party modeling package and is composed from vertices (the plural of *vertex*), edges, and polygons. Most objects in 3D games are meshes. A building might be a mesh or several meshes, a character might be another, as might a gun, a tree, and so on. The term *static*, when prefixed to the word *mesh* in the UDK, refers to any mesh whose structure—its vertices, edges, and polygons—are not animated. Examples of static meshes include statues, architecture, doors, tables, chairs, and windows, among others. Examples of meshes that are not static include human characters, flags and other cloth objects, jelly, alien slime, etc.

Note

Static meshes are examined in more detail in Chapter 6, "Building Game Worlds with Static Mesh Actors."

The static meshes to be added to this level will be taken from the default assets that ship with the UDK. These have already been imported into the UDK and are available from the Content Browser for dragging and dropping into the level, like the materials in the previous section. Feel free to drag and drop meshes of your own choosing into the level for decoration and stylization. The following steps however detail both my choices for the meshes and my reasons for choosing them.

1. Open the Content Browser and click the All Assets button in the top-left corner. Type `static meshes` in the Search and Filter pane's Search field to see only static meshes assets in the Asset pane. Be sure to remove any checkboxes from other filters, such as the material filter you checked in the previous section. (See Figure 2.30.)

2. Create a suspended walkway above the ground plane. The player will use an elevator to travel to this walkway, which will lead to a button on the wall that, when pressed, will open or close the sliding doors over the hole in the floor. (The doors themselves will be added to the level as static meshes in a later step.) To find the flooring for this walkway, check the Deco checkbox in the Content Browser's Search and Filter pane to limit the static meshes shown. These static meshes are labeled as "decorative" items. Scroll through the list until you find the static mesh named S_HU_Floors_SM_FireEscape_Straight256; then drag and drop this mesh into the level. (See Figure 2.31.)

3. A single instance of the fire-escape floor mesh is added to the level. It is aligned to the grid, but it is neither positioned nor scaled appropriately for the level.

Figure 2.30
Search the Content Browser for static meshes.

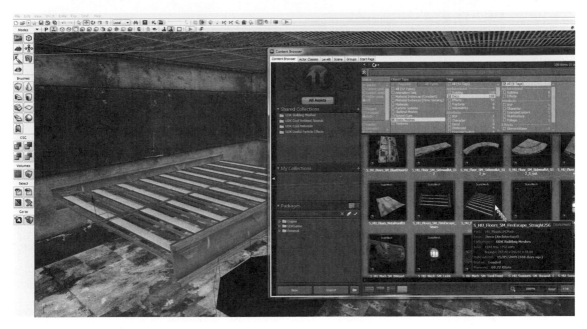

Figure 2.31
Find the walkway floor mesh and drag and drop it into the level.

The flooring is too large in terms of its width, length, and height—that is, too large in all three axes to be credible. To solve this, the overall size of the floor mesh must be reduced. That is, it must be scaled down by a specific scaling factor—in this case to half its original size in all three axes. To achieve this, select the floor mesh (if it is not selected already). Then type 0.5 in the DrawScale field in the UDK Editor's status bar in the bottom-right area of the screen (see Figure 2.32), and press the Enter key. This scales the floor mesh to half its original size. Fractional values in this field between 0 and 1—such as 0.5 and 0.25—reduce the size of the mesh, while values greater than 1 increase the size of the mesh. A value of 1 would have kept its original size, a value of 2 would have doubled its size, and a value of 4 quadrupled its size, and so on.

Note

The scale of a static mesh can also be changed through the mesh's Properties panel. To access this panel, either double-click the mesh or press the F4 key with the mesh selected. In the Properties panel, open the Display section and adjust the DrawScale decimal value to set the mesh scale.

4. Use the Move/Translation tool (click the Move button on the toolbar) to position the walkway mesh about halfway up the height of the room and flush against its corner, touching both the back and left walls. You can move, rotate,

Figure 2.32
Scaling the walkway mesh to half its original size.

and scale meshes in the level using the same transformation methods as with BSP Brushes. Do not be concerned in this case if parts of the walkway mesh—such as its corners—intersect the walls of the level. This will not affect the performance or stability of the game. The question is whether the arrangement looks acceptable to the eye. The Level Editor and its viewports are intended to give the level designer a reasonably accurate preview of how the level will appear to the gamer. For this reason, when positioning and orientating meshes, assume that if it looks acceptable in the viewports, it will look acceptable in the game. (See Figure 2.33.)

5. The walkway is positioned and scaled appropriately in the corner of the arena. The problem is, the walkway is not long enough to warrant its name. It should span most of the length of the arena, but it does not. It spans only a fraction of that distance, as can be seen in the Top viewport. There are at least two solutions to this problem. One is to scale or stretch the walkway mesh non-uniformly along its length until it is of the length required—that is, to scale it in only one axis. The chief disadvantage of this solution is that both the mesh and the pixels of its material will be scaled disproportionately, changing their appearance dramatically and for the worse. The other solution is to duplicate the walkway twice and to position and tile each duplicate flush against the previous

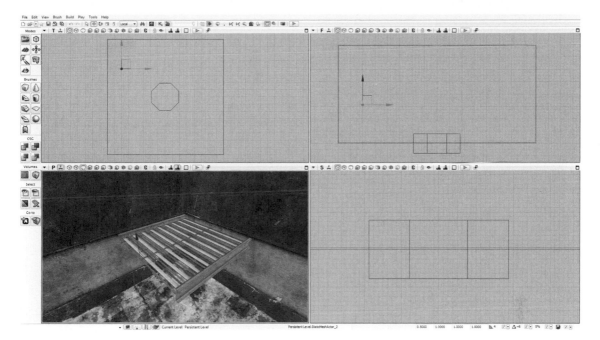

Figure 2.33
Position the walkway at the corner of the room.

one so that together, all three meshes create the appearance of one continuous walkway across the length of the room. To achieve this latter solution, select the walkway mesh and duplicate it once. (For help duplicating the mesh, see the upcoming sidebar.) Then, position the duplicate in front of the original so that their ends are touching. Next, duplicate again, and position this second duplicate in front of the first, again with their ends touching. (See Figure 2.34.)

Duplicating Meshes

Duplicating a mesh creates a new and duplicate instance of a mesh object in the level. The duplicate becomes a new actor in its own right and can be positioned, scaled, and rotated independently of any other actor.

The UDK Editor offers three methods for creating duplicates from a selected mesh actor:

- Open the Edit menu and choose Duplicate.
- Press the Ctrl+D keyboard shortcut.
- Press and hold down the Alt key on your keyboard while moving the mesh using the transformation widget. This will keep the original mesh in its existing position and will position a new and duplicate mesh in the area you designate.

6. The walkway now reaches across most of the length of the arena, thanks to the duplicate-mesh technique. However, a square gap should be left at one end to

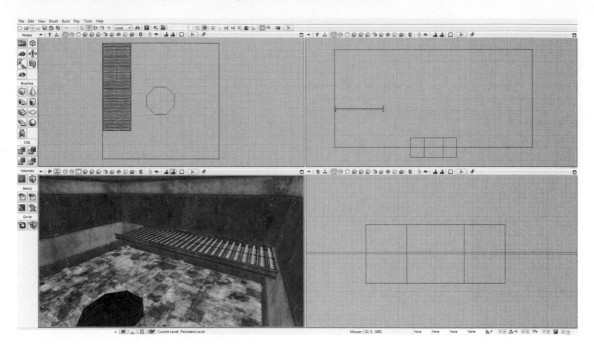

Figure 2.34
Using duplicates to add detail.

leave room for an elevator platform that will raise and lower the player between the ground and the walkway. (This platform will be added later in the chapter.) Here, you will add chain-link fencing on the long edge of the platform farthest from the wall to protect the player from falling off. To do this, type chain link in the Content Browser's Search and Filter pane; then drag and drop the chain-link mesh named S_HU_Deco_SM_ChainLink02 into the level, scale it uniformly to 0.5, duplicate it twice, and position all three instances along the length of the walkway to build the fence. (See Figure 2.35.)

7. The walkway leads to a wall-mounted switch whose purpose is to open and close a pair of sliding doors covering the hole at the center of the floor. The doors and the logic governing their behavior will be added later in this chapter using the Kismet Editor. For now, you will add the wall-mounted switch as a static mesh. To begin, filter the Content Browser for static meshes with the Deco tag and scroll the Asset pane for a mesh named S_HU_Trim_LowProfileE_corner. Then, drag and drop the mesh into the level and size it appropriately using the scaling tools, if required. Use a combination of both the Translate and Rotation tools to position the mesh on the far wall of the walkway. Note that pressing the spacebar with the mesh selected in the level will cycle you among the Translate, Rotate, and Scale modes. See Figure 2.36 for reference.

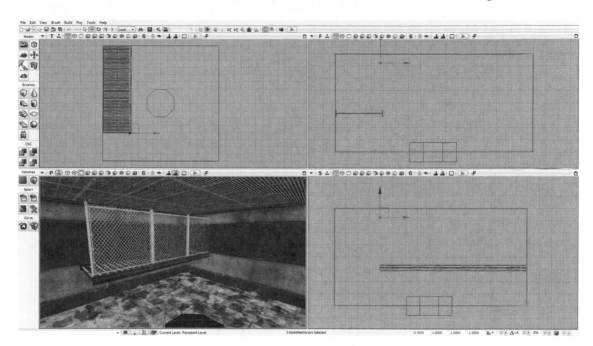

Figure 2.35
Creating the chain-link fence.

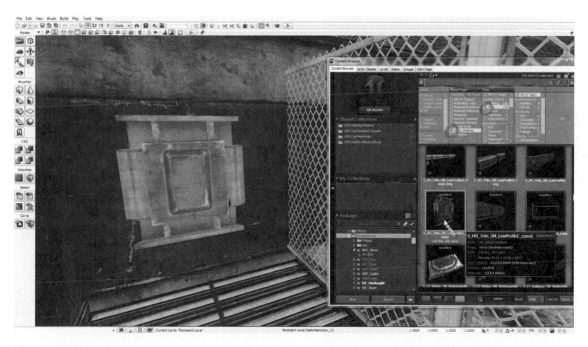

Figure 2.36
Adding a switch to the walkway.

8. Use the Content Browser to place the remaining static meshes in the level. These include the pipe (S_HU_Deco_Pipes_SM_PipeSet_B05), tanks (S_HU_Deco_StorageTanks_03), machine (S_HU_Deco_SM_HydraulicSupport_C), wall lights (S_HU_Light_SM_WallLight01), and swirling portal meshes (S_NEC_Base2_SM_Vortex), as shown in Figures 2.37 through 2.41. Each should be positioned, sized, and duplicated appropriately using the techniques mentioned

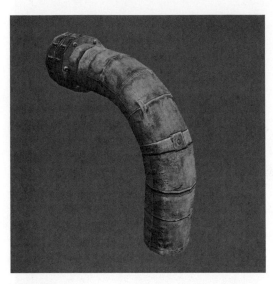

Figure 2.37
The pipe mesh, duplicated and added to the far wall.

Figure 2.38
The tanks, added beneath the walkway.

previously in this section. Figure 2.42 shows the level after all the meshes have been added.

Note

The level created so far can be found in the companion files under Chapter2\DM-Void_Level_04_ StaticMeshes.udk.

Figure 2.39
The machine, added opposite the tank.

Figure 2.40
The wall lights, duplicated across all four walls.

Figure 2.41
The swirling portal, added to mark the player's start location.

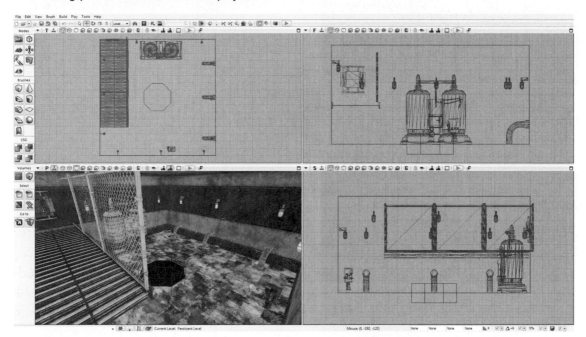

Figure 2.42
The level after all static meshes have been added.

ADDING LIGHTS

The arena created so far features no lighting at all, except for the default lighting provided by the UDK Editor to help level designers see the contents of their level in the viewports. Lighting is critically important in a UDK level. To demonstrate why, I

Figure 2.43
Testing the level.

encourage you to test-play the level so far to observe how it appears without lighting—that is, to preview the level in the editor from the perspective of the gamer and play it as though it were final. To do so, right-click the arena floor in the Perspective viewport and choose Play from Here in the menu that appears (see Figure 2.43). This launches the level in a separate window in game mode, with the player appearing in the spot you right-clicked.

As you can see, the level is almost entirely black, due to the absence of lights in the scene. There are some exceptions, such as the Unreal Console, which prints an error message on the screen. In addition, some meshes might be visible due to special properties that exempt them from lighting calculations. But most of the level, including the floor, walls, and ceiling, are lost in total darkness, as shown in Figure 2.44. Without a light source in the level, there is no light cast to make things visible to the eye. The primary lesson to be learned here is that levels without lighting will typically produce a flood-filled black screen when played by the gamer. Close the window containing the playable level by clicking the Close button in its upper-right corner. This will return focus to the UDK Editor.

Your next step in creating the level, then, is to add lighting. Here, you'll use the UDK Editor to drag and drop lights into the scene and to configure some basic lighting properties to get your lighting up and running.

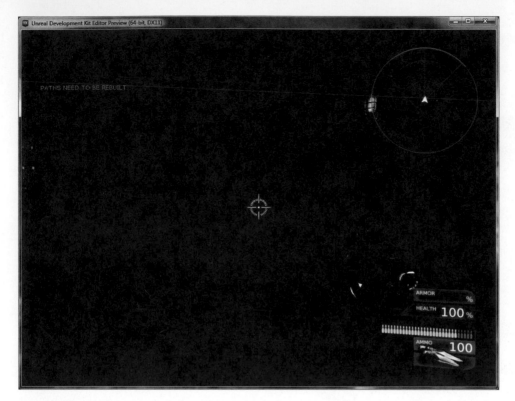

Figure 2.44
Test-playing a level without lights.

Note

The UDK supports an indirect-illumination lighting model, called Lightmass. Using the Lightmass system to light your level is processor intensive, requiring both time and system resources to calculate the final lighting model of the level. Lighting calculations—such as shadow and occlusion—are made on the basis of the static meshes in the level and on their orientation, scale, and position. That means lighting must be recalculated whenever the state of the meshes in the level changes. To avoid unnecessary and repetitious calculations, designers typically set up lighting toward the end of level creation, after the position, scale, and orientation of static meshes have been finalized. The workflow for the level created in this chapter does not entirely abide by that rule; this is partly to demonstrate how lighting can be calculated and recalculated as well as the benefits of calculating lighting later rather than sooner.

1. The UDK offers three basic light types: the *point light*, for simulating light bulbs and other lights that cast illumination in a spherical pattern; the *spotlight*, for lights casting illumination in narrow cones; and the *directional light*, for large light sources, such as the sun, that cast a sheet of light in a single direction. This level will use point lights only. To access point lights for dragging and dropping into the level, open the Content Browser and click the Actor Classes tab. The

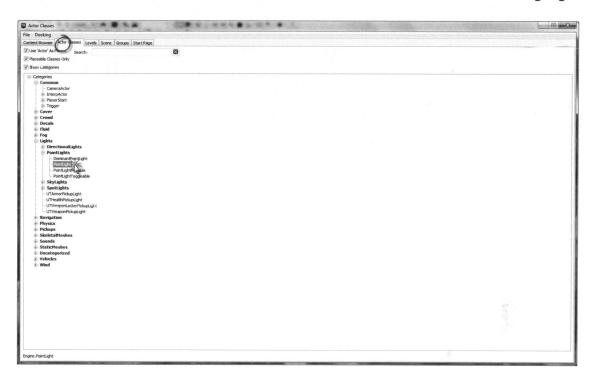

Figure 2.45
Finding lights in the Actor Classes Browser.

Actor Classes Browser opens; in the tree view, click Lights and then Point Lights to find the point lights available (see Figure 2.45).

2. The level created so far features duplicated meshes on the walls that represent lights in the arena. These duplicates are based on the template mesh named S_HU_Light_SM_WallLight01. As you have seen, the meshes themselves do not actually emit light in the level. That's because meshes are not recognized as light sources in the UDK. The next step, then, is to configure point-light actors in the level over the light meshes on the walls to simulate the light that those meshes would cast if they were real light sources. Start by dragging the point-light item from the Actor Classes Browser to the Perspective viewport. This creates a point-light actor in the level, which will appear as a large letter S surrounded by a sphere widget. In addition, as the editor detects the addition of a light, it switches the Perspective viewport from unlit mode to lit mode, displaying the level with preview lighting—that is, a rough estimation of how the lighting will appear when it is fully calculated using Lightmass (see Figure 2.46). You can toggle between unlit and lit mode by clicking the Unlit Mode and Lit Mode toolbar buttons, as shown in Figure 2.47, or by pressing the Alt+3 or Alt+4 keyboard shortcut for unlit mode and lit mode, respectively.

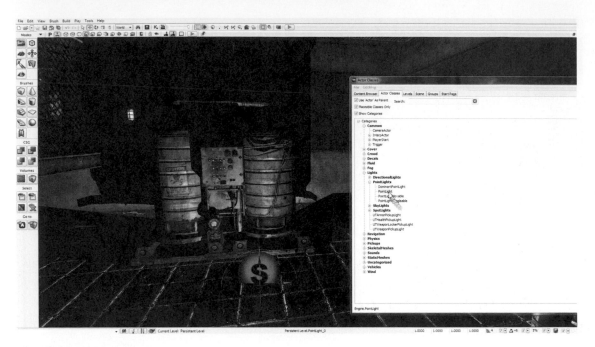

Figure 2.46
Adding a light to the level.

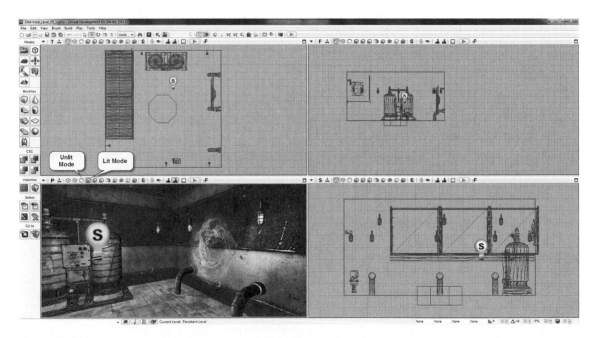

Figure 2.47
Changing between unlit mode (Alt+3) and lit mode (Alt+4).

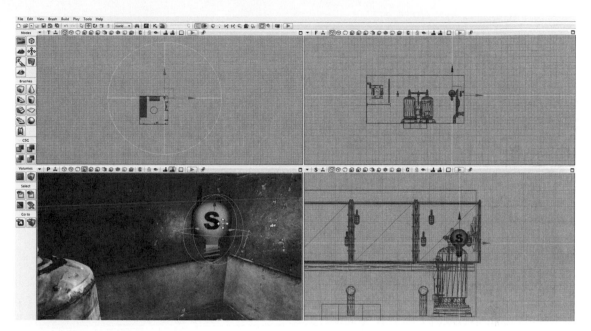

Figure 2.48
Positioning a point light inside a light mesh.

3. Use the transformation widget to position the point light inside one of the light meshes on the wall (see Figure 2.48).

4. Note that the center of the point-light sphere widget marks the source of the light—that is, the point from which illumination emits. A point light casts linear rays of light in all directions throughout its sphere of influence. Zoom out in the Top viewport to see the blue sphere surrounding the light, marking its sphere of influence. The light rays of the point light do not stretch beyond the sphere. Here, the light's sphere of influence is too large, almost encompassing the entire level. The size of the sphere must be reduced. To fix this, begin by displaying the light's Properties dialog box (see Figure 2.49) by first selecting the light in the viewport and then pressing the F4 key on the keyboard or right-clicking light and choosing Properties from the menu that appears.

5. To reduce the radius of the light's sphere to limit the light's range, click Light, Light Component, and then Point Light Component; then adjust the Radius setting, which controls the radius of the light's sphere of influence. You can enter a numerical value directly into the Radius field or drag the scrollbar to adjust the sphere size. As shown in Figure 2.50, I set the radius to 351 world units.

6. In addition to adjusting the radius of the point light's sphere of influence, you must change the color of the light to resemble the yellowish hue of a standard

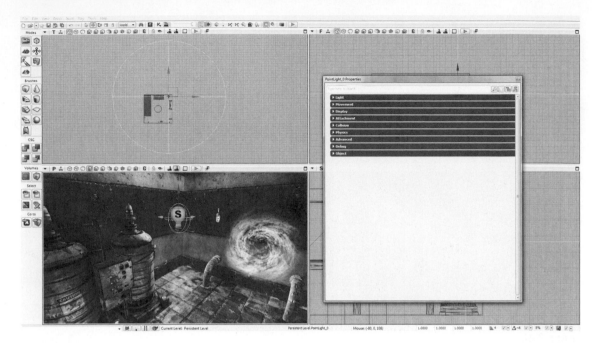

Figure 2.49
The light's Properties dialog box.

Figure 2.50
Set the point-light radius.

Figure 2.51
Set the point light's color and brightness.

tungsten bulb. To do so, click the Light Component sub-entry under the main Light Component entry in the Properties dialog box. Enter the value of 0.8 in the Brightness field; then click the color swatch to open the Select a Color dialog box. Change the color of the light to a tungsten yellowish hue, entering 0.99 in the R field, 1.00 in the G field, and 0.87 in the B field, as shown in Figure 2.51. When you're finished, click the OK button.

7. Because the point light is inside rather than outside the light mesh, its light-casting properties are diminished by the containing polygons of the light mesh. In addition, because the light meshes on the wall represent the level's source of illumination, they are not likely to cast shadows, nor be obscured by them. To address these issues, you must adjust the light meshes' shadow-casting properties. Begin by Ctrl-clicking each light mesh in the level to select them all. Then, with all the light meshes selected, press F4 to show a Properties dialog box for all the selected objects. In the Properties dialog box, click Static Mesh Actor, click Static Mesh Component, and then click Lighting. Then uncheck the Cast Shadow, Cast Dynamic Shadow, and Cast Static Shadow checkboxes, as shown in Figure 2.52.

8. Duplicate a point light from the original for each additional light mesh in the level using any of the aforementioned duplicate techniques. Position each

Figure 2.52
Disable shadow-casting settings for light meshes.

duplicate inside a unique light mesh so that it has one point light inside. This configures the lighting for the level. Figure 2.53 shows the arrangement of point lights across the level.

9. The lighting configuration in the level is now final in the sense that no further lights will be added and none of the existing lights will be tweaked in terms of position, size, or brightness. For this reason, now is an appropriate time to start thinking about building the final lighting of the level using the UDK's Lightmass system. This will transform preview lighting into final, high-quality lighting by way of further calculations to account for a lighting phenomenon called global or indirect illumination. However, to build the final lighting, more must be done in the way of preparation. Specifically, a light importance volume must be created. Here, the Builder Brush will be used to create an invisible volume surrounding the entirety of the level. *Invisible* is used here to mean that the created volume will be seen in the editor at design time but will not be seen in game mode by the player. The purpose of the volume is to focus the attention of Lightmass so that its calculations are based on only the essential effects of light within the level and not on those beyond the level boundaries. In short, the light importance volume ensures that Lightmass does not waste time and processing power calculating lighting effects in regions of the level that cannot

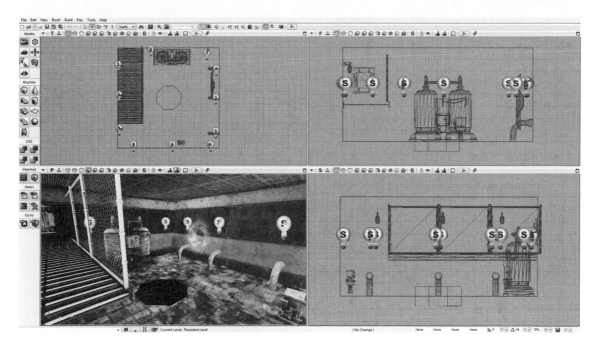

Figure 2.53
The final point-light configuration in the level.

and will not be seen by the gamer. To create a light importance volume, select the BSP Brush tool and create a cube that completely contains the level, as shown in Figure 2.54.

10. The BSP Brush is now configured as the template from which a light importance volume will be constructed. To construct it, right-click the Add Volume button in the Volumes section of the toolbox and choose Lightmass-ImportanceVolume from the menu that appears, as shown in Figure 2.55.

11. Click the Build All button to build the lighting in the level (see Figure 2.56). Then go take a tour of your level!

Note

As shown in Figure 2.57, clicking the Build All button might produce an error message that lists build errors—that is, errors found by the UDK compiler while building the level. Some of these errors might mention the absence of a player start location and a KillZ plane. For now, these can safely be ignored.

Note

Remember, changing the position and properties of lights and/or meshes in the scene after a build will require the level to be re-built.

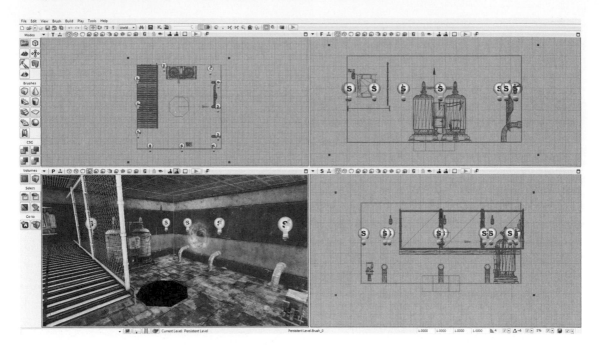

Figure 2.54
Build a BSP Brush containing the level.

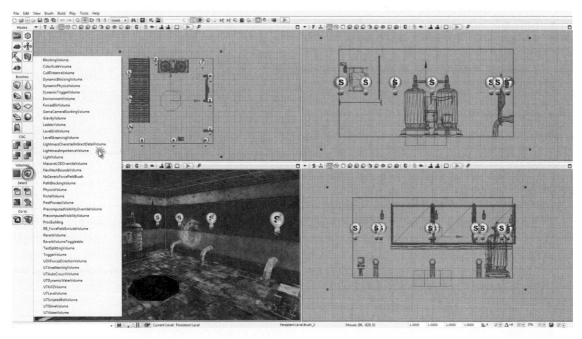

Figure 2.55
Adding a light importance volume from a BSP Brush.

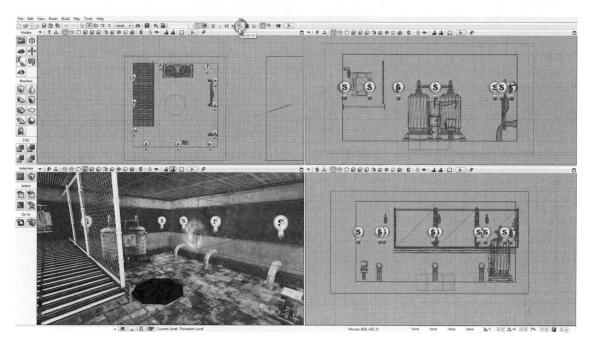

Figure 2.56
Click Build All to generate final lighting.

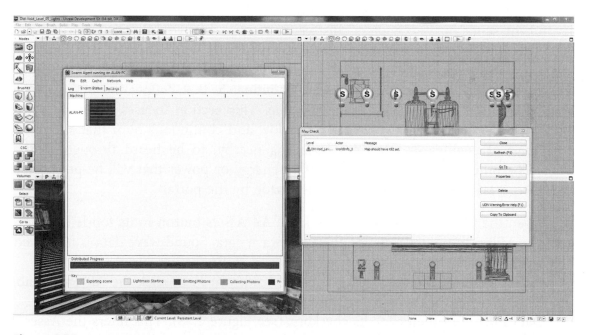

Figure 2.57
The Lightmass window and error dialog box.

Note

The level created so far is in the companion files under Chapter2\DM-Void_Level_05_Lights.udk.

Note

The subject of lighting and its application in the Unreal Engine requires much discussion and explanation. This is reserved for Chapter 8, "Lighting."

ADDING SOUNDS

As mentioned, *sound* refers to any audible content in a level, from door-open sound effects to full musical scores. Those who have taken the level for a test-play will no doubt have found that the level already contains a selection of sound effects—specifically, a gunshot sound played whenever the user fires a weapon, footstep sounds played as the gamer moves the game character, and breathing and bumping sounds played as the player runs, jumps, and falls. These sounds were not added manually via the Content Browser, but were included as defaults by the UDK from the moment you began developing the level.

You can remove these default sounds from the level, but doing this requires work beyond the scope of this chapter. This section focuses on using the Content Browser to add sound effects to complement the defaults already present. Sounds in the UDK work similarly to lights in that each sound has a position in 3D space and a set of properties applied to it, such as a sphere of influence that defines the range of the sound as well as a volume or intensity value. This section focuses on adding two sounds to the level created so far. One is a low and continuous hum that simulates the sound of engines or machines operating nearby, to be heard throughout the arena. The other is the ethereal sound of an energy or power that will be positioned over the portal mesh to simulate the noise made by the portal.

1. Open the Content Browser and click the All Assets button in its top-left corner. Then filter the Asset pane for all sound wave data. Sound wave data is not listed with the other filters—such as materials and static meshes—in the Favorites section of the Search and Filter pane. Instead, you must click the All Types tab next to the Favorites tab, scroll the list that appears to locate the Sound Wave Data filter, and then click its checkbox (see Figure 2.58). This filters the Asset pane to show only sound wave data—that is, sound assets. Figure 2.59 demonstrates how to do this.

2. Type `machine` in the Content Browser's Search and Filter pane to limit the sound-wave assets shown. Then select the Machine_Engine01 sound asset (see

Figure 2.58
Filter the Asset pane for sound wave data.

Figure 2.59) and drag and drop it into the level, positioning it at the center of the arena. Next, test-play the level to hear the sound played in-game.

3. Next, add the sound for the portal. Type `portal` in the Content Browser's Search and Filter pane. Then select the Portal_Loop01 sound asset (see Figure 2.60) and drag and drop it into the level. Position the sound over the portal mesh at the corner of the level.

4. Select the portal sound in the level (if it is not selected already) and press the F4 key to display its properties. Zoom out in the Top viewport to see the blue outline for the sound's sphere of influence. The sound is located at the sphere center, and its volume falls off from the center to the circumference of the sphere. That is, the sound is set to 100% at the center and to 0% at the circumference. At present, the range of the sound is larger than the size of the level, meaning the sound can be heard throughout the level. To tweak the sound so that it can be heard only when the player is standing close to the portal, click Ambient Sound Simple in the Properties dialog box, click Ambient Properties, and click Attenuation. Then change the Radius Min setting to 100 and the Radius Max setting to 200 (see Figure 2.61). Test the level; the portal sound should now fall off into silence as the player steps away from the portal.

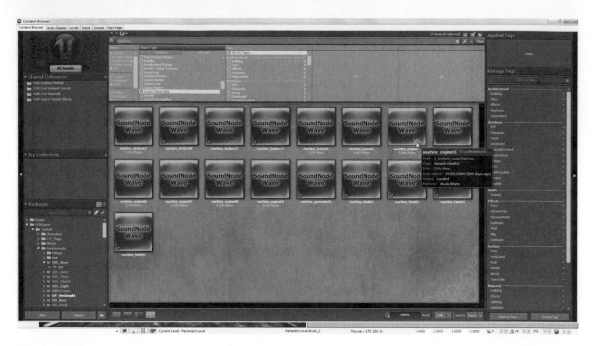

Figure 2.59
Select the repeated engine sound.

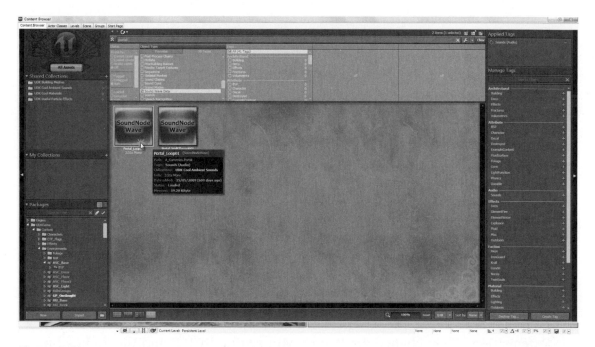

Figure 2.60
Select the portal sound.

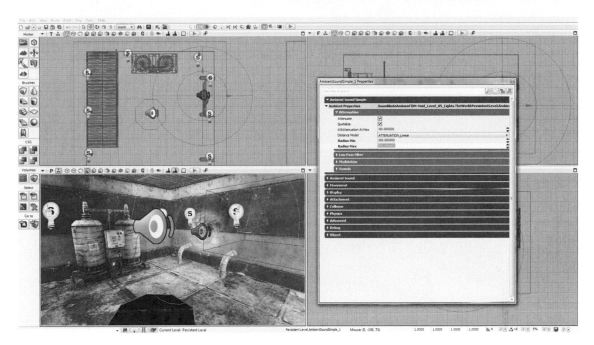

Figure 2.61
Set the portal-sound falloff.

Note

The level created so far is in the companion files under Chapter2\DM-Void_Level_06_Sounds.udk.

PLAYERSTART, KILLZ, AND A BLOCKING VOLUME

This section examines various separate and miscellaneous issues pertaining to the level, namely the player's start location, the KillZ plane, and blocking volumes (also called *collision volumes*). Each of these is considered in turn, starting with the player's start location.

1. The player's start location is the 3D location in the level at which the player will spawn (begin) by default when the level is played. This location will always apply unless some other overriding position is explicitly specified. Until now, when test-playing the level, you could specify a start location manually in the viewport by right-clicking and choosing Play from Here from the menu that appeared (refer to the section "Adding Lights" for more information). If, however, you clicked the standard Play button on the toolbar, an error message would appear indicating that the level could not be started due to a missing player start location. It is now time to add that location. To do so, open the Content Browser and click the Actor Classes tab to open the Actor Classes

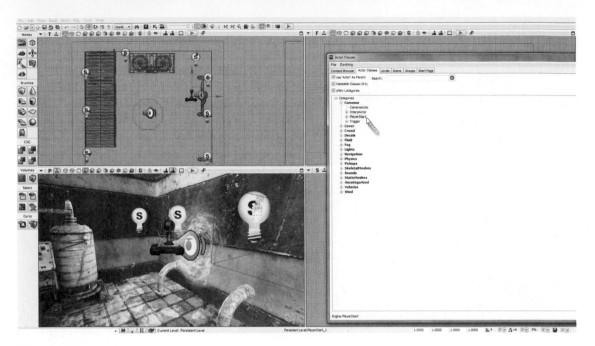

Figure 2.62
Creating a player start location.

Browser. Then click Categories, Common, and PlayerStart. Finally, drag and drop the PlayerStart actor into the level and position it in front of the portal, as shown in Figure 2.62. Give this a test run by clicking the standard Play button in the toolbar.

2. The KillZ plane is an infinitely wide 2D surface that marks the bottom-most extent of the level. It is not technically the same as the ground floor of the level, however, which is either a mesh or CSG and is visible. The purpose of the KillZ plane is to tell the UDK the universal y position below which nothing can exist. Anything in the level that hits or falls below the KillZ plane will be destroyed and removed immediately. The level so far does not have a KillZ plane. To witness the effects of its absence, start the level and fall through the hole at the center of the floor. When this happens, the player falls into a bottomless black pit, and the level will end only when you press the Esc key. Most level designers want to avoid the possibility of this type of infinite drop in levels where falls are possible. Thus, they will need to use a KillZ plane. To create one, zoom out in either the Front or Side viewport so the whole level is visible. Then open the View menu and choose World Properties (see Figure 2.63). The World Properties dialog box opens, displaying a set of properties that apply to the level generally.

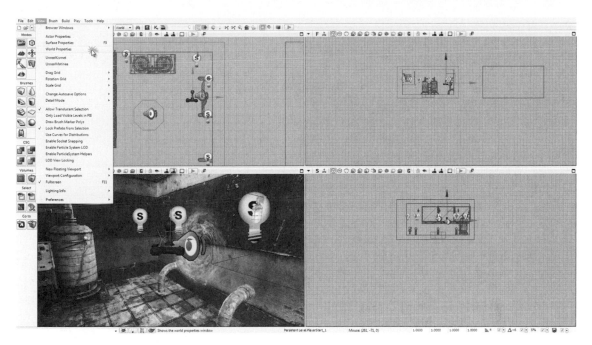

Figure 2.63
View the world properties.

3. In the World Properties dialog box, select Zone Info. Then use the up and down arrows in the KillZ field to adjust the position of the KillZ plane. The KillZ plane appears as a red line in the viewport; set it a little below the floor of the arena (see Figure 2.64). To test it, enter the level and jump into the hole in the floor. If the player dies soon after entering the hole, then the KillZ is set correctly in place.

4. A level might have none, one, or many blocking volumes. Each blocking volume marks a volume of space that is off limits to the player. That is, the blocking volume acts like an invisible wall or barrier to prevent the player from entering its boundaries during gameplay. The level in this chapter does not have a desperate need for a blocking volume, but I do want to include one around the portal mesh to prevent the player from walking through the portal. You create blocking volumes using the same method as that for creating light importance volumes. Start by creating a BSP Brush that surrounds the portal mesh, taking care to ensure that it does not also contain the player's start location. Then right-click the Add Volume button in the toolbox and choose BlockingVolume from the menu that appears (see Figure 2.65). A blocking volume now surrounds the portal and prevents the player from walking through it.

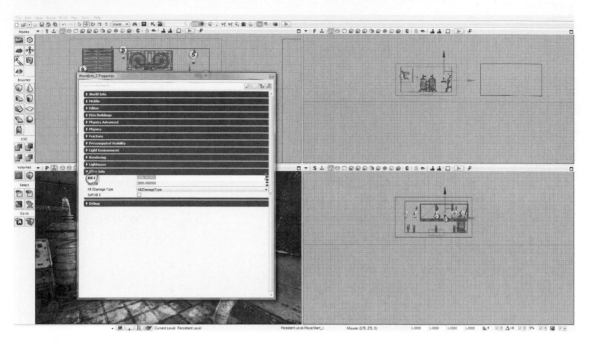

Figure 2.64
Setting the KillZ plane.

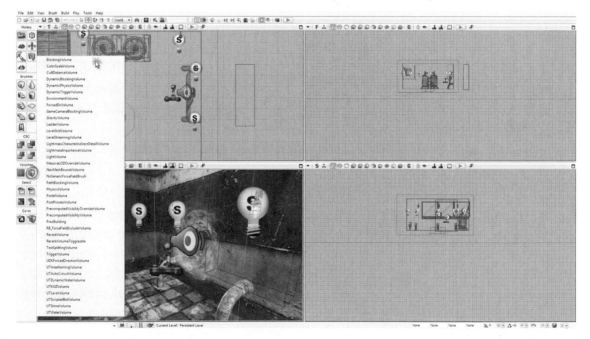

Figure 2.65
Adding a blocking volume.

Note

The level created so far is in the companion files under Chapter2\DM-Void_Level_07_Misc.udk.

VISUAL SCRIPTING WITH THE KISMET EDITOR

Before proceeding through this final section of the chapter, let's review what you have achieved thus far. At this stage, the level features many elements:

- CSG architecture for walls, a ceiling, and a floor with a hole at its center
- Static meshes for furnishings, machines, and special effects
- Lights for illumination and atmosphere
- 3D positional sounds to enhance the believability of the industrial/sci-fi environment
- A range of invisible but functional objects to define some behaviors in the level, such as a KillZ plane, a player start location, and a blocking volume

In summary, the level is completed except for one aspect: its underlying logic or rule set. The purpose of this rule set is to define the context-specific behavior and relationships of actors in the level.

As mentioned at the outset of this chapter, the player will be able to raise and lower himself or herself to and from an upper-floor platform by way of an elevator. Once on the platform, the player will be able to reach out and press a wall-mounted switch that opens and closes two sliding trap doors covering the hole at the center in the arena floor. From this description, at least two separate relationships between actors can be identified: the relationship between the elevator and the player actors and the relationship between the wall switch and the sliding trap-door actors. Neither of these relationships nor their attendant logic have been established or implemented in the level so far; it is time do so now.

At present, the level knows nothing about how these actors—the elevator, switch, and doors—are to behave. It does not know that the elevator (which you will add soon) should come into motion when stood upon by the player, or that the wall switch has any effect on the sliding doors (also added soon) at the center of the arena floor. To define their behavior, level designers can use either UnrealScript or the higher-level Kismet Editor, the latter being our choice in this chapter. So let's get started with the Kismet Editor and complete the level.

Note

Do not be concerned if the purpose of some or most steps in this section is not entirely clear or immediately obvious. There are many things to cover concerning the Kismet Editor and scripting; these will be detailed later in this book. For now, it is enough to follow the steps listed here to get a feel for the Kismet Editor and its workflow.

1. Before defining the logic for the level, both the elevator and sliding door meshes must be added. Add these now by dragging and dropping them from the Content Browser. Be sure to filter the Asset pane for static meshes and to position, scale, and rotate the meshes as appropriate. The elevator mesh used in Figure 2.66 was S_HU_Deco_SM_Metalbase01, and the mesh used for both sliding doors was S_HU_Doors_SM_BlastDoor02.

2. Right-click the elevator and choose Convert, then Convert StaticMeshActor to Kmover from the menu that appears, as shown in Figure 2.67. This converts the elevator mesh from a static mesh to a specialized version of a dynamic mesh. Put simply, static meshes are meshes that do not move during gameplay under any circumstances—for example, statues, walls, and lampposts. Dynamic meshes are meshes that can potentially move—for example, elevator platforms, doors, and cars.

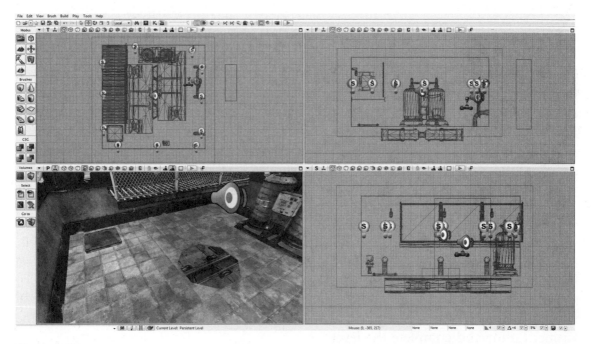

Figure 2.66
Add both the elevator and sliding doors to the level. Position the doors horizontally beneath the hole at the center of the floor. Remember to rebuild the lighting after adding the new meshes.

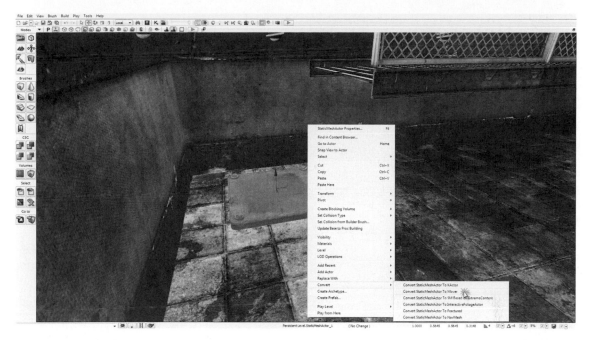

Figure 2.67
Convert the static elevator mesh to a dynamic mesh.

3. Select the elevator in the Perspective viewport (if it is not selected already) and press F4 to display its Properties dialog box. Then click Collision and, in the Collision Type drop-down list, choose COLLIDE_BlockAll (see Figure 2.68).

4. With the elevator selected, click the Open Unreal Kismet button (the green K button in the toolbar) to open the Kismet Editor (see Figure 2.69). You can also launch the Kismet Editor by opening the View menu and choosing Unreal Kismet. The Kismet Editor is used to create UnrealScripts via a mouse-driven graphic user interface.

5. You will use the Kismet Editor to define the behavior and logic for two different game elements: the elevator platform that will raise and lower the player to and from the upper platform in the level and the switch the player will use to open and close the trap doors on the floor. To start defining the behavior for the elevator, right-click anywhere in the Kismet Editor's Graph pane and choose New Event Using InterpActor_0 and then Mover from the menu that appears (see Figure 2.70). Two Kismet nodes will appear in the graph: InterpActor Mover and Matinee (see Figure 2.71). Notice that these two nodes are connected in the graph by wires. Specifically, the outputs of the InterpActor Mover node lead to the inputs of the Matinee node. Arrows on the wires indicate the direction of the connection or current.

Figure 2.68
Manually configure the collision information for the dynamic elevator mesh to make sure the player does not walk through it.

Figure 2.69
The Kismet Editor, empty and ready for work.

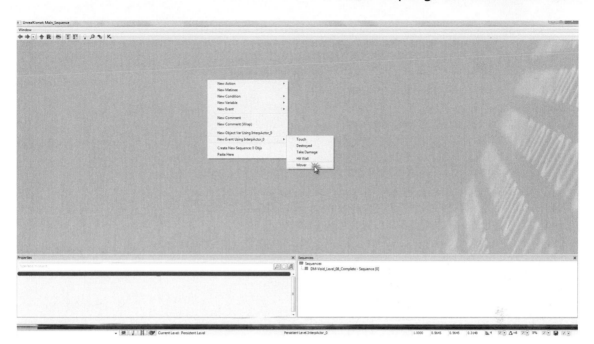

Figure 2.70
Right-click the Graph pane and choose from the menu that appears to create new nodes in the graph.

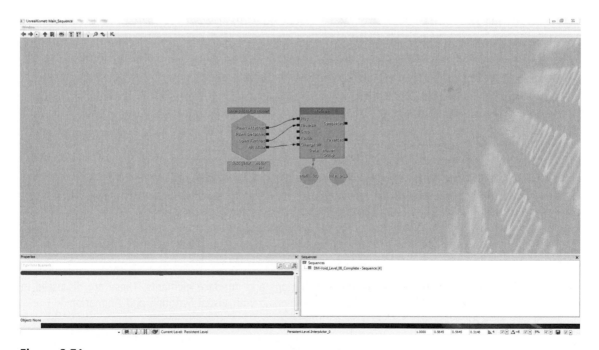

Figure 2.71
Mover nodes are added to the Kismet graph to define the behavior for a mover object in the level (in this case, the elevator). This graph contains two connected nodes: an InterpActor Mover node and a Matinee node.

Figure 2.72
The Unreal Matinee Editor.

6. The InterpActor Mover node in the Kismet Editor's Graph pane is an event node, and it is attached to the elevator mesh in the level. Whenever player-interaction events occur to the elevator mesh—for example, when the player stands on it—the corresponding event nodes in the graph are triggered. Information about the event leaves the event node via the output connection and travels to the input connections of any connected nodes, where the event is executed. In this case, when the player stands on the elevator, the InterpActor Mover node registers the event, after which the Matinee node is activated. The Matinee node defines the animation that must play for the event. In this case, the elevator must move either up or down, depending on its starting state. To create the elevator-up animation, double click the Matinee node in the Kismet Editor's Graph pane to open the Matinee Editor, shown in Figure 2.72.

Note

The Matinee Editor features a vast selection of buttons and interface elements. These are discussed in more detail in Chapter 9, "Kismet and Matinee: Beginning with Visual Scripting and Animation."

7. The elevator-up animation will be generated by the Matinee Editor on the basis of two key frames. The first key frame defines the position of the elevator mesh in its starting (bottom-most) state—that is, when the elevator is lowered

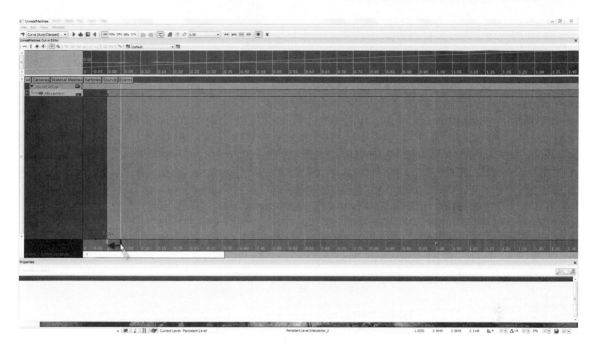

Figure 2.73
Creating the first key frame of the elevator-up animation.

on the ground. The second key frame defines the elevator position in its top-most state—that is, when the elevator is level with the upper platform. The Matinee Editor will then interpolate between these two key frames to produce an elevator-up animation. To define the first key frame of the animation, click and drag the Time slider at the bottom of the Matinee Editor timeline to the left-most position, at time 0 (animation start). Then press the Enter key on the keyboard to insert the first key frame of the animation at time 0, as shown in Figure 2.73.

8. Click and drag the red arrow at the end of the timeline toward the left to shorten the total length of the animation from five seconds to two seconds, as shown in Figure 2.74.

9. Drag the Time slider to the animation end time (at 2 seconds) and press the Enter key to insert the final key frame at the end of the animation, as shown in Figure 2.75.

10. Click the red arrow at the top of the timeline to select the second and final key frame. Then reduce the size of the Matinee Editor window and reposition it so that both the Matinee Editor and the Perspective viewport can be seen side by side. You should see the words UnrealMatinee in one corner of the viewport,

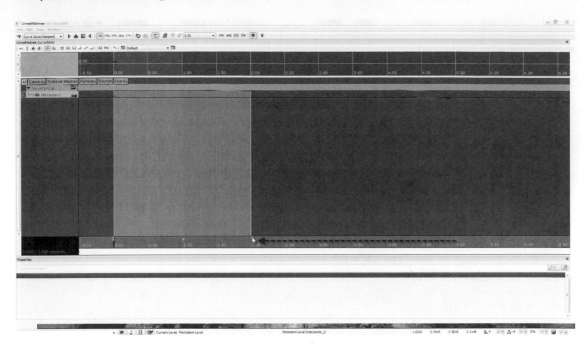

Figure 2.74
Drag the right-most marking arrow to adjust the end time of the animation.

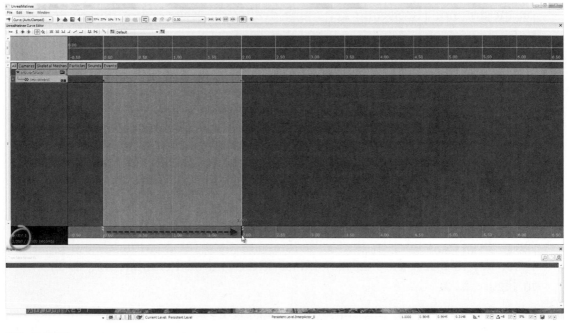

Figure 2.75
Set the second and final key frame of the animation.

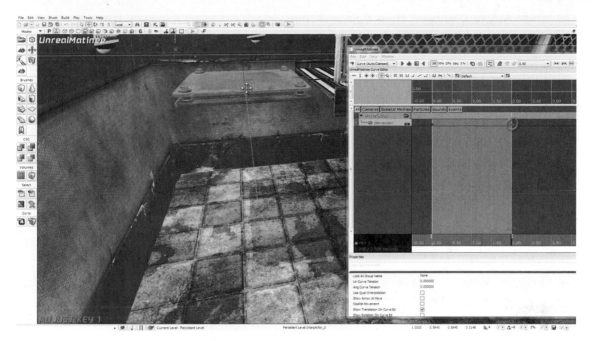

Figure 2.76
Select key frames using the key frame upper-arrow in the timeline. Move the elevator mesh in the viewport to record its position for the selected key frame.

and Adjust Key 1 in the opposite corner; these indicate that the Matinee Editor is in Record mode. That is, the Matinee Editor will record the position of the elevator mesh in the level and use it as the position of the elevator for the final key frame.

11. Use the transformation widget to move the elevator in the viewport to its top-most position, level with the upper platform. Notice the yellow line that appears in the viewport (see Figure 2.76); it represents the interpolated path the elevator will travel when the animation is played.

12. That's it—you're finished! Close the Kismet and Matinee Editors. Now the level contains an elevator that both raises and lowers appropriately when touched by the player. Try the level in game mode to see the elevator in action. Notice that you did not use the Matinee Editor to create an elevator-down animation. Instead, the Matinee Editor and Kismet automatically generated this animation by playing the up-animation in reverse.

13. The final task for this level is to define the behavior for the wall-mounted switch on the upper platform. When the switch is pressed, the trap doors on the floor should slide open or closed, depending on their starting state. To create the behavior for this switch, right-click a trap-door mesh in the Perspective viewport

and choose Convert, then Convert StaticMeshActor to Kmover from the menu that appears. Repeat this step on the other trap-door mesh. This will convert the static mesh actor to a dynamic mesh recognized by the Kismet and Matinee Editors—specifically, a Kmover dynamic mesh. Finally, select the doors and press F4 to open their Properties dialog box; then click Collision and change the Collision Type setting from COLLIDE_NoCollision to COLLIDE_BlockAll.

14. Before the switch behavior can be defined using the Kismet Editor, you must add a new, invisible actor to the level, called a trigger. A *trigger* is an invisible and cylindrical volume that is typically positioned near or around interactive elements such as switches to detect the actions of the player and trigger the appropriate event nodes in the Graph pane of the Kismet Editor. To create and add a trigger to the level, open the Content Browser and click the Actor Classes tab to open the Actor Classes Browser. Then click Categories, Common, and Trigger. Drag and drop the trigger actor from the Actor Classes Browser into the scene, and then position and scale it to contain the wall-mounted switch, as shown in Figure 2.77.

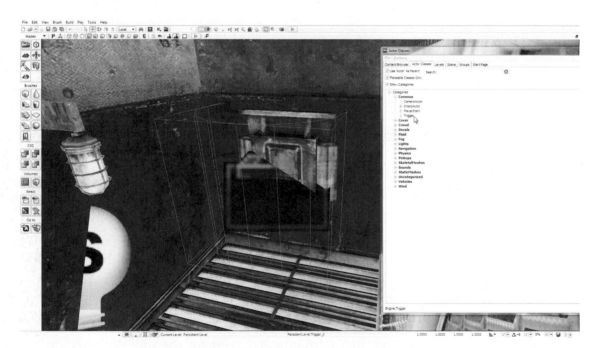

Figure 2.77
Triggers are volumes that surround interactive elements in a level, such as switches. Their purpose is to trigger events in the Kismet Editor's Graph pane when the player attempts to perform actions while standing inside the volume.

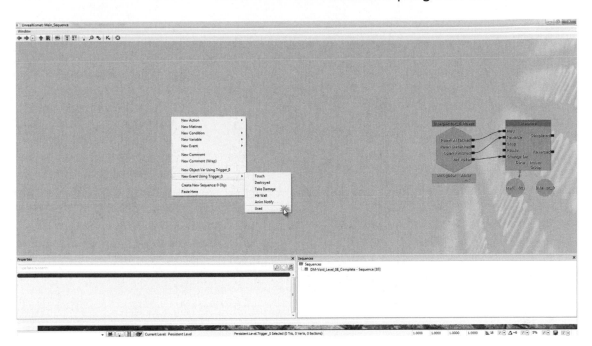

Figure 2.78
Creating a new Kismet event from a trigger in the level.

15. Select the trigger in the level, and then open the Kismet Editor. The Graph pane displays the Kismet nodes defining the behavior for the elevator. These can be ignored. Drag on any vacant space inside the Kismet Editor's Graph pane to move away from the existing nodes and to bring empty space into view. Then right-click this empty space and choose New Event Using Trigger_0 and then Used from the menu that appears (see Figure 2.78). This constructs a new Kismet event node that will be triggered when the player presses the action button (specifically, the E key on the keyboard) while standing within the volume of the trigger, close to the wall-mounted switch.

Tip

You can Ctrl-click and drag Kismet nodes to different positions in the Graph pane if required. This does not affect the logic of the sequence, but only the appearance of the nodes. It is good practice to arrange the nodes in such a way that sequences are easy to read and follow, as you shall see later.

16. Select the trigger event in the Kismet Editor's Graph pane and, in the Properties panel (found in the bottom-left corner of the Kismet Editor), under Sequence Event, change the Max Trigger Count setting to 0, as shown in Figure 2.79.

17. Right-click an empty area of the Kismet Editor's Graph pane and choose New Matinee from the menu that appears to create a new animation (see Figure 2.80).

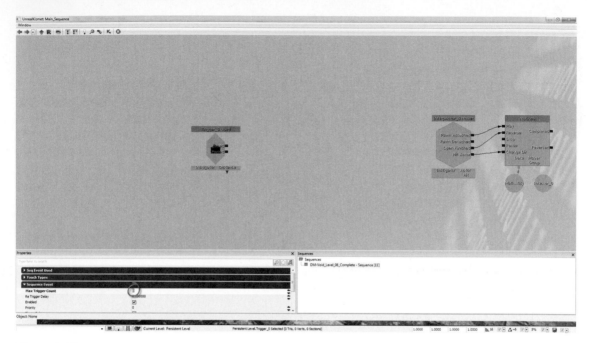

Figure 2.79
Change the Max Trigger Count setting to 0 to prevent the trigger from dying after one use.

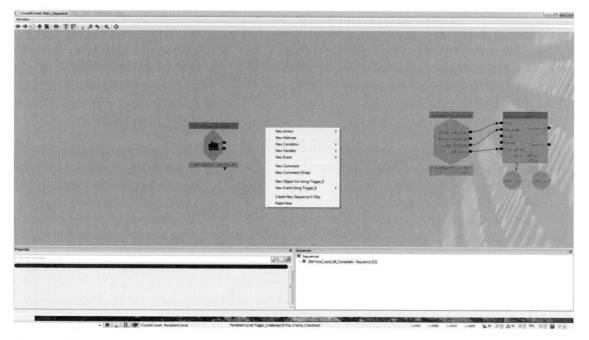

Figure 2.80
Create a new Matinee sequence.

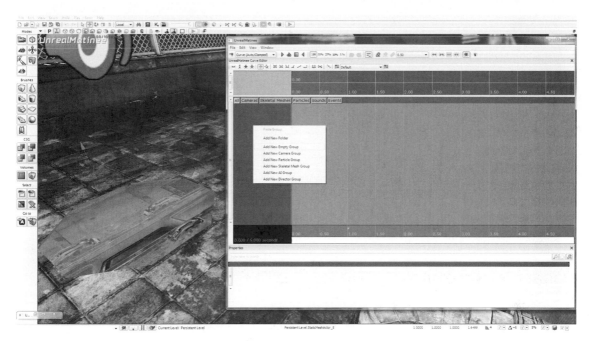

Figure 2.81
Create a new empty animation group for the selected actor in the scene.

18. Select one of the two sliding doors in the Perspective viewport; then double-click the Matinee node in the Kismet Editor's Graph pane to open the Matinee Editor. Then right-click anywhere in the grey column on the left side of the Matinee Editor and choose New Empty Group from the menu that appears (see Figure 2.81). Name the group Door01 and click OK to create a new animation group that will control the animation for one of the two sliding doors.

19. Right-click the new group and choose Add New Movement Track from the menu that appears (see Figure 2.82).

20. Repeat steps 18 and 19 for the second door. Both door meshes in the scene now have an associated Matinee group and a movement track to record their animation and key-frame properties (although no animation has yet been defined).

21. Each of the two doors will have one animation attached to its movement track. That is, there will be one animation for the left door and one for the right. Like that of the elevator, the animation for each door will consist of two key frames. The first defines the state of the door at the animation start (closed), and the second defines the state of the door at the animation end (open). The Matinee Editor will then interpolate a continuous animation between these start and end frames. To create the animation for the first door, begin by creating its first key

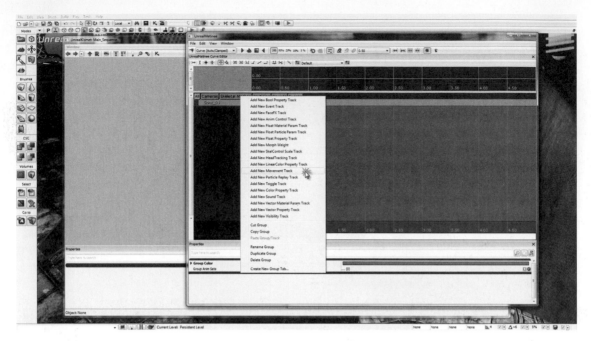

Figure 2.82
Add a new movement animation track to the empty group.

frame. Select the movement track in the Matinee Editor, drag the Time slider to time 0, and press the Enter key to insert a new key frame. Do the same for the movement track for the other door. (See Figure 2.83.)

22. Create a key frame for each door at the end of the animation by dragging the Time slider to meet the red arrow marker for the animation end and pressing the Enter key after selecting each movement track. Both doors now have start and end key frames, one end key frame per movement track.

23. Next, define the state of the doors on each final key frame, one door at a time. Select the final key frame on one of the movement tracks and move the door in the Perspective viewport to its open position. Then do the same for the other door. (See Figure 2.84.) The animation is created, and the Matinee Editor can be closed.

24. The animation for both sliding doors has been defined using the Matinee Editor. At present, however, the animation does not play when the gamer presses the switch on the wall because no relationship has been established in the Kismet Editor between the Trigger node and the Matinee node. The Trigger node is responsible for detecting when the player presses the wall-mounted switch, and the Matinee node is responsible for initiating playback of the animation. To

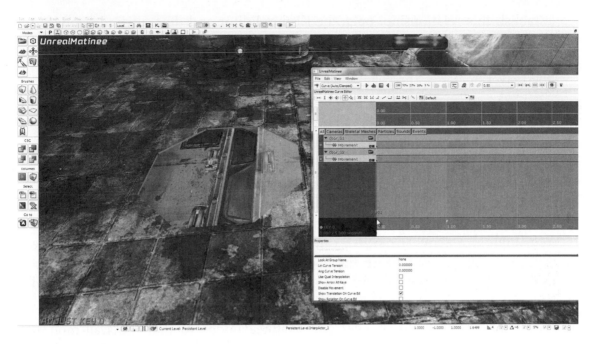

Figure 2.83
Creating start key frames for both doors.

Figure 2.84
Creating end key frames for each door.

establish this relationship, open the Kismet Editor and drag a wired connection between the Touched output of the Trigger node and the Play input of the Matinee node. This connection is equivalent to the following statement: "When the player activates the trigger, play the Matinee animation."

Tip

You can Alt-click a connection between Kismet nodes to break it.

25. Run the level in game mode and press the E key to activate the wall switch. Then use the elevator to return to the ground floor and confirm that the doors have opened in response. The switch appears to be working, but there is one remaining problem: The switch cannot be used to *close* the doors. That is, the switch is configured to open the doors if they are closed, and not to close the doors if they are open. Before you proceed to the next step, save the level and attempt to resolve this problem on your own in the Kismet Editor.

26. You can configure the Trigger and Matinee nodes so that the wall-mounted switch behaves as a toggle, opening and closing the sliding doors alternately with each press. To achieve this, insert a Switch node between the Trigger node and the Matinee node—that is, connect the trigger output to the switch input, and connect the switch output to the Matinee input. To do this, right-click any vacant space in the Kismet Editor's Graph pane and choose New Action, then Switch, and then Switch again from the menu that appears. Then Ctrl-drag to position the nodes such that the Switch node sits between the Trigger and Matinee nodes. Alt-click to break any connections between the Trigger and Matinee nodes in the graph, and then connect the Trigger node's Touched output to the Switch input. (See Figure 2.85.)

27. Select the Switch node in the Kismet Editor's Graph pane. Then, under Seq_Act Switch in the Properties panel, change the Link Count setting to 2 and check the Looping checkbox. Next, connect the Link 1 output to the Play input of the Matinee node, and the Link 2 output to the Reverse input of the Matinee node, as shown in Figure 2.86. The Switch node acts like a switcher or alternator in that it fires the next link output in the sequence each time its input is activated. Furthermore, the Switch node repeats this process on a loop, meaning the first link output of the node will be the next to fire when the sequence has reached its end. In short, the Switch node is what makes it possible for the wall-mounted switch in the level to toggle the door open and closed. Opening the door involves Kismet technology playing the open animation forward, and closing the door involves Kismet technology playing the open animation in reverse.

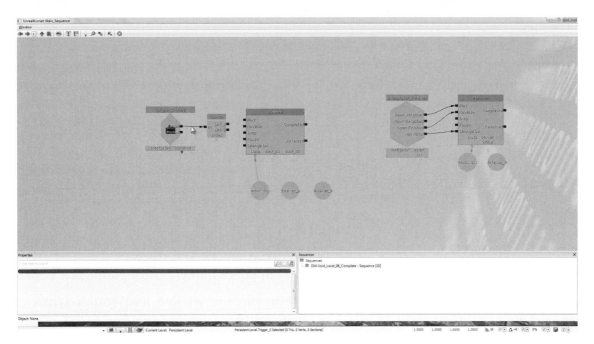

Figure 2.85
Connecting a trigger to a Matinee node via the Switch node.

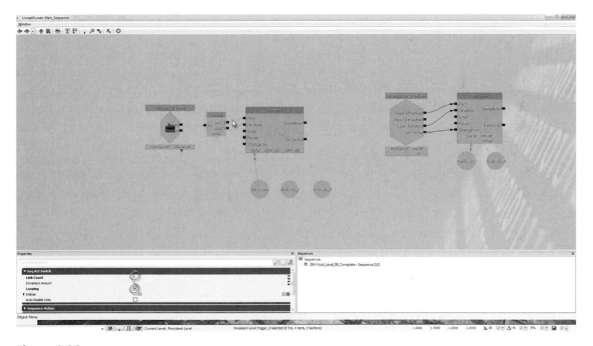

Figure 2.86
Use a switch to alternate in a loop between playing forward and backward.

Note

The completed level is in the companion files under Chapter2\DM-Void_Level_ 08_Complete.udk.

CONCLUSION

This chapter covered a lot of ground, providing a tutorial on how to create a complete level using the UDK. The level created can be considered complete in the sense that it conforms to all aspects of the plan stated at the beginning of the chapter. In creating the level, many techniques, tools and concepts were used, including BSP Brushes and CSG, the Content Browser, static meshes, the Kismet and Matinee Editors, sound and lighting, the Actor Classes Browser, and non-visible actors such as blocking volumes, KillZ planes, light importance volumes, and triggers. All these subjects and more are considered in greater detail in later chapters throughout this book.

The primary purpose of this chapter is not to offer a detailed and comprehensive explanation of all the tools and features discussed and used, but to offer an introductory glance at the UDK and its workflow for designing and building real-time 3D games. For this reason, readers should not worry themselves unduly if they have burning questions for which they do not have clearly formulated answers. There is much more to be said about everything covered here, and indeed more will be said. For now, take the level created here for a few test runs and make some attempts at tweaking the level based on your knowledge so far.

The next chapter is the first among many that take a more focused, systematic, and in-depth look at the UDK tools. Specifically, it examines the UDK basics—the fundamental concepts, features, and ideas that are relevant to all projects created in the UDK.

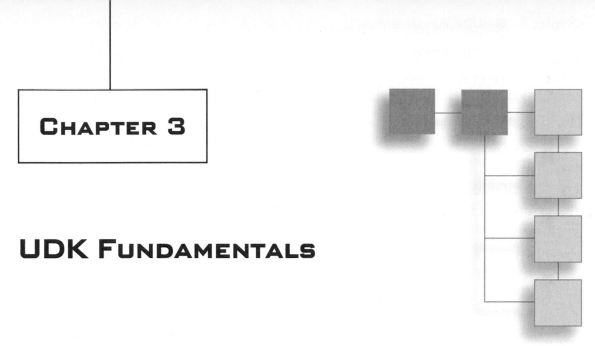

CHAPTER 3

UDK FUNDAMENTALS

Learn the rules so you know how to break them properly.

—The Dalai Lama

By the end of this chapter, you should:

- Understand the basic concepts underpinning the Unreal Engine.
- Feel confident using the main UDK Editor and tools.
- Be able to quickly navigate viewports and manipulate actors.
- Be familiar with a variety of keyboard shortcuts.
- Feel able to explore the UDK and its features independently.

The previous chapter was a tutorial that described how to use the UDK to construct a completely playable level from scratch. In constructing that level, you used a wide range of development tools and features, including (in no particular order) viewports, the Kismet and Matinee Editors, sounds, lighting, Lightmass, volumes, BSP Brushes and CSG, and static meshes to mention only a few. After considering these features generally, one might detect an abstract hierarchy or chain of dependency between the features. Specifically, some features were used more than others, some proved more critical than others, and some were based on others. The point here is that there are a whole range of UDK features (such as the Kismet Editor, materials, and static meshes) that cannot be used effectively (or at all) without first having an understanding of a more basic and critical set of features (such as viewports, 3D space, the transformation widget, and others). This set of core features and concepts is what I term the UDK fundamentals. In short, the UDK fundamentals are those essential features and ideas that all (or almost all) UDK users will need to call upon to get things done effectively with the UDK, even for the simplest of projects.

The UDK fundamentals consist of three constituent pieces. Because the whole is equal to the sum of its parts, understanding the UDK fundamentals involves understanding these three key aspects.

■ **The UDK Editor interface.** You must become familiar with the reasoning behind the main GUI layout, the purpose of specific groups of buttons and menus, and the kinds of things they achieve.

■ **The UDK keyboard shortcuts.** You must get into the habit of pressing a selection of key combinations on the keyboard for quick access to the UDK feature set. Although keyboard shortcuts are not essential (that is, the UDK can be used without them), the word shortcut hints at the speed and productivity gains to be had by using the keyboard shortcuts frequently. Using the keyboard shortcuts instead of the mouse can both speed up the UDK workflow and enhance the overall user experience.

■ **The jargon and concepts underpinning the Unreal Engine.** You must understand ideas such as 3D coordinate systems, transformations, and local and world space, as well as UDK jargon terms such as actor, widget, and console.

The primary purpose of this chapter is to examine the UDK fundamentals by detailing all three of their constituent aspects: the interface, the keyboard shortcuts, and some of the jargon and theoretical ideas on which the UDK and its tools are based. These aspects will be discussed not in the order in which I have listed them here, but in the order in which a new user is likely to encounter them. The chapter begins with an overview of the UDK interface and ends with a consideration of some important theory underpinning 3D real-time games generally and the Unreal Engine more specifically.

The UDK Editor Interface

The UDK Editor is the primary—but not the only—tool in the Unreal Development Kit. There are other important and useful tools in the kit, including SpeedTree, the Unreal Frontend, the UDK Mobile Editor, and the UnrealScript Compiler. However, the UDK Editor is considered the main tool in the UDK in the sense that it is where most developers will spend most of their time when developing most of their games. For this reason, the focus of the majority of this book is on the UDK Editor and its attendant tools and interface components.

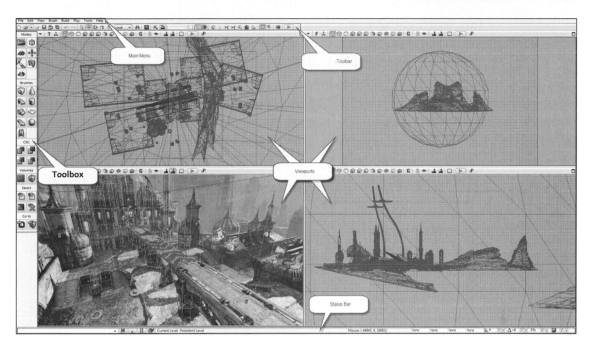

Figure 3.1
The UDK Editor interface: the main menu, toolbar, toolbox, viewports, and status bar.

The UDK Editor interface consists of five distinct components. The design of each of these components is not arbitrary; rather, it is intentional and structured. Each component contains a set of related buttons, drop-down menus, checkboxes, and other GUI gadgets to help developers get things done in an intuitive way. These five interface components, illustrated in Figure 3.1, are as follows:

- The main menu
- The toolbar
- The toolbox
- The viewports
- The status bar

The Main Menu

The UDK Editor's main menu appears along the top of the editor's window. It consists of several clickable words, or menus. Together, these menus provide access to all the global or application-level features of the UDK—those features that apply to the application and its behavior and in a general way to the level being created in the editor. For example, the main menu offers a means to open and save projects and to import and export level-specific data in a variety of file formats.

At the time of this writing, there are eight menus: File, Edit, View, Brush, Build, Play, Tools, and Help. As with most application menus, these menus lead to additional options and sub-menus when clicked. Although this book could go on to exhaustively consider every menu item in sequence, giving for each item a detailed and comprehensive explanation, but such an approach would likely prove tiresome for most readers and get in the way of understanding the UDK as a game-development tool. For this reason, it is enough to consider here the general purpose of the items associated with each of the top-level menu options as a group rather than individually. The purpose and usefulness of specific menu items will emerge later throughout our work in the book.

- **The File menu.** As with most applications, the left-most menu is the File menu. This menu is home to a set of project-management features that enable developers to create new levels, load and save levels, import and export data to and from levels, and exit the application.

- **The Edit menu.** This menu contains a selection of features for selecting, editing, and adjusting content in the level. From the Edit menu, users can copy, cut, paste, and duplicate actors (such as meshes and lights) in the level. In addition, users can use the Edit menu to select, deselect, delete, and find actors.

- **The View menu.** This menu is useful for both displaying and hiding a range of user interface (UI) elements and for controlling the visibility and detail level of actors and objects in the viewports. The View menu provides access to the Content Browser (and other browsers), the Search tool, and various editor settings, as well as the ability to toggle the visibility of viewport elements and to control the level of detail at which viewports render.

- **The Brush menu.** This menu is associated with the BSP Brush tools and with the CSG they produce. In short, every item in this menu is represented in quick-access form in the BSP and CSG sections of the toolbox, as you shall see.

- **The Build and Play menus.** These aptly named menus are reserved for all the compilation and play functions of the Unreal Engine, respectively. These build and play functions enable a developer to compile, debug, analyze, and run the current level. The Play menu specifically offers options for running the level in a separate window, in a viewport, or as a standalone application.

- **The Tools menu.** This menu provides access to a set of miscellaneous utilities and programs. Some of these can scan the level for potential problems and issues, while others are helpers for creating terrain meshes.

■ **The Help menu.** As in most applications, the final menu—the one farthest to the right—is the Help menu. The Help menu provides access to both the online UDK documentation in the Unreal Developer Network and the community forums on the official UDK Web site. It can also be used to view a range of useful hints and tips on using the UDK Editor and for viewing the version number of your editor. (Each release of the UDK features an editor with a unique version number.) You may need this information when seeking support and advice from other users on the forums.

The Toolbar

The toolbar sits directly beneath the main menu and is a graphical abbreviation of it. That is, all options on the toolbar can also be found in the main menu. Some can also be accessed by way of keyboard shortcuts. The purpose of the toolbar is to save you time. It does this by providing a constantly accessible and graphical strip of buttons that serve as shortcuts to the most frequently used menu options. The buttons are arranged horizontally from left to right, and the position of each button on the toolbar reflects the order of the corresponding menu group to which it belongs. That means the file and save options found in the File menu appear among the left-most toolbar buttons, while options from the Build and Play menus appear among the right-most toolbar buttons. In general, the toolbar offers quick-access buttons for creating new levels, for load and save operations, for selecting and editing actors, for building and playing levels, among other options. To determine the purpose of any button on the toolbar, simply hover the mouse cursor over the button; a tooltip with the name of the button appears, as shown in Figure 3.2.

Keeping It Simple

I like to keep my life as simple as possible, so I seek to find the shortest and quickest ways for doing things in the UDK. For this reason, I follow this general three-part rule:

■ I use keyboard shortcuts for all options that have them, especially to perform Cut (Ctrl+X), Copy (Ctrl+C), and Paste (Ctrl+V) operations.

■ I use the toolbar for all available options without keyboard shortcuts, such as Load, Save, and New.

■ I use the main menu as a last resort, when an option has no shortcut and is not represented on the toolbar.

As a result, I use the keyboard almost constantly, the toolbar frequently, and the main menu occasionally. I recommend trying my three-part method for a few days to see if it works well for you too.

Figure 3.2
Tooltips offer guidance as to the function of a toolbar button.

The Toolbox

The toolbox, which is aligned vertically along the left edge of the UDK Editor, offers the developer quick access to tools for building and editing levels. The toolbox is distinct from the toolbar. Whereas the toolbar is an abbreviation of the main menu, providing access to application-level features—such as tools for loading and saving new levels—the toolbox provides access to tools and features that are used for working in the current level.

All the buttons in the toolbox provide access to tools used or deployed in the viewports of the editor. That is, the developer will typically click a tool in the toolbox and then apply that tool in the viewport. These buttons are divided by type into six main sections:

- **Modes.** The Modes section contains buttons designed to switch the UDK Editor and its interface into one of several editing modes. A *mode* defines both how the GUI will appear and how the UDK Editor will behave in response to user input. When switched to different modes, the editor will behave slightly differently, as you shall see. For example, in Camera mode the editor expects the designer to adjust the position, rotation, and orientation of the viewport camera and to perform standard editing operations such as moving, scaling, and rotating level actors. In contrast, in Texture Alignment mode, the editor freezes the positions

and transformations of actors and permits only the adjustment of materials and mapping information. That is, it permits only adjustments
relating to how materials are applied across the surface of the 3D models in the level.

- **Brushes.** The Brushes section contains buttons for shaping the BSP Brush into one of a number of 3D geometric primitives, such as cubes, spheres, cylinders, and others. The buttons in this section also offer secondary functions, which you can access by right-clicking the button. When you do, a pop-up window appears, displaying a variety of numerical inputs that you can change to tweak the shape of a primitive.

- **CSG and Volumes.** The CSG and Volumes sections are related insofar as both offer buttons for constructing scene actors and elements with the BSP Brush. The tutorial in the previous chapter demonstrated the use of tools in the CSG section to construct static geometry (often used for floors and walls) and tools in the Volumes section to build non-visible volumes (such as collision and lighting volumes) in the shape of the BSP Brush.

- **Select and Go To.** These sections offer tools for quickly selecting, deselecting, and zooming in on actors in the level.

The Viewports

The viewports dominate the UDK Editor in the sense that the greater part of the editor GUI is taken up by viewport components. The screen space consumed by the viewports is reflective of their importance in the UDK workflow. Their primary purpose, as the tutorial in the previous chapter probably made clear, is to provide a real-time view of the level being created. Much more on the viewports will be said later in this chapter, in the upcoming section titled "Viewports." It is sufficient here to state that the viewports are critically important for getting things done in the UDK, and much development time will be spent using them.

The Status Bar

The status bar is an informative and functional panel aligned horizontally along the bottom of the UDK Editor. It is informative insofar as it provides information about the current state of the level, such as the grid-snapping options (discussed later), the current position of the mouse cursor in terms of Unreal world units, and the current auto-saving options. It is functional in the sense that it features buttons and input boxes for specifying ranges of values that affect the way the editor works. More will be said later in this chapter on the status bar.

UNDERSTANDING FILE-BASED VERSUS PROJECT-BASED APPLICATIONS

Game development is a multi-disciplinary field. Developers must use a variety of skills and software to be successful. Some of that software includes Photoshop, Microsoft Word, Microsoft Excel, Microsoft Project, 3DS Max, Maya, Blender, Notepad, and of course the UDK.

One might break these programs down into at least two types of software: file-based and project-based. Photoshop, Word, and Excel might be said to belong to the former group, with 3D applications such as Max, Maya, and the UDK belonging to the latter.

File-based applications are ones in which users open, work with, and save individual files, such as documents or photos. For example, in Microsoft Word, users can add text and pictures to compose a document. Once saved, all the information relevant for the document—the text and pictures—is embedded and written to a single document file. This gives users peace of mind, knowing their documents can be transported to a different computer and opened successfully in the same version of the application. The disadvantage of this method becomes apparent, however, when many different files or documents need to reference the same data and must update themselves to always contain the latest version of that data.

To illustrate, consider what might be the implications for the UDK if it were to use a file-based system—that is, a system in which the entire contents of a level, including its meshes, animations, materials, and scripting, were written to a single and portable map file. Suppose a new game-development studio decided to use a file-based version of the UDK to create a 3D platform game. This game consists of 10 levels, each featuring many of the same enemies and obstacles for the player to conquer. Each of the 10 levels is saved as a separate file, with each file containing all the mesh, lighting, sound, material, and scripting data for that level. Two problems will inevitably arise. First, each level file is needlessly larger because it contains embedded copies of meshes, materials, and other data that is repeated in other levels. Second, if any of the artists on the team decide to change the original asset, then the assets featured in level files will not update automatically to reflect the change. This is because the assets in the files are not externally referenced, but are rather embedded duplicates of the original asset.

Thankfully, UDK users need not concern themselves with these problems. That's because the UDK is a project-based application. In contrast to a file-based application, a project-based application works not with a single file, but with a collection of related and cross-referenced files, with all the files in the project being interdependent. In the UDK, this project-based workflow manifests itself in that game-asset data, such as meshes, textures, sounds, materials, and scripting, are stored in files (package files) separately from map data. *Map data* defines the arrangement of assets in the level, not the assets themselves—the positional, scaling, and rotational data that is applied to meshes and other actors to compose them into a level. This separation of map data from asset data means that artists and content creators can change and update assets without affecting or needing to change the map file for a level, and level designers can change map-related data without affecting assets. The methods for saving and loading map and asset data in the UDK are also separate. Maps are loaded and saved via the File menu, while asset packages are loaded and saved via buttons and menus in the Content Browser.

The implication of this separation is that it is possible to save one set of data without saving the other. Sometimes, this can be a useful feature—particularly when you want to keep the changes made to a specific map but to disregard the changes made to its referenced assets, or vice versa. However, it can also lead to confusion and unexpected issues for those not familiar with a project-based workflow. Specifically, it is important to keep in mind that opening the File menu and choosing Save or clicking the Save button on the toolbar saves only the map, not its referenced assets in the Content Browser. If a user were to open the File and choose Save, and do nothing else upon exiting the UDK, he or she would in fact save only the map, not the assets. If this saved level were then loaded back from the file into the UDK, the developer would see the latest version of the level using the older versions of the assets. See Figure 3.3 and Figure 3.4 for a graphical illustration of the fundamental conceptual differences between file- and project-based workflows.

File-Based Saving

Map

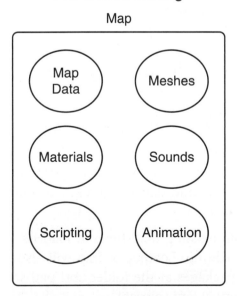

Figure 3.3
A file-based workflow. All relevant data is embedded into the file.

Project-Based Saving

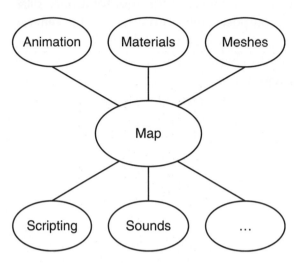

Figure 3.4
A project-based workflow involves a collection of cross-referenced files.

In short, the UDK is a project-based application. Being project-based means potentially dealing with multiple files across multiple folders, all interrelated. The UDK draws a distinction between map data and asset data, the former relating to the arrangement of actors in a 3D environment and the latter relating to the material, mesh, and other imported data used to construct those assets. This separation of data across multiple files means that developers must be careful to clearly understand what is happening when performing both save and load operations. Specifically, maps are loaded and saved via the UDK Editor's File menu into files whose format is UDK, and assets are loaded and saved into referenced packages via the Content Browser into files whose format is UPK. So, UDK files are map files, and UPK files are asset package files.

For your reference, some options found in the File menu include the following. (The Content Browser is covered later in this chapter.)

- **New.** Choosing the New option in the File menu creates a new and empty map file. That is, it clears the editor of any existing level and data and creates a new and blank level for editing.

- **Open.** The Open option enables you to open an existing map file and load its contents and data into the viewport, ready for editing. Loading a map will also prompt the UDK to seek out referenced asset packages at the folder and paths specified and to load their contents into memory as appropriate.

Note

An error message is displayed if a package could not be loaded or found at the specified path, and the user is given the opportunity to find the asset package file at a different location. The level can also be loaded without the asset package in question, but all related actors in the level will be removed.

- **Save.** Choosing the Save option saves the current level as shown in the viewports. This option does not save asset packages in the Content Browser.

- **Save All.** Choosing the Save All option will save all changes across the project, including changes to the map and to asset packages. Select this option when you know that all changes should be committed.

VIEWPORTS

As mentioned, the majority of GUI space in the UDK Editor is reserved for the four viewports, reflecting their importance in the UDK workflow. Put simply, the viewport enables you to see what you are doing. It shows you what your level looks like. To elaborate, the purpose of the viewport is to offer a real-time, director's eye, moveable view of the level from a given camera point.

These properties of a viewport are worth further consideration:

- **Viewports work in real time.** A viewport can be said to work in real time in two distinct senses. First, a viewport can display animations, motion, and special effects at their intended speed, just as they will appear in the game. Second, viewports provide a real-time response to the actions of the designer in the editor. For example, if a level designer deletes or moves a mesh actor, the viewport updates immediately to reflect that change.

- **Viewports offer a director's eye.** The viewport can display the level in a way that is very similar to how it will appear to a gamer during gameplay. More importantly, however, the viewport offers a director's eye view—an enhanced viewing mode intended to meet the needs of developers rather than reflect the experience of gamers. A director's eye view enables the designer to see a range of helper objects that define how the level works, but that are not visible to the gamer. These include objects such as lights, sounds, volumes, path-finding objects, collision boundaries, and trigger points. At this point, you need not have a complete understanding of what these objects do; just realize that they help define how the level works, and that although it is not necessary or even desirable for the player to see them, their size and position information are important to the designer. In addition, a director's eye view offers designers a free, out-of-body view of the level. The game camera is typically fixed to display game-relevant actors and action, with a first-person camera following the movement of the player and offering a view through the player character's eye and a third-person camera typically fixing itself at a specified distance away from the game character and following his or her movements through the game. In contrast, the viewport camera is not fixed at any specified position, height, or orientation. It enables the designer to move through walls, to move inside static meshes, and to enter far-off regions beyond the level's collision boundaries, if the designer so wishes.

■ **Viewports are positioned and movable.** It was hinted at in the previous list item that viewports work like cameras in that they have a position in 3D space, they have a focus, and they can be moved to new positions to bring new elements of the level into view. The key point to keep in mind is that viewports do not merely offer static views of the level. They can and must be moved to work effectively in the UDK.

Understanding and Switching Viewport Types

The UDK has four separate viewports, each offering a slightly different view of the same level. The style of view shown in a viewports depends largely on the viewport type. Any one of the four viewports in the UDK can belong to one of two types:

■ **Perspective.** A Perspective viewport (see Figure 3.5) works like a game camera. It offers a true 3D view of the level. You can pan, move, and rotate a Perspective viewport just like a first-person camera to look at almost any point in the level. A Perspective viewport is particularly useful for previewing the look and overall design of the level from the perspective of the gamer—for seeing how the level is likely to appear in its final form. Most of your development work in the UDK will take place in the Perspective viewport.

■ **Orthographic.** There are three orthographic viewports: the Front, Side, and Top viewports. Unlike a Perspective viewport, the orthographic viewports are not truly 3D; rather, they are 2D. Their purpose is to offer a blueprint view of the level from a fixed perspective (see Figure 3.6). The orthographic views can be panned and zoomed, but not rotated to view the level from different angles and perspectives. The primary purpose of the orthographic views is to offer precision to enable designers to avoid the kinds of mistakes that result when trying to be precise in perspective. The orthographic views are ideal for precisely positioning, scaling, and rotating actors in the level, as well as for performing other editing tasks that require measurement and exactness.

Figure 3.5
Perspective viewports work a lot like standard movie cameras.

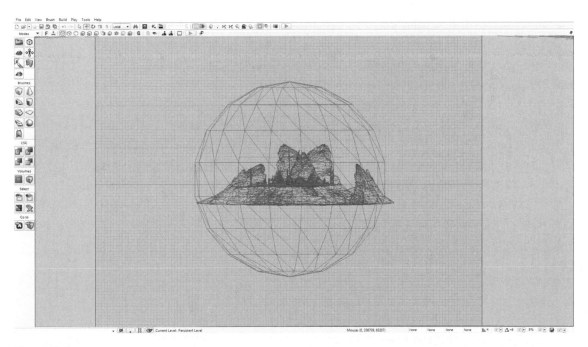

Figure 3.6
An orthographic viewport is for precision, measuring, and careful placement and transformations.

Figure 3.7
Switching the viewport type.

By default, the UDK Editor displays three orthographic viewports (Top, Side, and Front) and one Perspective viewport. Remember, though, that you can maximize any one viewport to full screen and then restore it to its standard size using the viewport's Maximize/Restore button (respectively) in the top-right corner of the viewport. Note, too, that for any of the four viewports in the UDK Editor, you can change the viewport type between perspective, front, side, and top. One way to do this is to right-click the Viewport Type button in the viewport's toolbar and choose a different type from the menu that appears (see Figure 3.7). This button displays the first letter of the name of the current viewport type—P for Perspective, F for Front, T for Top, or S for Side. You can also click the button to cycle through the viewport types, or even use keyboard shortcuts to switch types. Table 3.1 contains these keyboard shortcuts.

Table 3.1 Viewport Type Shortcuts

Type	Shortcut
Perspective	Alt+F
Top	Alt+G
Side	Alt+J
Front	Alt+H

Customizing the Viewport

The UDK Editor offers a range of options for customizing, tweaking, and changing the way a level appears in the viewports. (Note that these options change only how the level appears in the editor, not how the level appears to the gamer.) These viewing options fall into two broad categories. The first contains options for showing and hiding elements or actors such as meshes or brushes in a level so that developers can better focus their attention on specific elements. The second contains features, called *viewing modes*, that radically alter how the level appears generally in the viewport in terms of color. Both categories of features are designed to help developers work more effectively, diagnose potential problems, and preview the level at production-quality detail.

Showing and Hiding Actors

The first group of features enables developers to toggle the visibility of specific elements in the viewport—that is, to show or hide any combination of actors such as all meshes, all BSP Brushes, or all volumes. You can find these options in the Viewport Options menu, which you access by clicking the left-most arrow button on the viewport toolbar. As shown in Figure 3.8, the options in the menu are organized into three main groups: Show, Show Volumes, and Show Groups.

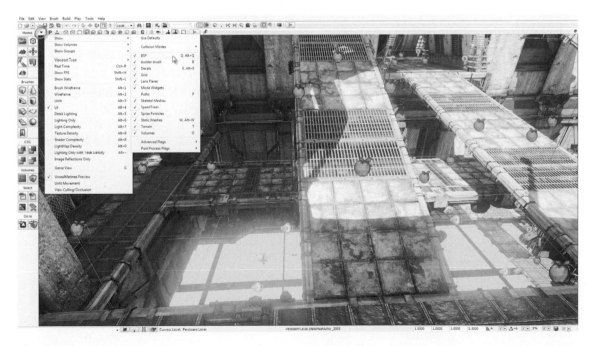

Figure 3.8
Viewport options for showing and hiding actors—including brushes, meshes, volumes—and groups of actors.

The Show menu houses all show/hide options pertaining to specific types of level actors —that is, all options for showing and hiding all actors of a particular kind. From this menu, you can show or hide all static meshes, all BSP Brushes, all volumes, or all terrains, among others. These options are useful if you want to hide everything in the viewport except one specific kind of actor. For example, if you want to tweak the positioning of static meshes, you could hide all types of actors except meshes to avoid accidentally selecting and transforming a non-mesh actor in the viewport.

All options on the Show menu are of an indiscriminate and global nature. That is, each option toggles the visibility of all actors belonging to a specific kind, regardless of any qualities that may distinguish the actors from each other. This can sometimes prove problematic. It might be the case that a developer wants to hide a variety of actors on the basis of some criteria other than their kind, such as their purpose or position in the level. Perhaps the developer wants to hide only weapon meshes, or only enemy meshes, or only collision volumes (but no other volumes), or only blue-colored lights. In these cases, the developer needs finer control over the criteria used to show or hide viewport elements. That is the rationale behind the other two menu options, Show Volumes and Show Groups. The Show Volumes menu provides access to options that enable developers to toggle the visibility of particular types of volumes in the viewport. These include all collision volumes, all blocking volumes, or all post-processing volumes, among others. The Show Groups option offers the ultimate in control over the visibility of elements in the viewport, enabling developers to show or hide custom-made groups of actors. The term *group* in the UDK refers, as you shall see later, to a user-defined collection of actors in the level—that is, a collection of actors (perhaps some meshes and lights and volumes) that the user has explicitly indicated as belonging to the same group. Details for creating and managing groups are found later in this chapter, in the section "The Groups Browser."

Note that some of the most common hide/show features have an associated keyboard shortcut, as shown in Table 3.2.

Table 3.2 Show/Hide Shortcuts	
Type	**Shortcut**
Meshes	W
BSP Brush	B
CSG	Q
Volumes	O

Viewing Modes

A *viewing mode* is a sort of visual theme—a color scheme, layout, and style—that can be applied to a viewport and its contents to change how the level appears in the viewport to the developer. The purpose of a viewing mode is not to style the level in an arbitrary way or according to aesthetic considerations. That is, its role is not to make the level look good. Rather, the purpose of a viewing mode is to style the level in the viewport so it more clearly shows useful diagnostic information. Viewing modes use color, shapes, and other visual clues to convey information. This is to help the developer identify relationships between actors, properties of the level and its structure, or features that could lead to problems and performance issues.

Every viewport in the UDK can be set into any one of 12 viewing modes.

- Brush Wireframe
- Wireframe
- Unlit
- Lit
- Detail Lighting
- Lighting Only
- Light Complexity
- Texture Density
- Shader Complexity
- Lightmap Density
- Lighting Only with Texel Density
- Game Mode

You can access these modes by using keyboard shortcuts, as outlined in Table 3.3, or from menu options via the viewport toolbar, as shown in Figure 3.9.

For more on each of these modes, read on.

Note

Coverage of Lightmap Density mode has been omitted here. This topic is discussed in Chapter 8, "Lighting."

Brush Wireframe Mode Versus Wireframe Mode   The first two viewing modes, Brush Wireframe and Wireframe, are related but distinct. As shown in Figure 3.10 and Figure 3.11, the modes look similar. In addition, both hide the material and

Table 3.3 Viewing Mode Shortcuts

Type	Shortcut
Brush Wireframe	Alt+1
Wireframe	Alt+2
Unlit	Alt+3
Lit	Alt+4
Detail Lighting	Alt+5
Lighting Only	Alt+6
Light Complexity	Alt+7
Texture Density	Alt+8
Shader Complexity	Alt+9
Lightmap Density	Alt+0
Lighting Only with Texel Density	Alt+−
Game Mode	G

Figure 3.9
Viewing Mode buttons on viewport toolbar. Most viewing modes are used for diagnostic purposes. Many developers use Wireframe, Brush Wireframe, Unlit, and Lit in most cases.

Figure 3.10
Brush Wireframe mode displays the wireframe of meshes but not the wireframe of CSG. Instead, it displays the BSP volumes that compose the CSG.

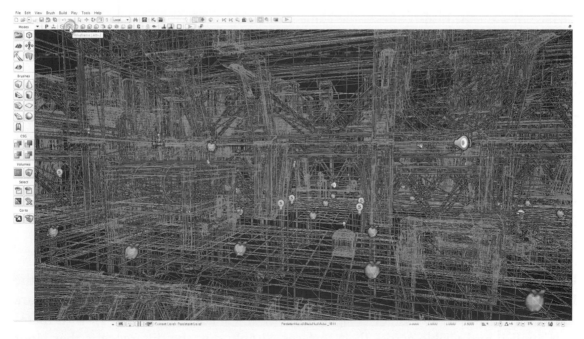

Figure 3.11
Wireframe mode displays wireframe for all geometry, including the CSG that results from BSP Brushes.

surface data of meshes and geometry, instead displaying their structure or skeleton, known as topology. *Topology* is used here to refer to the polygonal constitution of a mesh—the way the polygons are arranged to create a model.

As you will see in the next chapter, the key difference between Brush Wireframe mode and Wireframe mode is in how both the BSP Brush and CSG are shown in the viewport. As you learned in the previous chapter, a BSP Brush is used to define a volume in 3D space, and CSG refers to the polygonal geometry that is constructed on the basis of a BSP Brush. In Brush Wireframe mode, everything polygonal in the viewport is shown in wireframe except for the CSG. Instead of the CSG, the viewport displays the BSP Brush volume on which the CSG is based. In contrast, in Wireframe mode, the viewport shows everything in wireframe, including meshes and the CSG that resulted from the BSP Brush. This distinction will be clarified further in the next chapter, which focuses on BSP Brushes and CSG.

This begs the question, why would you want to see the level in any kind of wireframe mode at all? There are many reasons, two of which are mentioned here. First, these wireframe modes act as a sort of diagnostic tool, enabling developers to examine the topology of meshes to make informed decisions about whether they are appropriate for the level and for real-time 3D applications generally. This is useful because the topology of a mesh has important ramifications for a game. Specifically, the topology influences how easily a material can be applied across the surface of a mesh. It also affects the game's run-time performance in terms of frame rate. In short, a mesh with more polygons places greater demands on system hardware than a mesh with fewer polygons. The specifics of these considerations are primarily for graphic artists and are thus beyond the scope of this book, although they are discussed briefly in Chapter 6, "Building Game Worlds with Static Mesh Actors." The second benefit of wireframe modes is that they enable developers to see through the surface of meshes in the level, allowing them to select actors in the level that are behind walls or contained inside other meshes. Of course, the developer could use the standard textured viewing modes to select such awkwardly placed objects by simply rotating or moving the viewport to bring them into view, but wireframe modes sometimes make the selection process a lot simpler and quicker.

Unlit Mode Versus Lit Mode   Like the Brush Wireframe and Wireframe modes, the Unlit and Lit modes—perhaps the most commonly used modes by developers—are related but distinct. Both modes display meshes in a shaded style—that is, with materials applied and visible across their surfaces. Simply put, the difference is that Unlit mode does not feature lighting, whereas Lit mode does.

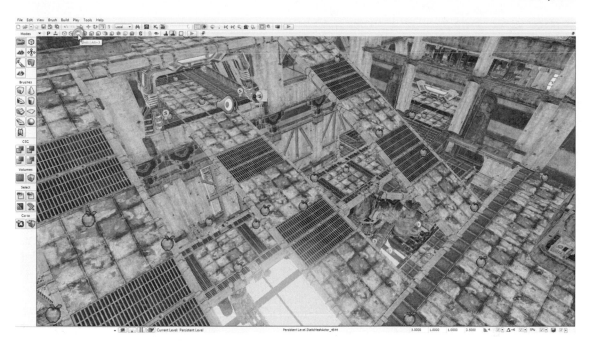

Figure 3.12
Unlit mode displays meshes with materials applied, but no lighting.

Although this simplification does capture the difference between these two modes, it also touches on a potential confusion—one that might easily arise out of the unfortunate name Unlit mode. As shown in Figure 3.12, Unlit mode does not display the level without lighting. After all, a level without lighting—without a light source—would appear completely black. Instead, Unlit mode simply ignores all lights that were manually created and positioned by the designer, and instead illuminates the level using a single, global ambient light. This light casts white light of a single intensity infinitely in all directions, ignoring shadow casting and other light-specific effects. The result is that all surfaces in the level appear to receive an equal amount of light and are thus equally visible in the viewport. In contrast, Lit mode, relies entirely on the light actors added to the level by the designer to illuminate the scene (see Figure 3.13). Lit mode more or less represents how the level will appear to the gamer. For this reason, it is one of the most commonly used viewing modes in the UDK.

So, why the need for Unlit mode, anyway? Why not just ignore Unlit mode altogether and stick with Lit mode? After all, Lit mode offers a more accurate representation of how the level appears to the gamer. In fact, the benefits of using Unlit mode are two-fold. First, Unlit mode offers developers a performance enhancement over Lit mode. Because Unlit mode bases its lighting calculations on only one, non-shadow-casting light, the editor runs more smoothly, the controls respond more swiftly, and the

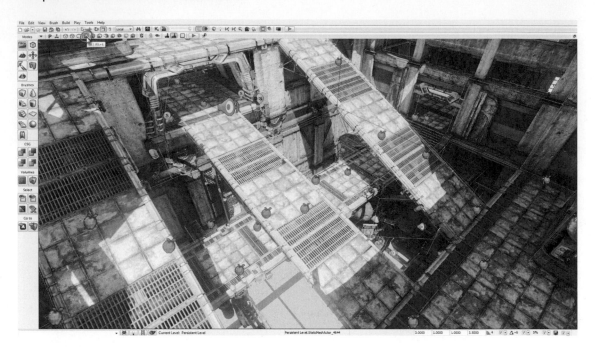

Figure 3.13
Lit mode displays the level in a way that resembles what the gamer will see during the game.

GPU and hardware are placed under less stress than with Lit mode. This can be desirable when you're working on non-lighting elements in the level, such as placing sounds and mapping static meshes. Second, in Unlit mode, developers can more clearly observe the mapping and tiling of materials and textures across the surface of meshes. In short, both Unlit and Lit mode offer many benefits, and I find myself switching between them most of the time while working with the UDK Editor.

Detail Lighting Mode   The Detail Lighting mode is a diagnostic viewing mode. That is, its purpose is to tell the developer something useful about the level—something informative that may influence the developer's design decisions. Detail Lighting mode graphically illustrates how the lighting of the level brings out the roughness or smoothness of materials applied to the geometry. As shown in Figure 3.14, this mode hides materials' diffuse and color data, instead presenting the mesh surface in a neutral, clay-like grey color. This enables the developer to visually isolate the effects of the bump and normal mapping (bumpiness and smoothness) as they appear under the current lighting conditions.

Lighting Only Mode   The Lighting Only mode does exactly what it says: It shows the effects of lighting in the level in isolation by substituting all the materials with neutral, grey, and clay-like versions. These materials enable developers to more

Figure 3.14
Detail Lighting mode shows the effects of lighting on selected material channels. Notice the clay-like grey appearance of the surface of meshes.

closely observe the effects of lighting on the geometry of the level. Specifically, in Lighting Only mode, designers can clearly see the effects of lighting on the surfaces of models based on the position, size, direction, and color of the lights in the level, as well as the effects of shadow casting (see Figure 3.15). Unlike Detail Lighting mode, Lighting Only mode does not show the roughness and bumpiness of surfaces.

Light Complexity Mode   A diagnostic mode, the Light Complexity mode automatically shades all surfaces of the level using a limited traffic-light color scheme to convey information about the lighting in the level. Every surface in the viewport is assigned a color from a range of hues that include black, green, orange, and red. (See Figure 3.16 for a black-and-white rendering of the Light Complexity mode in action.)

The color assigned to a surface is not arbitrary. That is, the color assigned to a surface is used to describe the number of lights (light complexity) in the level currently affecting that surface. In general, the colors of this scheme can be plotted to form a linear spectrum with green on the left, red on the right, and many gradations between. Green represents "few lights" or "low complexity," and red represents "many lights" or "high complexity." Some surfaces, however, are shaded outside the traffic-light color scheme, appearing completely black. Black surfaces are exempt

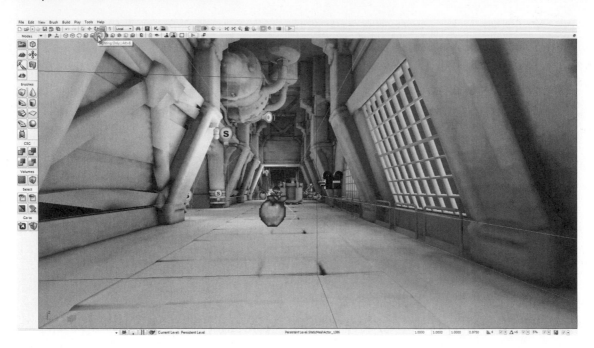

Figure 3.15
Lighting Only mode displays the effects of lighting, separate from materials. It shows the size, brightness, and coloration of light, as well as the position, shape, and intensity of shadows cast.

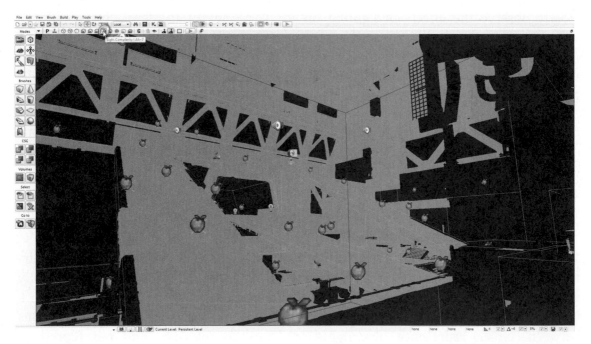

Figure 3.16
Light Complexity mode shades the viewport using a traffic-light, or hot-and-cold, color scheme to express lighting information.

from standard or dynamic lights or lighting in some way. This might be because the surface itself is a light source (such as a fluorescent tube), because its material overrides or customizes the scene lighting, or because of some other special properties that remove the surface from the UDK lighting system.

So how is this information useful? What kinds of decisions can be informed by light-complexity information? Put simply, light complexity has implications for both the amount of time taken by Lightmass to calculate a final lighting solution and the run-time performance of the level on most hardware. In many aspects of game development, the general rule of thumb is to keep things simple where possible. For this reason, most (preferably all) surfaces in a UDK level should appear green or close to green in Light Complexity mode, unless there is a compelling developmental reason for them to be otherwise—perhaps for special-effects purposes.

Texture Density Mode   Similar to Lighting Complexity mode, Texture Density mode styles all visible polygonal surfaces of the viewport using a temperature color scheme—that is, a spectrum of colors ranging from blue to red. As shown in Figure 3.17, every surface or mesh in the viewport is assigned a color that describes the mesh's texture density. Low-density surfaces appear in colder colors, beginning with blue; higher-density surfaces appear in warmer colors, ending in red. This color scheme helps developers quickly identify the texture density of any given surface in the level.

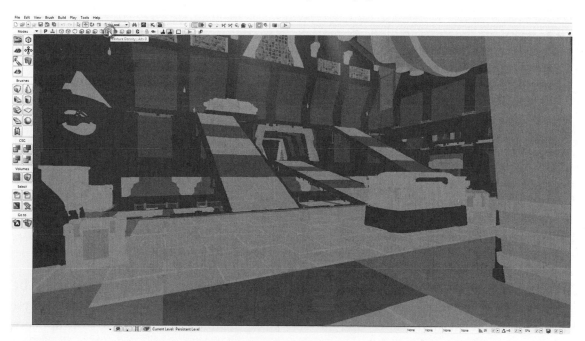

Figure 3.17
Texture Density mode uses a temperature color scheme to express texture information.

To understand why Texture Density mode might be useful, you first need a firm grasp of texture density. To explain, when textures are mapped onto surfaces, their texels change depending on the size of the surface—its width and height. That is, the texels either shrink or expand to fit the surface, depending on whether the surface is smaller or larger than the texture. (*Texel* is short for *texture pixel*; its plural form, *texels*, refers to all the pixels in a texture.) If the surface is large and the texture is small, the texels must be expanded to fit across the surface, creating a low texel density. In contrast, if the surface is small and the texture is large, then the texels must be squashed onto the surface to fit within it, creating a high texel density.

Texture density is important in game development for two main reasons. First, surfaces with a low texture density are at risk of appearing blurry or pixelated because the texture's texels are stretched to fit a larger surface area. The risk of distortion is proportional to how low the texture density is, meaning that very low-density surfaces look ugly and of low quality. Second, surfaces with a high texture density are at risk of reducing the performance of the game. That's because high-density surfaces are packed with an excess of texels, which is burdensome on both the CPU and the GPU. In theory, the ideal scenario for the level developer is to have a level in which all or most surfaces are optimized with regard to texel density. Such surfaces would appear green in Texture Density mode.

Note

As mentioned, Texture Density mode illustrates the relationship between the size of a surface in terms of width and height and the size of its textures in terms of number of texels. You can therefore adjust the texture density of a surface by changing the size of the surface, the size of its textures, or both.

Shader Complexity Mode   Shader Complexity mode is another of the UDK's diagnostic viewing modes. Like Texture Density mode, Shader Complexity mode uses a temperature color scheme to convey information about the level. Unlike Texture Density mode, however, Shader Complexity mode illustrates the complexity of the material's structure or composition (see Figure 3.18). In Shader Complexity mode, every visible surface in the viewport is assigned a color to describe shader complexity. Simple materials appear in colder colors, beginning with blue; more-complex materials appear in warmer colors, ending in red.

Material refers here to an algorithm or a recipe that defines how a surface should be shaded—that is, how it should appear. If a polygon surface is supposed to represent a brick wall, then the material of that surface is responsible for shading it so it appears to be made of brick. Materials use texture maps and other parametric data to define the appearance of a surface, including its diffuse appearance, its shininess, and its

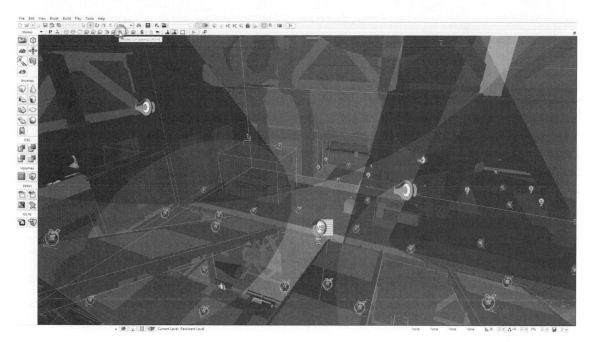

Figure 3.18
Shader Complexity mode illustrates the complexity of materials in the level using a temperature color scheme, ranging from blue to red.

bumpiness, among other characteristics. The more ingredients it uses to define this appearance—and the more complex those ingredients—the more processor intensive that material is, and thus the more complex that material is said to be.

In general, the degree of realism and detail in a material is proportional to its material's complexity, with more-complex materials generally being more realistic. However, more complex materials place a greater burden on the CPU and GPU than do less complex materials. Therefore, for the sake of performance, developers often seek to strike a balance or compromise in the complexity of their materials.

Lighting Only with Texel Density Mode   Lighting Only with Texel Density is yet another diagnostic mode (see Figure 3.19). Like Lit mode and Lighting Only mode, Lighting Only with Texel Density mode enables lighting and displays its effects on the surfaces of the level. This mode is distinguished from others, however, in that it substitutes the materials for all surfaces with a checkered material. The purpose of this material is to offer a graphic illustration of the mapping and tiling of the surface, as well as an alternative way to visualize texel density. More will be said about this mode in Chapter 5, "Materials, Textures, and UV Mapping."

Figure 3.19
Lighting Only with Texel Density mode enables developers to explore the mapping coordinates of geometry as well as to visualize the tiling and density of texels.

Game Mode   Game mode hides all level elements that would normally be visible to the designer in the viewport, but should not be visible to the game camera. These include such elements as sounds, lights, volumes, and other visual guides and references intended for developers.

Developers can use a feature called *real-time effects* to complement Game mode. Using real-time effects further reduces the difference between the view of the level in the viewports and the view of the level from the game camera. When the real-time effects feature is turned off, the contents of the level—waterfalls, water, clouds, birds, machines, and others—appear static and motionless, even though these elements might be animated in the game. Enabling real-time effects enables these animations—that is, it causes them to play back in real time, just as they would appear to the game camera. (To enable real-time effects, press the Ctrl+R keyboard shortcut.) The developer will see water flowing, birds flying, and machines moving wherever they should be moving during the game. In short, Game mode, together with real-time effects, can be useful for previewing how animated special effects, like particle systems and animated textures, will appear in the level without having to play the level (see Figure 3.20).

Figure 3.20
Enable Game mode with real-time effects to see a more accurate preview of the final game graphics in the editor, complete with animations and particle effects.

Viewports: Navigation and the Grid

Viewports are used not only to see the level and its contents, but also to move around and explore the level, also known as navigating. As you learned in the previous chapter, navigating with the viewport works much like controlling a first-person camera, like the kind found in most first-person shooter (FPS) games. The difference is the viewport camera can be moved up and down, left and right, and forward and backward, without being affected by enemies, dangers, solid objects, or other environmental forces that might exist such as gravity or inertia. The viewport camera can be navigated to bring any place in the level into view. It can travel through walls, up stairs, beyond crevices, and inside tunnels.

Because the level and viewport camera and all other game objects exist within a single 3D space, positions and sizes within that space can be specified, measured, and compared using a 3D coordinate system. The purpose of the 3D coordinate system is to enable developers to assign a unique number to any given position within that system, such as (0,0,0) or (5,4,3). This allows any given point to be identified immediately and systematically by its number. In addition, it enables you to perform arithmetic with the numbers—adding, subtracting, multiplying, and dividing them—to produce values that have meaning and relevance within the same coordinate system. For example, adding together two points, A and B, will result in a third point, C, that is a specified distance from the first point, A. Subtracting point B from A will also result in a third point, C, that represents the difference between A and B, or the amount of space to travel from A before reaching point B.

The UDK Coordinate System

This might all be well and good when speaking in the abstract, but how exactly does the 3D coordinate system work in the UDK? The UDK uses a 3D coordinate system consisting of three potentially infinite axes or straight lines that all intersect at a center point, called the origin. The origin is represented by the number—or coordinate, or vector—(0,0,0). One of the three axes (colored green in the UDK) extends from left to right and is known as the y axis. The second axis (colored red) extends forward and backward, and is known as the x axis. The third axis (colored blue) extends up and down and is known as the z axis. Together, these axes extend to match the limits of the level and can be used to describe any point within that space. Review Figure 3.21 to see how the UDK coordinate system and its axes are structured.

The 3D coordinate system enables the expression of positions and distances in the level as a three-component number in the form of (x,y,z). As mentioned, the origin is a point at (0,0,0). Any other point in the coordinate system can be expressed as a measured offset from the origin. For example, you can find a point expressed as (5,3,1) by starting at the origin, moving five units along the x axis, then three units along the y axis, and

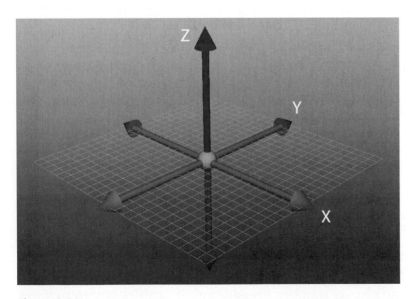

Figure 3.21
The UDK 3D coordinate system. (0,0,0) represents the origin, the center point at which all three axes (x, y, and z) intersect.

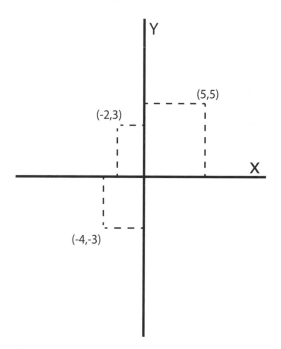

Figure 3.22
Finding positions in a coordinate space. (Diagram not drawn to scale.)

finally one unit up the z axis. Similarly, you can find the point (–3,–2,–1) by starting at the origin, moving three units in the opposite (negative) direction along the x axis, two units along the negative direction of the y axis, and then 1 unit down the z axis. See Figure 3.22 to visualize how points are located within a coordinate space.

World Space and the Grid

A coordinate space such as the one described in the preceding section in which positions can be identified absolutely and without discrepancy throughout the entire level is known as *world space*. This is because positions defined in that coordinate space have authority throughout the entire level. Each of the three axes in world space is divided into equally sized segments or notches called units. In the UDK, these are referred to as *Unreal world units*. If an infinite and straight line were cast from each notch on each axis, they would together form a grid of cubes that filled the volume of the entire level, with each cube in the grid being a cubic unit. These cubes compose the grid system in the UDK.

The main purpose of the grid is to help developers make informed judgments about the size of actors in the level, and to help them precisely position, scale, and rotate those actors. It is also used, as you shall see, for snapping actors to the

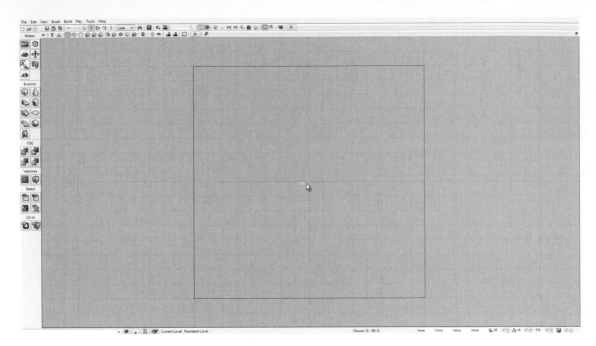

Figure 3.23
Measuring distances with the Measure tool.

grid—that is, for aligning the edges and extents of actors to the grid lines. The grid is visible by default in all orthographic viewports; if you prefer, you can switch it off in the viewport preferences. In addition, you can show and hide the grid via the Show menu, discussed earlier in this chapter in the section "Showing and Hiding Actors."

Another tool the UDK provides for working with the grid is the Measure tool. This tool, which works only in the orthographic viewports, is used to measure the straight-line distance between any two points in the viewport, in Unreal world units. To use this tool, click and hold the middle mouse button at point A, and then drag the mouse over to point B. This results in the creation of a red line that states the distance in Unreal world units between the two points A and B, as shown in Figure 3.23.

Note

How large is an unreal world unit, anyway? In the Unreal Engine 3, the height of an "average person" is between 88 and 92 Unreal world units.

Configuring the Grid

You can customize the appearance of the UDK grid in the viewport. Specifically, you can change the number of Unreal world units between each grid line. You can configure the grid such that a line appears for every world unit or for a variety of other

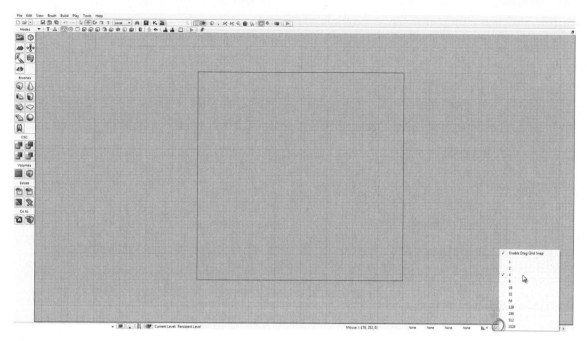

Figure 3.24
Configuring the grid.

sizes such as 4, 16, 512, or 1,024 world units. For example, if the grid were configured to display a line every 16 units, then every cubic division in the grid would represent 16 cubic units. Similarly, if each division were drawn every 4 units, then each cubic division would represent 4 cubic units. As you shall see, this can be a useful tool for reducing the density of the grid in the viewport, making it easier to see geometry, and also to position actors at specific increments and in the level. To configure the grid, click the Transform Snapping button on the status bar and select the desired value from the menu that appears (see Figure 3.24).

WORLD ACTORS

One of the fundamental UDK concepts is the concept of the actor. Actors are the constituent pieces of a level, meaning that a level cannot exist without actors. In many respects, the process of constructing a level is the process of adding, positioning, and arranging actors in 3D space.

Put simply, an actor is any gameplay object—a static mesh, a light, a sound, a start location, a volume, a particle system, among others. A typical level contains many gameplay objects, and thereby contains many actors. Saying that an actor is a gameplay object, however, is not precise; as you have seen, gameplay objects can be many kinds of things, each very different from the other. For example, a light is not like a sound, and a mesh is not like a particle system. So, when the term *actor* is defined as a gameplay object, it could be taken to mean almost anything at all. Hence, it is necessary here to be more precise about exactly what an actor is or is not.

Every gameplay object classified as an actor shares a common set of attributes and features that make it an actor. These properties are the essential properties of an actor—that is, they make an actor what it is. An actor cannot lose any one of these properties without ceasing to be an actor. So what are these properties? Well, it turns out that there are a great many of them—too many to list and detail here individually, although we will return to this subject in more depth in Chapter 12, "Scripting with UnrealScript." The next section considers three properties common to all actors and details how the values of these properties can be changed. A later section explains how you can display a Properties dialog box for any actor—that is, a dialog box that displays all editable properties for an actor.

Transforming Actors

Three of the properties common to all actors are numerical and decimal properties: position, rotation, and scale. That is, every actor in a level has its own position in world space as represented by a coordinate, its own orientation represented as an angle in degrees, and its own scale defined by three scaling factors. The position defines where in the level the actor will exist, the rotation defines the amount of turn applied to that actor at its position, and the scale defines the amount by which the actor will be stretched or shrunk to a new size (if at all). For example, a car mesh might begin in the level at a specified 3D position, and might later be rotated to face a specific direction, and might be scaled to a size that is appropriate for the level in relation to the size of other actors, such as buildings and people.

Changing the value of any one or more of these three properties of an actor—position, rotation, and scale—is known as *transforming*. Transforming an actor involves moving it (also known as *translating*), rotating it, or scaling it, or any combination of the three. You can achieve transformation in the UDK using any of the transformation tools, which are accessible via their toolbar buttons on the main toolbar. Whenever you need to change the position, rotation, or scale of any actor in the level, you will need to call upon these transformation tools (see Figure 3.25).

Tip

You can change between the transformation tools whenever an actor is selected by pressing the spacebar on the keyboard. Assuming the Translation tool is selected, a spacebar press will change it to the Rotate tool, a second press will change it to the Scaling tool, and a third press will revert it back to the Translation tool.

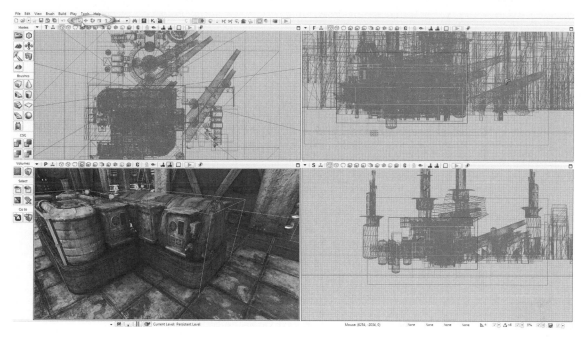

Figure 3.25
The transformation tools. From left to right: the Select tool, the Translate tool, the Rotate tool, the Uniform Scaling tool, and the Non-uniform Scaling tool. You use the Select tool to select actors in the level. (Other transformation tools can also be used to select actors, but the Select tool protects you from accidentally transforming actors during the selection process.)

Local Versus World Space

Before we get further into transforming actors, it is necessary to discuss transformation axes. Whenever you transform an actor in the level, you can perform that transformation using one of two coordinate systems: world space or local space. The world space coordinate system is a 3D coordinate system for defining and measuring positions uniquely throughout the level. The local space is also a coordinate system but is separate in that it is actor specific. That is, it is local to the actor. As with almost every 3D coordinate space, the origin of local space is (0,0,0). But this local origin is at the center of the actor, not at the center of the world. That means the same coordinate, such as (7,7,7), can refer to two different places in the different coordinate systems, world space and local space.

To visualize local space, imagine three axes—x, y, and z—extending in all three directions from the center of the actor. If the center of the actor (its local origin) is positioned at the center of the world, then the local and world origins will refer to the same position in world space. But if the actor is translated or offset to a new world position, away from the world origin—say, to (5,5,5)—then that position will be the

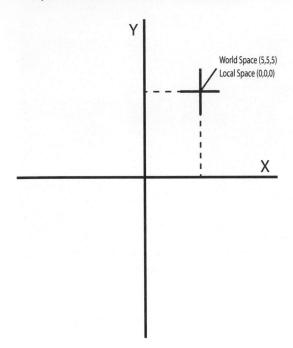

World Space (5,5,5)
Local Space (0,0,0)

Y

X

Figure 3.26
World space versus local space. Local space is a separate, actor-specific coordinate system within world space. An actor's world-space position actor represents the origin (0,0,0) of its local space.

actor's (0,0,0) origin in local space (see Figure 3.26). In this case, (1,1,1) in local space might have an equivalent world-space position of (6,6,6).

Some might question the usefulness of local space for transforming actors, perhaps wondering whether it might bring more confusion than it is really worth. After all, with the introduction of local space, it is now possible to specify a single position or coordinate that in fact refers to two completely different locations in the level, depending on the coordinate system used. So how does local space help you, and when is it appropriate to use it? To explain consider a situation in which the level designer positions an enemy character in the level. The local-space axes of this character are arranged so that the y axis extends outward from the character's eyes, representing the direction in which the character is looking. At first, the local y and world y axes correspond with each other. But suppose the level designer decides to move the character forward along the world y axis into the distance and to the world origin (see Figure 3.27).

Then the designer decides to rotate the character 45 degrees to the right about the world origin so that he faces a new direction in world space. Rotating a character involves rotating the mesh object; as the mesh object rotates, its local coordinate system will follow. The result is that after the rotation, the local y axis no longer

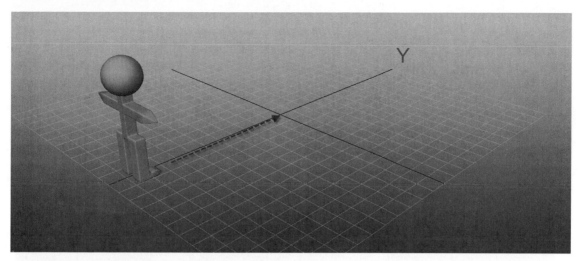

Figure 3.27
The character is positioned in the level and moved forwards along the world y axis to a new position.

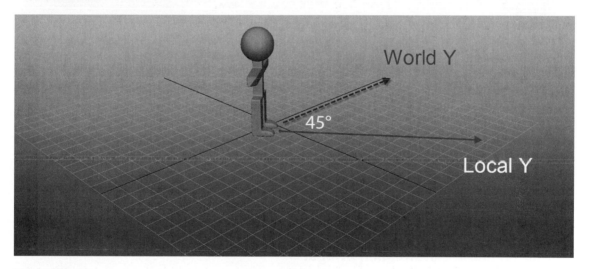

Figure 3.28
The character after rotation. Local and world axes cease to correspond.

corresponds with the world y axis. Specifically, the local y axis is 45 degrees away from the world y axis and facing in the direction in which the character is looking. That means to move the character forward along their look-at direction, the designer must translate the character on the local y axis, not the world y axis (see Figure 3.28).

Note

Whenever you want to position an actor at a specific location, scale, or rotation in the level, you should use world space.

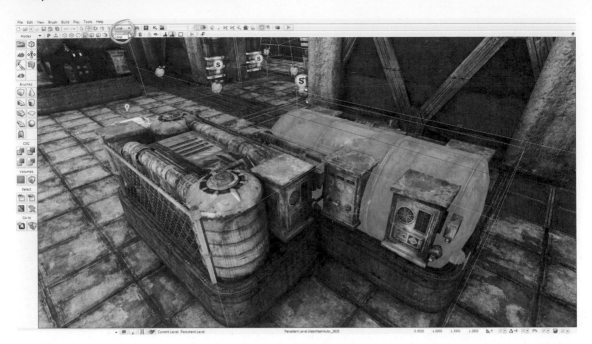

Figure 3.29
Changing the transform coordinate system between world and local.

Setting the Transformation Coordinate System

You can switch between the world and local coordinate systems by using the Coordinate System drop-down menu on the main toolbar. Select the actor to transform, select the transform tool you want to use from the toolbar (Translate, Rotate, or Scale), and then use the Coordinate System drop-down menu to select the appropriate coordinate system for the transformation (see Figure 3.29).

Translation and the Translation Widget

Translation is the act of moving an actor in the level to a new x, y, z world position. In the UDK, translation is performed using the Translate tool from the main toolbar. Once active, the Translate tool appears at the pivot point of the selected actor in the viewport as a multi-colored gadget or widget (see Figure 3.30). The translate widget displays x, y, and z axes that correspond to the local or world axes, depending on the transformation mode selected from the Transformation Mode drop-down box. The x axis appears in red, the y axis in green and the z axis in blue. You perform transformations on the selected actor by clicking and dragging on the specified axes. For example, to move an actor along the x axis, hover the mouse cursor over the red x axis (it will turn yellow), and then click and drag the mouse. The same process applies for the other axes.

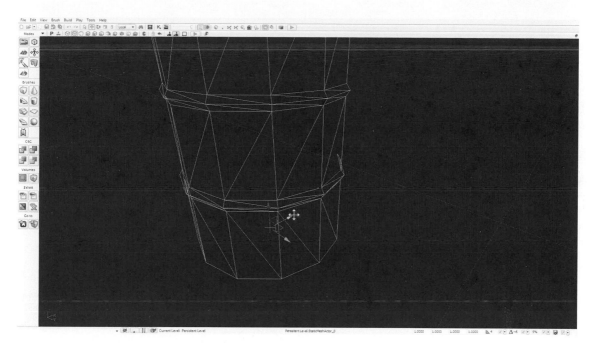

Figure 3.30
Restricting translation to a specified axis.

It is also possible to translate an actor on two axes simultaneously. To do this, make use of the right-angled shapes that appear where any two axes meet on the widget. Click and drag over the right-angled shapes to constrain movement on a plane, along any of the two selected axes (see Figure 3.31).

You can enable translation snapping by checking the Drag Grid Snapping checkbox in the status bar. This ensures that the selected actor is moved in constrained and specified increments that conform to the grid lines of the viewport. While snapping is active, the actor cannot be moved by fractions of an Unreal world unit; it can only be moved by whole units or groups of units. When snapping is disabled, actors can be moved in a continuous and unrestrained way without regard to the position of grid lines. Figure 3.32 shows how snapping can be toggled. Similar snapping settings are available for rotation and scaling.

Rotation and the Rotation Widget

Rotation involves changing the orientation of an actor—turning it about an axis. As an actor is rotated, its local coordinate space is also rotated. You perform rotation using the Rotation tool, which you can access from the main toolbar. When activated, the rotation widget appears in the viewport at the pivot point of the selected actor (see Figure 3.33). The rotation widget is divided into three color-coded sections,

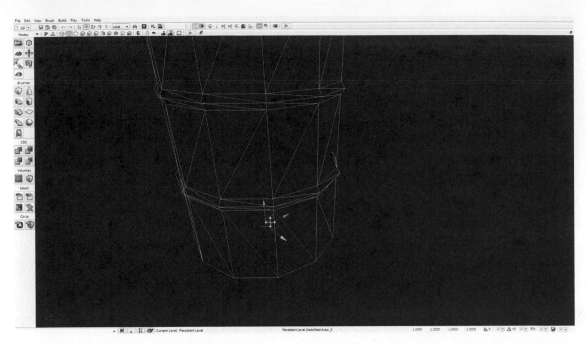

Figure 3.31
Restricting translation to a specified plane.

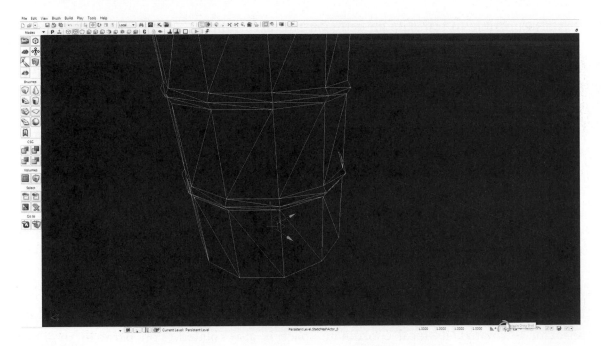

Figure 3.32
Toggle translation snapping to change the way actors are moved. When snapping is enabled, actors are moved in increments as determined by the spacing of grid lines. When disabled, actors can be moved free-form, without regard to grid spacing.

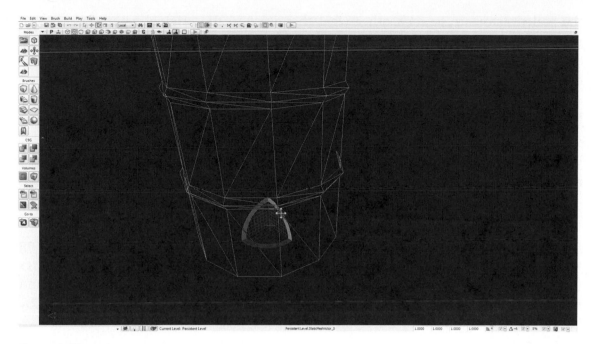

Figure 3.33
Rotating an actor with the rotation widget.

each representing a rotation around one of the three axes (x, y, and z). The red section represents rotation around the x axis, green around the y axis, and blue around the z axis. To perform a rotation, hover the mouse cursor over any of the three rotation handles (it will turn yellow). Then click and drag to rotate around the selected axis. While rotating the actor, the appearance of the widget changes in the viewport to display the angle and direction of rotation.

Scaling and the Scaling Widget

Scaling involves increasing or decreasing the size of an actor by a specified amount, called a scaling factor. For example, an actor scaled by a factor of 2 is made twice as large, and an actor scaled by a factor of 0.5 is shrunk to half its original size. An actor scaled by 1 maintains its original size, and an actor scaled by –1 maintains its size but is reversed or mirrored.

Scaling comes in two main forms: uniform and non-uniform scaling. Uniform scaling is a form of scaling whereby the actor is scaled by a single factor on all three axes. For example, an actor that is uniformly scaled by a factor of 2 is stretched to twice its size on all three axes. The result is an object that is twice as large in all its dimensions. Uniform scaling is *proportion preserving* because the relationships between the dimensions of the scaled actor do not change. That is, the width, height, and depth of the scaled actor are to each other what they were in the original actor. In contrast, non-uniform scaling is not proportion preserving because it enables developers to scale an object by different factors on different axes. With non-uniform scaling, for example, it is possible to scale an actor by a factor of 2 on the x axis, by a factor of 1 on the y axis, and by a factor of 0.5 on the z axis. The result of such a scale would be an actor that is twice as wide, just as long, and half as tall as the original.

You perform scaling in the UDK through the scaling tools—namely, the Uniform Scaling tool and the Non-uniform Scaling tool. You can access these tools via the main toolbar. Both scaling tools show an almost identical-looking widget in the viewport, positioned at the pivot of the selected actor. The uniform-scaling widget shows three red blocks, at the end of each of the three axes (see Figure 3.34). You scale with this by clicking and dragging anywhere over the widget. The non-uniform scaling widget shows three uniquely colored blocks, one at the end of each of the three axes (see Figure 3.35). The red block corresponds to the x axis, the green to the y axis, and the blue to the z axis. With this widget, you achieve scaling on a per-axis basis by clicking and dragging over the appropriate block. It is also possible to scale in two axes simultaneously, just as it was possible to translate in two axes simultaneously; simply click and drag over the right-angled symbol that appears on the widget where any two axes meet.

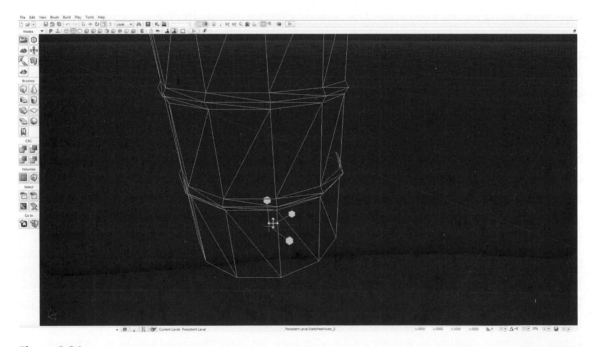

Figure 3.34
Uniform Scaling tool. This scales an object by one scaling factor in all three axes. It is proportion preserving.

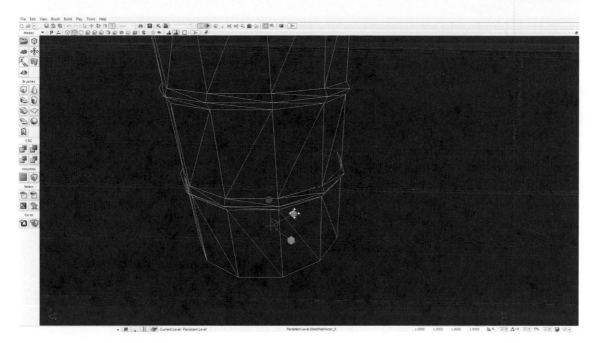

Figure 3.35
Non-uniform Scaling tool. This scales an object by one scaling factor per axis. This method of scaling is not proportion preserving.

Scaling by Specified Scaling Factors

The uniform and non-uniform scaling widgets are useful when you are not concerned with the exact scale of actors but intend only to scale by eye—that is, to scale them until they look appropriate. However, there might be times when your scaling must be more precise, such as when you are scaling two different mesh actors to fit them together precisely. In this case, you can manually type the specific scaling factors to be applied to the actors using the four Scaling Transformation fields in the status bar (see Figure 3.36). In the left-most box, named DrawScale, you can type a numerical value and press Enter to apply a uniform scaling factor to the selected actor. Alternatively, you can use the remaining three fields—DrawScale3D X, DrawScale3D Y, and DrawScale3D Z respectively—to enter non-uniform scaling values for specific axes of the selected actor.

Actor Properties

As mentioned, every actor in the level—from lights and sounds to meshes and volumes—shares a common set of essential properties. These properties make an actor what it is. Three of these actor properties are position, rotation, and scale. Each actor has a position within the world space of the level, as well as an orientation and a scale.

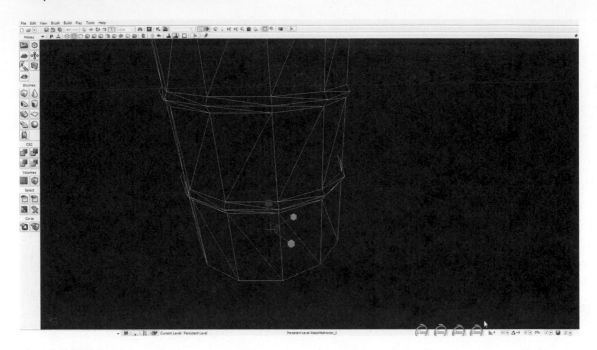

Figure 3.36
Use the Scaling Transformation fields in the status bar to enter specific scaling values for the selected actor.

In addition to these, actors typically have many more editable properties than this. For example, lights have brightness and color properties, meshes have material and mapping properties, and sounds have volume and effect properties, to mention just a few. The UDK offers a quick and easy way to view and edit all the properties of a selected actor: the actor's Properties dialog box (see Figure 3.37). You can access this page by one of three main methods: by selecting the actor in the viewport, opening the View menu, and choosing Actor Properties; or by selecting the actor in the viewport and pressing the F4 key on the keyboard or by double-clicking the actor.

The Properties dialog box consists of a collection of headings, each of which can be clicked to show or hide a set of related properties. For example, properties grouped under the Movement heading relate to the position and rotation of the selected actor; similarly, properties grouped under Collision relate to the size of the actor and how other actors should react if they collide with the actor. Other headings include Display, Physics, Advanced, Debug, Object, and others. The properties are too numerous to discuss them all in detail, but some of them are covered throughout this book and in particular contexts, as later examples will demonstrate.

Framing Actors, Locking Targets, and Others

The previous sections covered what actors are and some of their associated properties. This section considers some of the features and tools offered by the UDK Editor

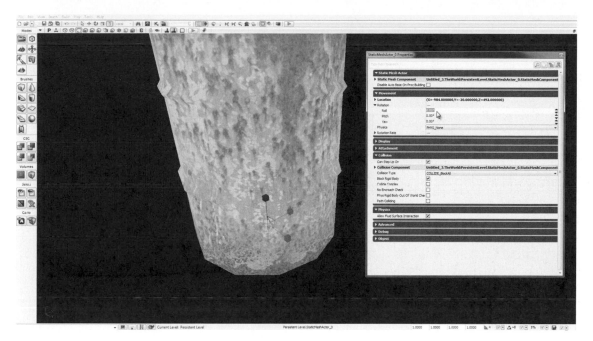

Figure 3.37
Use the Properties dialog box to view and edit the properties of a selected actor.

for working with actors in the level, in addition to the Translate, Rotate, and Scaling tools.

Framing Actors and Locking Viewports

As more actors and duplicates of actors are added, levels grow in complexity and density. When a level becomes complex, it can become easy to lose yourself in it and its details, and to lose track of the location of the currently selected actor. To focus all four viewports on the currently selected actor, you can simply press the Home key on the keyboard.

This homing feature is all well and good, but what if you want to center only one or a selected number of viewports (but not all viewports) on the selected object? To do this, click the Lock button in the toolbar of any viewport in which you *don't* want to center on the currently selected actor, as shown in Figure 3.38. (The Lock button is the one that features a padlock icon.) Despite what its name suggests, you can still move a locked viewport manually—that is, you can still pan, rotate, and zoom the viewport camera just as you could before. The lock feature simply prevents automatic adjustments or automatic moving of the viewport camera, such as the movement that occurs when you press the Home key to view the currently selected actor. Give this a try in the UDK Editor. (Be sure to deactivate the lock mode when you're finished to avoid confusion.)

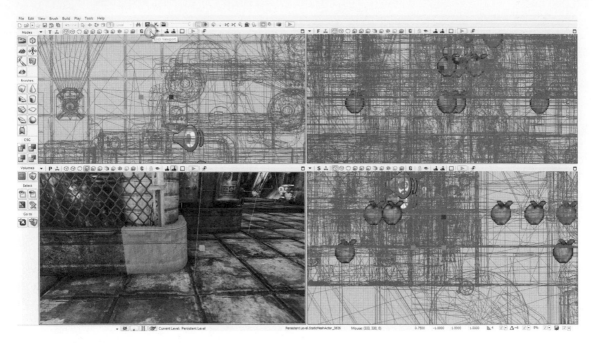

Figure 3.38
Lock specified viewports to prevent them from homing in on the selected actor.

Lock Actor to Camera

Every viewport toolbar contains a button with an eye icon, known as the Lock Selected Actor to Camera button (see Figure 3.39). You use this button primarily in conjunction with the Perspective viewport. When you click it, nothing seems to happen. The button appears depressed to indicate that a mode is active, but there is no other visible indication that anything has occurred or is occurring. That is, nothing happens until you select an actor in the viewport. When you do, the viewport camera is locked to, or aligned with, that actor.

More specifically, the viewport camera is aligned to the local axis of the selected object. The origin of the local coordinate system (the actor's position) becomes the position of the viewport camera, and the local y axis of the actor represents the direction (or look-at vector) in which the camera is looking. Furthermore, the viewport camera is locked to the selected actor, meaning that as the viewport camera is moved or rotated, the selected actor will be moved or rotated correspondingly. Clicking the Lock Selected Actor to Camera button will break the relationship between the viewport camera and the selected actor, enabling you to transform each one transformed independently as before.

Figure 3.39
The Lock Actor to Camera button aligns the viewport camera to the local axis of the selected actor. The origin represents the camera position, and the y axis represents the camera look-at direction.

At first, this mode might seem like an obscure and alternative method for transforming actors in the level. Although it can indeed be used to transform actors of any kind, it is especially useful for camera actors. (Camera actors are considered later in this book.) Lock Selected Actor to Camera mode offers a convenient way to see what the camera can see, and to position and move cameras on the basis of what they are viewing.

Maya Style Controls

In the world of computer graphics, Maya is a 3D modeling, texturing, rendering, and animation application, alongside other products including 3DS Max, SoftImage, LightWave, and Blender, among others. Like the UDK, Maya uses a 3D coordinate system and features viewports for previewing the contents of the 3D scene. To help the user navigate the viewports faster and to better examine the objects in the scene, it offers some keyboard shortcuts and controls. These popular controls have been ported to the UDK, where they are available for controlling UDK viewports. The Maya controls in the UDK are useful for rotating around selected objects. To use them, select an actor in the Perspective viewport, hold down the L key on the keyboard, and then drag the mouse to rotate around the actor.

CONTENT BROWSER AND OTHER MENUS

Levels begin their life in the UDK as a *tabula rasa*—an empty, black, three-dimensional space. You define levels by adding detail in the way of content—meshes, materials, sounds, and others. Content is added through the Content Browser. As such, the Content Browser is a fundamental component of the UDK for creating levels. It can be accessed from the UDK interface in any one of several ways:

- By clicking the Unreal logo button on the main toolbar (refer to Figure 2.22 in Chapter 2, "Building a First Project: A Tour of the UDK")

- By opening the View menu, choosing Browser Windows, and selecting Content Browser

- By using the Ctrl+Shift+F keyboard shortcut

The Content Browser is a digital asset manager in that it enables developers to manage and work with game content or assets—that is, with game-related data such as textures, materials, meshes, sounds, and almost anything else that can feature in the game. Specifically, the Content Browser enables developers to achieve a number of distinct but related tasks with assets. These include the following:

- It provides tools for importing content created in third-party software into the UDK system as a compatible asset.

- It enables developers to organize and arrange imported assets into an asset database that consists of packages and groups, and offers tools for tagging assets with content-specific keywords to make them easier to filter and search.

- It features searching and browsing tools to simplify the process of finding and previewing assets—and once an asset is found, it can be dragged and dropped into the level.

As such, the Content Browser has a pivotal role in the game-content workflow. It acts in some senses as a mediator between the Unreal Engine and the third-party content, enabling developers to import their externally created content into the engine as an engine-compliant asset. As shown in Figure 3.40, the Content Browser consists of seven unique parts. The first is the series of tabs along the top of the window. In these tabs, only the first refers to the Content Browser; all others display different screens, each serving their own purpose. The remaining elements refer specifically to elements in the Content Browser tab, which these are now considered in more detail.

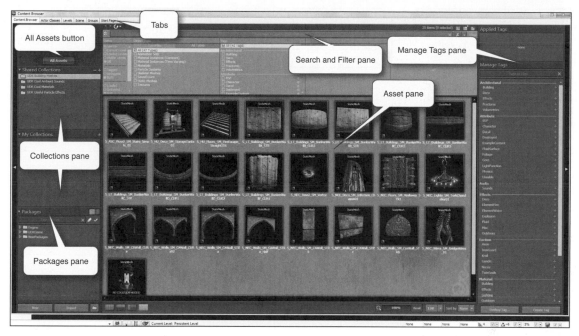

Figure 3.40
The Content Browser is a digital asset manager—a repository of imported assets that can be added to the level. Assets include textures, materials, meshes, sounds, particle systems, animations, and interface elements.

Packages and Groups

Meshes, materials, textures, audio files, particle systems, animations, and other game-related data are examples of assets or content. These are typically created in third-party software, such as Maya or 3DS Max. Then they are imported into the UDK via the Content Browser, where they are automatically converted and configured to be game-compliant assets. A *game-compliant asset* is any asset available in the Content Browser—an asset that the UDK has imported, converted, and configured successfully to work correctly with the Unreal Engine.

Note

The processes of importing assets are discussed at later points in the book on a per–asset-type basis. Chapter 5, "Materials, Textures, and UV Mapping," discusses exporting and importing material assets; Chapter 6, "Building Game Worlds with Static Mesh Actors," discusses mesh assets; and Chapter 7, "Music and Sound" discusses sound assets. This section considers assets generally, after they have been imported into the Content Browser.

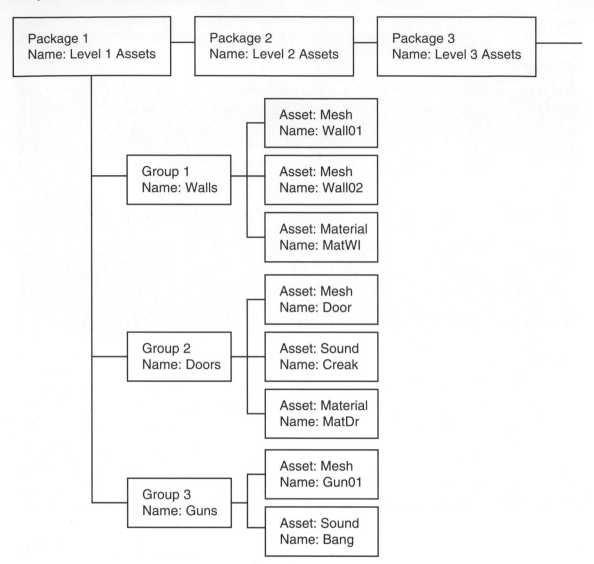

Figure 3.41 ■
You use the UDK asset hierarchy to organize assets. The hierarchy contains packages, groups and assets. Packages can contain one or more groups, and a group can contain one or more assets.

The imported asset—whatever it is—is brought into a relationship with the Unreal Engine and is arranged, like a file in a folder, in an asset hierarchy. The top-most nodes of the hierarchy are called *packages*. A package can be further subdivided into sub-folders called *groups*, and groups can contain one or more *assets*. The purpose of the hierarchy is to aid developers in arranging and organizing their assets to best suit the needs of their games and their workflow. For example, a designer might arrange packages and groups such that each package contains all the assets for a specific level, and each package is subdivided into groups to further organize those assets within the group. There might be one group for all floor meshes, another for all wall meshes, another for all character meshes, another for all sounds, and so on. (See Figure 3.41.)

The features and tools available for managing assets, packages, and groups are collected in the Content Browser's Packages pane, in the bottom-left corner of the window (refer to Figure 3.40). From here, users can explore the asset hierarchy, create new assets from scratch, import assets from external files, and import complete UDK packages filled with assets, as shown in Figure 3.42.

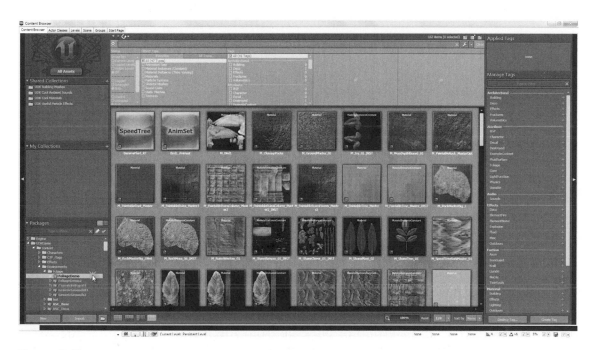

Figure 3.42
Clicking the nodes of the hierarchy—groups and packages—updates the Asset pane, showing thumbnails for all assets attached to the selected node.

Tip

You can use the Filter field on the Packages pane to search for a package or group with a specified name.

Notice that clicking a package or group in the asset hierarchy limits or filters the assets shown in the Assets pane to only those assets within the selected package or group. That means when you click an item in the asset hierarchy, you can see only the thumbnails for the assets associated with the selected item. To clear that filter and view all assets again, click the All Assets button in the top-left corner of the Content Browser (refer to Figure 3.40).

Importing Assets

The Import button in the Packages pane enables developers to import new assets from third-party packages. Table 3.4 lists the accepted file formats for specific asset types. Be sure to convert your assets to these formats as appropriate before attempting to import them into the UDK.

Table 3.4   UDK Asset File Formats

Type	Extension
Mesh	FBX, DAE, PSK, ASE, T3D
Sound and music	WAV
Texture	BMP, FLOAT, PCX, PNG, PSD, TGA
Movies and GUI elements	BIK, SWF
Material	T3D

Collections

A *collection* contains one or more assets. But wait—doesn't that sound like a package or a group? A collection is to the asset hierarchy what a virtual folder is to the file system: a pseudo-folder containing shortcuts to assets that are really contained elsewhere in the hierarchy. A collection acts like a package or a folder in the UDK interface to the extent that selecting a collection in the Collections pane (refer to Figure 3.40) will limit the Asset pane to show only those assets belonging to the collection, just as clicking a group or package from the hierarchy will filter the Asset pane. However, a collection does not actually contain assets the way a package or a group does. Rather, a collection contains shortcuts or references to assets that are stored elsewhere among the groups and packages of the hierarchy.

Deleting a collection or deleting individual assets from a collection removes only the asset references, not the assets themselves. That means collections act like custom-made filters, or like a Favorites bar or a quick-search feature. You can add a shortcut to one or more assets to any collection. It does not matter if the assets added are contained within the same package or group; a single collection can contain shortcuts to many different assets stored over many different groups.

In short, collections are useful in cases where developers want to quickly and frequently restrict the assets in the Asset pane to see a specific set of assets that are not stored in the same package or group. For example, a level developer might have arranged his or her assets so that walls, doors, floors, and ceilings each have their own group and package. In designing a particular room—say, a mad scientist's lab—the designer might call upon specific wall meshes, floor meshes, and other assets specific to that room. To browse those room-related assets—and only those assets— together in the Content Browser's Asset pane, the developer could add them to a custom collection called Lab_assets. Clicking the Lab_assets collection in the Collections pane will filter the Asset pane to show only the lab-related assets.

Adding and Removing Collections

To create a collection, add some assets to that collection, and then remove that collection, follow these steps:

1. Click the All Assets button in the top-left corner of the Content Browser to reset the Asset pane.

2. Click the Create Private Collections button (the one marked with a plus sign) in the Collections pane. Then assign a name to the collection and click the OK button (see Figure 3.43). Next, click the collection in the Collections pane; this will display an empty Asset pane because no assets have yet been assigned to the collection. Finally, click the All Assets button to reset the Assets pane.

3. Add an asset to the collection by clicking it in the Asset pane and dragging it to the collection in the Collections pane and dropping it there (see Figure 3.44). A shortcut to the asset is

Figure 3.43
Creating a new named collection.

automatically created. Repeat as needed until all assets have been added. Finally, click the collection in the Collections pane to show only the assets in the collection.

4. To delete the collection, select it in the Collections pane and click the Remove button on the Collections toolbar, marked with a minus sign, as shown in Figure 3.45. Confirm the removal by clicking the Destroy button. The collection is removed from the hierarchy, but the assets belonging to the collection are not deleted. These remain in their respective packages and groups.

Figure 3.44
Adding assets to a collection.

Asset Pane

The Content Browser's Asset pane contains a list of thumbnail images arranged in rows and columns. Each thumbnail represents a unique asset in the hierarchy—a texture, a material, a mesh, or a sound, among others. The number and type of assets shown in the list varies, depending on the group, package, or collection selected, or on the search and filtering options specified in the Search and Filter pane at the top of the Content Browser. These features limit the assets shown in the list so that developers can more easily reach the assets they are seeking. However, if you click the All Assets button, applying no filtering, the Asset pane will list all assets currently available to be edited or dropped into the level.

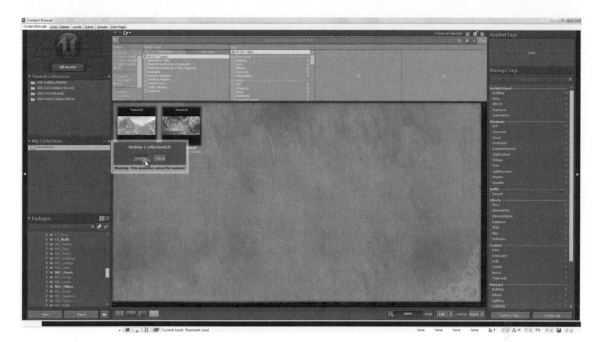

Figure 3.45
Destroying a collection.

Through the Asset pane, developers can do the following:

- Inspect assets.
- Edit and manage assets.
- Add assets to the level.

Inspecting Assets

The Asset pane offers a variety of features for changing the way Assets are arranged. You access these features through the buttons and drop-down menus aligned horizontally at the bottom of the pane. Specifically, the pane offers buttons for changing the viewing modes, changing the zoom level, and accessing the sorting options.

Changing the Asset Pane's Viewing Mode   As shown in Figure 3.46, the Asset pane's viewing modes control how much (or little) asset-related information appears in the Asset pane at any one time. This includes information such as asset size in memory, asset name and type, and the asset's path in the asset hierarchy. You can change the viewing mode by clicking any one of the four buttons in the bottom-left portion of the Asset pane.

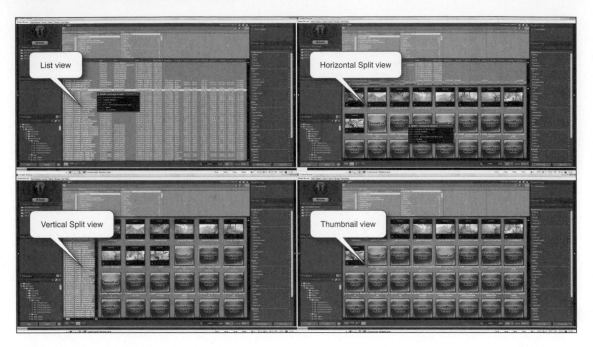

Figure 3.46
The four viewing modes of the Asset pane. The viewing mode determines the amount of asset information displayed in the list at any one time.

■ Clicking the left-most button sets the viewing mode to List view; in this mode, image thumbnails are replaced with a detailed list of assets, with each asset listed on a different row. Each row is divided into columns, with each column showing a specific property of the asset: its name, its path, its size, its dimensions, its type, and other data, depending on the asset type.

■ Clicking the second button from the left sets the viewing mode to Horizontal Split view. This view splits the Asset pane into two horizontal sections, with a detailed list of assets appearing in the upper half and thumbnails of the assets appearing in the lower half.

■ Clicking the third button from the left sets the viewing mode to Vertical Split view. This works like Horizontal Split view, except that it splits the view vertically.

■ Clicking the right-most button sets the viewing mode to Thumbnail view, which is the default mode. This view hides the detailed asset list, revealing only the thumbnails of the assets.

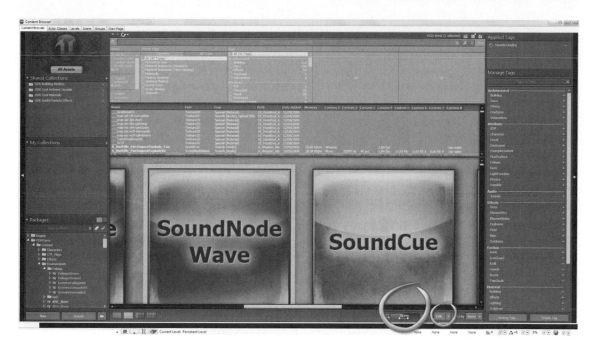

Figure 3.47
Zoom settings enable you to control the level of zoom applied to the thumbnails in the Asset pane.

Note

Which viewing mode should you choose? Whichever one you prefer. There is no right or wrong way to work here. I often like to use a Vertical Split view, with the detailed section being shorter than the thumbnail list. However, readers should choose the mode they like best, or the mode that best suits their situation.

Changing the Asset Pane's Zoom Level   As shown in Figure 3.47, the Asset pane offers two zoom controls to adjust the size of the thumbnails in the thumbnail list: the Zoom slider and the Size Setter drop-down list. To adjust the zoom using the Zoom slider, simply drag the slider from left to right or right to left to continuously expand or shrink the size of the thumbnails, respectively. (An alternative way to do this is to hold down the Ctrl key on the keyboard and scroll the middle mouse button, ensuring that the Content Browser has input focus.) To adjust the zoom using the Size-Setter drop-down list, simply click it to open it and choose from the list of preset sizes that appears to precisely set the size of thumbnails in pixels. The pixel sizes are 64, 128, 256, 512, 1,024, and 2,048.

Sorting the Asset Pane   When you sort items in the Asset pane, you define the order in which assets are listed. You can sort assets in the Asset pane by name,

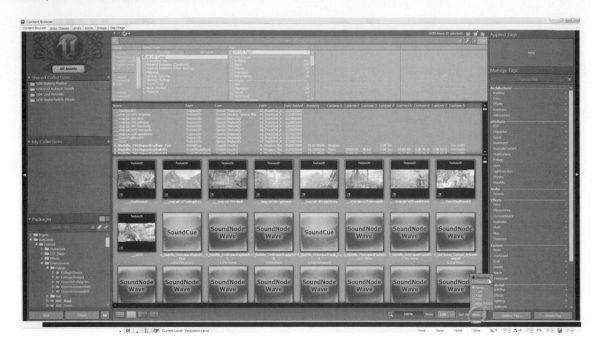

Figure 3.48
The sorting features control the order in which assets are listed in the Asset pane, regardless of viewing mode.

type, memory (size), tags, and date added in ascending or descending order. To access these sorting options, click the right-most drop-down list along the bottom of the Asset pane, as shown in Figure 3.48.

Editing and Managing Assets

The Asset pane enables you to do more than just inspect assets; you can both edit and manage them, too. Editing an asset involves changing the constitution or make-up of an asset. For meshes, editing involves changing the mesh's polygonal structure—that is, its topology. For sounds, editing involves mixing or applying special effects. The features for managing assets enable developers to change how assets exist in relation to other assets within the asset hierarchy. This involves deleting assets, moving them to new packages, renaming assets, creating duplicates of an asset, and exporting the asset to an external file.

You access the features for editing and managing assets by right-clicking any asset in the Asset pane. As shown in Figure 3.49, this displays a menu listing all asset-specific options for its editing and management. The options that appear on this menu differ to some extent, depending on the type of asset selected. For example, you'll see one

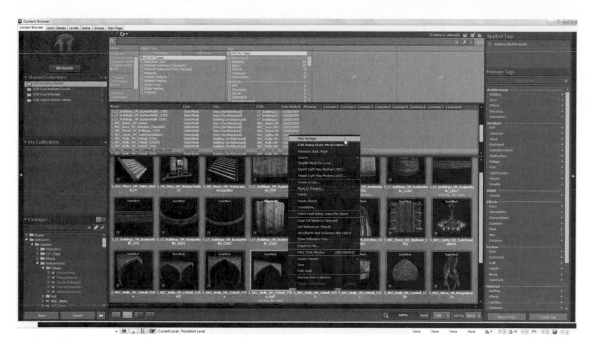

Figure 3.49
Right-click an asset in the Asset pane to show editing and managing options.

set of options for meshes, another for sounds, etc. That said, almost all versions of this menu have some options in common:

- **Find Package.** Choosing this option selects in the packages hierarchy the package and any sub-groups to which the selected asset belongs. This can be useful for identifying the owning package of an asset, something you might do to ensure that all the appropriate and required packages are distributed with your application.

- **Edit Using *Editor*.** Selecting this option opens the selected asset in a separate editor window that is tailored specifically for editing that type of asset. For example, the Static Mesh Editor will open if the selected asset is a mesh, the Sound Editor will open if the selected asset is a sound, and so on. The selected asset in the Asset pane can be one of several types: sound, sound cue, static mesh, skeletal mesh, texture, material, particle system, or movie, among others. (Later chapters consider each of the specific editor types in more detail; for now, it is enough to say that the UDK offers a range of editors and options for changing or tweaking assets, and that you select this option to access these editors.)

Note

Double-clicking an asset in the Asset pane of the Content Browser will open the default editor for that asset.

■ **Select Level Actors Using this Object.** There might be times during the development of a level when you want to select all actors in the level that are based on the same asset—for example, all duplicate mesh actors of a tree asset, or all duplicate sound actors of a sound asset. Choosing the Select Level Actors Using this Object option selects in the viewport all level actors associated with the asset selected in the Asset pane.

■ **Copy Full Name to Clipboard.** The names of assets in the UDK are often long and complex. This is because assets are typically named to express information not only about the asset itself, including its type, but also about its relationship to other assets and its position in the asset hierarchy. For example, one mesh asset that ships with the UDK is named as follows:

StaticMesh'LT_Buildings2.SM.Mesh.S_LT_Buildings_SM_BunkerWallA_STR'As

Although these long asset names do enable assets to easily be uniquely identified, they are difficult to remember and to type manually. Fortunately, you can select the Copy Full Name to Clipboard option to copy the name of the selected asset to the Clipboard, after which you can paste it into any application that accepts the pasting of text.

Note

Having the full name of an asset can be useful for search purposes. If you enter the full name of an asset into the Content Browser's Search field, the Asset pane will show only the assets with a matching name. Passing the asset name to other members of the development team means those members can quickly find the appropriate asset.

Adding Assets to the Level

One of the main functions of the Asset pane is to enable you to select assets and add them to the level as actors. There are two main methods by which you can add an asset to the level from the Asset pane. The first is the drag-and-drop method. Using this method, you simply need to select one or more assets in the Asset pane and then drag and drop them into any one of the four viewports. The selected assets will be positioned and centered at the world-space position that most closely corresponds to the cursor position in the viewport when the asset was dropped. The second

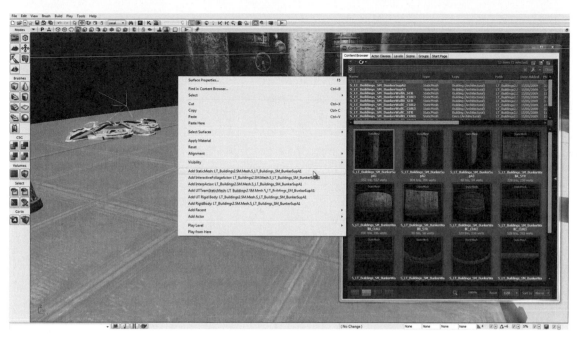

Figure 3.50
Adding assets from the Content Browser to the level as actors. Notice how the Packages, Collections, Search and Filter, and Tags panes have been collapsed to make more room for the Asset pane. You achieve this by clicking the Minimize arrow icons at the edge of each pane.

method is to select the asset in the Asset pane, close the Content Browser (optional), and then right-click the destination point in the viewport and choose Add *Asset* from the menu that appears, as shown in Figure 3.50. (The exact name of this menu command varies, depending on the type of asset selected in the Asset pane.)

Tags, Filtering, and Searching

The number of assets associated with and used by a video game will vary from game to game. Generally, however, most games will use hundreds or even thousands of different assets, from meshes and materials to sounds and particle systems. Because of the sheer number of assets used by a game, there is a developmental need to manage assets—to sort them, arrange them, search them, and filter them. This helps developers quickly find specific assets from among the many that exist, separating the relevant asset from the irrelevant, or the foreground from the background.

The Content Browser supports three main methods for searching assets: searching by name, filtering by type, or using tags. These methods are complementary; you need not choose one or the other, but can combine these methods to search for assets.

Figure 3.51
Searching all assets by name for the word *weapon*.

Searching By Name

To search assets by name, you use the Search and Filter pane along the top of the Content Browser (see Figure 3.51). Simply enter the full or partial name of an asset into the Search field; as you type, the contents of the Asset pane change to show only those assets matching the search criteria. Keep in mind that the Search and Filter pane works in combination with the filter and tag features, discussed next.

Filtering by Type

Filtering can restrict the type of asset listed in the Asset pane. For example, you can filter assets by type to view only static mesh assets, only sound assets, only material assets, and so on. You can also specify combinations of filters to view two or more types of assets together in the Asset pane, such as only static meshes and materials, or only sounds and particle systems.

You set filters in the Search and Filter Pane using the checkboxes beneath the Search field (see Figure 3.52). When you check a checkbox beneath the Search field, the assets shown in the Asset pane will automatically update to match the filter. You can also use filters to specify a range of assets to search. For example, if a filter for static meshes is applied, then any subsequent searches for assets by name will occur across only static mesh assets—at least until you disable filtering by checking the All checkbox on the Search and Filter pane.

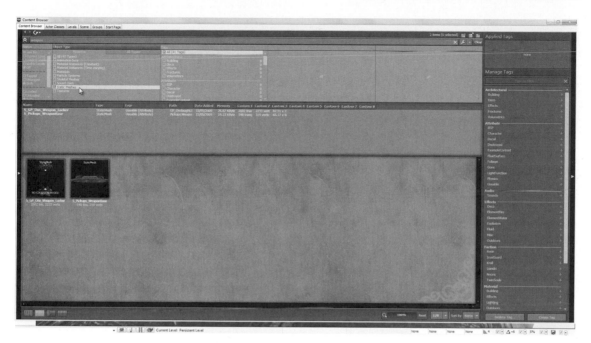

Figure 3.52
Filtering by the static mesh type. Notice how the Asset pane is further filtered based on the search and the filter. In short, the results shown here are for a search of static meshes associated with the word *weapon*.

Using Tags

Tagging in the UDK works much like tagging for photos and other files. The purpose of tagging assets is to enable them to be indexed—that is, to enable developers to search and filter assets by their tags. Tagging can make it easier and faster to locate assets.

A *tag* is a keyword that can be attached, or *tagged*, to an asset to describe that asset. For example the tag *weapon* might be attached to a weapon mesh to index or mark that mesh as a weapon. Similarly, the tag *explosive* might be attached to that same weapon to further indicate that it is an explosive weapon. Every asset in the UDK can have none, one, or many tags applied. In theory, there is no limit to the number of tags that can be attached to an asset.

You tag assets using the Tags pane on the right-hand side of the Content Browser. The Tags pane is divided into two areas: Applied Tags at the top and Manage Tags below. As shown in Figure 3.53, the Applied Tags area lists all tags applied (if any) to the selected asset in the Asset pane. It also enables you to remove tags from the selected asset by clicking the minus symbol beside the tag (see Figure 3.54).

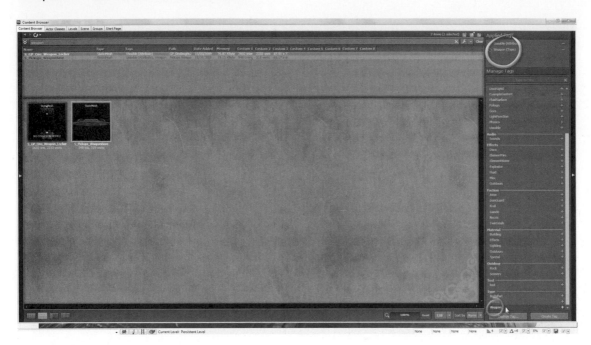

Figure 3.53
The Tags pane.

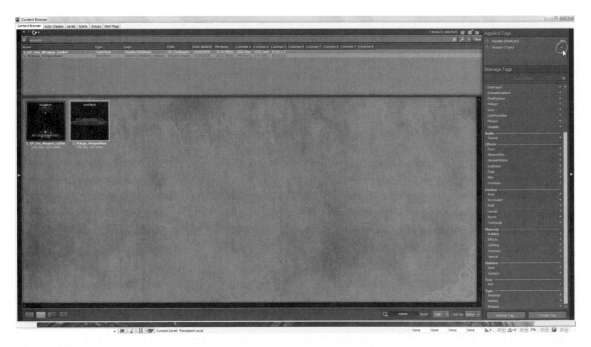

Figure 3.54
Removing tags from an asset.

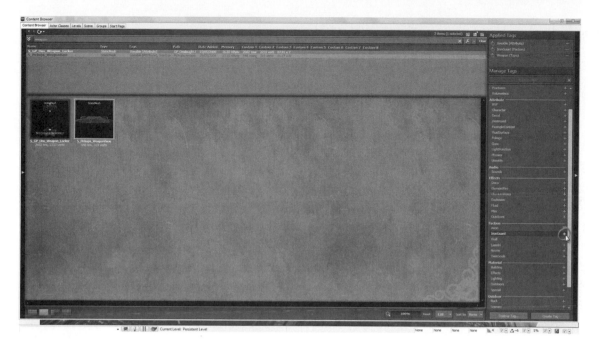

Figure 3.55
Applying tags to the selected asset.

Note

The Content Browser's Tags pane can be collapsed and expanded. To toggle between these states, click the arrow at the right edge of the Tags pane. In an open state, the arrow will point to the right, and in a collapsed state, the arrow will point to the left.

To apply a tag to the selected asset, use the Manage Tags area. Simply click the plus symbol beside the tag to apply it, as shown in Figure 3.55. You can also create and apply new and custom tags. To do so, click the Create Tag button at the bottom of the Tags pane; then enter name for the tag and the group under which the tag will be classified in the Manage Tags area (see Figure 3.56). After the tag is created, it can be applied to the selected asset just like any other tag.

Just as the assets in the Asset pane can be filtered by type, they can also be filtered by tags. To filter assets by tags, check the checkboxes next to one or more tags in the Tags section of the Search and Filter pane (see Figure 3.57). This restricts the assets in the Asset pane to those assets associated with the matching tags.

Browsers

As mentioned, the Content Browser is used to import and manage assets and to add assets to the level as actors. It is now time to move discussion away from the Content

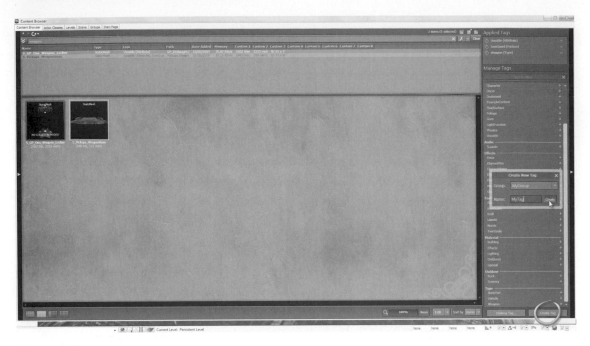

Figure 3.56
Creating new tags.

Figure 3.57
Filtering by tag.

Browser and to consider a selection of other browsers, which are accessible via the tabs at the top of the Content Browser window. These include the Actor Classes Browser, the Scene Browser, and the Groups Browser.

The Actor Classes Browser

The Actor Classes Browser is similar to the Content Browser in that it displays a list (albeit a non-thumbnail list) of objects that can be dragged and dropped into the level as actors. It is distinguished from the Content Browser in one fundamental respect, however. Rather than displaying a list of assets (such as meshes, sounds, or materials) that can be dropped into the level as actors, it displays a list of pre-baked, or ready-made, actors—that is, highly customized and specialized actors whose behavior and constitution have been pre-scripted in the UnrealScript language (see Figure 3.58). This list includes actors such as weapons, medi-kits, lights, vehicles, and other game-specific objects. Typically, you will use the Actor Classes Browser to drag and drop lights into the level, as well as the PlayerStart location—that is, the object defining the world-space position at which the player will be standing when the level begins.

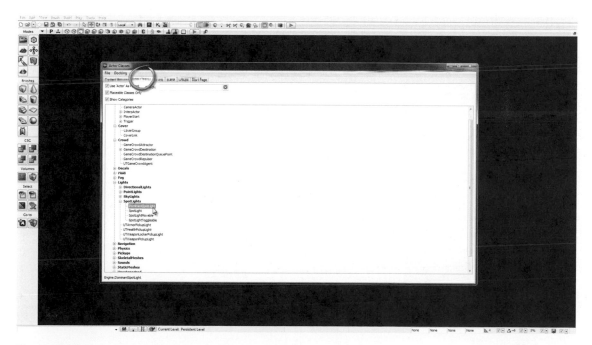

Figure 3.58
The Actor Classes Browser, used for adding specialized level actors.

Every actor listed in the Actor Classes Browser corresponds to a class in the UnrealScript language. That is, every actor listed is a self-contained unit of behavior and assets. You can tweak their properties to varying extents via their Properties dialog box (which you access by pressing the F4 key on your keyboard), but their fundamental behavior and structure can be defined only through the UnrealScript language. Later chapters discuss this browser in more detail.

The Scene Browser

The Scene Browser serves one main and critical purpose: to provide a searchable and ordered list of all visible and non-visible actors in the level. This list is especially useful when you need to search the level for an actor by name or to select an actor that is difficult to see or is hidden entirely. The list of actors in the Scene Browser is arranged in rows and columns, with each row representing a unique actor in the level. For each actor, the list states its name, its user-defined tag, its type, whether it belongs to a group, and its position in the level, among other properties. Selecting one or more actors in the list will also select that actor in the level, as well as display its Properties page (which is identical to the dialog box you open when you press F4) on the right side of the Scene Browser, as shown in Figure 3.59.

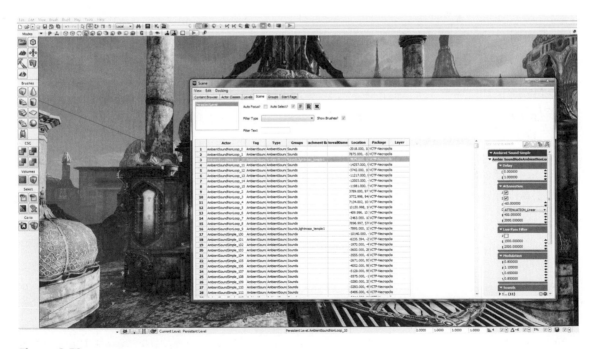

Figure 3.59
The Scene Browser lists all actors in a level.

Tip

Searching and browsing level actors by name in the Scene Browser is useful only if you've given those actors meaningful names. Names such as Mesh_1, Mesh_2, and Mesh_3 are not typically meaningful because they tell the designer nothing about the properties of those meshes. A designer cannot, from those names alone, determine what those meshes look like, where they might be positioned in world space, or the purpose those meshes serve. To know that, the designer would need to locate the mesh in the level for further inspection. To improve the speed at which a designer can work and to make the levels more accessible to other developers in the team, it is good practice to assign the actors of the level descriptive names, such as mesh_BlueEnemy, mesh_Telephone, and sound_Explosion. Unfortunately, the UDK does not enable you to change the name of actors per se. It does, however, enable you to add a tag to an actor, and this tag is searchable via the Scene Browser. To assign a tag to an actor, select the actor in the viewport and press F4 to display its Properties dialog box. Then click Object and enter a name in the Tag field.

Note

Every actor in the scene has a Tag property (singular). This property has no relation to the tags (plural) that can be applied to assets in the Content Browser. Assets in the Content Browser can be assigned one or more tags for categorization and searching purposes. The Tag property for an actor is a single string value that can be assigned to an actor and which works as a name for that actor.

The Groups Browser

The number of actors in the level typically rises very quickly as development progresses. Usually, it isn't long before a level is filled with hundreds of meshes, sounds, lights, and other actors. When a level reaches this stage of complexity, it can sometimes be a chore to find and select specific actors among the plethora of level actors, or to find and select multiple actors that are related in some way or by some criterion. For example, a designer might find it necessary to select all lights, enemy meshes, or architectural actors in the level. Although the designer could select these actors one by one, searching throughout the level for all relevant actors, doing so would be time-consuming and tedious if it were necessary to make these selections more than once.

To solve this problem, and to help organize the actors in a scene generally, the UDK offers various group features, which you can access via the Groups Browser, shown in Figure 3.60. To open the Groups Browser, click the Groups tab in the Content Browser window. The group features enable developers to create as many groups as they need, and to add one or more actors to a group. Actors that are grouped together can be selected and deselected together, hidden and shown together, transformed together, and deleted together if necessary.

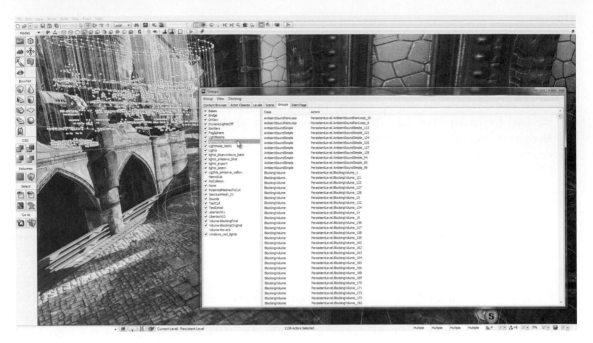

Figure 3.60
The Groups Browser is used to organize the actors in the level.

Creating Groups and Adding Actors to a Group　To assemble a set of actors in the level into one new group, first select all actors in the level that are to be grouped. (Remember, you can Ctrl-click to select multiple actors.) Then, in the Groups Browser, open the File menu and choose New. Name the group and click OK; the group is created, and the actors you selected are added to it.

To add actors to an existing group, first select all actors in the level that you want to add to the group. Then, in the Groups Browser, select the group to which the actors should be added. Next, open the File menu and choose Add Selected Actors to Group, as shown in Figure 3.61. The selected actors are added to the group.

Selecting All Actors in a Group　You can assign actors to groups. This can be useful for organizing actors in the scene—that is, for keeping related actors together such as all the trees, enemies, or weapons in a level. Sometimes, developers will likely want to select actors based on their relationship to each other, and thus will want to select all actors in a specified group. There are two ways to select all actors in a group. One is to select the group from the Groups Browser, and then open File menu and choose Select Actors. The other is to double-click the group name in the Groups Browser list.

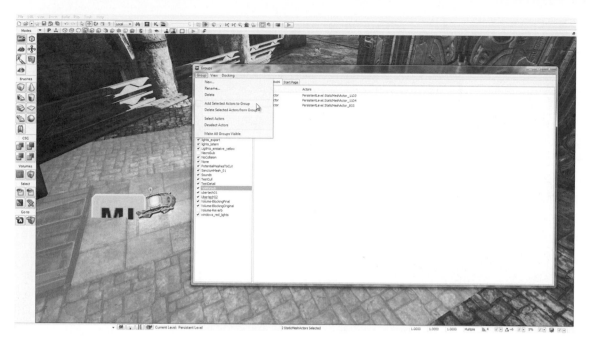

Figure 3.61
Adding actors to a group.

THE TOOLBOX

The toolbox, shown back in Figure 3.1, is a vertical bar of buttons that runs along the left side of the main UDK Editor window. The toolbox is distinct both in its appearance and in its function from the toolbar that runs horizontally along the top of the window. Generally speaking, the purpose of the toolbar is to provide access to application-level features such as Load and Save commands; to tools available through the UDK Editor, such as the Kismet Editor and the Matinee Editor; and to level-wide features such as Build Lighting and Build Geometry, the details of which will be given in later chapters. In contrast, the toolbox provides access to a range of features that aid the developer in defining, editing, or arranging level content, such as changing the mapping coordinates of mesh actors or building and adding special volumes, including collision and light volumes.

As shown in Figure 3.62 the toolbox's buttons are divided by type across six sections, which are discussed next:

- Modes
- BSP Brushes
- CSG
- Volumes

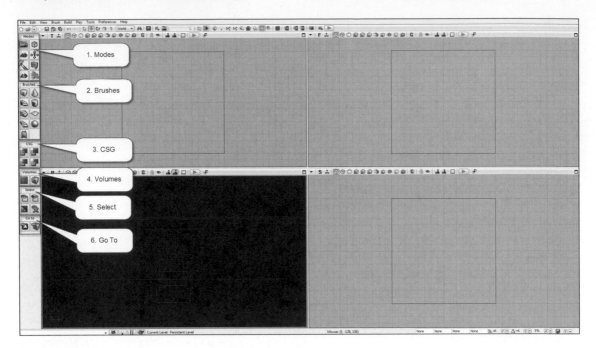

Figure 3.62
Toolbox buttons.

- Select
- Go To

The Modes Section

The Modes section of the toolbox, shown in Figure 3.63, contains a series of buttons that can be used to set the UDK Editor in a specific mode. *Mode* refers to a specific GUI layout and a collection of behaviors that define how the editor displays the level and how it responds to user input. Each mode helps you achieve different things. Following is an overview of each mode. (Most of the modes are discussed in more depth later in the book.)

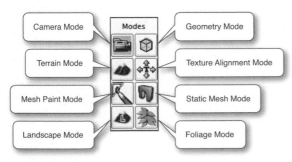

Figure 3.63
Mode buttons.

Camera Mode

Camera mode is the default mode. That is, the UDK Editor starts in this mode. If you switch away from this mode, you can access it again by either clicking the Camera Mode button or pressing the Shift+1 keyboard shortcut. Camera mode is the mode used by most developers, most of the time. This mode enables you to construct and edit the level in the most common sense. That is, in Camera mode, developers can navigate the viewports using the standard viewport navigation controls and can edit and transform scene actors using the standard transformation tools (Translate, Rotate, and Scale).

Geometry Mode

Geometry mode, which you access by clicking the Geometry Mode button (the one with a cube on it) or by pressing the Shift+2 keyboard shortcut, is used for high-level modeling control over BSP Brushes (see Figure 3.64). That is, Geometry mode is for defining and editing the shape of a BSP Brush at the component or sub-object level in terms of vertices, edges, and faces. In Geometry mode, the UDK enables developers to navigate viewports and to transform actors just as they can in Camera mode, but it also displays an additional toolbox of modeling controls, which developers can use to modify the internal structure of BSP Brushes. Geometry mode is discussed in more depth in the next chapter.

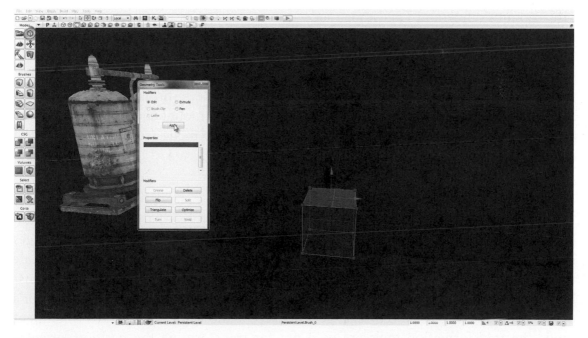

Figure 3.64
Geometry mode.

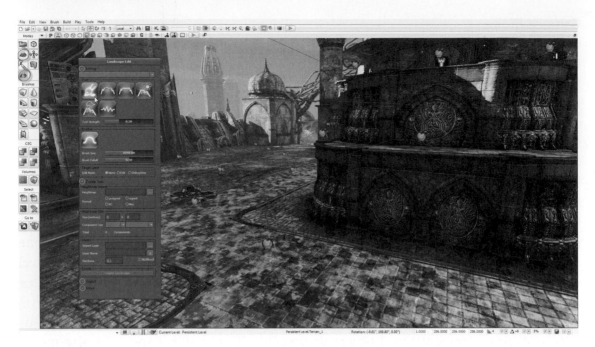

Figure 3.65
Landscape mode in action.

Terrain Editing Mode and Landscape Mode

The Terrain Editing and Landscape modes enable developers to use paint-deformation techniques to sculpt or deform the terrain of the level into shape. *Paint deformation* refers to a polygonal modeling technique that enables developers to use the mouse or a pressure-sensitive graphics tablet to paint detail and extrusions onto polygonal geometry. *Terrain* refers to any polygonal geometry that defines the terra-firma or ground plane of a level. This might include bumpy soil, rocky planes, or mountainous landscapes. The purpose of the Terrain Editing mode and the Landscape mode (see Figure 3.65) is to define the structure and appearance of terrain in the level.

Texture Alignment Mode

Texture Alignment mode, which you access via the Texture Alignment Mode button (the one with a cross-hair icon) or the Shift+4 keyboard shortcut, radically changes how the transformation tools work. In other modes, the Translate, Rotate, and Scale transformation tools are used to transform actors in the level. Specifically, the Translate tool adjusts an actor's world-space position, the Rotate tool changes the actor's orientation, and the Scale tool changes the size of the actor. In Texture Alignment mode the transformation tools are used not for transforming the position, orientation, and scale of actors (specifically meshes), but rather for transforming the texture alignment applied to meshes. In Texture Alignment mode, for example, the Translate tool does not move a selected mesh, but it does move the material applied to that mesh across its surface, as the loosened skin of an orange might be rotated separately around the fruit pieces inside. Similarly, the Rotate tool is used not for changing the orientation of the selected mesh, but for changing the orientation of the material applied to the mesh. Likewise, the Scale tool does not scale the mesh, but it does change the scaling and tiling of the material applied to the mesh. In short, Texture Alignment mode is for defining the texture coordinates of mesh actors by way of the transformation tools. More will be said about Texture Alignment mode in Chapter 5.

Mesh Paint Mode and Static Mesh Mode

The Mesh Paint and Static Mesh modes are designed exclusively for mesh actors in the level. The Mesh Paint mode is for applying texture and material effects, and the Static Mesh mode is for quickly and easily scattering multiple copies of a mesh throughout the level. (Mesh Paint mode is discussed further later in the book.)

Static Mesh mode is useful when you need to quickly drop many copies of the same mesh into different places in the level and at varying sizes and scales. These meshes might include rocks, trees, wood, rubble, flowers, foliage, hordes of creatures, etc. Although you could position, rotate, and scale duplicates of these meshes about the level by dragging and dropping them from the Content Browser, this approach can be both time-consuming and tedious. Using Static Mesh mode instead will make your life much easier!

Give Static Mesh mode a try:

1. Open the Content Browser and select a mesh for which many copies must be added.

2. Click the Static Mesh Mode button in the toolbox or press the Shift+7 keyboard shortcut.

3. While holding down the S key on the keyboard, click in the viewport at the position where you want to add a copy of the selected mesh. A duplicate of the mesh is added.

4. Repeat as many times as needed to add more duplicates.

As shown in Figure 3.66, in Static Mesh mode, a Properties dialog appears, displaying a range of properties that will be applied to the next mesh created. This dialog enables developers to randomly vary the appearance of each mesh by adjusting the minimum and maximum ranges for the Rotation and Scale properties. When you specify minimum and maximum values for these two transformation properties, the

Figure 3.66
Static Mesh mode.

UDK will randomly apply different rotation and scaling values within the range to the newly created mesh. It will do this automatically for each new mesh created.

The BSP Brushes, CSG, and Volumes Sections

The BSP Brushes, CSG, and Volumes sections of the toolbox, shown in Figure 3.67, are related. The BSP Brushes section is concerned with modeling the BSP Brush, while the CSG and Volumes sections are concerned with producing CSG and volumes on the basis of the brush. For more information about BSP Brushes, CSG, and volumes, refer to the section "Creating an Arena with BSP and CSG" in Chapter 2.

To summarize, the BSP Brushes section contains a set of buttons designed for automatically shaping or modeling the BSP Brush into any one of a standard set of geometric primitives. For example, the Cube button shapes the brush into a cube, the Sphere button shapes the brush into a sphere, and so on. The primitives available are as follows: cube, sphere, cone, cylinder, curved stairs, linear stairs, spiral stairs, plane, and cards (two intersecting planes). Each of these buttons also features an alternative menu for parametrically customizing the shape, which you can access by right-clicking the button.

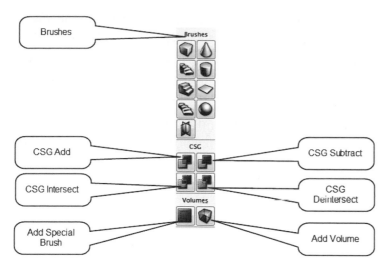

Figure 3.67
BSP Brushes, CSG, and Volumes buttons.

When the BSP Brush is shaped as designed, the designer then typically proceeds to build either CSG or a volume from the BSP Brush. To construct or edit CSG from the BSP Brush, click any one of the four CSG buttons: Add, Subtract, Intersect, or De-Intersect. These buttons are considered further in the next chapter. To construct volumes from the brush, any one of the two volume buttons can be clicked.

The Select and Go To Sections

The final two sections of the toolbox are the Select and Go To sections (see Figure 3.68). The Select section provides four different buttons for managing selections in the level—that is, selections of actors. Clicking the top-left button, Show Selected Only, hides all unselected actors in the level, enabling developers to focus their attention on the selected actor. Clicking the top-right button, Hide Selected Only, does the reverse. That is, it hides the selected actors, enabling developers to focus on the unselected actors. Clicking the bottom-left button, Invert Selection,

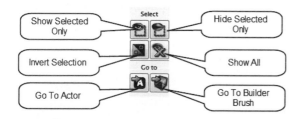

Figure 3.68
The Select and Go To sections.

selects all non-selected actors and deselects any selected actors. This can be useful when you need to select every actor except a few; rather than selecting all desired actors one by one, it can be quicker and easier to select the few you don't want and then to invert the selection. Clicking the bottom-right button, Show All, reveals all hidden actors, ensuring that all scene actors are visible in the viewports.

The Go To buttons relate to the actor that is centered in all four viewports. Clicking the left button, Go To Selected Actor, centers all four viewports on whichever actor is currently selected in the level. Clicking the right button, Go To Builder Brush, centers all four viewports on the red BSP Brush.

Conclusion

This chapter—which covered a lot of ground, both theoretical and practical—marks the end of Part I, "UDK Getting Started," and makes way for Part II, "UDK Essentials." The aim of both this chapter and of Part I as a whole is to detail the fundamental components of the UDK to establish a firm foundation for the work that will follow in the rest of this book. Indeed, you must understand the material covered in this chapter to fully appreciate and use the tools considered throughout Part II, "UDK Essentials." The features and concepts discussed here are the foundation, or infrastructure, on which other UDK tools, concepts, and features are constructed.

Having reached this point, you should have a firm grasp of the basics of the UDK Editor interface, including its tools for navigating viewports and for transforming level actors. Furthermore, you should be familiar with using the Content Browser to manage, organize, and add assets to the level. You should also be familiar with complementary browsers such as the Scene Browser, the Actor Classes Browser, and the Groups Browser.

I suggest that you play around with the UDK and create some levels of your own using the tools mentioned in this chapter before proceeding to Part II to consolidate your understanding of the materials covered so far.

The next chapter focuses on BSP Brushes and CSG. It explains how to model and create geometry using the BSP Brush, and further explains when to and when not to use the BSP Brush and CSG tools.

Part II

UDK Essentials

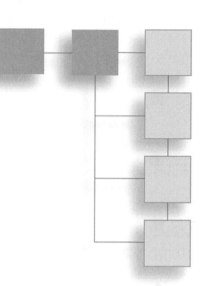

CHAPTER 4

BSP Brushes, the Builder Brush, and CSG

The essence of mathematics is not to make simple things complicated,
but to make complicated things simple.

—S. Gudder (Attributed)

By the end of this chapter, you should:

- Understand the relationship between the Builder Brush, BSP Brushes, and CSG.
- Be able to perform modeling operations in Geometry mode.
- Understand the geometric concepts of vertices, edges and faces.
- Recognize when it is and is not appropriate to use BSP and CSG in a level.
- Understand the BSP Wireframe shading mode for viewports.

The focus of this chapter is Geometry mode. This feature that stands apart from most other UDK features in that its purpose is asset creation more than it is asset placement or amendment.

A *mode* is a state of affairs. More specifically, in UDK terms, a mode is a unique configuration of features, shortcuts, tools, behaviors, and GUI layout into which the UDK Editor can be set on demand. The UDK Editor supports a range of different modes, including Geometry mode, Texture mode, Terrain mode, Camera mode, and others. (Refer to Figure 3.64 and the section "The Modes Section" in Chapter 3, "UDK Fundamentals.")

You can activate each of these modes with the click of a button in the UDK toolbox. Only one mode can be activated at any one time; activating one mode will automatically deactivate any other mode. That is, the UDK Editor can be set to Geometry mode or Camera mode or Texture mode or another mode, but it cannot be set to both Geometry mode and Camera mode, for example.

Each mode is unique and is distinguished from other modes by how it makes the UDK Editor behave and by the kinds of things it allows to happen when the mode is activated. For example, Camera mode allows users to navigate the coordinate space of viewports and to transform actors in viewports. Texture mode allows users to manipulate the tiling and alignment of texture maps on the surfaces of actors in the viewport. Geometry mode, by contrast, allows users to work with the geometry of the level.

In mathematics, the term *geometry* refers to land measure, and is concerned with the measurement of space and distances and with using numbers to describe shapes and sizes. In the UDK, the term *geometry* is defined more narrowly. That is, it refers collectively to all the 3D volumes, shapes, models, and meshes in the level. Any visible and tangible three-dimensional entity in a level, from cars to characters, is considered part of the geometry of that level.

Every piece of geometry in a UDK level—whether a character mesh, a gun, a tree, or something else—is categorized in one of two ways: as mesh geometry (which can be further subdivided into two groups, static and skeletal) or constructive solid geometry (CSG). The differences between mesh geometry and CSG are technical in that they relate not to the appearance of the geometry in the level but in the way they are constructed and in the way the Unreal Engine processes and understands them. That is, a gamer or developer cannot reliably determine whether any piece of geometry is a mesh or is CSG solely on the basis of its appearance in the level. To reliably distinguish the difference, a developer would need to use the UDK Editor and its tools to examine the properties and settings of the geometry. That being said, the majority of geometry in most levels will be meshes. That's because these are often easier to model in third-party applications and the Unreal Engine is optimized for rendering them. CSG accounts for the minority of geometry in the level (at least, in most levels), and is used primarily for creating 'simple geometry', including: walls, floors, ceilings and other flat and planar surfaces.

You might ascertain from its name that Geometry mode is concerned with the geometry of the level. This definition, however, is not quite specific enough to capture its meaning correctly. Geometry mode is in fact concerned only with CSG, not with mesh geometry. It would therefore be more accurate to rename Geometry mode "CSG mode." The purpose of Geometry mode is to provide the developer with tools for creating, deleting, and editing CSG in the level.

CSG is constructed on the basis of a skeleton or wireframe network called a BSP Brush. In turn, a BSP Brush is constructed on the basis of the Builder Brush, a red gizmo object that is visible in most viewports of the UDK Editor unless expressly hidden. These elements—CSG, BSP Brushes, and the Builder Brush—are the raw materials of Geometry mode. They are the elements with which a level designer must work to get things done. These elements and their relationship to each other are considered in more detail throughout this section, starting with the Builder Brush.

Note

Be sure to enable Wireframe Brush mode for all viewports when working in Geometry mode. (Refer to the section "Customizing the Viewport" in Chapter 3.) To enable Geometry mode, click the Geometry Mode button in the toolbox. (Refer to the section "The Modes Section" in Chapter 3 for more information on setting modes.)

THE BUILDER BRUSH

As mentioned, the three elements of Geometry mode are the Builder Brush, BSP Brushes, and CSG. These exist in relation to one another. That is, there is a direction of causation between them. This direction might be represented in the following way: Builder Brush > BSP Brushes > CSG. Put another way, the Builder Brush is used to construct BSP Brushes, and BSP Brushes produce CSG as an output.

The Builder Brush, then, is a tool used for the first step in the process of generating CSG. So what exactly is the Builder Brush, and how does it work? The Builder Brush appears in the viewport by default as a red cube or wireframe (provided it is not set to be hidden in the viewport options and provided its shape has not been changed). It is distinct from BSP Brushes and CSG, as well as any geometry of the level, in that it is visible in the viewport but does not exist as part of the level.

A Builder Brush does not belong to the level in the same way that characters, guns, walls, houses, and trees and other meshes belong to the level. Those elements belong to the level by being situated in the level coordinate space; by having a position, scale, and orientation in that space; by having a unique name among other uniquely named actors; and by having a presence in the level. In contrast, the Builder Brush acts more like the transformation gizmo or the viewport grid in that it is a design-time tool used by developers in the viewport for modeling and defining the shape of BSP Brushes.

The Builder Brush cannot be seen by the game camera when the level is played, and it does not appear as an entity belonging to the level when the Scene Browser tool is used. It can, however, be selected and, like most geometry in the level, moved, rotated, and scaled using the standard UDK transformation tools. Further, its shape, size, and structure can be changed and modeled into different forms, including spheres, planes, spirals, and all kinds of other volumes.

Note

You can toggle the Builder Brush into view in the viewport via the B keyboard shortcut. You can also show and hide it by opening the Viewport Options menu, choosing Show, and selecting Builder Brush. (Refer to Figure 2.6 in Chapter 2, "Building a First Project: A Tour of the UDK.")

The purpose of the Builder Brush (also known as the Red Builder Brush), shown in Figure 4.1, is to act as a template or a stamp for creating one or more BSP Brushes in its own image (see Figure 4.2). Developers typically shape and model the Red Builder Brush (hereafter referred to as RBB) into the form required—a cube, sphere, cylinder, or other volume—and then click the Add Static Geometry button in the toolbox. This stamps, or inserts, in the level an independent BSP Brush that is a clone of the RBB, added to the level at the same position, rotation, and scale as that of the RBB. After a BSP Brush has been added, the RBB can then be shaped and remodeled to create more BSP Brushes, without affecting the existing BSP Brushes.

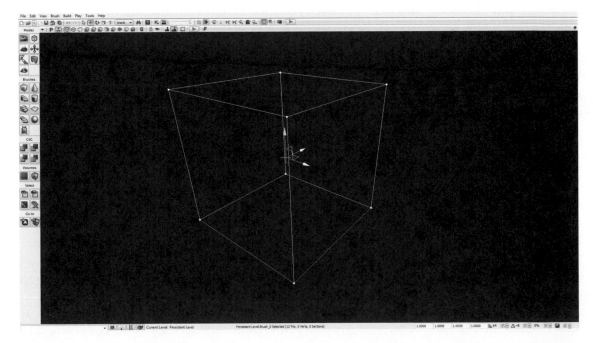

Figure 4.1
The Red Builder Brush.

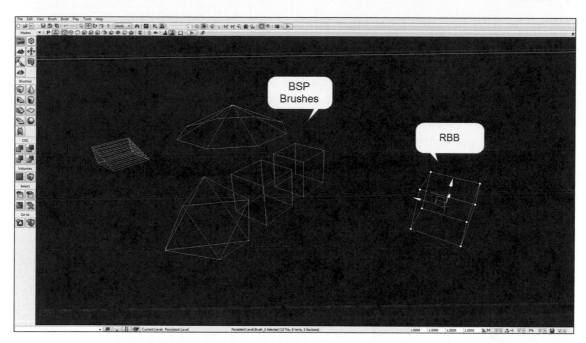

Figure 4.2
Adding many BSP Brushes to the level on the basis of the RBB. Remember: CSG results directly from BSP Brushes. Adding a BSP Brush is equivalent to adding CSG.

In short, the RBB is a 3D brush and is responsible for defining the initial shape, position, rotation, and scale of a new BSP Brush, just as the Brush tool in Adobe Photoshop is responsible for defining the shape, position, orientation, and scale of the brush marks added to the canvas. The output from the RBB is a BSP Brush. These appear as blue clones of the RBB in the viewport.

Note

BSP is an acronym for binary space partition. It refers to a rendering optimization technique. The details of this technique are not relevant to the successful use of BSP Brushes in the UDK, and are beyond the scope of this book.

BSP BRUSHES

As you've learned, BSP Brushes are inserted into the level on the basis of the RBB. The RBB can be used to create as many unique BSP Brushes as are necessary for the level. A BSP Brush appears as a wireframe in the viewport when the viewing mode is set to Brush Wireframe mode, although it does not appear in the game camera when the level is played.

Unlike the RBB (but like most other kinds of geometry), BSP Brushes do exist in the level insofar as each BSP Brush exists within world space; has a position, scale, and orientation; has a unique name; and goes on to have tangible results in the level geometry. A BSP Brush is like a geometric algorithm for producing CSG. That is, add a cube-shaped BSP Brush to the level, and the result will be cube-shaped geometry. Similarly, and add a sphere-shaped BSP Brush to the level, and the result will be sphere-shaped geometry. The CSG that results in the level is a product of the BSP Brushes.

BSP Brushes come in two forms (although both forms are created from the RBB).

- **Additive brushes.** Additive brushes add CSG to empty regions of the level in the shape of the brush.

- **Subtractive brushes.** Subtractive brushes remove CSG, or *subtract* a volume of space, from existing geometry in the shape of the brush, just as a hole punch cuts an identically shaped hole in a sheet of paper.

Figure 4.3 shows additive and subtractive brushes at work.

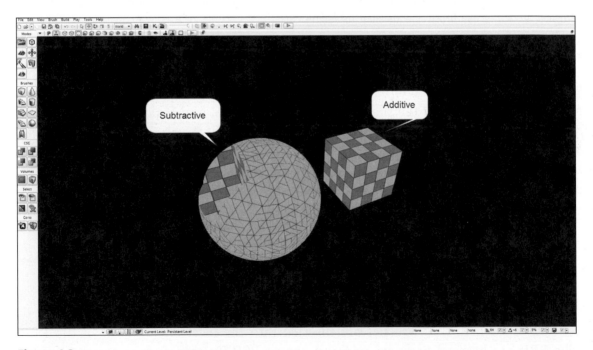

Figure 4.3
The additive brush sits alone in empty space and is cube shaped. It has resulted in cube-shaped CSG. The level also features a sphere-shaped additive brush that has been combined with an overlapping cube-shaped subtractive brush to produce CSG that appears as a sphere with a cube cut out, or removed.

What the additive and subtractive features of BSP Brushes demonstrate is that BSP Brushes need not work alone. They can work together—that is, compounded to produce a more complex brush network. The CSG that results in a level is not the product of individual brushes, such as an individual cube brush, but of *all* brushes in the level taken together as one complete geometric algorithm. An additive cube-shaped brush taken in isolation will produce CSG that is identical in shape and form to the brush. But if an additive sphere-shaped brush intersects with the original cube-shaped brush, then the two brushes are automatically combined into a brush network that results in more complex CSG. Many additive and subtractive BSP Brushes can be combined through Boolean operations into complex brush networks that have the potential to generate very detailed and complex CSG.

Creating Additive and Subtractive Brushes

To create an additive brush from the current RBB, click the Add CSG button in the toolbox. To create a subtractive brush, click the Subtract CSG button in the toolbox. (Figure 4.4 shows both buttons.) Note that it is good practice to add subtractive brushes *after* adding additive brushes. Adding a subtractive brush to empty space has no effect because such spaces contain no geometry to subtract.

The toolbox also contains Intersect and Deintersect buttons, also shown in Figure 4.4. These buttons produce a new BSP Brush on the basis of *both* the RBB and any other BSP Brushes it intersects in the

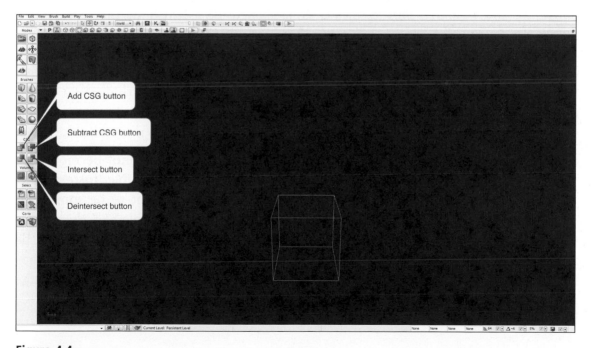

Figure 4.4
The toolbox's CSG section is used for creating additive and subtractive brushes. Brushes can also be produced from intersections.

level. Clicking the Intersect button produces a single BSP Brush, with the shape and form of the brush matching the volume of only the intersection between the RBB and other brushes. Clicking the Deintersect button produces a brush whose shape and form match the volume outside the intersection region. Why not give them all a try right now?

CSG

CSG, short for constructive solid geometry, is what results in the level from BSP Brushes when those brushes are taken as a totality—that is, when all the brushes are considered together as part of a brush network. CSG is *not* the same as BSP Brushes, however. BSP Brushes appear only in Brush Wireframe mode in the viewport, cannot be seen by the game camera, are combined with other brushes to define the topology or structure of geometry, and *can* be moved and transformed like the RBB using the transformation tools. In contrast, CSG appears to the game camera and in the viewport in shaded modes such as Lit mode, but cannot be moved, edited, or transformed. CSG is the static mesh or immovable polygonal data that is generated from BSP Brush wireframes.

To get a clearer idea about CSG and its relationship to BSP Brushes, try adding some CSG to the level. Start by creating a cube Builder Brush; then click the Add CSG button in the toolbox. This creates a cube-shaped BSP Brush in the level. Next, switch the Perspective viewport between Brush Wireframe mode (Alt+1), Wireframe mode (Alt+2), and Unlit mode (Alt+3). Notice that in Brush Wireframe mode, the structure of the cube-shaped BSP Brush is clearly visible (see Figure 4.5). In Wireframe mode, both the BSP Brush outline and the resultant CSG (polygonal mesh) are visible (see Figure 4.6). Finally, in Unlit mode, notice that only the resultant CSG is visible in the viewport, not the BSP Brush (see Figure 4.7).

As mentioned, the CSG in a level is static in the sense that it cannot be moved or edited after it is created from a BSP Brush network. It is not possible, for example, to select the CSG in the viewport and to rotate, move, or scale it to be something other than what it is. Does that mean you are stuck with immovable and changeable CSG in your level after the CSG is created? No. It is true that CSG itself cannot be moved or edited. But, CSG is generated on the basis of BSP Brushes and is permanently linked to them—and BSP Brushes *can* be changed, via Geometry mode. Editing the BSP Brushes that compose CSG is tantamount to editing the resultant CSG, because the CSG in the level is always linked to the underlying BSP Brushes.

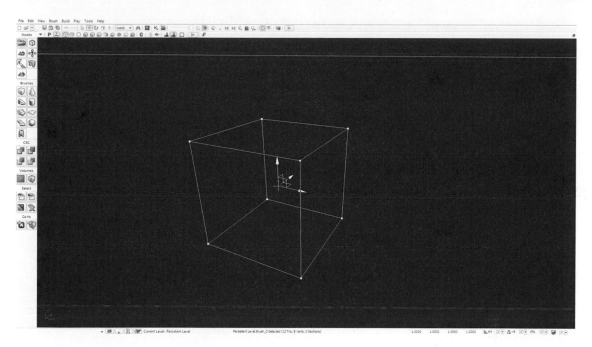

Figure 4.5
A cube-shaped BSP Brush in Brush Wireframe mode.

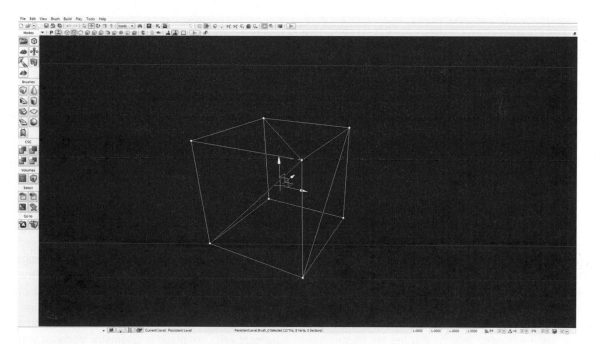

Figure 4.6
A cube-shaped BSP Brush alongside a CSG mesh in Wireframe mode.

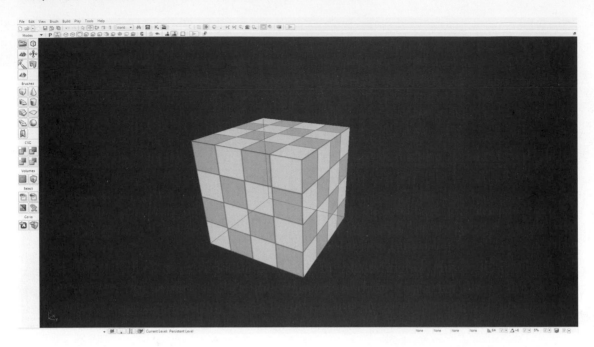

Figure 4.7
A cube-shaped CSG in Unlit mode.

Editing CSG

Create a cube BSP Brush on the basis of the RBB and then observe the cube-shaped CSG that results in the level. Use the Perspective viewport's Unlit mode to examine the CSG (refer to Figure 4.7).

Now suppose you want to move the cube CSG to a different location in the level. You cannot select the cube CSG directly to achieve this, but you can change the position of the underlying BSP Brush. To do so, switch the Perspective viewport to Brush Wireframe mode to see the BSP Brush; then select the transformation gizmo to translate the BSP Brush to a new position in the level.

Next, switch back to Unlit mode in the Perspective viewport and see what happens. The result is that the Brush Wireframe mode and the Unlit mode suddenly become out of sync with each other. Specifically, the Brush Wireframe mode shows the BSP Brush in its new and different position, but the Unlit mode continues to show the old CSG at its original position, as though the BSP Brush had never been moved at all. This might seem to prove that CSG cannot be moved or changed once added, or it might seem like an error or a bug. In fact, however, it is the result of how the Unreal Engine processes geometry. The BSP Brush has indeed been moved, but the Unreal Engine has not detected that this movement of the Brush has implications for the CSG in the level. To update the CSG in the level to bring it in line with the underlying BSP Brushes, you must rebuild the geometry of the level. This rebuild process must occur whenever existing Brushes are transformed or whenever edits are made in Geometry mode, as you shall see. To rebuild the level, click the Build Geometry for Visible Levels button on the application toolbar (see Figure 4.8). When you do, the UDK updates the CSG of the level to reflect the changes

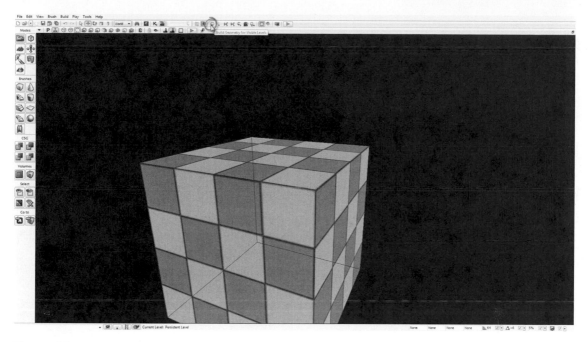

Figure 4.8
Be sure to update CSG by clicking the Build Geometry for Visible Levels button whenever changes are made to BSP Brushes in the level.

> made to the underlying BSP Brush. In other words, the CSG cube has moved! (Note that a dialog box might appear listing some errors relating to the absence of a KillZ plane; these errors can be ignored.)

Note

> You will have plenty of opportunity later in this chapter to combine BSP Brushes and rebuild level geometry.

COMPONENTS OF GEOMETRY

It has been said that geometry is an umbrella term referring to all the tangible elements of a level—all the things a gamer will see and recognize as having a material existence. This includes walls, floors, characters, guns, vehicles, and many other things. All the geometry in a level, whether CSG or meshes, is more appropriately named *polygonal geometry*. This is because without exception, all geometry in the Unreal Engine is composed of polygons—that is, triangles (tris) or quadrilaterals (quads). Although it might seem difficult to believe that organically shaped 3D meshes such as spheres, people, and trees could be formed from shapes with straight edges and right angles, Figure 4.9 demonstrates how this can be so. It shows a sphere

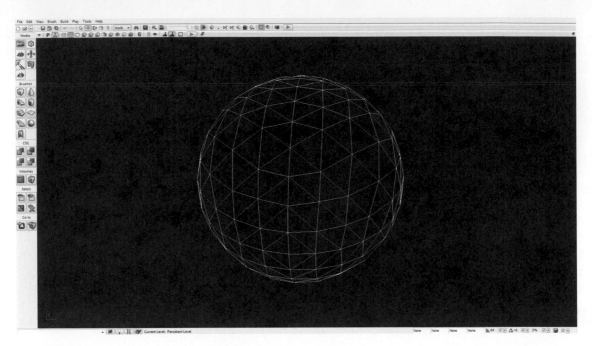

Figure 4.9
A sphere composed of a network of triangle polygons. This was created using the RBB with the Tetrahedron button selected and the Extrapolation option set at 2.

and its topology. Specifically, it demonstrates how a sphere is composed of a network of connected and appropriately angled polygons.

The polygons themselves—whether tris or quads—are composed of even smaller pieces or constituents. A tri, for example, is built from three corner points connected by three lines, one line between each pair of points. A quad has four corner points connected by four lines, one line between each pair of points (see Figure 4.10). In the world of games and graphics, the points are called *vertices* (the singular form is *vertex*) and the lines connecting the vertices are called *edges*, because they constitute the edges of the polygon. Thus, geometry in the Unreal Engine is composed of three kinds of components, or sub-objects: vertices, edges, and polygons, also called *faces*.

The UDK's Geometry mode is for modeling. *Modeling* is the process of adding, removing, and editing vertices, edges, and faces. Together, those components define the form of the geometry. This section covers using Geometry mode for modeling. Before continuing, switch to Geometry mode by clicking the Geometry Mode button in the UDK toolbox. Also ensure the Perspective viewport is switched to Brush Wireframe mode (Alt+1), as shown in Figure 4.11.

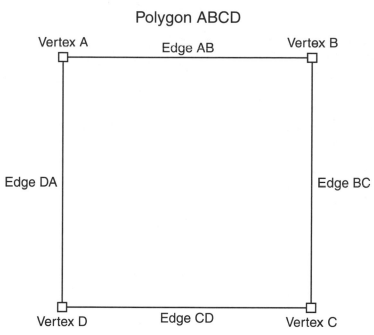

Figure 4.10
A quad composed of four corner vertices, ABCD, connected by a sequence of edges: AB, BC, CD, and DA.

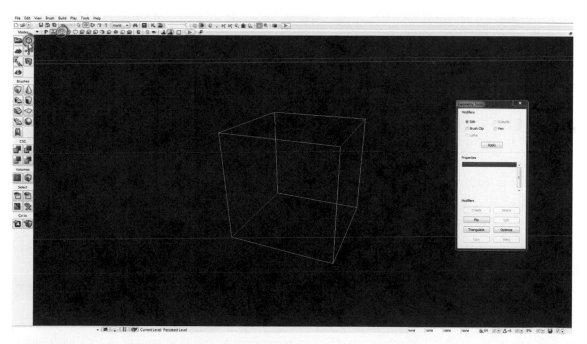

Figure 4.11
Geometry mode enables you to add, remove, and edit the components of CSG: vertices, edges, and faces.

Vertices

A vertex is the simplest piece of geometry, in that it does not depend on any smaller or simpler pieces for its existence. Geometrically, a vertex cannot be broken down into smaller pieces in the same way a shape can be broken down into vertices and edges. A vertex just is.

A vertex is almost identical to a point. Both a point and a vertex define a position in 3D space, such as (5,10,15) or (0,0,0). The difference between them is in their usage. A point exists in isolation—one point here and one point there, etc. In contrast, a vertex is a point that exists in relationship to other vertices, edges, and faces to form geometry.

The UDK gives you access to the vertices of both the Red Builder Brush and BSP Brushes through Geometry mode and the Brush Wireframe viewport mode. When both modes are enabled, and when either the RBB or any BSP Brush is selected, it is possible to access the vertices of the selected object. Try it now by selecting the RBB in the Perspective viewport. When the RBB is selected, the vertices are represented by small red squares (see Figure 4.12). Having access to the vertices of an object enables you to do two different but related things: to select one or more of

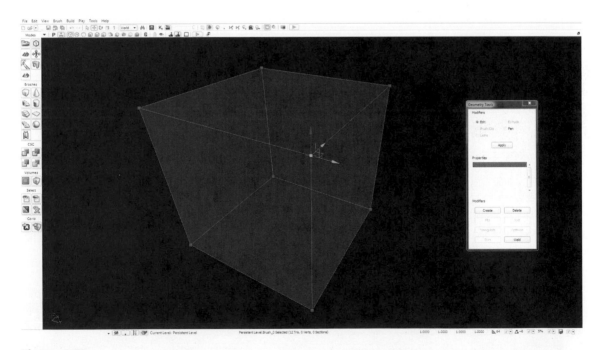

Figure 4.12
Vertices can be accessed in Geometry mode. They are represented by small red squares. A cube has eight vertices, one at each corner.

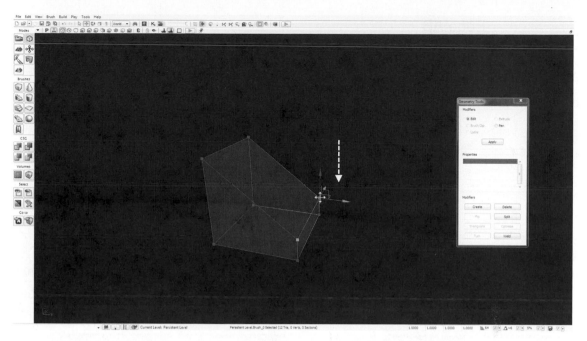

Figure 4.13
The top-left vertices are translated downward to change the shape of the RBB into a wedge.

the vertices with the Selection tool and to transform the selection using the Translate, Scale, and Rotate transformation tools (see Figure 4.13).

Edges

Edges are to lines what vertices are to points. In isolation, a line remains a line and nothing more. A line becomes an edge, however, when it is brought into relationship with other vertices and lines to form a polygon and, at a higher level, geometry. An edge is unlike a vertex in that it is a complex object, defined by two end vertices (v1 and v2), as shown in Figure 4.14. As with vertices, UDK Geometry mode allows you to select edges and transform them using the standard selection and transformation tools (see Figure 4.15).

Tip

Because edges are a type of line, and they have no width (except the width given to them by the UDK for the purposes of display in the viewports), they can be difficult to select. Fortunately, there is a technique that can make it easier to select the edges of geometry: clicking on them from inside the mesh. That is, to select an edge, move the viewport camera into the interior of the mesh and select the edge from within.

Edge AB

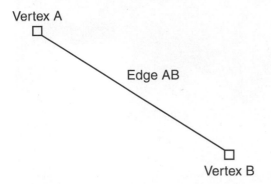

Figure 4.14
An edge is a line formed between two vertices. A connected sequence of enclosed edges forms a polygon.

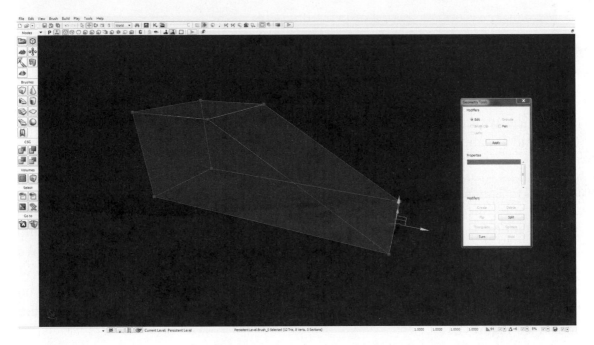

Figure 4.15
A line is selected and translated to elongate a cube.

Faces

A series of connected and enclosed edges form a face (see Figure 4.16). That is, a face, or shape, is produced when a series of connected edges makes an enclosed space, such as a triangle, rectangle, or other shape. An enclosed space is one in

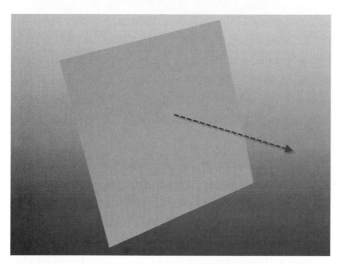

Figure 4.16
A face composed of vertices and edges. Faces are shaded (visible in the viewport and to the game camera) and contain a normal.

which each edge of the shape is connected to the next by way of a common vertex, and the final vertex of the final edge connects back to the first vertex of the first edge. This, in short, describes the geometric composition of a face, as it might be related in a mathematics textbook, and applies here too. However, in the case of games and the UDK, there are at least three additional properties, features, and conditions relating to faces that set faces apart from both vertices and edges and from the traditional mathematical concept of a face.

- In mathematics, a face can have almost any number of sides, from three onwards. In games, however, faces must be either three- or four-sided—either tris or quads (with tris preferred in most cases). Nothing more is acceptable. This restriction on the number of edges a single face can have exists for many different reasons, chief among them being the performance benefits.

Note

Some game engines support four-sided polygons and others support only three, depending on the rendering technology used. The Unreal Engine uses DirectX when rendering games on the Windows platform, and this technology does not support four-sided polygons directly. That is, four-sided polygons are assembled from two triangles aligned together.

- Unlike vertices and edges, faces are shaded and renderable, meaning the area of space enclosed by the edges will appear shaded and visible both in the viewports *and* to the game camera. The way in which the surface appears to the camera (its shininess, smoothness, roughness, etc.) is defined by its material. (Materials are discussed further in the next chapter.) By default, a checker-pattern material is applied to all faces whose material is not defined explicitly.

■ Every face has a normal vector (often simply called a normal). A *normal* is a vector (like an invisible arrow) that sits perpendicular to the face and points away in a straight line in one direction or the other. The main purpose of the normal is to define which way the polygon is facing. This matters because polygons are one-sided, meaning only one side of the polygon will be visible to the camera. The other side will appear completely transparent. The normal of the face determines which of the two sides is visible. That is, the normal points in the direction of the visible side and not the non-visible side. The visible side of the polygon can be changed by flipping the normal, as you shall see later in this chapter.

Like vertices and edges, polygons can be selected and transformed using the UDK selection and transformation tools. Figure 4.17 shows how the shape of the cube RBB can be adjusted by reducing the scale of one of its faces.

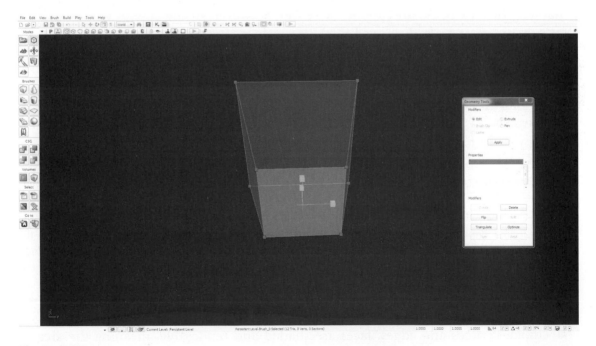

Figure 4.17
Reshaping a cube by scaling its faces.

Modeling in Geometry Mode

The polygonal geometry of a level consists of all the faces in the level, composed of vertices and edges. Geometry mode offers a set of tools for modifying geometry through its vertices, edges, and faces.

Remember: Geometry mode is for creating, editing, and removing CSG specifically, not other kinds of geometry, such as static meshes. Static meshes are similar to CSG in that they consist of vertices, edges, and faces, but they differ in the way the Unreal Engine processes, stores, and understands them. The Unreal Engine is optimized for the rendering of static meshes in a way that it is not for CSG; as a result, static meshes are preferable over CSG where possible. That does not mean CSG has no role to play in the creation of Unreal levels, only that its role is severely limited.

The purpose of CSG is primarily to create simple elements of geometry—that is, geometry with few faces such as flat surfaces for walls and floors, and simpler geometric primitives such as cubes and boxes, which are often used for stairs, crates, or paths. Geometry mode offers a set of modeling tools for creating such geometry as this—*not* for more complex static-mesh geometry such as characters, guns, and other detailed structures. The latter kind of geometry is modeled by artists using third-party modeling applications.

Geometry mode offers two main sets of tools (one set of which you have seen already): selection tools and transformation tools. Transformation tools are used to modify the vertices, edges, and polygons of geometry, both the RBB and BSP Brushes. Geometry mode also offers an additional toolbox of modeling commands called the Geometry tools group, which appears automatically whenever Geometry mode is activated, as shown in Figure 4.18. You can use this toolbox to add, remove, and change the geometry of the selected element in the viewport.

The Geometry Tools Group

The Geometry tools group (refer to Figure 4.18) is a floating window of options and features that appears automatically whenever Geometry mode is activated. The options in the Geometry tools group are divided into three groups: Modifiers, Properties, and Modifiers. (Yes, there are two groups called Modifiers. In my view, Modes would be a more appropriate term for the top-most group.)

The Geometry tools group is context sensitive in that the availability of options (the options that you can click) depends on both the kind of object selected in the viewport (vertices, faces, or edges) and the various other buttons in the tools group that might also be clicked. The top-most group of buttons, called Modifiers (but which I call Modes), set Geometry mode into a set of sub-modes. That is, they do nothing immediately upon being clicked, but change the way Geometry mode behaves and responds when working with vertices, edges, and faces, as you shall see. The middle Properties group displays a set of properties and values that are associated with the selected mode. Finally, the bottom-most Modifiers group provides access to a set of quick, one-click actions and operations that can be applied to the selected elements of geometry in the viewport.

Figure 4.18
The Geometry toolbox offers tools for adding geometry (adding faces), editing geometry, and removing geometry.

The Edit Sub-Mode

The Edit sub-mode of the Geometry tools group is the default sub-mode insofar as it is active when the Geometry toolbox first appears, after you enter Geometry mode. There is not, in fact, much to say about Edit sub-mode that has not already been said; this sub-mode has already been covered in this chapter, although it was not mentioned explicitly. In short, the Edit sub-mode enables you to select and transform the vertices, edges, and faces of the selected object in the viewport using the UDK selection and transformation tools, including Translate, Rotate, and Scale. The purpose of Edit sub-mode is to enable you to amend (shape and reshape) the *existing* topology of the geometry—the mesh as it stands. It does not allow you to add or remove detail. That function is the remit of other sub-modes, starting with the Extrude sub-mode.

The Extrude Sub-Mode

You can activate Extrude sub-mode only when one or more faces are selected in the viewport. This sub-mode does not apply to vertices or edges. That is, the Extrude sub-mode checkbox will appear disabled when any geometry component other than

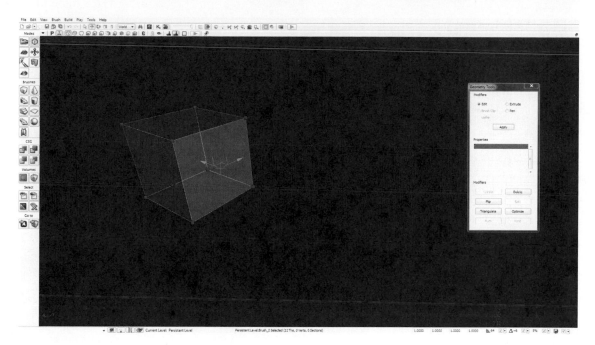

Figure 4.19
Using extrude in Geometry mode. Cube RBB before extrusion.

a face is selected. The Extrude sub-mode works in conjunction with the Translate tool and is a means of *adding* new faces to the geometry. When Extrude sub-mode is activated, users can move the selected face using the translate gizmo, similar to how it can be used to move faces in edit mode. In Extrude sub-mode, however, translating the selected face has the effect not of moving it, but of creating a new face at the destination location. This destination location is connected by adjacent faces to the original geometry, as though the original face had been extended outward. Figure 4.19 and Figure 4.20 show a before and after illustration of the extrude process.

To use the Extrude sub-mode, follow these steps:

1. Select a face.

2. Click the Extrude option button in the Geometry toolbox to enable the Extrude sub-mode.

3. Select the Translate tool.

4. Move the face as required. Geometry mode will automatically extrude the original face outward to the destination position.

The Extrude sub-mode will not allow you to *move* faces; the Edit sub-mode must be used for that. Each new and separate translate operation made while the Extrude

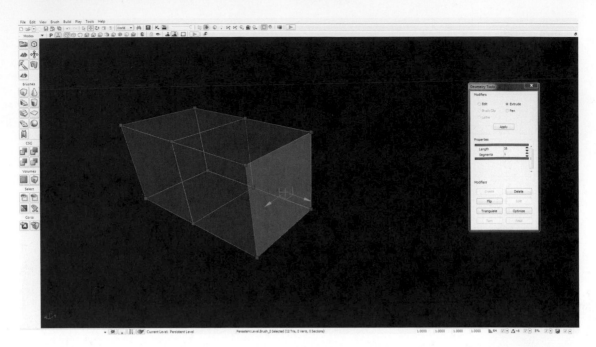

Figure 4.20
Using extrude in Geometry mode. Cube RBB after extrusion.

sub-mode is active will be considered a new and separate extrude, and will therefore create new and more complex geometry (more faces), as shown in Figure 4.21.

Extrude Options

The Extrude sub-mode has a number of parametric options that can be set and applied to all subsequent extrusions. These options appear in the Properties panel of the Geometry toolbox when the Extrude checkbox is checked, and are applied when the Apply button is clicked. The properties are Length and Segments. The Length property defines the length of extrusion to make from the selected face in Unreal world units, and the Segments property defines the number of divisions to make along the extrusion. The greater the number of segments, the greater the number of faces there will be along the extrusion. Both the length of the extrusion and the way in which it is divided can be controlled manually using the translate gizmo while in Extrude sub-mode, but the parametric options are offered from the Geometry toolbox both for those who prefer working with numbers when modeling and for those who require greater precision or control over the size of extrusions.

The Brush Clip Sub-Mode

The Brush Clip sub-mode is distinct from both the Edit and the Extrude sub-modes in that it is intended to work in an orthographic view and mainly with BSP Brushes rather than with the RBB. That is not to say that it cannot work with the RBB—it

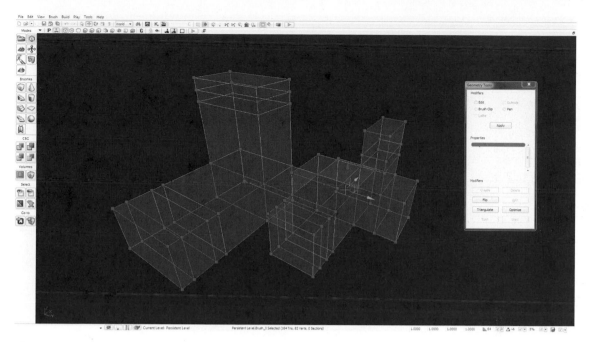

Figure 4.21
The RBB after many extrusions are applied to many different faces.

can, to some extent—only that its full potential can be realized with BSP Brushes. The Brush Clip sub-mode sets Geometry mode into a state that allows you to define a plane surface that intersects the volume of one or more brushes, and then to use that surface as a blade or cutter to slice the selected BSP Brushes along the intersection. In short, it allows you to slice apart a BSP Brush using a plane surface like a razor, much like an apple can be sliced in two by a knife. The Brush Clip sub-mode is useful when you need to create a BSP Brush whose shape is only half of a specific geometric primitive—for example, half a sphere, half a cone, or half a pyramid. Perhaps the best way to illustrate the Brush Clip mode is by an example. Try the following:

1. Start by creating a BSP Brush on the basis of the RBB. To do this, shape the RBB into a geometric primitive—say, a cube—and then click the Add CSG button in the toolbox to add a new BSP Brush to the level (see Figure 4.22). Move the RBB out of the way to see the BSP Brush more clearly.

2. Click the Brush Clip option button in the Geometry toolbox to switch to Brush Clip mode.

3. Focus on the top orthographic viewport. To create the clipping plane against which the brush will be sliced, press the spacebar twice, with the first press marking one point on the plane and the second press marking the second point

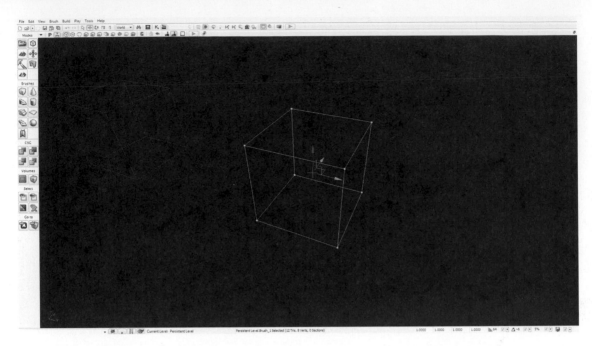

Figure 4.22
Create a cube BSP Brush from the RBB.

on the plane. From these two points a plane of infinite width and height can be constructed that passes through the two plotted points. This plane is constructed with the second spacebar press, and is visible in the viewport as a line and a normal (see Figure 4.23). The normal indicates the direction in which the plane is facing.

4. The slicing plane is created as a temporary object. It does not slice the plane. To perform the slice, you must click the Apply button in the Geometry toolbox. First, however, notice the options that appear in the Geometry toolbox's Properties group: Flip Normal and Split. These control how the slice will be performed when you click the Apply button. If you select the Flip Normal checkbox, the slicing plane normal will be flipped to the other side of the plane, meaning that the opposite side of the selected BSP Brush will be deleted when you click the Apply button (see Figure 4.24). If you select the Split checkbox, the selected BSP Brush will be sliced along the intersection with the clipping plane, and each side will become a separate and independent brush (see Figure 4.25). Clicking the Apply button without checking either of these two options will cut the selected BSP Brush along the intersection with the plane and delete the half of the BSP Brush that is on the side of the plane normal, leaving the other half

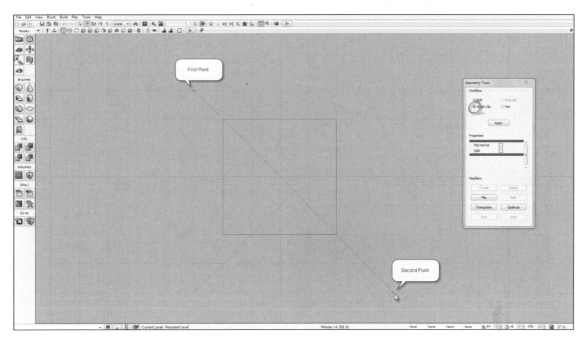

Figure 4.23
Slicing a plane constructed in Brush Clip sub-mode using the top viewport. The plane intersects the diagonal of the cube BSP Brush.

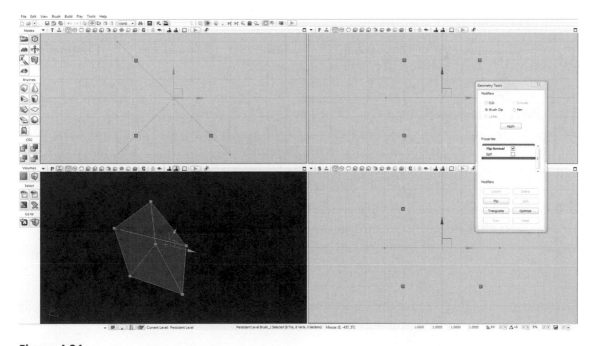

Figure 4.24
The slice plane normal is flipped, and the opposite side of the cube is deleted after the slice.

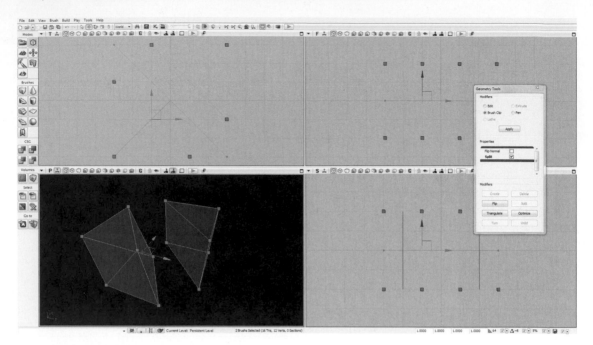

Figure 4.25
The cube is sliced according to slice plane, and each side of the BSP Brush is separated as a unique brush.

intact. That is, the Brush Clip sub-mode will delete the half of the BSP Brush that is on the same side as the normal perpendicular to the slicing plane, as shown in the viewport (see Figure 4.26).

The Pen Sub-Mode

The Pen sub-mode works by creating planar shapes or polygon profiles (such as squares, circles, stars, kites, etc.) in orthographic viewports. These profiles can then go on to be used to create the following:

- Shape objects, or 2D outlines, which are useful for performing lathe operations (as you shall see in the next section)

- A profile that can be extruded (pulled upward or downward into three dimensions) to create a Builder Brush

This section considers only the latter use—specifically, how to use the Pen sub-mode to create an RBB (see Figure 4.27).

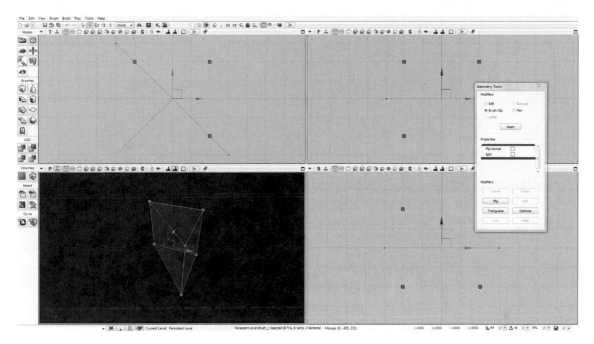

Figure 4.26
The cube BSP Brush, sliced according to slice plane.

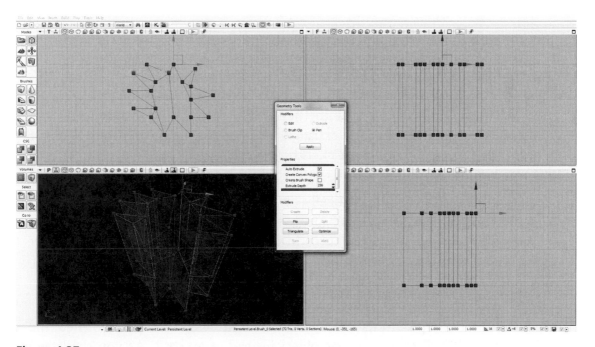

Figure 4.27
The Pen sub-mode, used to create an irregular star profile in the top viewport, which is then extruded to create an RBB.

When it comes to creating RBBs, the Pen sub-mode is a creative force rather than an amending one. That is, it is used to create new RBBs, not to modify existing ones. This is important because it means that the Pen sub-mode is involved with creating new RBBs and with discarding any existing RBBs, because there can be only one RBB in the level at any one time.

The Pen sub-mode works in orthographic viewports only. It allows you to draw planar shapes by plotting a series of connected vertices one by one using the spacebar on the keyboard. Each subsequent vertex will be connected automatically to the one plotted before. The Pen sub-mode recognizes a shape as being completed when it consists of three or more vertices and when the final plotted vertex connects or intersects with the first plotted vertex to make an enclosed space. For example, a rectangle shape is completed when five vertices have been plotted and when the fifth and final vertex is plotted over the first such that vertex one and five become fused together, leaving a rectangle shape with four vertices for the corners.

Tip

When plotting vertices in the Pen sub-mode, you can press the Esc key on the keyboard to undo the most recent plotted vertex.

When the Pen sub-mode detects that a shape has been completed, it refers to the properties as specified in the Properties group of the Geometry toolbox to determine how to respond—that is, whether it should create a shape or an RBB. These properties, shown in Figure 4.28, are as follows:

- **Auto-Extrude.** If this checkbox is checked when a shape is formed, the Pen sub-mode will automatically extrude the newly created shape according to the Extrude Depth parameter. The extruded shape is then converted into the RBB (unless the Create Brush Shape checkbox is checked).

- **Create Convex Polygons.** If this checkbox is checked when a shape is formed, the Pen sub-mode will automatically divide the shape into its simplest arrangement of polygons as required, ensuring that no polygon in the shape is concave. A concave polygon is one that turns in on itself, as opposed to a convex polygon, which turns out on itself. Figure 4.29 shows the distinction between concave and convex. In computer graphics, concave polygons can cause performance issues.

- **Create Brush Shape.** If this checkbox is checked when a shape is formed, the Pen sub-mode will create a shape object instead of an RBB. As you shall see in

Figure 4.28
The Geometry toolbox in the Pen sub-mode. Note the Auto-Extrude, Create Convex Polygons, Create Brush Shape, and Extrude Depth options.

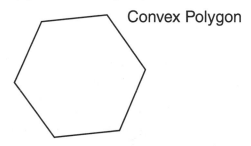

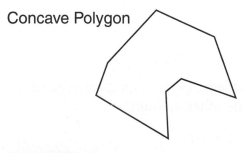

Figure 4.29
Concave polygons turn in on themselves. In contrast, convex polygons turn out on themselves.

the next section, shape objects are two-dimensional profiles that can be spun or revolved around an axis (lathed) to create three-dimensional objects.

■ **Extrude Depth.** This is a decimal parameter that defines the height in Unreal world units of the extrusion to be applied to a completed shape profile intended to be an RBB.

The Lathe Sub-Mode

The Lathe sub-mode works in conjunction with the Pen sub-mode. Like the Pen sub-mode, the Lathe sub-mode works only in orthographic viewports, and is a creative force in the sense that it is used to create RBBs only—not to modify RBBs or BSP Brushes.

As mentioned, one purpose of the Pen sub-mode is to create shape profiles in the form of shape objects. A shape object is simply a way for the Unreal Engine to remember a two-dimensional shape independently of the Builder Brush and outside of the Pen sub-mode. A shape object is a free-floating and selectable object that represents a planar shape such as a star, a circle, a box, an octagon, or many others. Like a Builder Brush, a shape object is not visible to the game camera and does not exist in the level in the same way that a mesh, light, or sound does. It exists for developmental reasons—for the benefit of the developer.

The Lathe sub-mode works with shape objects to create Builder Brushes. It does this by revolving (lathing) a selected shape object around a pivot point, just as a cup or vase is spun on a potter's wheel. The Lathe sub-mode is especially handy for creating Builder Brushes with circular cross sections—cylinders, cups, tubes, rings, lampposts, pedestals, and others. It is important to note, however, that as powerful as lathing might be as a modeling technique, its power in the UDK is severely limited. This is because lathing can produce geometry that is complex and organic, both of which are qualities to be avoided in CSG and are reserved instead for static meshes. For this reason, The Lathe sub-mode is not one you're likely to use frequently.

The Lathe sub-mode involves revolving a shape object about a pivot point for a specified amount of turn. From this sentence, it is possible to identify three properties or elements necessary for a lathe:

■ The shape object to be lathed

■ The pivot point to act as the center around which lathing will occur

■ The amount of revolution to be applied to the lathe (should the profile be lathed a full 360 degrees, or only 90 degrees, or some other amount?)

These three properties are now considered in more detail.

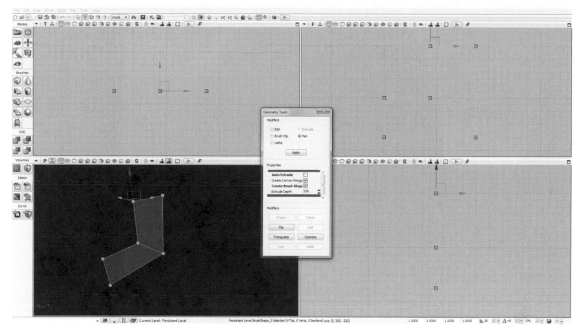

Figure 4.30
A brush shape object is created using the Pen sub-mode. Ensure that the Create Brush Shape option is checked before the brush shape is completed; otherwise, the Pen sub-mode will create a Builder Brush instead of a brush shape.

Shape Profile

The Lathe sub-mode expects the shape object (the shape profile to be lathed) to have been created previously using the Pen sub-mode, with the Create Brush Shape option checked in the Pen sub-mode properties. Creating a shape profile in Pen sub-mode with this option checked will create a brush shape object that can be selected and transformed in the viewports using the transform tools—Translate, Rotate, and Scale—just as the Builder Brush can be transformed (see Figure 4.30).

Pivot Point

Every actor in a UDK level has one and only one pivot point—the world-space coordinate about which transformations for that actor are centered. When an actor is selected in the viewport for transformation, the transformation gizmo appears at the location of the actor's pivot. The pivot point of an object affects how transformations are applied to that object.

The pivot point applies to all three forms of transformation (translate, rotate and scale), but is perhaps most useful and notable in the case of rotation. The rotation of an actor always occurs about its pivot point, and the location of the pivot point

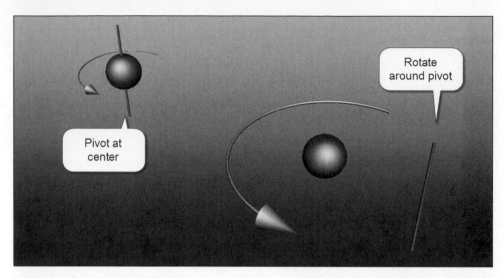

Figure 4.31
The location of an actor's pivot point dictates how it is affected by transformations.

influences the orientation and position of the actor after transformation. That means two identical actors—say, two cubes—with different pivot points will appear at different orientations and positions in world space even when the same amount of rotation is applied to each. In short, the pivot point marks the center of the rotation—the point at which an invisible axis or pole is created around which the object will spin when rotated. By default, the pivot point is assigned to the center of the object. That is, an object is rotated by default around its center, just as the earth spins on its own center axis. But the pivot point can be moved and an object rotated around a different center. For example, the pivot points of planets in a heliocentric solar system are centered outside of themselves and on the central sun, the point around which they rotate. See Figure 4.31 to visualize the concept of pivots more clearly.

The UDK allows the pivot point of any actor to be changed from its default, either temporarily or permanently. To change the pivot point of an actor temporarily, follow these steps:

1. Select the actor in the viewport.

2. Right-click the position to which the pivot point should be moved.

3. In the menu that opens, choose Pivot and select Move Here (see Figure 4.32) or Move Here (Snapped). The latter option moves the pivot point to the grid line nearest to the clicked point.

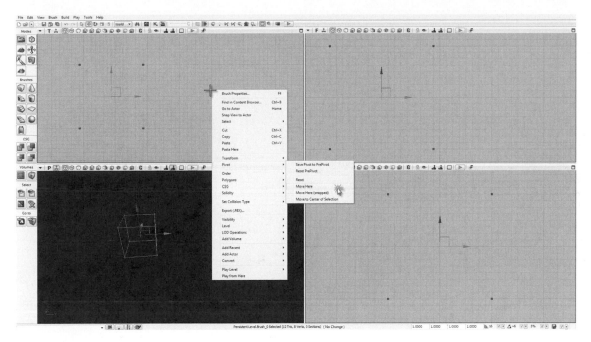

Figure 4.32
Temporarily changing the location of the pivot.

This changes the location of the pivot point only temporarily. That is, the location of the pivot point will be reset to its default after the actor is deselected in the viewport. To permanently change the pivot point so that it remains in place even after the selected object is deselected, you must complete one additional step after you set the new pivot point: Right-click the new pivot point and, in the menu that appears, choose Pivot and then choose Save Pivot to PrePivot (see Figure 4.33). The new pivot point will now be the default pivot point for the selected actor. You can restore the previous pivot at any time by right-clicking the pivot point and, in the menu that appears, selecting Pivot and then Reset PrePivot.

Lathe Revolution

The Lathe sub-mode is for creating complex-shaped Builder Brushes. As mentioned, it works by revolving a brush shape object about its pivot point for a specified amount of turn, generating a continuous Builder Brush volume throughout the rotation. You can specify the amount of turn applied to the brush shape object in relative and fractional terms using the Properties group in the Geometry toolbox while in the Lathe sub-mode—namely, via the Total Segments and Segments properties (see Figure 4.34). Together, these properties determine the number of sides generated for the

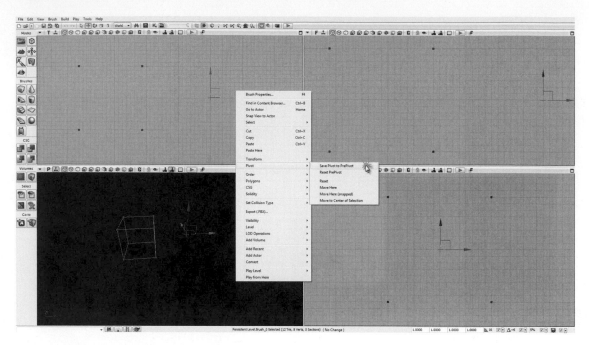

Figure 4.33
Saving the pivot point.

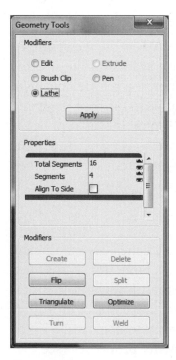

Figure 4.34
Lathing properties, used to specify the amount of rotation applied to a shape.

brush shape object by the lathe. The higher the value for both these properties, the greater the number of sides generated. The higher the number of sides, the smoother and rounder the brush shape object will appear; the lower the number of sides, the more jagged and polygonal the brush shape object will appear.

The total amount of turn that can be applied to the shape profile in the lathe is 360 degrees (one complete revolution), and the Total Segments property is an integer value that refers to the total number of sides distributed equally across a complete revolution. That is, it refers to the maximum number of sides that the Builder Brush could have from the lathe. It could have as many sides or fewer, but not more. The Segments property refers to the number of sides the Builder Brush will *actually* have once the lathe is completed. This value must be an integer that is equal to or less than the Total Segments property. Thus, the Segments property in combination with the Total Segments property expresses a fraction of a 360-degree turn, representing the total amount of turn to be applied to the shape profile when lathed. See Figure 4.35 to see how an L-shaped figure is lathed around its pivot for a fraction of a complete revolution to create a circular-like Builder Brush.

Clicking the Apply button while in the Lathe sub-mode applies the lathe to the selected shape profile, based on its current pivot point and on the Total Segments

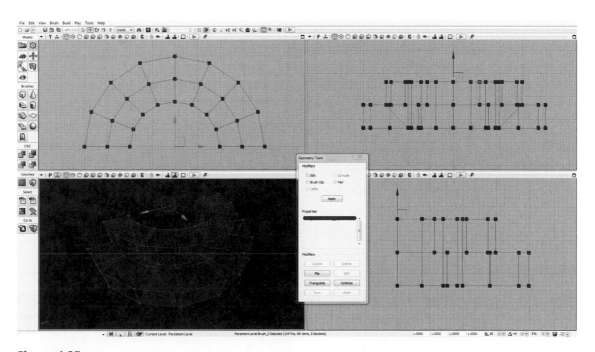

Figure 4.35
Lathing an L-shaped profile around its pivot to create a Builder Brush.

and Segments properties in the Properties group of the Geometry toolbox. The active viewport at the time the lathe is performed is also significant because it defines the axis around which the lathe occurs. A box-shaped profile, for example, can be lathed around a vertical axis to create a ring or hoop aligned to the ground, or it can be lathed around a horizontal axis to create an archway or a hole, aligned upright. In short, the lathe will be performed around the look-at axis of the active viewport. That is, the selected shape profile will be lathed around an axis that matches the viewing direction of the viewport. For this reason, lathing should be performed only when an orthographic viewport is active—either the top, side, or front.

Note

> If the lathe operation fails because the active viewport does not define a valid lathe axis, then an error message will appear notifying you of the failure and a valid Builder Brush will not be created. That means you should use a different profile or a different lathe axis for the lathe.

The Modifiers

Eight modifiers appear in the bottom group of the Geometry toolbox: Create, Delete, Flip, Split, Triangulate, Optimize, Turn, and Weld. All eight of the modifiers are quick one-button operations. In addition, all—except perhaps Create and Delete—are true modifiers in a sense in which the aforementioned sub-modes are not. That is, they work on existing geometry in the level rather than creating new geometry. To be more exact, the modifiers work at the component level and not at the object level of geometry. That is, they work on the vertices, edges, and faces of particular actors, and not on the actors as a whole. *Geometry* here is taken to mean both the RBB and its components, as well as the BSP Brushes and their components. Thus, the modifiers apply to the vertices, edges, and faces of either the RBB or particular BSP Brushes.

Like the sub-mode checkboxes in the Geometry tools group, the modifier buttons below them are context sensitive, meaning that their availability (the ability to click them) depends on the selection in the viewport. One button that is available in one scenario might not be available in another.

Create and Delete

The Create and Delete modifiers are true to their names to some extent, Delete more so than Create. When clicked, the Delete modifier deletes all the selected edges, vertices, or faces of the selected actor in the level. To use this modifier, simply select the components of the object to delete in the viewport and then click the Delete button in the Geometry toolbox. The Create modifier, on the other hand, does not create

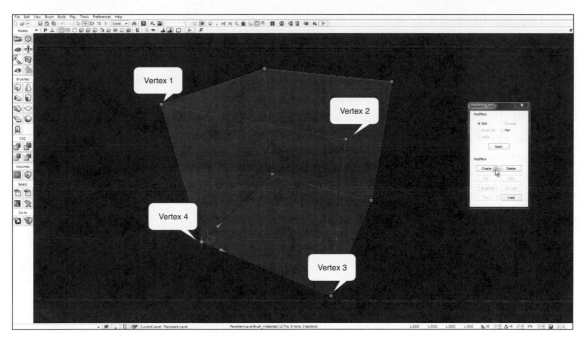

Figure 4.36
Cap an open border with the Create modifier. Start by selecting each of the vertices on the open border in sequence, clockwise or anti-clockwise, and then cap the border by clicking the Create button in the Geometry toolbox.

individual vertices or edges, as the name might suggest. Rather, it is used to cap open borders—that is, to insert polygons as a cap or a lid into empty areas of the geometry where polygons can be accepted. For example, suppose the Delete modifier is used to remove one of the six faces of a cube, leaving a gap or open area in its place. The Create modifier can then be used to remedy this situation by capping or filling up that gap again with a new face. To use the Create modifier, select all four of the vertices in sequence that surround the empty space, and then click the Create button (see Figure 4.36).

Flip and Split

The purpose of the Flip modifier is to invert the normal of the selected polygon, and thereby to change the direction in which the polygon is facing. As mentioned earlier in this chapter, a polygon is formed by an enclosed border of edges and has a normal, which is an invisible vector that reaches out as a perpendicular from the surface of the polygon. The normal can reach in one of two directions: either to the front or to the back of the polygon. The direction of the normal determines which side of the polygon is visible to the camera. Flipping the normal of a polygon causes the normal to point in the opposite direction.

The Flip modifier can be useful for ensuring that faces are aligned toward the camera. It can also be used in combination with the Create modifier. That is, the Create modifier generates a polygon inside an open border, but the direction in which that polygon is facing depends on whether the user selected the vertices on the border in a clockwise or anti-clockwise direction. Vertices around a border that are selected in a clockwise direction cause the Create modifier to produce a face whose normal points outward; vertices selected in the opposite direction lead to a face whose normal points inward. If you accidentally produce a polygon facing in the wrong direction, you can use the Flip modifier to solve the problem by changing the direction of the face normal.

The Split modifier is available only when an edge is selected. Its purpose is to add or insert detail into the geometry—that is, to add more vertices, edges, and faces. Technically, the Split modifier inserts a connected loop of edges (an *edge loop*) through all edges in the edge ring to which the selected edge belongs. To visualize this, imagine a sheet of letter-sized paper. Fold it in half such that a vertical crease is formed through the center, from top to bottom. The top and bottom edges of the paper exist in the same edge ring, and the perpendicular crease connecting them represents the edge loop that has been inserted using the Split technique (see Figure 4.37).

If this technique were applied to the front face of a cube and then repeated upward and downward along all connected faces, a complete and connected loop of edges would cut through the middle of the cube, effectively dividing it into two halves— those on the left side of the edge loop and those on the right. The cube is not literally cut in half; that is, its two halves are not separated from each other. Rather, it is cut metaphorically in that an additional series of edges runs through the middle of the

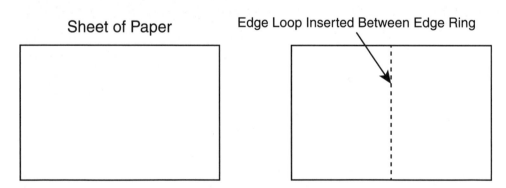

Figure 4.37
Inserting an edge loop on a sheet of paper.

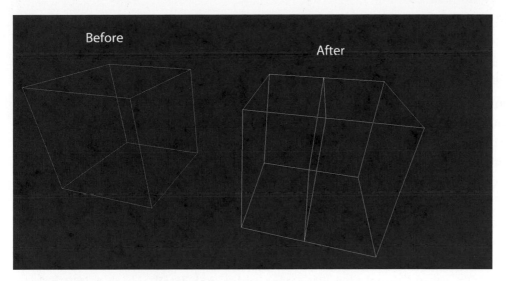

Figure 4.38
Inserting an edge loop into a cube.

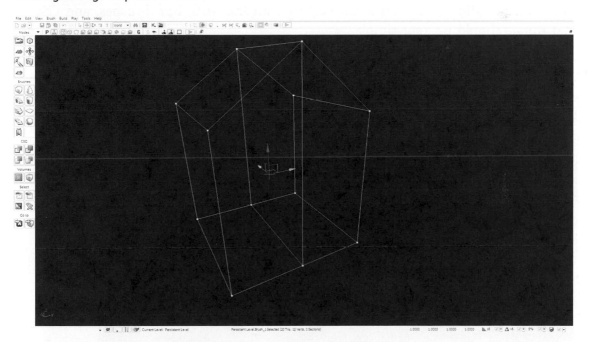

Figure 4.39
Creating a house model from a cube, using detail added by an edge loop.

cube. Thus, the Split modifier inserts an edge loop into geometry, and an edge loop is a form of subdivision—a means of adding more detail to geometry. Figure 4.38 shows the topology of a cube after an edge loop is added through the center. Figure 4.39 shows a sample modification that can be made to the cube only after the edge loop is inserted.

Triangulate and Optimize

The Triangulate and Optimize modifiers affect the complexity of the geometry—the number of polygons that compose the geometry. Triangulate makes the geometry more complex, while Optimize makes the geometry less complex.

The Triangulate modifier is accessible at both the object level and the face level, meaning you can click its button in the toolbox when the whole actor is selected in the viewport or when particular faces of the actor are selected. When the whole actor is selected, the Triangulate modifier will apply to all faces of the selected object, as opposed to only the selected faces. When clicked, the Triangulate modifier subdivides the selected faces into triangles (polygons with three sides). That is, it inserts and arranges additional edges into the selected polygons as necessary so that they are composed entirely of triangles. Figure 4.40 shows a cube that has been triangulated. The triangulation of geometry results in new geometry that has more faces than the version before. These additional faces represent additional detail, which might be useful for shaping and sculpting purposes (as it is in the case of edge loops). Remember: One of the guiding principles when dealing with the RBB, BSP Brushes, and CSG is that things should be kept simple.

The Optimize modifier works at the object level. It is the antithesis of the Triangulate and Split modifiers insofar as its purpose is to reduce and remove detail from geometry rather than to add and insert detail. To be more exact, the chief purpose of the Optimize modifier is to remove all unnecessary detail from geometry—that is, the

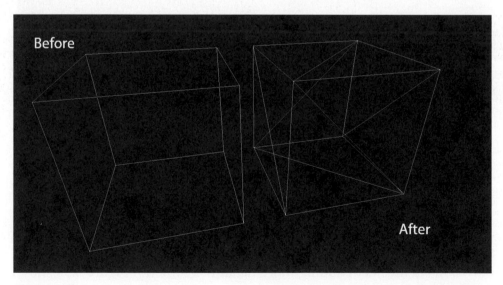

Figure 4.40
A cube before and after triangulation.

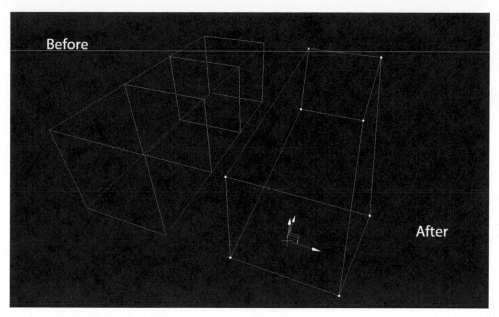

Figure 4.41
Simplifying geometry with Optimize. A box shape composed of a cross-section of edge loops is reduced by Optimize to a six-sided structure.

edges, vertices, and faces that can be removed from geometry without changing the overall form or topology. The unnecessary details of a cube, for example, are all the faces, vertices, and edges that can be removed from it without its changing what the cube essentially is—that is, without destroying the cube shape. The Optimize modifier works by removing the common edges between any two or more neighboring polygons that exist on the same plane. Figure 4.41 shows the Optimize modifier in action. In short, the Optimize modifier is useful because it strives for simplicity—and simplicity is the aim when working CSG.

Turn and Weld

The final two modifiers in the Geometry toolbox are Turn and Weld. Turn (see Figure 4.42) applies to the edges of triangulated polygons only, and the latter to vertices only. When a polygon, such as a rectangle, is triangulated, it is divided into two right-angled triangles sharing a common edge running diagonally from one corner to the opposite one. For a rectangle, the diagonal can run in one of two ways: from the top-left corner to the bottom-right corner or from the bottom-left corner to the top-right corner. (The diagonal might be able to run in many other different ways on more complex shapes.) When it triangulates a polygon, the Triangulate modifier will automatically choose a direction for the edges created, but that direction might turn

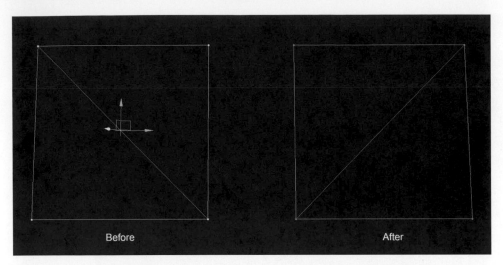

Figure 4.42
Turning edges with the Turn modifier.

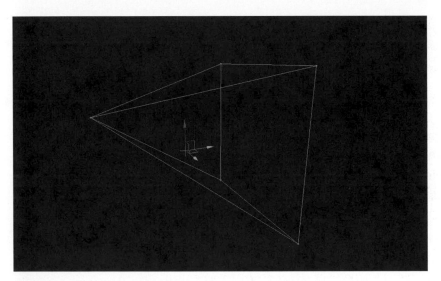

Figure 4.43
Creating a pyramid from a cube by welding together four vertices on one side.

out to be different from the one intended. To resolve this issue, you can use the Turn modifier to rotate and change the direction of the diagonal in the triangulated region. Simply select the edge to be turned and click the Turn button.

The Weld modifier shares the simplifying role of the Optimize modifier to the extent that both modifiers reduce the total number of vertices in the geometry. But whereas the Optimize modifier works at the object level, the Weld modifier works at the vertex level. The purpose of the Weld modifier is to merge two or more vertices that share a common edge. If you select a vertex (the first vertex as the destination point), and then go on to select more vertices, clicking the Weld button will merge all vertices into the first vertex. Figure 4.43 shows an example of the kinds of things that can be achieved with Weld.

Project: Creating a CSG Environment Using BSP Brushes

Each chapter in this part of the book concentrates both the theory and practice of a particular aspect of the UDK, such as Geometry mode, Kismet, or the Material Editor. For this reason, each of these chapters contains both a theory section and a practical section. The theory section focuses on the ideas, concepts, and background underpinning the UDK aspect in question. The practical section focuses on applying the theory, tools, and features related to that aspect by putting them to use in creating a playable project of some kind.

Note

It is useful to consider both the theory and the practice of a tool or group of features. It might be interesting to know, for example, that the Builder Brush is in theory a template style tool that can be used to define 3D volumes in a UDK level. But if the theory behind the Builder Brush is given without reference to a concrete example, it can be difficult to appreciate the tool's full versatility and power. In contrast, a practical example of the Builder Brush—the Builder Brush at work—given without reference to any theory about how it works or why it is useful can leave the student at a loss to explain the purpose of the tool. Theory and practice are complementary In that the theory can help justify and explain the practice, and the practice can help consolidate and clarify the theory.

This section discusses in a tutorial style how to complete a project that makes use of the many different tools discussed in the theory section of the chapter. Specifically, it discusses using Geometry mode, including BSP Brushes, the RBB, the Extrude and Pen sub-modes, and others. The project detailed in this section demonstrates a number of different ways to use the Geometry mode tools, though it by no means demonstrates all possible usages. Its aim is to create a CSG environment featuring a long, thin corridor leading to an atrium containing a gable ceiling and a cross-shaped hole at the center of the floor. The project will be playable in the sense that it can be executed and explored by the gamer, but it will not feature gaming elements such as enemies, lighting, materials, scripted actions, sound, or other qualities.

The purpose of the project is to demonstrate Geometry mode at work, and you are encouraged to follow along with the instructions to re-create the project step by step. Having said that, the book companion files do contain a series of map files that

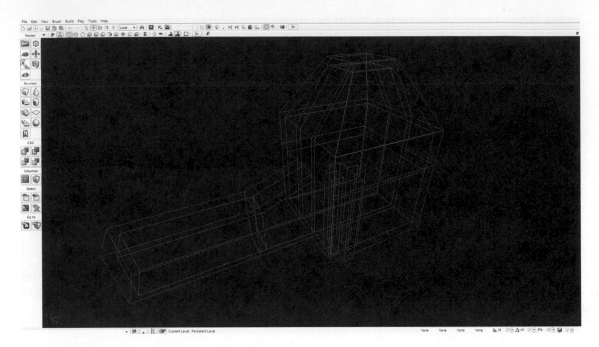

Figure 4.44
The completed project: a corridor connected to an atrium.

represent the project at various stages of completion. These are provided for both
your convenience and inspection, but it is recommended that you begin from an
empty map file and work alongside me step by step toward completion. The result
of the project should look something like Figure 4.44.

Note

This tutorial assumes you will be starting the project from a blank slate—that is, from a new and empty
project, and using the default viewport and visibility settings as detailed in the "Showing Viewport
Information" section of Chapter 2. You should ensure that snapping is enabled and that drag-grid
snapping is set to 16 Unreal world units. (You can change this from the status bar.) It is recommended
that you snap to the grid whenever possible to simplify the aligning and positioning of geometry and
actors.

Shaping the Environment

There are many ways in which a level designer might approach a project such as this,
depending on time, needs, and the purpose of the level, as well as other factors. The
point is, there is no universally right or wrong method for approaching this task.
Some methods might be faster, simpler, or more precise than others, depending on

the circumstances. Some designers might start by creating the corridor and then proceeding onward to create the atrium, and then finally connecting them together. This book, however, will start by creating the overall shape of the complete environment—both the corridor and the atrium (and its ceiling)—as seen from the outside, and then work toward hollowing out that shape to carve out an interior. The following steps demonstrate how to do this:

1. Maximize the top viewport. Then create a cube Builder Brush at the center of the level that's 256 × 256 × 256 Unreal world units. (Right-click the Cube Brush button in the toolbox to manually enter the dimensions of the cube Builder Brush.) This cube will represent the starting point from which the environment will be sculpted (see Figure 4.45).

Note

The name given to this technique—whereby complex objects are modeled through the subdividing and adjusting of the vertices, faces, and edges of simpler geometric primitives—is called *box modeling* or *polygonal modeling*. This technique will be used to shape the CSG environment for this level.

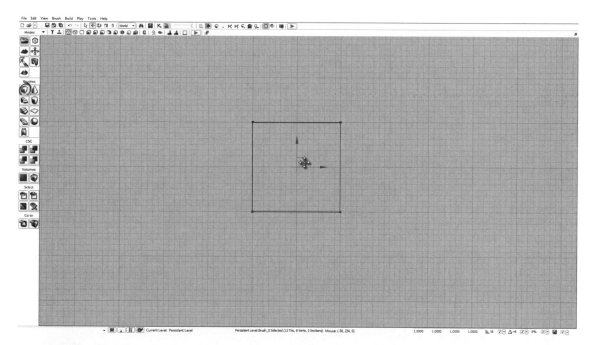

Figure 4.45
Start the polygonal modeling process with a cube builder brush.

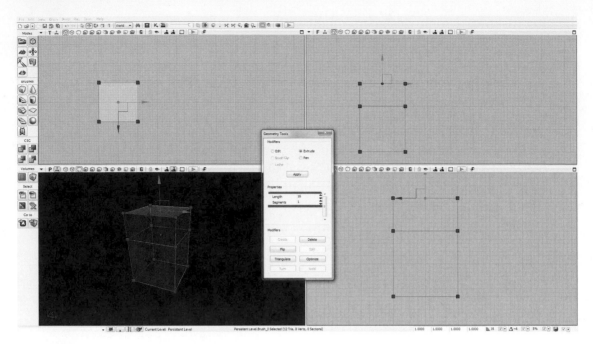

Figure 4.46
Extrude the top polygon of the cube to create space for the roof.

2. Extend the height of the box to make room for the ceiling region. To begin, switch to a four-viewport arrangement and click the Geometry Mode button in the toolbox to switch to Geometry mode. Next, switch to the Extrude sub-mode and use the Perspective viewport to select the top polygon of the cube RBB. Finally, use the Translate tool to extrude the top polygon upward by 128 Unreal world units (that is, up to the next major grid line), as shown in Figure 4.46.

Note

The level created so far can be found in the companion files under DM-Void_Level_01_CSG.udk.

3. Switch from the Extrude sub-mode to the Edit sub-mode and shape the roof further by selecting the top polygon of the RBB and using the Uniform Scaling tool to reduce its size, giving it a gable look. The polygon does not need to be scaled to exact values in this case; it is enough that it simply looks right (see Figure 4.47 for a guide).

Note

The level created so far is in the companion files under DM-CSG_Project_02_roof_created.udk.

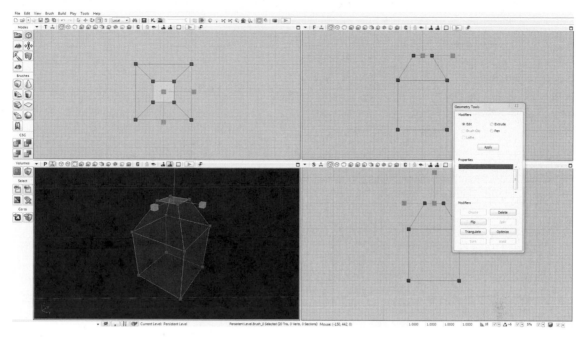

Figure 4.47
Scale the top polygon to shape the environment's roof region.

4. The shape of the main environment—the floors, walls, and ceiling—is now created. It is now time to create the entrance and the corridor. To create the entrance, which will extrude outward from one of the walls of the environment, more detail must be added. Select any one of the edges running around the front of the RBB and click the Split button in the Geometry toolbox to insert a vertical edge loop around the front, back, top, and bottom faces of the RBB (see Figure 4.48).

5. The edge loop inserted to create the entrance runs vertically through the middle of the environment. This edge loop is meant to represent the right side of the entrance (another edge loop will be inserted for the left side). Thus, it must be moved toward the right side. To do this, marquee-select (window-select) all the vertices of the newly inserted central edge loop. (Hold down the Ctrl and Alt keys on the keyboard and then click and drag over the edge loop to select all its vertices.) Then use the Translate tool to slide the vertices toward the right. Next, create the edge loop for the left side of the entrance using a similar procedure: Select any one of the edges running around the RBB and click the Split button in the Geometry toolbox to insert the second edge for the left side of the entrance. Marquee-select the vertices of this loop and slide them toward the left as required. See Figure 4.49 for the result of this process.

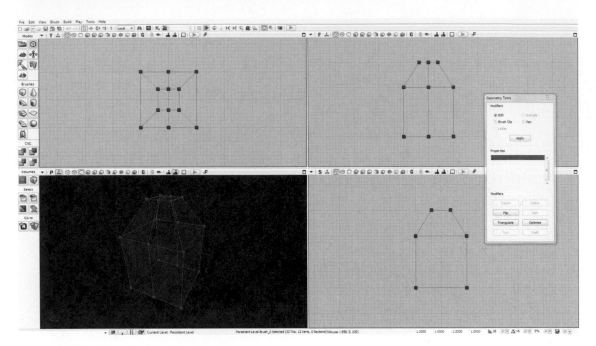

Figure 4.48
Split the environment vertically through the middle with an edge loop.

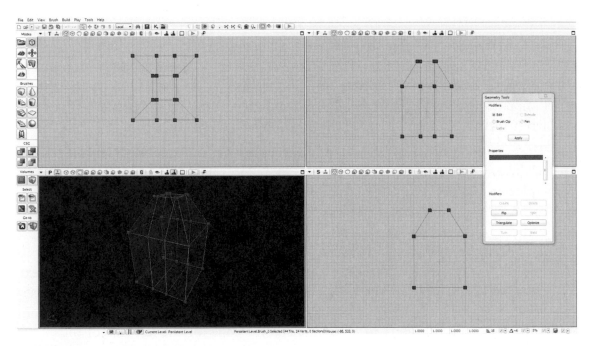

Figure 4.49
Insert edge loops for the left and right side of the entrance.

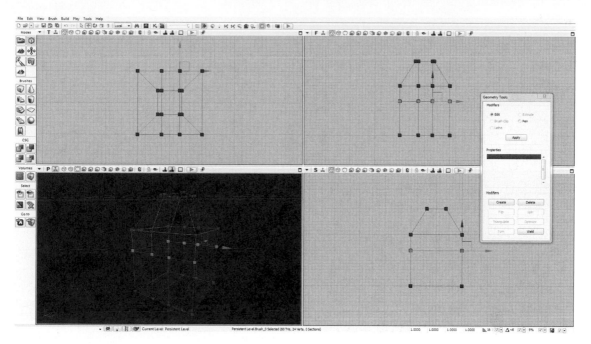

Figure 4.50
Insert a horizontal edge loop to mark the height of the entrance.

6. Create a horizontal edge loop running around all four walls of the environment to add enough detail to mark the top of the entrance. To do this, select any vertical edge in the lower half of the environment and then click the Split button in the Geometry toolbox. Use the marquee-selection method on the vertices of this edge loop to raise or lower the loop to set the height of the entrance (see Figure 4.50). There is now a single polygon at the front of the environment that will act as the entrance to the corridor.

Note

The level created so far is in the companion files under DM-CSG_Project_03_entry_loops.udk.

7. Switch to the Extrude sub-mode and select the entrance polygon at the front of the RBB in the Perspective viewport. The corridor must now be extruded outward from this polygon. Select the Translate tool and extrude the selected polygon outward in the top viewport by 128 Unreal world units (one major grid line). Then extrude it outward again by 256 Unreal world units (two major grid lines). The length of the corridor should now be 384 Unreal world units (three major grid lines), as shown in Figure 4.51.

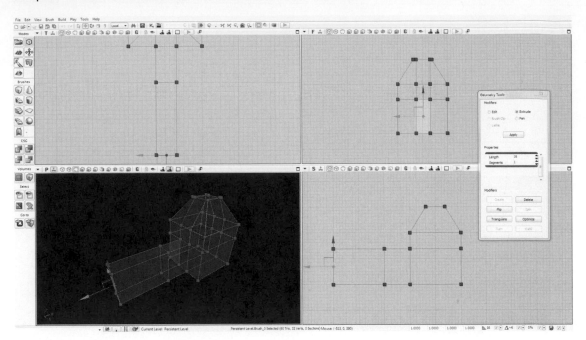

Figure 4.51
Extrude a corridor outward from the entrance polygon.

Note

The level created so far can be found in the companion files under DM-CSG_Project_04_corridor.udk.

8. Switch back to the Edit sub-mode. Select the largest ceiling polygon of the corridor and move it downward in the side viewport to shape the corridor further. Next, click the Optimize button to simplify the RBB. Figure 4.52 shows the result.

9. Click the Add CSG button in the application toolbox to create an additive BSP Brush in the shape of the RBB in the level. The viewport mode of the Perspective viewport switches to Unlit mode, and the environment becomes visible from the outside with a checkered material applied, as shown in Figure 4.53. The problem is, the newly constructed environment exists only from the outside as a solid mass of polygons; it has no interior. That is, the environment can be seen and understood from the outside, but not from the inside. Move the viewport camera inside the environment and notice how everything inside the brush appears black in Unlit mode.

10. To create an interior, you must hollow out the environment. That is, an interior and smaller volume of matching shape must be subtracted from the

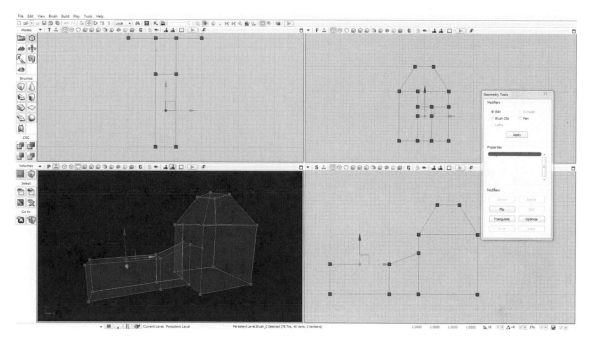

Figure 4.52
Reshaped corridor and optimized RBB.

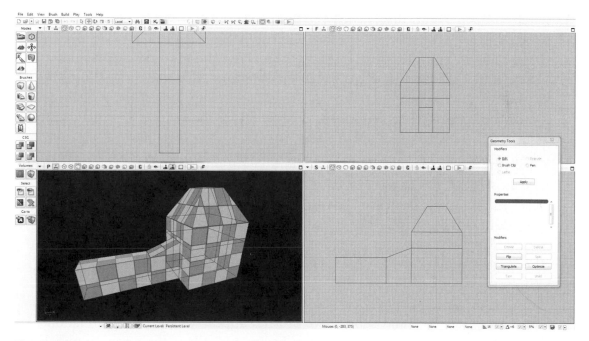

Figure 4.53
The atrium and corridor from the outside.

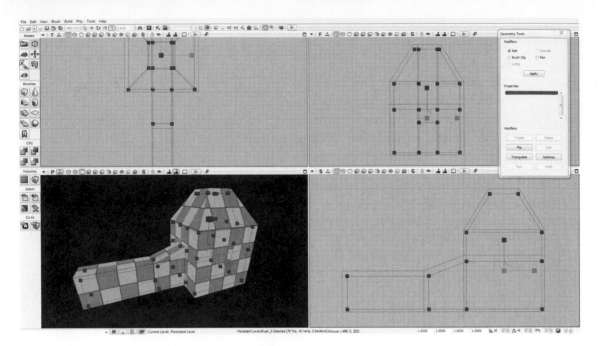

Figure 4.54
The scaled-down RBB should be a smaller version of the environment.

environment. To do this, switch the Perspective viewport into Brush Wireframe mode (press Alt+1 on the keyboard) and scale the Builder Brush downward marginally so that the RBB represents a smaller version of the environment BSP Brush. This difference in size between the RBB and environment BSP Brush represents the thickness of the walls, floors, and ceiling. Adjust the position and tweak the vertices of the RBB if required to ensure the smaller RBB sits comfortably inside the larger BSP volume and matches its topology. (See Figure 4.54.)

11. Click the CSG Subtract button in the application toolbox. A subtractive BSP Brush is added to the level in the shape of the RBB, inside the previously inserted additive BSP Brush. The subtractive BSP Brush intersects the volume of the additive BSP Brush. Thus, it subtracts geometry, leaving its interior hollowed. Move the viewport camera inside the environment and look around in the Perspective viewport. Then switch the Perspective viewport back to Brush Wireframe mode and move the RBB out of view, either moving it into the distance or pressing the B key on the keyboard to hide it. Notice that additive brushes appear blue and subtractive brushes appear yellow. Congratulations! The environment is now created. (See Figure 4.55.) It is time now to punch a hole through the floor.

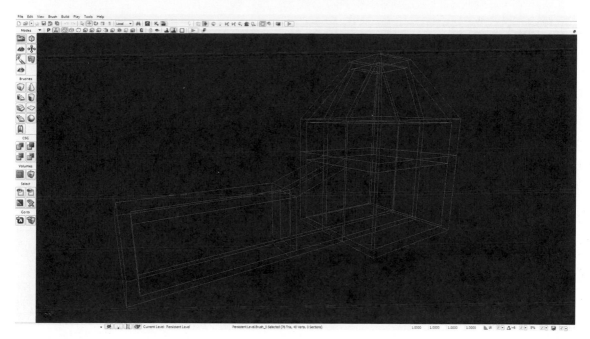

Figure 4.55
The exterior and interior BSP Brushes, with the interior subtracting from the exterior.

Note

The level created so far can be found in the companion files under DM-CSG_Project_05_env_created.udk.

Making a Hole in the Floor

The hole in the floor of the atrium is to be cross-shaped. You will form this shape using the Pen sub-mode. The hole itself will be made in the floor by way of a cross-shaped subtractive brush (although the brush will begin as an additive brush, as you shall see).

1. Maximize the top viewport, ensure the RBB is visible, and switch to Geometry mode and select the Pen sub-mode. Use the Pen tool to draw a cross-shaped Builder Brush that is smaller than the floor region of the atrium. Create this shape outside the atrium region in the viewport. Finally, click the CSG Add button in the application toolbox. (See Figure 4.56.)

2. The cross-shaped brush will work like a cookie cutter, punching a similarly shaped hole through the floor of the atrium. Switch the Perspective viewport into Brush Wireframe mode and then move (translate) the additive cross-shaped

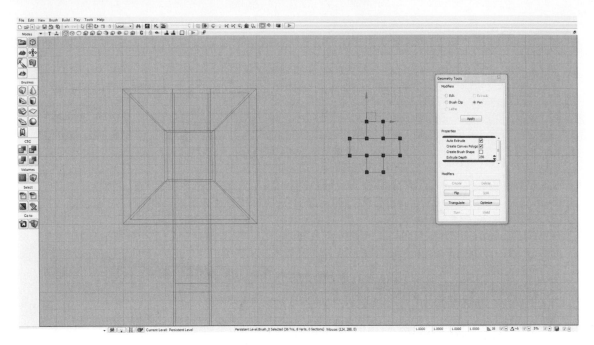

Figure 4.56
Creating an additive brush from a cross-shaped Builder Brush.

brush into the atrium so that it intersects the center of the floor.
(See Figure 4.57.)

Note

You could have punched this hole directly into the floor more easily by creating the brush inside the atrium and clicking the CSG Subtract button, but I wanted to work this way—the longer way around —to demonstrate the BSP and CSG workflow in more detail. Specifically, I wanted to show you three things. First, I wanted to show you that the brush type (additive or subtractive) can be changed after the brush is created. Second, I wanted to show you that a brush can be translated in the level just as though it were a mesh. Third, I wanted to show you that it is sometimes necessary to manually rebuild the geometry of the level to observe the results of the BSP Brushes in the level CSG.

3. Select the cross-shaped brush in the viewport and press the F4 key on the keyboard to display the Brush Properties panel (see Figure 4.58). From the panel, open the Brush group and change the Csg Oper value from CSG_Add to CSG_Subtract to change the brush type. In Brush Wireframe mode, the brush should change from blue to yellow to reflect the change in type.

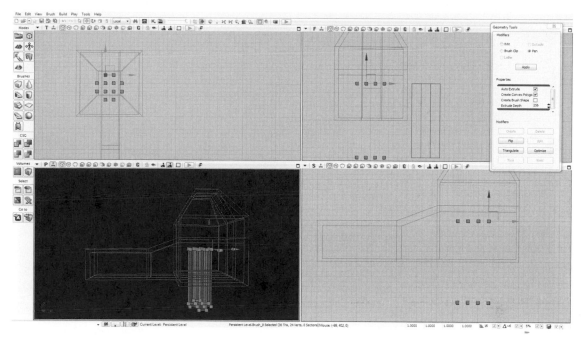

Figure 4.57
Translate the cross-shaped brush over the center of the atrium floor in preparation for subtraction.

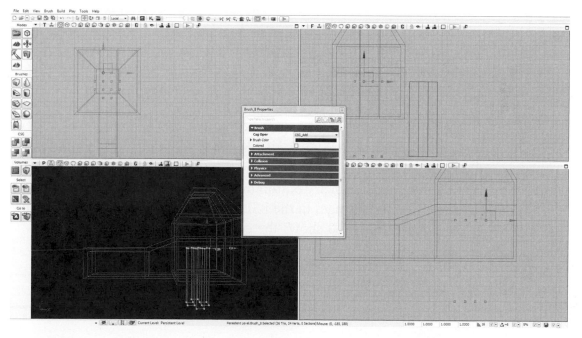

Figure 4.58
Changing the brush type from additive to subtractive in the Brush Properties panel.

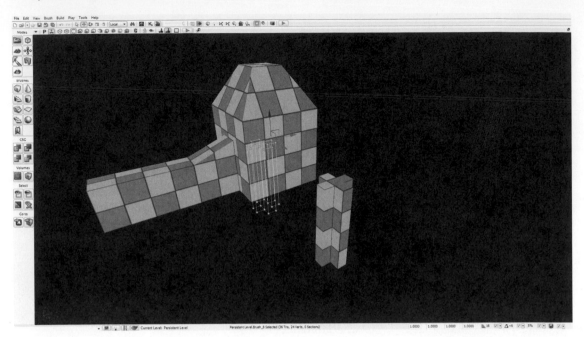

Figure 4.59
The level CSG is out of sync with the BSP Brushes.

4. Switch the Perspective viewport back to Unlit mode. Notice that the level CSG has
   not updated to reflect the changes that have occurred to the BSP Brushes.
   Specifically, the cross-shaped CSG still appears as it did when it was first added to
   the level as an additive brush outside the atrium. It does not appear as it should do,
   as a subtraction from the atrium floor. (See Figure 4.59.) This is because the UDK
   has not detected the changes in the BSP Brushes and therefore has not anticipated
   their implications on the level CSG. To rectify this, you must regenerate the level
   CSG by clicking the Build Geometry button in the toolbar. When you do, the level
   CSG updates to reflect the changes in the BSP Brushes, and the cross-shaped hole
   appears in the floor. Figure 4.60 shows the completed project.

Note

The level created so far can be found in the companion files under DM-CSG_Project_06_finished.udk.

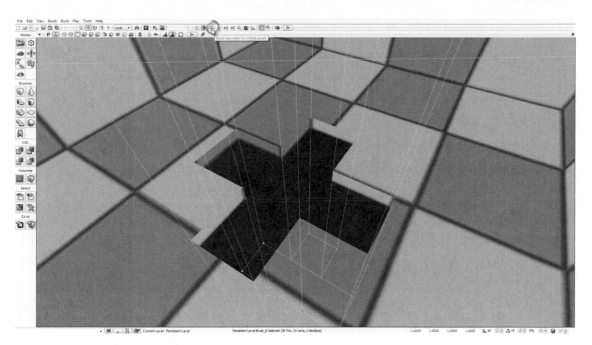

Figure 4.60
Update the level CSG by rebuilding geometry.

CONCLUSION

The focus of this chapter has been on Geometry mode and on three critical elements associated with it: the Red Builder Brush, BSP Brushes, and CSG. These three elements constitute the geometry of a level. Geometry mode offers a range of tools for adjusting the structure constituent pieces of geometry. These pieces are vertices, edges, and faces.

There are three important tips to keep in mind when working with Geometry mode and with CSG specifically:

- **Use meshes over CSG.** Use meshes for all detailed geometry, including characters, weapons, architectural details, clothes, and other details. Meshes offer performance benefits over CSG. That is, use of CSG incurs heavier performance penalties than the use of meshes.

- **Keep CSG simple.** Use CSG only for planar surfaces such as platforms, walls, floors, and ceilings. Avoid using complex brushes such as spheres, cylinders, and cones.

- **Remember to rebuild the level geometry.** You must do this whenever the type of a brush is changed or a brush is transformed.

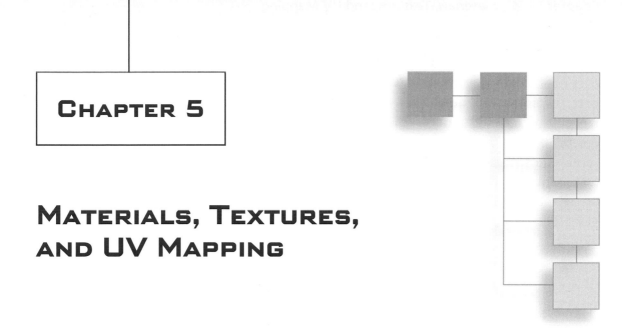

CHAPTER 5

MATERIALS, TEXTURES, AND UV MAPPING

> The computing scientist's main challenge is not to get confused by the complexities of his own making.
>
> —Edsger W. Dijkstra

By the end of this chapter, you should:

- Understand the difference between materials, maps, and textures.
- Appreciate how mapping relates to materials.
- Understand the concepts of material channels and material expressions.
- Be familiar with the Material Editor interface.
- Be able to use the Material Editor to create, edit, and apply materials to objects.

The previous chapter discussed not only the Builder Brush, BSP Brushes, and CSG, but also the general theory behind 3D geometry. In particular, it explained that any unit of geometry in the Unreal Engine (that is, any mesh object) is constructed from three basic pieces: vertices, edges, and faces. A face (such as a rectangle or triangle) is a polygonal surface that is formed by an enclosed sequence of connected edges, and an edge is a line segment drawn between any two vertices (points).

Unlike edges and vertices, faces are visible to the game camera. That is, a face can be seen by the gamer, whereas vertices and edges cannot. The developer can see representations of vertices and edges when any of the editor viewports are set to Wireframe mode, but their visibility in these cases is for the benefit of the developer, not of the gamer. Faces, however, can be seen by both developer and gamer; thus, their appearance is especially important.

Faces come together to form a mesh, and meshes come together to form the greater part of almost any UDK level. The appearance of faces, then, contributes to the realism of a level. To be more exact, the way the faces of a mesh are shaded determines the material from which the mesh appears to be made. For example, a mesh whose faces are shaded with a tiled brick pattern takes on the look of a thing that is made from brick, such as a wall or a fence. In contrast, a mesh whose faces are shaded with a misted transparency might take on the look of a thing made from glass. The focus of this chapter is how faces are shaded to appear to be made from real-world materials. To that end, this chapter discusses materials (or shader networks), textures, and mapping.

MATERIALS AND TEXTURES: WHAT ARE THEY?

The terms *material* and *texture* are sometimes used interchangeably, but they refer to different—though related—concepts. To summarize their relationship, a material can contain one or more textures, just as a restaurant menu can contain one or more dishes. To define them more fully, a material is an algorithm or a procedure for specifying how a face will appear to the game camera under various lighting conditions. This touches on three important concepts relating to materials:

■ Materials define how faces appear.

■ Materials are algorithms.

■ The appearance of faces varies with lighting conditions.

Materials Define How Faces Appear

To say that a material defines the appearance of one or more faces is to say that it defines how those faces will look to the game camera at any one time. Like any regular surface in the real world—such as a floor, wall, table, or what have you—the look of a face or surface can often be described by different qualities, including the following (to name a few):

■ Color

■ Bumpiness

■ Shininess

■ Transparency

- Glossiness
- Reflectivity

These qualities are defined by a material through its channels. A material has a number of different channels, each corresponding to a unique quality. For example, a material's bump channel defines the material's bumpiness, its diffuse channel defines its color, and so on. These channels are discussed in more detail later in this chapter. The important point to keep in mind here is that the overall appearance of a surface is the product of a number of different qualities, of which color and bumpiness are two. A material defines the appearance of a surface by controlling each of its qualities by way of material channels.

Materials Are Algorithms

Merriam-Webster defines the word *algorithm* as follows:

> ...a step-by-step procedure for solving a problem or accomplishing some end especially by a computer.

Likewise, a material is a set of clearly defined steps—in this case, one that contributes toward producing an output of pixels that shades the surface of a face.

Because a material can be thought of as an algorithm, it can also be conceived of in a graph or diagram form (see Figure 5.1). Its structure says something that is true not only of that particular material, but of all materials generally. Specifically, at the lowest level of the graph, a material is composed from a network of different textures or maps, all of which eventually feed into one or another of the higher level material channels. The textures (also known as *texture maps* or *maps*) are typically 2D images, such as JPG or PNG files. The pixel outputs from these textures are fed into the material channels, and the output from all the channels are then combined with other parameters and lighting conditions to produce a final output for the material. This final material is used to shade the surface of one or more associated faces.

The Appearance of Faces Varies with Lighting Conditions

The purpose of a material is to define the appearance of one or more faces, subject to lighting conditions in the level. This highlights an important point: Materials work not in isolation but in collaboration with lighting to define the appearance of a face. That is, lighting and materials interact to shade faces. The material of a face responds to incident light, and the reflection of light as it strikes a surface is determined in part by the properties of that surface.

Material (As Output)

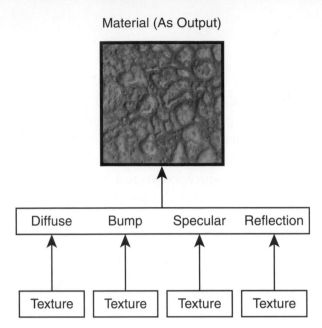

Figure 5.1
A material expressed as a graph.

Note

This chapter covers lighting only briefly. Chapter 8, "Lighting," discusses the subject in more detail.

MATERIAL CHANNELS

As mentioned, the appearance of any object or surface that is conceived—from wooden tables to glass windows—can be described by referencing a number of different qualities, such as color, roughness, shininess, transparency and others. The appearance of any object or surface in the UDK is defined by an algorithm called a *material*. Each material is composed at the highest level from a set of material channels, each channel defining how a surface appears with regard to one of its unique qualities—one channel for defining the color of an object, another for defining its roughness, another for its transparency, and so on.

To say this, of course, is all well and good. But, the question remains as to *how* the channel achieves its purpose. How does a channel go about its business of making a surface look the way it does? The short answer is, it does so by making use of maps, and thus by making use of pixels.

Every material in a material channel corresponds to a rectangle or map, of pixels, and each pixel in the map corresponds to a particular integer value (see Figure 5.2). An

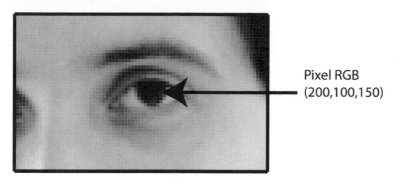

Pixel RGB
(200,100,150)

Figure 5.2
A map is a grid of numbers, whether gray-scale or color.

integer is a number with no fractional component. In gray-scale images, each pixel of the map corresponds to an integer value along a scale of grayness between 0 (black) and 255 (white), with intermediate values being a tone between the two extremes. In color images that use the RGB (red, green, blue) color space, like most images for video games, pixel values correspond to a three-dimensional vector—that is, a three-component number, such as (0,128,200). In this number, red corresponds to the first component, green to the second, and blue to the third.

Color is created when the values of the three components are combined. Each component in the number ranges from 0 to 255 and describes the strength or degree of contribution to the composite color made by that component. A pure red color should be 100 percent red, 0 percent green, and 0 percent blue. Likewise, a pure blue color would be 100 percent blue, 0 percent red, and 0 percent green. Table 5.1 lists some primary colors and their RGB representations.

Table 5.1   RGB Colors

Color	Value (RGB)
Red	(255, 0, 0)
Green	(0, 255, 0)
Blue	(0, 0, 255)
White	(255, 255, 255)
Black	(0, 0, 0)
Magenta	(255, 0, 255)
Yellow	(255, 255, 0)
Cyan	(0, 255, 255)

There are two key points to keep in mind. First, a material channel is a map of pixels that can be either gray scale or color. Second, the map's pixels are ultimately numerical values. That means a map is in essence a grid of numbers. The map's numerical values define how the material channel contributes to the shading of a surface or object. The meanings of the values in the channel (the way the pixels affect the surface) vary depending on the type of channel.

Note

Because colors in the RGB color space can be expressed as three-component numbers, in which each component is an integer, it is possible to perform arithmetical operations with the colors. That means colors can be added, subtracted, multiplied, and divided together to produce a third color. This is considered in more detail later in this chapter.

The Diffuse Channel

The diffuse channel is responsible for shading a surface with what most people would describe as the surface color, or look (see Figure 5.3). For example, the diffuse channel for a surface meant to depict a brick wall might contain a map of pixels arranged to mimic a brick wall. This would shade the surface in its likeness, making the surface appear to be made from bricks.

Note

The diffuse channel takes its name from the study of optics and light, specifically from the concept of a diffuse reflection. A diffuse reflection occurs when a ray of light—say, from the sun or from an artificial light—strikes a surface and is bounced or reflected, resulting in many more rays of light, some of which eventually make contact with the eye of an observer. These rays make it possible for that observer to see the object from which the light bounced.

Figure 5.3
A cube object with checkered material applied via the diffuse channel.

The diffuse channel, unlike many other channels, typically uses color images rather than gray-scale ones because most developers want their games to appear in color. The diffuse channel is perhaps the most important of all material channels. Although many material channels are optional, almost all materials have a diffuse channel.

The Specular Channel

The specular channel defines the specularity of a material—that is, its shininess. Some objects are shiny; this quality of shininess exists in addition to the object's diffuse properties (see Figure 5.4). Shiny objects include metal, glass, chrome, plastics, wet surfaces, and others.

All these shiny surfaces have at least four properties in common:

- Their shininess depends on the location and strength of the surrounding lighting.
- They all have a shining region or a place that shines, also known as a specular highlight, which changes depending partly on the position of the observer.
- The specular highlight has a color.
- The specular highlight has an intensity—a strength of shine—that is controlled in part by lighting conditions.

In the UDK, these last three properties—location of shine, color of shine and strength of shine—are controlled by the pixels in the material's specular channel.

Figure 5.4
A sphere with a bright white specular highlight.

The color of the shine at any one place on the surface is determined by the composite RGB color of the corresponding pixels in the specular channel—red pixels result in a red shine, blue pixels in a blue shine, etc. The location and intensity of shine on the surface are defined only by the brightness values of the pixels in the channel. In the RGB color space, each of the three color components can be any value between 0 and 255, between black and white, reflecting the strength or degree of contribution made to the color by each channel. The brightness value of any RGB pixel is equal to the value of the highest component. Thus, the brightness value of the color (233,110,52) is 233, because the red component has the highest of the three values. The brightness value of (10,10,25) is 25 because the blue component has the highest value. The degree of shine for any pixel on a surface is directly proportional to the corresponding pixel in the specular channel of the material. Pixels with a brightness value of 0 do not shine at all under any lighting conditions, and pixels with a brightness value of 255 make the boldest kind of shine possible under almost all lighting conditions.

The Normal Channel

The normal channel refers to a normal map—an RGB rectangle of pixels. Normal maps can be used to create bumpy effects on a surface. They can also be used to add surface detail to low polygonal models (that is, models with few polygons) to make them appear higher res (that is, like models with more polygons). Using normal mapping, an artist can export or *bake* the surface details of a high-resolution model into a map of pixels. This map can then be applied as a normal map to a low-resolution version of the model to make it appear to have the details of the high-resolution version (see Figure 5.5).

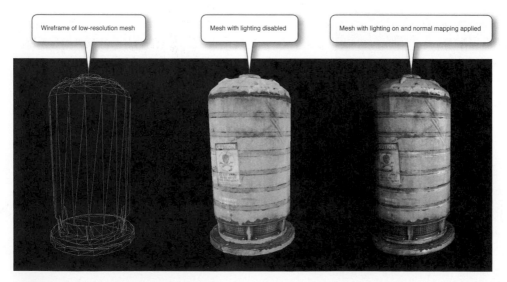

Figure 5.5
Applying a normal map.

Note

As you shall see later in this book, normal mapping and bump mapping are distinct forms of mapping. Normal mapping is in many respects a refinement or enhancement to the older bump-mapping technique.

Note

For those interested in how normal maps work under the hood, see Chapter 8, on lighting. For now, it is enough to know that normal maps can be used to create bumpiness on a surface, as well other kinds of perturbations and details.

The Emissive Channel

The emissive channel is an RGB rectangle of pixels that defines the amount and size of glow that is applied to a surface. It is useful for creating objects that are supposed to be illuminated, such as fluorescent tubes and fire. Unlike other material channels, the emissive channel works independently of the lighting in a scene. That is, the brightness of the emissive regions remains unaffected by lighting. Emissive regions of a material will continue to glow even in cases where there is no lighting at all.

Three properties relate to the emissive channel. These are defined by way of the pixels in the emissive map. The properties are as follows:

- The position of the glow within the material
- The amount of glow to be applied to the glowing regions
- The color of the glow

The position and color of the glow on a surface are defined by the corresponding pixels in the RGB emissive map. Red pixels glow red, blue pixels glow blue, etc. The intensity of the glow applied to any one pixel in the map is defined by that pixel's brightness value. The higher the brightness value, the stronger the glow will appear. The strongest kinds of glow are surrounded by a similarly colored halo, as shown in Figure 5.6.

The Opacity Channel

The opacity channel is a gray-scale map whose pixels act like a mask, controlling the extent to which parts of a surface appear opaque or transparent. The opacity channel is typically used to create transparent or semi-transparent materials—for example, materials for glass, fences, holes, smoke, fog, and other surfaces with similar properties (see Figure 5.7).

Figure 5.6
The emissive channel is used to provide objects with a glow.

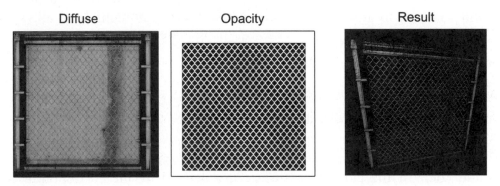

Figure 5.7
The opacity channel uses a gray-scale map whose color values define opaque, transparent, and semi-transparent regions of a surface.

Every pixel in the opacity channel ranges from 0 (black) to 255 (white), where black is interpreted as fully transparent and white is interpreted as opaque or solid. Values between these two extremes represent degrees of transparency, with pixels closer to white appearing more opaque and those closer to black more transparent.

It is important to emphasize that the opacity channel itself is never visible in the material, at least not in the same way the diffuse channel or the specular channel is. Only the results or effects of the opacity channel can be seen in the final, composite material. The opacity channel acts as a mask, or stencil, that defines the visibility not of itself but of the other channels in the material. More accurately, the gray-scale value of pixel in the opacity channel defines the degree of transparency to be applied to every corresponding pixel in the other channels. In this way, the properties of the opacity channel are mapped onto the other channels.

MATERIALS AS ALGORITHMS

Materials bring polygonal surfaces to life in 3D graphics. They make the difference between a polygon with a default checkerboard material applied and a polygon that appears to be made from real-world stuff such as bricks, sand, flesh, water, concrete, stone, glass, metal, and anything else that goes toward composing a material object.

As you have seen, you can think of a material as an algorithm or a function. Like most algorithms and functions, materials have an output. The output of a material is essentially the rectangle of pixels that will be applied to the surface of one or more polygons. This output is produced by combining all the channels of the material—the diffuse channel, the specular channel, the opacity channel, and all the others—in a particular way.

The channels themselves turn out also to be a rectangle of pixels. The diffuse channel is a rectangle of pixels defining the color of a surface, the specular channel specifies the extent to which a surface will be shiny, and the opacity channel is a rectangle of pixels that acts as a mask for the other channels. Being rectangles of pixels, all the channels are in turn the output of lower-order maps (other rectangles of pixels) that can be combined, blended, and connected in various ways. Thought of from the bottom upward, a material is essentially a network of connected maps that combine at many levels. These combinations produce outputs that are themselves independent maps, and these outputs are cascaded upward iteratively through the network to high-order processes, where eventually they feed into the channels of the material and are combined one final time to result in the final material (see Figure 5.8). The process of constructing a material, then, must also be the process of constructing a network or graph. The UDK Material Editor works very much within this graph paradigm, as you will see later in this chapter.

UV MAPPING

In the UDK, the purpose of a material is to shade the surfaces of polygonal geometry to make it appear to be made from real-world materials. There is, however, an intervening process between the creation of a material and its assignment onto the surfaces of a model. That stage is called *mapping*.

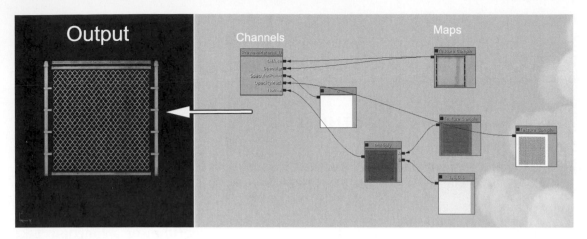

Figure 5.8
A material results in pixel output, constructed from a set of channels and lower-order maps (also known as *material expressions*).

Mapping is designed to solve a problem. Specifically, the output of a material is a flat, two-dimensional rectangle of pixels, while polygonal geometry exists in three dimensions and is rarely flat or rectangular. There is no obvious one-to-one correspondence between the two-dimensional material and the three-dimensional object to which it should be applied. How, then, should the material be applied to the surface of a model? In other words, which subset of pixels in the material should be associated or mapped to a subset of pixels across particular polygons of the model? For example, a material for a character mesh might contain pixel data for the face, arms, hands, legs and torso. But when this two-dimensional material is assigned to a three-dimensional character mesh, how will the UDK know that the pixels for the face should be applied to the polygons representing the face, as opposed to the polygons for the feet or hands? The answer is mapping, also known as mapping coordinates.

Mapping refers to the mathematical instructions that explain how a two-dimensional set of pixels relates to the geometry of a model—that is, how the pixels of a material are distributed across the surface of a model. The way in which any material should be applied to a model (the mapping) differs from model to model. For this reason, mapping information is embedded into the model, not into the material. The material can be applied to many different models according to very different mapping coordinates. Figure 5.9 shows an example of a material that must be mapped carefully onto a model to appear correctly across its surface.

Material

Material Mapped onto Model

Figure 5.9
A material is packaged and arranged for mapping onto a model.

How does the mapping information embedded into the model work? How is it possible to map a two-dimensional space onto a three-dimensional one? Mapping works by allowing artists to first express pixel positions within the material in terms of two-dimensional coordinates, and then to embed that coordinate information into the vertices of polygons so that corresponding sections of the material are interpolated (or spread) across the polygon between the vertices.

Let us consider this in more detail. Every material, being a rectangle of pixels, consists of four corners, or vertices—one at the top left, one at the top right, one at the bottom left, and one at the bottom right. The two-dimensional space of a material can be described and measured using a coordinate space, called UV space. UV space consists of two axes, U (horizontal) and V (vertical), leading off from an origin at the top-left corner. In UV space, values range as decimals from 0 to 1. The top-left corner of the material is the origin of the coordinate system; its coordinate is thus UV(0,0). The bottom-right corner represents the furthest extremity of UV space, and its coordinate is UV(1,1). Any point inside the material can therefore be expressed in terms of a UV coordinate, the center point being UV(0.5,0.5) (because 0.5 is halfway between 0 and 1) and the top-right corner being UV(1,0). (See Figure 5.10.)

Note

It is also possible to express UV coordinates using negative values such as UV(−1,−1) or (0,−1). Such coordinates refer to a mirrored version of the material.

Mapping information in the form of UV coordinates is embedded into a mesh by way of its vertices to define how a material should be applied across its surfaces.

UV SPACE

(0,0)   (1,0)

(0,1)   (1,1)

Figure 5.10
UV space for a material.

Every polygon of a model is defined by its edges and vertices, with the vertices representing the polygon's corners. Each vertex in a polygon carries within itself a UV coordinate that maps into its associated material, meaning that each vertex corresponds to a particular position within the material. Mapping, then, works by filling in the pixels of the polygon with the corresponding pixels in the material that fall within the UV range specified by the vertices (see Figure 5.11). Thus, a rectangular polygon with a top-left vertex of UV(0,0) and a bottom-right vertex of UV(1,1) will be filled with all pixels from the material. It will in effect match the material exactly. By contrast, a rectangular polygon with a top-left vertex of UV(0,0) and a bottom-right vertex of UV(0.5,0.5) will show only half the material.

Note

What do you think a rectangle between (0,0) and (2,2) would look like? A rectangle with UVs between (0,0) and (2,2) would tile the material twice across the width and the height of the polygon.

Note

Artists typically specify the UV coordinates for a model not in the UDK, but in third-party modeling software, prior to the model being imported into the UDK.

Mapped Polygon

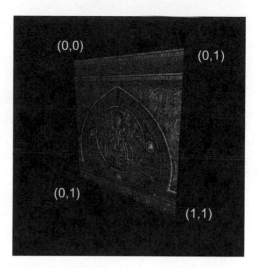

UV SPACE

(0,0)   (1,0)

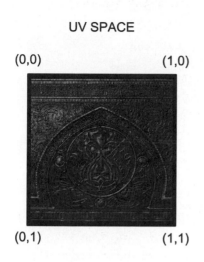

(0,1)   (1,1)

Figure 5.11
A material mapped between the vertices of a polygon using UV coordinates.

PROJECT: MATERIALS AND MAPPING

This section marks the beginning of the project-based work for this chapter, and it picks up where the work in the previous chapter left off. It seeks both to apply the information on materials and mapping discussed so far in this chapter and to introduce new topics and techniques. Some of the new topics that will be discussed include the following:

- How to create materials using the UDK Material Editor
- How to adjust the mapping coordinates on CSG
- How to import images as texture maps
- How to create material instances based on materials

The main aim of this project is to demonstrate how to create new materials and how to apply them to the floors, walls, and ceiling of the atrium map created in the previous chapter. The completed project is shown in Figure 5.12.

It is worth mentioning here that it is not essential that the project from the previous chapter be completed for you to get started with this project. The concepts discussed here are general, and can be applied in all other cases in which materials come into play. For the purposes of applying materials, however, it is necessary that there be

Figure 5.12
A view of the completed material project.

something—some kind of geometry—to which they can be applied. This chapter uses the CSG created in the previous project as the geometry to which materials must be assigned, but you can use CSG from your own work if you prefer.

Note

This chapter does not consider the issue of lighting, which is reserved for Chapter 8. For this reason, some material effects, such as normal maps (bumpiness), will not be visible even when the project for this chapter is completed. This is because those material effects depend on there being at least one light source in the level, beyond the default ambient light used for the Unlit mode of the viewports.

Applying Pre-made Materials via the Content Browser to Atrium Walls

The first main objective of this project is to use the Content Browser to browse for an appropriate and existing (pre-made) material, and then to apply that material to all the walls of the atrium level. To begin this project, open the completed project file from the previous chapter, located in the file DM-CSG_Project_05_finished.udk. Alternatively, you can create a new UDK level from scratch and add the necessary CSG, or open another existing level featuring CSG that is eligible for receiving

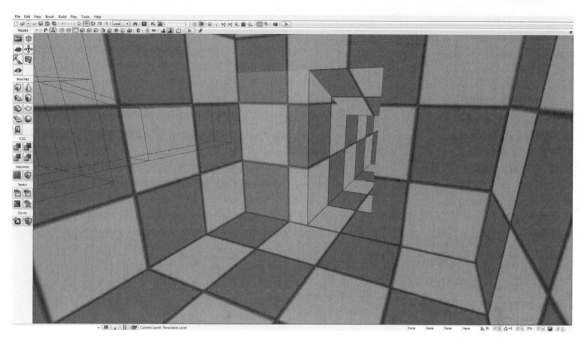

Figure 5.13
Before you start the material project, you must have CSG for the walls, floors, and ceiling of an atrium. This project was loaded from the file DM-CSG_Project_05_finished.udk.

materials. (More information on building CSG can be found in the previous chapter.) The starting project should look something like Figure 5.13.

1. Open the Edit menu and choose Select None or press the Shift+N keyboard shortcut to deselect all actors in the level.

2. Press Ctrl+Shift+F to open the Content Browser and click the All Assets button to view all assets.

3. Select the Materials checkbox in the Search and Filter pane to ensure that only assets that are materials appear in the Preview pane. This displays a list of all materials available (see Figure 5.14).

4. Browse or search the material thumbnails in the Preview pane to locate a wall material consistent with the atrium's theme or style. The style I have chosen is an industrial/mechanical style M_HU_Walls_SM_FlatWall (see Figure 5.15).

5. After you select the material to be assigned to the walls in the Content Browser, you're ready to specify which walls in the level should receive the selected material. To do this, reduce the Content Browser to an intermediate size and drag to it one side of the editor so that the Content Browser and the perspective

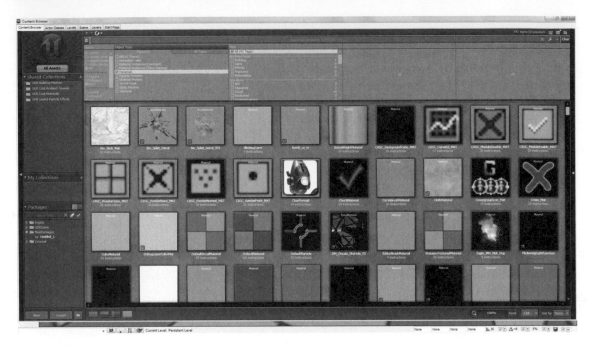

Figure 5.14
Filter the Content Browser to view all material assets.

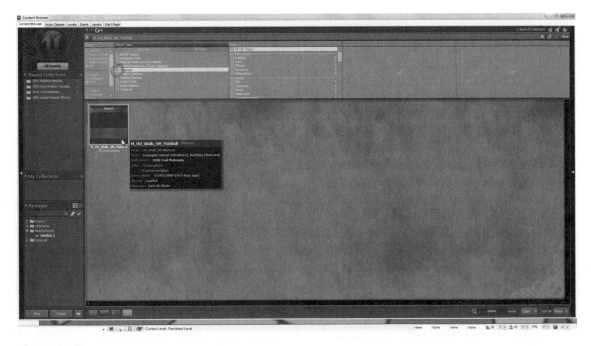

Figure 5.15
Finding a suitable material for the atrium walls.

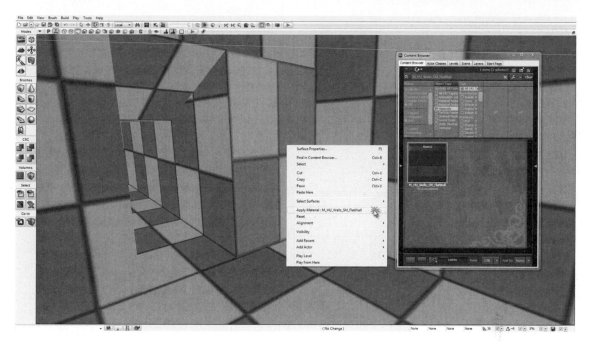

Figure 5.16
Applying a material to a selected face. Notice that the left and right sides of the Content Browser have been collapsed. This can be a useful technique for gaining screen space for the Preview pane.

viewport can be viewed together. Then, right-click a wall polygon and choose Apply Material from the menu that appears. The UDK applies the material selected in the Content Browser to the selected polygon using a default mapping (see Figure 5.16).

6. Another way to apply a material to a surface is via drag-and-drop. Try this method using a different wall surface, clicking and dragging the material thumbnail from the Content Browser onto a surface in the viewport.

7. There is no restriction on the number of surfaces that can be selected in the viewport at any one time; likewise, there is also no restriction on the number of surfaces to which a material can be applied at once. Try selecting multiple surfaces and then applying the material to them using the technique described in step 5 (see Figure 5.17). Remember, you can Ctrl-click to select multiple surfaces.

8. Yet another alternative is to copy and paste materials from one surface to another. Use this method to apply the material to the remaining wall surfaces of the level. To do so, select a wall surface with a material applied, and press the

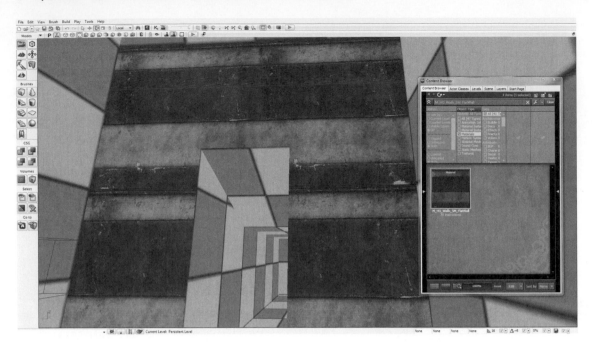

Figure 5.17
Applying a material to multiple surfaces.

Ctrl+C keyboard shortcut to copy it. Next, use the Ctrl-click method to select the remaining wall surfaces. Finally, once they are selected, press the Ctrl+V keyboard shortcut to paste the copied material onto the selected surfaces. This will paste not only the material, but also the mapping information that was assigned to the surface from which the material was copied. (See Figure 5.18.)

Note

In a case such as this one, where a material must be assigned to all walls, the optimal strategy would probably have been to first select all walls in the level and to then apply the material to them in one fell swoop by right-clicking a selection and choosing Apply Material from the shortcut menu, as in step 5. I deliberately avoided that method here to demonstrate some alternative methods for applying materials.

Note

The level created so far can be found in the companion files under DM-Mat_Project_01_wall_start.udk.

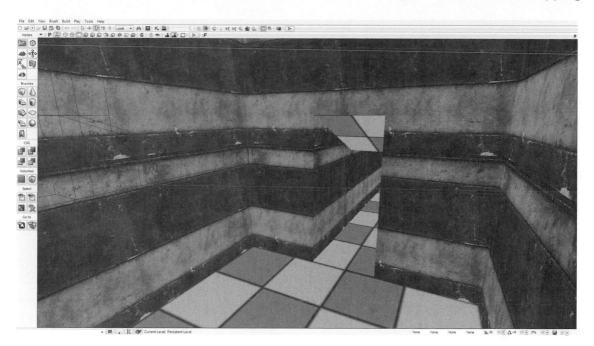

Figure 5.18
Copy and paste materials and mapping information.

Adjusting the UV Mapping Coordinates on the Walls Using the Surface Properties Dialog Box

Each of the atrium wall faces has the wall material applied using its default mapping information. *Default mapping* refers simply to the mapping that the UDK has assigned to the face automatically, rather than to mapping specified manually by the user. In this case, the default mapping is acceptable; the walls look better now than they did when the checker pattern was applied, and the wall surfaces are reasonably convincing in that they are quite clearly identifiable as walls. That being said, the vertical tiling of the wall material is not only noticeable, but is striking. As you can see in Figure 5.19, the material is tiled twice along the height of the wall, with the details of the wall repeated.

You can solve this problem in many different ways, one being to change the UV mapping of the affected CSG surfaces. The UDK offers two tools for changing this: Texture Alignment mode and the Surface Properties dialog box.

One aim of this section is to reduce the vertical tiling of the wall material on all the atrium wall surfaces. Another is to adjust the vertical positioning of the material on the wall surfaces so that one of the material's border elements rests close to the floor

Figure 5.19
The wall material is tiled twice vertically along the wall.

and another rests close to the ceiling. This will give the wall a finished and integrated appearance. To achieve this, you can use the Surface Properties dialog box.

The Surface Properties dialog box (see Figure 5.20) offers control over the UV mapping and the lighting properties of a surface. It is divided into sections, each devoted to adjusting either UV mapping or lighting properties. The UV-mapping options are as follows:

- **Pan.** You use the buttons in the Pan group to offset or slide the material up, down, left, or right along the surface by a specified number of texels (texture pixels). The U buttons offset the material horizontally and the V buttons offset it vertically. Clicking the buttons will offset the material in a positive direction, and Shift-clicking the buttons will offset the material negatively. In effect, the Pan buttons increment and decrement the UV coordinates of the vertices.

- **Rotation.** You can use the buttons in the Rotation group to turn, flip, or rotate the material across the surface. You can rotate materials by a set increment of 45 or 90 degrees, or by any custom angle. Materials can also be flipped (or mirrored) to face the opposite direction, as though they were rotated 180 degrees about their local x or y axis.

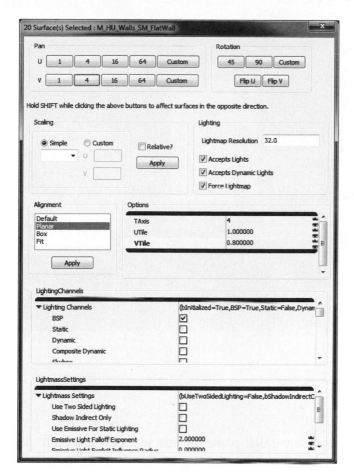

Figure 5.20
The Surface Properties dialog box.

- **Scaling, Alignment, and Options.** The Scaling, Alignment, and Options groups affect the size of the material on the surfaces and the extent of its tiling. Materials are tiled across the U (horizontal) and V (vertical) axes. The greater the amount of tiling, the greater the amount of material repetitions there are across the surface.

Use of the Scaling, Alignment, and Options settings, in combination with the Pan setting, is demonstrated in the following steps:

1. Ctrl-click to select all wall surfaces in the level. Then right-click a selected surface and choose Surface Properties from the menu that appears (see Figure 5.21).

2. Start tweaking the mapping of the wall surfaces by changing the alignment and tiling of their material. First, make sure the Alignment setting is set to Planar to

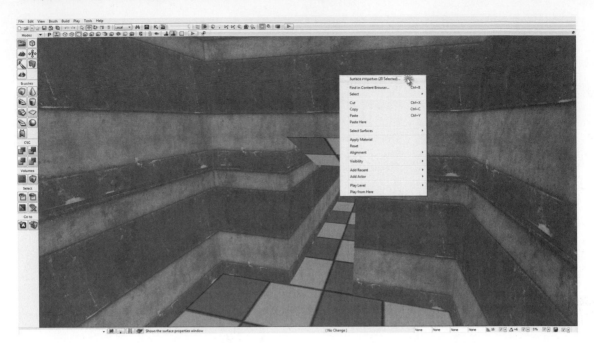

Figure 5.21
Accessing the Surface Properties dialog box.

ensure the material is projected from a parallel plane as one seamless material across all faces of the wall. Then reduce the vertical tiling of the material by setting the VTile parameter in the Options group to 0.8, as shown in Figure 5.22. This stretches the material such that only 80 percent of it will fit across the height of the walls.

3. The vertical tiling of the walls has been reduced by 20 percent, but the border (or trim) features of the wall texture do not align appropriately with the floor and ceiling. To resolve this problem, you must pan the material vertically across the surface—that is, shift the material up or down to bring the trim features in better alignment with the floor and ceiling. To do so, click the 4 button in the V row in the Pan section to lower the material into place; then click the 1 button to control the alignment more precisely. (See Figure 5.23.) Remember, you can Shift-click these buttons to reverse the direction of the pan. When you're finished, close the dialog box; the material is now aligned correctly with the wall surfaces.

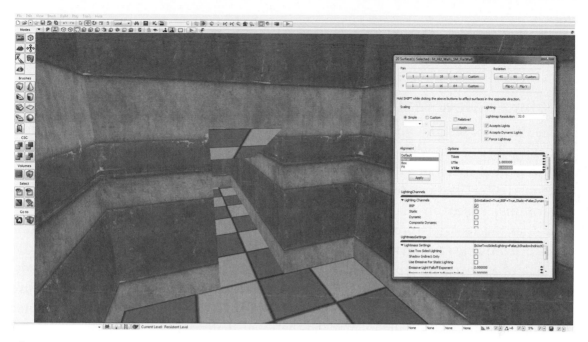

Figure 5.22
Reducing the vertical tiling of the walls.

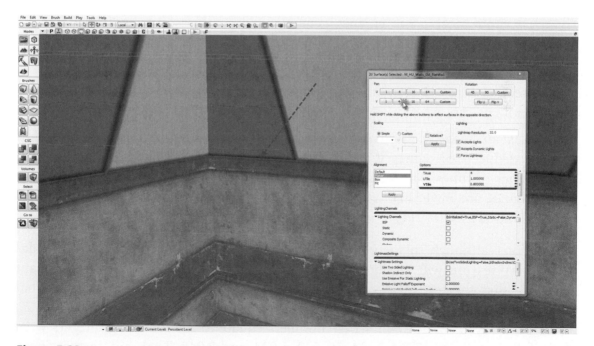

Figure 5.23
Reducing the vertical tiling of the walls.

Note

The level created so far can be found in the companion files under DM-Mat_Project_02_walls_comp.udk.

Creating a New Material for the Floor

In the previous section, you dragged a pre-made material from the Content Browser and applied it to the walls of the atrium. In this section, the floor of the atrium will receive a new material created from scratch using the UDK Material Editor. The Material Editor is the interface used by developers to construct material networks (algorithms) based on material channels, texture maps, and other kinds of maps. Note that the term *texture map* refers to a rectangle of pixels. A material is distinguished from a texture map in the same way that a body can be distinguished from any one of its parts. A typical body contains arms, legs, a torso, a head, feet, hands, and so on. Similarly, a material (the whole) is composed from one or more texture maps (parts). Refer to the section "Materials Are Algorithms" earlier in this chapter for more information on the relationship between materials and textures.

The material created here will be based on a number of texture maps that are provided with the UDK, but users can also import their own maps from standard image files.

The UDK and most game engines generally place at least two requirements on textures:

- A texture filename cannot contain spaces, although it can contain the underscore character (_) to separate multiple words.

- A texture can be imported only from a lossless image file format—in other words, an image file format that would *not* cause the original image data to be lost, reduced, or damaged if the file were subsequently saved an indefinite number of times. The image formats meeting this description and accepted by the UDK are BMP, FLOAT, PCX, PNG, PSD, and TGA. Note that image formats such as GIF, JPG, and TIF are not supported.

In addition—although this is not so much a requirement as a strong recommendation—every texture will ideally have a width and height that is power 2 compliant to ensure that the texture is optimized for processing by graphics hardware. That means the width or height of a texture can be any of the following values: 2^1, 2^2, 2^3, 2^4, 2^5, 2^6, 2^7, 2^8, 2^9, 2^{10}, 2^{11}.... These numbers equate to the following integers written in full: 2, 4, 8, 16, 32, 64, 128, 256, 512, 1,024, and 2,048. That said, textures need not have an aspect ratio of 1—that is, they need not be square—so the following width and height combinations are equally valid: 64×128, 512×32, 1,024×256, etc.

Note

Textures for mobile devices must be square. That is, the width and height of a mobile texture in pixels must be equal.

Importing Texture Maps

Textures must be imported into the UDK as part of an asset package that can be viewed through the Content Browser. To import a texture, right-click any vacant space in the Content Browser's Preview pane and choose Import from the menu that appears. Alternatively, click the Import button at the bottom of the Packages pane. (See Figure 5.24.) An Open dialog box appears, prompting you to select a file to import. After you select a file, the Import dialog box opens. Here, you specify which package and group is to be the owner of the texture. The Import dialog box, shown in Figure 5.25, specifies a package name and group to which the asset will be imported. If the package and group names match those of any existing packages or groups, then the imported asset will be inserted as a member of that package and group. If the package and group names do not match any existing packages and groups, then a package and group of the same names will be created, and the asset will be added to them. (Refer to the section "Packages and Groups" in Chapter 3, "UDK Fundamentals," for more information on packages and groups.)

Figure 5.24
Start the import process.

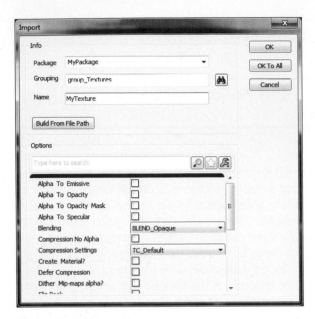

Figure 5.25
Importing a texture asset into a package and group.

Follow these steps to create a new material using the Content Browser, which you will go on to construct and define in the Material Editor. The result of this construction will be a material that can be applied to the floor of the atrium.

1. To get started, press Shift+N to deselect everything in the viewports. Then press Ctrl+Shift+F to open the Content Browser. Click the All Assets button and ensure that no search filter is active in the Search and Filter pane. If you wish, enable the Material filter to restrict the Asset pane to display material assets only. Finally, click the New button in the bottom-left corner of the Packages pane to create a new material. (See Figure 5.26.)

2. The New dialog box opens (see Figure 5.27). Specify the name of the package (in this example, MyPackage) and the group in the asset hierarchy to which the newly created material asset should belong (here, Materials) in the Package and Grouping fields, respectively. In the Name field, enter a descriptive name for the asset—in this example, `atrium_Floor`. In the Factory list, specify the type of asset to be created—in this case, Material. Finally, click the OK button to create the material.

The Content Browser is updated to feature the newly added material and its package and group in the Packages pane. The Material Editor is also opened in preparation

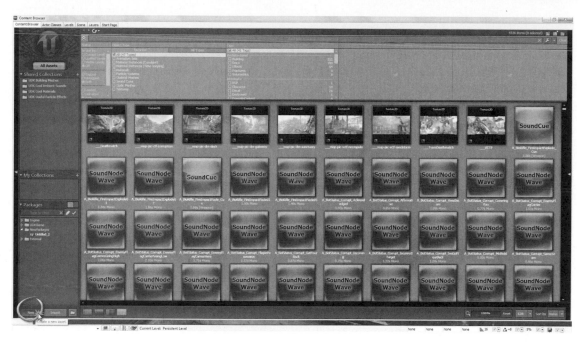

Figure 5.26
Creating a new material using the Content Brower's Packages pane.

Figure 5.27
Parameters for the material asset.

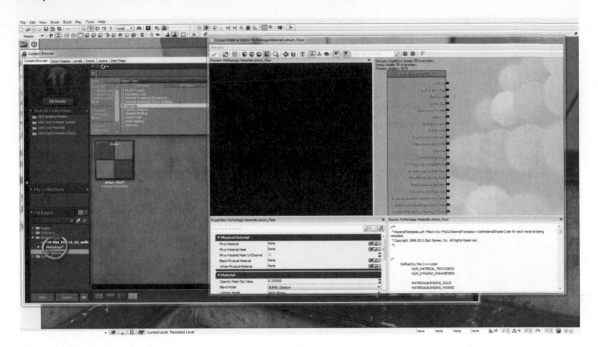

Figure 5.28
A new material is created.

for creating a new material; this window can be closed for the moment. Notice that the new package and group have been created in the asset hierarchy and that the new material has been added as a member of that group, and thereby as a member of the package. (See Figure 5.28.)

Note

Double-clicking any material asset in the Content Browser Preview pane will open it for inspection in the Material Editor. Materials are in this sense "open for viewing." Examining materials in this manner is a useful way to understand how materials are composed—by learning how UDK developers created them.

Note

As you learned in the section "Understanding File-Based Versus Project-Based Applications" in Chapter 3, level and asset packages each have their own save status, meaning that each can be saved independently of the other. Saving the level does not necessarily save the changes made to the level assets, and vice versa. (You can resolve this issue by choosing Save All from the File main menu.) A similar but distinct relationship exists between asset packages and the individual assets themselves. In short, the save status of individual assets—such as materials, textures and meshes—depends on the save status of the asset package containing them. That means it is possible to edit and commit changes to specific assets within a package and then to lose those changes on exiting the UDK because the package containing those assets was not saved. The point is that the save status of an asset does not cascade upward to a package, but the save status of a package cascades downward to all its contained assets. To commit changes made to any specific asset, it will be necessary to also save the changes to the containing package. To save the package, right-click the package name in the Content Browser's Asset Hierarchy pane and choose Save from the menu that appears.

The Material Editor

As mentioned, you can think of a material as an algorithm or a hierarchy of maps that eventually feeds upward into a set of channels whose final output is a rectangle of pixels. The newly created material is empty in the sense that it contains nothing but a set of empty channels whose output is a rectangle of black pixels, because black pixels have the value of 0 (nothing).

To define the appearance of this new material, you must use the Material Editor, which you can access from the Content Browser by double-clicking any material in the Preview pane or right-clicking a material and choosing Edit Using Material Editor from the menu that appears. The main purpose of the Material Editor is to enable developers to construct materials, which consist of a graph or network that results in the output of a rectangle of pixels. The Material Editor interface, shown in Figure 5.29, is divided into five main elements:

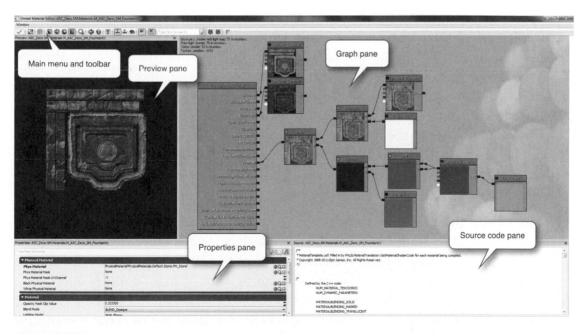

Figure 5.29
The Material Editor GUI.

Figure 5.30
All panels are visible in the Material Editor, except the Material Expressions panel.

- **The main menu and toolbar.** The main menu contains only the Window option, used to show and hide specific panels of the interface. If your version of the Material Editor looks different from the one in Figure 5.29, it might be because you have different panels displayed. To achieve the layout shown in Figure 5.29, check the options in the Window menu as shown in Figure 5.30. The Material Editor toolbar offers a range of useful features, which will be introduced as required during the project.

- **The Preview pane.** The Preview pane is tantamount to a miniature viewport. This pane displays the current output of the material in real time on a mesh object, either a primitive (such as a cube or a sphere) or a custom mesh object selected from the Content Browser. The controls for the Preview pane are similar to (but distinct from) the controls for standard viewports. Clicking and holding the left-mouse button while dragging the mouse will rotate the Preview pane around the mesh focused at its center, and clicking and holding the right-mouse button while dragging the mouse will zoom the Preview pane closer to or further from the mesh. Using a combination of these controls, it is possible to completely navigate the Preview pane to observe the effects of the material on the object. You can also hold down the L key on the keyboard while moving the mouse to position the light source in the Preview pane; this enables you to observe the effects of the material under different lighting conditions.

- **The Graph pane.** The Graph pane is the main working area of the Material Editor. It works similarly to the Kismet interface, which was discussed briefly in Chapter 2, "Building a First Project: A Tour of the UDK," and is detailed further in Chapter 9, "Kismet and Matinee: Beginning with Visual Scripting and Animation." You use the Graph pane to both construct and describe a material by way of a network of connected nodes. The output of the material seen on the mesh in the Preview pane is entirely the product of the network of nodes featured in the Graph pane. Constructing the graph (and thus the material) is a matter of dragging and dropping various nodes into the Graph pane and joining them together in specific and calculated ways by drawing wires between their input and output connectors. Each node contains at least one input connector and one output connector. Some nodes correspond to textures; their output is a rectangle of pixels. Some nodes are used to perform various kinds of mathematical operations, such as combining two inputs to produce a single output— for example, blending two textures to produce a resultant texture as an output. The outputs of various nodes can go on to be the inputs for various other nodes; thus, the chain goes on toward the final node. In general, the Graph pane is read from right to left, tracing along the connections until all the nodes eventually feed into the primary node on the left. The input connectors of this node correspond to the different material channels, and the output of this node is the final output of pixels representing the material seen in the Preview pane.

- **The Properties pane.** The Properties pane is typically found at the bottom-left corner of the Material Editor window. It is a context-sensitive panel in that its content changes depending on the node that is selected in the graph. Its purpose is to show and allow users to edit all the parameters associated with the selected node.

- **The Source Code pane.** The Material Editor works much like an HTML editor such as Dreamweaver. That is, an HTML editor's GUI is really a front end for automatically generating a document that is written in HTML and CSS. Likewise, the Material Editor and its mouse-driven Graph pane is, in fact, a front end for generating a material algorithm behind the scenes that is eventually written to a file in High Level Shader Language (HLSL). The HLSL script that is generated is the file that the UDK uses to run on the graphics processing unit (GPU) to make the material work. In other words, the UDK recognizes materials under the hood not as a graph or a network but as an HLSL script. The Source Code pane, featured in the bottom-right area of the Material Editor, updates in real-time to show the contents of the HLSL file that is being generated on the basis of the material graph.

Building the Floor Material

The aim of this section is to detail how the Material Editor can be used to construct a material for the floor. Creating the material will involve creating a network of connected nodes, or *material expressions*. In the UDK, this term is used to refer to any kind of node in the material graph, including textures (texture samples). The following steps detail the process of creating a material:

1. Open the Content Browser (if necessary) and double-click the newly created material to load it into the Material Editor. (Note that the Preview pane of the

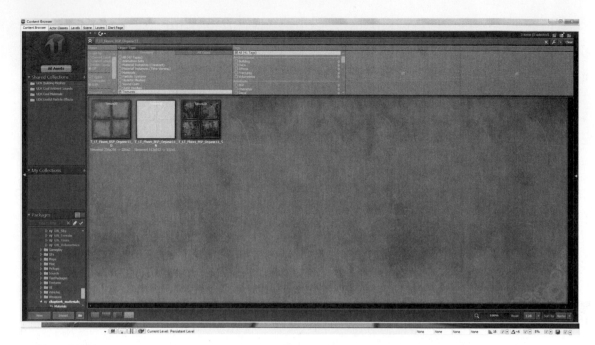

Figure 5.31
Searching for texture assets to be included into the floor material.

Material Editor will appear completely black because the material graph is currently empty.)

2. Back in the Content Browser, find all the texture samples that will be included in the floor material. Click the All Assets button, select the Textures checkbox in the Search and Filter pane to restrict the content of the Preview pane to textures only, and type T_LT_Floors_BSP_Organic11 in the Search field (see Figure 5.31).

3. Drag the T_LT_Floors_BSP_Organic11_D *and* T_LT_Floors_BSP_Organic11_N texture samples into the Material Editor window one at a time. As shown in Figure 5.32, a separate texture sample node is created for each one in the graph. The first sample represents the texture to be used for the material's diffuse channel (the color) and the second sample represents the texture to be used for the normal channel (the bumpiness and roughness).

Note

Notice that the Preview pane of the Material Editor is still black, even though texture-sample expressions have been added to the Graph pane. This is because the expressions are not yet connected to the graph and to the material channels by way of wires. For a material expression to exist within the graph, it must be connected to the material channels.

Figure 5.32
Dragging and dropping texture samples from the Content Browser window to the Material Editor window creates texture-sample expressions in the Graph pane.

4. Start creating the material by positioning the two material expressions neatly in the Graph pane. (You can drag material expressions around the Graph pane by holding down the Ctrl key on the keyboard while clicking and dragging the selected expression.) Place the diffuse texture sample at the top of the Graph pane beside the Diffuse input socket of the primary node, and place the normal texture sample beside the Normal input socket. To create a quick and rough material for the floor that you can see in the Preview pane, click and drag to create a connection between the output socket of the diffuse texture sample and the input connection of the diffuse channel. Sockets are represented as square shapes attached to the edge of the node. Try the same for the normal texture sample and the normal channel. (See Figure 5.33.) Also, try clicking the primitive buttons (box, sphere, cylinder, and plane) in the Material Editor to see the floor material applied to different 3D objects in the Preview pane. Finally, click the Apply button (the one with a green checkmark) in the toolbar to apply the changes to the current material in the package.

Note

Multiple nodes can be selected via marquee (or window) selecting. To do this, hold down the Ctrl+Alt key combination and then click and drag to draw a rectangle around the nodes to be selected. You can move multiple nodes using the aforementioned Ctrl-drag method.

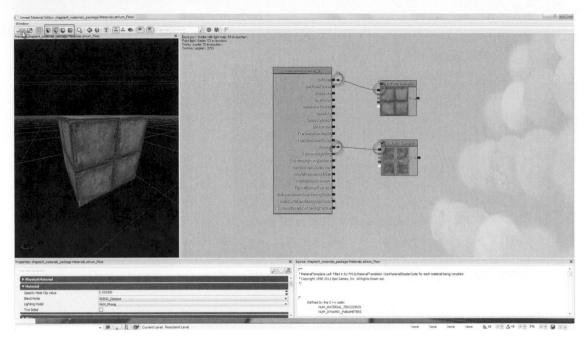

Figure 5.33
The diffuse and normal samples, connected to their respective channels on the primary node.

5. The material created so far features two separate texture samples: one feeding into the diffuse channel and the other feeding into the normal channel. That means both the diffuse and normal channels are determining the rectangle of pixels output by the graph. The problem is, the current material lacks a specular channel. Most real-world materials have some degree of specularity (shininess), however subtle—even materials such as concrete and brickwork. You could add a specular channel to the material by adding a new and independent texture sample dedicated to specularity to the graph. (A texture sample that defines specularity just as the diffuse texture defines the diffuse channel and the normal texture defines the normal channel.) However, this solution is suboptimal because the extra subtle realism gained from the specular channel cannot be justified considering the extra time lost creating the specular map and the extra memory used by the UDK to hold the pixels of the map. A "cheaper," or more optimal, way to create specularity is to define a specular channel on the basis of a modified diffuse map. To start, right-click any vacant space in the Graph pane and choose Math and then Power from the menu that appears (see Figure 5.34). This creates a mathematical power expression, which can (like all the mathematical nodes) be used to perform real-time mathematical operations to the pixel values of connected texture samples.

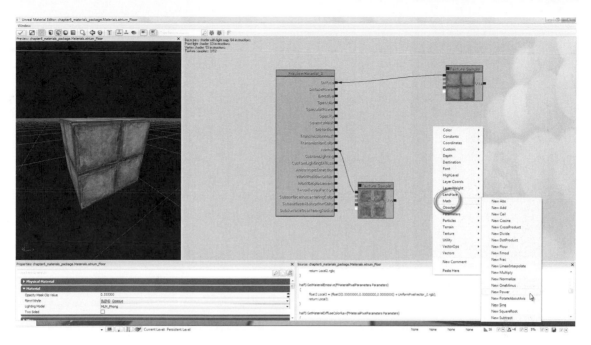

Figure 5.34
Creating a mathematical power node to increase the contrast of the Diffuse texture sample.

6. You can use the power node to increase or decrease the contrast of a connected texture sample—that is, to increase or decrease the connected texture's luminance levels. Changing the contrast of an image does not affect the hue of an image (the colors themselves) but does affect their brightness. Increasing the contrast makes darker colors darker and brighter colors brighter, which increases the intensity of an image by making edges more pronounced. (This is because edges in an image are the result of differentials in values, or brightness, between neighboring pixels.) The power node accepts two inputs: Base, which expects to receive an image whose contrast is to be changed, and Exponent, which expects a single decimal value that defines the extent to which the contrast of the image plugged into the Base node is to be adjusted. The power node offers one output. The output represents a rectangle of pixels that is the result of the contrast adjustment. This will eventually feed into the specular channel (although not directly, because there is more work to do beyond this step). To work with this node, plug the diffuse texture sample into the Base socket (see Figure 5.35). Notice that the diffuse texture sample can connect both to the diffuse channel and to the power node; that means the diffuse texture sample is acting as an input to both the diffuse channel and the power operation. The power operation *does not* affect the original diffuse texture sample, but rather accepts that

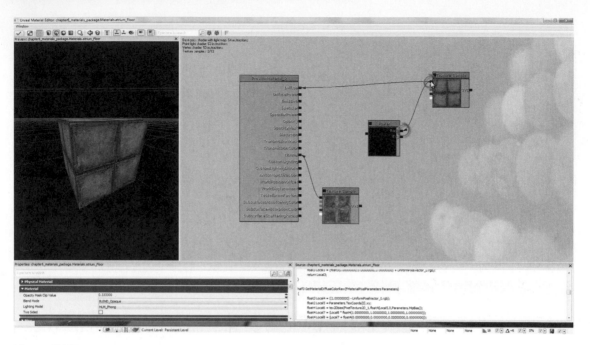

Figure 5.35
Creating a mathematical power node to increase the contrast of the diffuse texture sample.

as an input and outputs a completely separate sample. This output sample can then be passed on as an input to other nodes.

7. At present, nothing is connected to the Exponent socket. This socket expects not a texture sample (a grid of numbers), but a single decimal number that defines the amount of change to be made to the contrast of the image. A value of 1 retains the existing contrast; a value less than 1 reduces the contrast; and a value greater than 1 increases the contrast. To increase the contrast of the image, create a constant node by right-clicking a vacant area of the material graph and choosing Constants and then New Constant from the menu that appears. Alternatively, hold down the 1 key on the keyboard and click in any vacant space. Then select the constant node in the graph and attach it to the Exponent input socket of the power node. Finally, use the Properties pane at the bottom of the Material Editor to adjust the value of the constant to 2 (to double the contrast of the image). To preview the effects of your changes in the power node, click the small dark square to the left of the node name.

8. As you can see in Figure 5.36, increasing the contrast using the power node appears to have darkened the image overall. This is inconsistent with a specular highlight, which must be bright. For this reason, the brightness of the power

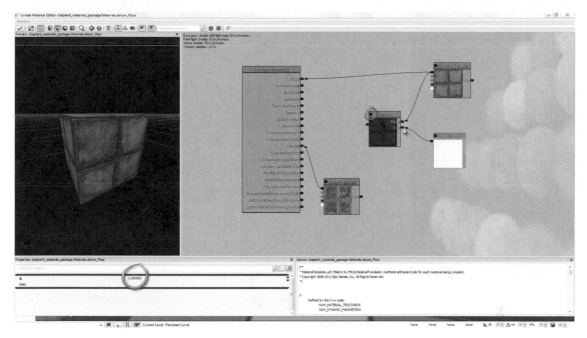

Figure 5.36
Wiring up the power node to increase the contrast of the diffuse texture sample.

node's output will need to be increased. To achieve this, you can use a multiply node, which performs multiplication. To add a multiply node to the material graph, right-click any vacant space in the Graph pane and choose Math followed by Multiply from the menu that appears. Alternatively, hold down the M key on the keyboard and click any vacant space.

Note

Color multiplication in the UDK differs from color multiplication in the conventional sense because typically it is used for darkening, not brightening. In the UDK however, it can do both. As mentioned, an RGB color can be reduced to a three-component number, with each component having a range of 0 to 255 (0 being black and 255 being white). In the UDK, these extremes are represented by the decimal range of 0 to 1. Multiplication is the act of scaling one number by another number. Because colors in the RGB space can be reduced to numbers, color multiplication is therefore the act of scaling one color by another color, or value. Traditional color multiplication works according to the following formula: Color 1 × Color 2 / 255. According to this formula, any color *x* multiplied by black (0) will always result in black, and any color *x* multiplied by white (255) will always result in *x*. In short, the product of any two colors is always the darker of the two colors. For this reason, traditional color multiplication can be used only to darken and never to brighten colors. In the UDK, however, it is possible to multiply a color by a value greater than 1 (255)—that is, by a value in a high dynamic range—resulting in a color that is, in fact, brighter and not darker. This technique will be applied to brighten the darkened output of the power node.

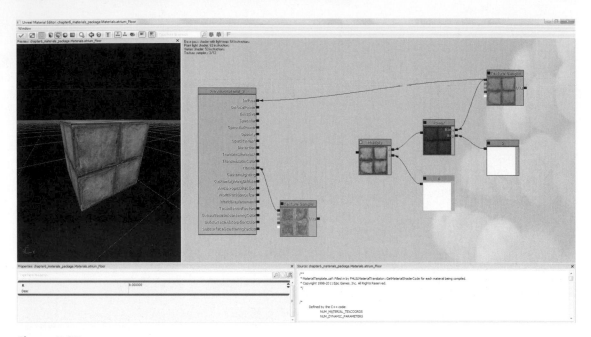

Figure 5.37
Multiply nodes can be used for brightening and darkening texture samples.

9. The multiply node accepts two inputs—one for each multiplicand A and B—and the output node is for the pixels that constitute the product. Input A should be connected to the output of the power expression, and input B should be connected to a new constant value above 1 that will be multiplied with all the pixels in A to increase their brightness. You can create the new constant value using the technique described in step 7, setting its value to 8 (see Figure 5.37). Remember to adjust the positions of all the expressions in the graph to accommodate the new additions and to increase readability.

10. The specular map for the floor material is almost complete; there remains but one problem. Specifically, the shine, or specularity, of an object typically appears as a grayscale or desaturated color, often as a white highlight. The specular map created so far, however, actually colored much like the diffuse sample. It will therefore be necessary to remove or neutralize the colors of the diffuse sample, effectively bringing it closer to a black-and-white image. The process of neutralizing the colors of an image is called *desaturation*. Desaturation can be achieved through a desaturation node. To add this node, right-click any vacant space in the Graph pane and choose Color followed by New Desaturation in the menu that appears. Next, plug the output of the multiply node into the top socket of the desaturation node; then create a new constant to plug into the bottom socket of the desaturation node. The constant will control the

degree of desaturation to be applied to the texture sample. A value of 1 results in complete desaturation, and a value of 0 results in no desaturation. Set this value to 0.5, and then connect the output of the desaturation node into the specular channel to observe the effects on the material of the specular highlight. Congratulations! This material now has a convincing specular channel, created not from a separate specular map but by reusing the diffuse map in combination with mathematical operations. See Figure 5.38 and Figure 5.39.

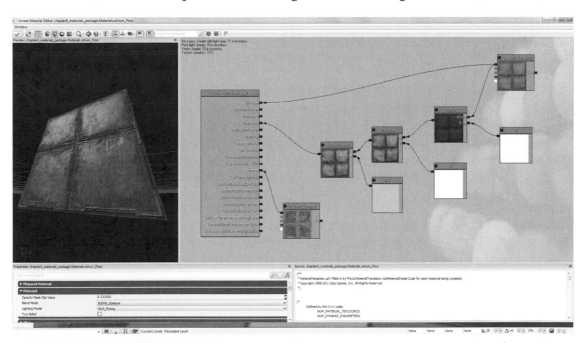

Figure 5.38
The final floor material, complete with a specular highlight.

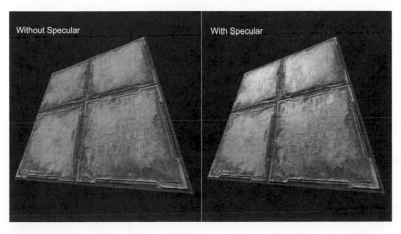

Figure 5.39
Comparing two versions of the floor material, one with a specular highlight and one without.

Commenting Materials

The practice of commenting materials is much like the practice of commenting source. Just as responsible programmers insert human-readable text into their source code, so should responsible material developers insert human-readable text into their material graph.

The purpose of the comment, when used appropriately, is at least two-fold:

- It makes the material clearer to read and easier to understand for developers on the team who were not involved in the material's creation.

- It acts as both a reminder and guide for the creators of the material. This is especially so in cases where the creators must revisit the material many weeks or months after its creation.

The Material Editor supports two types or levels of comments (see Figure 5.40):

- **Node-specific comment.** A node-specific comment is a human-readable string that can be attached to a specific node in the material graph. A node-specific comment can be assigned to a node by way of its Desc property (an abbreviation

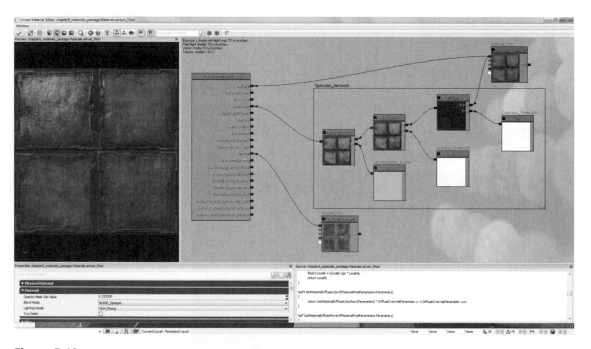

Figure 5.40
The floor material has been commented using both node-specific comments and group comments. One group comment labels the specular network of nodes, and various node-specific comments are used to clarify the function of the node.

of Description). Every node has its own Desc property. To assign a description to a node, select the node in the graph and edit its Desc value.

■ **Group comment.** A group comment is a comment that applies to a group of nodes in the material graph. To create a group comment, select two or more nodes. Then right-click any vacant space in the material graph, select New Comment from the menu that appears, and enter a comment in the dialog box that opens.

Applying the Floor Material

It is now time to apply the newly created floor material to the floor CSG in the level, and then to adjust the UV mapping of the floor so that the material tiles and aligns appropriately across the floor's surface. You can adjust the UV mapping of the floor in one of at least two ways: using the Surface Properties dialog box (discussed earlier in this chapter in the section "Adjusting the UV Mapping Coordinates on the Walls Using the Surface Properties Dialog Box") or using Texture Alignment mode (discussed in this section).

1. To assign the floor material to the floor, select all polygons of the floor, including the narrower hallway polygons. Then open the Content Browser and select the newly created material in the Preview pane. Next, right-click the floor polygons in the viewport and choose Apply Material from the menu that appears. The selected material will be applied to the floor polygons (see Figure 5.41).

2. Adjust the tiling of the floor material so that the tiles more closely fit the floor—that is, so the edges of the tiles align to the edges of the floor. One way to specify the alignment and tiling of the material is through the Surface Properties dialog box, which you access by right-clicking the floor polygons in the viewport and selecting Surface Properties from the menu that appears. You can also specify it using Texture Alignment mode. To access Texture Alignment mode, click the Texture Alignment Mode button in the main UDK toolbox (see Figure 5.42) or press Shift+F4.

3. In Texture Alignment mode, the UDK Editor is no different from when it is in the standard Camera mode, except that the Texture Alignment Mode button in the toolbox appears depressed instead of the Camera Mode button. The distinguishing feature of Texture Alignment mode relates to the way in which the editor responds to the Translate, Rotate, and Scale tools. In Texture Alignment mode, these tools do not affect the position, orientation, and scale of selected

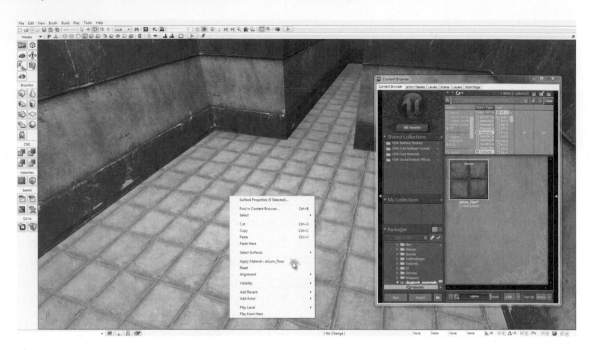

Figure 5.41
Applying the floor material to the floor of the atrium.

Figure 5.42
Selecting Texture Alignment mode from the UDK toolbox.

Figure 5.43
Scaling the floor texture into alignment with the floor.

actors, but instead affect the position, rotation, and scale of the material on the selected actors. Put another way, they control the UV mapping of materials. Specifically, the Translate tool affects the horizontal and vertical position of the material across the surface; the Rotate tool rotates the material over the surface; and the Scale tool increases and decreases the tiling of the material. The uniform Scale tool adjusts both the U and V tiling simultaneously, while the non-uniform Scale tool affects tiling in one direction only. Use these tools to adjust the tiling of the material as shown in Figure 5.43. Be sure to return to Camera mode when you are finished.

Note

Beware: Texture-alignment operations in Texture Alignment mode cannot be undone. You cannot undo or redo texture-alignment operations.

Note

The level created so far can be found in the companion files under DM-Mat_Project_03_floor_comp.udk.

Creating a Ceiling Material

So far, the only element of the level that remains without a material is the ceiling. It is now time to address this. You could pursue at least two different strategies here:

- You could create a completely new material with completely new maps and apply it to the ceiling.

- You could apply a variation of an existing material to the ceiling in the same way a variation of the diffuse map was used for the specular channel in the material for the floor.

This section focuses on the second of these two strategies for two reasons: first, to demonstrate the Material Instances feature, and second, to reiterate the importance of gaining as much detail and realism as possible from as few resources as possible.

Material instances differ from materials in that they are a derivative asset type rather than an original asset type. That is, they are created not from scratch but on the basis of an existing asset—namely, a material asset. A material instance is treated by the UDK as a separate, independent material asset. Nevertheless, it is created from an existing material. It recycles the texture samples of that material and enables developers to modify or tweak some of its mathematical parameters, allowing the instance to appear very different from the original.

In this case, the material instance to be applied to the ceiling will be based on the floor material. The ceiling material will be identical to the floor material, except for the color of the tiles.

1. Before you create a material instance from the floor material, you must first make some minor adjustments to the floor material. These adjustments relate to the diffuse channel. To begin, open the floor material in the Material Editor and Alt-click on the diffuse channel input socket or on the diffuse sample output socket to disconnect the diffuse texture sample from the diffuse channel. (See Figure 5.44.) You must disconnect the diffuse sample from the diffuse channel to adjust its wiring—that is, its connection to the diffuse channel.

2. Add a vector parameter node to the graph. To do so, right-click a vacant area in the material graph and choose Parameter New Vector Parameter from the menu that appears (see Figure 5.45). The vector parameter node consists of a three-component number and can be used to define a color in terms of its RGB values. This color can be multiplied with the diffuse texture sample by way of a multiply node to tint or color that texture sample.

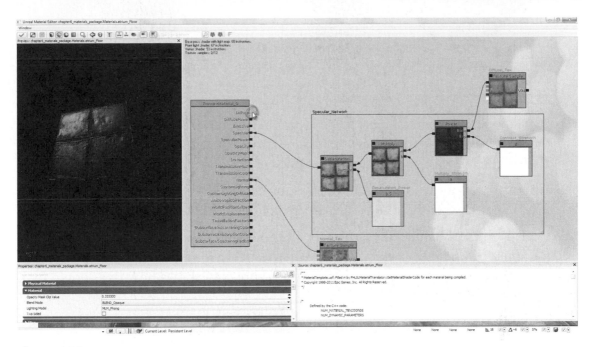

Figure 5.44
Disconnecting the diffuse texture sample from the diffuse channel.

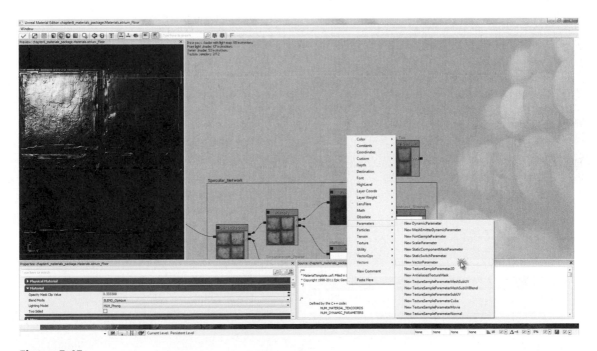

Figure 5.45
Parameters can be accessed and edited through Material Instances. Vector Parameters are three component numbers that can be used to represent RGB colors.

Note

Any node described as a parameter in a material can be accessed, edited, or tweaked in all derived material instances. This is what allows a material instance to differ substantially from the original material.

3. All unique parameters must have a unique name. To specify the name for a parameter, you use the Parameter Name property, accessible from the Material Editor's Properties pane. Name the newly created parameter Diffuse_Tint.

4. Choose a default color for the tint. In this case, I have chosen pure white (RGB: 1,1,1). This leaves the diffuse texture sample unaffected for the floor material.

5. Add a multiply node and connect both the diffuse texture sample and the parameter node into sockets A and B respectively. Then connect the output of the multiply node to the diffuse channel. Figure 5.46 shows how this should look in the graph.

6. The addition of the vector parameter to the floor material means that the material is now fully configured for instancing. That is, a material instance for the ceiling can now be created and adjusted on the basis of the floor material. Close

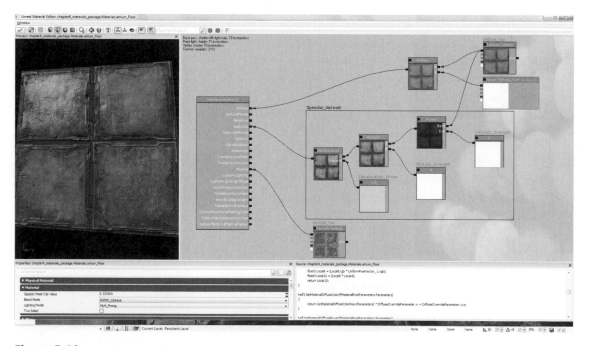

Figure 5.46
The diffuse texture sample is tinted white. The material can now be instanced and tweaked for the ceiling.

Figure 5.47
Creating a material instance.

the Material Editor and save the changes to the floor material, if required. Next, find the floor material in the Content Browser Preview pane, right-click it, and choose Create New Material Instance (Constant) from the menu that appears (see Figure 5.47).

7. In the Material Instance Creation dialog box, give the material instance a name and click OK.

8. A new material instance is created in the Content Browser and is opened automatically in the Material Instance Editor. In Material Instance Editor's Properties pane, under Vector Parameter Value, select the parameter checkbox. Then adjust the color as appropriate for the ceiling. I have selected the RGB color (0.533527,1.000000,0.744625). The material instance preview updates to show the newly colored variation of the material for the ceiling (see Figure 5.48).

9. You can apply material instances to CSG surfaces as though they were standard materials. Find the material instance in the Content Browser and apply it to all the polygons of the ceiling, adjusting the UV mapping as required using either the Surface Properties dialog box or Texture Alignment mode. *Voilà!* The walls, floor and ceiling of the level not only have materials applied, but have them

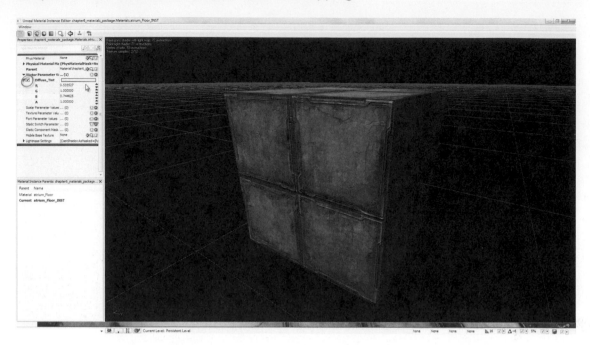

Figure 5.48
Tweaking the diffuse color parameter for the ceiling material instance.

applied in such a way that their diversity and detail is created from only a handful of resources combined using mathematical operations. (See Figure 5.49.)

Note

The completed materials project can be found in the companion files under DM-Mat_Project_04_mat_comp.udk.

Conclusion

The focus of this chapter was on materials, mapping, textures, and material instances. A *material* is an algorithm whose output is a rectangle of pixels used to shade the surfaces of geometry. *Mapping* refers to the instruction set used by the UDK to wrap a rectangle of pixels around a three-dimensional object. These subjects were not by any means covered in a way that can be considered comprehensive. You should think of the material covered here as an introduction rather than as a

Figure 5.49
The ceiling with a material instance applied.

complete reference. You are advised to spend some time practicing with materials by creating your own, using your own assets and texture samples. The next chapter puts materials and mapping behind us and enters the world of static meshes, the most common form of geometry found in a UDK level.

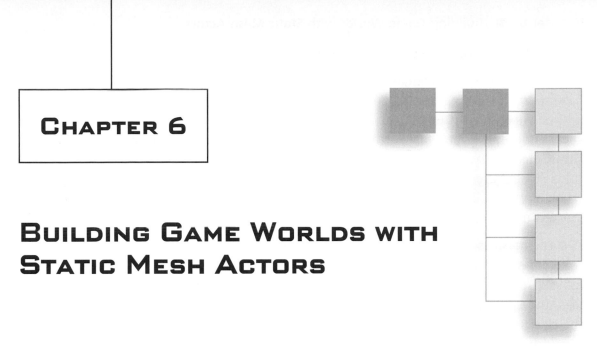

CHAPTER 6

BUILDING GAME WORLDS WITH STATIC MESH ACTORS

> Everybody at the party is a many-sided polygon.
>
> —They Might Be Giants

By the end of this chapter, you should:

- Understand the differences between static meshes, CSG, and skeletal meshes.
- Become more familiar with collision meshes and lightmaps.
- Understand the building-block technique of working with static meshes.
- Be able to create static meshes, lightmap UVs, and collision meshes.
- Be able to align meshes in the level using the Unreal Grid.

This chapter builds on the foundation laid by the previous two in considering the static mesh, a form of geometry that, like CSG, relies on the concepts of vertices, edges, and polygons, as well as on the concepts of materials, mapping, and coordinates. You should be familiar and comfortable with these concepts before proceeding with this chapter.

The static mesh is a critical or fundamental concept in the UDK. Instances of static meshes (static mesh actors) probably account for around 90 percent of the visible geometry in most UDK levels. *Static mesh* refers to any 3D model imported into the UDK from a third-party modeling application. This model acts as an abstract template or stamp from which instances or clones are made. Static meshes themselves are *not* inserted into a level, but are used to create clones or instances that are, with each clone or instance being called a *static mesh actor*. This chapter considers static meshes and static mesh actors further.

THE ANATOMY OF A STATIC MESH

A static mesh is an arrangement of polygons, edges, and vertices imported from a third-party modeling application into the UDK to represent the geometric detail of a level. As shown in Figure 6.1, static meshes are used to represent most level objects such as doors, statues, tables, chairs, cars, swords, weapons, armor, computers, spaceships, etc. Really, they're used for almost every kind of tangible thing except for terrains (which are created using the UDK Landscape tool), some architectural elements (such as flat walls and floors, created with CSG), and animated characters (which are created using skeletal meshes).

A static mesh is a versatile object. There is almost no limit to the number of different things a static mesh can be used to represent. Consider a mesh used to represent a table. It contains a number of object-specific properties, such as the number of table legs, the color of the table, the physical material from which the table is made, and the size in terms of width and height. These properties are specific to the table. They would have no relevance if the mesh were used to represent a chair, a car, or lamppost instead, because the properties of those objects are different from the properties of the table.

That being said, there is a set of essential components common to all meshes. This set of properties is intrinsic to a static mesh. Specifically, a static mesh consists of

Figure 6.1
Static mesh actors.

three core components: the mesh component, the collision mesh component, and the UV sets component.

The Mesh Component

The *mesh component* is the channel or section of the static mesh that contains the vertices, edges, and faces of the visible geometry used to represent objects (see Figure 6.2). This component is typically the first component that comes to mind (at least to most minds) when the term *mesh* or *static mesh* is used. Its purpose is to define the geometry of the mesh. This geometry will have initially been created by an artist in a 3D modeling package, such as 3DS Max, Maya, ZBrush, Mudbox, Blender, or others.

Figure 6.2
The mesh component of a static mesh.

A mesh for a game will usually differ from a movie or television mesh in that its polycount, short for *polygon count*, will be lower. The polycount of any specific mesh is the total number of polygons in that mesh. A mesh loaded and shown in a UDK level has its polygons loaded into memory, where they are processed by the graphics processing unit (GPU) for rendering to the display. A mesh x with a greater polycount than mesh y is more detailed, more complex, and thus computationally more expensive to process. Statements about the complexity of a mesh are equivalent to statements about the number of polygons in a mesh; a complex mesh is a mesh with lots of polygons.

One of the aims of a game developer who wants his game to perform well on most hardware is to maintain a balance in the polycounts of his meshes, considering detail on the one hand and simplicity on the other. There is no hard and fast rule about how many polygons is the right number for any specific mesh. The number of polygons suitable for any given mesh depends on many factors, including the following:

■ The hardware for which the game is intended

■ The number of other meshes in the scene

■ The importance of the mesh

■ The object being represented by the mesh (for example, character faces are often more detailed than tables or chairs)

■ The lighting conditions under which the mesh will appear

■ Whether the mesh will be seen in detail by the player or appear only as a background object

Regardless of how the polycount is calculated, it is the responsibility of developers to ensure their static meshes are of an *appropriate* level of detail.

The Collision Mesh Component

Static meshes are commonly used to represent solid objects. Tables, chairs, walls, floors, and doors are just a few examples of objects that are solid. In the context of game development, solid objects are defined by their function—by what they *do*. Specifically, solid objects act as blocking volumes—that is, they act as barriers, preventing other solids from passing through. Most walls are solid in that the player and other solids cannot pass through them.

Most static mesh actors are supposed to be solid. There are some exceptions, such as volume light effects, cobwebs, magical barriers, and holograms. But in general, static meshes are designed to be impenetrable.

Note

Static meshes are generally impenetrable, and are always immovable and unbreakable. Fractured static meshes, in contrast, are a type of static meshes that can be broken into parts to simulate destruction effects, such as when a wall breaks apart from an explosion or gun fire. Fractured static meshes are considered in further detail in the appendix, "Q&A: Taking It Further with the UDK."

A static mesh's collision mesh component ensures that the mesh acts as a solid in the level. It does this with a completely self-contained arrangement of polygons whose purpose is to tightly enclose the mesh component. It is a simpler arrangement of polygons that acts as a non-visible approximation of the mesh component, defining the mesh boundaries and extents that are significant for calculating collisions. Figure 6.3

Figure 6.3
The collision mesh component of a static mesh. The collision mesh appears as a cage of connected edges completely enclosing the mesh component.

compares and contrasts a mesh component with its surrounding collision mesh component, shown in wireframe.

You might reasonably wonder why the lower-fidelity collision mesh must be used at all. Why not use the more detailed and accurate mesh component? It would no doubt lead to better, more accurate collisions. The reason, as is often the case in gaming, relates to performance. The process of ascertaining when collisions occur is called *collision detection*. Collision detection works by cycling through all the vertices, edges, and polygons of one mesh and comparing them to those of another mesh to check for overlaps. By extension, the process of collision detection throughout the level works by comparing all the vertices, edges, and polygons of all meshes. That means the complexity and computational cost of the collision-detection process is proportional to the complexity of the meshes being compared. Because the level of detail required for achieving graphical realism in a mesh is higher than the level of detail required for achieving believable collisions, you can separate the mesh seen by the gamer from the mesh used for collision detection. The collision-detection mesh should be the simplest mesh possible for closely approximating the overall shape of the more detailed mesh component. The ideal collision mesh is a primitive, such as a box, pyramid, or cube.

The UV Sets Component

As mentioned in the previous chapter, mapping coordinates are mathematical instructions that explain how a particular rectangle of pixels, produced by a material, should be projected over the three-dimensional surface of a model or a mesh. Through mapping coordinates, there is a two-way correspondence between pixel positions in the material and pixel positions on the surface of the mesh. That is, pixel positions in the material correspond to particular positions on the polygons of the mesh, and positions on the polygons of the mesh correspond to positions within the material.

Mapping coordinates are not part of the material, but are part of the mesh. Specifically, they are embedded in a mesh through UV sets—one complete set of mapping coordinates per UV set. A mesh can contain as many as four UV sets and thereby as many as four mapping coordinates. Each UV set is known as a UV channel. These sets begin at the number 0; thus, a mesh can have information in channels 0, 1, 2, and 3. A typical mesh contains two UV sets (channels 0 and 1). The first UV set defines the mapping coordinates used by default with any associated material—that is, how a material is mapped onto the mesh in most circumstances. The second UV set defines the mapping coordinates for a lightmap. (See Figure 6.4.) Every static object in a level—that is, every object that does not move—features a UV set of

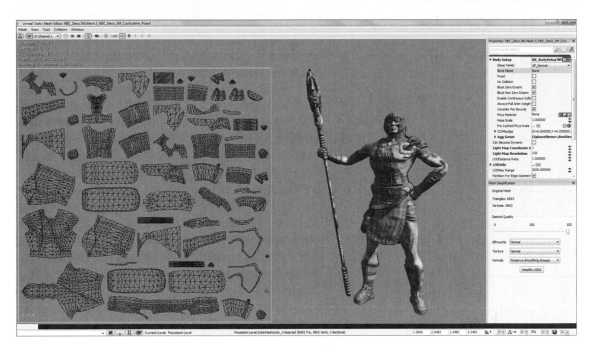

Figure 6.4
Static meshes feature at least two UV sets, one defining the mapping coordinates for the associated material and the other defining the mapping coordinates for a lightmap.

mapping coordinates for its own lightmap. A *lightmap* is an RGB texture sample that is automatically generated at development time by the UDK Lightmass system on a per-object basis, with one lightmap of a specified size per object. The sample is used to store all the pixel information about how the lighting conditions affect the surface of the model in terms of shading, shadows, and color. The UDK uses the lightmap at runtime to blend its effects onto its associated surface to make that surface appear lit without having to repeatedly perform expensive lighting calculations. The lightmap's mapping coordinates must be separated from the mapping coordinates used for the material for the same reason the collision mesh component must be separated from the mesh component. Lightmapping and its importance in the UDK are discussed further in Chapter 8, "Lighting."

STATIC MESHES VERSUS CSG

Both static meshes and constructive solid geometry (CSG) are geometric constructs. They are composed from the same basic kinds of pieces: vertices, edges, and faces. The difference between them relates not to their geometric composition but to the specific ways the Unreal Engine recognizes, stores, and processes them. This difference has appreciable performance implications, and informs the kinds of developmental tasks for which each is most suited in specific circumstances. Table 6.1 lists some

Table 6.1 Static Meshes Versus CSG

Object	Most Suited Geometry
Planar surface (wall, floor, ceiling)	CSG
Surface with finer mapping control in UDK	CSG (via Texture Alignment mode)
Complex object (statue, car, building)	Static mesh
Geometric primitives (box, pyramid, etc.)	CSG
Meshes that are simple to transform (move, scale, rotate)	Static mesh
Meshes that can be animated via the Kismet and Matinee Editors	Static mesh

common objects and, for each object, notes the most appropriate geometry form, either CSG or static mesh.

STATIC MESH ACTORS

As mentioned, a static mesh has three core components: the mesh component, the collision mesh component, and the UV sets component. Together, these three components constitute a static mesh, which is imported into the UDK as a template object from a third-party modeling application.

You can insert specific instances or clones of a static mesh into a UDK level as static mesh actors using the Content Browser. Each actor is a separate level entity, with its own position, orientation, and scale within the world coordinate space. You can use static mesh actors for at least two different but related purposes: to insert discrete, self-contained objects into a level, and to create composite objects.

Static Mesh Actors for Discrete Objects

Perhaps the most obvious (though not necessarily the most common!) use for static mesh actors is to create discrete and self-contained objects in a level. For example, one static mesh actor might equal one table, one chair, one weapon, or what have you. Almost all such discrete objects are added to a level by way of static meshes. These objects are termed discrete here because they are countable; one can be easily and visually distinguished or separated from the other. Figure 6.5 shows three separate and discrete buckets (one, two, and three), each being a static mesh actor that is a unique instance of the bucket static mesh. The three buckets would not typically be confused as being only one bucket or as being a part of something larger. Creating

Figure 6.5
Static mesh actors can be used to add discrete elements to a level—weapons, statues, trees, elevators, and other clearly demarcated objects, like the three separate and discrete buckets shown here.

single and discrete units of detail in this way about the level is one of the purposes of the static mesh.

Static Mesh Actors for Composite Objects

A second (and perhaps the most common) way static mesh actors can be used in a level is to construct composite objects. A *composite object* is a whole formed from an arrangement of two or more static mesh actors. That is, multiple static mesh actors can be translated, rotated and scaled into a configuration with others to produce a more complex object, just as multiple Lego bricks can be connected and combined to form constructions greater than themselves—houses, cars, tanks, trees, and others. A composite object in a level that is constructed in this way has individual static mesh actors as its constituent pieces. A house object, for example, might be formed from multiple static mesh actors—several for the windows, one for the front door, another two for each half of the roof, six for the walls, several to construct a picket fence around the perimeter, and so on. This method of combining static mesh actors to form a composite object is known by many in UDK circles as the modular method, because in a composite object, every static mesh actor represents a unique module or ingredient (see Figure 6.6 and Figure 6.7).

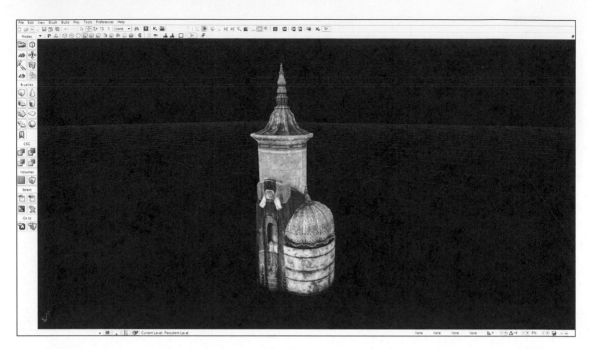

Figure 6.6
A tower structure seems to be one discrete mesh.

Figure 6.7
In fact, the tower structure is a composite object made from an arrangement of several mesh actors.

Why would a developer bother with the modular building method? What can be gained by importing all these different bits and pieces of a composite object as unique static meshes, as opposed to creating a composite object in modeling software and importing it whole into the UDK? For example, why not just model a complete house or a complete car in modeling software and then import it whole? Surely, that would save a lot of time, effort, and work. The modular building method is preferred in most cases for three main reasons: flexibility, versatility, and performance.

Flexibility

In this context, flexibility refers to the extent to which developers can change or adjust their constructions without having to leave the UDK Editor. Objects made with the modular method are the product of the configuration of their mesh pieces. That is, they are produced by the meshes that compose them. As such, they are altered by changes in their configuration, with different configurations resulting in different composites. Because the configuration of complex objects can be specified in the UDK Editor through the translation, rotation and scaling of static mesh actors, the modular method is considered flexible.

Developers can tweak composite objects without having to leave the UDK Editor. That is, a designer can create a building by assembling multiple static meshes, and can then tweak the building by adding, removing, or changing those static meshes. The designer can change the doors by replacing the door meshes, remove windows by deleting the window meshes and replacing them with wall meshes, and so on. If the same building were made first in a modeling package and then imported whole into the UDK, the construction would be fixed; the UDK would recognize it as a self-contained unit whose parts were immutable. To make changes to the model, the designer would have to leave the UDK and return to the modeling software. Once there, the designer would have to make the appropriate changes, and then re-import the model whole again into the UDK, carefully replacing the original.

Versatility

An entity x is said to be more versatile than an entity y when x can be used for more unique purposes than y. So x is more versatile than y because it can do more varied things. It follows, then, that the modular building method is more versatile than other methods because any given set of mesh pieces can be combined and recombined in different configurations to produce very different kinds of objects. In other words, the same parts can be used to make different things.

The total number of complex objects that can be made in a level from any given set of mesh parts equals the total number of different ways in which those parts can be combined. That means any set of static meshes can be instanced into static mesh actors any number of times and combined in different ways to produce an astonishing number of complex and unique objects. For example, with a set of, say, 30 architectural meshes (pillars, windows, doors, walls, arches, pedestals, etc.) it would be possible to construct a level that was grand in size and contained many different buildings, and for all of those buildings to be constructed from actors based on the same set of architectural meshes. The amount of variation and difference between the buildings in that level would represent a difference not in the kinds of pieces from which they were made, but in the ways in which those pieces were combined. The point is, a single set of meshes can produce many different complex objects. The set is said to be versatile because instances of those meshes can be brought into unique configurations to make many different things.

Performance

To appreciate the performance benefits offered by the modular method, you can compare some of its performance implications with those of the alternative, importing whole meshes. The general workflow for the modular method consists in importing a finite set of static-mesh pieces and then using many *instances* of those pieces to assemble complex objects. In contrast, the "importing whole" method involves importing larger and more complex meshes that are already the product of smaller pieces. The typical result of this is that levels using the modular method contain fewer static meshes but more static mesh actors, while levels made from the "import whole" method contain more static meshes but fewer static mesh actors.

It is important to recall here the technical distinction between the static mesh and the static mesh actor. The static mesh is the actual mesh—the vertices, edges, and polygons—imported into the UDK that acts as a template from which clones or instances are derived and inserted into the level at their own unique positions, rotations, and scales. These instances are called static mesh actors. Thus, the term *static mesh actor* can be taken as equivalent to *instance of a static mesh*. Levels built using the modular method tend to use exponentially more static mesh actors than static meshes because the complexity of the level is made through the arrangement of many copies of the same basic and small set of static mesh pieces. In contrast, levels constructed using the "import whole" method tend to rely on a larger and more varied set of static meshes. This is because the complex detail of the level is imported in terms of whole objects and has an almost one-to-one correspondence between the number of static meshes and static mesh actors. That is, a complex object in the level usually occurs only once; also, because it is imported pre-made, it is not composed through the repetition of smaller static mesh actors.

The fact that modular levels contain a small set of static meshes compared to the counterpart method has implications on performance. Specifically, every unique static mesh in a level places appreciable demands on system resources, whereas static mesh actors make no comparable demand. This is because static mesh actors are references to, not complete duplicates of, static meshes. For this reason, modular levels fare better in terms of performance than counterpart levels. Although they might use many static mesh actors, they use comparatively few static meshes.

Using Static Meshes

Creating meshes to work with the modular method is an exercise in reducing the complex to the simple—that is, in defining the complex elements in terms of their simpler units. Doing this successfully depends primarily on the developer having a firm idea or plan of the level to be created. That is, the level designer must know what the level is going to be like. Once that level plan is finalized, the developer proceeds with reductionism by first dissecting the complex elements of the level into their constituent pieces and then testing every one of those pieces to see whether it is suitable for being made into an independent static mesh. These two steps translate into two questions that a developer must ask about the things in his level. About the complex things—such as houses, cars, garages, weapons, tunnels, bridges, ships, towers, and more—the developer must ask, "From what sort of pieces is this thing made?" And about the pieces themselves—such as walls, pillars, iron bars, girders, struts, supports, doors, nuts and bolts, and more—the developer must ask, "Should I create a separate static mesh for this piece, or should this piece be imported into the UDK as a building block?"

Whether a particular constituent piece should be made an independent static mesh in the context of the level demands a yes or no answer. To reach a decision about this, a developer can test the piece against some criteria in the form of a set of four questions, which I shall list in a moment. If any of these questions about any particular piece can be answered in the positive, then that piece can warrant being an independent static mesh. If no positive answer can be given, then that piece should not be independent. Instead, it should instead be part of a larger and more complex piece.

The four questions a designer should ask about constituent pieces are as follows:

- **Is the piece sufficiently general?** Questions about the generality of a piece are related to versatility. To ask whether a piece is sufficiently general is to ask whether that piece can be used to build a sufficient variety of different things— that is, whether that kind of building block would be sufficiently common among the structures of the level. The concept of sufficiency differs from level to

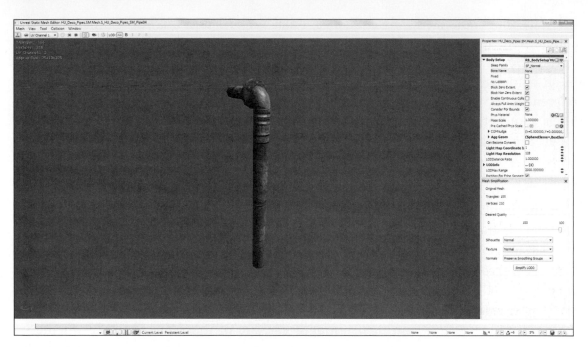

Figure 6.8
A pipe is a general piece in that it can have many different purposes in a level. It could run along a wall, connect to a tank or boiler, lie on the floor as debris or wreckage, etc.

level and game to game. Developers must use both their judgment and their experience to reach a decision as to the degree of versatility that is "sufficient" in a piece. (See Figure 6.8.)

■ **Is the piece part of a symmetrical or reflected object?** There are many complex objects that are symmetrical, mirrored, or in some way the same on multiple sides or in multiple sections. Such objects might include a domed ceiling with an identical pattern in each quadrant or a car that is identical on both sides, to name but a few. These kinds of objects are typically assembled from many identical pieces that are the reverse, flip side, or inverse of each other. For this reason, they lend themselves especially well to the modular method of building, which is based on repetition and mirroring. Each unique (not flipped or mirrored) side or segment of the model can be identified as a separate piece; assembling the complex whole in the UDK is a matter of duplicating, assembling, and mirroring the symmetrical pieces as appropriate, as shown in Figure 6.9.

■ **Is the piece repeated many times throughout the object?** Questions of repetition in a level have important implications for whether a piece is classified as an independent mesh. Repetition and patterns are typically seen in many

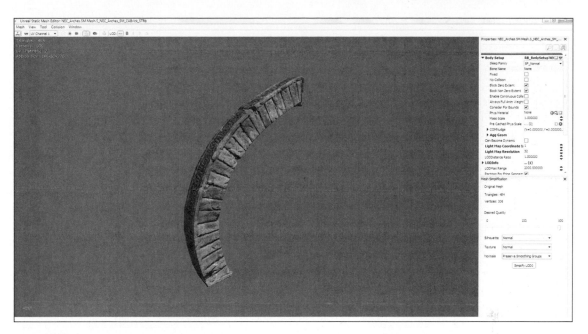

Figure 6.9
This is part of a symmetrical arch. It can be assembled beside a reflected copy of itself to form the complete arch.

places and structures, both naturally and artificially. For example, houses are assembled from many similar architectural elements: cornices, alcoves, walls, roofs, and so on. Public buildings are supported by many similar columns or pillars (see Figure 6.10), and interior environments feature many similar light fixtures, doors, and staircases. A constituent piece that is repeated sufficiently throughout one or many complex objects should be separated as an individual static mesh. Its value as such is proportional to the extent to which it can be repeated.

- **Could the piece ever feature in the level on its own as an independent object?**
  Any object that both acts as a constituent piece for a more complex object and can be a significant and relevant object on its own should be created as a separate mesh. Objects of this kind might be barrels, control panels, pillars and columns, statues, wooden beams, ropes and wires, and pipes, to mention but a few. (See Figure 6.11.)

PROJECT: A BRIDGE BETWEEN TWO ISLANDS

This section moves away from the world of theory and enters the world of practice to apply the concepts explained so far. In this section, you will work along with me, step by step, to use the modular building technique in the UDK to construct a level made

Figure 6.10
This column could be repeated many times throughout a building.

Figure 6.11
A lantern is not only a general-purpose piece as well as one that could be repeated and mirrored as part of a more complex piece, but is also a piece that can stand alone as a separate object.

Figure 6.12
The completed static mesh project: a complex bridge object connecting two complex islands. It's a world created from a set of static mesh actors.

entirely from static mesh actors. As with other practical sections of this book, this static mesh project will use only resources and assets supplied with the UDK.

The objective of this project is to construct a playable level that features two separate islands connected by two central bridges suspended over a pool of water (see Figure 6.12). All these will be created from static mesh actors (except for the water, which will be created from a CSG plane). The player will be able to walk between the islands via the bridges. Note that the UDK does not offer a bridge mesh asset, nor does it offer an island mesh asset. For this reason, you will use the modular building technique to assemble a bridge and an island from small, simple mesh pieces.

In addition to illustrating that technique, the project will also introduce and explain some new topics related to static meshes. These include the following:

- **The Static Mesh Editor.** You can use this editor interface, which you can launch from the Content Browser, to preview and customize any static mesh asset. It is used to customize not a particular static mesh *actor* that might happen to exist in the level, but the static mesh itself, whose properties cascade downward to all static mesh actors based on that mesh.

- **Prefab asset.** A prefab asset is a special asset type designed for the modular building method. Its main purpose is to enable developers to save specific arrangements of static mesh actors (particular complex objects) so that they can be dragged and dropped into the level from the Content Browser many times, as though they were one static mesh actor.

Exploring the Static Mesh Editor

As mentioned, a static mesh consists of three main components: the mesh component, the collision mesh component, and the UV sets component. The purpose of the Static Mesh Editor is to enable developers to view and change these three components. It should be emphasized here that the Static Mesh Editor is used not for editing *particular* static mesh actors in a *particular* level, but for editing more general and abstract static meshes—the actual mesh data that is imported into the UDK and used as a template from which instances are made. For this reason, edits made to a static mesh with the Static Mesh Editor will cascade downward to *all* actors based on that mesh.

The Static Mesh Editor consists of three main parts (see Figure 6.13):

- **The toolbar.** The purpose of the toolbar is to control the kinds of information and properties shown in the Preview pane.
- **The Preview pane.** The Preview pane is a viewport that can be rotated and zoomed to view the static mesh loaded into the Static Mesh Editor. (Note that only one static mesh can be loaded into one instance of the Static Mesh Editor at any one time.)

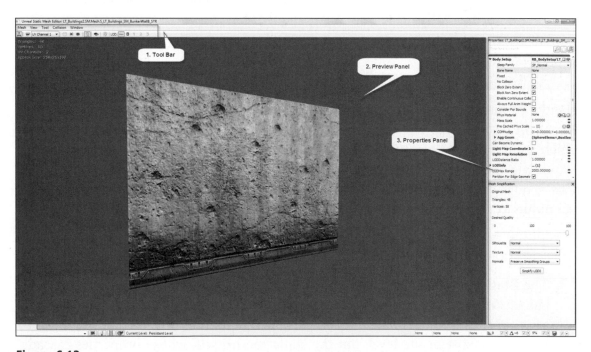

Figure 6.13
The Static Mesh Editor is used for both viewing and changing static meshes. It consists of three main user interface components: the toolbar, the Preview pane, and the Properties panel.

■ **The Properties panel.** The Properties panel displays many of the editable values and fields that apply to the static mesh. Changing these values can have a substantial effect on the mesh and how it works in the level.

Preparing the Level Foundation with CSG

As mentioned, the static mesh level will feature two artificial islands connected by as many bridges, each bridge suspended over a pool of water. To prepare for this level, you must create the ground geometry—the *terra firma* that will support the entire level. This section briefly describes the steps involved in doing that. The ground geometry will be created as CSG using the Geometry mode tools, both of which were covered in more depth in Chapter 4, "BSP Brushes, the Builder Brush, and CSG."

1. In the main UDK Editor window, open the File menu and choose New to create a new map. The New Map dialog box opens (see Figure 6.14), enabling you to generate a new map from a number of basic map templates. Click the Midday Lighting to produce a map with a ground plane, a cube, preconfigured lighting, and a midday sky.

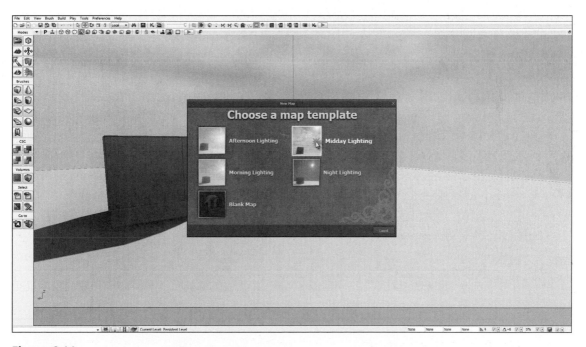

Figure 6.14
Generate a new map from the New Map dialog box.

Figure 6.15
Click the Build Lighting button in the main application toolbar to update the lighting for the level.

2. The preconfigured lighting, ground plane, and surrounding midday sky will come in useful for the map, but you don't need the cube mesh. To remove it from the scene, select the cube in the Perspective viewport and press the Delete key on the keyboard.

3. Notice that although the cube mesh is deleted from the scene, the shadow it casts remains on the ground plane as though the cube were still there. (See Figure 6.15.) To correct this problem, you must recalculate the lighting of the level. This is akin to updating the lighting; it causes the UDK's Lightmass system to perform the necessary lighting calculations to determine which objects receive light and which objects cast shadows. To recalculate the lighting, click the Build Lighting button in the application toolbar (also shown in Figure 6.15). The cube shadow disappears.

Note

Chapter 8 explains in more depth why shadows cast by objects remain in the scene even after those objects have been deleted—at least until the lighting solution for the level is recalculated.

4. The next step is to start creating the main world CSG geometry—that is, the geometry that will act as the foundation on which the level will be built. The

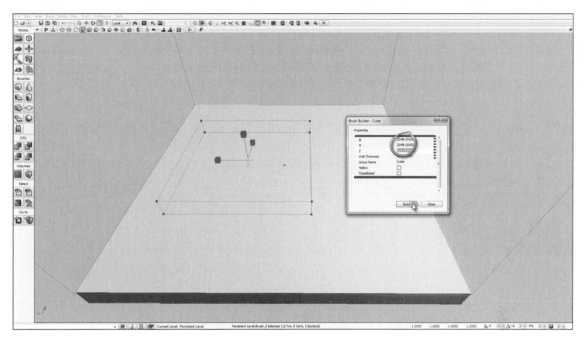

Figure 6.16
Creating the 2,048 × 2,048 × 256 *terra firma* cube primitive for the level.

CSG will be a short box primitive with a large rectangular recess extruded downward from its top-most polygon, hollowing out much of the box. The box's top-most polygon will represent ground level. The extruded recess will define the volume of the pool of water that will exist beneath the bridges. The two upper edges of the box running parallel to the width of the pool will mark the edges of the islands. To get started, create the box primitive by right-clicking the Box Primitive BSP Brush tool in the UDK toolbox. Set the width and length of the box to 2,048 Unreal world units, and set the height of the box to 256 Unreal world units, as shown in Figure 6.16. (To get some idea of the size and proportions of this box, remember that the height of an average male character is approximately 96 Unreal world units.)

5. Use the Translate tool to ensure the newly created box is snapped to the grid—that is, that every edge of the box rests exactly on a grid line.

6. You'll need to make some tweaks to the box using the Split and Extrude tools, available from the toolbox in Geometry mode. To switch to Geometry mode, click the Geometry Mode button in the application toolbox (see Figure 6.17) or press Shift+2.

7. You'll use the Geometry mode tools to hollow out a region of the box. That region will become the volume for the watery pool that will exist beneath the

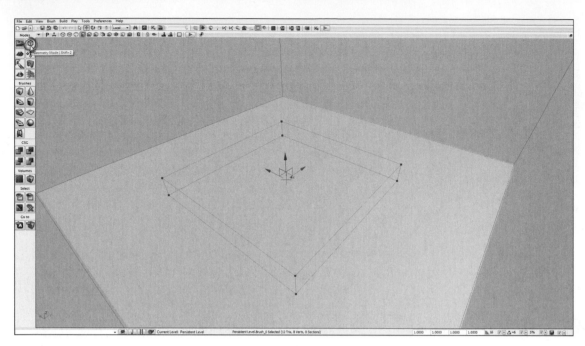

Figure 6.17
Click the Geometry Mode button in the toolbox to switch to Geometry mode.

bridges. To create this hollowed region, you'll first divide the box so that the top polygon is split by four new edges, one on each side, creating a smaller polygon at its center. This center polygon will then be extruded downward for the depth of the pool. To divide the box, hover the perspective camera over the interior of the box and select one of its edges. Then click the Split button in the Geometry toolbox to insert a loop of edges that bisects the selected edge. Repeat this process for the three remaining sides of the box. Finally, use the marquee selection technique (Alt+Ctrl-click and drag) to select and move the vertices into position, as shown in Figure 6.18.

8. The center polygon at the top of the box marks the total width and height of the pool of water. But it is still a two-dimensional area; it lacks depth. You will now add depth by way of a negative extrusion. Extrude the polygon downward and create a volume for the pool of water. Be sure not to extrude the top polygon below the bottom-most polygon of the box. (See Figure 6.19 for a reference.) When you're finished, click the Add CSG button in the toolbox to commit the changes and to print or stamp the Builder Brush into the level in the form of CSG. (Note that you can safely delete the box object that was created with the level if you find that it obstructs your view when working.)

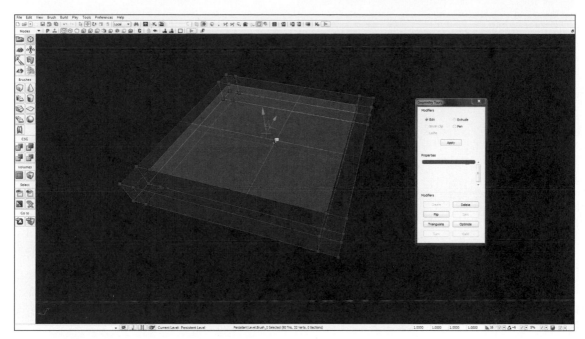

Figure 6.18
Clicking the Split button inserts edge loops into a model. It is used here to add a smaller polygon to the top polygon of the box, ready for a negative extrusion.

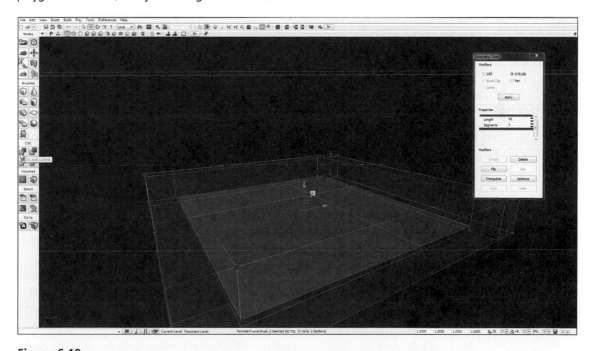

Figure 6.19
Shape the Builder Brush to contain a hollowed region for the pool of water. Then add the Builder Brush to the level in the form of CSG.

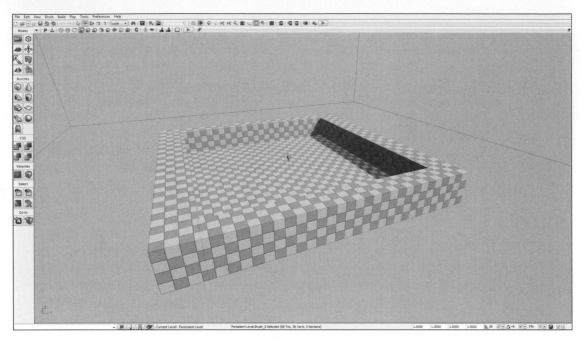

Figure 6.20
The CSG acts not only as a ground surface and foundation for the level, but also as a plan or guide in that its shape, size, and position map out the level to be made.

Note

The level created so far can be found in the companion files under DM-Mesh_Project_01_start.udk.

Creating the First Island

The mesh level's CSG was created from a box-shaped Builder Brush, which you modified using the Split and Extrude tools in Geometry mode. The CSG serves two main functions for the level (see Figure 6.20):

■ It acts as the *terra firma,* or the solid foundation on which all other objects in the level will ultimately rest. In this sense, the CSG is the floor, or the bottom-most surface. That is to say, it can support the weight of anything standing on it and will allow nothing to pass beneath it. In addition, it is not affected by gravity, meaning that it can never fall from its current position.

■ It acts as a guide or aid to the level developer. The shape, size, and position of the CSG approximates the level to be created, giving the level designer a rough picture of the level layout; an understanding of where actors will be positioned, an idea as to the appropriate sizes and scales for objects, and a picture of the extents of the level.

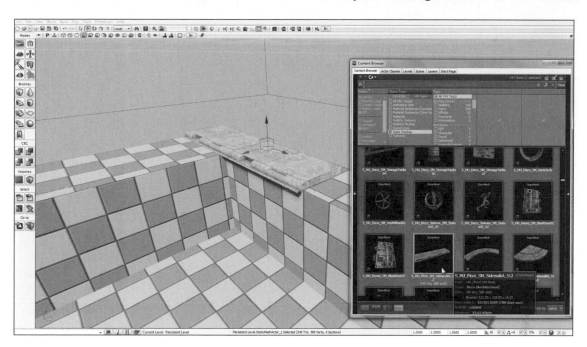

Figure 6.21
Drag and drop the static mesh edge trim from the Content Browser.

The next step in the construction of the level is to create the two islands from static meshes. These islands will be connected by two bridges. The construction process for the islands is detailed in the steps that follow.

1. Begin constructing the first island by adding the edges of the island where it meets with the water pool. For this purpose, I have selected the following mesh: S_HU_Floor_SM_SidewalkA_512. To find this mesh, use the Content Browser's Search and Filter pane, ensuring that the Static Mesh filter is checked to restrict what kinds of assets appear in the Preview pane. Then drag and drop the mesh from the Content Browser to the Perspective viewport to create an instance of it in the level. Using the Translate and Rotate tools, respectively, position and rotate the mesh to place it at the edge of the water pool (see Figure 6.21).

2. Notice that the island is far wider than the edge trim mesh. Fortunately, the modular building method presents a possible solution: positioning several instances of the edge-trim mesh side by side, tiled across the width of the island. To duplicate the static mesh actor, select the actor in the Perspective viewport, and then hold down the Alt key on the keyboard while translating it sideways. This moves not the original mesh, but a newly created duplicate. Create several duplicate meshes in this way and position them side by side along the edge of the water pool, as shown in Figure 6.22. Notice how the edge-trim mesh is tiled and repeated to construct a larger and more complex object.

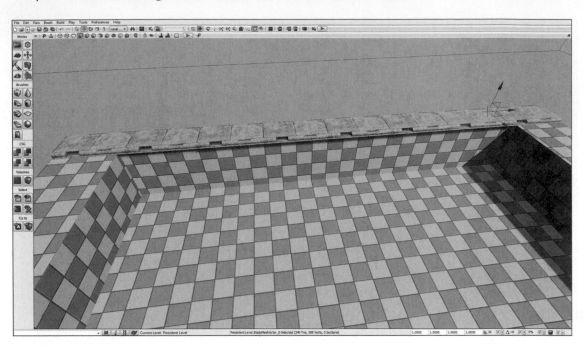

Figure 6.22
Use the modular building method to tile the edge-trim meshes in a line at the edge where the island meets the pool.

3. Turn your attention to creating the main body of the island floor—the largest section of floor that runs away from the edge trim and into the distance. This section of the floor should appear to be made from concrete. It will be constructed using the modular building technique that was used to create the trim. Specifically, many cloned instances of the same mesh will be tiled and arranged together to form a larger and more complex whole. To achieve this, open the Content Browser and search for the mesh named S_LT_Buildings_SM_Bunker-WallB_STR (see Figure 6.23). This mesh will be used to create the larger section of the island floor, even though its name suggests that it is intended to be used for walls. This mesh is one among many that exhibit the property of generality; it can be used successfully as a building block for many different and perhaps unforeseen purposes.

4. Double-click the S_LT_Buildings_SM_BunkerWallB_STR mesh in the Content Browser to preview it in the Static Mesh Editor. You can also access this interface by right-clicking the mesh asset and choosing Edit Using Static Mesh Editor from the menu that appears. The Static Mesh Editor enables developers to both inspect and change the properties of their static meshes. There are no specific changes to apply to the S_LT_Buildings_SM_BunkerWallB_STR mesh, but I wanted to introduce the Static Mesh Editor nonetheless.

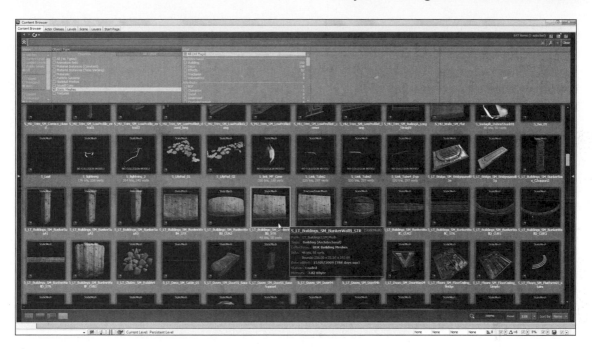

Figure 6.23
Use the Content Browser to find a general-use mesh for the island floor.

Viewing the Collision Mesh and UV Sets of a Static Mesh

A static mesh's collision mesh is not typically created in the UDK via the Static Mesh Editor. Instead, it is usually created in modeling software and imported into the UDK along with the mesh component and UV sets. For this reason, the Static Mesh Editor offers limited functionality for *creating* collision meshes. It does, however, offer some features for generating collision meshes, as well as a means for previewing the collision mesh component of a static mesh. To view a collision mesh in the editor's Preview panel, open the editor's View menu and choose Collision. As shown in Figure 6.24, the collision mesh appears as a green wireframe surrounding the mesh component.

The Static Mesh Editor also offers some features for generating collision meshes either from a set of creation parameters (for example, the 6DOP Collision option produces a box collision mesh that is sized to completely contain the static mesh component). It can also be used to generate collision meshes from what the UDK regards as the best fit, based on the mesh component of a static mesh (for example, the Auto-Convex option generates a best-fit collision mesh that is convex in shape and that completely surrounds the mesh component). The details of each option are beyond the scope of this book, but you access these features from the Collision menu.

Like collision meshes, the UV sets for a static mesh are typically defined in third-party modeling software such as 3DS Max and Maya prior to import into the UDK. The Static Mesh Editor is not intended for creating UV sets, and therefore offers no mapping-creation features. It does, however, enable developers to view the UV sets attached to a particular mesh. To view a mesh's UV sets, click the UV Set button (the one with the letters "UV") in the editor toolbar, shown in Figure 6.25. You can use the UV Set drop-down list box beside this button to select the channel to view. The UV mapping information appears in the Preview pane as a black wireframe, drawn in front of the mesh object.

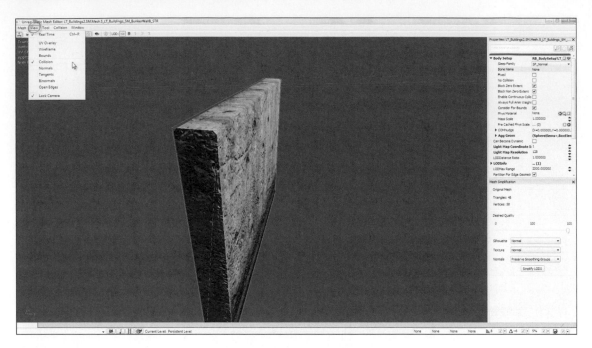

Figure 6.24
Viewing the collision mesh component of a static mesh.

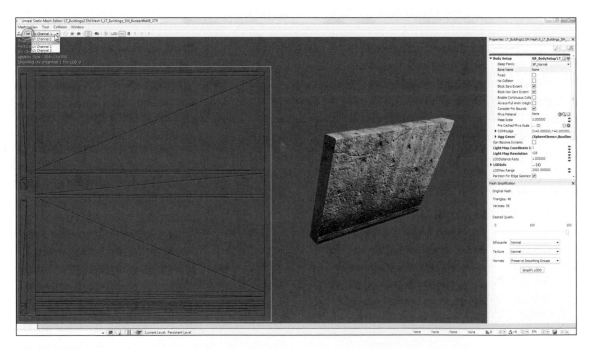

Figure 6.25
Click the UV Set button to toggle the visibility of UV sets. When UV sets are visible, use the drop-down to select the UV set to view.

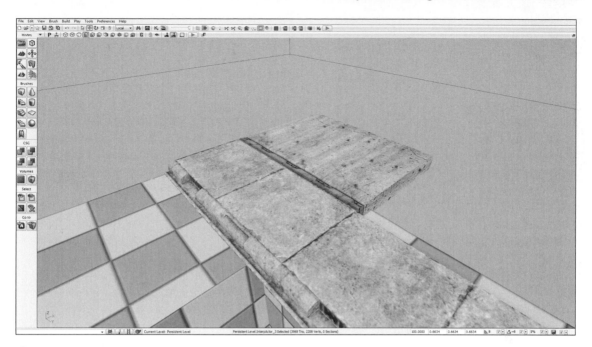

Figure 6.26
Transform the mesh to act as a tile for the island floor.

5. Close the Static Mesh Editor and drag and drop an instance of the S_LT_Buildings_SM_BunkerWallB_STR mesh from the Content Browser into the level. Next, rotate and scale it so that it rests flat horizontally and aligns neatly with the edge trim (see Figure 6.26).

6. Using the Alt+drag method (holding down Alt and dragging with the transformation widget), duplicate and tile the mesh across the width of the island to fill out the floor, ensuring that each edge-trim piece neighbors a floor piece (see Figure 6.27).

7. A large part of the island floor has now been filled using the modular building method. The problem—which becomes more apparent when the Perspective viewport is moved such that the whole of the island floor is visible from an aerial vantage point—is that the tiling and repetition among the floor tiles is noticeable. This is because all the bunker floor tiles are identical in terms of their mesh topology and their materials, as are edge-trim tiles. One way to make this less noticeable is to flip or reverse the orientation of a few of the tiles. To do this, select a few of the floor tiles and the edge-trim pieces, right-click one of the selected items, and choose Transform followed by Mirror Y Axis from the menu that appears (see Figure 6.28). Each of the selected pieces will be flipped or reversed around the y axis. (In addition, the position of some of the piece might

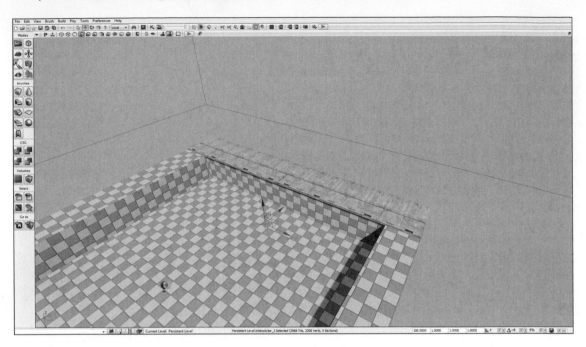

Figure 6.27
Filling out the island floor with floor pieces.

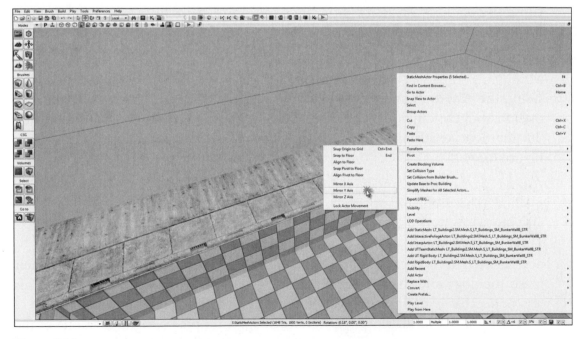

Figure 6.28
Mirroring selected floor tiles to break repetition.

Figure 6.29
Blocking the open areas of the island with rock structures.

change, making it necessary to move a few pieces back into position.) The result of this process will be a tiled island floor composed from many copies of only two different pieces, with the inversion of some pieces greatly reducing the tiled look and increasing the realism.

8. The floor of the island is completed, but there is still work to do to finish the island. At present, gamers can run over the edge of the island floor and drop to their deaths into nothingness because there are no fences or obstacles to restrain them. To prevent this, you can add large rock and mountainous structures to surround the floor whenever there is an opening that can lead to death. Some appropriate rock structures can be found as static meshes in the Content Browser, including SM_CastleRock_01, SM_CastleRock_02, SM_CastleRock_03, SM_CastleRock_04, and SM_CastleRock_06. Add some of these structures to complete most of the island, as shown in Figure 6.29.

Note

Notice in the Content Browser that some thumbnails for rock meshes feature the phrase "No Collision Model!" A mesh with no collision model lacks a collision mesh component. In other words, that mesh will not resist collisions, will not act as an obstacle, and will allow other solids to pass through it. A rock mesh without a collision model cannot act as a suitable barrier, protecting the player from falling off the island edge. There are at least three different solutions to this problem. One is to ensure that the player can come into contact only with those rock meshes that have collision models. Another is to use the Static Mesh Editor to generate basic collision models for all the rock meshes. A third solution is to surround the mesh with a collision/blocking volume. (Refer to the section "PlayerStart, KillZ, and a Collision Volume" in Chapter 2, "Building a First Project: A Tour of the UDK.")

Note

The level created so far can be found in the companion files under DM-Mesh_Project_02_island_01.udk.

Creating the Second Island Using a Prefab Asset

As mentioned, this project will feature two islands connected by two bridges suspended above a pool of water. The previous section focused on the creation of the first island. (Figure 6.30 shows the work completed so far.) This section focuses on creating the second island, which will appear opposite the first.

There are a number of ways in which a level designer could create the second island. One would be to create the second island from scratch, just as you constructed the first island. Although there is nothing wrong with that method, this section will demonstrate a different method: reusing the first island to create the second, by way of a

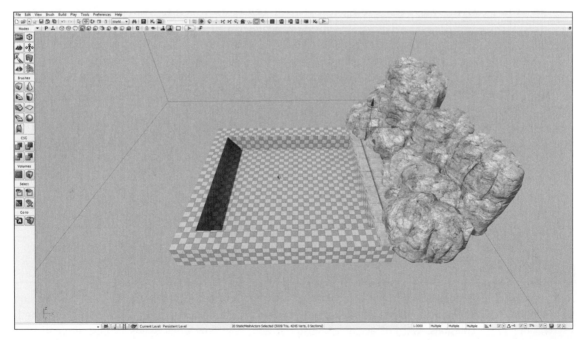

Figure 6.30
Preparing to create the second island.

UDK asset type called a *prefab asset*, sometimes called simply *prefab* for short. So what is a prefab asset?

The term *prefab* is an abbreviation of the term *prefabrication*. In the UDK, a prefabrication is designed to solve problems specific to the modular building method. That is, a prefab is designed to address issues that arise because of the nature of the modular building method. As mentioned, the modular building method involves assembling and arranging many unique static mesh actors to create larger and more complex objects, such as when walls, floors, windows, and ceilings are brought together to make a house. The problem is, it can be troublesome to work at the level of complex objects. Because complex objects are composed from multiple and separate parts, it can be difficult to select a complex object in its entirety or to transform or clone a complex object as a whole. Clicking with the Select tool to select a complex object in the viewport will not, in fact, select all the pieces of the complex object, but will instead select the single and constituent piece of that object that happened to be beneath the mouse cursor at the time of the selection. To select and transform the complex object in its entirety, the user must select each and every one of its constituent pieces. Consequently, complex objects that have many constituent pieces can be both troublesome and tedious to select and work with. To resolve this problem, the UDK enables you to select all the constituent pieces of a complex object and save that selection as an asset or template in the Content Browser. Dragging and dropping this prefab asset from the Content Browser into the level creates instances of the complex object, which can be selected and manipulated as discrete objects rather than terms of their pieces.

Follow these steps to create a prefab asset from the first island and to use that prefab asset to create a cloned second island on the opposite side of the level:

1. Select all static meshes that compose the first island, including the floor and rock meshes. Use the Wireframe viewing mode and the Show/Hide features of the Perspective viewport to assist in the selection. You can also use the Scene Browser. When the island is selected, right-click the selection and choose Create Prefab from the menu that appears, as shown in Figure 6.31.

2. The Package Creation dialog box opens (see Figure 6.32). This dialog box is shown whenever a new asset is imported or created. (Refer to the section "Packages and Groups" in Chapter 3, "UDK Fundamentals," for more information on packages.) In the Package field, you specify either the name of an existing package to which the prefab asset should be added or the name of a new package that should be created to contain the prefab asset (in this case, MyAssetPackage). In the Grouping field, you specify the name of the group to

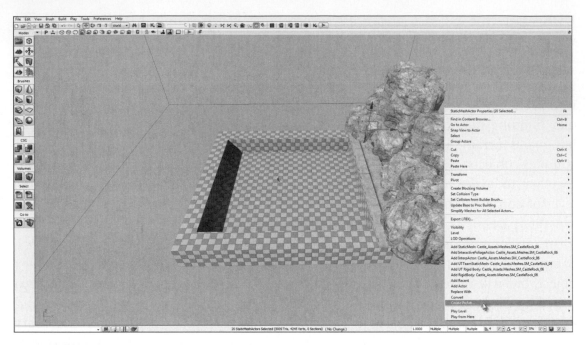

Figure 6.31
Create a prefab from a selection.

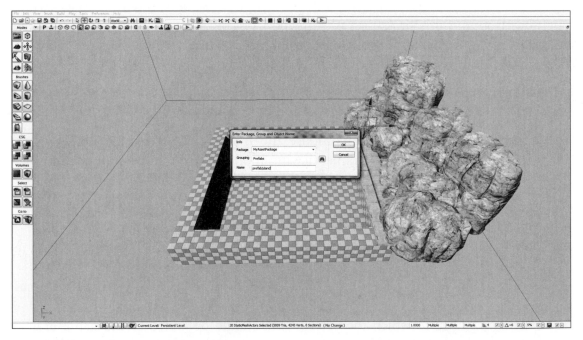

Figure 6.32
Creating a new Package for the Prefab Asset.

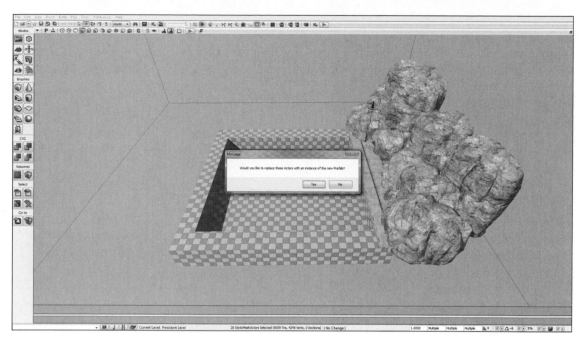

Figure 6.33
Click Yes to replace scene actors with a prefab asset.

which the prefab asset will belong (here, Prefabs). In the Name field, you type a name for the prefab asset (in this example, `prefabIsland`).

3. As shown in Figure 6.33, the UDK asks whether the actors (the floor and rocks) that currently comprise the complex object in the level (the island) should be replaced by an instance of the newly created prefab. Click Yes. Notice that the floor and rock pieces are removed from the level and are replaced by an instance of the prefab. This prefab, representing a complex object, can be selected and transformed whole. It can also be duplicated whole in the same way that static meshes can be duplicated, by Alt-dragging.

4. To create the second island for the level, open the Content Browser and filter the Preview pane to see the prefab island (see Figure 6.34). Then drag and drop it into the level, positioning it at the far end of the pool, opposite the first island.

Note

The level created so far can be found in the companion files under DM-Mesh_Project_03_island_02.udk.

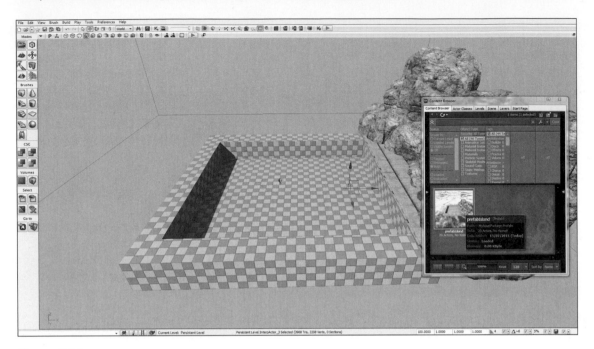

Figure 6.34
Selecting prefab assets from the Content Browser.

Creating the Bridges

As shown in Figure 6.35, the level created so far contains two islands at each end of a CSG volume reserved for a pool. Each island is a prefab object. The two islands will be connected by as many bridges, which will be constructed in a similar way to the islands. That is, the first bridge will be modeled from scratch using the modular building method, and the second bridge will be created as a cloned prefab object based on the first bridge.

1. Start by building the first of the two bridges. This bridge will be formed from a number of identical segments repeated along its length, with each segment being composed of several meshes. These include two reflected instances of S_NEC_Trims_SM_Vertebral_T01 placed side by side for the main floor of the bridge (see Figure 6.36); two instances of S_HU_Trim_SM_LowProfileA_closed_long, one running horizontally at each side of the bridge to act as a fence (see Figure 6.37); and one instance of S_HU_Trim_SM_LowProfileE_long to act as the support for the bridge (see Figure 6.38). These components will be arranged through translation, scaling, and rotation to make a bridge segment, which will be repeated to form the length of the bridge, reaching from one island to the other. Drag and drop these meshes now into the level and arrange them as shown in Figure 6.39 to create the segment.

Figure 6.35
The level so far....

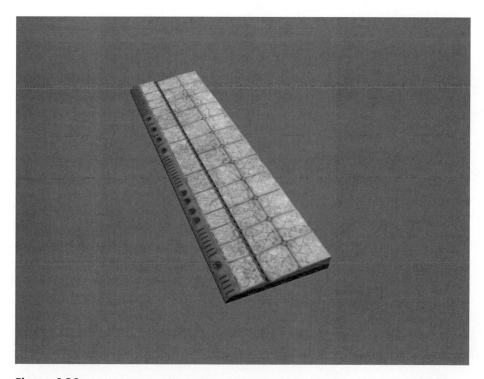

Figure 6.36
The bridge floor: S_NEC_Trims_SM_Vertebral_T01.

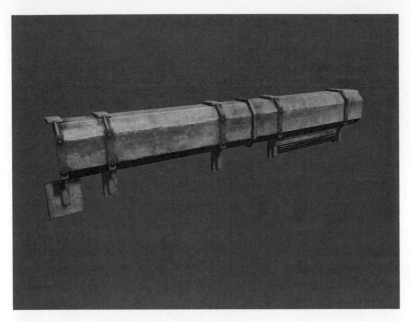

Figure 6.37
The bridge fence: S_HU_Trim_SM_LowProfileA_closed_long.

Figure 6.38
The bridge support: S_HU_Trim_SM_LowProfileE_long.

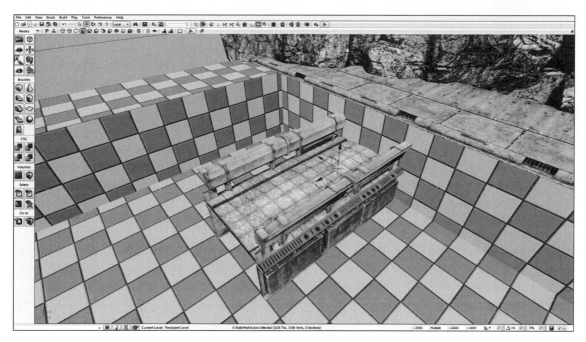

Figure 6.39
The bridge segment.

2. Repeat the bridge segments across the length of the pool to form the first bridge, carefully positioning each segment next to the one before, as shown in Figure 6.40.

3. The second bridge will be constructed from a prefab asset, created from the first bridge. To create the prefab asset, select all the mesh pieces in the existing bridge; then right-click the selection and choose Create Prefab from the menu that appears. Name the prefab accordingly (for example, `Bridge_Prefab_01`), replace the first bridge with a prefab version, clone it to create a second bridge, and move the second bridge into position (see Figure 6.41).

Note

The level created so far can be found in the companion files under DM-Mesh_Project_04_bridges.udk.

Applying the Remaining Materials

The level now consists of two separate islands connected by two bridges, but there is no pool of water between them. This must now be created. First, the five CSG polygonal faces that constitute the bottom of the pool—the four side faces and the one bottom face—must receive an appropriate material. Next, a CSG plane must be

Figure 6.40
The bridge is formed from many segments.

Figure 6.41
Cloning the second bridge as a prefab.

Figure 6.42
Selecting a material for the five underwater faces.

created above the pool but below the bridge using the Builder Brush. This plane must then be assigned an animated water material. Follow these steps:

1. Begin by finding a suitable material for the five underwater faces. You can find your own material in the Content Browser, or use my selection, M_Ground-Master_01. Be sure to enable the Material search filter in the Content Browser's Search and Filter pane. Select the material, as shown in Figure 6.42.

2. Close the Content Browser and select all five underwater faces. Then right-click the selection and choose Apply Material from the menu that appears to assign the selected material in the Content Browser to the selected faces in the viewport (see Figure 6.43). Use Texture Alignment mode or the Surface Properties dialog box to adjust the mapping of the faces as required. More information on mapping can be found in the sections "Adjusting the UV Mapping Coordinates on the Walls Using the Surface Properties Dialog Box" and "Applying the Floor Material" in Chapter 5, "Materials, Textures, and UV Mapping."

3. Next, create the plane of water CSG using the Red Builder Brush. The plane will be created above the bottom-most underwater surface but below the majority of the bridge and ground level. Using the appropriate tools in the application toolbox, convert the Builder Brush into a plane primitive shape, as shown in Figure 6.44.

Figure 6.43
Applying a material to the underwater faces.

Figure 6.44
Convert the Red Builder Brush into a plane primitive.

Figure 6.45
The water plane is added to the level, above the lower levels of the water volume and below the bridge.

4. Use Geometry mode to resize the width and height of the plane to match or exceed the dimensions of the water volume, completely obscuring the bottom-most underwater polygon from any viewer standing on the bridge or islands. Then click the Add CSG Button to add the water plane. (See Figure 6.45.)

5. Next, you must apply a water material to the water plane. To begin, open the Content Browser and use the Search and Filter pane to search for the term *water*, restricting the search results to materials. A selection of water materials appears in the Content Browser's Preview pane (see Figure 6.46).

6. Select the water material M_UN_Liquid_BSP_BlueWater02; then drag and drop it from the Content Browser onto the water plane surface to apply it (see Figure 6.47). Adjust the mapping as appropriate using the Surface Properties dialog box or Texture Alignment mode.

7. The level is now almost complete. It features two islands, two bridges, and a pool of water. There remains, however, open space on both sides of the bridges and in the areas where there are no islands. You can fill these spaces with the appropriate filler meshes. There is no right or wrong here; feel free to experiment. I added more rocks, some foliage, and other meshes.

8. When you're finished, rebuild the lighting for the level and then give it a test run. Splendid work! (See Figure 6.48.)

Figure 6.46
Searching for a water material using the Content Browser.

Figure 6.47
Applying the water material to the water plane.

Figure 6.48
Exploring the island level.

Note

The level created so far can be found in the companion files under DM-Mesh_Project_05_complete.udk.

CONCLUSION

Like the ones before it, this chapter covered a lot of ground, both theoretical and practical. Most of the theory outlined here—such as mesh construction, UV mapping, and collision detection—applies not only to the Unreal Engine but to almost all real-time 3D game engines, including Source, Unity, Torque 3D, Shiva, and DX Studio. In that sense, the concepts presented here are transferable. An additional and important transferable idea outlined here is the modular building method, which involves using smaller mesh pieces to construct a more complex whole.

These concepts and techniques were put to use in a mesh project that required you to create an environment featuring two islands, two bridges, and a water plane. This project introduced you to two additional features of the UDK: the Static Mesh Editor and the prefab asset. The former enables developers to edit and preview the three core properties of a static mesh: the mesh component, the collision mesh component, and the UV sets. The latter enables developers to save and template a selection of multiple meshes so that complex arrangements can be reused and transformed as though they were a single and independent mesh.

In the next chapter, you leave the world of static meshes, which is concerned with visual detail and realism, and enter the world of sound and music, which is concerned with audible detail and realism.

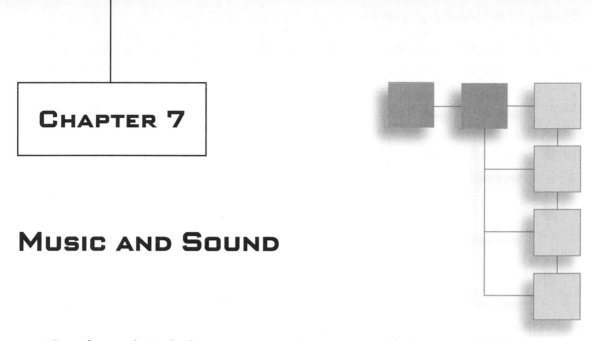

CHAPTER 7

MUSIC AND SOUND

After silence, that which comes nearest to expressing the inexpressible is music.

—Aldous Huxley

By the end of this chapter, you should:

- Understand the conceptual differences between music and sound.
- Be familiar with sound wave data and sound cues.
- Be confident in using the Sound Cue Editor.
- Understand concepts such as attenuation, falloff, pitch, and low pass filter.
- Be able to create levels with both music and sound using sound actors.

This chapter focuses on sound and music and on their application to the UDK and to UDK-based games. Like graphics, sound and music are features of a game that probably need no justification in the contemporary games industry. Their importance is now unanimously accepted except among a minority of developers working largely on fringe and experimental games. Even so, this chapter will devote some space to providing a rudimentary justification for sound and music, partly to reinforce the reasons they are important and partly to help you distinguish between situations in which sound and music are appropriate and situations in which they are not. From here on, the term *audio* will be used to refer to sound and music together; the difference between them is discussed later in this chapter.

Audio is justified because it enables developers to achieve one of their primary goals when designing a game: creating an atmospheric and immersive environment—that is, a believable environment that captures gamers' imaginations and makes them care about its characters, places, and goings-on. Such an environment reaches out to the gamer, acting as the foundation on which the gamer can make an emotional investment in the game.

Creating such an environment depends on appealing in an appropriate way to the gamer's five senses: sight, hearing, taste, touch, and smell. Due to technological limitations, the latter three senses cannot at present be appealed to; smell-o-vision, taste-o-vision, and touch-o-vision are either not available or not sufficiently developed to integrate into a game that can run on most hardware. That means if these three senses can be accessed at all, it must occur indirectly via the imagination and the other two senses—sight and hearing—to which video games do have a direct line (at least in most cases). So it is by appealing to sight and hearing that video games must captivate the gamer. Graphics and animation appeal to sight (animation is considered in a later chapter), and audio appeals to hearing. Imaginative combinations of graphics and audio can produce atmosphere and immersion, making these features essential to a video game.

Audio in Video Games

There are six main ways in which audio can be used in a video game to create immersion and atmosphere. They are as follows:

- **Audio as music.** One of the most notable and obvious ways in which audio is used in a game is to provide music. Music serves two main purposes. First, it acts as a backing track on a menu or an options screen to set a theme for the game (hence, such tracks are often called *theme tunes*). Chanting monks and choir voices, for example, might set the theme for a gothic-style game featuring vampires, dungeons, and dark nights. In contrast, flutes, harps, and harpsichords might set the theme for a medieval tale featuring a mystical fairy garden. Second, music sets the mood. That is, it complements the action or events occurring in the game. This form of music plays in the background as an underscore or accompaniment to game events. It provides emotional commentary in that it can cause the gamer to feel certain things or to experience particular emotions in response to game events. An example of mood setting at work is when a gamer explores an enchanted forest alongside the gentle and whimsical backing track of violins—and then suddenly, an evil warlock springs from nowhere and fires a thunderbolt toward the gamer, causing the musical track to change into an intense and battle-like war song. The change in music signals a change both in mood and in the kinds of emotions the gamer might experience.

- **Audio as sound effect.** The term *sound effect* typically refers to a unit of sound—a gunshot, button click, footstep, crunch, crack, whoosh, or bang. Each unit is a separate sound effect and may be used independently or in combination with other sound effects to produce even more complex sound effects. Most sounds in a game that are not music or part of an ambient or a spoken track are classified as sound effects.

- **Audio as ambience.** Audio can be used to set ambience—that is, the character and mood of a place—but in a way that is distinct from music. Ambient audio is used to make places sound believable—to make swamps sound like swamps and space stations sound like space stations. Ambient audio can be distinguished from music by at least two key properties. First, ambient audio is not typically rhythmic or instrumental in the way that music is. That is, it does not contain rhythm, repetition, a chorus, or a verse. Its sounds are created not so much by musical instruments as by other real-world actors—natural forces like wind and fire or mechanical objects such as cars and machines. Second, ambient audio exists in the space and time of the game, meaning that its sounds trace their origins to events happening in the environment. The sound of fire is heard because there is fire in the environment; the sound of birds is heard because there are birds in the environment; etc. In contrast, music exists in a nowhere place (even though it can and does change based on events happening in the game). Violins, pianos, guitars, and other instruments are strongly present in musical tracks, but they exist to set mood, not because those instruments are necessarily in the environment. The music is not something typically recognized as being heard by the characters in the game (except when used for comedic effect). Ambience, on the other hand, *is* usually something heard by characters. Ambient tracks are typically music-length tracks that sound like recordings of natural or everyday environments. They can be thought of as compositions of sound effects: motorways, forests, warehouses, industrial environments, seaside resorts, desolate landscapes, crowded pedestrian zones, etc.

- **Audio as dialogue.** The main purpose of a dialogue track is to provide spoken words, usually to act as a voice for an animated game character. The volume of a dialogue track is typically higher than the volume of all other audio to ensure that the spoken words are not overshadowed. There are two defining qualities of dialogue tracks that result from their containing spoken words, and that have technical implications on how the tracks should be integrated into the game. The first is that a dialogue track is language specific. The spoken word must occur in one particular language (such as English, German, or French) unless the speaker is speaking nonsense (*The Sims*) or a fictitious language (*Klingon*). Consequently, dialogue tracks have both localization implications *and* lip-synching implications, meaning they have a bearing on how easy and cost-effective it will be to convert the game to additional languages. Developers hoping to localize will need to take special care when deciding how to integrate voice into their games so that it can be easily substituted when producing versions in other languages. The second defining feature of a dialogue track is that it can contain offensive material, including profanity, sexual content, and drug and alcohol references. These factors have implications on the age classification for the game.

Note

Some games feature options to disable offensive material. The availability of these options depends on developers having tagged or labeled specific dialogue tracks, so that those tracks can be omitted or censored when offensive material is disabled.

- **Audio as feedback.** One important (and often overlooked) use of audio is as feedback. In computer software, the term *feedback* refers to how software responds to the user's actions or how software tells the user that specific operations have (or have not) occurred. Perhaps the most famous example of audio feedback is the beep, played by some of the earliest home computers whenever an error occurred. In games, click or zap sounds are often heard whenever the gamer clicks a button on a menu. Similarly, other such sounds are heard when gamers complete or fail their mission or achieve a high score. These are examples of audio feedback because the audio is used as a signal to the gamer that a significant event has occurred.

- **Audio as a communication tool.** Audio can be used as a communication tool— that is, a tool that enables gamers to communicate with each other via microphones in multiplayer gaming. This use of audio enables gamers to talk to and hear one another during gameplay in live multiplayer sessions. Such features in a game, if they are to be used, require additional hardware from the gamer, including a microphone and an Internet connection capable of streaming live audio.

Music and Sound: Is There a Difference?

The previous section identified six main uses of audio in games. It also mentioned that the term *audio* should be taken to mean *music* and *sound* together. When these two words are used separately, a question arises: Is there a difference between them? Traditionally, game developers have made some kind of distinction between them—and the distinction has been a technical rather than a philosophical one. That is, game developers have not attempted to make claims about what music and sound are and what the conceptual differences between them might be, but have made a distinction between them for technical reasons—to make it easier for them to integrate audio into games. Music is often identified as a composition of sounds that lasts for longer than, say, a minute, and must be streamed into memory rather than loaded whole. Such audio includes music tracks, dialogue tracks, ambient tracks, communication streams, and others. In contrast, sounds are shorter than a minute in length, can be loaded whole, and are usually played repeatedly. These include sound effects and feedback sounds.

The UDK, however, does not—at least on the surface—make any distinction between music and sound. It uses only one term—*wave sound data*—to refer to any unit of audio, whether sound or music, and it expects users to import all their wave sound data using the same method and in the same file format (WAV). Under the hood, the Unreal Engine compresses imported sound data to the open-source OGG format, and may or may not distinguish between music and sound along the lines mentioned previously when playing them via the audio hardware. In summary, then, although many game developers draw a distinction between music and sound on the basis of duration, file size, and the number of repeated playbacks, the UDK makes no such distinction. The UDK expects audio to be imported in WAV format, and for each unique file to be imported as a unique wave sound data asset in the Content Browser. Thus, a wave sound asset can be a sound effect, a musical track, an ambient track, a dialogue track, or a feedback track.

WAVE SOUND AND SOUND CUES

The UDK can accept any number of WAV files for import, and each file will be imported as a unique and independent wave sound asset, accessible from the Content Browser like most other assets. The wave sound asset, however, is not the only kind of audio asset supported by the UDK. The UDK also supports the sound cue asset, a composite asset type. The sound cue asset stands to wave sounds as materials stand to textures. That is, sound cues can contain wave sounds, or can be the parent of wave sounds.

Figure 7.1 illustrates the structure of a sample sound cue. Just as Unreal materials refer to a network of material expressions (a configuration of texture samples and mathematical nodes) that combine to produce a unified output, so the sound cue asset can contain a network of sound cues and mathematical nodes to produce a unified audio output. Thus, the sound cue asset depends on wave sound assets and can combine those assets in a network that produces an output greater than the sum of its wave sound parts. In this sense, the wave sound asset is a basic or fundamental asset, and the sound cue asset is a complex or composite asset. Similar to the material

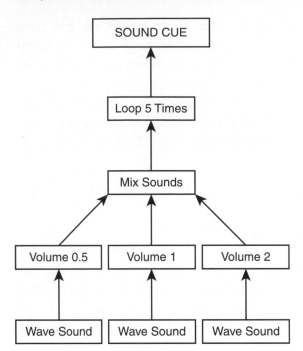

Figure 7.1
Sound cues can contain wave sound data.

asset, the sound cue asset is created using an editor interface—specifically, the Sound Cue Editor. The Sound Cue Editor is discussed later in this chapter.

PROJECT: ADDING AUDIO TO THE BRIDGE LEVEL

The majority of this chapter focuses on project work. This is because the UDK audio feature set is far more limited than the feature sets for meshes, materials, and brushes. Note that *limited* does not necessarily mean *inferior* or *lacking power*. This is especially true in the case of the UDK feature set for audio. This feature set is comparatively limited in terms of the number of buttons, nodes, and interfaces the developer must use, but the features that do exist allow for a wide range of customization and control over the audio that can be included in the game.

In the project to be completed for this chapter, you'll add audio to the level you created in the previous chapter (see Figure 7.2). This project assumes that you have completed the mesh project in the previous chapter. However, the completed mesh project is provided for you in the book companion files, found at the following location: /Chapter7/DM-Audio_Project_06_start.udk. This file can be used as the starting point for the work in this project.

Figure 7.2
The static mesh network for this level was created in the previous chapter.

The mesh project in the previous chapter involved creating an outdoor level from static mesh actors using the modular building method. The level featured two islands connected by two bridges suspended over a pool of water. The level was enhanced through the addition of trees, foliage, rocks, and other items. The main aim of the audio project in this chapter is to add atmosphere and immersion to the bridge level by inserting a number of different sounds. Specifically, this project involves adding three different sounds: two wave sounds and one sound cue. One wave sound and one sound cue will together act as an ambient track for the level, containing the sound of lapping water, chirping birds, and the relentless hissing of crickets. The second wave sound will act as a sound effect—the repetitious sound of throbbing energy that will become audible whenever a player moves close to a specific static mesh. In this project, several features of the UDK are demonstrated. These include the following:

- Adding wave sounds to a level using sound actors (particular instances of a sound in a level)

- Controlling and adjusting the properties of sound actors to enhance the realism of the level

- Using the Sound Cue Editor to create sound cues from multiple wave sounds

- Creating sound actors on the basis of sound cues

Adding a Sound Effect for an Energy Device

One static mesh feature of the level that was not created in the previous chapter was an energy device—a collection of static meshes arranged together to create a science-fiction machine on one of the islands. This device has an unknown purpose and is of unknown origin. It will be added exclusively for the purpose of demonstrating certain audio features. The energy device, shown in Figure 7.3, can be found in the DM-Audio_Project_06_start.udk level, which is the starting point for this project. If you prefer, you can also create it manually from the static meshes shown in Figures 7.4 through 7.6.

The energy device is *obviously* a hazardous perpetual motion machine powered by zero-point energy! For this reason, it should be associated with a constant, pulsating hum or buzz sound effect, to make it sound alive. This repeating sound effect should increase in audibility the closer the gamer moves to the device. The sound effect should be heard at full volume when the gamer is standing beside the device, and it should be inaudible when the gamer is beyond a specified distance away. The following steps will make this possible.

1. Press Ctrl+Shift+F to open the Content Browser, and click the All Assets button. Using the Search field, search for the term "energy." Select the Sound Wave

Figure 7.3
Static mesh actors are arranged to create an energy device.

Figure 7.4
The base mesh for the energy device: S_Pickups_Base_Health_Large.

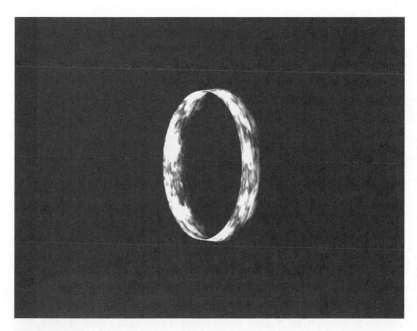

Figure 7.5
The surrounding energy field: S_warp_ring_out.

Figure 7.6
The beam for the energy device: Mesh.S_Pickups_Base_HealthGlow01.

Data checkbox to restrict the content in the Preview pane to wave sound assets. If the Sound Wave Data checkbox is not visible, click the All Types tab in the Search and Filter pane, as shown in Figure 7.7.

2. Double-click the Energy43 sound wave asset in the Content Browser's Preview pane to preview it. To stop playback, right-click the sound asset and select Stop Sound from the menu that appears, as shown in Figure 7.8. With the Energy43 sound—a humming sound suitable for the energy device in the level— still selected, close the Content Browser.

3. Like a static mesh, sound wave data is a template—a sound in the abstract. Thus, it cannot itself be inserted into the level. Instead, the template acts as a basis from which particular instances are derived in the form of actors in the level. Consequently, to add the Energy43 sound into the level, you must create a *sound actor*, which will be an instance of the Energy43 sound wave data. To create a sound actor from the selected Energy43 sound, right-click the energy device mesh in the level and, from the menu that appears, select Add Actor, followed by All Templates, and then Add AmbientSoundSimple, as shown in Figure 7.9.

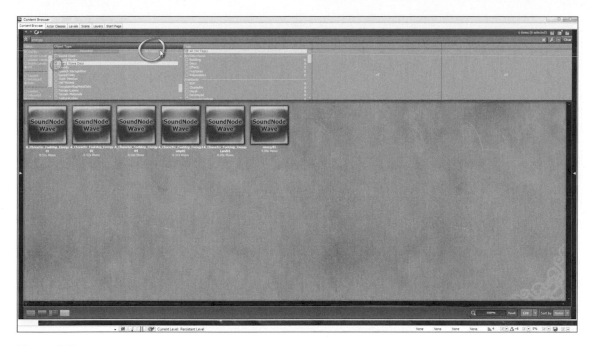

Figure 7.7
Filter for sound wave data.

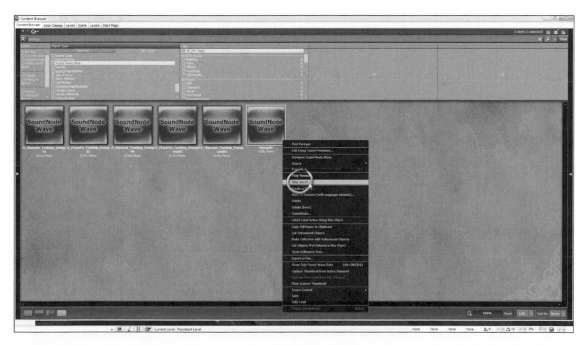

Figure 7.8
Stop the playback of sounds from the context menu.

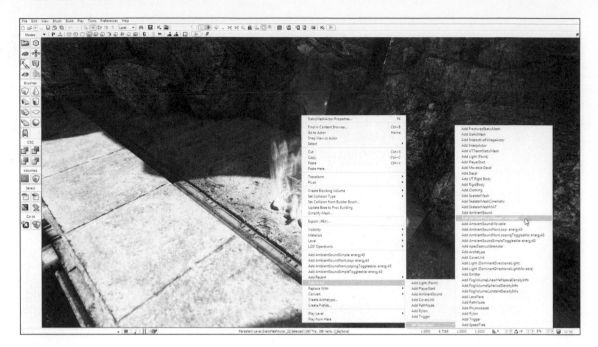

Figure 7.9
Creating a sound actor.

Note

The context menu mentioned in step 3 includes an option for adding a selection of different sound actors on the basis of the Energy43 sound selected in the Content Browser. The difference between them is subtle but important. These actors include the following:

- **AmbientSoundSimple.** AmbientSoundSimple is a form of sound actor that plays a sound wave sample in an infinite loop. That is, the sound plays through completely and then begins again after each completion, repeating indefinitely. Whether a sound is loopable depends in part on the content of the sound file. Specifically, a loopable sound must end in the way it begins for the repeat to be seamless. AmbientSoundSimple is the most appropriate choice for the energy device because the humming or buzzing sound should repeat endlessly in this way.

- **AmbientSoundNonLoop.** AmbientSoundNonLoop is an actor that plays a sound sample once or a specified number of times—not an infinite number of times. AmbientSound-NonLoop actors do not play continuously. For this reason, they are not appropriate for the energy device.

- **AmbientSoundSimpleToggleable.** Like AmbientSoundSimple, AmbientSoundSimple-Toggleable plays a sound sample an infinite number of times, but its toggleable property means the actor can be started and stopped (or enabled and disabled) at run-time through script or Unreal Kismet. This additional functionality would be wasted on the energy device, because it will repeat infinitely and never need to be stopped.

- **AmbientSoundNonLoopingToggleable.** AmbientSoundNonLoopingToggleable is a toggleable version of the AmbientSoundNonLoop actor, a sound actor that plays a specified sound once or a specified number of times. The toggleable property allows the sound to be started or stopped on demand through script or Unreal Kismet. This sound actor is perhaps the most inappropriate of the actors for the energy device because it does not loop infinitely and contains a toggleable feature that is not necessary.

4. An Actor Factory dialog box opens (see Figure 7.10). Click OK to insert the sound actor into the level. As shown in Figure 7.11, a blue speaker icon appears to indicate the position of the sound. Like meshes, the sound can be transformed using the standard transformation tools: The Translate tool can be used to adjust the position of the sound.

5. Exactly one ambient sound actor should now exist in the bridge level at the location of the energy device. The sound actor represents a particular instance of the sound wave data, Energy43. To preview it in the editor, click the Toggle Real Time Audio button in the toolbar, as shown in Figure 7.12.

Editing Ambient Sound Actor Properties

The ambient sound actor offers a range of editable properties that control how the sound is heard by the gamer at run-time, all of which are accessible from the sound actor's Properties panel, under Ambient Properties. These properties fall into three

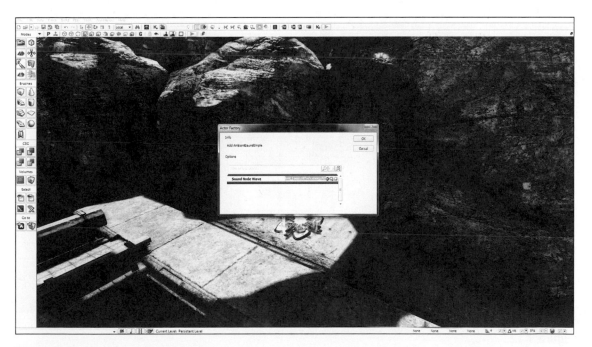

Figure 7.10
Confirm the creation of ambient sound actors.

Figure 7.11
AmbientSoundSimple actors are represented by blue speaker icons in the viewport.

Figure 7.12
You can toggle audio on and off in the editor using the Toggle Real Time Audio button, which features a speaker icon and appears on the UDK Editor's main application toolbar.

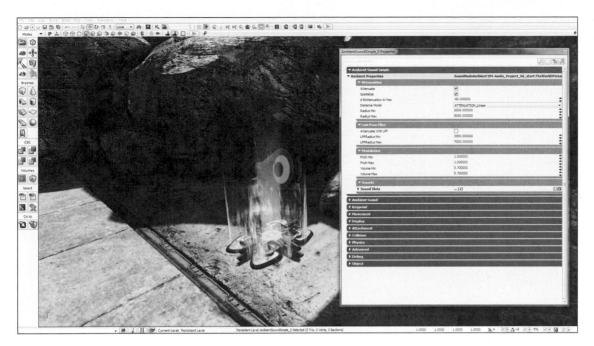

Figure 7.13
The Properties panel for an ambient sound.

distinct groups: Attenuation, Low Pass Filter, and Modulation. With the sound actor selected, press F4 to open the Properties panel and access these properties (see Figure 7.13).

Setting Sound Wave Attenuation

The properties in the Attenuation group are used primarily to mathematically specify the relationship or ratio between the volume of the sound and the distance of the gamer from the sound. That is, these properties determine how the volume of the sound decreases from a maximum to a minimum the farther the gamer moves from the sound, mimicking the way sounds closer to the listener are typically louder than sounds that are farther away. This decrease in volume over distance is known in video gaming as a *falloff*, and is controlled in the UDK by a selection of properties, including Attenuate, Distance Model, Radius Min, and Radius Max (refer to Figure 7.13).

Let us first consider the latter two properties: Radius Min and Radius Max. Figure 7.14 helps illustrate them. It shows the selected sound actor surrounded by two concentric wireframe spheres, one inside the other. The small, inner sphere has a radius matching Radius Min, and the larger, outer sphere has a radius matching Radius Max. This setup was created by selecting the sound actor in the Perspective

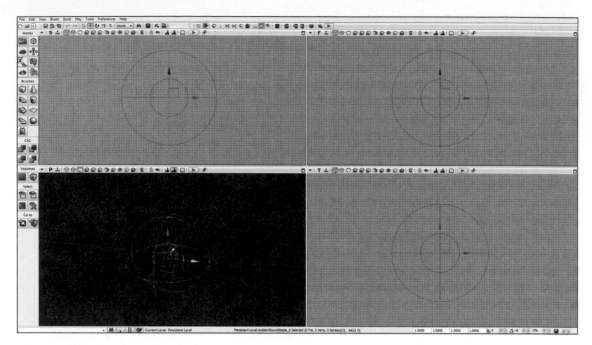

Figure 7.14
The sound actor surrounded by two spheres corresponding to the Radius Min and Radius Max properties.

viewport, pressing Alt+2 to switch to Wireframe mode, and using the viewport's Show/Hide menu to hide all meshes, all terrains, all volumes, all brushes, and the Builder Brush. (For more on showing and hiding actors, refer to the section "Customizing the Viewport" in Chapter 3, "UDK Fundamentals.") You do not need to hide these elements to see the spheres (they are visible in Lit mode), but it does make them clearer to see in illustrations.

The sound actor's two concentric spheres are for diagnostic purposes; they exist for the benefit of the level designer. That means they are visible in the editor's viewports but not to the game camera. The purpose of the spheres is to illustrate the space inside which the sound can be heard—that is, inside which the volume of the sound will be greater than 0. The inner sphere (Radius Min) defines the interior space, inside which the sound will be heard at its maximum volume. The outer sphere (Radius Max) defines the space outside which the volume will be 0 (completely inaudible). The space between the inner and outer sphere is where the volume will fall off continuously from its maximum at the inner sphere to its minimum at the outer sphere. So, increasing the size of the outer sphere while keeping the inner sphere constant will increase the distance over which the falloff occurs. Likewise, increasing the size of the inner sphere while keeping the outer sphere constant will increase the region inside which the sound will be heard at its maximum volume.

The final properties to consider in the Attenuation group are the Attenuate and Distance Model properties. The Attenuate property is a Boolean (true/false) value that specifies whether the volume of the sound should fall off at all. A value of false means that the sound will be heard throughout the level at constant volume, regardless of the gamer's position. This can be useful for music or ambient track sound actors. The second property, Distance Model, refers to the formula used to calculate the falloff in volume between the inner and outer sphere. A value of ATTENTUA-TION_Linear causes the volume to fall off linearly between the inner and outer spheres, meaning the volume of the sound between the inner and outer spheres is inversely proportional to the distance of the gamer from the sound. Thus, the volume decreases by a uniform increment the farther away the gamer moves. Try experimenting with this setting to observe the effects.

To set the attenuation properties for the sound actor associated with the energy device, follow these steps.

1. In the sound actor's Properties panel, ensure that the Attenuate checkbox in the Attenuation group is checked and that Distance Model is set to ATTENTUA-TION_Linear, as shown in Figure 7.15.

2. The sound actor currently features a minimum and a maximum radius that is far too large given the size of the energy device. To correct this, zoom out in the

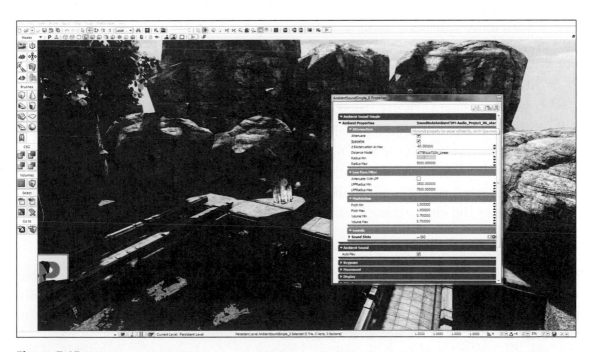

Figure 7.15
Preparing to change the attenuation for the sound.

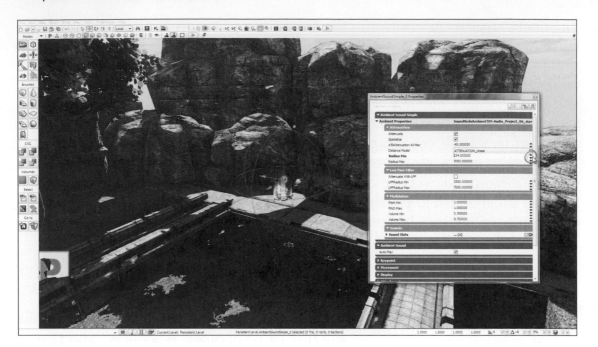

Figure 7.16
Adjusting the size of the inner sphere.

Perspective viewport to get a clear view of the inner and outer spheres for the sound's attenuation. Then, in the sound actor's Properties panel, adjust the sound actor's inner sphere by clicking and dragging between the upper and lower arrows in the Properties panel's Min Radius field (see Figure 7.16). This technique enables you to interactively reduce the size of the inner sphere, keeping a watch on the sphere as it changes in the Perspective viewport. The sphere should completely contain the energy device mesh and some of the surrounding environment. This marks the space in which the sound will be heard at maximum volume.

3. Repeat this process to reduce the size of the outer sphere, as shown in Figure 7.17. Both spheres together define the attenuation for the sound actor. Give the level a test to ensure the sound actor works as intended, growing louder in volume the closer the gamer moves to the energy device.

Low Pass Filter and Modulation

The Low Pass Filter and the Modulation properties—which are summarized here, but require no modifications for the energy device sound actor in this level—differ from the attenuation properties in that they do not relate to the position of the listener in the level. That is, they do not affect the volume or properties of the sound based on the distance of the listener from the sound. Rather, they apply as a constant to the sound, affecting it uniformly.

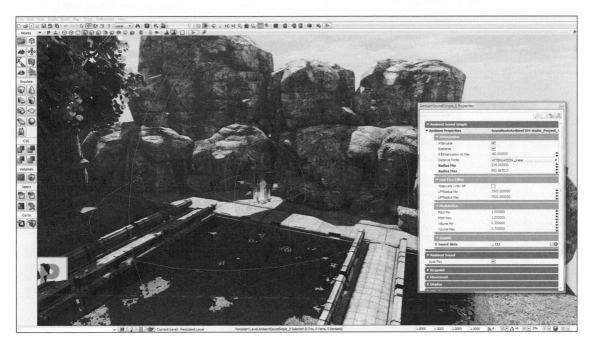

Figure 7.17
Setting the sound actor attenuation.

As mentioned, the Low Pass Filter property refers to a formula that works on the raw sound data (sound waves) to clip or reduce the amplitude (strength) of signals above a specified frequency, known as the *filter frequency* or *cutoff frequency*. The usual result of the application of a low pass filter is a sound that is more muffled or more diluted than the original one. Consequently, the effect is often applied to sounds that are supposed to originate from behind walls, under floors, or in areas that prevent the sound from being heard at full strength. Because there are no such inhibiting factors acting on the energy device sound, a low pass filter is not required here. All you need to do is ensure the Attenuate with LPF checkbox in the sound actor's Properties panel's Low Pass Filter group is unchecked, as shown in Figure 7.18.

Note

> The minimum and maximum radius values for the Low Pass Filter, available from the Properties panel, determine the distances at which the Low Pass Filter effect is applied. The minimum radius indicates the distance at which the Low Pass Filter effect begins to be applied, and the maximum radius indicates the distance at which the Low Pass Filter is applied at its maximum.

The Modulation group consists of four properties arranged into two pairs: Pitch Min and Pitch Max, and Volume Min and Volume Max. Each pair specifies the minimum and maximum of a range, with the Pitch values defining the range of possible pitches

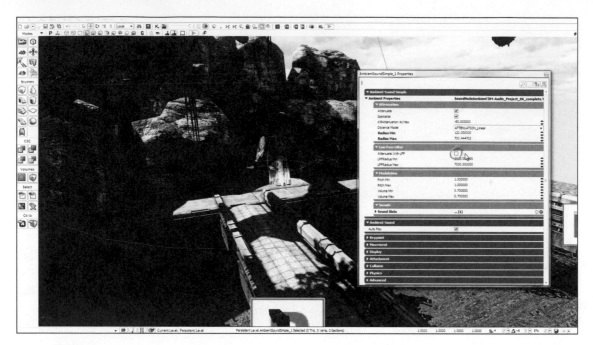

Figure 7.18
Ensure the Attenuate with LPF checkbox is not checked for the energy device sound actor.

for the sound and the Volume values defining the range of possible volumes for the sound. When the Min and Max values differ, a value between them is generated at random and applied to the sound every time it is played or restarted. When the Min and Max values are identical, the range is limited to only one possible value (the Min and Max values), and this value is applied to the sound on each playback or restart.

You can use the Modulation properties to add variation to the sound—that is, to make it sound slightly different on each playback. The energy device is a perpetual motion device, forever looping and cycling; thus, the Modulation properties are not appropriate for this sound. For this reason, ensure the Min and Max values for both pitch and volume are identical. (Refer to Figure 7.18.)

Note

Both the Pitch and Volume values in the Properties panel—and elsewhere in the UDK—are multipliers. They are not absolute values measured in decibels. A volume value of 1, for example, does not set the volume of the sound to 1dB (decibel), but *multiplies* the default volume of the sound by a value of 1. That means a volume value of 1 will always play the sound at its default volume. Similarly, a volume value of 0 will silence a sound because the product of the default volume multiplied by 0 is 0dB. A volume value of 2 plays a sound at twice its default volume, and a volume value of 0.5 plays a sound at half its default volume.

Ambient Tracks from Sound Wave Data

You have created the throbbing sound effect for the perpetual motion energy device using sound wave data and a sound actor. You have also tuned the actor's attenuation properties to ensure the volume of the sound reduces (attenuates) with distance. This section moves away from sound effects, to creating an ambient track for the level.

Remember, the main purpose of an ambient track—a loopable track that plays continuously—is to set character and mood for an environment. Ambient tracks have the quality of being situated in the game environment. They do not feature instrumental music—that is, music produced through musical instruments—but are rather composed of environment-relevant sound effects.

The ambience for the bridge level will consist of several fundamental audio elements, including lapping water, bird song, and some crickets. You will add these elements into the level by way of two main UDK sound assets: a sound wave data asset for the water-lapping element and a sound cue asset for the remaining ambience. This section focuses on adding the water-lapping ambience with a sound wave asset. The process for doing so closely resembles that of adding the energy device sound effect, explained in the previous section. The fundamental difference relates to the sound actor's attenuation properties.

1. Press Ctrl+Shift+F to open the Content Browser, and click the All Assets button. Using the Search field, search for the term "water." Select the Sound Wave Data checkbox to restrict the content in the Preview pane to sound wave assets. Double-click some of the assets listed to test them, and find a water-lapping sound appropriate for the level. I have chosen mono_water02. (See Figure 7.19.) With the water-lapping sound asset still selected, close the Content Browser.

2. As before, you must add a sound actor to the level for the selected sound. To do so, right-click in the Perspective viewport and, from the menu that appears, select Add Actor, followed by All Templates, and then Add AmbientSoundSimple. Position the newly added actor in the air above the water plane, as shown in Figure 7.20. (Its position in the level will not affect how the sound is heard during gameplay, but placing it over the water might be helpful to the developer, to visually affirm that the sound is associated with the water.)

Note

With a Sound Wave object selected in the Content Browser, you can also add a sound actor to the level by right-clicking in the Perspective viewport and selecting Add AmbientSoundSimple from the menu that appears.

Figure 7.19
Find a lapping water sound wave asset in the Content Browser.

Figure 7.20
Adding a sound actor to the level for the water-lapping sound.

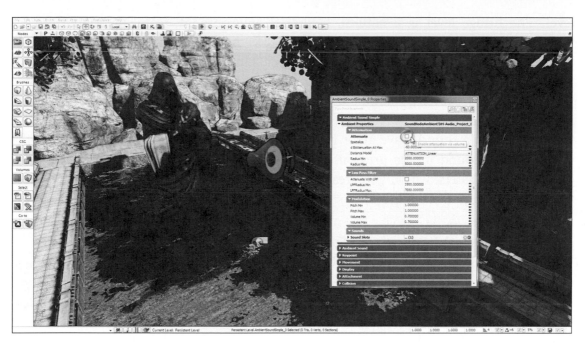

Figure 7.21
Disabling attenuation ensures that a sound is heard uniformly at its specified volume throughout the environment. That means its volume will not change with the position of the gamer.

3. Select the sound actor in the Perspective viewport and press F4 to open its Properties panel. At present, the sound actor attenuates just as the energy device sound effect attenuates—that is, its volume will vary depending on the distance of the player from the location of the sound. Although this volume-changing behavior is suitable for sound effects with an easily identifiable source in the level, it is not suitable for sound effects that are ambient—that is, sound effects that pervade the environment, like the pool of water at the center of the level. This pool of water is a defining feature of the environment; it can be seen from almost every position in the level and it spans the largest surface area of the level. For this reason, the water-lapping sound should be heard throughout the level at constant volume. To achieve this, uncheck the Attenuate checkbox in the ambient sound's Property panel's Attenuation group, as shown in Figure 7.21.

Creating an Ambient Track with Sound Cues

The previous section focused on creating ambience for the bridge level by adding a water-lapping sound wave asset, played on a loop, and without attenuation properties. The water-lapping sound however, while important for ambience, is not the only kind of environmental and ambient sound that a visitor could expect to find at the bridge level. The bridge level is a natural, terrestrial environment, featuring islands, rocks, water, trees, foliage, and a surrounding blue sky. As such, the environment is likely to prove hospitable to life of various kinds, including birds and insects—creatures whose activities are not always seen but are typically *audible*. You can further enhance the realism of the level by adding a variety of ambient sounds to represent these life forms and to signify their presence. You could add these sounds to the level one at a time by adding a sound wave actor for each individual sound, the way you added the water-lapping sound in the previous section. A more flexible method, however, is to add sound cue assets, which you create using the Sound Cue Editor. The next few sections demonstrate this method.

Sound Cues and the Sound Cue Editor

The UDK offers two different but related kinds of audio assets: the basic sound wave data asset and the more complex sound cue asset. The terms *basic* and *complex* are used here to indicate not how difficult sound waves and sound cues are to understand, but the nature of the relationship between them. That is, the complex sound cue asset depends on the more basic sound wave asset; it might be said that sound waves are a *dependency* of sound cues.

To introduce and justify the concept of sound cues and to highlight their importance, it can be helpful to list some of the tasks that sound cue assets can achieve but that sound wave assets cannot—or at least, not without a lot more work. Following are four scenarios in which a sound cue asset represents a more appropriate solution than a sound wave asset. In short, a sound cue asset is more appropriate when:

- One or more sounds should be played either simultaneously or in sequence, and when the developer wants to treat all those sounds as a single asset or a prefab—that is, as a collective or whole.

- The developer needs finer control over how a sound or a group of sounds is played. This includes control over looping, the order in which sounds are played, and the intervals of time or pauses between sounds.

- The developer wants to either mix multiple sounds together or play a selection of different sounds at random.

- The developer needs to apply special effects to one or more sounds over time, such as attenuation, low pass filters, delays, loops, modulation, oscillation, and fades.

The sound cue asset makes completion of these audio tasks possible because of its structure and architecture. The sound cue is in many respects the audio version of a

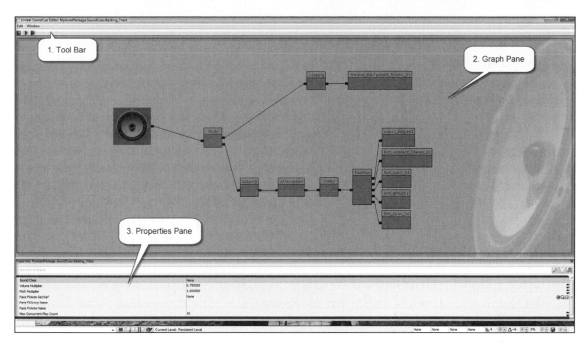

Figure 7.22
The Sound Cue Editor featuring the graph for the ambient track to be created. The editor consists of three main sections: the toolbar, the Graph pane, and the Properties pane.

material, if such an analogy is possible. Materials contain textures, and sound cues contain sound waves. Further, just as a material is a network of connected texture and mathematical nodes, so the sound cue is a network (or composition) of connected sound wave and mathematical nodes. The product of a material is a rectangle of pixels, and the product of a sound cue is a continuous piece of audio.

The audio produced by a sound cue is the result of its graph. The purpose of the Sound Cue Editor—which you open by right-clicking any sound cue asset in the Content Browser and choosing Edit in Sound Cue Editor from the menu that appears—is to offer developers the tools to construct and edit that graph. As shown in Figure 7.22, the Sound Cue Editor consists of three main elements:

- **The toolbar and main menu.** The Sound Cue Editor's main menu features a limited set of options, mainly for copying (Ctrl+C), cutting (Ctrl+X), and pasting (Ctrl+V) the selected node in the Graph pane, and for showing and hiding the Properties pane at the bottom of the editor window. The toolbar features even fewer buttons and options, all of which are nonetheless important. The left-most button is the Stop button; like the Stop button on most media players, clicking this button stops the playback of whatever audio is playing. Clicking the second button, Play Selected, plays not the complete sound cue (the graph) but only the selected node in the graph (provided the node is playable). Clicking the final button, Play, plays the complete sound cue.

■ **The Graph pane.** The Graph pane is the Sound Cue Editor's main working area, in which a graph of nodes is constructed. Like a material graph in the Material Editor, a sound cue graph in the Sound Cue Editor can be read from right to left, and the nodes of the graph have both input and output sockets that can be connected using wires. The Graph pane in the Sound Cue Editor also uses the same paradigm and keyboard and mouse controls as the Material Editor. That means you can drag and move nodes using the Ctrl-click technique, marquee-select multiple nodes with the Ctrl+Alt-click-and-drag technique, and add nodes to the graph by right-clicking in graph background and choosing a node from the menu that appears, as shown in Figure 7.23. (See the section "The Material Editor" in Chapter 5, "Materials, Textures, and UV Mapping" for more information on the Material Editor.) All nodes in the graph must eventually connect in some way to the left-most speaker node. This is the primary node of the graph, representing the graph's output. Nodes that connect to the speaker node

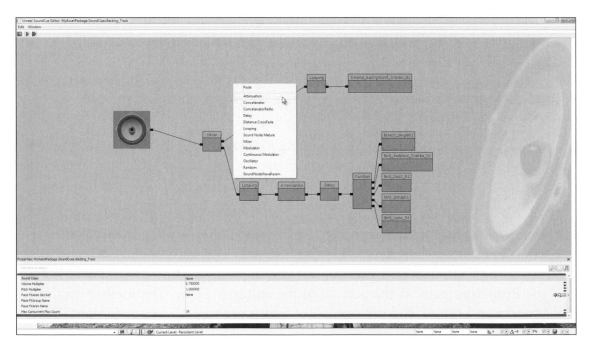

Figure 7.23
Adding new nodes to the sound cue graph.

are output from the sound cue to the PC speakers—that is, they become audible. Creating a sound cue is therefore a matter of constructing a graph, which involves wiring both sound wave and mathematical nodes together.

■ **The Properties pane.** The Properties pane is context sensitive in that its content changes depending on the node selected in the graph. This panel acts much like the editor's F4 Properties panel, providing access to all the editable properties associated with the selected node. You will make frequent use of the Properties pane in your work constructing a graph for the ambient sound cue for the bridge level.

Creating a Sound Cue

Having formally introduced the sound cue and the Sound Cue Editor, it's time to attend to the task at hand: creating an ambient sound cue for the bridge level. This sound cue will complement the existing water-lapping sound wave with the sound of birds, crickets, insects, and other life forms. You will add the sound cue asset as a new asset of the MyAssetsPackage created for the mesh prefabs in the previous chapter. The following steps detail how to create a new sound cue asset.

1. Press Ctrl+Shift+F to open the Content Browser. Then select MyAssetsPackage from the package hierarchy, as shown in Figure 7.24.

Figure 7.24
Selecting MyAssetsPackage from the package hierarchy.

Figure 7.25
Creating a new sound cue asset.

2. Click the New button in the bottom-left corner of the Content Browser. The New Asset dialog box opens; fill it out as shown in Figure 7.25 to create a new, named sound cue asset. Enter MyAssetsPackage in the Package field, Sound Cues in the Grouping field, and the sound cue name (Ambient_Sound_Cue) in the Name field. Also, be sure to set the Factory parameter to the Sound Cue type. As shown in Figure 7.26, the sound cue asset is created and available in the Content Browser.

3. Save the package by right-clicking it in the package hierarchy and choosing Save from the menu that appears.

Sound Waves for Sound Cues

As you have seen, sound waves are raw materials for sound cues. A sound cue will not be audible nor will it work correctly unless it contains at least one sound wave asset in its graph. This is because sound wave assets represent audible data, whereas the remaining mathematical nodes of sound cues (such as modulation and mixing nodes) *work on* sound waves. That is, they process sound waves and combine them in various ways to produce audible results. For this reason, you must first find *all* the sound wave assets to be included as part of the sound cue ambient track.

Figure 7.26
The sound cue is created and almost ready for editing.

The sound cue track will be an ambient complement to the water-lapping sound wave that currently repeats in the level. That is, the purpose of the sound cue will be to further enhance the water sound. I want to add two different kinds of sounds to the ambient track. They differ not so much in their audible content as in the way I want them to work.

- I want to include the constant and repeating hissing sound of crickets to add a sense of vibrancy and animation to the environment.

- I want the sound of birds or other insects to play occasionally and at random. The randomness of the sounds will enhance the realism of the level by reducing the regularity and uniformity of the track.

To get started, find the appropriate sounds in the Content Browser. (There will be six of them.)

1. Press Ctrl+Shift+F to open the Content Browser. Then find the newly created sound cue asset in the Preview pane, right-click it, and choose Edit in Sound Cue Editor from the menu that appears. The Sound Cue Editor opens; except for the speaker node, the graph for the current sound cue appears empty (see Figure 7.27).

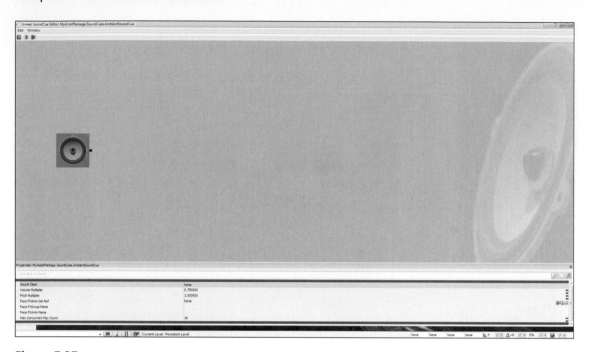

Figure 7.27
Opening the new sound cue in the Sound Cue Editor.

2. Without closing the Sound Cue Editor, return to the Content Browser and click the All Assets button. Click the All Types tab and check the Sound Wave Data checkbox to restrict the content in the Preview pane to sound wave data only. Search for the term "ambient"; then, in the Preview pane, Ctrl-click to select the following six sounds (see Figure 7.28): Swamp_Background_Stereo_01, Insect_single01, Bird_Ambient_Stereo_01, Bird_Duck_01, Bird_group01, and Bird_Loon_01.

3. Right-click any vacant space in the Graph pane of the Sound Cue Editor and choose SoundNodeWave from the menu that appears (see Figure 7.29) to add all six sounds to the graph as separate nodes. You can play any selected node in the graph by clicking the Play Selected button on the Sound Cue Editor toolbar (see Figure 7.30). Now that the six sounds have been added, you are ready to construct the graph of the sound cue. This will involve wiring the nodes together in combination with other nodes to link their output to the speaker node, as discussed in the next section.

Building the Sound Cue Graph

The Sound Cue Editor contains a graph with six sound wave nodes, each node representing a unique wave sound. These nodes represent the six sound waves to be incorporated into the environment ambient track. These nodes, however, are not yet

Figure 7.28
Selecting six sound wave assets for the sound cue.

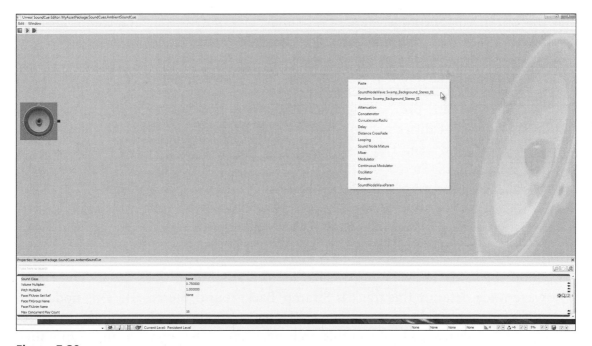

Figure 7.29
Adding sound wave nodes to the Sound Cue Editor graph.

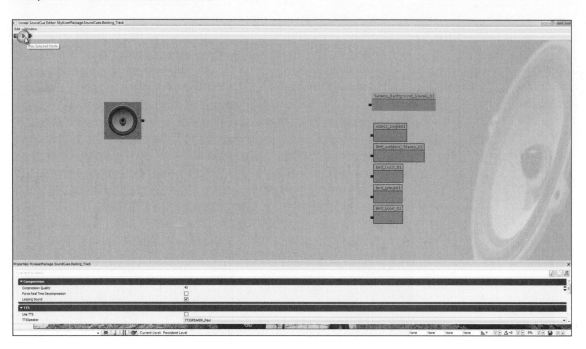

Figure 7.30
Playing the selected node with the Play Selected command.

connected in any way—either to each other or to the primary speaker node—meaning that the sound cue currently outputs no audio data. Playback of the sound cue will result in nothing but silence, even though it contains six sound wave nodes. Constructing the sound cue graph involves connecting these nodes to produce a meaningful and useful output.

As mentioned in the previous section, the sound cue will contain two types of sounds—sounds that differ not so much in their content as in the way they will be played in the sound cue. The first sound is a constant and looping crickets track (Swamp_Background_Stereo_01), and the second sound consists of Insect_single01, Bird_Ambient_Stereo_01, Bird_Duck_01, Bird_group01, and Bird_Loon_01. From among the latter five sounds, the sound cue will, at various intervals, select one at random to be played. The following steps explain how to construct a sound cue that is consistent with that design.

1. Build the node network responsible for the looping crickets track. The sound wave node data for this track is Swamp_Background_Stereo_01. This node must be connected to some other mathematical nodes to play as intended. Use the Ctrl-click method to drag this node apart from the others in the graph, then right-click a vacant area of the graph and choose Looping from the menu that appears (see Figure 7.31) to add a Looping node to the graph. The Looping node

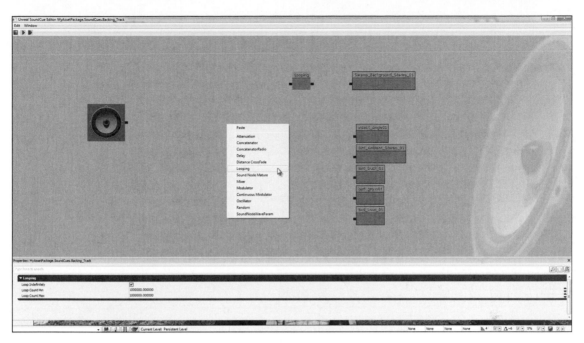

Figure 7.31
Adding a Looping node to the graph. Looping nodes repeat their inputs.

will repeat its input (whatever is plugged into its input socket) according to a set of parameters.

2. To repeat the crickets audio, wire the output of the crickets node to the input of the Looping node. To do this, click and drag from the crickets node's output connector to the Looping node's input connector (see Figure 7.32).

3. Select the Looping node in the graph and notice the properties associated with it in the Properties pane. Specifically, the Looping node features three properties, outlined in Table 7.1. In this example, you can leave the Looping node with its default properties to loop its input infinitely.

4. To test the sound cue so far, wire the output of the Looping node to the input of the speaker node, and then click the Play Sound Cue button in the toolbar (see Figure 7.33). Alternatively, select the Looping node in the graph and click the Play Selected button. This sends the output of the selected node to the speakers.

5. Having successfully created the looping cricket track in the graph, it's time to add the second element: a track that repeatedly selects an animal sound at random and at specific intervals from among five sound waves. This is a complex process, with multiple stages. The first stage involves repetition. That is, the process of randomly selecting a sound for playback must occur repeatedly throughout the duration of the ambient track; otherwise, it will happen only

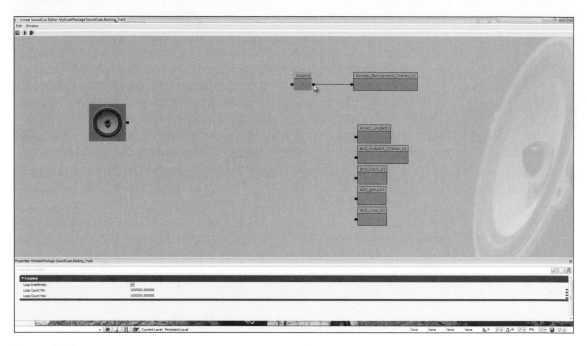

Figure 7.32
Looping the crickets audio infinitely using the Looping node.

Table 7.1	Looping Node Properties
Property	**Description**
Loop Indefinitely	This true or false value specifies whether the input should loop infinitely.
Loop Count Min*	If Loop Indefinitely is false, this specifies the minimum number of repeats.
Loop Count Max*	If Loop Indefinitely is false, this specifies the maximum number of repeats.

*Both the Loop Count Min and Loop Count Max values are relevant only if Loop Indefinitely is set to false. If Loop Indefinitely is set to false, then a repeat count for the input is selected at random from within the range specified by the Min and Max values. If Loop Count Min and Loop Count Max are identical, then this value specifies an exact repeat count.

once. That means a Looping node will be required, and that it should be set to loop indefinitely to repeat the selection process for as long as the sound cue plays. Add this node now by right-clicking a vacant area of the graph and choosing Looping from the menu that appears. The sound cue graph will look something like the graph in Figure 7.34.

6. The second stage of the process involves not selecting a sound at random from among the five sound waves, but a time delay—a waiting period, so that an

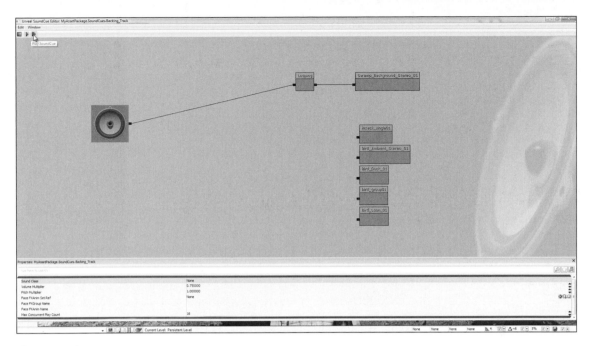

Figure 7.33
Previewing the cricket loop in the Sound Cue Editor.

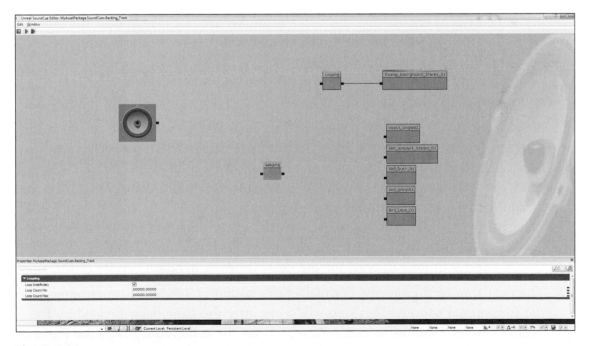

Figure 7.34
Building the random-selection process: adding another Looping node.

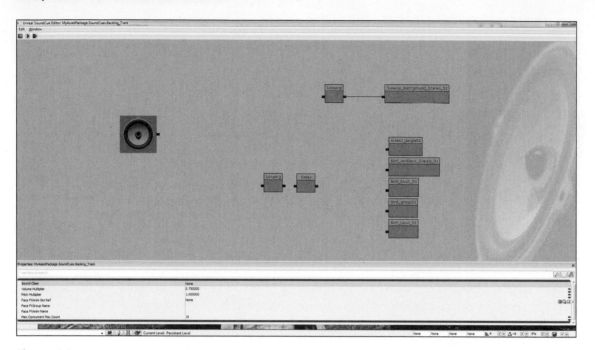

Figure 7.35
Delay nodes are used to delay the playback of their inputs by a specified interval measured in seconds.

interval of time passes before another sound is selected and played. The purpose of the delay is to ensure that the selected sounds are not played one immediately after the other in an unbroken and unrealistic sequence. You can add a time delay to the graph by way of a Delay node. To add a Delay node to the graph, right-click any vacant space in the graph and choose Delay from the menu that appears. Position this node beside the Looping node, as shown in Figure 7.35.

7. Notice that the Delay node contains Delay Min and Delay Max properties measured in seconds to specify a range for the time delay. These properties work much like the corresponding Min and Max properties for the Looping node, specifying a range from which a value is selected at random. If the Delay Min and Delay Max values are identical, then that value is used as the time delay. To add variation in the delay for the sound cue, enter the value 2 in the Delay Min field and the value 5 in the Delay Max field, as shown in Figure 7.36. This will randomly select a unique interval for the delay on each iteration (cycle) of the loop.

8. The next step in the process is to select one sound at random from among the five animal sounds. This step will occur after the time delay created by the previous node. Random selection of sounds can be achieved through the Random node. Add one of these nodes to the graph now by right-clicking a vacant area of the graph and choosing Random from the menu that appears. (See Figure 7.37.)

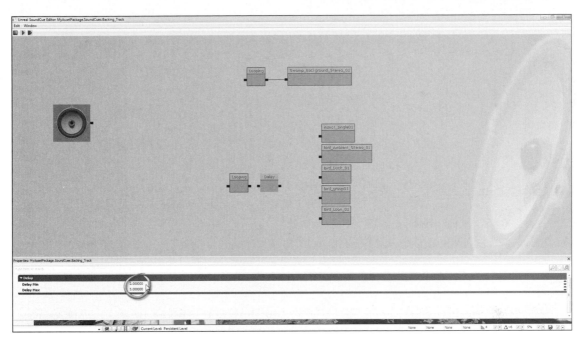

Figure 7.36
Changing the delay interval for the Delay node in the Sound Cue Editor.

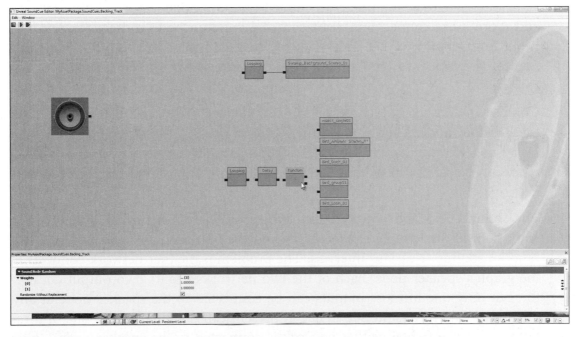

Figure 7.37
The Random node randomly selects an input to use as its output.

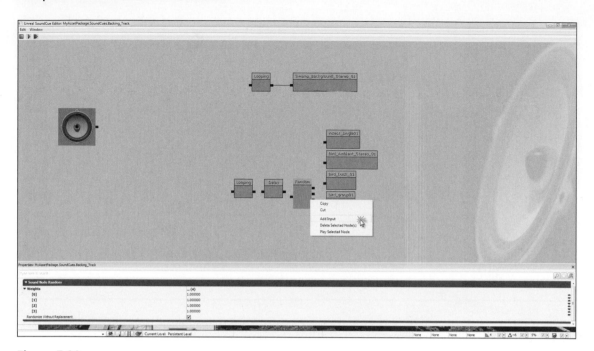

Figure 7.38
Adding inputs to the Random node.

9. The purpose of the Random node is to randomly select one of its inputs to use as its output. Notice that the newly added Random node features two inputs. To add more input connections, right-click the Random node and choose Add Input from the menu that appears (see Figure 7.38). Use this technique to add a total of five inputs to the Random node, to match the number of available sounds.

10. Connect the output of each of the five sound wave nodes into a unique input of the Random node. Then connect the Random node to the Delay node, and the Delay node to the Looping node. This completes the network of nodes that will randomly select and play an animal sound. Figure 7.39 shows the connected network.

11. The sound cue graph now contains two separate mini-networks. The top network defines the looping crickets track and the bottom network plays various random sounds at various intervals. The problem is, neither network connects to the graph's speaker node. Each of the two networks has its own output connector, but only one of those outputs can be connected to the speaker node at any one time. That means the sound cue at present can potentially have one of three outputs: silence (when neither network is connected to the speaker node), the sound of crickets (when the top network is connected to the speaker node), or

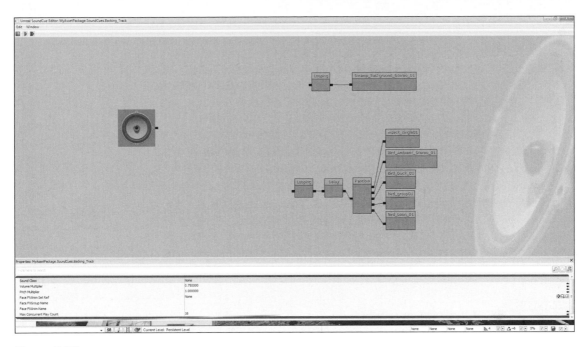

Figure 7.39
The connected random play network.

the random playback of various animal sounds (when the bottom network is connected to the speaker node). For all the sound waves to play as intended, you must add an additional node, a Mixer node, to combine the two networks into one output that connects to the speaker node. The Mixer node accepts two or more inputs and collapses them into a single output, just as Adobe Photoshop can flatten a multitude of layers into a single composition. To add the Mixer node, right-click a vacant area of the graph and choose Mixer from the menu that appears. Then connect the Mixer node's output to the speaker node to complete the sound cue network, as shown in Figure 7.40.

Adding the Sound Cue to the Level

You have created the ambient sound cue by constructing a graph network of sound wave nodes and mathematical nodes. To test the sound cue, click the Play Sound Cue button in the Sound Cue Editor's toolbar. The sound cue should produce a track in which the sound of crickets are heard constantly and in a loop, and in which the sound of birds and other animals play randomly at various intervals. The final step in completing the sound level is to add the sound cue to the level via an ambient sound actor (see Figure 7.41). The following steps explain how to do this, and raise

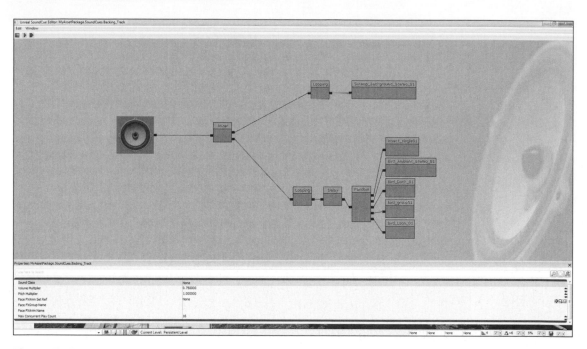

Figure 7.40
Using the Mixer node to reduce two audio inputs into one output.

Figure 7.41
The sound cue is now completed and can be added to the level via an actor.

Figure 7.42
Using the Content Browser to save changes to your asset package.

an important issue regarding the customizability of sound cue actors in terms of modulation, attenuation, and low pass filters.

1. Close the Sound Cue Editor.

2. Save the changes to your asset package to preserve the sound cue edits. To do so, open the Content Browser, select the package in the package hierarchy, right-click the selected package, and choose Save (see Figure 7.42). Alternatively, open the File menu in the main UDK Editor and choose Save All.

3. Select the sound cue in the Content Browser Preview pane. Next, close the Content Browser, returning to the main UDK Editor. In the Perspective viewport, right-click the spot where the sound cue should be inserted as an actor and, in the menu that appears, choose Add Actor, then All Templates, followed by AmbientSound. The sound cue is inserted into the level, and the level is ready for testing. (See Figure 7.43.)

Note

The completed level can be found in the companion files under DM-Audio_Project_06_complete.udk.

4. The sound cue's AmbientSound actor is different from the AmbientSoundSimple actor for sound waves. Specifically, it features no modulation, attenuation, or

Figure 7.43
Insert the sound cue into the level, and then take the level for a test run.

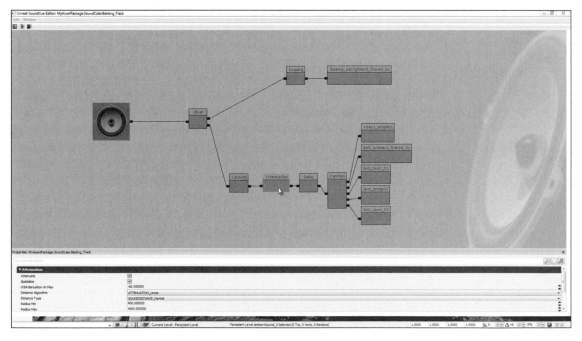

Figure 7.44
An Attenuation node added to the sound cue graph.

low pass filter properties in its Properties panel (accessible via the F4 key). That's because sound cues typically have their attenuation, modulation, and low pass filter properties set in the sound cue graph using the correspondingly named nodes. The sound cue created in this project features no such nodes, so the sound cue can be heard uniformly throughout the level in the same way as a sound wave actor whose attenuation properties have been disabled. To add these properties to the sound cue, return to the Sound Cue Editor and add the appropriate nodes: the Modulator node (to affect the starting volume of a sound node), the Attenuation node (to affect the volume of the sound cue over distance), and the Low Pass Filter node (to apply muffled effects to the sound node). The properties for these three nodes are identical to the properties discussed for modulation, LPF, and attenuation earlier in this chapter. Figure 7.44 shows the sound cue graph with an Attenuation node added.

CONCLUSION

The focus of this chapter has been primarily—though not exclusively—audio in video games. Not exclusively, because many of the audio concepts and categories introduced here, such as ambient tracks, music tracks, and sound effects, pertain less strictly to music production and implementation than they do to the field of game design more generally. This chapter discussed not only the significance of audio to games, but the distinctions and terms used by the UDK when working with audio. Specifically, it explained how and why the UDK distinguishes between sound wave and sound cue assets. It further explored how sound cues are created through the Sound Cue Editor.

The next chapter enters the world of lighting in video games. In so doing, it also revisits and revises some subjects covered in previous chapters, including the subjects of materials and static meshes.

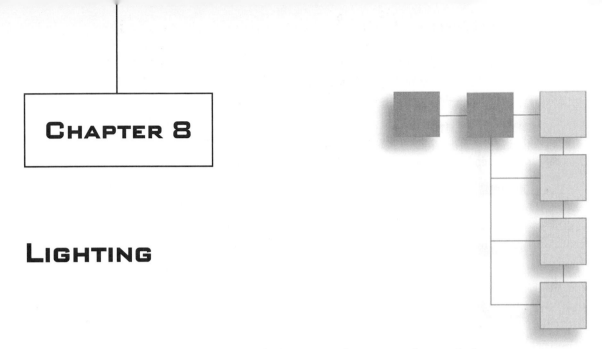

CHAPTER 8

LIGHTING

What is true by lamplight is not always true by sunlight.

—Joseph Joubert

By the end of this chapter, you should:

- Understand the fundamentals of light theory.
- Understand concepts such as indirect illumination and lightmapping.
- Be able to use the UDK light actors, including spot lights, directional lights, and point lights.
- Be able to use emissive channels in materials to create light sources.
- Understand the basics of using Unreal Lightmass.

This chapter concentrates on the subject of lighting. Lighting poses more technical problems and obstacles to achieving realism in real-time games than any other aspect of game creation. This is due primarily to the computational expense of calculating or simulating accurate lighting in real-time conditions, on a frame-by-frame basis. For this reason, most new, major innovations for video-game graphics tend to be related to lighting—typically new algorithms or techniques for faking lighting effects or for improving the way lighting is calculated.

Understood loosely in its scientific sense, the term *lighting* refers to electromagnetic radiation whose basic unit is a *photon*, which travels in the form of rays, and which makes sight and vision possible whenever it meets an eye.

Note

Objects that reflect light into an eye are said to be visible to that eye. The way in which an object reflects light affects how that object appears. Objects that reflect only light in the red color spectrum will appear entirely red. Those that reflect only light in the blue spectrum will appear entirely blue. Those that reflect only light in the green spectrum will appear entirely green. If an object only absorbs and does not reflect light, that object appears black. Lastly, if an object could somehow deflect and bend light such that the light hit surrounding objects instead, that object would be invisible.

Sight as a sense depends therefore on the existence of both light and eyes. Thus, an environment that lacks either or both of these things can allow for no kind of sight. Figure 8.1 is a demonstration of this principle: It shows a UDK level that features no light source at all. Figure 8.1 is intended to be a non–text-based justification of lighting—an explanation of how lighting is critically important to video games and, more specifically, to video-game graphics. In short, no amount of graphic detail and artistic ability can be seen or witnessed in a game without the presence of a light source.

The terms *lighting* and *illumination* are often used interchangeably in everyday language to refer to the totality of lights in an environment and to their effects. In computer graphics, however, their meanings are more restricted. The term *illumination* refers strictly to the ability of light to make things visible or brighter. Thus, a light bulb (when switched on) is said to *illuminate* the room because it makes the objects of the room visible. The extent to which an environment is

Figure 8.1
This is what a level without lighting looks like.

illuminated is the extent to which it is made visible by its light sources. In contrast, the definition of *lighting* is wider in scope, referring to illumination *plus* the aesthetic and artistic qualities that result from the configuration of lights—that is, the way in which the properties of light (lights and darks, brightness, angles, color, shadows, etc.) can create mood and atmosphere and can evoke emotions and feelings. Based on these definitions, then, not all environments with illumination have lighting, but all environments with lighting have some degree of illumination.

Before you can progress further with lighting and create UDK levels that have lighting, you must consider light theory in more detail as it relates to computer graphics. The next section starts to focus on that theory.

The Additive Color Space (RGB)

In the UDK and in computer graphics in general, the term *light source* refers to any object that can and does cast light into a scene in the form of rays. Examples include light bulbs, light tubes, the sun, lamps, candles, and more. Those rays leave their source of illumination in a straight line and have the ability to illuminate any surfaces with which they come into contact. (More details on how light rays work are considered in the next section of this chapter.)

Any light source can cast an illumination of a specific color. In computer graphics, the color cast by any light is represented by the additive color space, in which red, green, and blue are the primary colors. A *color space* is a mathematical model or system that defines a range of colors in which each color can be uniquely identified using a number. A simple color space (not the one used by computer lighting) might define four colors, with each color numbered sequentially using the cardinal numbers—for example, red=1, blue=2, green=3, and yellow=4.

An *additive color space* is one in which colors are produced by way of addition. Additive color spaces are suitable for lighting because lights give out color, or *add* color to an environment. The additive color space used by almost all video games is the RGB color space, so named because the core colors (primary colors) of the space are red, green, and blue. To say that these colors are the primary colors is to say that every other color in the color space is derived from these three. That is, the three primary colors can be combined in varying degrees to produce all the other colors in the color space. That means the color of light has three components. It is the result of the mixing of three primary intensities. The first is the red intensity, the second is the green, and the third is the blue. For this reason, every color in the RGB space can be expressed numerically as a ratio of intensities—the ratio of red to green to blue.

Numbers in the RGB space are therefore three-component numbers in the form (R, G, B). Table 5.1 in Chapter 5, "Materials, Textures, and UV Mapping," lists some of the most common colors in RGB form.

In an additive color space, rays from lights of different colors can be mixed together to produce light of a different color. For example, if three equally sized light bulbs of different color (one red, one green, and one blue) were overlapped exactly at the center of a room and cast their illumination with equal intensity, the resultant light would be white because white is represented in RGB as (255,255,255). (See Figure 8.2.) If the blue bulb were suddenly extinguished, the light color in the room would turn yellow (255, 255, 0). That's because the blue component was removed and because red mixed with green results in yellow. If the red bulb were then extinguished, the light would become green (0, 255, 0). And if the green bulb were extinguished, the room would turn dark from a lack of illumination (0,0,0), as shown in Figure 8.1. The point is, light sources emit their illumination in color, and they tint and shade the surfaces that they intersect. Further, their intensity can be blended with illuminations from other lights, and this blending changes the color of the illumination. The colors of lights are mixed and blended together in RGB in exactly the same way as RGB colors can be created through the mixing of channels and the blending of layers using Photoshop and other pixel based photo-editing applications.

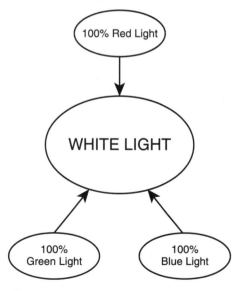

Figure 8.2
The color space of computer-generated lighting.

ILLUMINATION: DIRECT AND INDIRECT

Earlier, the term *illumination* was defined as the capacity of light to make things visible. Thus, an object that can be seen is said to be illuminated. That object can be seen because RGB-colored rays of light emitted from a light source have come into contact with the object and eventually bounced their way to the light-receptive cells of the eye, which the brain then translates and processes into the phenomenon of vision, or sight.

The mathematical models—the sets of algorithms—used to calculate the way in which light rays bounce around the surfaces of an environment after being emitted from a light source and before reaching the eye are known as *illumination models*. The purpose of an illumination model is *not* to determine what an observer can actually see in an environment from a particular position or perspective. Rather, its purpose is to determine at a global and impersonal level the extent to which every surface (whether in the line of sight or not) is illuminated based on all the light sources and the trajectories of the rays from those sources. The illumination model is in essence a simulator. First, it accepts all light sources as its input. Second, based on its inputs, it calculates which surfaces are illuminated given the position of the lights and the position and sizes of other surfaces, taking into consideration the shadows they might cast as well as the light rays they might obscure or block. Third, it outputs the results of its work as a comprehensive record or map that details the luminosity of the environment (the illumination of all surfaces). Figure 8.3 illustrates how an illumination model works.

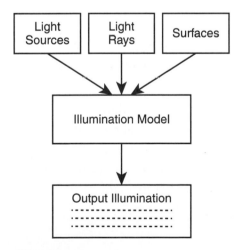

Figure 8.3
The illumination model calculates the extent to which surfaces are illuminated based on the trajectories of all light rays in the environment.

Video games (and, more generally, computer graphics) feature two main and mutually exclusive models of illumination: direct illumination and indirect illumination (also known as global illumination). The phrase *mutually exclusive* is used here to mean that a video game will not typically use both models to calculate illumination, but will use either one or the other depending on its needs and on the level of realism required. The point is that a game will make a decision to use one of these two models to generate an illumination solution for the surfaces, meshes, and actors in the game environment. As you shall see, the UDK allows developers to choose either a direct illumination model or an indirect illumination model for their level. The default (and recommended) model is indirect illumination.

Direct Illumination

One of the first illumination models used in video games, the direct illumination mode was designed with performance in mind. In other words, it was intended to offer a fast lighting solution that could run with as few performance penalties as possible on the majority of consumer hardware available at the time of its design. Consequently, a direct illumination model can calculate an illumination solution faster than most alternatives, but its results are among the least accurate when compared to real-world lighting.

In this model, the only surfaces that can be visible (that can receive illumination) are those that are *directly* accessible to the rays of light emitted from a light source. That is, the rays of light from a light source (the *incident rays*) must be able to make direct (non-bounced) contact with a surface for that surface to be visible. That means only surfaces that are facing the light source (that is, surfaces whose normals point toward the light source) and that are not obscured by other objects can receive illumination. All other surfaces appear completely black because they never make contact with an incident ray.

The direct illumination model differs dramatically from real-world lighting in that it allows for no bounced light (see Figure 8.4). That is, it does not allow light rays to reflect off surfaces to indirectly illuminate a scene. Although there are techniques that can be used in conjunction with direct illumination to simulate the effect of bounced light, the Unreal Engine uses the more realistic indirect illumination model by default. This model is considered next.

Indirect Illumination

As mentioned, the direct illumination model differs from real-world lighting primarily because it does not allow for bounced light. But what is bounced light? To

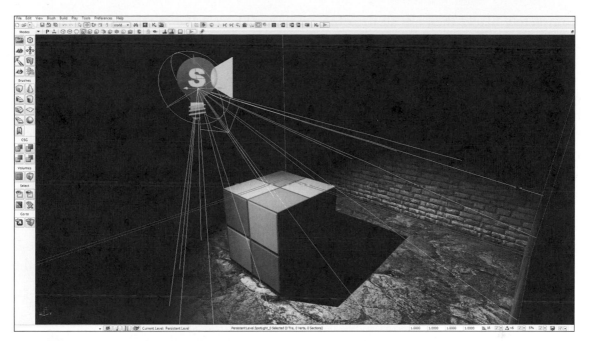

Figure 8.4
Direct illumination does not allow for light bouncing. In this model, only surfaces struck directly by rays from a light source are visible.

understand bounced light in more detail, consider a real-world environment in which the sun casts its golden, ultraviolet rays through the window of a restaurant and illuminates its interior. The interior consists of tables, chairs, menus, customers, meals, waiters, chefs, and so on. The interior contains two kinds of spaces that are not directly accessible to the sunlight—that is, regions that are not in the way of the sun:

- All the spaces that are *permanently* obscured from the sun due to the architecture of the restaurant or to the arrangement of its interior. Such spaces include the floor under the tables and chairs, the drawers and shelves behind the bar, the interior of cupboards, and the ceiling of the restaurant.

- All the spaces that are *temporarily* obscured from the sun due to the activity and movement in the restaurant, such as when the waitress casts a shadow over a table as she passes by the window.

Despite the many differences that exist among these spaces, there is a quality that all of them share (apart from their being out of the sun). Specifically, none of these spaces appears completely black. True, some spaces appear darker than others do because some are in shadow more than others are. But none (or almost none) are completely black; they are all to some extent visible. All the spaces in the restaurant interior not directly in the sunlight can still be seen, meaning they are still *illuminated*. It follows, then, that all visible surfaces in the restaurant interior are coming into contact with rays from a light source. Those spaces that are not directly in the sun but that are still visible are receiving their illumination indirectly, from rays that have been bounced, reflected, or refracted from the surrounding surfaces. These include surfaces commonly thought of as non reflective, such as brick walls, tables, chairs, and people.

The way in which a ray of light reacts when it strikes a surface depends on the angle at which the intersection occurs (see Figure 8.5) and on the type of surface it intersects (as defined by its material). Light can be either reflected or refracted from a surface. The latter means that the light will bend or change direction as it passes *through* a surface (such as glass or crystal), which will affect how objects behind the transparent surface are illuminated. Light is mostly reflected (bounced), however.

Reflections come in two forms:

- **Specular.** A specular reflection occurs when a ray of light strikes a smooth and reflective surface, such as a mirror or polished chrome. This type of reflection tends to produce a single ray of white light.

- **Diffuse.** A diffuse reflection occurs when a ray of light strikes a diffuse surface— that is, a surface that is rougher, such as wood, plastic, leather, some metals, food, organic materials, bone, flesh, cotton, wool, and others. Rays of light that strike diffuse surfaces tend to produce many other scattered and reflected rays due to the surface's rough form. These reflected rays are called *diffuse interreflections*.

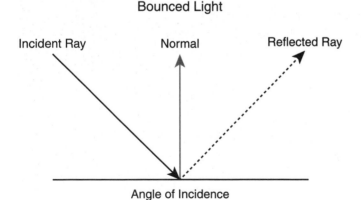

Bounced Light

Figure 8.5
Incoming light is known as an *incident ray*. It creates a bounced ray of light, known as *reflected light*. The intersection of the two rays is known as the *angle of incidence*.

Diffuse interreflections have two main properties:

- They are less intense than the original incident ray from which they branched.

- They inherit a subtle degree of the color of the surface from which they were reflected.

For these reasons, diffuse interreflections not only illuminate surrounding surfaces with less intensity than their parent ray, but they subtly color the surfaces with their inherited color. This explains why many pale white floor surfaces often appear to be colored close to their edges, where they meet a wall of different color. For example, the edges of a white floor that neighbor a red brick wall will often appear to be subtly shaded with red.

In short, then, indirect illumination can achieve greater realism in 3D scenes than direct illumination because it allows for reflected and refracted light. That is, the indirect illumination model calculates an illumination solution for an environment by considering not only the rays emitted directly from a light source, but also the illumination created by way of refractions and reflections, both specular and diffuse. (See Figure 8.6.)

Figure 8.6
Indirect illumination allows for light bouncing, meaning that light can bounce around an environment and illuminate surfaces not directly accessible to light sources. This increases realism.

The disadvantage of using an indirect illumination model is its price in terms of performance—that is, the time needed to reach an illumination solution. This is proportional to the complexity of the environment and to the total number of ray reflections that factor into the calculation. Most of the details of these lighting calculations are hidden from the developer by the Unreal Engine and Lightmass system; they calculate an illumination solution for you. Nevertheless, an understanding of indirect illumination can help you better use Lightmass to control the lighting in your levels.

Fakeiosity

It is often suggested that because direct illumination cannot allow for bounced light, it cannot hope to achieve any of the bounced lighting effects produced through indirect illumination (also called *radiosity* or *global illumination*). This, however, is false, as demonstrated by the bounced lighting effects in the many movies and games that were created before indirect illumination was widely available.

Games using a direct illumination model can take advantage of that model's properties to fake the effects of radiosity using a technique known as *fakeiosity*. Its performance benefits can be impressive. In short, fakeiosity requires the developer to insert into the level not only many lights where there should be light sources, but also many additional less-intense lights throughout the level to simulate bounced light. Fakeiosity is, in effect, a DIY global illumination.

Fakeiosity has been used in many games and for many reasons, but it does typically have the disadvantage of requiring a lot of tweaking and adjustment to produce the intended results. For this reason, many UDK developers stick with the Unreal Lightmass system. Fakeiosity is not considered further in this book; those interested in learning more about this technique might consider reading *Essential CG Lighting Techniques with 3ds Max* by Darren Brooker.

NORMAL MAPPING: DETAIL LIGHTING

As mentioned, the Unreal Engine can help increase the realism of the lighting in game levels by way of the indirect illumination model, which more closely approximates the effects of real-world lighting than the direct illumination model. The indirect illumination model calculates the extent to which every surface in a level is illuminated (or not), taking into consideration the position and orientation of all light sources, the trajectories of light rays, and the positions, sizes, and orientations of all surfaces. The primary challenge facing a programmer of such an illumination model is calculating the illumination of all surfaces without placing unrealistic demands on the computing hardware. For example, what is the optimal way to determine whether a surface comes into contact with light rays? What is the optimal way to calculate the variation in shading across a surface, taking into consideration the illumination, occlusion, and shadow casting of the environment? These questions are critical for an illumination model aiming to simulate real-world lighting.

It is important to remember that the illumination of a surface is not an all-or-nothing matter. A surface is neither completely illuminated nor completely *not* illuminated. Illumination is a matter of degree, and not kind. Illumination is a *continuous* rather than a discrete property insofar as some surfaces can be more or less illuminated than others. For example, the roof surface of a house can receive more illumination than the walls that are in shadow, but both the roof and the walls are still said to be illuminated. Not only that, different parts of the same surface can be more or less illuminated than other parts. For example, some parts of a wall can be in shadow while others are not. In short, shading across a surface can vary dramatically and is a function of the light sources, light rays, and other surfaces in the environment. The illumination model must calculate this shading for every surface as realistically as possible, in a way that is feasible given current computing hardware.

One of the earliest solutions to the problem of calculating a continuous illumination across the surfaces of 3D video games was vertex-based lighting. *Vertex-based lighting* is a system or an algorithm that can work in conjunction with either the direct or the indirect illumination model. It tries to determine how much light is received by a polygonal surface through its vertices. Specifically, the vertex-based lighting method works by cycling through every vertex of a polygon, testing for the total number of intersecting light rays. The algorithm considers both the intensity and the origin of those rays. The result of this process is that each vertex of every polygon is assigned a decimal value between 0 and 1 (known as a *weight*) that describes the vertex's exposure to light—that is, how much light reaches the vertex. The value 0 indicates black (no light), and 1 indicates white (fully bright). Each surface is then shaded through a method of linear interpolation, known as *Gouraud shading*. This shading acts as the illumination for the surface. That is, the surface is shaded (or illuminated) continuously using a gradient fill that blends between each of the polygon's vertices, as shown in Figure 8.7. In this way, the shading for every polygonal surface in the level is generated.

Vertex-based lighting presents two problems in achieving realistic lighting, both intimately related to the fact that surfaces in video games are fundamentally distinct in their composition from real-world surfaces. (Specifically, surfaces in video games are either three- or four-sided, and are composed entirely from vertices and edges.) The first of the two problems is that the exposure of a surface to light can be measured only at the surface's vertices, or corners. This is a problem because there are many different ways in which a light source can illuminate the central regions of a surface

Vertex Based Lighting

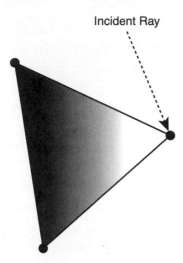

Figure 8.7
Calculating surface shading through vertex-based lighting and Gouraud shading.

without illuminating its corner points—for example, a torch light shining at the center of a wall, as illustrated in Figure 8.8. Surfaces that receive no illumination at the vertices will render entirely black because their shading is a gradient fill between only black and non-illuminated end points.

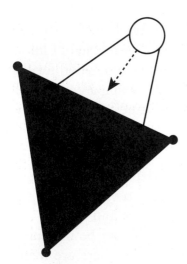

Figure 8.8
The problems of vertex-based lighting. Light that does not intersect the vertices of a polygon will cause that polygon to render black.

The second problem is that Gouraud Shading, being a method of gradient fill, does not closely approximate real-world shading. Additionally, polygonal surfaces, being the construction of a mathematical model, do not closely approximate real-world surfaces. Polygonal surfaces are blind to the details and texture present in a real-world surface because the computer-generated surface produced by edges and vertices is perfectly flat. Gouraud shading, too, is blind to the details and texture of a surface in that it calculates a surface's shading exclusively based on its vertices. It does not consider any of its intervening details. In contrast, the shading of a real-world surface is the product not of its corner points, but of the way in which light rays strike across every part of the surface at a practically limitless number of incident angles. The texture of a surface—its tiny notches and chinks and its roughness and angularity—means that no two parts of the surface ever receive illumination at the same angles, no two parts of the surface ever receive the same amount light, and light bounces differently from part to part. Consequently, real-world lighting produces practically limitless and continuous variation in the shading of a surface.

Computer-generated lighting must aim to approximate that non-uniform variation in lighting across a surface. Gouraud shading was one attempt to do that, but another and more recent and successful attempt is through the technique of normal mapping *and* per-pixel lighting. These techniques represent more recent attempts by game developers and mathematicians to overcome some of the main problems in achieving realistic lighting in games. These problems arise from vertex-based lighting and more generally from the way in which polygonal surfaces are constitutionally distinct from real-world surfaces.

Per-pixel lighting differs from vertex-based lighting in that it calculates the illumination of a surface by comparing light rays not to the vertices of the surface, but to every one of the rendered pixels on the surface. That means surfaces illuminated by the per-pixel lighting model are sensitive to light at a pixel level. It follows, then, that the shading for a surface in this model is not the result of Gouraud shading, which blindly interpolates between vertices to create a gradient, but is the result of a lighting calculation made on a pixel-by-pixel basis. For this reason, per-pixel lighting does not share the interpolation problems inherent to vertex-based lighting. Let's return to the example of a torch shining a small cone of light at the center of a wall. The vertex-based lighting model was found to be lacking in this case because it would render the wall entirely black because the torchlight does not intersect any of the wall's corner vertices. The per-pixel solution, however, is immune from this problem because lighting is calculated for each pixel of the surface. That means surface pixels intersecting the torch light will be illuminated, and those not intersecting will not be illuminated. From this, it can be concluded that the per-pixel model can allow for more realistic lighting, but with a computational expense. Per-pixel lighting is more computationally expensive than vertex-based lighting because there are typically many more pixels per surface than vertices.

Because per-pixel lighting calculates the illumination for a surface on a per-pixel basis, it can read from or work with the pixels of the material that are applied to the surface. This is significant because it means that additional information can be encoded into the pixels of material channels to further influence the way in which lighting shades a surface—that is, the way lighting reacts to each pixel. This concept is the driving idea behind normal mapping, which can work only with per-pixel lighting methods. The purpose of normal mapping is to allow developers to use a map to define the details of a surface—its roughness, jaggedness, its dents and notches, and so on—without having to actually model that detail with polygons. The Unreal Engine supports normal mapping. That means each material has a *normal channel* (alongside its other channels, such as the diffuse and specular channels), which can be connected to a 2D texture map, known as the *normal map*, as shown in Figure 8.9.

The purpose of the normal map (see Figure 8.10 for an example) is to define the surface detail of a surface or mesh. It is much like any other texture map in that it

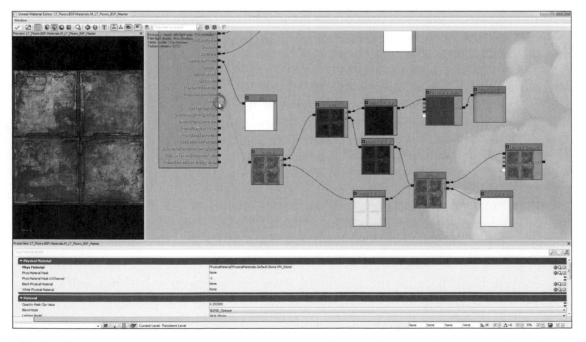

Figure 8.9
The normal channel being connected to a normal map using the Unreal Material Editor.

Figure 8.10
A normal map approximating the surface detail of a wall.

is a two-dimensional rectangle of RGB pixels. But it is also distinct in that, unlike the diffuse map, it is not intended to be viewed by gamers on its own. Rather, the RGB values for every pixel in the normal map define the XYZ components, respectively, of a normal vector, one normal vector per pixel of the map. These pixels (normals) are mapped onto the associated geometry through mapping coordinates and define the normal vector at the mapped position on the mesh. Each pixel (normal) of the normal map represents the three-dimensional direction in which the corresponding pixel is facing, which affects how much light it can receive (given the position of lights sources in the level). Pixels that point toward a light receive more illumination than those pointing away. Indeed, the brightness of a pixel is to some extent an expression of how far its normal is orientated toward an incident ray. In short, normal maps offer developers per-pixel control over the way light reacts to a surface. Specifically, developers can set some pixels x in the normal map to point in one direction, and can set other pixels y to point in a different direction. This difference in direction between set x and set y means that set x will receive a different degree of illumination from set y.

This power to set normals and to change levels of illumination can be harnessed to create the *appearance* of details on a flat polygonal surface where no such details exist.

Figure 8.11
A material without normal mapping.

Figure 8.12
A material with normal mapping.

This is because much of the detail on a surface is created through contrast in luminance—that is, contrast between lights and darks. Lights and darks are created by lighting, with dark areas being those areas less accessible to light and light areas being those more accessible to light. See Figure 8.11 and Figure 8.12 for a comparison between the light effects created by a material without normal mapping and the light effects created by a material with normal mapping.

The chief purpose of this section was to define what normal mapping is, how it works, and why it is necessary. Normal mapping is a texturing technique that works with per-pixel lighting. It follows, then, that a scene without per-pixel lighting cannot support normal mapping. For a game to have normal mapping, its lighting system must be able to support per-pixel lighting, and for that per-pixel lighting to be realistic, the lighting system must support indirect illumination.

Having accepted this, another question might arise: How is it possible, given the limitations of consumer hardware, for a video-game engine to calculate indirect illumination using a per-pixel lighting system on a frame-by-frame basis? Surely, so many frequent calculations (30 times per second or more) would bring the game to a grinding halt and perhaps even crash on most home computers or gaming consoles. Lighting systems such as these must exist only in the dreams of game developers and technology evangelists! The answer to this question is, in fact, yes. Most contemporary consumer hardware *cannot* support an indirect illumination model with per-pixel lighting on a frame-by-frame basis. But, not all lighting calculations need to occur on a frame-by-frame basis. It is, in fact, possible to pre-calculate most of the level lighting at design time in one long pass, before the game is even played. This is the job of Lightmass, which makes indirect illumination and per-pixel lighting possible in UDK games. This component is the focus of the next section.

UNREAL LIGHTMASS: LIGHTMAPPING

Unreal Lightmass is the official name given to the UDK software component responsible for calculating a lighting solution for a level using indirect illumination and per-pixel lighting. The term *Lightmass* in essence refers to a set of algorithms and processes that together accept a UDK level as their input (including the level's lights, actors, CSG surfaces, and so on) and calculate the illumination, shadows, and occlusion of all surfaces in that level.

Lightmass is not intended to provide a real-time lighting solution. It is not intended, for example, to be run on every frame of a game to calculate the latest lighting solution for the level being played. Doing that would be prohibitive in terms of performance due to the quantity, complexity, and frequency of the calculations that must be made. Rather, Lightmass is almost always run by developers at design time from the UDK Editor to pre-calculate the level lighting—that is, to calculate the lighting for the level *before* the game is played. That means a game ships not with the Lightmass system itself, but with its output as an asset within the game.

Note

> Pre-calculating the level lighting in this way is known in the industry as *baking*; thus, the lighting data that results from Lightmass is said to be *baked* into the level.

As mentioned, the purpose of the Lightmass system is to calculate a complete lighting solution for a level based on its inputs. This involves working out the extent to which every pixel of every surface receives illumination—that is, the extent to which each surface comes into contact with light rays. The output of the Lightmass system is the solution itself—the data that constitutes the illumination for the level. This data should be everything that makes it possible for the Unreal Engine to convert a level from a non-illuminated form to an illuminated form. This data (the output of Lightmass) takes on a pixel-based form, being the result of per-pixel lighting. Specifically, the Lightmass system outputs a set of 2D RGB texture maps called *lightmaps*—one lightmap per actor.

To understand lightmaps and their role in baked lighting, it is necessary first to consider how the graphical appearance of an object in a level—such as a wall, door, creature, and so on—is produced. At least three main factors determine how an object appears in a level:

- **The geometry of the object.** *Geometry* here refers to the object's composition in terms of vertices, edges, and faces, which define its structure or form.

- **The object's material.** This is composed of a network of texture maps and nodes, which define how the surface of an object should be shaded under lighting neutral conditions. The purpose of the material is to define all the graphically significant features of a surface that are the result of the object's intrinsic properties—that is, the things that *belong* to the surface. The roughness of a brick wall in a material, for example, is the result of the physical properties of the brick—the result of both how the brick is made and the materials from which it is made.

- **How light rays are cast about an environment from light sources.** This factor affects the shading of a surface in terms of lights and darks. It differs in a fundamental respect from the previous two factors (mesh and material) in that it describes a phenomenon *external* to the object itself—an influence that is not *part of* the object but that *acts on* the object. In essence, lighting is an environmental influence on the appearance of the object, affecting the object's appearance in three main ways:
  - Lighting affects the color of pixels on a surface. Red lights affect the brightness of a surface in the red channel, green in the green channel, and blue in the blue channel.
  - Lighting affects the illumination of a surface in terms of lights and darks. Areas of a surface that receive more intense illumination appear brighter than areas that receive less intense illumination.

- Lighting casts shadows—or rather, shadows (a lack of illumination) appear on an object when other objects obscure or block rays from a light source.

So What Is a Lightmap?

The work of the lightmap is equivalent to the third factor affecting the appearance of a surface (along with an object's constitution and its material): lighting, or the external or environmental influence on an object. A *lightmap* is a two-dimensional color texture—a rectangle of RGB pixels with no alpha channel or transparency. It defines all of the graphical detail *added* to a surface by the culminative effects of lighting in the level. These details take the form of coloration, illumination, and shadowing.

How Does Lightmapping Work?

The term *lightmapping* refers to the practice of using lightmaps to create the lighting for a level. The ultimate goal of lightmapping in a game is to blend each lightmap as a layer onto its corresponding surface and over its material to make that surface appear affected by lighting (see Figure 8.13).

Every object in the level typically has its own lightmap. Thus, every object is typically affected by lighting. Like a material, the lightmap is associated with a surface or mesh through its mapping coordinates. Generally, each mesh has two sets of mapping coordinates: one for a material and one for a lightmap. The lightmap mapping coordinates detail how the pixels of a 2D lightmap correspond to the pixels of the three-dimensional surface.

Both the Unreal Lightmass system and the Unreal Engine use lightmapping. Lightmass uses lightmapping to *output* its results to a set of lightmaps by way of lightmap mapping coordinates; the Unreal Engine uses lightmapping to input the same set of

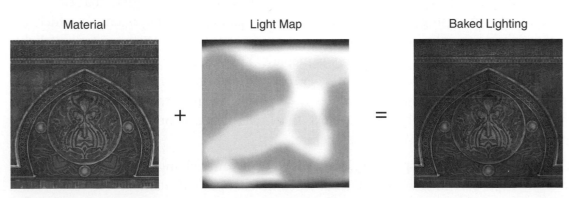

Figure 8.13
A lightmap applied to a surface.

lightmaps onto the same set of surfaces through their coordinates to make them appear illuminated in the game.

In short, lightmaps act as a second, specially blended material that shades surfaces to make them appear illuminated. Both the Unreal Engine and Lightmass use lightmapping. The ultimate purpose of Lightmass is to output a set of lightmaps. Because the lighting of a level is baked in this way through mapping, it is possible to achieve indirect illumination and per-pixel lighting in games.

STATIC, DYNAMIC, AND COMPOSITE DYNAMIC LIGHTING

With lightmapping, the majority of expensive lighting calculations can be avoided on a per-frame basis. That's because it allows a set of pre-baked lightmaps from Lightmass to be blended onto the surfaces of a level to make the surfaces appear illuminated. A technical problem arises with such pre-calculated (or baked) lighting, however: Lighting calculated before gameplay through lightmaps cannot easily account for dynamic changes in lighting conditions during gameplay.

Lightmaps generated in advance by Lightmass might be accurate and realistic at the time of their generation, but will become invalidated the moment events occur during gameplay that change the way light affects the level. For example, some artificial lights can be turned on and off to add and remove illumination to and from a level. Further, some lights, such as torch lights and car headlights, can move, casting new illumination and shadows in new directions. Some lights, such as disco lights and siren lights, can change color, affecting the hue of their illumination. Furthermore, changes in the position, orientation, and shape of objects can have implications for lighting because objects can influence the shadows cast and the way light rays bounce around a level.

The point is, a slew of changes can happen in a level during gameplay that can invalidate the lightmapping that was generated prior gameplay. The extent to which the baked lighting is invalidated is to some degree proportional to the extent of light-relevant change that occurs during gameplay. You could argue that any extent of physical change in the level is light relevant, however small. In fact, it could be said that any amount of change invalidates the *entirety* of any previous lighting solution that uses indirect illumination because the light rays no longer fall and reflect at exactly the same incident angles as before.

This is true technically speaking, but the *effects* of some changes are more noticeable to human observers than others. That is, some changes can damage the realism and believability of the level more severely than others. The shadow cast by a moving car, for example, is likely to be more noticeable than the subtle effects of light rays reflecting from a wall. So, while it is true that change in the level can invalidate the lighting solution, the extent to which a solution becomes invalidated to a game developer is the extent to which the lighting ceases to be *believable*.

To respond to the obstacles facing realistic pre-baked lighting posed by light-relevant changes in real time, UDK developers have introduced two additional types of lighting: standard dynamic lighting and dynamic composite lighting.

Static Lighting

Static lighting refers to the pre-calculated (baked) lighting generated by Lightmass through lightmapping. It is called *static* because it is especially useful for lighting objects that typically do not move: walls, floors, tables, chairs, trees, and more. The defining feature of static lighting is that it is calculated before gameplay, never during gameplay. It therefore has the potential of being the most realistic and accurate form of lighting that the Unreal lighting system allows.

Dynamic Lighting

Dynamic lighting stands in stark contrast to static lighting in that it is calculated not in advance but in real time, on a per-frame basis. Lighting that is calculated at run time on a per-frame basis is said to be calculated *dynamically*—hence the name *dynamic lighting*. It is important to mention that dynamic lighting is *not* intended to be a replacement for static lighting. Instead, it is intended to work alongside static lighting—to complement it. Dynamic lighting is used to patch up the lighting of a level in areas and for objects that require more than static lighting.

Dynamic light sources work much like static light sources, except they are calculated in real time and support the direct illumination model instead of the indirect illumination model. Dynamic lights can be used to realistically illuminate and cast shadows for moving objects, and can be used to represent lights that move, rotate, change color, and toggle off and on. Despite their advantages in terms of realism and their capacity for change, dynamic lights are computationally very expensive. Hence, for performance reasons, it is not recommended that any single object in a level be affected by more than two dynamic lights at any one time.

Dynamic Composite Lighting

The problem with using static lighting exclusively is that it does not allow for real-time changes in the lighting conditions of the level. Dynamic lights are one solution to this problem, but they are computationally expensive—so much so that very few of them can be used in a level that is intended to perform well on most computers.

The expense of dynamic lighting increases exponentially with the number of dynamic lights and with the number of objects to be affected by those lights. That means dynamic lighting is in practice a prohibitive lighting solution for levels that feature many moving or changing parts or that feature a lot of moving or changing light sources.

In an attempt to solve the performance issues associated with dynamic lighting, UDK developers have introduced dynamic composite lighting. This is an optimized, cheaper form of dynamic lighting that can be applied to all changeable objects in a level. It is meant to complement static lighting and, in most cases, to replace dynamic lighting.

Dynamic composite lighting is cheaper but less accurate than most other lighting forms. Specifically, it works to illuminate dynamic objects (objects that change) by using an approximation of the surrounding static light sources. It does this by effectively creating a moveable dynamic light that follows changeable objects and is an average of all the surrounding static lights.

Note

The under-the-hood details of the dynamic composite light are beyond the scope of this book.

In practice, most game developers always use static lighting for the majority of the level lighting, and then use dynamic composite lighting for objects and lights that must change. Dynamic lights are typically used as a last resort in cases where changeable objects must receive lighting that is more accurate than that achieved by dynamic composite lighting.

UDK LIGHT TYPES: POINT, SPOT, AND DIRECTIONAL

It is time to move away from light theory as it relates to game development and to look at the different kinds of light sources supported by the UDK (the objects used to cast light rays) and at how to add those sources as influential light actors to a level. Before moving on to that, however, it is worthwhile to summarize everything you've learned so far about light theory:

■ Levels without light sources appear completely black. Light sources make vision possible.

■ Light sources cast linear and RGB-colored rays of light into a level. These rays can bounce from diffuse and specular surfaces. Light sources are therefore emitters of light.

- The UDK lighting system supports three kinds of lighting models: static, dynamic, and dynamic composite. Static is preferred in most situations, dynamic composite is preferred in situations involving moving and changing actors, and dynamic is used only as a last resort.

- Unreal Lightmass is a set of algorithms and processes that bake realistic static lighting for a level in the form of lightmaps. Lightmass calculates lighting using indirect illumination and per-pixel lighting. Using normal mapping, the Unreal Engine blends lightmaps onto the surfaces of geometry to make them appear illuminated at run time.

- Every object in the level has its own lightmap, and a lightmap is associated with the surface of a mesh through mapping coordinates.

With that information in mind, press Ctrl+Shift+F to open the Content Browser. Then select the Actor Classes Browser, as shown in Figure 8.14. Notice the Lights option in the hierarchy. From here, you can drag and drop lights into the scene. (More details follow in upcoming sections.)

Figure 8.14
You can access lights from the Actor Classes Browser.

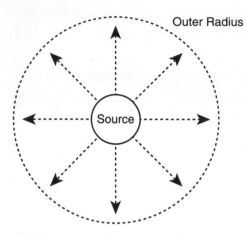

Point Light

Outer Radius

Source

Figure 8.15
Point lights, which cast light in all directions, are often used to simulate artificial light sources such as light bulbs.

Point Lights

The first light type to consider in the UDK is the *point light*, so named because it is an invisible spherical surface that casts rays of light outward in all directions, as shown in Figure 8.15. The point light has a position in 3D space, marking the center point of the source. Both its rotation and scaling values have no effect.

Figure 8.16 shows a point light's Properties panel. As you can see, the point features an extensive range of properties divided into several categories, including Point Light Component, Lightmass, and Light Component.

Note

When a light is dropped into the scene, the UDK illuminates the level using a preview lighting model to approximate how the final lighting will appear in the level (as shown in Figure 8.16). The final lighting for the level, complete with indirect illumination, can be generated using Lightmass. The steps for doing this appear later in this chapter.

As shown in Figure 8.17, point lights have several general properties, which apply to all other light types. These common properties are found in the Light Component section of the Properties panel. Some of them are listed and described in Table 8.1.

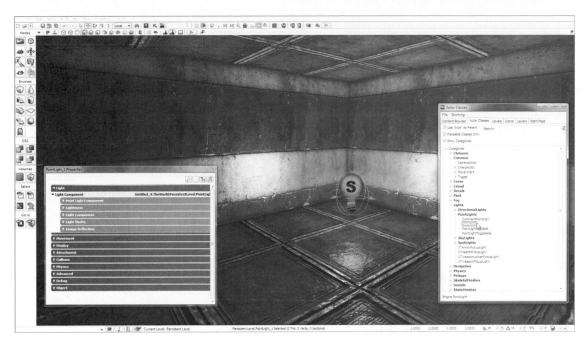

Figure 8.16
A point light, with its Properties panel open.

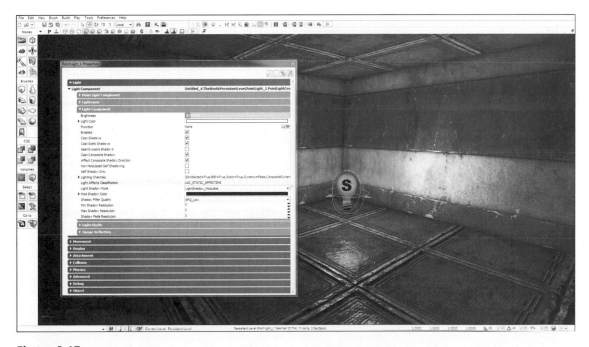

Figure 8.17
Common light properties.

Table 8.1   Common Light Properties

Property	Description
Brightness	A decimal multiplier value that controls the light brightness. The default setting is 1.
Light Color	An RGB value that specifies the color of light rays emitted from the source.
Enabled	A Boolean value. True means the light is on; false means the light is off.
Cast Shadows	A Boolean value indicating whether the light casts shadows.

Table 8.2   Point Light Properties

Property	Description
Radius	Specifies the radius of a surrounding sphere inside which light falls off to 0.
Falloff Exponent	Controls how light inside the sphere falls off from 100 percent to 0. The default is 2.

Note

Some of the properties for the point light—and for all lights—are *legacy* components, meaning they apply only to older versions of the UDK and are provided in the latest release only to support levels created in those versions.

The point light features a decimal Brightness property, which is a multiplier that sets the intensity of the rays emitted from the light source. The Color property can specify a bold RGB color to be applied to the rays, and the Enabled property specifies whether the light is switched on or off. The point light also has some specific properties not shared by other light types, which pertain to the structure of the point light. These properties, which appear in the Point Light Component section of the Properties panel, are described in Table 8.2.

Spot Lights

A spot light consists of two main components:

- **Light source.** As with the point light, the light source represents the surface that emits colored light rays into the scene.

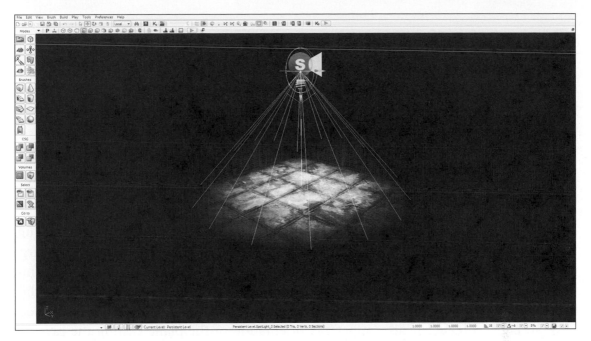

Figure 8.18
A spot light.

- **Light cone.** The light cone defines a conic volume extended from the light source that restricts or limits the rays cast by the source. In short, the light cone represents the volume inside which the spot light casts rays, with the rays terminating at the edges of the cone. In a direct illumination model, nothing outside the cone can be illuminated by the spot light.

Figure 8.18 shows a spot light. Notice that the region outside the cone is entirely black. This suggests that the scene (using the UDK preview lighting) features a direct illumination model.

The spot light is the cheapest of all light types in terms of computational expense. It has a position and rotation in 3D space, and its Properties panel features a range of properties for tweaking the light. The spot light can be controlled by a light component (featuring the properties common to all light types, listed in Table 8.1), a point light component (offering further point light–specific properties for defining the light source, listed in Table 8.2), and a spot light component, which includes properties specific to spot lights. The two main spot light–specific properties are detailed in Table 8.3.

Table 8.3 Spot Light Properties	
Property	**Description**
Inner Cone	Specifies the radius of the interior volume inside which light is at full intensity.
Outer Cone	Specifies the radius of outer volume inside which light falls off from 100 percent to 0 percent.

Directional Lights

Directional light is used mostly to simulate exterior light sources, including the sun, moon, and other celestial bodies. A directional light represents an infinitely large plane acting as a light source that casts parallel rays of light from its surface into the level. For this reason, the position and scale of the light are irrelevant; neither value changes how the light affects the level. The rotation of the light, however, does have an effect, because it determines the orientation of the plane casting the rays.

You can tweak directional lights via the Properties panel. It features all the properties shared by other types of lights as well as a specific directional light property: Trace Distance. The Trace Distance property is a decimal value that controls the length in Unreal world units of the parallel rays cast by the light. The default value for this property is 1000000000.000000, which is greater than the extents of almost any level that could be made in the UDK. Thus, in practice, the directional light casts its rays in parallel throughout the length of the level. Figure 8.19 shows a directional light.

PROJECT: LIGHTING CUBE PARK

The previous sections of this chapter concerned themselves mainly with the theoretical foundations of video-game lighting and with the different kinds of lights available in the Unreal Engine: point lights, spot lights, and directional lights. This section marks the beginning of the project work for this chapter. Here, the theoretical concepts are applied and your understanding of them is consolidated through their use.

The culmination of this project will be a Daliesque, abstract environment, called the *cube park*, featuring basic geometric primitives (see Figure 8.20). The work for this project consists in illuminating the environment using a variety of light types and lighting techniques. Specifically, the project will use a colored spot light, a directional light to represent moonlight, and indirect illumination to increase the realism of the level. This section will also introduce such features as light channels, light functions, and emissive lighting.

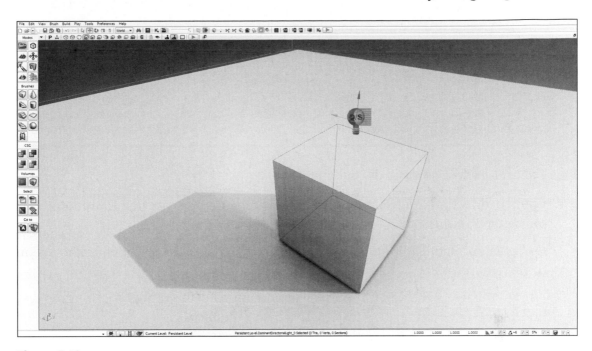

Figure 8.19
A directional light.

Figure 8.20
An aerial view of the completed level.

Note

Some of the lighting tasks performed in this level might seem contrived. That is, they are the kinds of tasks that belong in a tutorial or classroom, but not in a real game. Despite their simple or abstract nature, however, it is important to remember the purpose of these tasks: to demonstrate how to use lights to do things in a level. What you can do with lights varies from level to level, but the way of using lights remains unchanged. The skills for using lights are transferable; they can be absorbed here in a pure form by way of simple examples and then deployed elsewhere to achieve more specific ends.

This lighting project consists of four main steps:

1. Using a directional light to simulate moonlight for the exterior (outdoors) part of the environment

2. Using a spot light to illuminate and color part of the floor in the interior section of the environment

3. Using emissive lighting and indirect illumination to illuminate the interior section of the environment by way of an object's materials

4. Using a light function (that is, using a light as a projector) to project an image onto the wall of a cube primitive

Creating Moonlight

The lighting project will begin from a UDK level file that I have created, which can be found in the DM-Light_Project_01_start.udk companion file. This level, shown in Figure 8.21, represents the starting point from which work for the lighting project will begin. In essence, the project consists of adding lights to this level. The level contains static meshes with materials, BSP Brushes, and CSG, all covered earlier in this book.

The level features two sections: an outdoor environment and an interior environment. The outdoor environment consists of a large ground surface across which many giant cube meshes (TexPropCube) have been scattered, alongside a large shelter made from BSP Brushes. The interior of the shelter contains some wall light meshes (S_LT_Light_SM_Light01) and a pillar mesh (S_Column_01). This level is based on the standard moonlight template map. (If you prefer to create the map yourself as an exercise, you can do so. Open the File menu and choose the New command. Then, in the Choose a Map Template dialog box, click Night Lighting, as shown in Figure 8.22.)

The first lighting challenge for this map is to create the dominant light source for the exterior section of the map. This light source is known in the movie, photography,

Figure 8.21
Getting started on the lighting for the cube park. This level is loaded from the DM-Light_Project_01_start.udk file.

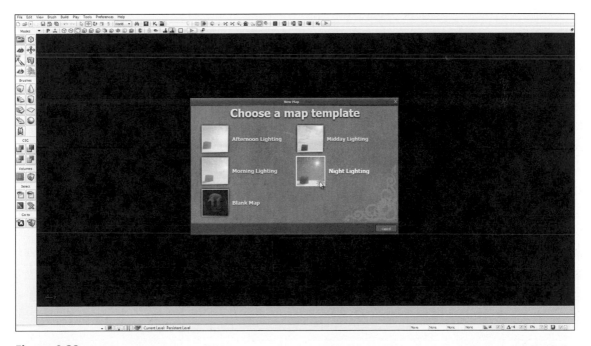

Figure 8.22
Creating the cube park map from scratch via the UDK night map template.

and games industries as the *key light* because it is the brightest, most prominent light source for a particular area. The key light is the main shadow-casting light, and determines the direction of the strongest shadows.

For this project, the key light source in the exterior section of the level will be the moon—or, more accurately, the indirect illumination of the sun, whose rays are reflected by the surface of the moon. The light actor to represent the moonlight—a dominant directional light—has already been created for you in the moon lightmap template. The dominant directional light, which is a type of directional light optimized for use as a key light source, is available from the Actor Classes Browser. It is not necessary to add a dominant light to this scene because one has already been created for you. You can, however, adjust the light's properties.

Note

No single area of a scene should be illuminated by more than one dominant light. That is, no two dominant lights should overlap in terms of their area of influence.

1. Select the dominant directional light using either the Perspective viewport or the Scene Browser (see Figure 8.23). Notice that the icon for the dominant light in the Perspective viewport features the letters D and S. The letter D indicates that

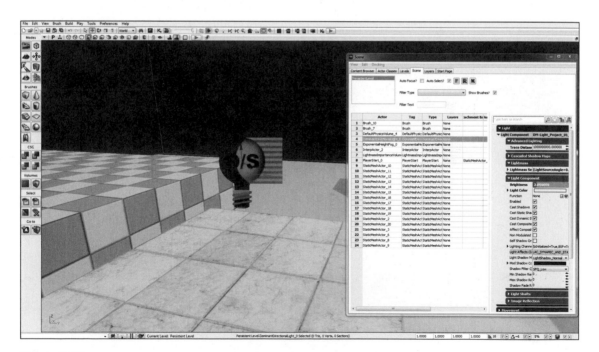

Figure 8.23
Selecting the key light source for the level exterior. This light represents the moon.

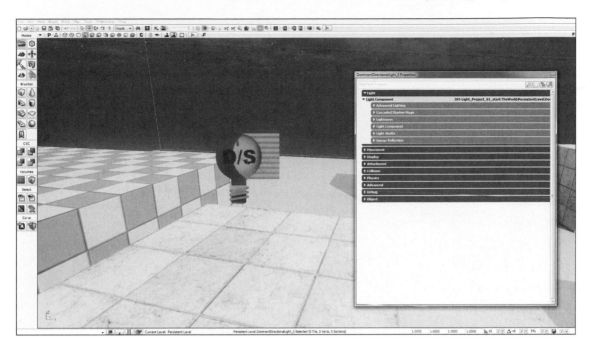

Figure 8.24
Examining the dominant directional light in the Properties panel.

the light affects dynamic objects (objects that move or change), and the letter S indicates that the light affects static objects (objects that do not move or change). That means this light will influence static objects with static lighting (through lightmapping) and will illuminate moving objects and cast shadows in real time through either dynamic lighting or dynamic composite lighting.

2. Press the F4 key to open the light's Properties panel, shown in Figure 8.24. Then click the Light Component bar. Notice that the Cast Shadows, Cast Static Shadows, Cast Dynamic Shadows, and Cast Composite Shadow properties are enabled, as shown in Figure 8.25. The three latter properties are dependent on the first property. That is, if the first property is false, then the remaining three are false regardless of whether they are enabled. The final three values specify whether shadow casting is enabled for static, composite dynamic, and dynamic lighting, respectively. When all three types are enabled, the light will not cast all three types of shadows for every object in its reach, but rather will cast the most appropriate of the three on a per-object basis. There is an order of preference among the options; that is, a light will prefer to cast static shadows where possible, then composite dynamic, and then dynamic.

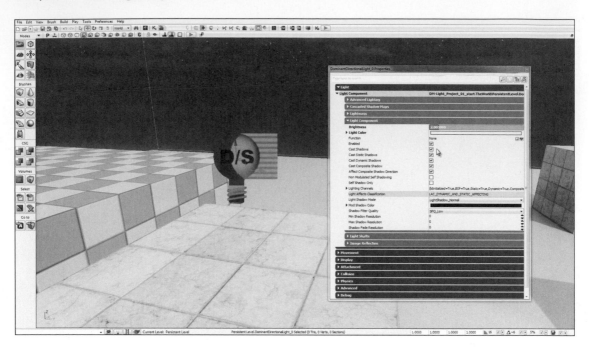

Figure 8.25
The shadow-casting properties of the dominant directional light.

Add a Spot Light to the Interior

In the next phase of the project, you will add illumination via a spot light to the interior of the shelter building. The shelter was constructed from a complex of two BSP Brushes. One, a hollowed box brush, acts as the shelter's walls, floors, and ceiling. The other, a subtractive brush, was used to punch a hole in one of the walls to act as the entrance and exit point. The shelter contains four mesh actors: three wall light meshes and one pillar mesh. As shown in Figure 8.26, the interior of the shelter is more or less dark except for the moonlight illumination that enters from outside through the open entrance. The purpose of the spot light to be added here will not be to illuminate the majority of the interior environment; that illumination will be added in a later section of this chapter through emissive lighting. Instead, the spot light will have a narrower and more eccentric purpose: coloring and illuminating the CSG surface directly beneath the pillar, without affecting the pillar itself.

This task presents a problem that is unique to video-game lights: selective lighting, or having a light affect only a subset of actors within its range. The solution to this

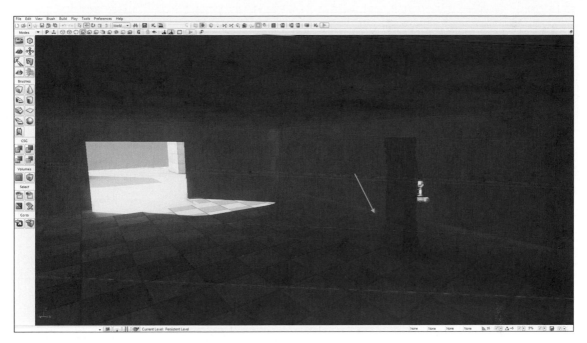

Figure 8.26
A spot light will be added to illuminate the floor surrounding the pillar but not the pillar itself. This will be achieved through light channels.

problem can be found in a UDK feature called *lighting channels*, as you shall see in the following steps:

1. Create a spot light in the scene. To do this, press Shift+N to deselect all actors and surfaces in the level. Then, press Ctrl+Shift+F to open the Content Browser. Click the Actors Classes tab and drag a spot-light object from the actor's hierarchy to the level through the Perspective viewport, releasing the mouse button over the point at which the spot light should be inserted. Using the transformation tools, adjust the position of the spot light so that it hovers above the pillar, casting its illumination downward onto the floor below (see Figure 8.27). Notice that the spot light illuminates the top of the pillar and casts a dynamic shadow on the floor. (It is currently a dynamic shadow because you have not yet used Lightmass to calculate static lighting through lightmaps.)

2. Open the spot light's Properties panel and tweak the light's cone size if required. The spot light must illuminate a circle of the floor around the pillar (refer to Figure 8.27). The color of the spot light is currently white, but it should be red. To change this, click the Light Color swatch to open the Select a Color dialog box, and choose the desired color, as shown in Figure 8.28.

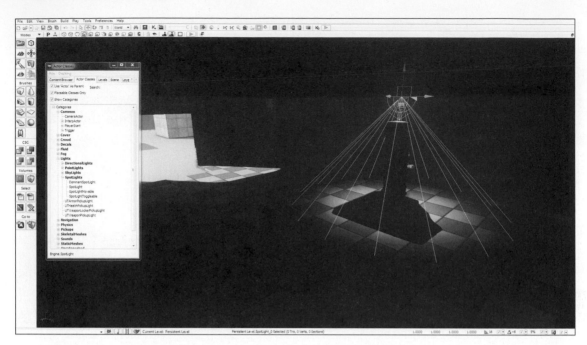

Figure 8.27
Positioning the spot light vertically above the pillar.

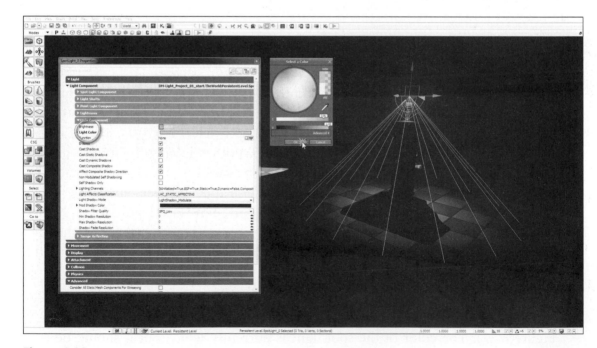

Figure 8.28
Changing the color of the spot light.

3. Currently, the light affects both the floor and the pillar, when it should affect only the floor. This is because both the floor and pillar fall within the cone of the spot light. To exclude the pillar from the spot light's influence, you can use light channels. Using light channels, both a light and an object can each be assigned one or more tags (that is labels, or identifiers). Only objects whose tags match those of the light will be affected by the light. So to exclude the pillar from the spot light through light channels, you must configure the tagging for both the spot light and the pillar to ensure that they do not match. To start, view the tags of the spot light. Open the spot light's Properties panel, click the Light Component bar, and click the Light Channels entry to reveal all the tags available. As shown in Figure 8.29, there is a wide selection of tags, most of which exist only to be checked or unchecked according to the needs of the developer. Tags assigned to the light are indicated with a checkmark. By default, the light is assigned to the BSP, Static, and Composite Dynamic tags. Leave the tagging alone for the spot light; the settings are fine as they are. Instead, you'll adjust the tagging for the static pillar mesh.

4. Select the pillar mesh. Then open its Properties panel, click the Light Component bar, and click the Light Channels entry to reveal the tagging options. That is, click Static Mesh Component, then Lighting, and then Lighting Channels.

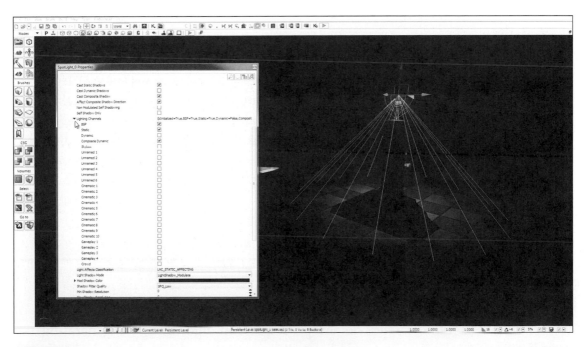

Figure 8.29
The light channels for the spot light.

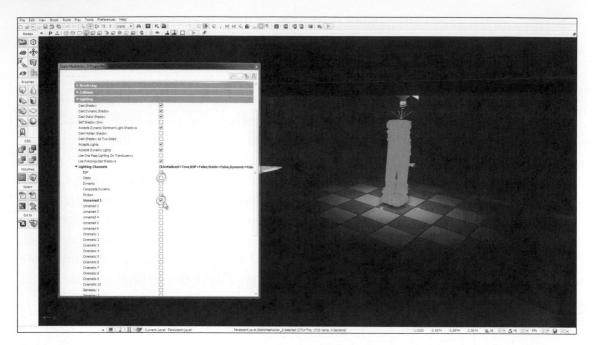

Figure 8.30
The pillar is excluded from the spot-light illumination due to a tagging mismatch.

5. Notice that both the spot light and the pillar mesh have the Static channel enabled; this is why the pillar is affected by the spot light. Note, however, that you cannot disable the Static channel right away. Objects must have at least one light channel enabled. Because the Static channel is the only channel enabled for the pillar, you must first enable a second channel before you disable it. Click the Unnamed 1 checkbox to select it; then uncheck the Static checkbox to disable that channel. This tagging mismatch between the spot light and pillar means the pillar will no longer be illuminated by the spot light, as shown in Figure 8.30.

Note

The level so far can be found in the DM-Light_Project_02_spot_chan.udk companion file.

Lightmass

As mentioned, *Lightmass* refers to the processes and algorithms for generating the static lighting of a level using an indirect illumination model and per-pixel lighting. The output of the Lightmass system is a set of pixel-based and color lightmaps describing the level illumination. These maps can be applied to all surfaces to make them appear illuminated at run time.

The Lightmass system is not a permanently active background process in the editor, and it is not run automatically. Instead, it must be invoked by the user when the static lighting for the level must be calculated. This is because Lightmass can take from a few seconds to a few minutes, hours, or even days to calculate the complete lighting for a level, depending on the complexity of the level and the power of the development hardware.

The fact that Lightmass does not run automatically, but must be run explicitly, means that the editor's viewports do not always display the final static lighting for a level. Instead, they often display rough, approximate preview lighting. The preview lighting is dynamic (calculated in real time) and uses a direct illumination model— hence it was possible to witness the illumination effects of the spot light (as added in the previous section) as soon as it was added to the scene. This was also why the static environment was not affected by the spot light's bounced light. The preview lighting exists primarily for the benefit of developers, to give them an idea of how the final lighting of the level might look without having to perform time-consuming Lightmass calculations. Preview lighting is, in essence, a draft form of lighting.

The level will not use its final, more realistic static lighting until Lightmass is run and its calculations are completed. The following steps discuss how to use Lightmass to build the static lighting for the level. Note that running Lightmass is typically one of the last things a developer does during level development. This is because every change to the level in terms of lights and geometry will invalidate the level's static lighting. Moving a light, adding a new light, deleting a light, moving a mesh, and adding a new mesh are all examples of actions that invalidate the static lighting for a level. If Lightmass were run *before* such actions occurred, it would have to be run again afterward to update the static lighting. Although Lightmass is typically run only at the end of level development, this lighting project will require you to run Lightmass several times, the first time being in this section. This is to more clearly demonstrate how changes to geometry in the level affect the final lighting solution produced by Lightmass.

Before running Lightmass, there are a number of recommended preparatory steps that can be taken. Notice I said the steps are recommended, not essential. That is, Lightmass could be run successfully right now without your having taken any one of these steps. Taking these steps, however, can help improve the performance of Lightmass in terms of the speed of its calculation and the quality of its results. It can also help reduce the number of times Lightmass calculations need to be made.

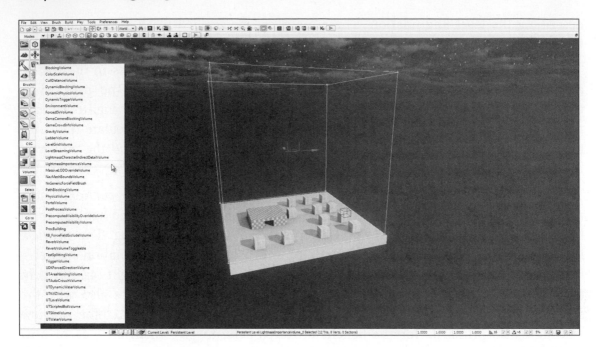

Figure 8.31
Creating a Lightmass importance volume.

The first step is to ensure that the level has one or more Lightmass importance volumes. Lightmass importance volumes are invisible volume actors (BSP Brushes) that are created using both the BSP Builder Brush and the Add Volumes button in the toolbox, as shown in Figure 8.31. (For more information, refer to Chapter 2, "Building a First Project: A Tour of the UDK"—specifically, the section on creating a collision volume.) Our cube park project already features a Lightmass Importance volume surrounding the level, as seen in Figure 8.32. The purpose of the volume is to define a region of space inside which indirect illumination will be allowed when Lightmass performs its calculations. Regions of the level outside of a Lightmass importance volume will support only direct illumination. This means that a level cannot support indirect illumination without a Lightmass importance volume.

The next preparatory step is to set an appropriate number of allowed light bounces for Lightmass's indirect illumination calculations. This step involves setting an integer value that specifies the total number of times any single light ray in the simulation may bounce (or reflect). In the real world, a light ray may bounce from surfaces an indefinite number of times. But the concepts of potential infinity and limitlessness cannot be considered acceptable values for parameters in a computer simulation that is expected to end. For this reason, the total number of times a light ray may bounce

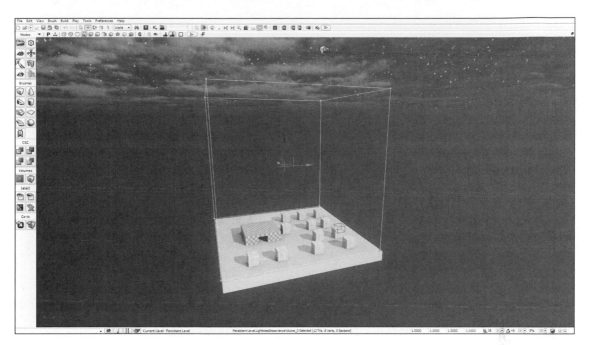

Figure 8.32
The level is surrounded by a Lightmass importance volume, ready to run Lightmass.

must be specified. Bounces above the specified limit will be ignored by Lightmass and will not factor into the illumination solution. To set this parameter, open the View menu and choose World Properties. Then, in the World Properties panel, click Lightmass and then Lightmass Settings. Finally, type a value in the Num Indirect Light Bounces field or leave it at the default value, which is 3 (recommend in this case), as shown in Figure 8.33. This value is proportional both to Lightmass's computation time and to the brightness of the level. Higher values result in longer solutions and brighter levels because the effects of more bounced rays must be calculated.

The final preparatory step for running Lightmass is to set the level of lighting quality to be generated by Lightmass. The lighting quality setting reflects the degree of realism that will be produced in the lighting, with higher quality outputs taking longer to generate. You can set the lighting quality from the main Editor toolbar. To do so, right-click the Lighting Quality button and select the desired quality setting from the menu that appears—here, Production, as shown in Figure 8.34. Production is the highest standard of lighting that can be achieved using Lightmass, and is typically the standard chosen for the final lighting build of a level.

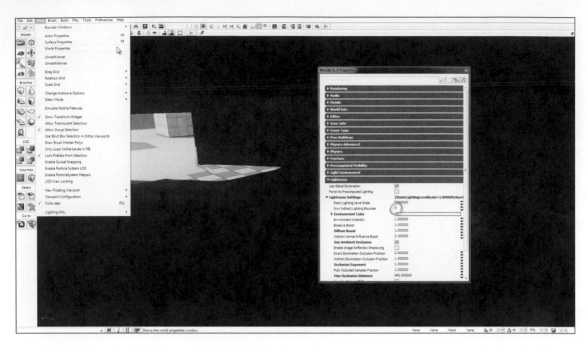

Figure 8.33
Setting the maximum number of allowed light bounces for Lightmass.

Figure 8.34
Setting the lighting quality.

It is now time to run Lightmass to build the lighting for the level. The following will apply:

- Indirect illumination will be applied to the whole of the level because it is enclosed within the Lightmass importance volume.

- The light will be production quality.

- The Lightmass system will trace out all light rays for a total of three bounces.

To run Lightmass, follow these steps:

1. Click the Build Lighting button in the main toolbar, as shown in Figure 8.35. The Lightmass settings dialog appears, as shown in Figure 8.36.

2. Ensure that the Build BSP, Build Static Meshes, and Use Lightmass checkboxes are checked. Then click the OK button. The Lightmass build process begins. When it does, the Swarm Agent appears (see Figure 8.37) and attempts to utilize the power of multiple PCs over a network to produce the lighting solution. When the build process is complete, the lightmaps are generated and are applied to the surfaces of all models in the level. In other words, the level contains static lighting.

Figure 8.35
Starting Lightmass.

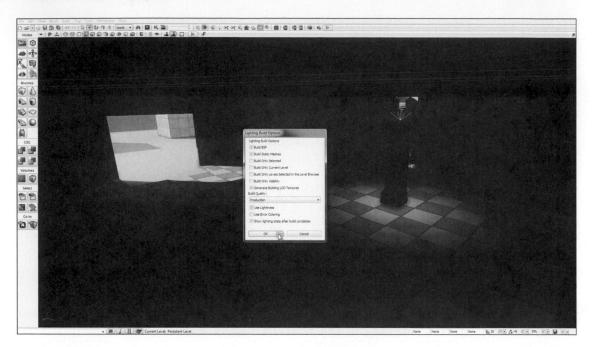

Figure 8.36
Finalizing Lightmass settings.

3. To view the lightmaps generated by Lightmass, open the Content Browser and, in the Packages pane, select the package whose name matches the level's file-name (in this case, DM-Light_Project_02_spot_chan). Then ensure the All or Texture checkbox is selected in the Filter pane to display the level lightmaps in the Asset pane, as shown in Figure 8.38. To open a lightmap, double-click it in the Asset pane as you would any other type of asset.

Emissive Lighting

The previous section detailed how to use the Lightmass system with Lightmass importance volumes to build the static lighting solution for the level, complete with indirect illumination and per-pixel lighting. Lights and geometry that are added, removed, or changed in the level *after* the lighting solution has been built will invalidate that solution, causing the UDK to revert to the preview lighting model that was used to illuminate the level before the solution was built. In such circumstances, it is necessary to rebuild the lighting solution. This section and the next involve adding new lights to the level—specifically, emissive and function lights. For this reason, this section and the next will invalidate the lighting solution built in the previous section, requiring you to build it again after the changes have been made.

Figure 8.37
The Lightmass Swarm Agent.

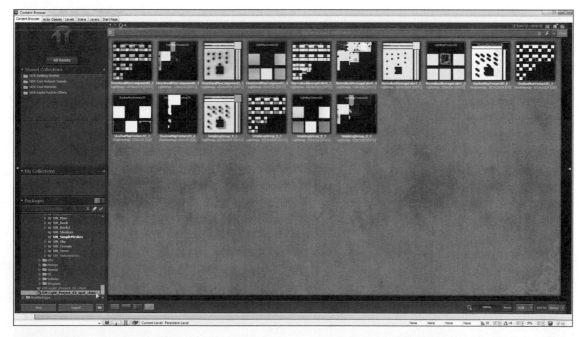

Figure 8.38
Viewing the level lightmaps generated by Lightmass.

The focus of this section is on emissive lighting. The purpose of emissive lighting—along with other light sources, such as point lights, spot lights, and directional lights—is to cast colored rays of light into the scene. Emissive lighting is distinguished from these other light sources, however, by the way in which a developer uses it. Unlike standard light sources, emissive light sources are not tangible actors that can be dragged and dropped into the level. Rather, emissive lighting is added indirectly to the scene through emergence. That is, emissive lighting can emerge from the emissive channel of materials. In short, emissive lighting makes it possible to use a static mesh as a light source—or more accurately, to use the emissive channel of the material across the mesh's surface as a means for casting light rays into the scene. That means light-source meshes such as lamps and neon signs can be used to cast light into the scene directly, which can spare you from having to create standard point lights or spot lights in the position of the mesh to simulate its illumination. The following steps demonstrate how to illuminate the interior of the level's shelter region using emissive lighting created from the three lamp meshes attached to the shelter wall.

1. Select one of the wall light meshes and open its Properties panel. Open the Static Mesh Actor section, click Static Mesh Component, click Lightmass, and click Use Emissive for Static Lighting checkbox to select it, as shown in Figure 8.39. This enables the mesh to act as a light source, casting light rays from its surface

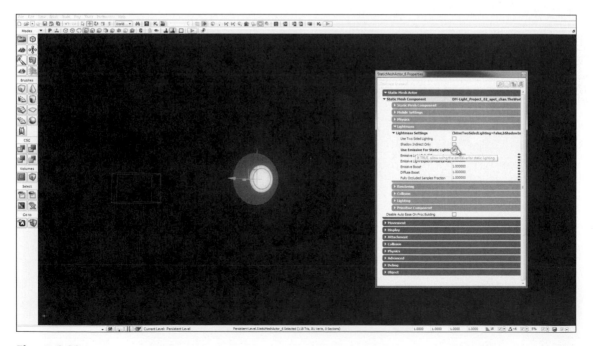

Figure 8.39
Flagging a mesh as an emissive light source.

using its material's emissive channel. If the mesh has no emissive channel, the mesh will cast black light, which is equivalent to no illumination.

2. Notice that emissive lighting is enabled for static lighting, but not for dynamic or dynamic composite. That means the emissive light will influence static lighting only. For this reason, their effects cannot be visible until Lightmass has been used to build the static lighting solution through lightmapping. Run Lightmass now to build the lighting solution and observe the effects of the mesh's emissive light. (See Figure 8.40.)

3. Compare Figure 8.39 with Figure 8.40 to observe the considerable difference in the lighting of the shelter that has resulted from emissive lighting. I would like to reduce the effects of this light—both its brightness and the distance over which it travels. To do so, press F4 to open the mesh's Properties panel. Then open the Static Mesh Actor session and click the Lightmass component. Notice that the default value for the Emissive Light Explicit Influence Radius is 0, meaning not that the emissive light has no influence, but that the radius of the influence sphere is controlled by the brightness of the pixels in the material's emissive channel. (The Emissive Light Explicit Influence Radius setting is a

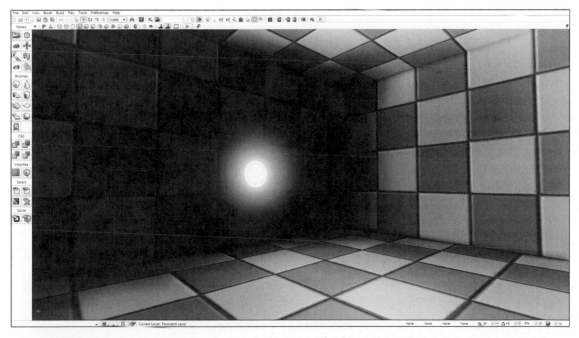

Figure 8.40
Run Lightmass to build the static lighting for the level and to view the effects of emissive lighting.

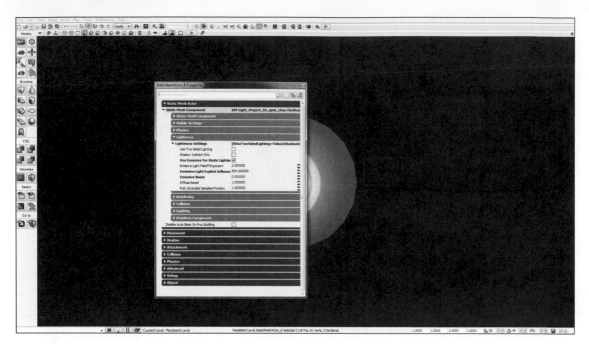

Figure 8.41
Tweaking emissive light settings, adjusting the brightness and range.

decimal determining the radius in Unreal world units of a surrounding spherical volume outside which the emissive light has no effect.) To reduce the brightness of the light, change the Emissive Boost parameter to 0.5. To reduce the influence of the light, change the Emissive Light Explicit Influence Radius setting to 500. (See Figure 8.41.)

4. Run Lightmass to observe the new effects of the emissive light, shown in Figure 8.42.

5. Duplicate the light mesh twice, replacing each instance for the other two light meshes in the shelter. This ensures that all three light meshes in the shelter will cast emissive light.

6. To observe the effect, run Lightmass once more. Figure 8.43 shows the final shelter interior illuminated using emissive lighting.

Note

The level so far can be found in the DM-Light_Project_03_emis.udk companion file.

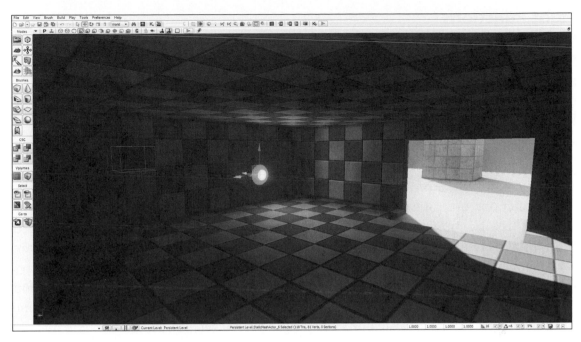

Figure 8.42
Rebuild the lighting solution to see the latest changes to the emissive lighting.

Figure 8.43
The interior of the shelter, illuminated with emissive lighting.

Light Functions

The last lighting subject to consider in this chapter is the light function, or function light. The light function is not a light source type itself, but is a special property of various types of light sources. Specifically, *light function* refers to the ability of a standard light—such as a point light, spot light, or directional light—to act as a projector by casting a specified material as an illumination into the scene. More precisely, it refers to the ability of a light source to cast the pixels from the emissive channel of a specified material as matching colored light rays into the scene.

Light functions support animated materials, and thus support animated projections. Light functions are often used to simulate animated shadowing affects, such as the shadows cast by moving clouds onto the ground or the shadows cast onto a sea bed by rippling water above. Because light functions support animated materials, they are always calculated dynamically. Therefore, lights that use light functions are always dynamic lights. For this reason, light functions should be used sparingly. This section details how to use light functions to create an animated projection on the side of one of the cubes in the exterior region of the cube park level.

1. Press Ctrl+Shift+F to open the Content Browser, and click the Actor Classes tab. From there, drag and drop a toggleable spot light into the Perspective viewport next to one of the cubes to add the light to the level, as shown in Figure 8.44.

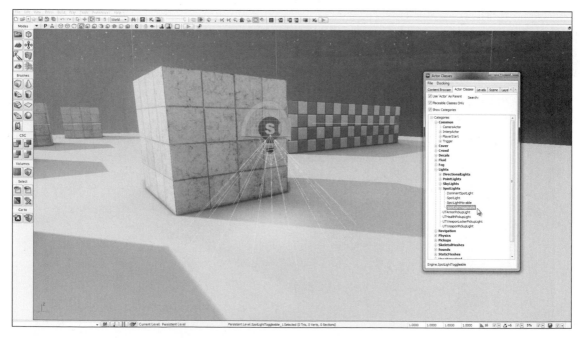

Figure 8.44
Drag and drop a toggleable spot light into the level.

Figure 8.45
Positioning the spot light.

(Toggleable spot lights are spot lights that can be toggled on and off, and thus are a form of dynamic light. Only the toggleable and moveable versions of lights support light functions.)

2. Position the spot light so that its cone projects rays onto the side of the cube, as shown in Figure 8.45. Notice that Figure 8.45 shows the scene in the Lighting Only view (Alt+6). As mentioned in Chapter 3, "UDK Fundamentals," this mode enables developers to hide the surface details of materials to concentrate on illumination. When the light is positioned, press Alt+4 to switch the back to the standard Lit mode.

3. Before a light function can be assigned to the light, an appropriate and specialized material must be created for the purpose. In this example, the material will be an animated cloud effect. Open the Content Browser and create a new material named CloudAnim. (For help creating the material, refer to Chapter 5.) Then look in the Content Browser for a texture asset named T_UDK_Cloud_Noise01. This texture represents a cloud pattern. Drag and drop this asset into the Material Editor and connect it directly to the emissive channel, as shown in Figure 8.46. Note that only the emissive channel factors into light functions, meaning that other channels will be ignored.

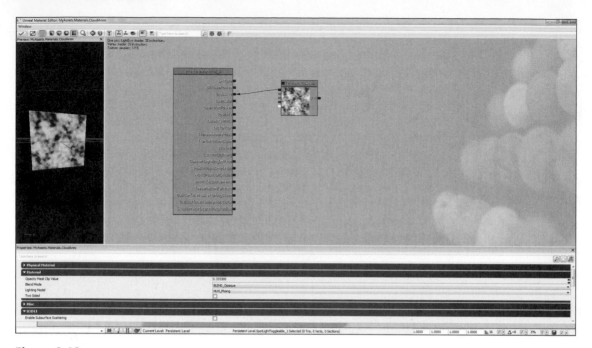

Figure 8.46
Creating a light function material.

4. Animate the material using a Panner coordinate node. To do this, right-click a vacant space inside the material graph and choose Coordinates, then New Panner from the menu that appears. Connect this node into the UVs input of the cloud emissive map. Select the Panner node in the graph and assign a value 0.3 to the SpeedX and SpeedY properties. Notice in the Preview pane that the material is now animated (see Figure 8.47).

5. To make the material compatible with light functions, two properties must be set. Select the primary node in the graph. Then, in the Properties panel, open the Material section and set the Lighting Model parameter to MLM_Unlit. Next, open the Mutually Exclusive Usage section and select the Used as Light Function checkbox. (See Figure 8.48.) Finally, save the material and exit the Material Editor.

6. Select the newly created light function material in the Content Browser's Preview pane. Then return to the Perspective viewport and open the Properties panel for the spot light. Open the Light Component section and click the blue down arrow in the Function field, and choose Light Function from the menu that appears (see Figure 8.49) to add light function support to the spot light.

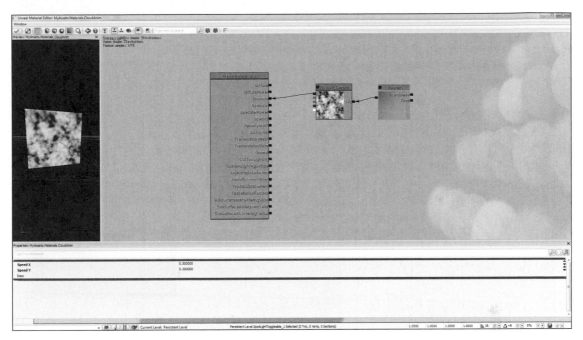

Figure 8.47
Animating the clouds material using a Panner coordinate node.

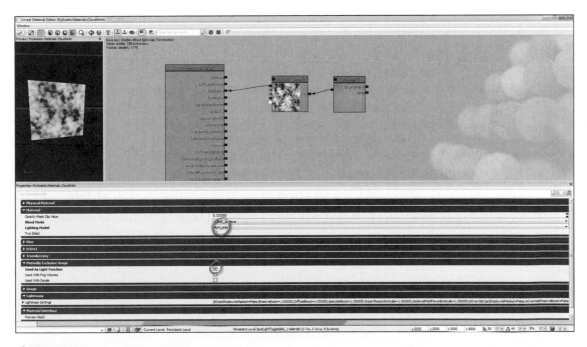

Figure 8.48
Configuring the material for use as a light function.

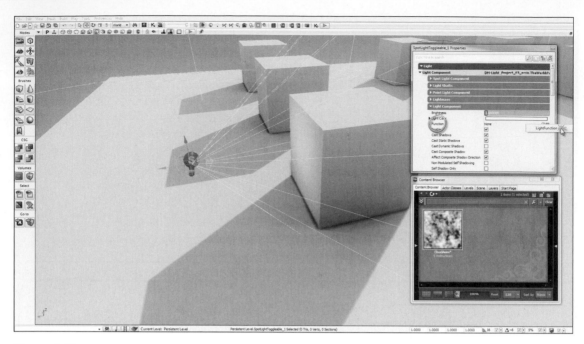

Figure 8.49
Adding light function support to the spot light.

7. Click the green left arrow in the Source Material field. This will set the material selected in the Content Browser to act as the material for the light function. The spot light in the viewport will also update to reflect the changes, and the material will be projected onto the side of the cube. (See Figure 8.50.) The spot light now acts as a projector, projecting the animated cloud material onto the side of the cube.

8. Ensure that the Real Time Preview setting is enabled in the Perspective viewport's toolbar to observe the animation effects (see Figure 8.51). Note that it was not necessary to rebuild the lighting to see the light function at work. This is because Lightmass pertains to static lighting, whereas light functions are dynamic.

Note

The completed level can be found in the DM-Light_Project_04_Complete.udk companion file.

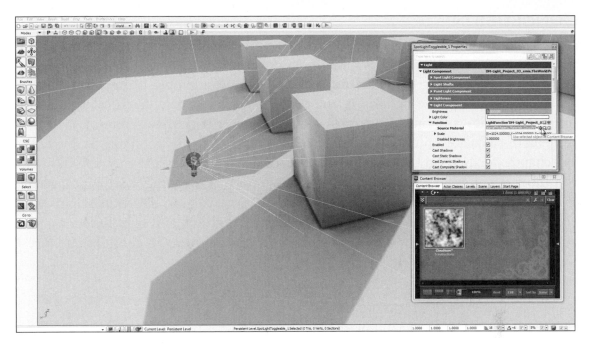

Figure 8.50
Adding the selected material to the light function.

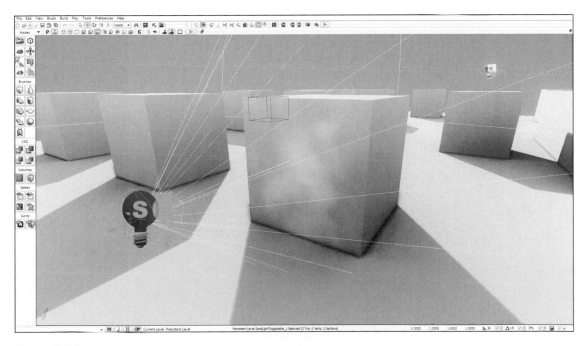

Figure 8.51
The completed projector light, and a completed project.

Conclusion

Lighting in video games and in real-time 3D graphics generally is a broad field with a long history. Attempts to improve the realism of 3D graphics and their real-time performance on consumer hardware have often involved attempts to improve lighting systems. This is because lighting is one of the most noticeable graphical features of an environment—and one of the most computationally expensive game-relevant phenomena to calculate. In considering the subject of lighting as it pertains to the UDK, this chapter focused on the additive color space of light, direct and indirect illumination models, vertex-based and per-pixel lighting, normal mapping, and lightmapping, as well as the more practical features of point lights, spot lights, directional lights, and Lightmass. It also considered the subject of emissive lighting and light functions. The next chapter enters the world of animation and visual scripting in considering Unreal Kismet and Unreal Matinee.

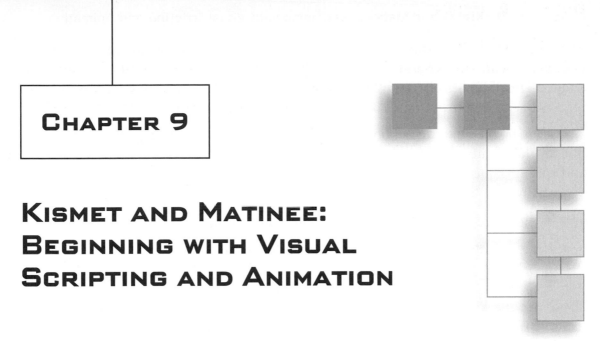

CHAPTER 9

KISMET AND MATINEE: BEGINNING WITH VISUAL SCRIPTING AND ANIMATION

Solve the problem and then write the code.

—Anonymous

By the end of this chapter, you should:

- Understand the Kismet and Matinee systems.

- Be able to use Kismet to define game logic and behavior.

- Understand the concepts of key frame animation and interpolation.

- Be able to use Matinee to create key frame animations.

- Understand the Matinee Director mode.

This chapter is dedicated to two unique UDK features: Kismet and Matinee. These two distinct but related features, each with their own editors, are used to create assets that cannot be seen or heard directly but that play a fundamental role in the way a game works. Together, these two features operate behind the scenes to define the game logic, the rules, and the way in which actors in the level move and change over time. Specifically, Kismet enables developers to define and customize the logic or rules governing a game, and Matinee enables developers to plan the animation and motion aspects of a game.

UNREAL KISMET

The term *kismet* is the Anglicized form of a Turkish word roughly meaning *fate* or *destiny*. The term conjures up the idea of determinism—the idea that all actions are the result of previous causes, and that the future is thereby predetermined. The UDK feature called Unreal Kismet—Kismet for short—is appropriately named because Kismet, along with UnrealScript, defines *all* the behaviors and events that can happen in a level. This includes all the different ways in which actors in a level can behave and respond according to timing, conditions, and a gamer's actions.

Kismet is not used to define only the events that will certainly happen in the game, but all the events that could happen in the game given the appropriate conditions and circumstances. The following statements, or rules, are a few examples of the potentially limitless numbers of rules that might be defined for a level using Kismet:

- If the player is standing over a trap then initiate the trap.
- If the countdown has completed, then detonate the bomb.
- Play an alarm sound whenever the player comes into view of the security cameras.

These are the kinds of statements that can be made about a level and implemented using Kismet (as well as UnrealScript; see Chapter 12, "Scripting with UnrealScript"). All these statements have some abstract properties in common that make them statements about rules, or logic. That is, all these statements are composed from a set of common and abstract ingredients. These ingredients form the raw materials of statements about rules, and are thus the raw materials of Kismet. Specifically, each of the three statements is formed from four different and abstract ingredients:

- Variables
- Actions
- Events
- Conditions

Variables

The bold words in the following sentences represent the variables in those sentences. Notice that the variables correspond to nouns.

- If the **player** is standing over a **trap** then initiate the **trap**.
- If the **countdown** has completed, then detonate the **bomb**.
- Play an **alarm** sound whenever the **player** comes into view of the **security cameras**.

A *variable* is any value that can change or vary. In algebra, the use of a letter (such as x) signals a variable. Its value cannot be known in advance because any number or value can be substituted for x. Thus, the first statement could be written in algebraic form as follows: "If *x* is standing over *y*, then initiate *y*." The word *player* in the first statement is a variable because it represents not a specific player that is known in advance (for example, Player 1), but any player that may happen to stand on the trap (Player 2, or Player 3, or Player 4, and so on). Similarly, the word *trap* in the first statement is a variable because it refers not to a specific trap that is known in advance of gameplay, but to whatever trap the player happens to be standing on at any one time (if the player is standing on a trap at all).

A variable might be said to have four essential properties:

- A name, such as *x*, *player*, *trap*, or something else
- A value, such as *x* = 5, *player* = Player 7, *trap* = Trap9, or something else
- The value of a variable can change
- The value of a variable cannot be known in advance

Actions

The bold words in the following sentences represent the actions in those sentences:

- If the player is standing over a trap then **initiate** the trap.
- If the countdown has completed, then **detonate** the bomb.
- **Play** an alarm sound whenever the player comes into view of the security cameras.

Notice that the actions correspond to verbs—to *doing* words. This is because actions are an active force; they cause things to happen. Examples of actions include *play sound, set variable, detonate bomb, initiate trap, fire gun, jump the barrel, run to the finish line, open the door, punch the monster,* and so on.

An action has two properties: the action to be performed (such as open, initiate, or detonate) and the parameters of the action. The latter defines the object or variable affected by the action, or the way in which the action is to be performed (for example, detonate *the bomb* or initiate *the trap*).

Events

The bold words in the following sentences represent the events of those sentences:

- If the **player is standing over a trap** then initiate the trap.
- If the **countdown has completed**, then detonate the bomb.
- Play an alarm sound whenever the **player comes into view of the security cameras.**

Notice that the events correspond to a statement about a state of affairs and can evaluate to either true or false. For example, it can be either true or false at any one time that a player is standing over a trap, or that a countdown has completed, or that a player is in view of the security cameras. When statements described as events evaluate to true (that is, when they accurately describe a state of affairs in the game), those events are said to have occurred.

The event is related to but distinct from the action in that it does not perform actions itself but often leads to actions being performed. That is, an event is the trigger for an action. Actions are associated with events, and are performed when those events are true. For example, if it is true that countdown has completed (the event), then the bomb should be detonated (the action).

Conditions

The bold words in the following sentences represent the conditions of those sentences:

- **If** the player is standing over a trap **then** initiate the trap.
- **If** the countdown has completed, **then** detonate the bomb.
- Play an alarm sound **whenever** the player comes into view of the security cameras.

Notice that the conditions correspond only to the topic-neutral and syntactical words of the sentence. That means conditions are a syntactical, not a semantic, matter. That is, they relate not to the content or subject matter of a sentence but to the way in which propositions in the sentence relate to each other. Specifically, conditions define how events are related to actions. In the first sentence, for example, the condition specifies that the *initiate trap* action will be performed when the *standing over trap* event is true.

Kismet and UnrealScript

The purpose of Kismet is to enable developers to both state and uphold the game logic or rule set for a game using any number of combinations of variables, actions, events, and conditions. You might reasonably conclude from this description that Kismet is a programming language, since it involves building statements about rules and logic, and you wouldn't be entirely wrong. This, however, raises a question: How does Kismet differ from UnrealScript? If both are programming languages used to define the behavior of an Unreal Engine game, then both languages effectively do the same thing. Surely, one of the two must be redundant?

The answer to this question is that Kismet is not a programming language in the *traditional* sense of the word. Thus, there *are* important differences between Unreal-Script and Kismet. These differences generally influence the kinds of tasks for which they are typically used, one being more suitable than the other in particular circumstances.

Kismet Is a Visual Scripting System

Perhaps the most notable difference between Kismet and UnrealScript pertains to the way in which programs are made in those languages. Programs in UnrealScript are written in the conventional sense of the word into a third-party text editor according to the grammatical rules of the UnrealScript language, as shown in Figure 9.1. UnrealScript programs are written and processed on a line-by-line and statement-by-statement basis.

Kismet, in contrast, is a visual scripting system. Kismet programs (known as *sequences*) are constructed visually by building a graph of connected nodes (each node known as a *sequence object*) using a mouse-driven GUI editor that is part of the UDK suite of tools (see Figure 9.2). Kismet programs (sequences) can be made using drag and drop in the Kismet Editor, just as materials and sound cues can be made using drag and drop in the Material Editor and Sound Cue Editor, respectively. Kismet sequences, therefore, are constructed graphically, and are not written from source code entered into a text editor.

Figure 9.1
UnrealScript is a traditional scripting language, written via a text editor.

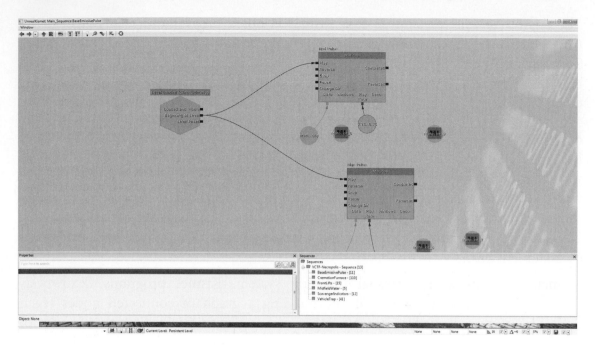

Figure 9.2
Kismet is a visual scripting system. Programs in Kismet are built using a mouse-driven editor interface.

Being graphical rather than text based, Kismet offers several advantages to developers:

- Developers need not learn a text-based, English-derived scripting language to make Kismet sequences.

- The flow and logic of Kismet sequences can be visualized more easily than the flow and logic of a text-based language.

- Kismet sequences are immune to syntactical, grammatical, and spelling errors.

Note

Although Kismet sequences are immune to syntactical, grammatical, and spelling errors, they are not immune to logic errors, because developers may be flawed in their logic and reasoning.

Note

Some developers of UDK games on the iOS platform (specifically on older devices) have reported performance issues when using Kismet. In the interests of performance, be sure to keep Kismet sequences as simple as possible. This recommendation of simplicity applies not only to Kismet, but to game programming generally.

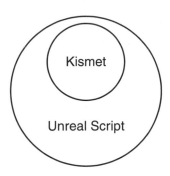

Figure 9.3
Kismet vs. UnrealScript.

UnrealScript is More Powerful and Flexible

The second fundamental difference between Kismet and UnrealScript is that Unreal-Script is wider in its scope than Kismet. That is, the range of UnrealScript both encompasses and exceeds the range of Kismet, as shown in Figure 9.3. That means that there are things that can be achieved in UnrealScript that cannot be achieved in Kismet, and that everything achievable in Kismet can also be achieved in Unreal-Script—hence UnrealScript sometimes being referred to as the big guns in relation to Kismet, or as the more powerful and flexible option.

Note

It should be stressed that Kismet and UnrealScript are not mutually exclusive features of the UDK. Developers need not make a one-time choice between using either Kismet or UnrealScript. Both can and typically are used in the development of the same UDK-based game, for different reasons and to achieve different purposes.

Why Use Kismet?

Developers can use either Kismet or UnrealScript when implementing any one feature of their game. For example, developers who want to show a greeting message to the player as the player enters the game will find they can implement this behavior using either Kismet or UnrealScript. The question arises, then, as to when it is or is not appropriate to use Kismet, if it is appropriate to use it all. This question takes on the more force when it is understood that the scope of UnrealScript both encompasses and exceeds the scope of Kismet.

The decision as to when to use Kismet or UnrealScript for a particular feature depends on the developer's preferences and on the particular needs of the project. Some developers prefer Kismet wherever possible, resorting to UnrealScript only as a last resort. Other developers recommend avoiding Kismet entirely, preferring to use UnrealScript for all their programming needs. In this book, I shall side with neither of these extremes, but will cite two of the main reasons people use Kismet to help you determine when Kismet will be most appropriate for the different features of your own projects.

Note

Some developers adhere to the following general rule when deciding whether Kismet or Unreal Script should be chosen for a specific task. Kismet is appropriate for triggering simple animations, such as door-opening, elevator rising, and portal spinning animations. Unreal Script is more suitable for complex behavior, such as creating new weapons, modifying game physics, and adding comprehensive artificial intelligence.

Kismet Requires No Recompilation

One of the main advantages of Kismet is that changes and edits can be made to Kismet sequences more easily than UnrealScript programs. You can make changes to Kismet sequences without ever leaving the UDK Editor, and you can observe their effects in the editor almost immediately, too. The same cannot be said for changes to UnrealScript programs, which must be made in a third party text editor and then recompiled to take effect.

For example, suppose a developer wants to increase the speed with which a door in the level opens whenever the player approaches it. Using Kismet, the developer can open the Kismet Editor, change the appropriate nodes in the graph, and observe the effects in game. In contrast, using UnrealScript, the developer must exit the UDK Editor, open a third-party text editor such as Notepad or a development environment such as Visual Studio, code the changes, recompile the code, and then return to the UDK Editor to run the level and observe the effects of the change. The difference in the number of steps that must be performed in Kismet versus UnrealScript can have both appreciable and dramatic consequences on the amount of development time lost in implementing changes. Kismet can typically save development time for programming actions whose parameters require a lot of tweaking.

Note

Compilation refers to the way in which the source code (the written programming) of a text-based programming language such as UnrealScript is translated into a different form that is simpler and easier for the computer to process and execute. In other words, compilation is a process in which the computer translates a human-readable language into a form that it can process more easily. Compiled languages have a performance advantage over languages that are not compiled.

Kismet Is More Accessible

Kismet is often said to be more accessible than UnrealScript in that Kismet sequences can be both read and created more easily and by more people than UnrealScript programs. That is, Kismet places fewer demands on the developer in terms of the technical knowledge and experience. Unlike UnrealScript, Kismet does not require the developer to know a programming language and its syntax and rules, nor does it require the developer to know about programming concepts such as compilation, or object orientation, or polymorphism. Kismet sequences are constructed entirely in the Kismet Editor using drag and drop, and the logic and flow of a Kismet sequence can be read visually from the nodes of the Kismet graph. The advantage of Kismet's accessibility is that UDK level files and the Kismet sequences inside them can be passed around to a greater number of people in the development team (coders, artists, designers, and so on), all of whom can read, understand, and edit the sequence.

Note

Some programmers argue that Kismet's accessibility is a disadvantage rather than an advantage. Why? Because it makes it harder for programmers to deliberately obfuscate their source code such that they are the only people who understand it, thereby protecting their jobs! This book, however, asserts that source code should be clear and concise, and that attempts to make game development easier for all are to be encouraged and not discouraged. For this reason, the accessibility of Kismet is viewed here as an advantage.

The Unreal Kismet Editor Interface

The Kismet Editor is a GUI, mouse-driven interface that supports drag and drop. It provides all the tools necessary for creating, editing, and organizing the Kismet sequences in a level.

The Kismet Editor and its workflow are in many ways similar to the Material Editor and the Sound Cue Editor. Kismet sequences are constructed from a graph of connected nodes, each called a *sequence object*. There is, however, an important difference between how the Material Editor and Sound Cue Editor are used and how the Kismet Editor is used. Specifically, the Material Editor and Sound Cue Editor are used to edit unique and individual assets. As a result, you can have multiple instances of each of those editors open at any one time, with each instance used to edit a single asset. In contrast, the Kismet Editor is used for viewing, managing, and editing *all* Kismet sequences in a level. That is, there can be only one running instance of the Kismet Editor open at any one time, and that instance is used for editing all Kismet sequences in a level. Kismet sequences are therefore not assets in the conventional sense of the word. That is, Kismet sequences are not viewable in the Preview pane

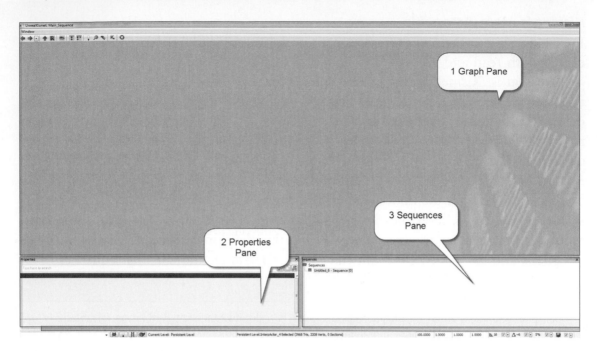

Figure 9.4
The Unreal Kismet Editor interface.

of the Content Browser in the same way textures, sounds, and meshes are. To access and edit the Kismet sequences of a level, you must open the Kismet Editor.

The Kismet Editor, shown in Figure 9.4, consists of three main parts or panes:

- **The Graph pane.** The Graph pane is the largest area of the Kismet Editor. It's where Kismet graphs are constructed. The mouse and keyboard controls for this space match the mouse and keyboard controls for the Material Editor and Sound Cue Editor. In particular, you can add sequence objects to the graph by right-clicking in a vacant space and choosing a node from the menu that appears, as shown in Figure 9.5. Further, you can use the Ctrl-click method to select and drag sequence objects around the editor. Multiple sequence objects can be selected and edited using a Marquee select (Ctrl+Alt+click and drag).

Note

Notice that the Kismet sequence objects are arranged on the menu according to the Kismet ingredients listed earlier in this chapter: variables, events, actions, and conditions.

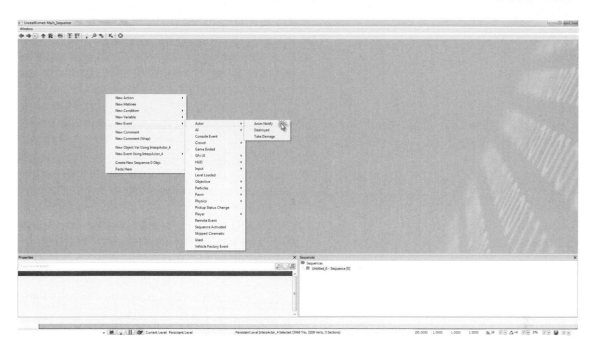

Figure 9.5
Adding sequence objects to the graph by right-clicking in the Graph pane.

- **The Properties pane.** The Properties pane, shown in Figure 9.6, is context sensitive. That is, it changes depending on the sequence object selected in the graph, much as Properties panes in the Material Editor and Sound Cue Editor change depending on the selected node. The Properties pane enables developers to tweak and adjust node-specific properties, as you shall see throughout this chapter.

- **The Sequences pane.** As mentioned, the Kismet Editor is used to edit and display all Kismet sequences in a level, not just one individual Kismet sequence. Considering that a level may contain many Kismet sequences, and that each sequence may contain many graph nodes, there arises the problem of managing all those sequences so they don't overcrowd the Graph pane. The Sequences pane solves this problem, enabling developers to divide their Kismet sequences into pages, each page having its own Graph pane and related nodes. Using the Sequences pane, developers can switch among pages. Selecting a page loads the contents of that page into the Kismet Editor's Graph pane, as shown in Figure 9.7.

Figure 9.6
Editing properties in the Kismet Editor Properties pane.

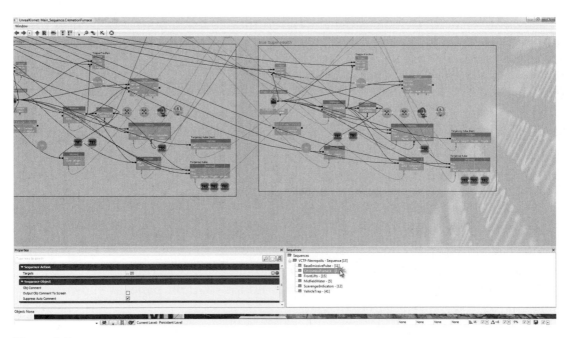

Figure 9.7
Switching between sequences using the Sequences pane.

UNREAL MATINEE

As mentioned, Unreal Kismet is a visual scripting system. Its purpose is to provide developers with a simple-to-use and accessible GUI system for defining the behavior of a level and of its constituent actors. Defining the behavior of a level involves specifying all the possible permutations of its constituent actors—that is, all the possible ways in which its actors can behave and respond to stimulus and events. In short, scripting a level with Kismet involves defining the when and the how of that level—when events occur, how the events lead to actions, and how the actions *do* things.

The how aspect of behavior requires further elaboration. Specifically, defining the how of a level involves specifying how actors do things. If a door is to open on its hinges, for example, then it is necessary to define how that door will open—the speed at which it opens and the angle at which it turns on its hinges. As another example, a car mesh that is to travel along the road must be told the speed at which it is to travel; whether it is to turn, swerve, or stop along the journey; and the route it will follow. Without these instructions, the actions will amount to nothing. The when and how of a level is defined for the most part by Unreal Kismet, but some of the how is delegated to a companion editor: the Matinee Editor, shown in Figure 9.8.

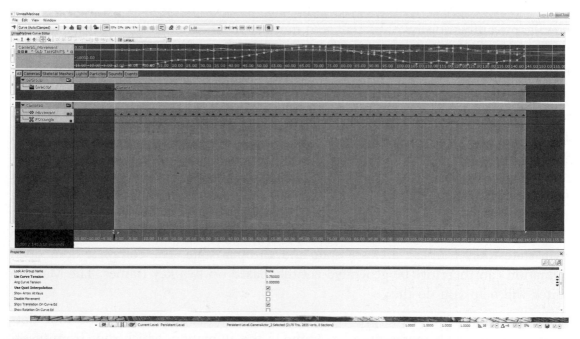

Figure 9.8
The Matinee Editor, used for creating key frame animations.

Kismet defines how events lead to actions and the general logic and flow of those actions. Some actions, however—such as doors being opened, cars being moved, handles being turned, buttons being pressed, wheels being rotated, and others—affect the position and motion of actors in the level. These kinds of actions involve making changes to actors over time, or animating them. The details of these animations are specified not by Kismet but by Matinee. Thus, the purpose of Matinee is to define all the animations that can be applied to actors in the level.

Matinee is not responsible for actually applying those animations to actors; that is the work of Kismet. But Matinee *is* responsible for specifying the details of the animation—the actual changes that should occur to an object over time, once the animation is set in motion by Kismet. The methods that Matinee uses to define animations are called *key framing* and *interpolation*.

Key Frames and Interpolation

As mentioned, animating an object involves changing the properties of an object over time. The properties of a UDK object such as an actor include its position, orientation, scale, visibility, speed, and others. For example, the properties of a door in a level include its three-dimensional world space position, its orientation as it pivots about the hinge, and its scale. The feature that these properties have in common is that they are expressed in terms of numbers, whether integers or decimals. Thus, video-game animation involves changing numbers over time—adding them, subtracting them, multiplying them, and dividing them.

Because animations can be thought of as the changing of numbers over time, and because computers can perform arithmetic with numbers, animations can therefore be defined using a system called *key framing*. Using key frame animation, developers can explicitly define the state of an object at specific times in the animation (that is, at key frames) through its numerical properties, and can then have the computer automatically calculate the states of the object on all remaining frames in a way that is consistent with the key frames. With key frame animation, all the intervening frames between key frames can be interpolated based on the key frames. In the case of a door-open animation, for example, the door rotates on its hinges between two main states (key frames): a closed state and an open state. The complete door-open animation can therefore be generated entirely based on two key frames. The Matinee Editor will help you do this.

Figure 9.9 demonstrates the process of key frame animation. Each of the four dots marked on the graph represents a key frame in the animation, which runs from 0 seconds to 15 seconds. The value at each key frame is connected to the value of the

Key Frame Animation Using Linear Interpolation

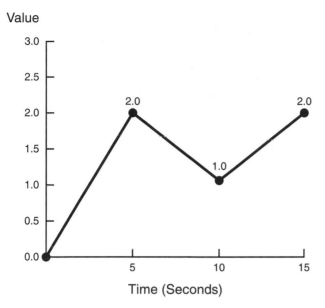

Figure 9.9
Mathematical representation of key frame animation, using *Linear Interpolation*.

previous key frame by a line, which determines the values of all the intervening frames —that is, of all the times between key frames. Thus, the time 2.5 seconds yields a value of 1.5, as does the time 12.5 seconds. In this way, the lines between key frames *interpolate*; that is, they produce interpolated values. How values between key frames are generated can vary. Figure 9.9 generates interpolated values using straight lines, known as *linear interpolation*. It is also possible to use curves for interpolation.

The Unreal Matinee Editor Interface

The Matinee Editor is where key frame animations are constructed. Using the Matinee Editor, developers can set key frame values and control the method of interpolation between key frames. As shown in Figure 9.10, the Matinee Editor consists of four main components:

- **The main menu and toolbar.** The Main Menu and toolbar enable developers to copy and paste data; to import and export key frame animation data to and from third-party applications; to insert, edit, and remove key frames; and to control the other editors and panes available in the editor interface. Later sections of this chapter will demonstrate the use of many of these features.

- **The Curve Editor.** The Curve Editor occupies a narrow region below the toolbar. The purpose of the Curve Editor, shown in expanded form in Figure 9.11, is

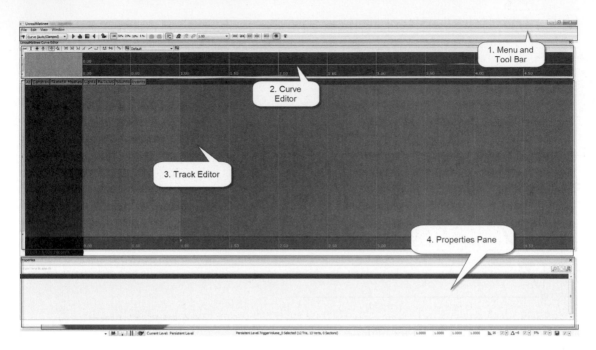

Figure 9.10
The Unreal Matinee Editor interface.

to display the line and curve graph charting the key frames of the animation, and to allow developers to control the lines or curves that are interpolated between key frames. This graph is similar in style to the graph in Figure 9.9.

■ **The Track Editor.** The Track Editor is typically the largest section of the Matinee interface. Shown in Figure 9.12, it's where developers plot, create, and edit the key frames of the animation—where they explicitly define the main states of their objects through the animation. The Track Editor can feature one or more tracks, each stacked vertically and representing a unique and individual property of the object that is to be animated. Thus, there might be a track for the visibility of an object, a track for its material, and a track for its position. Key frames are arranged across the timeline from left to right, charting the length of the animation, and appear as red triangles in the Track Editor.

■ **The Properties pane.** The Matinee Editor's context sensitive Properties pane acts much like similarly placed panes in the other UDK editors. The main purpose of the Properties pane is to show all editable properties for the selected object in the Matinee Editor—usually the properties of the selected key frame.

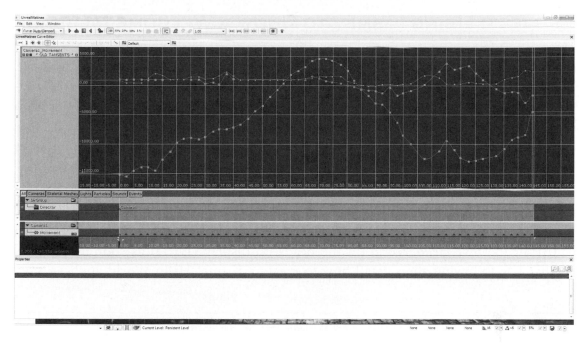

Figure 9.11
An expanded Curve Editor charts the frames of an animation in the form of a graph. The horizontal axis represents time, and the vertical axis represents value—that is, the height, width, color, and so on.

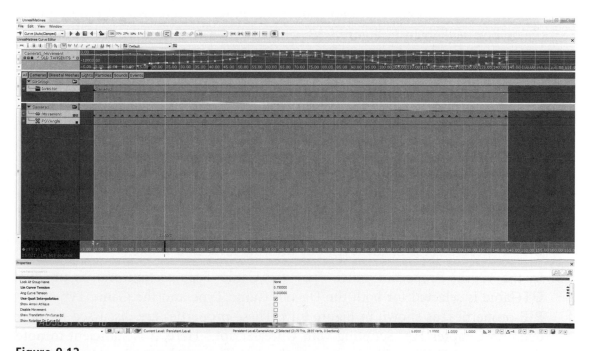

Figure 9.12
An expanded Track Editor allows developers to plot the key frames of their animation. Key frames can be plotted across one or more tracks, each track charting the changes in a unique and different property of the object.

PROJECT: USING KISMET TO SHOW A WELCOME MESSAGE

This section focuses on the first of three different projects in this chapter, each intended to demonstrate a particular and unique set of features for Kismet and Matinee. Together, the three projects comprise a practical overview of Kismet and Matinee, comprehensive enough to provide a strong foundational knowledge of those features—a knowledge that can be both extended and improved through self-learning, experimentation, and reading later chapters of this book. This first project involves creating your first Kismet program (sequence) and introduces the Kismet Editor.

Most programmers start to learn programming by coding a Hello World program—a program that does little or nothing besides print the text *Hello World* on the screen. For this reason, your first Kismet sequence will be a Hello World sequence, which will print the text *Hello World* on the heads-up display (HUD) as soon as the level begins. The following steps detail how to create a Kismet Hello World application:

Note

HUD refers collectively to all 2D graphical elements that appear on the screen in front of the level and game actors, including health bars, score readouts, ammo counters, crosshairs, mini-maps, and others.

1. Start a new UDK template project based on the morning level. To do this, open the File menu, choose New, and choose Morning Lighting from the New Map dialog box, as shown in Figure 9.13. This creates a level featuring a ground plane, a cube, and a dominant directional light configured to act as morning sunlight.

Note

Kismet can be used with any kind of level. This template was chosen because it will save you the work of having to manually create and configure level geometry and lighting. The Night Lighting, Midday Lighting, or Afternoon Lighting template would have served your purpose equally well.

2. Click the View menu and choose World Properties, as shown in Figure 9.14. The World Properties panel opens, listing a range of settings associated not with a specific actor in the level, but with the level as a whole.

3. In the World Properties panel, open the Game Type section and ensure that UTGame is selected for both the Default Game Type and the Game Type for PIE properties, as shown in Figure 9.15. These properties are discussed in more detail in Chapter 12, "Scripting with UnrealScript." Here, it is sufficient to note that the Default Game Type property determines how the level is played when run outside the editor on a standalone basis, and the Game Type for PIE

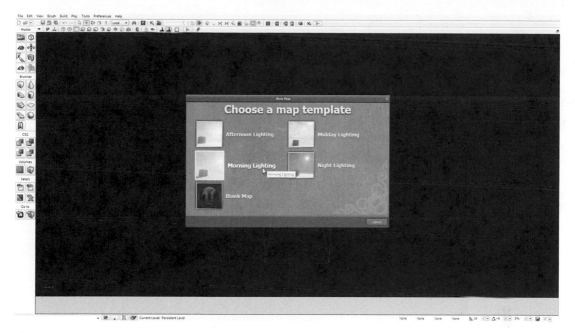

Figure 9.13
Creating a new level based on the Morning Lighting template.

Figure 9.14
Accessing the World Properties panel from the View menu.

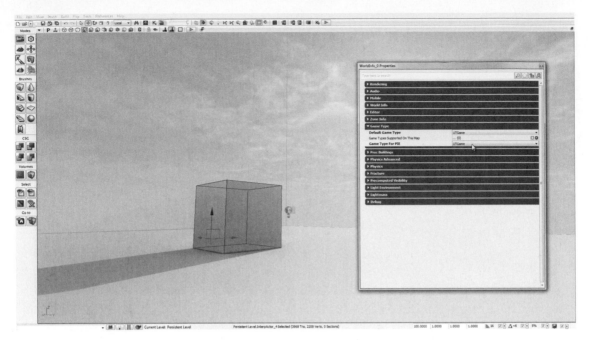

Figure 9.15
Setting the Default Game Type and Game Type for PIE properties to UTGame in the World Properties panel.

property determines how the level is played when run in the editor (hence the acronym PIE, for play in editor). The value UTGame indicates that the level should play as a default first-person shooter game, complete with a weapon and a HUD. Values other than UTGame will not necessarily allow a HUD to be shown by default during gameplay, meaning that any messages (such as "Hello World") that you choose to print there will not be seen.

4. It is time to start coding the Kismet Hello World application. Close the World Properties panel; then click the Open Kismet Editor button (marked with a green K, as shown in Figure 9.16) in the toolbar to open the Unreal Kismet Editor.

5. Take a moment before creating the Hello World sequence to identify the events and actions to be performed. Your intention can be stated as follows: "When the level begins, print the text *Hello World* to the game HUD." The event in this sentence is *level begin*, and the action to be performed is *print text* with a parameter of *Hello World*.

6. Create a Kismet sequence object to represent the event. To do this, right-click in the Graph pane and choose New Event and then Level Loaded from the menu that appears. This adds an event node to the graph that will be initiated when the level is loaded, or first run, as shown in Figure 9.17. The Level Loaded

Figure 9.16
Opening the Kismet Editor.

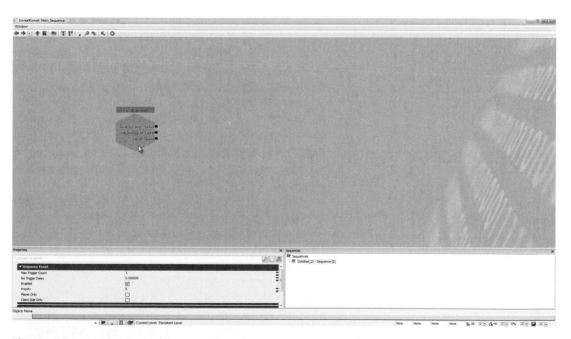

Figure 9.17
Adding a Level Loaded Event sequence object to the graph.

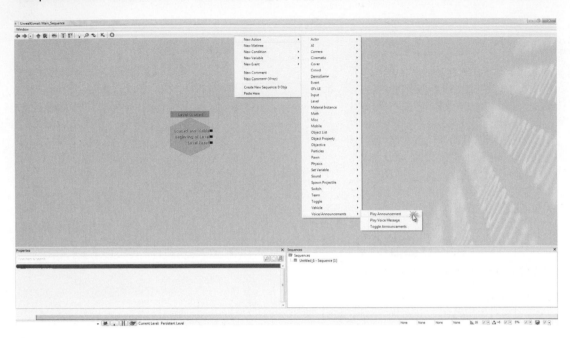

Figure 9.18
Creating an announcement action in the Graph pane.

sequence object has three output connections: Loaded and Visible, Beginning of Level, and Level Reset. Only one of these will fire at any one time, depending on the circumstances of the event. In this case, the text *Hello World* should appear at the beginning of the level, so you'll use the Beginning of Level output socket.

7. The action to be performed when the level begins is to print a welcome message to the user via the HUD. Messages can be printed to the HUD via the Announcement action. To add this action to the graph, right-click in a vacant space in the Graph pane and choose New Action, followed by Voice/ Announcements, and then Play Announcement from the menu that appears, as shown in Figure 9.18. This adds a Play Announcement node to the graph.

8. Click the Play Announcement sequence object in the graph to select it. Then, in the Properties pane, open the UTSeq Act Play Announcement section and type `Hello World` in the Announcement Text field, as shown in Figure 9.19. This instructs the Play Announcement action to show this text when the announcement is made.

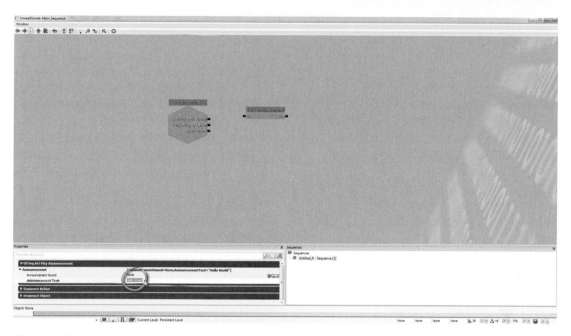

Figure 9.19
Assigning the string *Hello World* to the Announcement node.

Tip

You can assign a sound to the announcement, to play back alongside the text. To assign a sound, first select the sound in the Content Browser. Then, back in the Kismet Editor, click the green left arrow next to the Sound property in the Properties pane.

9. The graph now contains two sequence objects: one event and one action. Next, you must establish a connection between them so that the Play Announcement action is performed when the Level Loaded event is fired. To create this connection, use the mouse to drag a wire between the Beginning of Level output socket of the Level Loaded event to the input socket of the Play Announcement action, as shown in Figure 9.20. This will cause the Play Announcement action to be performed when the Level Loaded event is fired.

10. Take the level for a test drive to witness the effects of the Kismet sequence. Notice that the Level Loaded event is fired automatically as the level begins, and that the *Hello World* announcement appears as intended and then fades away. (See Figure 9.21).

Note

The completed level can be found in the companion files under DM-Kismet_Project_01_HWorld.udk.

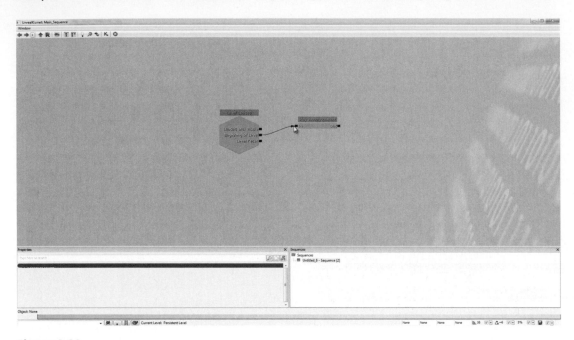

Figure 9.20
Connecting an event to an action.

Figure 9.21
Testing the Hello World level.

PROJECT: USING KISMET TO CREATE AN AUTOMATIC DOOR

The second of the three projects in this chapter involves using both Kismet and Matinee to create a set of double doors that will open automatically as the player approaches them, and will close automatically as the player moves away from them.

Figure 9.22
The door project involves using Kismet to automatically open a set of double doors as the player moves close to them.

You will use Kismet to define the relationship that exists between the event of "the player being near the door" and the action of "opening or closing the door." You will use Matinee to define the animation or the motion involved in the opening and closing of the door—that is, the transformation properties applied to the doors over time to make them move.

You can begin the work for this project from a file that I have prepared: DM-Kismet_Project_02_Door.udk. This level, shown in Figure 9.22, is based on the Morning Light template level, with some additional mesh actors: a CSG corridor and two door-mesh actors (the actors to be animated) in front of the corridor.

Note

It is not essential that you work from this file. You can create your own door setup to use as a starting point. This file is provided merely for convenience.

The following steps detail the work involved in creating an animated door using Kismet and Matinee:

1. Open the Kismet_Project_02_Door.udk level or a level of your own creation in the UDK Editor. Then select the mesh actors representing the left and right doors. At present, these two door meshes are static mesh actors, meaning they

Figure 9.23
Converting a static mesh actor to a KMover.

are not allowed to move or change during gameplay. Before you can animate these meshes through Kismet and Matinee, you must convert them from static meshes to dynamic meshes. Dynamic meshes take various forms, one of which is the Kismet Mover (KMover) mesh, which can be rotated, scaled, and translated. (The term *InterpActor* is sometimes used to refer to KMovers to emphasize the fact that these meshes can be interpolated, or changed over time.) To convert the static door meshes to KMover meshes, right-click the meshes in the Perspective viewport and choose Convert and then Convert StaticMeshActor to KMover from the menu that appears, as shown in Figure 9.23.

2. Define the relationship between the doors and the player that will enable you to determine whether the player is standing near the doors. To achieve this, you must use a *trigger volume*—that is, an invisible BSP volume that marks out a volume of space around the doors. Later, you'll use Kismet to configure the doors to open when the player enters this volume and to close when the player leaves it. To create the trigger volume, first select the BSP Brush in the Perspective viewport. Then click the Geometry Mode button in the toolbox to switch to Geometry mode. Finally, resize the brush by moving its vertices so that it marks out a cubic region around the doors, as shown in Figure 9.24. When you're finished, switch away from Geometry mode.

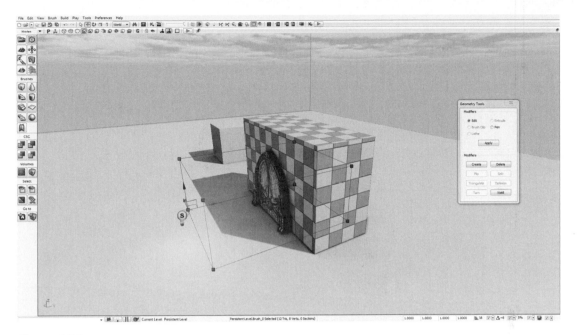

Figure 9.24
Shaping the BSP Builder Brush to create a trigger volume.

3. Add a trigger volume to the level in the shape of the Builder Brush. To do so, right-click the Add Volumes button in the toolbox and choose TriggerVolume from the menu that appears, as shown in Figure 9.25. A trigger volume is added to the level.

Note

The level so far can be found in the companion files under DM-Kismet_Project_02_Door.udk.

Scripting the Door with Kismet

The level now contains everything necessary to start creating a Kismet sequence that can open and close the doors as the player approaches and moves away from them. Specifically, it features two dynamic door actors in the form of KMovers, with a trigger volume surrounding the doors. Before you create the Kismet sequence, it is worthwhile to state more clearly what must be achieved with the doors to identify the relevant events and actions involved. The tasks might be stated in the following two sentences (the events are in italics and the actions in bold):

- When the *player enters the trigger volume*, **open the doors**.

- When the *player leaves the trigger volume*, **close the doors**.

Figure 9.25
Creating a trigger volume from a Builder Brush.

1. Click the Open Kismet Editor button in the main toolbar to open the Kismet Editor. The first step in creating a Kismet sequence object for opening the doors is to add a sequence object representing the event—*player enters the trigger volume*—to be fired when the player enters the trigger volume surrounding the doors. To add this sequence object, select the trigger volume in the Perspective viewport; then, in the Kismet Editor, right-click any vacant space in the Graph pane and choose New Event Using Trigger_Volume followed by Touch from the menu that appears, as shown in Figure 9.26. This creates a Trigger Volume Touch event not for all trigger volumes in the level, but for the *selected* trigger volume. Notice that the TriggerVolume0_Touch node that appears (see Figure 9.27) features three output sockets: Touched (fired when the player enters the trigger volume), UnTouched (fired when the player leaves the trigger volume), and Empty (fired whenever the trigger volume contains no player). Only one of these three sockets can be fired at any one time.

Note

In the UDK, the term *touch* refers to a collision or intersection. Thus, a Trigger Volume Touch event refers to an event that involves the player making contact with a collision volume.

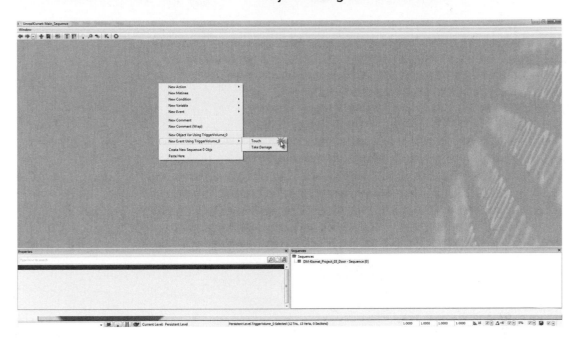

Figure 9.26
Adding a Trigger Volume Touch event to represent the *player enters the trigger volume* event.

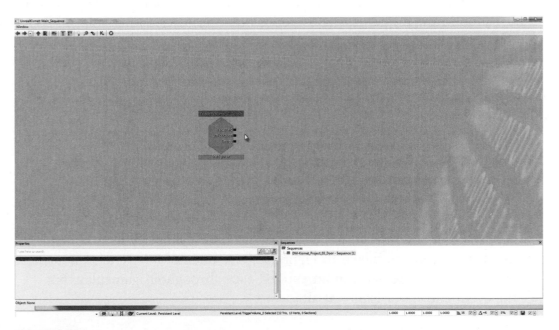

Figure 9.27
The three output sockets of the Trigger Touched Event sequence object.

Figure 9.28
Set the Max Trigger Count property from its default of 1 to 0 to prevent the selected event from expiring.

2. Click the trigger volume in the Graph pane to select it. Then open the Sequence Event section in the Properties pane. Notice that it features a Max Trigger Count property and that its default value is 1. This property defines or limits the total number of times the sequence object may be activated during gameplay before it expires. (An expired sequence object is deactivated for the rest of gameplay.) Here, a value of 1 means that the event will be triggered one time when the player enters the trigger volume, after which it will expire. It will not fire for any subsequent events. In other words, a value of 1 for this property will result in the doors opening once on the first Trigger Volume Touch event and then never closing or opening again because all subsequent events (Touch and Untouch) will be ignored. Our intention, however, is to have the doors open and close whenever the player enters or leaves the volume, regardless of how many times this happens. For this reason, the Max Trigger Count property should be changed from 1 to 0, as shown in Figure 9.28. A value of 0 here does not mean the event begins and remains in an expired state throughout gameplay, but that the event can never expire at all.

Tip

To deactivate an event entirely, uncheck the Enabled property.

3. With the Trigger Volume Touch event configured appropriately in the Kismet sequence, it's time to add a sequence object for the Door Open action. The Kismet Editor, however, does not feature a pre-made Door Open action because a game can contain a potentially unlimited number of different doors, and those doors can open in a potentially unlimited number of different ways. For example, a trap door looks and opens differently from a vault door, a revolving door, a car door, or the door of a jewelry box. To accommodate this variation and to allow developers to define the motion and changes specific to their objects and needs, the Matinee Editor is offered. In this example, the purpose of this editor is to create an animation sequence (specifically, a Door Open sequence) that can be launched from Kismet. To get started with Matinee, you must first add a Matinee sequence object to the Kismet graph. (This sequence object will be the Kismet representation of the door animation sequence that you will create.) To do so, right-click any vacant space in the graph and choose New Matinee. As shown in Figure 9.29, a Matinee sequence object is added to the Kismet graph. Double-click this sequence object to open the Matinee Editor, where the details of the animation sequence can be defined.

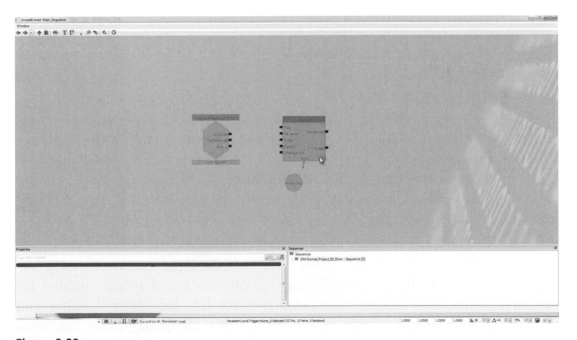

Figure 9.29
The Matinee sequence object.

Animating the Door with Matinee

In video games, the term *animation* typically refers to a change in parameters such as color, position, orientation, scale, and form over time. Such animations are often known as *parametric animations* because the changes that occur can be specified through parameters. There are two main kinds of parametric animations in video games. These might loosely—though not entirely appropriately—be named static and dynamic animation. Static animation is animation in a game whose details are known in advance by the developer—that is, whose details can be given by the developer in advance of gameplay. This includes animation that runs for a specified time, at a specified frame rate, and at a specified occasion, and involves a specified set of actors, motions, and timings. The key feature of these animations is that they can be planned and stated by the developer during the development of the game.

In contrast to static animation, there is dynamic animation. This latter term refers to animation that is brought about by the gamer as a result of his or her input and actions during gameplay. Examples of dynamic animation include navigating a character into a room, causing a character to jump to a specified location, and causing the game camera to zoom toward a specified location. To some extent, these animations are dependent on the actions of the gamer. For this reason, the details of such animations change frequently and cannot be known in advance by developers.

This section is concerned entirely with the first type of animation: static animation. It aims to define the changes that occur to a pair of doors as they open and close over time. These changes, which are the remit of Matinee, can be planned for and scheduled in advance.

The Unreal Matinee Editor, shown in Figure 9.30, offers developers a suite of tools for defining static, parametric, and planned animations for the actors in their level using key framing and interpolation techniques. In short, the Matinee Editor is the tool that developers typically use to tell Unreal how one or more actors in the scene change over time—how doors open, how platforms raise and lower, how bridges collapse, how propellers turn, how lights flicker and flash, and how cameras move and zoom, to name but a few examples.

The Matinee Editor is not the only way to define animations. It is possible, for example, to script such animations using UnrealScript. But the Unreal Matinee makes creating animations easier because it offers a GUI and dedicated system tailored for animation creation. The Matinee Editor works more like the Material Editor and Sound Cue Editor than the Kismet Editor. That is, it is designed to edit individual

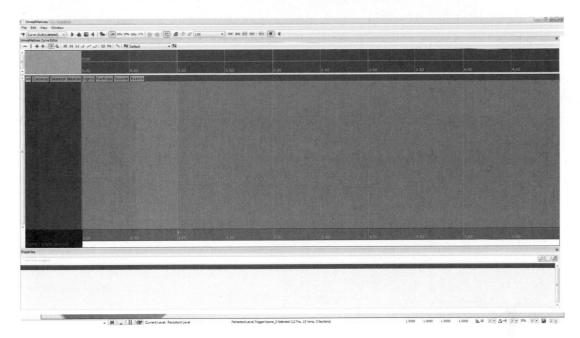

Figure 9.30
The Unreal Matinee Editor.

animations or individual groups of related animations, but not to show all animations that are part of a level.

The purpose of this section is to use the Matinee Editor to create a "door open" animation for the two doors in the level. This animation will be defined through key frames and interpolation. In this animation, both the left and right doors must rotate around their hinges (pivot) and open outward to allow the player through. Follow these steps:

1. Minimize the Matinee Editor and select one of the doors in the Perspective viewport. Then, select the Rotate transformation gizmo and rotate the door for test purposes. Notice that the door does not rotate around the point where the hinges should be (see Figure 9.31). This is because every mesh has a *pivot*—a point that determines its center of rotation. The pivot for each of the door meshes does not match the position of the hinges for the door; therefore, the door does not appear to rotate about its hinges. Press Ctrl+Z to undo the rotation and reset the door to its original orientation.

2. To move the door mesh's pivot to the hinge position, make sure one of the doors is selected. Then, right-click at the far edge of the door where the hinge should be and choose Pivot and then Move Here (Snapped) from the menu that appears (see Figure 9.32). This changes the location of the pivot to the spot on the mesh that you right-clicked.

Figure 9.31
Rotation troubles: The door does not rotate around the hinges. This is because a mesh rotates around its pivot, and its pivot does not match the position of the door hinge.

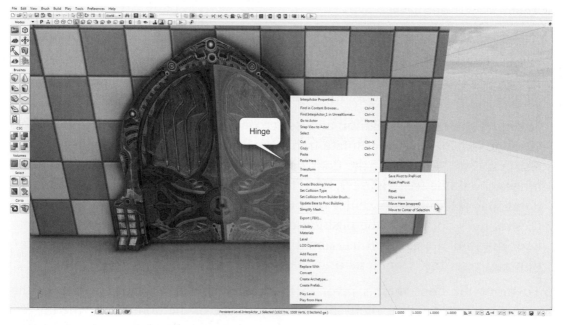

Figure 9.32
Setting the pivot.

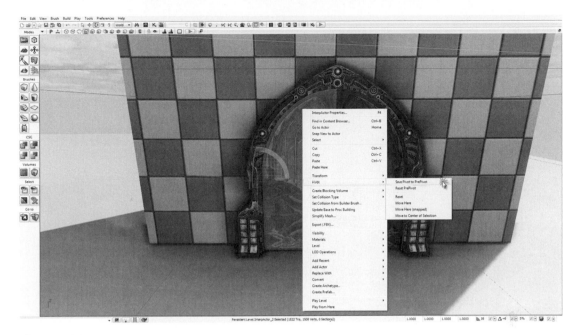

Figure 9.33
Saving the pivot.

3. The new pivot location is temporary, lasting only as long as the mesh remains selected. To save the pivot position, right-click anywhere in the door mesh and choose Pivot and then Save Pivot to Pre-Pivot from the menu that appears, as shown in Figure 9.33.

4. Repeat steps 2 and 3 for the other door mesh so both meshes pivot at their hinges. Each door can now be rotated in a way that is both appropriate and believable. Then select each of the two doors, right-click the selection, and choose Convert followed by StaticMeshActor to KMover from the menu that appears. This ensures the door meshes are converted into dynamic rather than static actors—that is, the kind of actors that can be animated at run time through Kismet.

5. Return to the Matinee Editor, where you'll script an open-door animation for each door. You'll handle each door separately, with one animation for the left door and one for the right. To get started, select one of the doors in the Perspective viewport. Then, right-click in the left-most gray margin of the Matinee Editor's Track Editor and choose Add New Empty Group from the menu that appears (see Figure 9.34). In the Group Name dialog box (see Figure 9.35), enter a name for the group (Such as LeftDoor or RightDoor) and then click the OK button. This creates a group to which all the animation properties for the selected door will be attached.

Figure 9.34
Creating an empty animation group for the selected door.

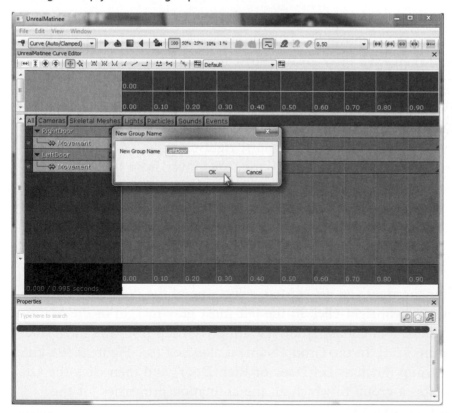

Figure 9.35
The Group Name dialog box.

Tip

Ensure that the door is selected *before* you create the group. Newly created groups are always associated with the selected actor in the level.

6. The newly created group in the Track Editor can contain one or more tracks, each corresponding to a specific property to be animated on the mesh. The purpose of the door-open animation is to rotate the door from its closed orientation to its open orientation. Thus, the door-open animation involves animating one property: the door's orientation. For this reason, you must create one track in the Track Editor that is associated with the mesh's transformation properties. To create this track as a child of the new group, right-click the group in the Track Editor and choose Add New Movement Track from the menu that appears, as shown in Figure 9.36. Movement tracks are used to animate all transformation properties of an object, including its position, orientation, and scale.

7. Using the scroll wheel on your mouse or the zoom controls in the editor toolbar, zoom out to see the full length of the animation in the Matinee Editor. Notice that the start of the animation is marked by a red flag to the left of the

Figure 9.36
Movement tracks are created as children of a group and allow the transformation properties of an object to be animated through key framing.

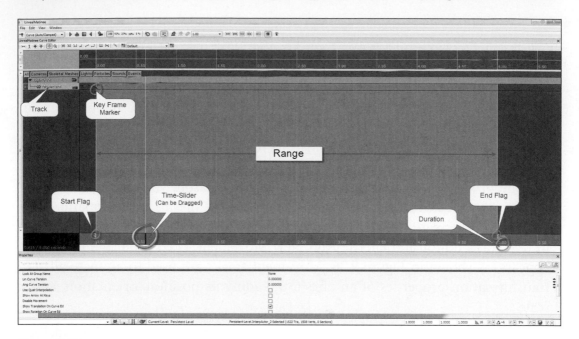

Figure 9.37
The timeline displays the length of the animation in seconds. The red flags on the timeline mark the start and the end of the animation, and the black bar represents the Time slider—the current position in the animation.

animation timeline, and that the end of the animation is marked by a red flag at the end of the timeline. (See Figure 9.37.) By default, the animation is five seconds long. (You can discern the duration of the animation in seconds using the timeline.) The animation also contains one pre-made key frame representing the door's current closed position at frame 0; this key frame is represented by a red triangle at the top of the Track Editor.

8. As mentioned, the duration of the animation is currently five seconds. I think this is too long—the door should open in one second. To reduce the duration of the animation, drag its End flag from the five-second point leftward to the one-second point on the timeline, as shown in Figure 9.38.

9. The animation is now one second long and has one key frame on the first frame. This key frame marks the initial state of the door before the door-open animation begins. On this frame, the door will be in a closed state. To complete this animation, a key frame must be created on the final frame, with the door in its open state. Matinee will then be able to generate the intervening frames between the closed and open states using interpolation. To create the final key

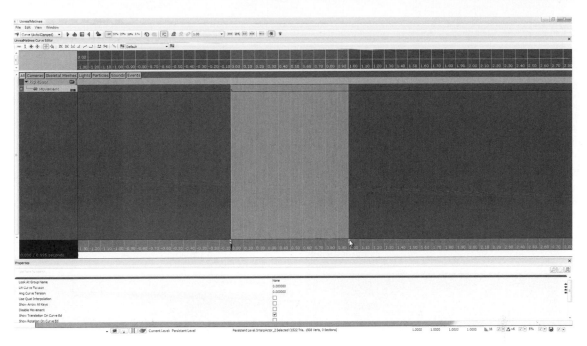

Figure 9.38
Drag the End flag to the left, along the timeline, to reduce the total length of the animation from five seconds to one second.

frame, make sure the Movement track is selected in the editor; then drag the Time slider to the final frame at one second. Finally, click the Add Key button in the Matinee Editor toolbar or press Enter. Figure 9.39. demonstrates the addition of a second and final key frame.

10. The second key frame of the door-open animation has been created, but the open state of the door has not been associated with the key frame. The door is closed both on the first and on the final key frame of the animation, meaning that the door will not move because it begins and ends in the same state. To address this, first reduce the size of the Matinee Editor window so that both the Perspective viewport and the Matinee Editor can be seen onscreen at the same time. Next, select the final key frame on the Movement track. Notice that the words UnrealMatinee appear in the top-left corner of the Perspective viewport, along with the words Adjust Key 1 in the bottom left, as shown in Figure 9.40. This indicates that Unreal Matinee is now recording *all* the transformations made to the selected door mesh using the transformation gizmo, and that the recorded data will be assigned to Key Frame 1, which is the final key frame. (Key frame numbering begins at 0.) Consider Figure 9.39.

Figure 9.39
Creating a second key frame.

Figure 9.40
Preparing to record the final key frame for a door mesh.

Figure 9.41
Rotating the door to its open state with Matinee.

11. Use the Rotation gizmo in the Perspective viewport to rotate the door to its open state, as shown in Figure 9.41. The rotation is recorded in the final key frame, meaning that the animation will automatically interpolate between the two states when played back. Drag the Time slider back and forth between the first and last frame to observe how the door smoothly rotates on its hinges between its closed and open state.

12. It's time to create the animation for the second door, which should open simultaneously with the first one. To begin, drag the Time slider back to the first frame of the animation. Next, select the *other* door in the Perspective viewport—the door that was not animated. With this door selected, create a new empty group in the Track Editor and name the group LeftDoor or RightDoor, as appropriate. (Refer to step 5 for help creating a group.) Figure 9.42. shows the result.

13. This door requires its own Movement track to store key frame data. Create the Movement track for this group using the technique described in step 6; then use Matinee to record the start and end frames for this door as described in steps 9, 10, and 11. Figure 9.43 shows the completed animation, with both doors rotating to an open state over the course of one second.

14. The door-open animation is now complete in that there is nothing further for the animation that needs to be created in Matinee. However, the Kismet

Figure 9.42
Creating a new animation group for the second door.

Figure 9.43
Double doors rotating from a closed state to an open state in a one-second animation.

sequence for the level does not currently connect the Trigger Touch and Trigger Untouch events to the Matinee node, meaning that the door-open animation will not play as the player approaches the doors. To address this, close the Matinee Editor and return to the Kismet Editor. Then create a connection between the Trigger Event sequence object and the Matinee node. To do so, begin by dragging a connection between the Touched socket of the Trigger Volume0_Touch node and the Play socket of the Matinee node to ensure that the animation plays as the player enters the trigger volume. Then drag a connection between the TriggerVolume0_Touch node's UnTouched socket and the Matinee node's Reverse socket to ensure the door-open animation plays in reverse as the player leaves the trigger volume. (That is, leaving the trigger volume will cause the door to close.) See Figure 9.44.

15. Give this Kismet sequence a test run. *Voilà!* The doors should open and close as the player approaches and moves away from the doors, as shown in Figure 9.45. The one disappointing thing is that doors are completely silent—they make no sound on their opening or closing. Let us return to Kismet and address this issue.

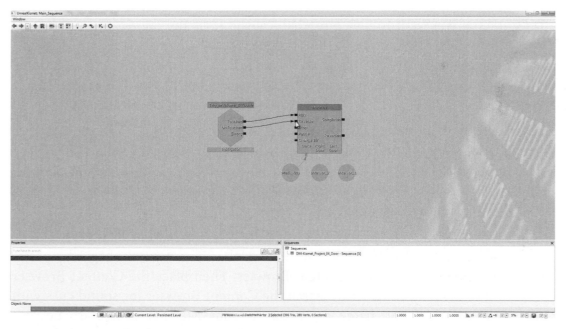

Figure 9.44
Configuring Kismet to play door-open and door-close animations based on the player's Touch status with a trigger volume.

Figure 9.45
Testing the Kismet sequence so far….

16. Let's assume you want to play a mechanical sound as the doors open to increase the realism of the scene. To do this, start by adding a new Kismet sequence object. Right-click a blank area in the Kismet Editor and choose New Action, then Sound, and then Play Sound from the menu that appears, as shown in Figure 9.46.

17. Move the Play Sound node between the TriggerVolume0_Touch and Matinee nodes. Then connect the Touch output socket of the TriggerVolume0_Touch node to the Play input socket of the Play Sound node, as shown in Figure 9.47. This ensures that the selected sound will play as the player enters or leaves the trigger volume. At present, however, no sound has been associated with the Play Sound node, meaning that the node will currently play silence.

18. To associate a sound with the sound node in the Kismet graph, begin by pressing Ctrl+Shift+F to open the Content Browser. Then place the Content Browser next to the Kismet Editor. Next, search the Content Browser for sound cues with the word "door" in their name. Select the A_Door_Metal03_CloseStartCue sound cue and return to the Kismet Editor. Finally, select the Play Sound node and click the green left arrow in the Properties pane's Play Sound field (found in the Seq Act Play Sound section) to insert the selected sound cue, as shown in

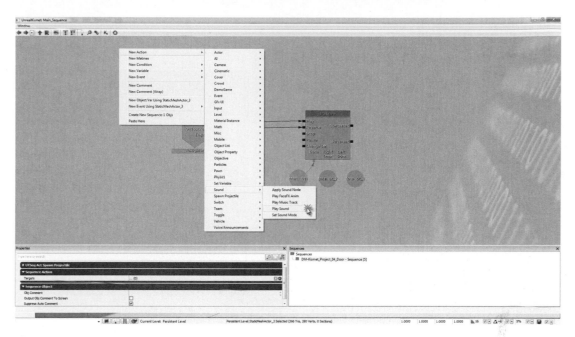

Figure 9.46
Play Sound sequence objects can play selected sound-cue assets from the Content Browser.

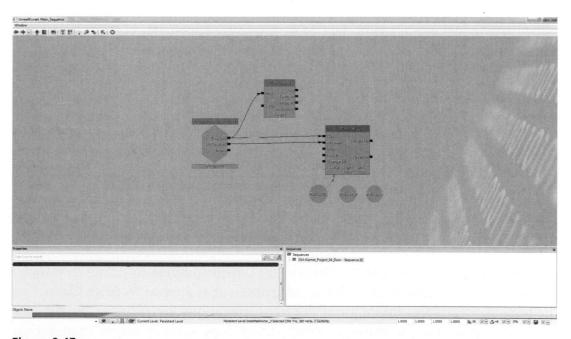

Figure 9.47
The nodes of the Kismet graph are connected, ready for playing a door-open and door-close animation.

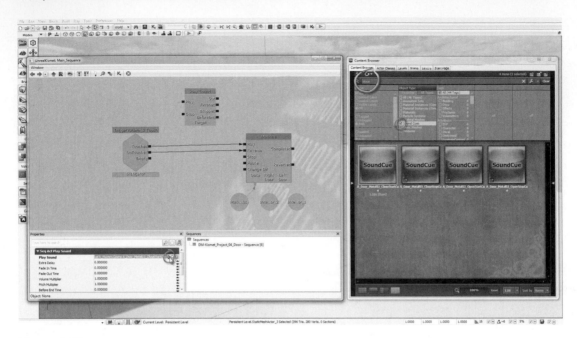

Figure 9.48
Associating a sound with the Play Sound node.

Figure 9.48. Congratulations! The door should now open and close on approach, and a sound should play in sync with the door-open animation.

19. Repeat steps 16 through 18 to add a sound for the closing animation. The door open-and-close project is now completed.

Note

The completed level can be found in the companion files under DM-Kismet_Project_04_Door.udk.

PROJECT: CREATING A CAMERA TOUR WITH DIRECTOR MODE

The previous project demonstrated the use of Unreal Matinee to create key frame animations on a per-actor basis—that is, animations that applied to particular actors the level. You can also use Matinee to create animations that work at the director actor-level animations, which define how specific actors change over or-level animations control how the level and its contents are shown or to the player through cameras over time.

Director-level animations consist of cutting or changing to different cameras over time to present the level from different perspectives to increase dramatic effect. For example, a 15-second director-level animation might instruct the engine to show the level from camera 1 for the first five seconds, then from camera 2 for the next five seconds, and then from camera 3 for the final five seconds. Director-level animations are not typically played during active gameplay, when the player has control. Rather, director-level animations typically apply during game cut scenes—that is, scenes in which the player has the passive role of a viewer or an observer. One of the most notable forms of cut scenes for a game is the introduction movie—the animation sequence intended to set the scene or atmosphere.

This section focuses on the third and final project for this chapter. Its aim is to use Matinee's Director mode (see Figure 9.49) to offer the gamer a cut scene tour of the level created in the previous section. Specifically, this section will demonstrate the creation of a 10-second animation in which two camera actors fly throughout the level, enabling the gamer to observe the tour from the perspective of the cameras as they move. The gamer will be able to see from only one camera at any one time. Director mode will be used to control the cuts between cameras over the course of the animation, with camera 1 being active for the first five seconds and camera 2 being active for the last five seconds.

Figure 9.49
Matinee's Director mode can be used to create director-level animations.

Note

This section continues from the level created in the previous section, although none of its Kismet or Matinee work is required for the Kismet and Matinee work here. The animation sequence created in this section is entirely independent of the door-open and door-close animation sequences.

1. To get started creating the camera animation, you must create two camera actors in the level. These will be the cameras from which the level tour will be seen, and to which the Matinee Editor will cut and change as the tour animation is played. To create these two cameras, press Ctrl+Shift+F to open the Content Browser; then click the Actor Classes tab. Next, drag two camera actors from the Actor Classes tab into the Perspective viewport of the level and position them at different locations in the level. As shown in Figure 9.50, I have inserted one in the sky for an aerial view of the level, and the other on the ground for a ground view of the level. Remember to use the Lock Selected Actors to Camera feature to position and orient the cameras appropriately. For more information on this feature, refer to the section "Framing Actors, Locking Targets, and Others" in Chapter 3, "UDK Fundamentals."

2. As mentioned, the player should not be able to control his or her character as the level begins, but should be treated to an automated cut scene in which his or

cameras in the level. Camera actors can be added to the level via the Actor Classes tab of the
ıvser.

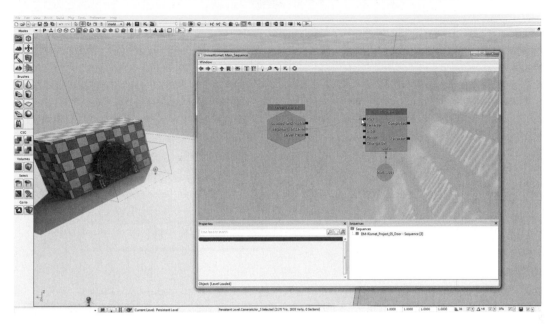

Figure 9.51
Connecting a Level Loaded node to a Matinee node.

her role is as passive viewer. The next step in creating this animation is to open the Kismet Editor and to create two nodes: a Level Loaded node and a Matinee node. Connect them together as shown in Figure 9.51.

3. Double click the Matinee node to open the Matinee Editor; then drag the animation End flag to set the animation duration to five seconds.

4. Create a new camera group for each camera, as shown in Figure 9.52. Be sure to select each camera one at a time and create a new camera group for each one.

Note

Notice that the group to be created here is not an empty group, but a camera group. Camera groups come pre-equipped with a Movement track (for key framing the motion of the camera) and an FOV track (for key framing the camera's field of view properties). The animation to be created in this section involves animating only the movement properties of the camera.

5. As before, each Movement track in each camera group features a pre-made key frame on the first frame of the animation, representing the starting state of the cameras. It is now time to key frame the motion for each camera separately so that each camera moves around the level on its own course throughout the animation. I want to circle the aerial camera around the level, and to move the ground-level camera on a path around the doors and around the cube actor.

Figure 9.52
Creating a Matinee camera group for each camera.

(The course for your own cameras need not be the same as mine.) To create the motion for these cameras, I pressed Enter to insert key frames at a number of points along the timeline, between the start and end frames of the animation. This is to ensure that the cameras move in a number of different ways: The aerial camera will orbit the level for the first five seconds, and then the ground-level camera will travel the level from the ground for the last five seconds. I have inserted key frames for the aerial camera at 0 seconds, 2.5 seconds, and 5 seconds, as shown in Figure 9.53.

6. Having inserted key frames into the animation, it's time to associate key frame data with them. That is, you must select each key frame in the Track Editor and then transform the associated camera in the viewport to record the transformation data into the key frame. The cameras can be moved as standard scene actors using the Transformation gizmo in the same way the doors meshes were transformed using Matinee in the previous section. However, the camera group in the Matinee Editor offers a Camera View button (see Figure 9.54) that enables developers to see through the lens of the camera in the Perspective viewport while it is being moved and transformed for the animation. In short, the Camera View button allows the viewport to become the camera—to display its contents from the perspective of the camera, based on its position and field of view. To animate the camera for each key frame, click the Camera View button and

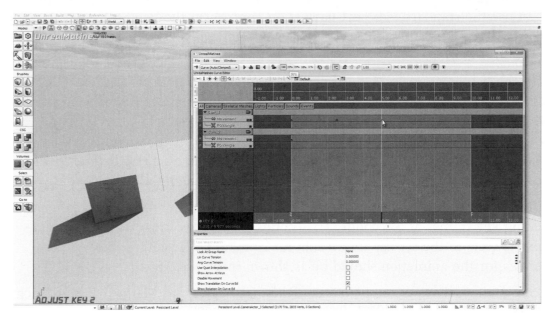

Figure 9.53
Creating key frames for the first camera.

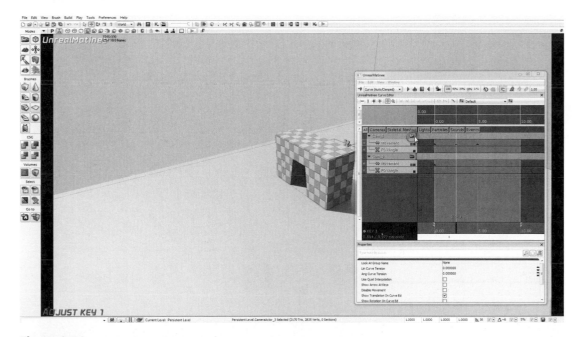

Figure 9.54
The Camera View button, available from the camera group in the Track Editor, offers developers a camera-centric view of the animation in the Perspective viewport.

then use the standard viewport navigation controls in the Perspective viewport to transform the camera to new positions around the level. See Figure 9.53 for more information.

7. Use the camera-centric Matinee view to position and animate camera 1 for all its key frames during the first five seconds of the animation. It will not matter to the animation that camera 1 is not animated for the final five seconds, just as it will not matter that camera 2 is not animated for the first seconds. You'll use Director mode later to ensure that camera 1 is the active camera for the first five seconds, and that camera 2 is the active camera for the final five seconds.

8. After creating the animation data for camera 1, repeat the process for camera 2, setting key frames at 5 seconds, 7.5 seconds, and 10 seconds. Use the camera-centric view to the set key frame data for camera 2. The complete set of key frames for the animation should be as shown in Figure 9.55.

9. Both cameras have a complete set of key frames in the Matinee Editor, each charting the camera's path during the fly-through. The Perspective viewport also shows this path graphically using curves that extend outward from the camera actors. Having created animation for the cameras, however, is not enough in itself to make the level complete. At present, when the player starts

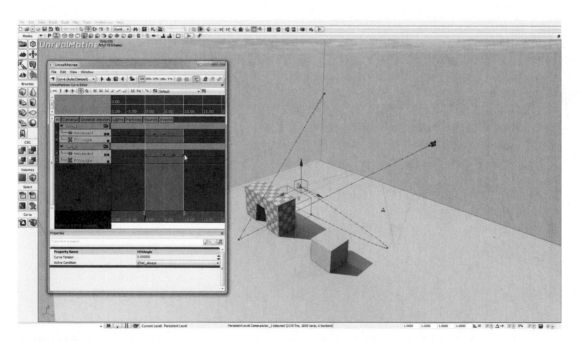

Figure 9.55
The complete set of key frames for cameras 1 and 2 during the course of the 10-second animation. Notice that the trajectories for the cameras are shown in the Perspective viewport as colored curves.

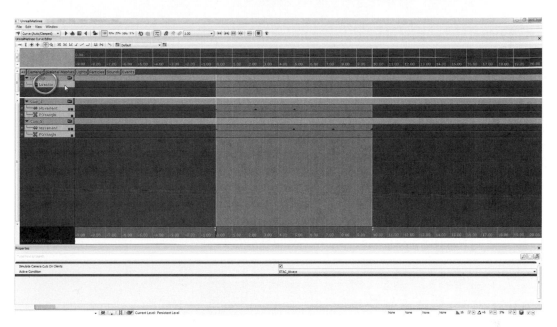

Figure 9.56
Create a new director group in the Matinee Editor.

the level, the animation will not be visible because Director mode has not been used to specify the camera from which the level is viewed, nor for how long. To use Director mode, open the Matinee Editor (if it is not open already), right-click in the margin of the Track Editor, and choose New Director Group from the menu that appears. This creates a new director group in a separate panel above the Track Editor (see Figure 9.56). The director group provides all the options required for setting and changing the active camera for the animation.

10. Select the director group in the Matinee Editor. Then use the mouse to drag the Track Editor's Time slider to the first frame of the animation. Next, press the Enter key to create a camera cut in the director group. (The purpose of the camera cut is to specify which camera in the level should be the active camera for the selected frame of the animation and for all subsequent frames until a new camera cut changes the active camera or the animation ends.) The New Cut dialog box appears, in which you can specify the active camera. Select Cam_1 for camera 1, as shown in Figure 9.57.

11. Move the Time slider to the five-second mark. Then insert a second camera cut in the director group to change the active camera from camera 1 to camera 2 at the five-second mark. Next, click the Camera View button in the director group and click the Play button in the toolbar to preview the complete animation from the Perspective viewport, complete with camera cuts. (See Figure 9.58.)

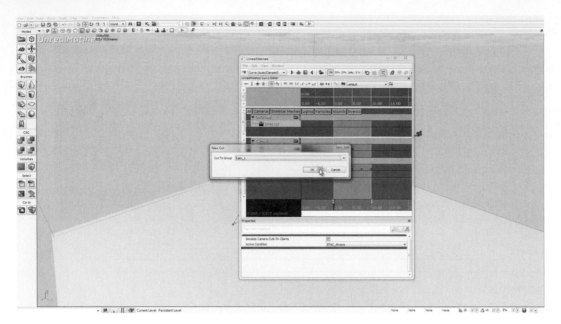

Figure 9.57
Creating a camera cut and selecting the active camera.

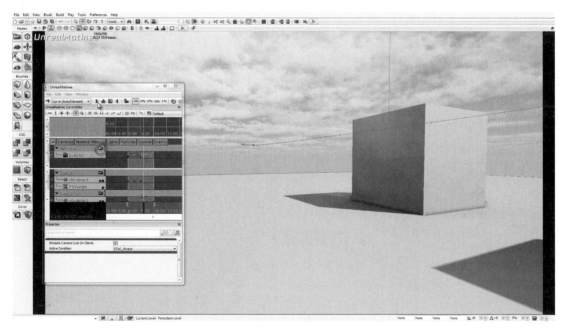

Figure 9.58
Previewing the complete director animation.

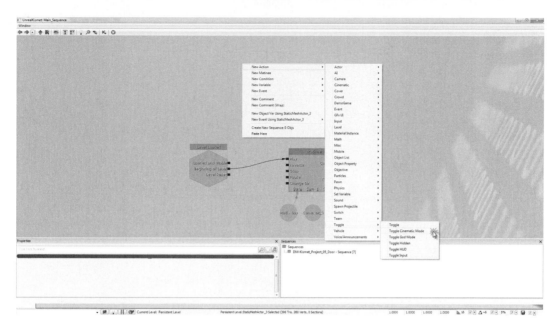

Figure 9.59
Toggle Cinematic Mode nodes can disable user input during the playback of cut scenes.

12. If the level were played right now, the animation would be seen as intended, but the gamer could continue to control the player character in parallel with the animation. To disable user input during cut-scene playback, and then re-enable it after playback of the cut scene is complete, open Kismet. Then, right-click on any vacant space in the Graph pane, and choose New Action, then Toggle, followed by Cinematic Mode from the menu that appears, as shown in Figure 9.59. This creates a Toggle Cinematic Mode node.

13. Connect the Beginning of Level output socket of the Level Loaded node to the Enable input socket of Toggle Cinematic Mode node. This enables Cinematic mode as the level begins. Then connect the Completed output socket of the Matinee node to the Disable input socket of the Toggle Cinematic Mode node. This disables Cinematic mode as the animation completes. See Figure 9.60.

14. Notice that the Toggle Cinematic Mode node has a Target socket. This is used to specify the player for whom input is to be disabled. If this parameter is left disconnected, then no player will be affected. To set Player 0 as the target (Player 0 is the only player in a single-player game, such as this one) you must create a variable object representing the player. To do so, right-click in the Kismet graph and choose New Variable followed by Player from the menu that appears. Then connect the Toggle Cinematic Mode node's Target socket to the Player 0 variable, as shown in Figure 9.61.

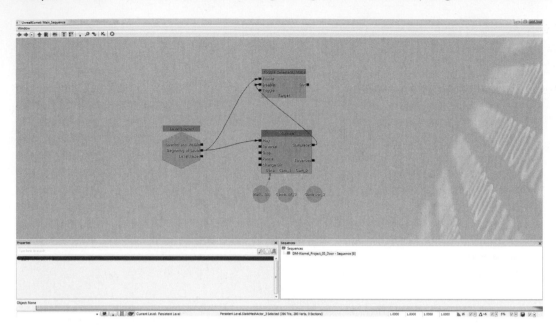

Figure 9.60
Connecting the Toggle Cinematic Mode node to the Level Loaded and Matinee nodes.

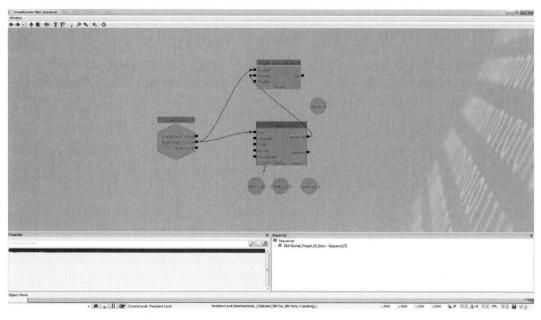

Figure 9.61
Connecting the Toggle Cinematic Mode node's Target socket to the Player 0 variable.

Figure 9.62
The completed project: camera in motion.

15. Congratulations! You're finished with the third and final project in this chapter, shown in Figure 9.62. I recommend taking it for a test run to make sure it works. I further recommend playing around and experimenting with other Kismet nodes to enhance the features of the level.

Note

The completed level can be found in the companion files under DM-Kismet_Project_05_Camera.udk.

CONCLUSION

There is so much to learn about Kismet and Matinee, a chapter of this size cannot hope to do them justice. The aim of this chapter was not so much to explain every feature of Kismet and Matinee, but to introduce their basic workflow to equip you to be a confident self-learner. Together, the three projects in this chapter demonstrated how to work with the four fundamental ingredients of Kismet: variables, events, actions, and conditions. This chapter also demonstrated how to create object-level and director-level key frame animations using Matinee. The next chapter enters the world of user interfaces by examining the Scaleform feature set.

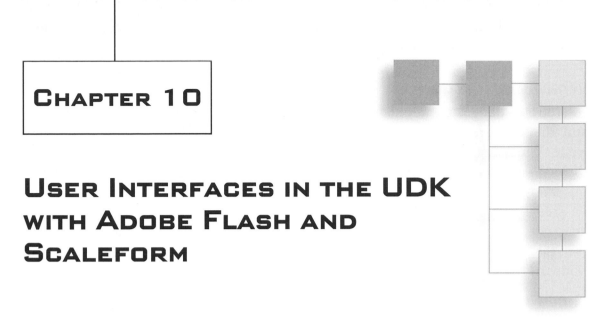

CHAPTER 10

USER INTERFACES IN THE UDK WITH ADOBE FLASH AND SCALEFORM

The function of good software is to make the complex appear to be simple.

—Grady Booch

By the end of this chapter, you should:

- Understand what Scaleform is and does.
- Be able to create basic GUIs with Adobe Flash.
- Be able to install the Scaleform GFX Flash Player.
- Understand how to import Flash SWFs into the UDK.
- Be able to use Kismet to display Flash-based GUIs in a level.

The title of this chapter includes a number of technical words whose meanings are related in the context of the UDK, and which must be defined here in order to proceed. These words are *user interfaces*, *Adobe Flash*, and *Scaleform*. They are defined in the sections that follow.

USER INTERFACE

The term *user interface* is used here to refer to a graphical user interface, or GUI. The terms do have distinct meanings in software design, but for the purpose of game development, their meanings are the same. *GUI* refers to the space where interaction between users and machines occurs. Thus, a GUI is a space of interaction between user and software. This definition, however, raises two key questions: What is interaction? That is, what does it mean for a game to be interactive? Secondly, where is this space of interaction, anyway?

What Is Interaction?

In software design, the term *interaction* refers to communication between the user and the software. Such events typically occur many times per second in a video game. The user communicates with the software by way of input—that is, by feeding the software instructions and commands through input devices such as keyboards, mice, joysticks, gamepads, and so on, using buttons, text boxes, and diagrams onscreen. For example, clicking a Reload button in a menu might cause the game character to reload his active weapon. Therefore, such an action is an example of the user communicating with the software—specifically, communicating an instruction (the player character should reload his active weapon immediately).

In contrast, software communicates with the user through output and response. For example, the game might inform the player of his or her health through an onscreen health meter bar, which reduces whenever the player takes damage. Further, a game can inform the player of his or her score via a real-time score counter, and can inform the player of his or her location in the level through a mini-map component. The mini-map, health bar, and ammo bar components in Figure 10.1 are examples of software communication.

Figure 10.1
GUI components featuring HUDs and game-related information.

Both the communications made by the gamer and those made in response by the software together fall under the umbrella of interaction. Therefore, a game that is said to be *interactive* is one that allows two-way communication between the user and software. That is, it allows the user a degree of influence and input over the game, and allows the game to act and to change in response.

Where Is the Space of Interaction?

The GUI has been termed a *space of interaction*. The word *space* is used here to mean not a physical space, such as the real-world room in which the game is played or the shopping mall in which the game was purchased, but a conceptual space. Specifically, it refers to a conceptual space that exists in the minds of game developers and in the plans and diagrams they make when planning and constructing the game. In particular, the term *space* is used here to indicate that not all components of the game software are related to interaction. Further, not all parts relating to interaction are necessarily a part of the GUI. Rather, the GUI refers to a particular set of software components within the game that relate to interaction.

Specifically, the GUI refers narrowly to two main types of spaces of interaction in a game:

- **Menus.** The game menus are both a space of interaction and a meta-gaming component. They are said to be the latter because they are not in the game in the same way that actors are a part of the level. Instead, they exist in a space outside the game world and game events (see Figure 10.2). The menus for most games include the following:

  - **The main menu.** This is where the player starts new games and exits the application to the desktop.

  - **The options menu.** Players use this menu to adjust the game volume, the resolution, and gamma correction.

  - **The controller menu.** From here, the player can define the controls for the game—for example, the keyboard and mouse bindings.

  - **The save and load game menus.** Players use these menus to retain and resume their progress in the game, respectively.

  - **A range of other game-specific menus.** Typical menus are full screen, require the player's undivided attention, are mouse driven, and are modal, meaning that gameplay pauses while the menu is active and does not resume until the menu is closed.

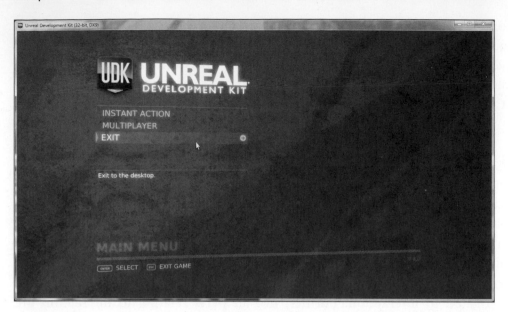

Figure 10.2
A GUI menu. Contrast this with HUD elements in Figure 10.1.

■ **HUDs.** Like menus, HUDs (short for *heads-up displays*) are a graphical meta-gaming component. That is, they do not exist in the game world and are not subject to the physics and forces of the environment. Unlike menus, however, HUDs are non-modal, run in parallel with gameplay, and are not full-screen but are instead shown as panels or 2D displays in front of gameplay. HUDs typically consist of all 2D graphical components that are shown onscreen during game-play at specified screen positions, and exist to provide the gamer either with information about the game or with opportunities to input instructions into the game. HUDs might include health bars, score counters, mini-maps, direction arrows, danger signs, subtitles, inventory panels, buttons, tips, messages, dialog boxes, and others.

In short, the GUI is a meta-gaming feature that the gamer uses both to get things done in the game (via input) and to view information about what is going on in the game (via output provided by the software, typically in response to input). Menus and HUDs are sometimes referred to as a form of augmented reality (AR) because they provide information that enhances or exists above and beyond what is happening in the game world. Think of the GUI as the space of interaction in the game that includes all the menu systems and HUDs, as well as all their attendant graphical widgets (buttons, drop-down menus, list boxes, checkboxes, images, text, and subtitles). The development of a GUI for a game involves the creation of menus and HUDs, as detailed in the next section of this chapter.

SCALEFORM AND FLASH

Like meshes, textures, and sounds, the user interfaces for most contemporary UDK games are created in third-party software.

They are then imported into the UDK using another third-party tool that is integrated into both the UDK and the Unreal Engine. Specifically, user interfaces for UDK games are created as Shockwave Flash (SWF) presentations in Adobe Flash or another Flash-compliant application, and are then imported into the UDK through an integrated technology known as Scaleform. (Actually, Scaleform is known more fully as Autodesk Scaleform because it is created not by Epic Games but by Autodesk, Inc.)

The Scaleform software is integrated into both the architecture of the UDK and the Unreal Engine in the same way a coffee shop franchise might integrate itself into a bookstore or airport. The purpose of Scaleform is to create a metaphorical bridge between a user interface created in Flash as an SWF file and an Unreal-powered game (see Figure 10.3). That is, Scaleform allows Flash presentations to be shown and played inside a UDK game, as though they were an intrinsic part of the game. In addition to allowing Flash presentations to be played in the game, Scaleform allows them to be integrated into the game in the sense that a channel of two-way communication can be made between the Flash presentation and the game. This

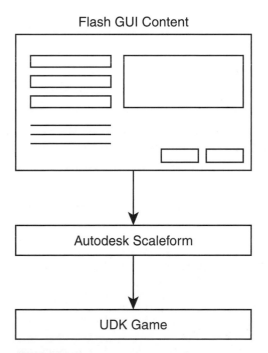

Figure 10.3
Scaleform integrates Flash content into UDK applications.

allows the game to call ActionScript functions and procedures within the Flash presentation, and allows the Flash presentation to call Kismet and Unreal Script functions within the game.

Note

ActionScript is the name of the scripting language used in Adobe Flash to code functionality for Flash presentations.

The rest of this chapter demonstrates by example how to use Adobe Flash and Scaleform together to create a basic menu interface for a UDK game. The version of Adobe Flash used for the following project will be Adobe Flash Professional CS5, and the images created there will be made in Adobe Photoshop CS5. These applications are not required, however; alternatives can be used to create both Flash presentations and images. Examples include SWiSH Max4, KoolMoves 7, Gimp, Paint Shop Pro, and others. The step-by-step instructions for subsequent sections, however, will be particular to Flash CS5 and Photoshop CS5.

PROJECT: CREATING A MENU USER INTERFACE

Your work in this project will involve creating an image in Photoshop, configuring Flash for use with Scaleform, creating a presentation in Flash, and then using the Scaleform feature of the UDK to connect that presentation with the game.

This project involves the use of tools and applications that are not themselves part of the UDK—namely, Adobe Photoshop and Adobe Flash. It is important to mention, however, that this project is not intended to be a tutorial for Adobe Photoshop or Adobe Flash. It is assumed that you are generally familiar with these tools and their use. Furthermore, the project is not intended to demonstrate all—or even most—of the features of Scaleform. Scaleform is a comprehensive tool, and a complete discussion of it would require a book of this size. Rather, the purpose of this project is to introduce the Scaleform component of the UDK through an example—to detail the basic workflow of Scaleform step by step by creating a simple presentation in Adobe Flash that should appear as a functional GUI in a UDK game. This GUI will feature one logo graphic and two separate buttons: one that exits the game when clicked and another that loads a specified map when clicked. Figure 10.4 shows the completed project.

Configuring Scaleform for Adobe Flash

The user interface project begins not with the UDK but with Adobe Flash because Adobe Flash is used to create the user interface. That is, Adobe Flash is the

Figure 10.4
The completed GUI project: Flash content up and running in a UDK application

content-creation tool. The mouse-driven Flash environment will be used to position, size, and orient the GUI components (such as buttons, text boxes, lists, and so on) in the user interface in the same way the UDK Editor is used to arrange sounds and meshes into a cohesive level. Because the development of the interface starts in Flash, the project begins by configuring the Scaleform software provided with the UDK for use with the Flash application—that is, to integrate Scaleform into the Flash development environment. This will make developing Scaleform-compliant Flash projects easier.

Configuring Adobe Flash for use with Scaleform involves installing a Scaleform plug-in into Flash. This plug-in, which ships with the UDK, enables developers to preview their Flash presentations directly from the Flash interface using a hardware-accelerated Scaleform renderer. That means developers can edit and change their Flash presentations and then see the results of their work as though it were running in a UDK game, without having to leaving the Flash interface. The developer need not repeatedly export data from Flash into the UDK simply to test the results of non-final changes.

1. To install the Scaleform Flash plug-in in Adobe Flash CS5, start Flash. Then, open the Help menu and choose Manage Extensions, as shown in Figure 10.5. The Manage Extensions Browser appears.

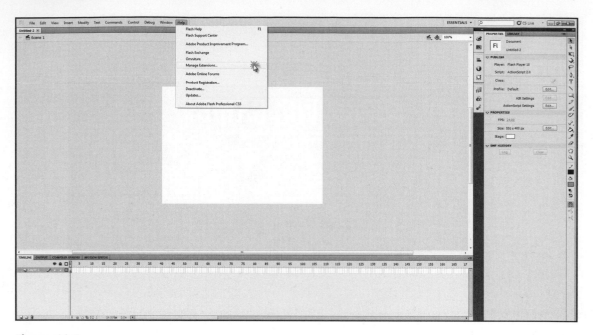

Figure 10.5
Installing the Flash Scaleform plug-in.

2. In the Products pane, located on the left side of the Manage Extensions Browser, click Flash, as shown in Figure 10.6. Then click the Install button in the top-right corner of the screen. From the dialog box that appears, select the folder in which the Scaleform plug-in is located. (By default, the Scaleform plug-in can be found in the UDK installation folder, located at \UDK\Binaries\GFx\CLIK Tools\ Scaleform CLIK.mxp.) Select this file and click OK. Then restart Adobe Flash.

3. The newly installed Scaleform plug-in takes the form of a Flash panel, meaning the plug-in's features can be accessed via the Scaleform Launcher panel in the Flash editor. To display this panel, open the Window menu, choose Other Panels, and select Scaleform Launcher, as shown in Figure 10.7.

4. The Scaleform Launcher panel can be docked as a permanently visible panel in the Flash interface, alongside other similar windows and panels. This panel includes a button that, when clicked, runs the active Flash presentation using a hardware-accelerated renderer. That means developers can preview their Flash representations with Scaleform. To ensure that the Scaleform Launcher works appropriately, developers must first create a Launcher profile, which is a collection of settings that dictate how the Scaleform Launcher should work. The most important of these settings is the fully qualified path to the Scaleform FX-MediaPlayer executable file—the software component actually responsible for running Flash presentations using Scaleform. To create a profile, click the Add

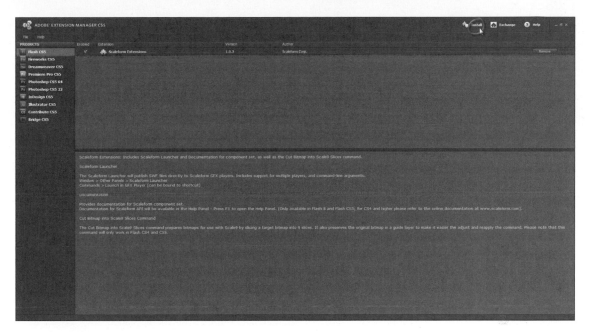

Figure 10.6
The Scaleform Media Player plug-in enables developers to preview Flash-based interfaces in a hardware renderer. The plug-in file is named Scaleform CLIK.mxp and is provided with the UDK.

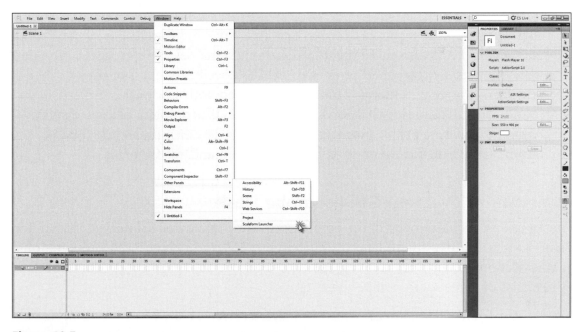

Figure 10.7
Displaying the Scaleform Launcher panel.

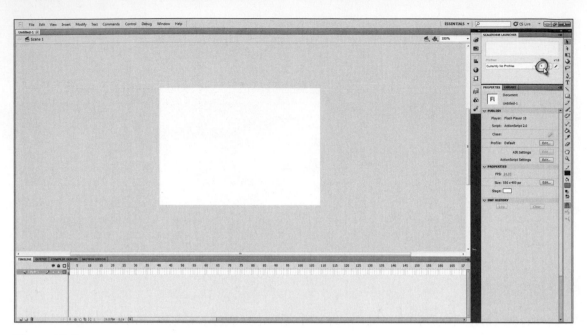

Figure 10.8
Creating a new Scaleform Launcher profile.

New Profile button (marked with a plus sign) in the Scaleform Launcher panel, as shown in Figure 10.8. The New Profile dialog box opens; here, you can specify a number of settings for the Scaleform Launcher.

5. Type a name—for example, Scaleform Player—for the profile in the Profile Name field, as shown in Figure 10.9. Then click the Select Path button (the one with the plus sign) by the Player EXE field to specify the path of the Scaleform Player executable. This file is provided with the UDK, and can be found at UDK\Binaries\GFx\FxMediaPlayer.exe. If prompted, enter a display name for the new profile (such as Scaleform Player); then click the OK button. The Scaleform plug-in is now configured and ready for use.

Preparing to Create a GUI in Adobe Flash

The previous section focused on configuring the Scaleform Launcher plug-in for Flash. This will prove useful later, to quickly preview and debug Flash presentations. In this section, you'll start creating the user interface for the project. This interface will consist of three main components:

■ **A logo image.** This image, which has already been created in Photoshop for you and is provided in the book companion files, states the name of a hypothetical game.

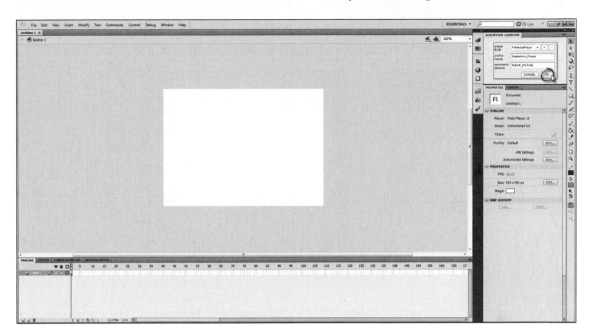

Figure 10.9
Configuring the Scaleform Launcher.

- **A Start or New Game button.** This will cause a specified map to load when clicked.

- **An Exit or Quit button.** This will terminate the UDK application when clicked.

You'll learn how to create both the Start and Exit buttons later in this chapter. This section focuses on guidelines for creating images for Flash presentations bound for UDK games via Scaleform. When it comes to creating images for this purpose, there are two main recommendations:

- **Save in PNG format.** Images to be used in Scaleform should be saved in the lossless PNG format rather than in other lossless formats such as TIFF or in other lossy formats such as JPG (even though Flash supports those formats). The Scaleform software imports Flash presentations into the UDK by extracting all their member images and resaving each one as a unique and independent texture 2D asset. For this reason, the PNG format is recommended for all images in a Flash/Scaleform presentation to ensure that the UDK imports images in an accepted format and without a loss of quality.

Figure 10.10
Quality loss due to JPG compression.

Lossy Versus Lossless Formats

Lossless file formats are designed to ensure that data can be saved without the reduction in quality, or *loss*, that is sometimes the result of specific compression and encryption methods. Lossless formats such as PNG retain the integrity of their data on each file-save operation. That is, a PNG file can be saved multiple times in succession without losing or damaging data in the file. In contrast, the JPG format, typically used to ensure smaller file sizes and a shorter loading time, is an example of a *lossy* format. With lossy formats, data is lost on each file-save operation due to the compression and encryption methods used. As a result, images lose more and more quality every time they are saved in the JPG format, and the extent of the loss is proportional to the amount of compression and encryption applied. That means the resulting image of a JPG-save operation is a lower fidelity version of the original (see Figure 10.10).

■ **Size images according to the power 2 rule.** Images used by Scaleform are imported into the UDK as texture 2D assets. Texture 2D assets—and therefore all Scaleform images—should be sized in terms of pixel width and height according to the power 2 rule. In short, this rule states that the width and height of a texture in pixels should be only values that can result from squaring any number whose previous squaring began from 2. Valid sizes are therefore 2, 4, 8, 16, 32, 64, 128, 256, 512, 1,024, 2,048, and so on. Note, however, that textures need not be square. For example, the following width and height combinations would be valid: 512 × 1,024, 256 × 64, 8 × 2,048, and so on. For more on the power 2 rule, refer to the section "Creating a New Material for the Floor" in Chapter 5, "Materials, Textures, and UV Mapping."

Note

The power 2 rule is not a requirement of UDK textures so much as a recommendation. It is possible, for example, to import a texture that is not power 2 compliant in its width and height. When this happens, however, the UDK will automatically up-scale the texture to the nearest power 2–compliant size. This resizing will result in a new texture of a different aspect ratio, leading to distortion and artifacting.

Building the GUI in Flash

As mentioned, the Flash-based interface to be created for this project, will consist of three parts: the logo, the Start button, and the Exit button. The logo image has been created in Photoshop and is available from the book companion files for this chapter. The image has been saved in the PNG format according to the power 2 rule (it is 1024 × 256 pixels). The work of this section will be to create and assemble all the interface elements into a single and complete working interface using Adobe Flash. The final step of this section will save the interface in the form of an SWF Flash file, configured and ready to be imported into the UDK via Scaleform.

Setting Up the Stage

The following steps detail the process of creating an interface in Flash, from start to finish. They consider how to configure the Stage component in Flash in preparation for working, how to add images and buttons as actors to the stage, how to code executable behavior for those buttons in ActionScript, and how to add a mouse cursor component.

1. Open Adobe Flash and click ActionScript 2.0 in the Create New section of the dialog box that appears at startup to create a new ActionScript 2.0 project, as shown in Figure 10.11. (At the time of this writing, Scaleform supports only ActionScript 2.0. ActionScript 3.0 applications are not supported.)

2. In Flash, the term *stage* refers to the canvas on which the presentation will be shown, and is where the user interface for this project will be constructed. By default, the stage is 550 × 400 pixels, with a white background. This default width and height is too small for a full-screen menu interface, which will likely appear in the game at an HD resolution. The dimensions of the stage should be changed to 1,920 × 1,080 pixels. To make this change, click the Edit button in the Properties panel and type the new values in the dialog box that appears. (See Figure 10.12.)

3. Depending on the resolution of your system, the resized version of the stage might be too large to fit inside the Flash workspace. If this is the case, zoom out to bring the whole of the stage into view at once glance. To do this, type a

Figure 10.11
Creating a new Flash ActionScript 2.0 project.

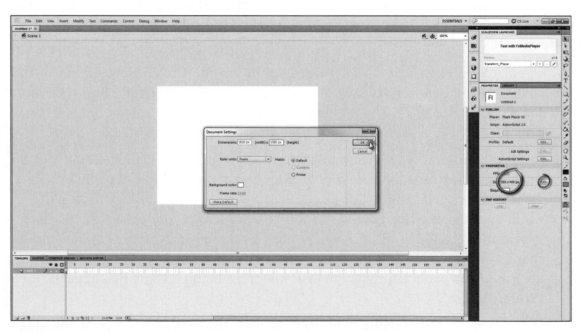

Figure 10.12
Changing the stage's pixel dimensions to 1,920 × 1,080.

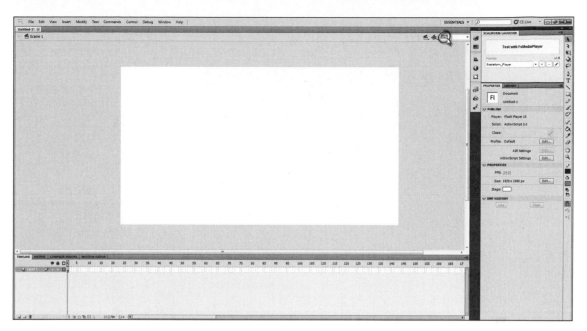

Figure 10.13
Zooming out to view the complete stage at 50 percent of its original size.

percentage value into the Zoom field, found in the upper-right corner of the stage. See Figure 10.13.

4. The background color for the user interface should be black, not white. To change the background to black, click the Stage color swatch in the Properties panel and choose black from the available colors. As shown in Figure 10.14, the stage will turn black.

5. The stage is now ready for the GUI elements. First, though, you should save the project. Begin by ensuring the appropriate compatibility and publishing settings have been applied to the project. To do so, open the File menu and choose Publish Settings, as shown in Figure 10.15, or press Ctrl+Shift+F12. The Publish Settings dialog box appears.

6. Click the Formats tab and remove the checkmark from the HTML checkbox, as shown in Figure 10.16. This will prevent Adobe Flash from generating an HTML file associated with the SWF document at build time. Selecting this checkbox might be useful when deploying SWF files for the Web, but it is unnecessary for building SWF files for Scaleform.

7. Click the Flash tab, click the Player drop-down list, and choose Flash Player 8, as shown in Figure 10.17. This indicates that your Flash presentation will be

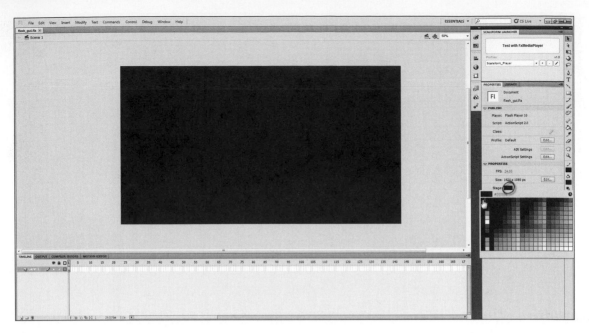

Figure 10.14
Using the Stage color swatch to change the stage background color from white to black.

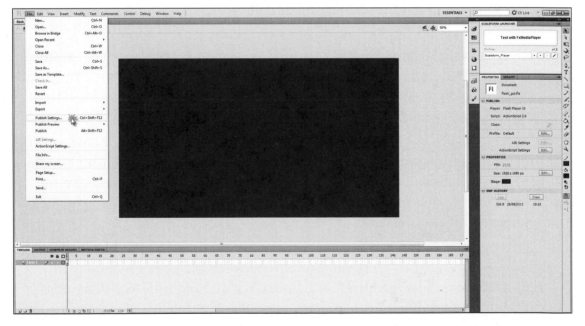

Figure 10.15
Editing the publishing settings for the Flash presentation.

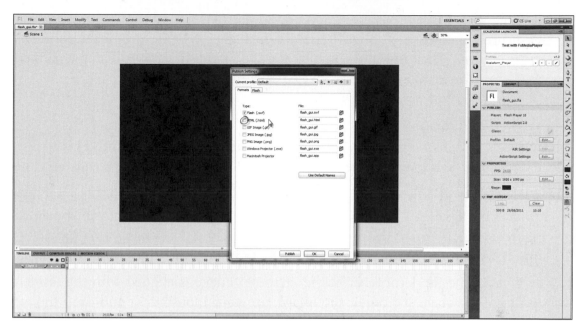

Figure 10.16
Uncheck the HTML checkbox on the Publish Settings dialog box's Formats tab.

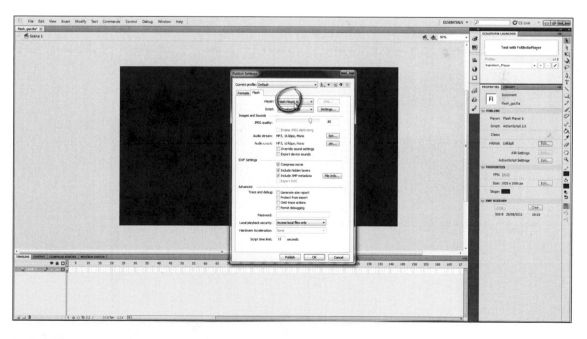

Figure 10.17
Selecting the Flash player version to compile the SWF file.

playable with Flash Player version 8 and lower. (At present, Scaleform supports Flash presentations in versions 8 and lower; higher versions are not supported by Scaleform.) Click the OK button to close the Publish Settings dialog box; then open the File menu and choose Save to save the Flash project.

Adding the Logo Image

The first step in constructing the GUI is to add the main logo graphic. This image, named Logo.png, was created already in Adobe Photoshop and is provided in the companion files. To add this file to the stage, follow these steps:

1. Open the File menu, choose Import, and select Import to Stage, as shown in Figure 10.18; alternatively, press Ctrl+R. In the Open File dialog box that appears, select the image file and click OK to import the image onto the stage.

2. By default, the top-left corner of the imported image is aligned with the top-left corner of the stage. To center the image, use your mouse drag and drop the image into place. Alternatively, click the image to select it; then open the Window menu and choose Align or press Ctrl+K. This opens the Align panel (see Figure 10.19), from which a series of alignment presets can be applied to the selected object on the stage. Click the Align to Stage checkbox to select it, and then click the Align Horizontal Center button to center the logo image.

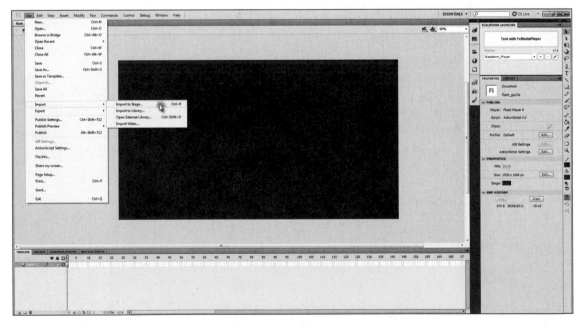

Figure 10.18
Importing a rasterized image onto the stage.

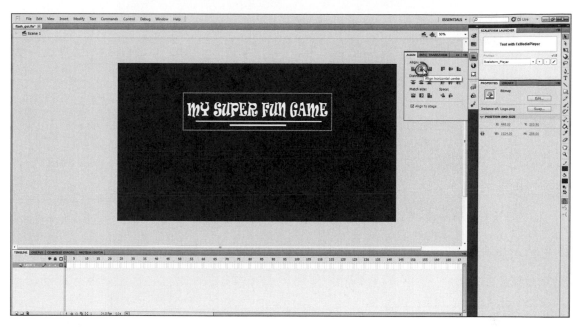

Figure 10.19
Aligning the logo image to the stage center using the Align panel.

Adding and Configuring the Buttons

It's time to add the menu buttons to the interface. To do so, follow these steps:

1. Click the Rectangle button in the toolbar. Then click and drag to create a button-sized rectangle on the left side of the stage, beneath the main logo, as shown in Figure 10.20.

2. If it is not blue by default, change the button's background color to blue. To do so, use the Select tool (to access it, press the V key on the keyboard) to select the button on the stage. Then click the Fill color swatch in the Properties panel and choose a blue from the available colors, as shown in Figure 10.21.

3. Copy the selected button, and then paste it onto the stage to create a duplicate. This will act as the Exit button. Drag and drop the duplicate to the right side of the stage to mirror the first button, as shown in Figure 10.22.

4. To label the left-most button, select the Text tool, and click and drag in the button to create a text box. Type Start in the text box; then use the color swatch in the Properties panel to ensure the text color is set to white. If you wish, increase or decrease the font size by typing a new value in the Size field in the Properties panel. Repeat this process for the Exit button, as shown in Figure 10.23.

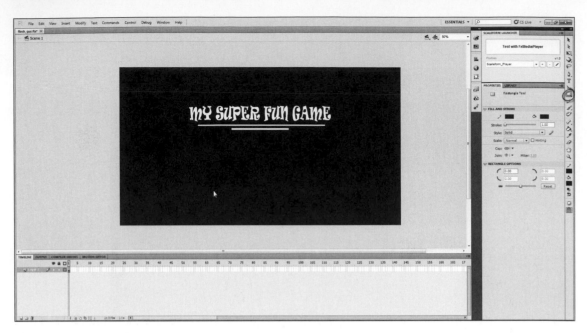

Figure 10.20
Creating a button with the Rectangle tool.

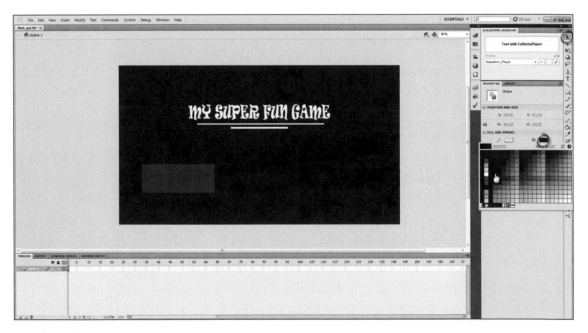

Figure 10.21
Choosing the fill color for the selected button.

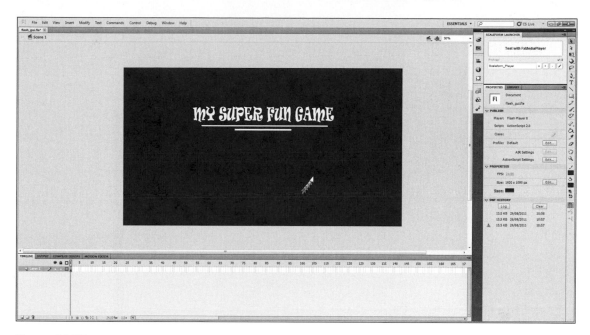

Figure 10.22
Creating an Exit button through duplication.

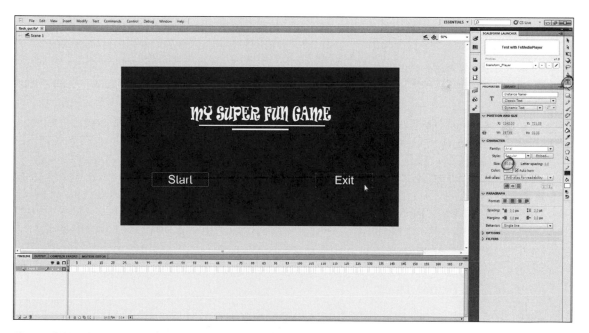

Figure 10.23
Setting the text for a button.

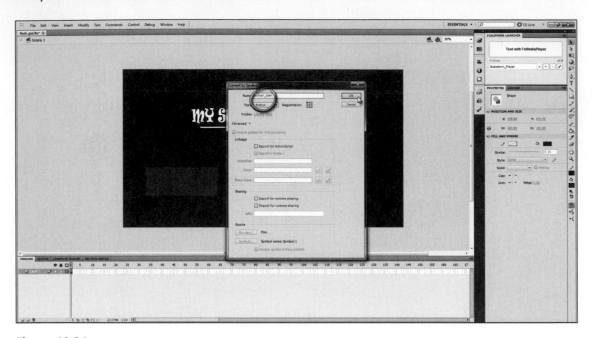

Figure 10.24
Converting the buttons to symbols.

5. So far, Flash does not recognize either button as a button. That is, Flash does not consider these rectangles to have a pushed, neutral, or rollover state, or any properties that are typically associated with buttons. To rectify this, use the Select tool to select one of the buttons and its text (marquee-select them both); then open the Modify menu and choose Convert to Symbol or press F8 to open the Convert to Symbol dialog box (see Figure 10.24). This dialog box enables you to convert objects such as rectangles and text into functional components such as buttons. Type a name for the button in the Name field; then click the Type drop-down list and choose Button. Finally, click OK to convert the rectangle to a button. Repeat this process for the other button.

6. Next, define the appearance of both buttons for each of their three main states: up (when the button is neither being pressed nor being hovered over), over (when the cursor is over the button), and down (when the button is clicked). To begin, right-click the Start button and choose Edit in Place from the menu that appears (see Figure 10.25).

7. Notice that the timeline lists four states (key frames) for the Start button: up, over, down, and hit. Of these four key frames, you will define the first three. The up state, being the button's default state, already features a key frame, which is defined as the button's initial and current state. To add a key frame for the over state, click the Over entry in the timeline, right-click it, and choose Insert

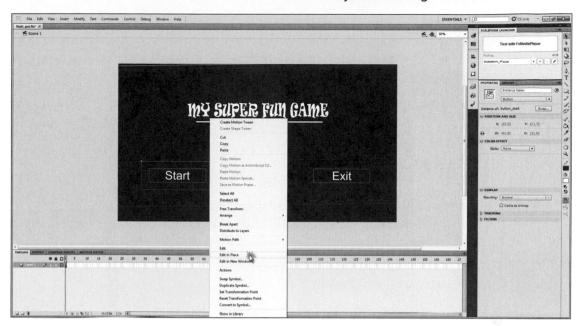

Figure 10.25
Creating and configuring text for the buttons.

Key Frame from the menu that appears, as shown in Figure 10.26. Repeat this process for the Down entry in the timeline.

8. Although the Up, Over, and Down key frames for the Start button have been created, the appearance of the button won't currently change when the Over or Down key frame occurs. (The same is true for the Up state, but as this is the default state, its appearance need not be changed here.) To set the button's appearance for the Over key frame, begin by selecting the Over key frame in the timeline; then select the Start button on the stage. With both these selected, use the Properties panel to change the color of the button from blue to green, as shown in Figure 10.27. When the button is in the up state, it will now appear green. To make sure things are working properly, click the Up key frame in the timeline; note that the Start button changes back to its original color. Repeat this process to define the color of the button for the Down key frame, changing the button to the color red.

9. To exit Edit in Place mode for the selected button, click the Scene 1 label in the top-left corner of the screen (see Figure 10.28). Then repeat steps 15 through 17 to define the key frame states for the Exit button.

10. Although the Flash presentation is not yet finished, take it for a test drive to preview it. To do so, click the Test with fxMediaPlayer button from the Scaleform Launcher panel. The results are shown in Figure 10.29.

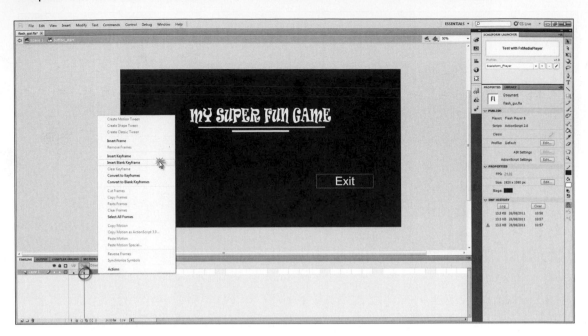

Figure 10.26
Creating key frames for the over and down button states.

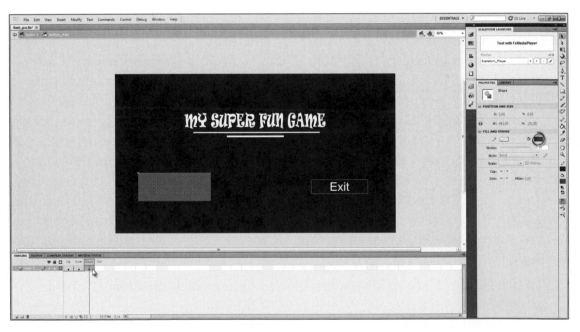

Figure 10.27
Setting the button appearance for the Over and Down key frames.

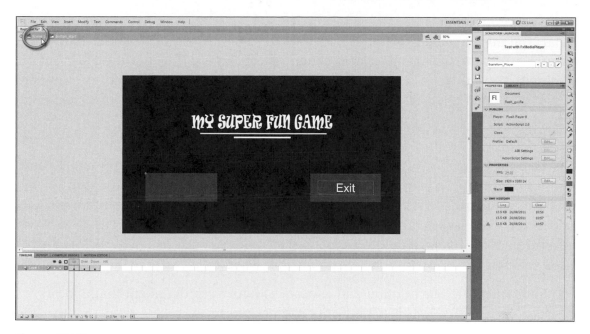

Figure 10.28
Exiting Edit in Place mode.

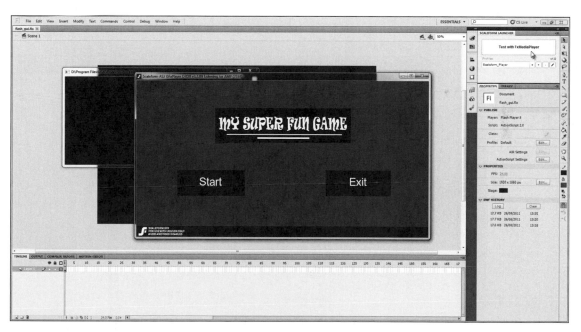

Figure 10.29
Testing the Flash-based interface in the Scaleform Launcher.

Coding the Buttons

So far, the buttons change appearance based on the cursor position, but they don't perform any particular game-related action when clicked. Clicking the Start button is supposed to initiate a level, and clicking the Exit button is supposed to terminate the application, but so far, none of these behaviors have been implemented in the game.

It will be Kismet's job to actually start a new level and terminate the application, but it is the responsibility of the Flash-based interface to set the appropriate Kismet behavior in motion whenever the buttons are clicked. That is, it is the duty of the interface to initiate the Kismet events that lead to specific actions. (See the previous chapter for more information on variables, events, actions, and conditions.) The work involved in Flash for fulfilling this responsibility will be coded in Flash's ECMAScript-based scripting language, known as ActionScript. Begin by coding the Start button.

1. Right-click the Start button and choose Actions from the menu that appears (see Figure 10.30). The ActionScript Editor appears.

2. The ActionScript Editor—part GUI and part text-based interface—enables developers to code ActionScript behavior for the selected object. In the Text pane of the ActionScript Editor, enter the following code (also shown in Figure 10.31).

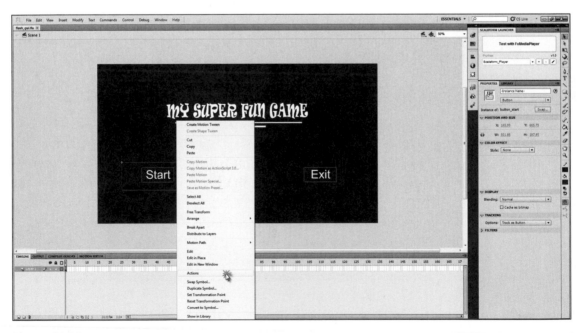

Figure 10.30
Opening the ActionScript Editor.

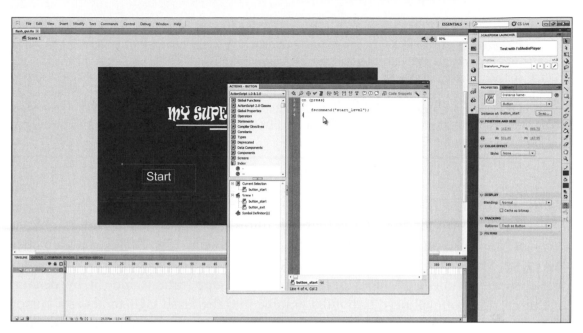

Figure 10.31
Coding a `press` event for a button. This code will be run whenever the button is clicked and will invoke a Kismet event.

```
on (press)
{
        fscommand("start_level");
}
```

This code is a function, which is simply a block of code designed to achieve a specific purpose. This function uses a special command called `fscommand`, which is a string parameter inside parentheses. The string is a user-defined instruction—in this case, `start_level`—that will be passed on to a Kismet event when the button is clicked (assuming the Flash GUI is integrated into the game using Scaleform). Kismet will accept that string as a parameter in an event, and will assess its content to determine the appropriate behavior.

3. Repeat step 3 to code the Exit button. The code for this button should be as follows:

```
on (press)
{
        fscommand("exit_level");
}
```

Note

Use of `fscommand` is generally discouraged by Epic Games. It is not intended for production use—that is, for use in commercial products. Instead, it is recommended that developers use either the ready-made CLIK components provided with the Scaleform software or UnrealScript to customize the GFx Kismet node. These two subjects are beyond the scope of this book; they are mentioned here to help guide you in learning more about Scaleform and its use with the UDK. The use of the `fscommand` here offers an introduction to Scaleform's general use with the UDK and provides a foundation from which you can proceed to explore the CLIK objects.

Adding a Cursor

The remaining issue for the GUI is that it features no mouse cursor—no graphic to represent the position of the mouse onscreen. Although the Scaleform Launcher plug-in for Flash uses the default Windows cursor for preview purposes, the Scaleform software in the UDK does not because UDK applications hide it by default. For this reason, you will need to build a graphic into the Flash GUI to act as a cursor when the GUI is run in a UDK application. The book companion files contain a 64×64-pixel cursor graphic (cursor.png). You can add this to the stage to act as a cursor in the same way you added the logo graphic to act as a title:

1. Open the File menu, choose Import, and select Import to Stage. Then select the cursor graphic, clicking OK to confirm the operation. As shown in Figure 10.32, the graphic is added to the stage.

2. Select the cursor graphic. Then, open the Modify menu and choose Convert to Symbol or press F8 to open the Convert to Symbol dialog box, shown in Figure 10.33. Type a name for the cursor object in the Name field; then click the Type drop-down list and choose Movie Clip. Finally, click OK.

Note

The cursor graphic must be converted into a Movie Clip object not because it will be animated on a frame-by-frame basis, but because ActionScript can be added to Movie Clip objects. You'll need to add ActionScript to the cursor to ensure that it moves according to the mouse.

3. If this interface were run in Scaleform, the cursor would not currently move with the mouse input. Indeed, it would not move at all. To fix this, right-

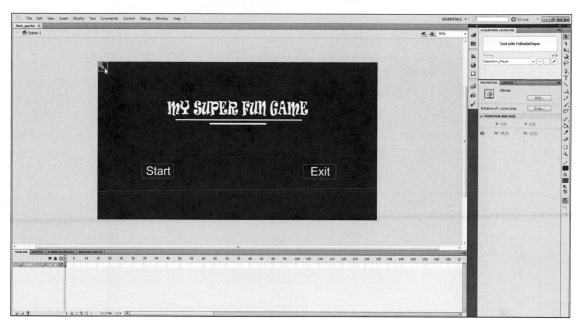

Figure 10.32
A cursor graphic is added to the stage from a PNG file.

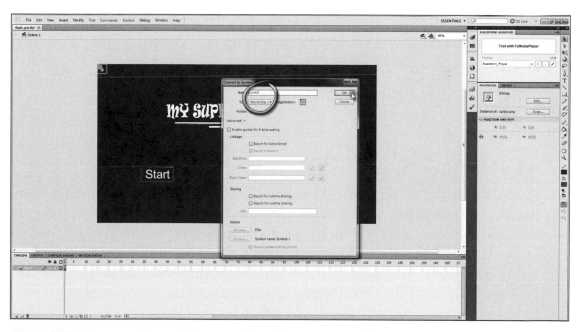

Figure 10.33
Converting the cursor to a scriptable object.

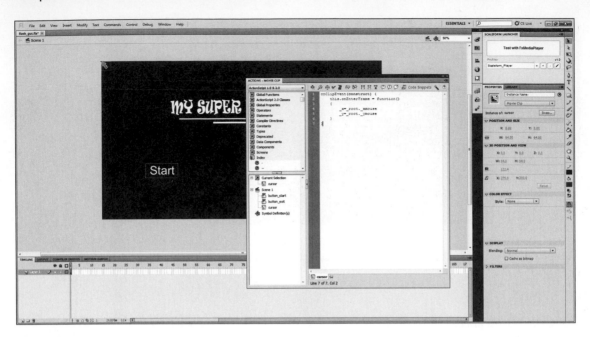

Figure 10.34
Coding in ActionScript to update the stage position of the cursor graphic.

click the cursor and choose Actions from the menu that appears to open the
ActionScript Editor. Then, in the ActionScript Editor, enter the following code.

```
onClipEvent(construct) {
            this.onEnterFrame = function()
            {
                    _x=_root._xmouse
                    _y=_root._ymouse
            }
}
```

This code assigns a function to the OnEnterFrame event of the cursor graphic,
which is called once per frame throughout the duration of the Flash animation.
Because the animation has a default frame rate of 24 frames per second, this
event is therefore called 24 times per second for as long as the Flash GUI is
active. On each frame, ActionScript will read the mouse position in terms of xy
screen coordinates (in pixels) from the mouse input device and will update the
xy stage position of the mouse cursor graphic accordingly. The lines
_x=_root._xmouse and _y=_root._ymouse are responsible for setting the
x and y position of the cursor graphic according to mouse input. See Figure 10.34.

4. Test the Flash GUI in Scaleform to confirm that the cursor moves according to
mouse input and that buttons react to the position of the cursor. Furthermore,

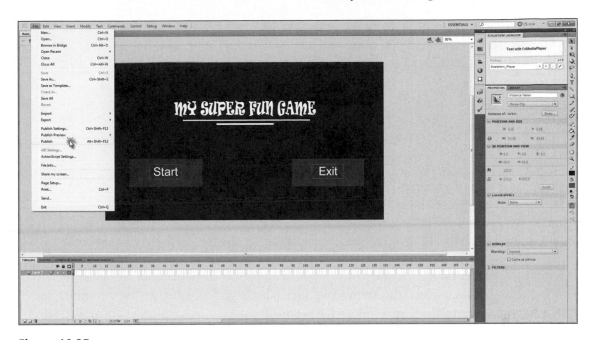

Figure 10.35
Publishing the project to an SWF is equivalent to compiling it.

make sure that clicking a button causes it to invoke a Kismet event, to which it will pass an appropriate string parameter.

5. The Flash GUI is now complete. To save the project, open the File menu and choose Save.

6. To compile the GUI into an SWF file, open the File menu and choose Publish (see Figure 10.35) or press Alt+Shift+F12. The SWF file for the project will be output in the same folder as the Flash project file.

Note

The completed Flash user interface can be found in the companion files. The project file is flash_menu.fla, and the compiled SWF is flash_menu.swf.

Importing the SWF into the UDK

You've created the Flash-based interface for the game. It consists of a logo image with the name of the game, a cursor image that moves according to mouse input, and a Start and an Exit button to fire events in Kismet that will start and terminate the game, respectively. This section concentrates on transferring, or importing, the Flash SWF project into the UDK as an asset. From there, it can be integrated into UDK levels.

1. SWF files to be imported into the UDK as assets must be located in the UDK installation folder—specifically, in any subfolder of the folder UDK\UDKGame\

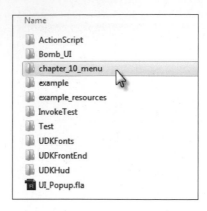

Figure 10.36
Creating a subfolder under UDK\UDKGame\Flash to house the SWF file for the interface to be imported.

Flash. The name of the subfolder should describe the contents of the SWF file. For this project, copy the menu.swf file, which was output in the previous section, into a subfolder of UDK\UDKGame\Flash named chapter_10_menu, as shown in Figure 10.36.

2. Open the UDK. Next, open the Content Browser and click the Import button. The Open dialog box appears; select the menu.swf file and click OK. In the Flash Import dialog box that appears (see Figure 10.37), accept all the default settings and click OK. The Flash file will be then imported into the UDK as a new package.

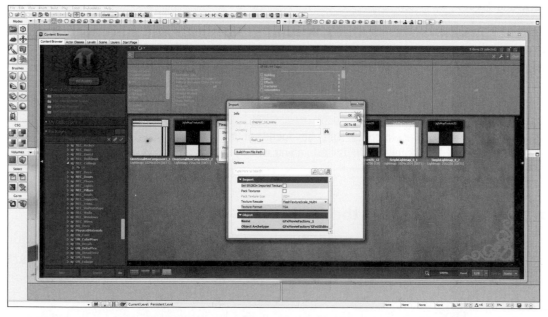

Figure 10.37
Importing the menu.swf file into the UDK via Scaleform.

Figure 10.38
Scaleform extracts the images from the SWF and imports them as texture 2D assets.

The UDK Scaleform software imports the SWF as an asset and extracts every image in the SWF, importing each as a separate asset. If you examine the Content Browser's Asset pane, you'll see three assets: the SWF asset and two texture 2D assets (one for the logo and one for the cursor). See Figure 10.38.

Creating a Menu Level

The previous sections demonstrated how to create a user interface in Adobe Flash and how to import that user interface into the UDK as an asset via the Scaleform software. The imported user interface should act as a main menu rather than as a HUD. That is, the menu should be shown full screen and in modal form, meaning that the player should not be able to move his or her character around the level while the menu is active. This section explains how to configure the level to support this kind of menu.

Note

In the UDK, all game content must be created as a level, regardless of its purpose. The purpose of this level is not to feature a world filled with meshes, sounds, lights, and animations, but to feature the minimum required to show a menu and to enable the player to use it to provide input.

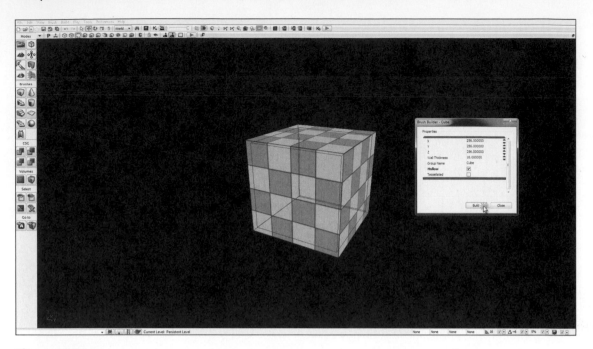

Figure 10.39
A hollowed cube at the center of the level.

1. In a new, blank map, use the Builder Brush to create a CSG hollowed cube (256 × 256 × 256 Unreal units) at the center of the level, as shown in Figure 10.39. This cube marks the extents of the level.

2. Open the Content Browser and click the Actor Classes tab. Then drag and drop a player start location into the interior of the cube to represent the location at which the player will begin when the level is run. (See Figure 10.40.)

Note

The project so far can be found in the companion files under DM-Scaleform_Project_01_Menu.udk.

3. To prevent the player from being able to move around in the level, you must disable user input for the player character. That way, the input for this level will control the user interface, not the player character. To create this behavior, open the Kismet Editor, right-click in the graph, and add a Level Loaded sequence object and a Toggle Cinematic Mode sequence object, connecting the former to the latter as shown in Figure 10.41.

4. As it stands, Kismet will disable user input as intended but will not display the user interface. To add this behavior, you must connect a new node, Open GFx Movie, to the Out socket of the Toggle Cinematic Mode node. This will open

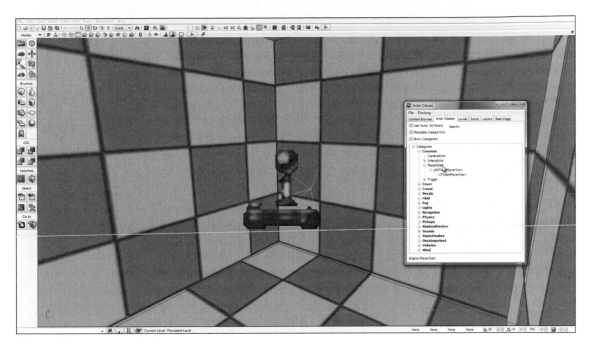

Figure 10.40
Inserting a player start location from the Actor Classes Browser.

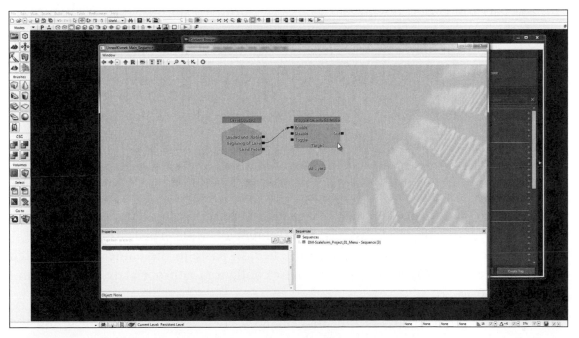

Figure 10.41
Enabling Cinematic mode from Kismet.

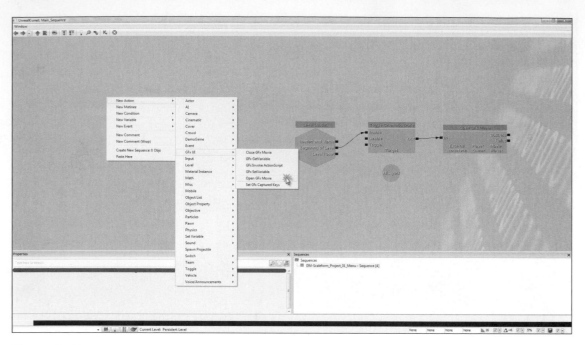

Figure 10.42
Wiring the Open GFx Movie node to display a Flash GUI.

and play the Flash presentation using Scaleform. To do this, right-click in the graph and choose New Action, then GFx UI, followed by Open GFx Movie from the menu that appears. Then connect the Out socket of the Toggle Cinematic Mode node to the In socket of the Open GFx Movie node, as shown in Figure 10.42.

5. Select the Open GFx Movie sequence object in the Kismet graph and enable the Take Focus checkbox in the Properties pane. This ensures that input focus is given to the Flash GUI when the level begins. That is, the GUI is activated to receive mouse, keyboard, and other input from the player. The Open GFx Movie node also has a Movie property in the Properties pane. This references the Flash asset to be loaded and played by the node when it is executed. To enter this property, select the Flash asset in the Content Browser. Then, back in Kismet, click the green left arrow by the Movie field to paste in the name of the selected Flash asset. The Open GFx node is now configured appropriately, as shown in Figure 10.43.

6. Test the level. You should find that the level loads with input disabled and the menu shown, but that clicking on the buttons of the interface has no appreciable effect. For example, clicking the Start button does not initiate a new level, and clicking the Exit button does not terminate the current level. This is because

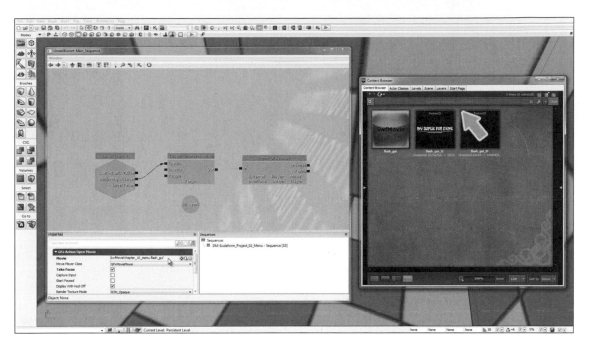

Figure 10.43
Configuring the Open GFx Movie node for playback.

although both of these buttons feed into Kismet by calling the fscommand, Unreal Kismet does not at present respond to their calls. To address this issue, configure Kismet to respond to the button actions. Start by creating two instances in the Kismet graph of the FsCommand node, one for each button, as shown in Figure 10.44. To create this node, right-click in the graph pane and choose New Event, then GFx UI, followed by FsCommand from the menu that appears.

7. Each FsCommand sequence event has a Movie property (which specifies the name of the Flash movie with which the command is associated) and an FSCommand property (which specifies the user-defined string naming the command) in its Properties pane. For the FsCommand node to fire, its FSCommand property must match the name of the parameter passed by the button to the fscommand function in ActionScript. That means each of the newly added FsCommand nodes should be associated with the same GUI interface referenced in step 5. However, the FsCommand node for the Start button should be associated with the start_level fscommand, and the Exit button with the exit_level fscommand. (Refer to the section "Coding the Buttons" earlier in this chapter for more information.) Figure 10.45 shows the complete properties for the FsCommand node associated with the Start button.

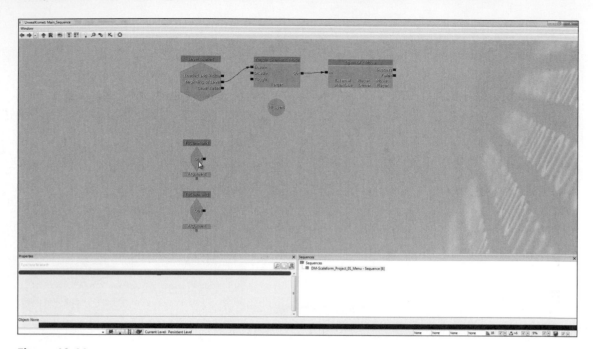

Figure 10.44
Creating FsCommand nodes, one for each button that calls `fscommand` in ActionScript.

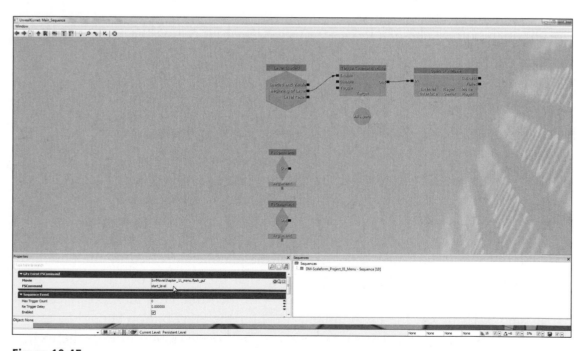

Figure 10.45
Creating FsCommand nodes, one for each button. The FSCommand property of each node should match the name of the parameter passed by its respective button in the Flash interface if it is to be activated in Kismet.

8. The Kismet Graph now features two separate FsCommand sequence objects: one fired when the Start button is clicked and the other when the Exit button is clicked. When clicked, the Start button should initiate a new level, and the Exit button should terminate the application. You can achieve both of these goals through Console Commands. These are English-like statements that can be sent to and passed by the Unreal Engine at run time to perform high-level game functions such as loading levels and exiting the game. Console Commands can be sent to the Unreal Engine via a Kismet node; one of these nodes should be attached to the Out socket of each FsCommand node. To create a Console Command node, right-click in the Kismet Graph and choose New Action, then Misc, followed by Console Command from the menu that appears. Repeat this procedure to create a second Console Command node. Finally, connect one Console Command node to each FsCommand node, as shown in Figure 10.46.

Note

Remember to attach the Player node to the target socket of each Console Command node. Player nodes can be created by right-clicking in the graph and choosing New Variable, then Player, followed by Player again from the menu that appears.

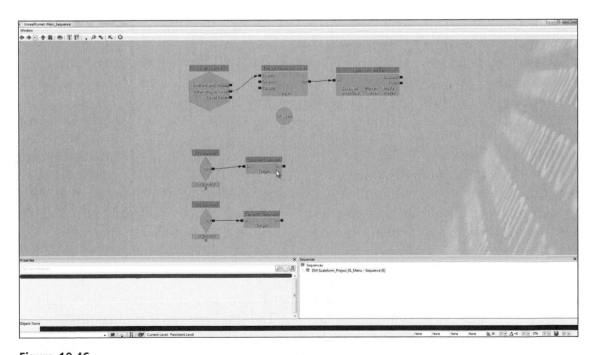

Figure 10.46
Console Commands can be sent to the Unreal Engine at run time via specialized Kismet nodes to perform game-level operations.

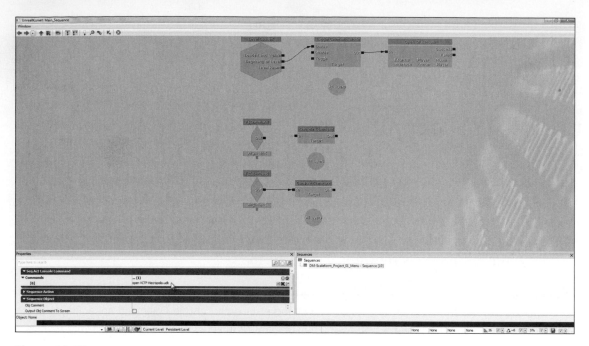

Figure 10.47
Opening maps with the Open Console Command.

9. Create the Console Command for the Start button. When clicked, this button will cause the VCTF-Necropolis.udk UDK map to open and run. (This map is provided with the UDK and can be found in the UDK\UDKGame\Content\ Maps\UT3 folder.) Select the Start button's Console Command node in the Kismet graph (the node attached to the Out socket of the Start button's FsCommand node). Then, in the node's Properties pane, set the Commands property to Open VCTF-Necropolis.udk, as shown in Figure 10.47.

10. The second Console Command is associated with the Exit button, which, when clicked, will cause the application to terminate. To achieve this, select the Exit button's Console Command node in the Kismet graph. Then, in the node's Properties pane, set the Commands property to Exit, as shown in Figure 10.48.

11. Test the level. To do so, close the Kismet Editor and, in the main UDK Editor, open the Play menu and choose On PC. The level runs as a standalone application, as though the game had been launched by the gamer. The level should work as intended. Congratulations!

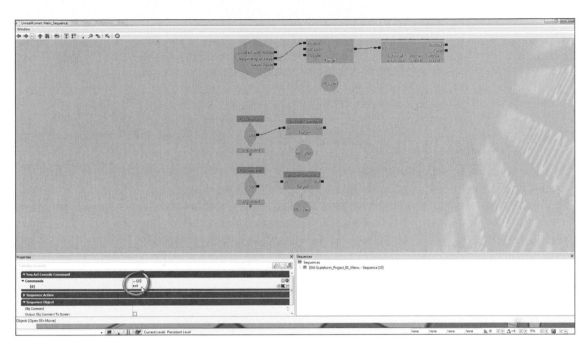

Figure 10.48
Configuring the Exit Console Command.

Note

You should run the level via this method rather than clicking the Play button on the UDK Editor toolbar. This is because many Console Commands cannot run while the game is being tested in the editor.

Note

The completed project can be found in the companion files under DM-Scaleform_Project_02_Menu.udk.

Conclusion

User interfaces and their development in Adobe Flash were the primary topics of this chapter. The Autodesk Scaleform software is the component responsible for bridging between Flash-created content and hardware accelerated games, making it possible to show Flash presentations in UDK games. This chapter demonstrated both how to import Flash content into the UDK via the Content Browser and how to play and connect with that content. It stepped you through the creation of a Flash-based main menu user interface that featured a logo, a cursor, and two buttons—one that launched a new map and one that terminated the application. The next chapter considers the issue of particle systems.

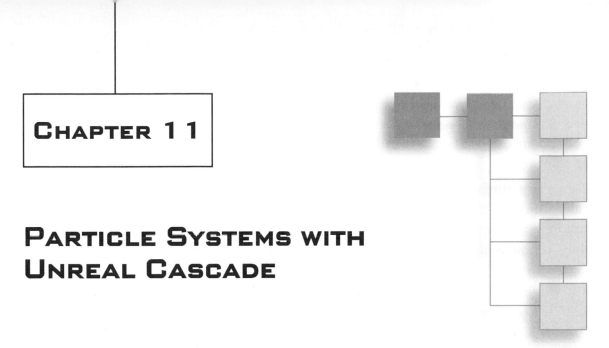

CHAPTER 11

PARTICLE SYSTEMS WITH UNREAL CASCADE

Don't wake me for the end of the world unless it has very good special effects.

—Roger Zelazny

By the end of this chapter, you should:

- Be able to create a particle system using Cascade.
- Understand the Cascade interface.
- Understand the concepts of emitters and particles.
- Understand emitter modules.
- Be able to use distributions to animate the properties of emitter modules.

Particle systems are probably best introduced by stating not so much what they are in terms of their constitution, but what they do in a video game. Specifically, particle systems are used to create animated effects that involve small and fuzzy entities, lots of entities, or both. These kinds of effects would prove difficult to create using traditional rendering techniques. Particle systems are used to create effects such as snow, rain, fairy sparkles, sparks, explosions, dust, smoke, fire, muzzle flash, heat shimmers, and swarms of bees, to name but a few. In the UDK, the editor interface and tools used to build particle systems are collectively named *Unreal Cascade* (often shortened to *Cascade*). Both particle systems and Cascade are the subjects of this chapter.

The Need for a Particle System

Some might argue that a particle system is redundant because it is entirely possible to create, for example, a swarm of bees in the UDK by duplicating many bee meshes and animating those meshes individually to produce a swarm through the Kismet and Matinee tools. Given that, the question arises why a particle system is necessary at all.

To answer this question, consider again the example of the swarm of bees. Specifically, consider the work involved in achieving this swarm. First, the developer must produce a polygonal bee mesh to act as a template for all bees in the swarm. Given that a swarm can contain hundreds of bees (if not more), the template mesh will need to be duplicated, or instanced, in the UDK Editor for as many bees as there are in the swarm. Further, although each bee in a swarm shares a range of visual characteristics with all other bees that make it recognizable as a bee, each bee differs from the others in a range of subtle ways—for example, in coloration or stripe patterning. Achieving such variation in detail while working this way would involve the UDK developer creating a set of material instances, each differing subtly from a template bee material. Then, each instance would be applied to a specific set of bees to differentiate them visually from the other sets in the swarm. Finally, each bee in the swarm would be located at a unique position in space and would follow its own, unique flight path over time, even though the positions and flight paths of all bees would be sufficiently similar to allow them to collectively be called a swarm. The upshot of this is that the developer would need to use Kismet and Matinee to create a key frame animation for every bee in the swarm, and to ensure that the animations worked in unison to make the swarm believable.

Two main technical problems arise for the developer when creating something as complex as a swarm using traditional UDK content-creation methods rather than a particle system:

- Both the developer and the game engine must invest considerable effort, time, and resources in creating the swarm of bees. This is true even in cases where the swarm is meant not as a main feature of the level but as a temporary sideshow that is visible in the background for only a few seconds, to enhance the realism of the level.

- Making changes to the bee swarm after its creation would be problematic. It would be possible but cumbersome, for example, to adjust the flight-path animation of a particular bee, to change the duration for which the swarm is visible, or to change the coloration and pattern for a particular set of bees.

Both of these problems are primarily workflow problems—problems that result largely from *how* the swarm is constructed. The game developer could have made his or her life easier had different tools been used. These problems arise because of the intrinsic unsuitability of the tools and working methods used for creating effects of this kind. Thus, they are not problems that will necessarily go away by using the same tools in different ways (even though those tools might be impressively versatile). Hence, there is a need for a different kind of tool in the UDK to make creating these kinds of effects simpler and more manageable. The Unreal Cascade Editor, for use with particle systems, is designed to answer that need.

THE ANATOMY OF THE PARTICLE SYSTEM

As mentioned, game developers use particle systems to create complex graphical effects that typically involve many small, unique pieces (*particles*), each having a finite lifespan, its own position, and its own scale, and following its own path over time. Particle systems can be further understood when broken down into their constituent pieces. Specifically, particle systems consist of one or more *emitters*, and each emitter is responsible for spawning one or more particles over time. As shown in Figure 11.1, the particle is the base unit and raw material of the particle system, and the emitter is responsible for creating particles.

Emitters

An *emitter* is a non-visible component that acts much like a garden hose. It is responsible for spawning clones of a particle into the system at a specified position and rate and for a specified duration. A particle system must have at least one emitter if it is to be effective, but it can have more. When it does, each emitter is responsible for spawning a different kind of particle into the system.

The term *spawning* is common in game development and video gaming, and refers to the act of creation or generation. An emitter that has spawned a particle into the system has thereby generated a new clone or instance of a particle at a specified position, orientation, and scale in world space. Thus, a particle that has been spawned has come into existence. Emitters, therefore, are responsible for bringing particles into existence—for defining their starting state.

Although emitters cannot be seen by the gamer during gameplay, their shape, form, and size are often approximated by developers using geometric primitives, such as cubes and cylinders, to influence the way in which its particles are spawned. For example, an emitter that is an infinitesimally small point in three-dimensional space

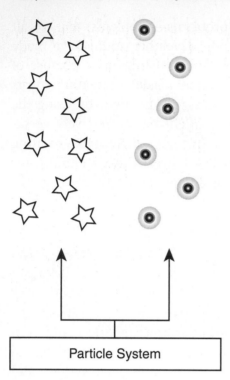

Figure 11.1
Particle systems are composed from one or more emitters that pour out particles of a finite lifespan at specified intervals.

will spawn all its particles at the same location in space, while an emitter that is approximated by a larger cylindrical volume will spawn each instance of a particle at a random and unique location inside the volume. (See Figure 11.2.)

Particles

Particles represent the base unit or raw materials of the particle system. There is no simpler entity in the particle system than the particle. In a particle system intended to simulate rain, for example, one particle would be equivalent to one raindrop. In a system designed to simulate snow, one particle would equal one snowflake. And in a system intended to simulate a swarm of bees, one particle would represent one bee.

Every particle in the system has a set of properties that together define how the particle will appear and behave within the system. Some of the properties defining how the particle is to behave include the following:

■ **Lifetime.** The lifetime of a particle defines how long in terms of seconds the particle is to exist after being spawned. That is, it defines how much time must

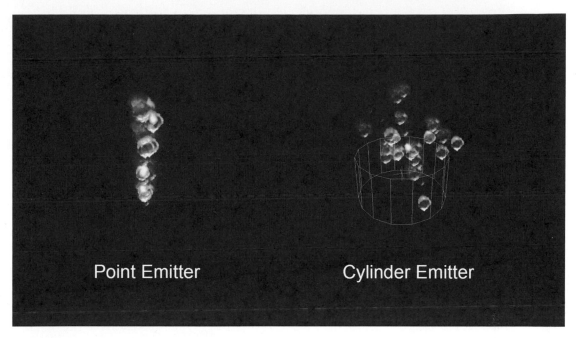

Figure 11.2
Emitters are responsible for spawning particles into the system. The shape of the emitter influences the way in which particles are spatially distributed when spawned.

elapse before the particle is removed from the system. For example, raindrops emitted into a rain system might take five seconds to fall from the sky to the ground; thus, five seconds in this system represents the time after which the particles should be removed.

- **Position.** The position of a particle defines its location at any one time relative to its spawn position (that is, the position at which it began its existence). Given that most particles move over time, the position of most particles is constantly changing according to their trajectory over their lifetime.

The mathematical information (the *curve*) that defines how the properties of a particle change over time (including its position property) is called a *distribution*. (See Figure 11.3.) A particle might have one distribution defining changes for its position and other defining changes for its orientation.

In addition to the properties that define how a particle behaves over time, there are properties that define how a particle appears both constantly and over time:

- **Material.** The material property specifies the material to be applied to all particles spawned by a given emitter in the system. For example, raindrop particles

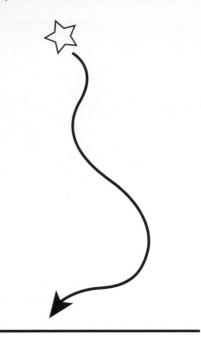

Figure 11.3
A particle following its position distribution as it falls from the sky to the ground during its lifetime.

will be assigned a raindrop material, bee particles will be assigned a bee material, and so on.

Quad Particles

The simplest kind of particle that can exist—and the kind most commonly used—is the quad particle, so named because it is a four-sided polygon with a material applied. It is not the only kind of particle that can be used, however. It is possible to have *n*Gon particles (many sided particles) or even complex mesh particles in which each particle in the system is a static mesh. This book, however, considers only the quad particle.

The key characteristics of the quad particle (other than being four-sided) are that it is always turned toward the viewer, no matter where the viewer is; and its material determines its appearance. That means quad particles are in effect two-dimensional rather than three-dimensional. Materials for quad particles act like pictures stuck on cards or sheets of paper (see Figure 11.4). Thus, a particle system that uses quad particles to create a swarm of bees would need to ensure that the material for those particles defined not the unwrapped skin of a bee in the way that a material often defines the skin of a mesh, but defined the whole of a bee as it will be seen in the level. This approach should not be problematic, provided the swarm of bees is seen in the distance and is not examined closely by the gamer.

Figure 11.4
A particle as a textured quad—a four-sided polygon with a material applied.

- **Scale.** The particle's scale defines the size of the particle at any one time. Like the particle's position, the scale can change over time according to the distribution. Some particles, such as bees in a swarm, would be unlikely to change their scale in a particle system because they neither grow nor shrink in an obvious way. Other particles, however—such as those defining smoke, fire, or force fields—might change their scale as they expand and contract according to atmospheric conditions.

The Cascade Editor

Unreal Cascade refers to the range of tools and options available in the UDK for creating particle systems. The Cascade Editor is the mouse-driven graphical user interface that makes those tools accessible. Using the Cascade Editor, developers can create new particle system assets and can edit and inspect existing particle system assets.

In the UDK, a particle system is considered an asset. Instances of those assets are added to a level as actors in the same way instances of a static mesh are added as static mesh actors. Because a particle system consists of emitters and particles and their attendant properties (such as distributions), creating and editing particle systems involves editing emitters and particles. The Cascade interface offers tools for creating particle systems through five distinct interface elements, as shown in Figure 11.5.

The Main Menu and Toolbar

Cascade's main menu and toolbar act much like the main menus and toolbars in the other UDK editors in that they enable users to show or hide various panes, provide

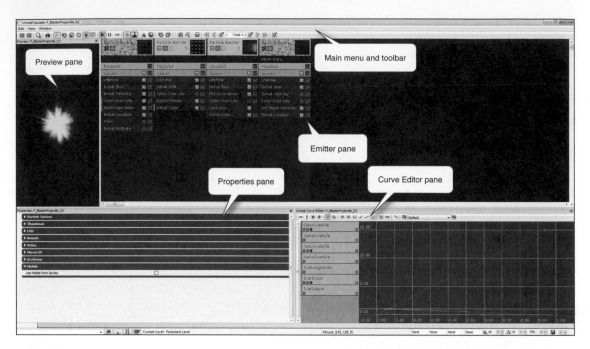

Figure 11.5
The Unreal Cascade Editor is a mouse-driven GUI used for creating and editing particle systems.

options for saving the project, and allow for the display of various information and diagnostics in the Preview pane. The toolbar, however, offers some options that are unique to particle systems and are especially noteworthy, as shown in Figure 11.6:

- **Sim options.** A particle system is sometimes referred to as a simulation because it simulates through animation how a collection of particles might behave under specified conditions. The sim options—sim being short for *simulation*—consist of two buttons: Restart Sim and Restart in Level. Clicking the Restart Sim button restarts the playback of the particle system in the Preview pane from the beginning. This option is equivalent to a Rewind and Play button, except that it restarts only the particle system being previewed in the editor. It does not affect the playback of particular instances of the particle system in the level. In contrast, clicking the Restart in Level button restarts the playback of the particle system in the editor and all its associated instances (actors) in the level.

- **Play options.** The play options are used to control the playback of the particle system in the Preview pane of the Cascade Editor. These options exist not only

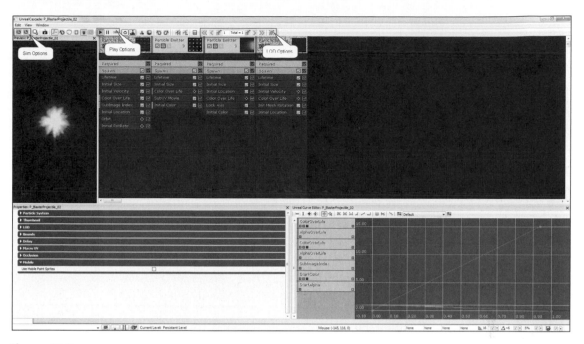

Figure 11.6
The Cascade menu and toolbar. Sim options are used to restart playback of the particle system in the level and editor. Play options are used to start, stop, and fast-forward playback of the particle system. LOD options are used to define multiple versions of the particle system for various levels of detail.

so that developers can start and pause the simulation through the Start and Pause buttons, respectively, but so that developers can better preview the animation and motion of particles via the Speed Control button, which is set to 100 percent by default. (The button is marked with the number 100 in Figure 11.6). This value indicates that the particle system is running at its standard speed. The button, when clicked, allows developers to reduce the speed of the particle system to a range of other speeds, including 1 percent, 10 percent, 25 percent, and 50 percent.

- **LOD options.** A particle system that has LODs—short for *levels of detail*—is one that contains multiple versions of its emitters, one version per LOD, each version being associated with a particular quality or level of detail (see Figure 11.7). For example, a particle system for a swarm of bees might have two LODs, each one associated with one emitter: a low-quality LOD and a high-quality LOD. The low-quality version emits fewer bees and uses a smaller material for each

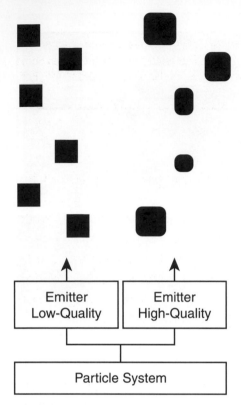

Figure 11.7
LOD allows multiple versions of a particle system to be defined, each differing in quality (level of detail). Notice that the high-quality version emits rectangles with rounded corners, and the lower quality version emits simpler rectangles. The version of the particle system shown during gameplay will depend on the distance between the gamer and the particle system, with high-quality versions shown when viewed up close and lower-quality versions shown when the gamer is further away.

bee, while the high-quality version emits the maximum number of bees that is appropriate and assigns the largest material appropriate to each bee. Game performance can then be increased if the game detects the distance of the player character from the particle system during gameplay and shows the LOD that is appropriate for that distance—the low-quality LOD when the particle system is far away and the high-quality LOD when the player moves close to the particle system. (Distance is defined numerically in Unreal world units.) The LOD options in the toolbar enable developers to create, delete, and change between LODs.

Note

LODs are not covered further in this book. It is recommend, however, that after reading this chapter, you open and examine some of the particle systems that ship with the UDK to better understand LODs. Some particle systems to consider include P_CTF_Flag_IronGuard_Idle_Red, P_FX_LinkGun_3P_Beam_MF_Red, and P_Pickups_Base_Health_Glow, accessible from the Content Browser.

The Preview Pane

The Preview pane shows a three-dimensional view of the particle system being assembled in the Cascade Editor. In this pane, the particle system is centered at the origin. The navigation controls enable developers to zoom and orbit this origin to inspect the particle system from different angles and distances. To zoom the Preview pane in and out, press the right mouse button and drag up or down. The view can be orbited or rotated around the X and Z axis by holding down the left mouse button and clicking and dragging. Finally, you can pan the view (move it vertically or horizontally) by holding down the middle mouse button while moving the mouse.

The Emitter Pane

In many respects, the Emitter pane is similar to the Graph pane in the Kismet Editor and the Material Editors. It offers a diagrammatic representation of the particle system being created and, along with the Properties pane and the Curve Editor pane, is where much of the creation work takes place. In the Emitter pane, developers can add, view, and remove the emitters in a particle system. Each emitter in the system appears as a separate column and can contain one or more modules, represented in the editor as blocks or rows inside the column. Each module defines a range of properties for the particles generated by the emitter, such as Lifetime, Initial Size, and Initial Location. You add modules to selected emitters by right-clicking a blank area in the Emitter pane and choosing the desired module from the menu that appears. (See Figure 11.8.)

The Properties Pane

The Properties pane, shown in Figure 11.9, appears by default in the bottom-left corner of the Cascade Editor. Its contents are context sensitive. That is, the Properties pane lists all the editable properties of the currently selected module in the Emitter pane. In other words, the Properties pane provides a means for editing the properties of the selected module.

The Curve Editor Pane

Typically, the particles in a particle system are in constant motion, always moving. The bees of a swarm are always flying, the raindrops of a shower are always falling,

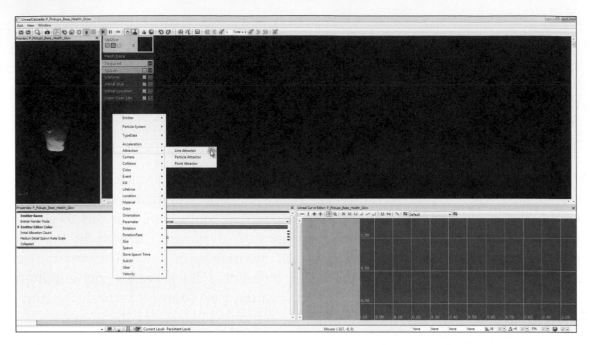

Figure 11.8
The Emitter pane shows the emitters that comprise the particle system. You can add modules to an emitter through a right-click context menu.

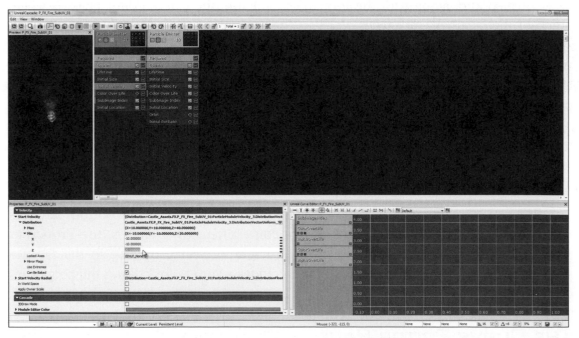

Figure 11.9
The Properties pane lists all the editable properties of the currently selected module in the Emitter pane.

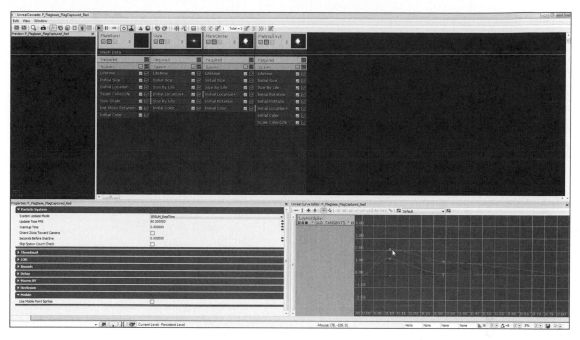

Figure 11.10
Editing curves in the Curve Editor pane.

the debris from an explosion are always scattering, and so on. A particle becomes the subject of perpetual change and motion from the moment it is spawned by an emitter. As mentioned, the emitter is responsible for spawning a particle, which involves assigning the particle a starting position, a scale, and an orientation. Once the particle is spawned, however, it takes on a life of its own. It springs into motion and becomes an active force. The mathematical information referred to as a *distribution* typically defines a curve that expresses how a range of numeric and key frame–amenable properties of a particle change and interpolate over time. The Curve Editor pane is used to create and edit these curve distributions (see Figure 11.10). For more information on key framing, refer to the section "Animating the Door with Matinee" in Chapter 9, "Kismet and Matinee: Beginning with Visual Scripting and Animation."

PROJECT: BALLOON TIME

In this project, you will create a particle system that continually releases party balloons into the air, as shown in Figure 11.11. (Fortunately, these are virtual balloons; otherwise, their gaseous releases and lack of biodegradability would likely wreak environmental havoc!) This project is based on the Morning Lighting map template. It will feature a particle system actor that repeatedly spawns balloon particles across a

Figure 11.11
The completed project. This level features a particle system launching a bunch of balloons into the sky.

large surface at ground level and allows the balloons to rise gently into the sky, where they will vanish from view.

Creating this particle system will involve two main stages. First, you will import a flipbook texture of a balloon and configure that texture as a material suitable for use in a particle system. Second, you will create a particle system actor in the level featuring one emitter that endlessly spawns upwardly mobile quads with a balloon material applied to simulate the effect of floating balloons.

Creating Flipbook Textures for Animated Balloons

A flipbook texture is not structurally different from any other texture; indeed, flipbook textures are like standard textures in that they are two-dimensional rectangles of RGB pixels loaded from industry-standard image files, such as PNG or TGA files. Flipbook textures differ from standard textures in their use.

As their name suggests, flipbook textures are reminiscent of the animation effect created when the pages of a book of sketches are flipped through quickly and in sequence, each page of the book representing a unique frame in an animation. Flipbook textures contain all the frames for an animation organized into equally sized tiles arranged in rows and columns. This grid-like arrangement into a finite set of frames enables the UDK to extract each frame from the texture based on its offset in the grid, and to show each frame in sequence at a specified frame rate to create an animated texture. This makes flipbook textures especially useful for creating textured animations that must loop repeatedly, ping-pong forward and backward, or play frames in a random order. Consequently, flipbook textures are often used to create explosion effects, flickering lights, twinkling stars, and noise effects, among others.

For the balloon project, a flipbook texture has been used to create an animated balloon texture. The texture shows a four-frame animation of a balloon whose string twitches or moves because of the breeze and atmospheric pressure. This effect will help to increase the realism of the balloon particles that will rise from the ground to the sky in a particle system. Figure 11.12 shows the complete four-frame balloon animation, complete with alpha channel. This image is provided with the book companion files as balloon.tga. This file is 1,024 × 1,024 pixels and contains a total of four frames, each frame being 512 × 512 pixels. The work of this section is to import the balloon image into the UDK Content Browser as a flipbook texture and then to configure the texture in a material that can be used for the particles of a particle system.

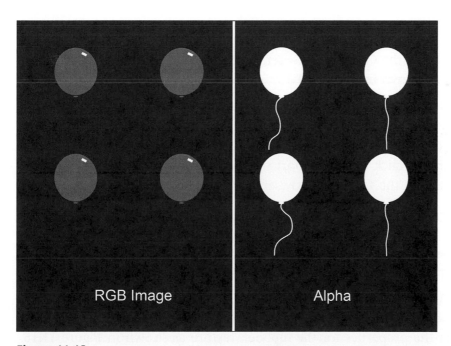

Figure 11.12
A flipbook texture featuring four variations of a red balloon divided across the image into four equally sized tiles, arranged in columns and rows. This flipbook texture, then, contains a four-frame animation.

Figure 11.13
Importing a texture via the Content Browser.

1. After creating a new level based on the Morning Lighting map template, press Ctrl+Shift+F to open the Content Browser. Then click the Import button in the Packages pane, as shown in Figure 11.13.

2. The Open File dialog box appears. Select the balloon.tga image file and click OK. In the Import dialog box that appears, type a name for the texture in the Name field. Then, in the Options section, check the Flip Book checkbox, as shown in Figure 11.14. Finally, click OK to import the flipbook texture. The flipbook texture will appear in the Content Browser's Preview pane.

Caution

You must configure a texture as a flipbook texture on import. A texture that is imported as a regular texture cannot later be converted to a flipbook texture.

3. Right-click the texture in the Content Browser and choose Properties from the menu that appears. The balloon texture's Properties panel appears. In the Flip Book section, set the properties for the flipbook texture as shown in Figure 11.15. Specifically, ensure that the Looping and Auto-Play checkboxes are checked to

Figure 11.14
Importing a texture as a flipbook texture.

ensure that the flipbook animation will loop endlessly and will play immediately. Further, set the Horizontal Images and Vertical Images settings to 2 to divide the frames of the animation into a maximum of two columns and two rows. The UDK will calculate the pixel dimensions of each frame in the texture by dividing the total texture width by the Horizontal Images setting, and by dividing the total texture height by the Vertical Images setting. Finally, ensure that FBMethod property is set to TFBM_UR_COL, and that the Frame Rate property (frames per second) is set to 16. That way, the balloon texture will play four times per second. (The animation contains four frames, and 4 × 4=16.) When you're finished, close the Properties panel.

4. Configure the flipbook texture into a material that can be used for a particle in a particle system. To begin, create a new material by clicking the New button in the Content Browser's Packages pane or right-clicking a vacant space in the Preview pane and choosing New Material from the menu that appears. In the Material Creation dialog box that opens, assign the material a name. Then open the newly created material in the Material Editor, as shown in Figure 11.16. The material is represented by the PreviewMaterial_0 node.

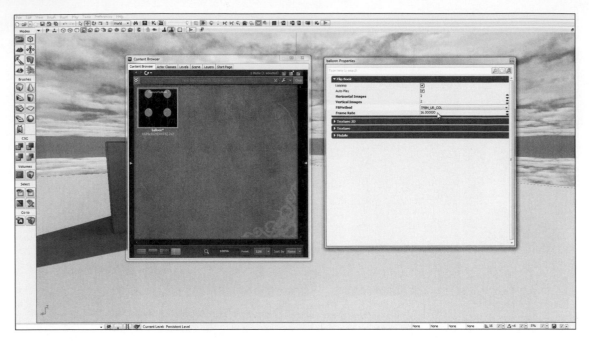

Figure 11.15
Configuring the flipbook texture via its Properties panel.

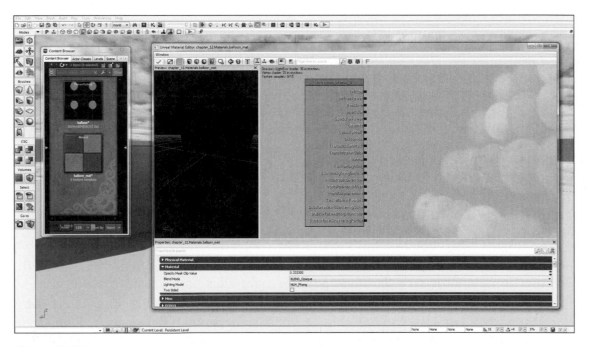

Figure 11.16
The Material Editor is open, ready to define a new material.

Note

More information on creating materials can be found in Chapter 5, "Materials, Textures, and UV Mapping."

5. Select the balloon flipbook texture in the Content Browser. Then, in the Material Editor, add a FlipBook node based on the balloon flipbook texture. To do this, right-click any vacant space in the Material Editor Graph pane and choose Texture, followed by New FlipBook Sample from the menu that appears. Assuming the texture properties were set as described in step 3, the preview thumbnail in the FlipBook node should show the first frame of the flipbook animation (rather than all four frames), as shown in Figure 11.17.

6. Click the PreviewMaterial_0 node in the Graph pane to select it. Then, in the Materials section of the node's Properties pane, ensure that the Blend Mode parameter is set to Blend Masked. This blend mode will ensure that black pixels in the alpha channel will be used to hide areas of the material outside the balloon pixels. Next, make sure the Lighting Model parameter is set to MLM_Unlit. This is to ensure that the material is not affected by scene lighting. Finally, check

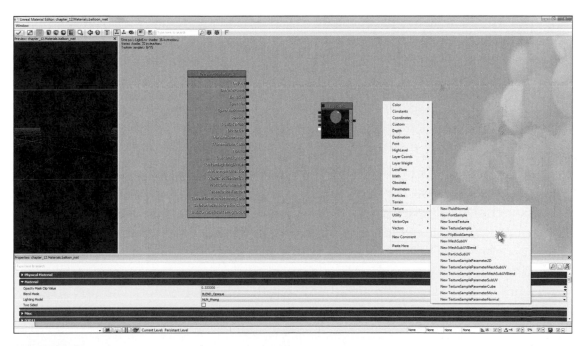

Figure 11.17
A FlipBook node created in the Material Editor Graph pane.

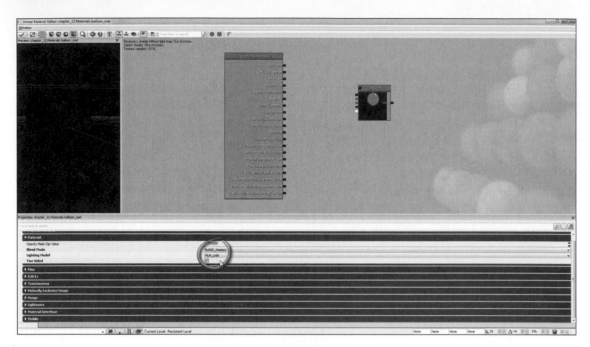

Figure 11.18
Configuring the properties for the primary material node.

the Two Sided checkbox to ensure that the material can be seen from the front and behind. (See Figure 11.18.)

7. In the Usage section of the PreviewMaterial_0 node's Properties pane, check the Used with Particle Sprites and Used with Particle Sub UV checkboxes, as shown in Figure 11.19. The former will allow you to apply the material to a quad particle (sprite), and the latter will allow you to animate the sprite using the flipbook texture. The material is now configured for use with a particle system.

8. All that remains is to connect the FlipBook node to the PreviewMaterial_0 node. To do this, connect the RGB output of the FlipBook node to the Emissive channel of the PreviewMaterial_0 node (rather than to the Diffuse channel) to ensure that the material is immune from lighting. Then connect the Alpha channel of the FlipBook node to the Opacity Mask channel of the PreviewMaterial_0 node to ensure the Alpha channel masks the material appropriately. (See Figure 11.20.) Save this material and exit the Material Editor. The first stage of the project is complete.

Note

The level so far can be found in the companion files under DM-Balloons_Project_01_MatComp.udk.

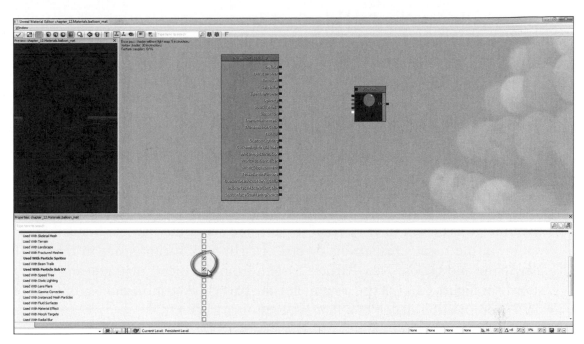

Figure 11.19
Configuring the Usage properties for the primary material node.

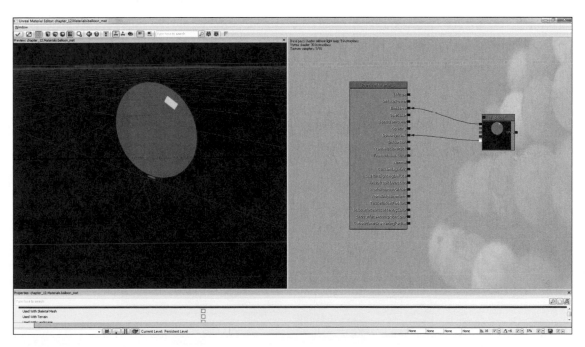

Figure 11.20
Completing the balloon material.

Using Cascade for the Particle System

The previous section detailed the creation of a particle system–compliant material featuring a four-frame flipbook texture of an animated balloon. The work of this section will be to integrate that material into a particle system. The particle system created here will feature one cylindrical-shaped emitter that will be placed at ground level and will continuously emit multiple balloon particles at a fixed rate. These particles will be textured quads that will gently float upward from the ground to the sky, where they will terminate and disappear from view. The following steps demonstrate how to build such a particle system using the Cascade Editor.

1. Open the Content Browser and create a new particle system. To do so, either click the New button in the Packages pane and select the Particle System option in the Asset Creation dialog box or right-click vacant space in the Preview pane and choose New Particle System from the menu that appears, as shown in Figure 11.21. Type a name for the particle system in the Name field of the Asset Creation dialog box that appears; then click OK.

2. The Cascade Editor should open automatically when you create a new particle system. If it doesn't, double-click the particle system thumbnail in the Content Browser's Preview pane. By default, the particle system contains a single emitter that spawns blank (null-material) particles. To assign the balloon material to the

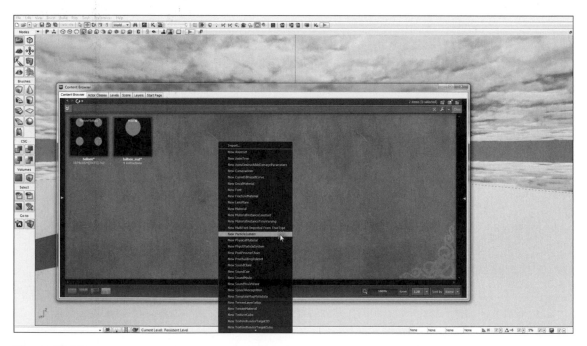

Figure 11.21
Creating a new particle system.

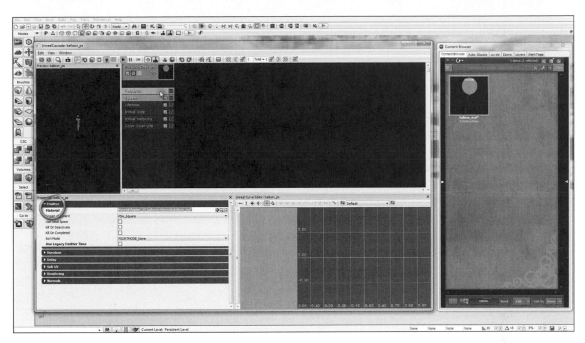

Figure 11.22
Applying the balloon texture to the particle sprites.

particles, select the balloon material in the Content Browser. Then, in the Cascade Editor, select the Required module in the Particle Emitter column. Finally, in the Emitter section of the Properties pane, click the green left arrow in the Material field, as shown in Figure 11.22. The particle emitter will now fire balloon sprites into the air.

3. Although the particle emitter will fire balloon sprites into the air, these will not be clearly visible in the Cascade Editor's Preview pane because of its background color. To fix this, click the Toggle Grid button on the toolbar to enable the grid in the Preview pane. Then click the Open Color Selection Dialog Box button on the toolbar to open the Select a Color dialog box, which you can use to change the background color to gray. See Figure 11.23.

4. As you can see in the Preview pane, the particle emitter is currently an infinitely small point in space, meaning all the balloons are generated from the same location. The emitter for this system should be not a point, but a cylinder—meaning that each emitted balloon will begin at any random location inside the cylindrical volume. To change the shape of the emitter, you must add a new module to the emitter to access the necessary properties. To begin, right-click any vacant space in the Particle Emitter column and choose Location followed

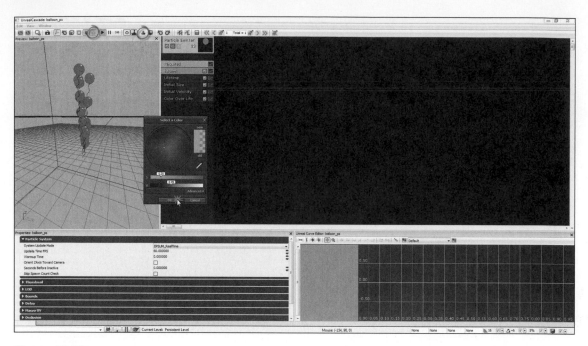

Figure 11.23
Setting the background color for the Cascade Editor Preview pane.

by Cylinder from the menu that appears. As shown in Figure 11.24, this creates a Cylinder module for the emitter and changes the spatial distribution of the balloon particles in the Preview pane.

5. It is difficult to visualize the cylindrical nature of the emitter. To resolve this, enable a wireframe preview of the emitter in the Preview pane by clicking the Cylinder module in the Particle Emitter column and checking the Draw 3D checkbox in the Cascade section of the Properties panel, as shown in Figure 11.25.

6. The cylinder radius for the emitter produces an acceptable result. But the cylinder is supposed to represent the floor plane, so it should be shorter than it is. To change the height of the cylinder, make sure the Cylinder module is still selected in the Particle Emitter column. Then, in the Location section of the Properties panel, change the Start Height/Distribution/Constant setting from 50 to 5 Unreal world units, as shown in Figure 11.26. (Distributions typically affect how values change over time, but the cylinder's start height is a constant value and a curve, meaning the value will remain constant throughout the simulation.)

7. The balloon particles are currently spawned from inside the volume of a shortened cylinder emitter and proceed to float upward into the atmosphere. To view the current lifetime of the particles in seconds, click the Lifetime module in the Particle Emitter column. Then open the Lifetime section of the Properties pane.

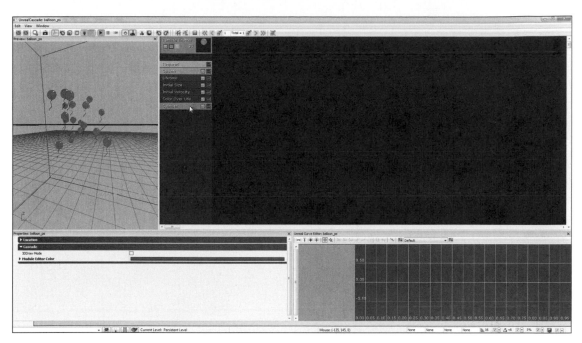

Figure 11.24
Adding a Cylinder module to the default emitter.

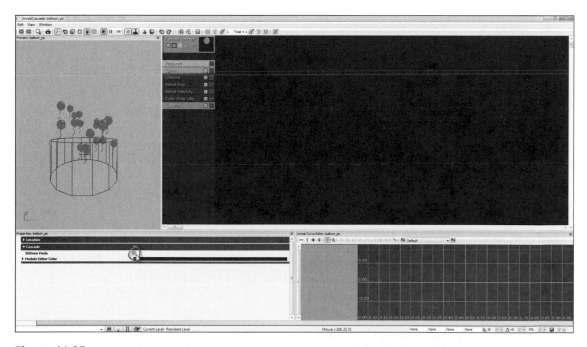

Figure 11.25
Showing a wireframe preview of the emitter.

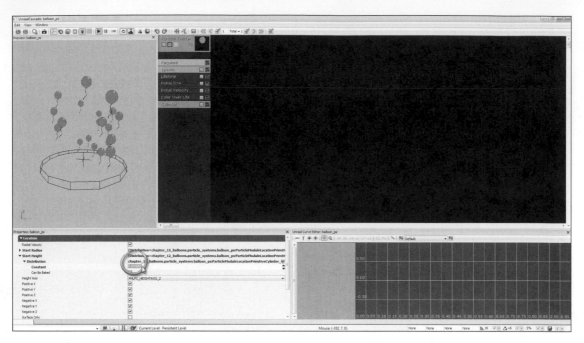

Figure 11.26
Reducing the height of the cylinder emitter.

The lifetime for the balloon particles is defined by the Lifetime/Distribution Min and Max settings. Both these parameters are currently set to 1, meaning that each particle survives for one second after it is spawned. Change the Min and Max values to 4 and 6, respectively, as shown in Figure 11.27. This way, any one particle in the system can have a lifetime that ranges from four to six seconds, allowing the balloons more time to travel upward into the atmosphere. Close the particle system now and save the changes if prompted.

8. The balloon particle system can now be deployed into the level as an actor. Adding a particle system as an actor is much like adding a sound, light, or static mesh as an actor. Start by selecting the particle system in the Preview pane of the Content Browser; then drag and drop it into the level at an appropriate location (in this case, on the ground plane). Notice that an icon appears in the level to represent the position of the particle emitter. Finally, click the Play button for the level and observe the particle system in action. (See Figure 11.28.) Splendid work!

Note

The completed level can be found in the companion files under DM-Balloons_Project_02_PSComp.udk.

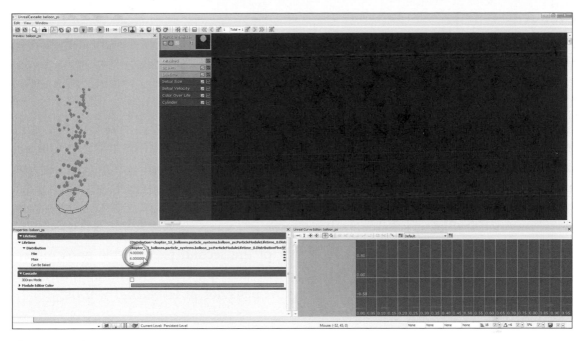

Figure 11.27
Setting the lifetime of balloon particles.

Figure 11.28
Celebrating with balloons: the particle system in action.

CONCLUSION

This chapter touched only the surface of the subject of particle systems. Certainly, much more lies beneath. It defined a particle system as a collection of one or more emitters that spawn particles. Once spawned, these particles seem to take on a life of their own through the mathematical structure of a distribution.

Before proceeding to the next chapter, I recommend that you spend more time exploring particle systems—specifically, experimenting with distributions and curves using the knowledge gained on curves in Chapter 9. I also recommend that you experiment with non–sprite based particles, including mesh particles, as demonstrated by a number of the particle systems distributed with the UDK (including the system named P_Pickups_Base_Health_Glow).

The next chapter, which is the final chapter of the second part of this book, enters the world of programming by considering UnrealScript, the powerful scripting language offered by the UDK for customizing the behavior of levels and worlds.

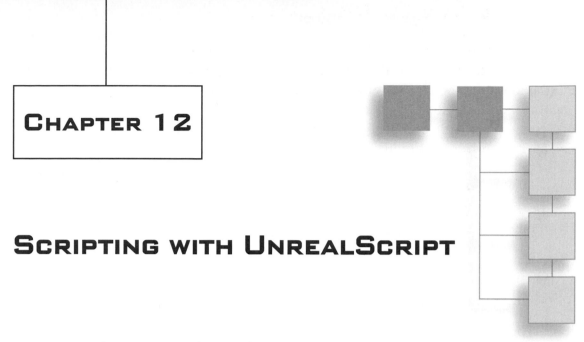

CHAPTER 12

SCRIPTING WITH UNREALSCRIPT

One of my most productive days was throwing away 1,000 lines of code.

—Attributed to Kenneth Lane Thompson

By the end of this chapter, you should:

- Be able to create simple applications using the UnrealScript language.
- Understand game flow in an UnrealScript application.
- Understand the Game Info, World Info, and Actor classes.
- Be able to extend new classes in the UnrealScript class hierarchy.
- Be able to edit UnrealScript config files with more confidence.

An introductory book on the UDK could take one of two approaches when discussing UnrealScript, the UDK's text-based scripting language for extending and customizing the Unreal Engine. The first approach is to assume the reader has no programming experience and to explain both the basics of programming and the UnrealScript language. The second is to assume that the reader already has knowledge of an established language but has not yet coded in UnrealScript. This book takes the latter of the two approaches. It assumes the reader has knowledge of fundamental object-oriented programming concepts such as variables, functions, classes, constants, data structures, inheritance, and polymorphism. This assumption has been made for two reasons. First, there are already many valuable books and tutorials that comprehensively discuss the basics of object-oriented programming. Second, the focus of this book is on the UDK and its tools, not on the basics of programming.

That being said, an understanding of programming will be required for this chapter and for the remaining chapters in this book. Readers who are not familiar with programming but who wish to proceed with this book should first consider reading one or more introductory titles on either C++ or Java. For C++, I recommend *Beginning C++ Through Game Programming*, 3rd edition, by Michael Dawson. For Java, I recommend *Beginning Java Game Programming*, 2nd edition, by Jonathan S. Harbour. (Both of these books are published by Cengage Learning.) If you are not familiar with programming but want to proceed with this book, attempting to pick up the knowledge as you proceed, I recommend that you first revisit Chapter 9, "Kismet and Matinee: Beginning with Visual Scripting and Animation."

WHAT IS UNREALSCRIPT?

UnrealScript is a text-based, object-oriented scripting language whose scripts (code files) can be parsed, compiled, and executed by the Unreal Engine and its associated tools. The purpose of the language is to offer game developers a flexible and powerful script-based means of extending and customizing both the behavior of the Unreal Engine and their games.

The UnrealScript language has several notable and distinguishing features:

- It is fully object oriented.
- UnrealScript coding involves deriving.
- It is based on C++ and Java.
- It has state programming features.

Note

Accessing NULL (or None) pointers in UnrealScript will not crash an application with an exception as it would were it built in the C++ language.

UnrealScript Is Fully Object Oriented

Programming languages that are object oriented are languages that support the concept of classes and a selection of class-related concepts such as class hierarchy and inheritance, member variables and functions, access specifiers, virtual functions, and polymorphism. A *class* in this sense can be defined as a container for a set of related code, including variables and functions. Both C++ and Java are examples of object-oriented languages because of their support for classes. The UnrealScript language also is object oriented because it supports classes, but it takes that object orientation a little further.

It is important for developers approaching UnrealScript from C++ to understand what object orientation involves in UnrealScript. Although C++ allows developers to create classes using the `class` keyword and to create variables and functions as members of a class, it is also possible to use C++ to code a range of variables and functions that do not in any way belong to a class. For example, C++ supports the use of global variables—that is, variables that are accessible to all code throughout the application, but outside the scope of any particular class. Similarly, C++ supports global functions that can be coded outside the scope of any particular class but that can still be accessed and called through the inclusion of header files. The following code demonstrates a C++ source file that contains a global variable and function:

```
//global variable
int g_Var;
int Add(int Number)
{
    g_Var += Number;
    return g_Var
}
```

Although C++ allows the creation of global functions and variables, they are inconsistent with the object-oriented paradigm because none of them depend on a class. In contrast, UnrealScript is fully object oriented, meaning it does not allow for the creation of global functions and variables. In UnrealScript, there is no such thing as a classless object or function. All variables and functions that can exist in UnrealScript must exist as members of a class. In short, UnrealScript supports only object orientation, including classes, inheritance, and polymorphism. In UnrealScript, variables that belong to a class are called *instance variables* rather than *properties*, and functions are called *member functions* rather than *methods*.

UnrealScript Involves Coding Through Deriving

As mentioned, UnrealScript is fully object oriented. It follows that developers must add their own functionality to the engine or to their games by deriving new classes from existing ones. The UDK ships with a range of pre-defined UnrealScript classes in both source-code and compiled form, all of which are essential to the workings of the UDK and the Unreal Engine. All these pre-defined classes exist in a class hierarchy whose ultimate ancestor class is known as the `Object` class. Figure 12.1 shows a sample schematic of the UDK class hierarchy. (Note that it does not reflect the actual UDK class hierarchy, but is intended to roughly illustrate how it is arranged.)

The classes that ship with the UDK define many of the common features available in the Unreal Engine and in the UDK Editor, including the camera actor, spot lights,

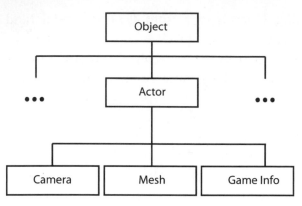

Figure 12.1
A rough illustration of the UnrealScript class hierarchy.

point lights, static meshes, materials, Kismet nodes, sound actors, and many more. Developers code their own functionality in their games and in the UDK not by amending existing classes but by creating new classes that are derived from them—that is, new classes that extend the existing ones. In UnrealScript, the word *extend* refers to the process typically known as *deriving*. Therefore, class A extends class B when A derives from B. For example, a developer who wanted to create a chase-view camera as opposed to a first-person camera for his or her game might create a new chase-view camera class that extended from the existing and default camera class.

Native and Non-Native Classes

UnrealScript supports two main kinds of classes:

- **Native.** Native classes are either wholly or partially coded in C++ and are built into the Unreal Engine, either by being compiled into the engine executable or by being integrated into the engine via an external binary library.

- **Non-native.** Non-native classes are defined entirely in UnrealScript.

Creating native classes depends on having access to the Unreal Engine source code, which is not available to UDK developers. That means UDK developers can create only non-native classes—that is, only classes that can be defined entirely in UnrealScript. This does not mean, however, that UDK developers cannot use or extend the pre-made native classes that ship with the UDK; it means only that they cannot create their own native classes.

UnrealScript Is Based on C++ and Java

UnrealScript is based on C++ and Java in that it shares most of their keywords, structure, and syntax. This makes UnrealScript especially easy to learn for programmers who know C++ or Java (or other languages that derive from them, including

JavaScript, PHP, Lua, and C#). Specifically, UnrealScript (as well as C++ and Java) supports the following keywords: `if`, `else`, `switch`, `for`, `while`, `int`, `break`, `continue`, and `float`, among others. Furthermore, UnrealScript supports use of the opening and closing braces (`{}`) to mark the beginning and end of sections of code, respectively.

UnrealScript Has State Programming Features

One feature of UnrealScript that distinguishes it from Java and C++ is that Unreal-Script supports states. That is, UnrealScript is based on the concept of a finite state machine (FSM), a system that supports many potential states but can exist in only one of those states at any one time. In particular, UnrealScript allows developers to effectively define multiple versions of a single class, each called a *state*, and to have UnrealScript switch back and forth between the different states at run time depending on specific conditions. The result is that a single class can make its functions and variables conditionally available—that is, a single class can have multiple implementations for the same function, making only one implementation available at any one time depending on the state of the class. For example, a game might feature a character with a set of specified moods: happy, angry, and sad. The character would be encoded as a class, and its three moods could be represented by three different states. The character might also feature a function named `SayHello`, and the implementation of this function would differ across states. This would make it possible for the character to say different things when `SayHello` was called, depending on his mood.

Note

Although Java and C++ do not have explicit features for states, they can be used to implement similar behavior. To highlight that UnrealScript features states is not to suggest that C++ or Java are lacking as languages.

GETTING STARTED WITH UNREALSCRIPT: PIXELMINE NFRINGE AND MICROSOFT VISUAL STUDIO

The UDK is often branded as a complete toolset for making games. Indeed, the UDK official Web site describes the UDK as "a complete professional development frame-work," with "all the tools you need to create great games." This is true, in a sense—a complete game *could* be made using only the tools provided by the UDK. But there is also a sense in which this is a little misleading: The UDK does not offer (among other things) an integrated code editor for creating and compiling UnrealScript programs even though most commercial-grade UDK games will require at least some coding in UnrealScript. That means developers who must code in UnrealScript must do so using a third-party tool, whether that tool is a text editor such as Notepad or an integrated development environment (IDE) such as Microsoft Visual Studio.

Note

If you use Notepad or another text editor to code in UnrealScript, you will need to manually launch the UDK compiler. To compile scripts, you must run the UDKLift.exe file with the `make-full` switch. Unreal-Script can also be compiled through the Unreal Front End. More information on this can be found at http://udn.epicgames.com/Three/UnrealFrontend.html.

Those who choose the latter option can download and install a Visual Studio add-in, nFringe, which provides syntax highlighting, compiling, and code-completion features for UnrealScript, as shown in Figure 12.2. The following sections detail how to download, install, and configure nFringe for use with Visual Studio. You'll finish with a Visual Studio project that is configured and ready for you to create and build UnrealScript code.

Note

The following sections also contain valuable information about UnrealScript generally. For this reason, it is recommended that you do not skip it, even if you plan to code in UnrealScript with Notepad or another text editor instead of Visual Studio and nFringe.

Figure 12.2
Microsoft Visual Studio used with nFringe to edit and compile an UnrealScript application.

Downloading and Installing nFringe

As mentioned, Microsoft Visual Studio can be used to code UnrealScript programs. This software comes in various versions, ranging from the free Express edition (available from www.microsoft.com/express) to the commercial Professional edition. Both of these versions can be used to create UnrealScript (even though the IDE is not intended for this purpose), and both are compatible with the PixelMine nFringe add-in. This add-in extends Visual Studio to make available for UnrealScript the syntax-highlighting and code-completion features that are available for the standard Visual Studio languages, such as C++, C#, and Visual Basic. The nFringe add-in also allows developers to compile UnrealScript programs at the click of a button, saving them from compiling scripts via the command line.

This book assumes you have either edition of the latest version of Microsoft Visual Studio (currently 2010) installed on your system. To download and install the latest version of nFringe on your system, navigate to http://pixelminegames.com and download and run the setup.exe nFringe installation file to install the program onto your computer.

Note

At the time of this writing, nFringe is not free if it is being used to make commercial games. Developers of commercial games should consider the nFringe pricing terms. For more information, visit http://pixelminegames.com/nfringe.

When it is installed to the computer, Visual Studio will automatically be configured to use nFringe. The next step is to set up a Visual Studio project configured to compile UnrealScript code. To do that, you need to understand how the UDK structures UnrealScript files, covered next.

Class Folders and Configuring nFringe

In the UnrealScript language, every class must have its own unique source file, one source file per class. The name of that file must match the name of the class contained inside. Hence, a class named MyClass must be stored inside a source file named MyClass.uc. (.uc is the file extension for UnrealScript source files.) In UnrealScript, it is not possible to have more than one class defined inside a source file. Two separate classes demand two separate files, three demand three, and so on. Thus, there should be as many UnrealScript source files as there are classes.

The source code for the classes shipped with the UDK are distributed throughout the subfolders of the Development\Src folder (*src* being an abbreviation of *source*), inside the UDK installation folder. (See Figure 12.3.) This folder is especially significant

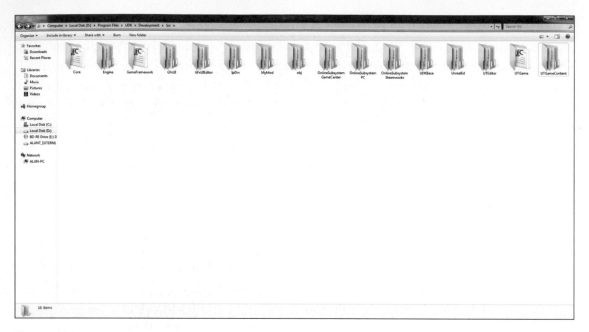

Figure 12.3
UnrealScript source files must be contained inside the Development\Src folder if they are to be compiled successfully by the UnrealScript compiler.

because it contains not only the classes that ship with the UDK, but all UnrealScript classes, including custom classes created by the game developer. Further, classes inside the Development\Src folder must be organized and arranged into further subfolders according to a predetermined structure. Specifically, each folder inside the Development\Src folder is used to group together related classes (source files). For example, all engine-related classes are found inside the Classes subfolder of the Engine subfolder; all classes related to the UDK Editor are inside the Classes subfolder of the UnrealEd subfolder; and so on. Figure 12.4 illustrates the UnrealScript folder structure in more detail.

In short, the Development\Src folder is the top-most folder in a hierarchy of folders that are together used to organize all the UnrealScript source files for a single and complete game, just as the UDKGame folder houses all the assets for a single and complete game. (Refer to Chapter 2, "Building a First Project: A Tour of the UDK," for more information). For example, a developer wanting to create a set of classes that define the behavior of different enemies in a game, one class per enemy, might collect together these classes in a folder named Development\Src\Enemies\Classes. It is important to emphasize that this folder structure for classes is not a recommendation of the UDK, but a requirement. Source files that do not conform to this standard will not be recognized and compiled by the UDK UnrealScript compiler.

Folder Structure of Development\Src Folder

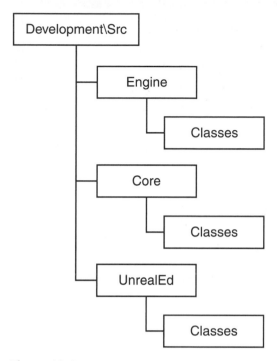

Figure 12.4
UnrealScript source files must be distributed across subfolders of the Development\Src folder. Subfolders of this folder organize related classes together. Each subfolder should keep its classes inside a Classes subfolder.

Adding functionality to the Unreal Engine and to UDK games through UnrealScript is the process of creating new classes and source files in the Development\Src folder according to the UDK convention. Visual Studio and nFringe, therefore, must be configured to facilitate this process. Specifically, a single Visual Studio project must be created (a *project* being a collection of related files and compilation settings). This project will enable you to view all the existing classes of the UDK as well as to add and amend new classes. There will not be a reason to create multiple Visual Studio projects for a single game; one Visual Studio project will serve your developmental needs. The details of creating and configuring this project are as follows.

1. Start Microsoft Visual Studio and choose New Project from the Project Template menu that appears at startup. The New Project dialog box opens; from there, select UnrealScript in the Installed Templates list, as shown in Figure 12.5. (This option appears because of the nFringe add-in.) Select the UnrealEngine Licensee project; then enter a name and path for the project in the Name and Location fields at the bottom of the dialog box and choose Development\Src for

Figure 12.5
Creating a new Visual Studio project with nFringe for UnrealScript.

the project location. Finally, click the OK button to confirm the details and create a new, blank UnrealScript project.

Note

If the UnrealScript option is not visible in the Installed Templates list, check to ensure the nFringe add-in was installed successfully. Troubleshooting information can be found at the official nFringe Wiki Web site (http://tiny.cc/3bp0y).

2. The project you just created currently contains no source files. The aim here is to populate the project with all the UnrealScript source files that are in the sub-folders under Development\Src. Eventually, the nFringe plug-in will do this for you automatically. The problem at present is that Visual Studio has created the project file in a subfolder of the Development\Src folder, meaning that nFringe cannot locate any of the other subfolders of Development\Src. To fix this, close Visual Studio. Then move the newly created Visual Studio project into the Development\Src folder, deleting the subfolder in which it was originally created, as shown in Figure 12.6.

3. After you shift the UnrealScript project files to the Development\Src folder, open the project in Visual Studio. nFringe has populated the project with all the UnrealScript files provided with the UDK. These files are now viewable and editable using Microsoft Visual Studio. Notice that the file hierarchy in the

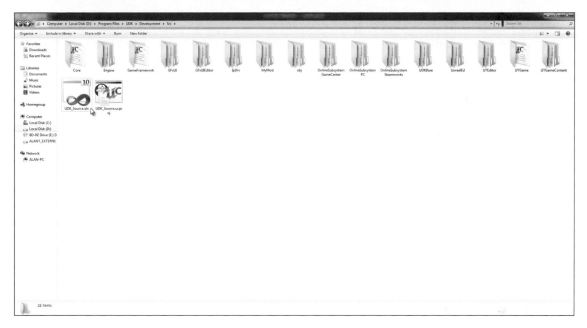

Figure 12.6
Moving the UnrealScript Visual Studio project into the Development\Src folder.

Visual Studio Solution Explorer matches that of the Development\Src folder. Notice too that the UDK class hierarchy can be viewed and inspected from the Class View tab. (See Figure 12.7.)

4. Although the project is now filled with source files from the Development\Src folder, it cannot at present be compiled because nFringe must be notified of the full file path of the UDK compiler executable. To do this, right-click the project name in the Solution Explorer and choose Properties from the menu that appears, as shown in Figure 12.8. The Properties panel for the current project opens.

5. Click the General tab in the Properties panel. Then specify the full path of the UDK UnrealScript compiler in the UCC Path field by clicking the Browse button and selecting the file Binaries\Win64\UDK.com (or Win32\UDK.com for 32-bit operating systems). (See Figure 12.9.)

6. Click the Debug tab in the Properties panel and type `Binaries\Win64\ UDK.exe` (or `Win32\UDK.exe` for 32-bit operating systems) in the Start Game Executable field. Next, ensure that Disable Sound, Disable Startup Movies, and Force Windowed Mode checkboxes are checked, as shown in Figure 12.10. The first checkbox disables audio when a UDK game is compiled and run from Visual Studio in Debug mode, the second checkbox disables

Figure 12.7
nFringe populates the project with UnrealScript source files.

Figure 12.8
Accessing the project properties from the Visual Studio Solution Explorer.

Figure 12.9
Selecting the UnrealScript compiler.

Figure 12.10
Specifying debug properties for the active UnrealScript project.

Figure 12.11
Compiling UnrealScript in Visual Studio.

startup cut scenes, and the third checkbox ensures that a UDK game is run in windowed mode as opposed to full screen mode. Finally, exit the panel by clicking its Close button. Visual Studio applies the settings you chose.

7. The project (meaning all UnrealScript source files) can now be compiled. That is, the source files can now be translated into a compiled form. To do this, open the Build menu and choose Rebuild Solution or press Ctrl+Alt+F7. Examine the compilation results from the Output pane at the bottom of the Visual Studio window, as shown in Figure 12.11.

8. The compilation of the UnrealScript source files in the Development\Src folder results in the creation of new, compiled files with a .u extension in the UDK-Game\Script folder. Each U file in the UDKGame\Script folder corresponds to a subfolder in the Development\Src folder and contains the compiled code for all classes in that folder. Notice in Figure 12.12 that the compiled files are named core.u, engine.u, unrealed.u, and so on. The purpose of compilation is to produce a set of optimized UnrealScript files that the engine will use at run time to parse and execute the UnrealScript. The Unreal Engine will use the compiled files only, not the source files, at run time. The source files are created for the purpose of compilation.

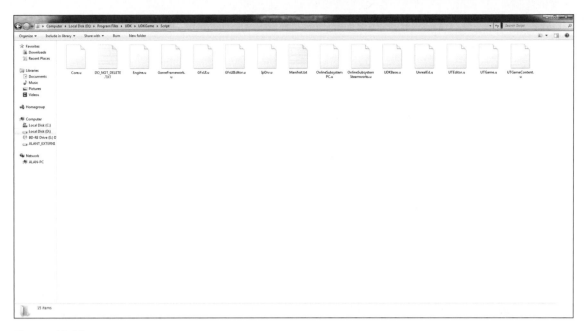

Figure 12.12
Compiled UnrealScript files. Compare the names of the compiled files to the names of the folders in the Development\Src folder, as shown in Figure 12.3.

THE STRUCTURE OF AN UNREALSCRIPT APPLICATION

You've learned how Visual Studio and nFringe can be used to write, compile, and debug UnrealScript applications. Whether you have chosen to use those applications or not, you should now be in a position to compile the UnrealScript source code. The purpose of this section is to outline the general structure of an UnrealScript application—to detail its general order of events. This is important because one of the first questions most developers ask when presented with the reasonably intimidating and extensive class hierarchy of UnrealScript classes is, where do I start with all this? Where does an UnrealScript application begin? If I wanted to print a message to the screen at the start of a level, where would I code this?

To answer this question, it is important to begin with the understanding that the phrase *UnrealScript application* is used here and in the UDK documentation in a loose sense. There is, properly speaking, no such thing as an UnrealScript application in that UnrealScript does not compile into a standalone executable file and it is not intended to be run on its own as an application. Thus, UnrealScript has no starting point function, like the `main` or `winmain` functions in C++. Rather, the Unreal Engine is the application that makes use of the UnrealScript class hierarchy by declaring instances of its classes as needed. Thus, to ask where an UnrealScript application begins is to ask either which of its classes is instantiated first or which member

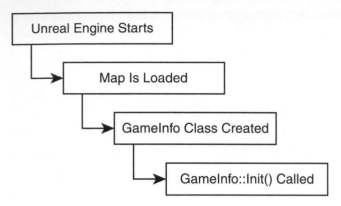

Figure 12.13
The flow of an UnrealScript application. The GameInfo class defines the main game logic of a level.

function of a class is called first. Figure 12.13 provides clues as to the answer. Before considering it further, however, first consider some of the most important and fundamental classes in the UnrealScript class hierarchy.

Note

Every class in the UnrealScript hierarchy descends either directly or indirectly from the ultimate ancestor class Object, whose instance variables and member functions are inherited by all other classes. Most (but not all) classes, however, are also descendents of the Actor class, which defines a thing that can exist in a game level (for example, a static mesh, sound, light, and so on). Static meshes, sounds, and lights are all examples of classes derived (extended) from the Actor class. See source files Object.uc and Actor.uc for more information. To see an overview of a class and its variables and functions, use the Visual Studio Class View panel.

WorldInfo Class (Source File: WorldInfo.uc)

The WorldInfo class corresponds to the game level that is loaded and currently being played. It is a singleton class in that there can be only one instance of a WorldInfo class active for one map. The Unreal Engine instantiates a single instance of the WorldInfo class whenever a level is loaded, and it destroys that same instance whenever the level ends.

Like the GameInfo class, discussed in a moment, the WorldInfo class is somewhat misnamed because its name implies that it is more of a database than a class—as though its purpose is only to store or contain information. In fact, the purpose of the WorldInfo class is not only to contain information about a specified map or level, but to do things to that level. It is an active as well as a passive force. It can be used both to read information about a level and to perform operations on a level.

The WorldInfo class is the UnrealScript representative or manager of a level. It enables developers to enumerate all actors in the level, to measure the time that has elapsed since the level began, and to perform level queries about distances, measurements, and volumes, among other things. The WorldInfo class is responsible narrowly for managing all the physical properties of a level—properties relating to world geometry, time, space, motion, distance, gravity, and so on. It is *not* the responsibility of the WorldInfo class to manage the game rules or game logic. The WorldInfo class does not keep track of whether the player has succeeded in his or her objectives, enemies have infiltrated the base, the player has achieved a high score, or the time limit has expired. These latter properties are the remit of the GameInfo class.

GameInfo Class (Source File: GameInfo.uc)

The GameInfo class is subordinate to the WorldInfo class in terms of the management hierarchy that exists among classes in an UnrealScript application. That is, the WorldInfo class owns the GameInfo class; its scope contains and surpasses the scope of the GameInfo class. A WorldInfo class can exist without a GameInfo class, but the GameInfo class cannot exist without a WorldInfo class.

In the order of class instantiation in an UnrealScript application, the WorldInfo class is created before and terminated after the GameInfo class. The GameInfo class stands in contrast to the WorldInfo class in that it acts as a manager not for the physical properties of the level, but for the abstract game-logic rules that govern how the game is to be played in the level. For example, the GameInfo class might keep track of the number of kills in a game, the time limit, or the synchronization of events, and will determine whether a win or a loss condition has been satisfied.

There is a functional separation between the WorldInfo and GameInfo classes because it is possible for one level to host many different types of games. For example, one map could be played with a death-match format or a capture-the-flag format. In this example, the physical properties of the world (its architecture, gravitational forces, lighting conditions, and size) will remain the same, but its game rules change—hence the reason for two distinct classes, GameInfo and WorldInfo. Because the rules of a game are game specific (they vary from game to game), developers are highly likely to extend and customize the GameInfo class for their games.

Note

Execution for an UnrealScript application begins in the GameInfo class—specifically in the GameInfo::Init() member function, called when a level is initialized. Overriding this function in an extended class therefore allows developers to customize startup behavior in a level, as you shall see.

The Player

One of the most important concepts in a game is the player. In UnrealScript, the player is represented by a collection of three separate classes, each corresponding to a particular aspect of the player.

The player in a UDK game consists of three main components:

- **Controller.** The controller represents the input or instructions provided by the gamer to the game through an input device such as a keyboard, mouse, or gamepad. Through these devices, the gamer tells the game his or her intentions—that is, what the player as both an actor and active force in the level should do. Those instructions might be to run, jump, punch, kick, shoot, hide, harvest wood, dispatch armies, or burst some floating blocks, depending on the game.

- **Pawn.** The pawn represents the player's physical presence in the level (if he or she has one). In a side-scrolling platform game, for example, the character mesh representing the player that responds to his or her input constitutes the pawn of the player. The pawn is an optional component. There are all kinds of games in which the player does not have a physical presence—strategy and God games, to name but two in which the player controls an overarching authority that dispatches instructions but has no physical representation in the world.

- **Camera.** The camera represents the vantage point from which the world is shown to the player onscreen. First-person games feature first-person cameras, while third-person games feature a camera at some location outside the player's body—perhaps from over the shoulder or an isometric view.

The three components of a player (controller, pawn, and camera) are encapsulated in the classes Pawn (Pawn.uc), Camera (Camera.uc), and PlayerController (Player-Controller.uc).

Printing a Message with GameInfo

Every level loaded by the Unreal Engine must have an associated GameType class. GameType is used to refer to any instance of a class that has been extended from the GameInfo class and that defines the rules and game logic pertaining to the level. Developers define the rules and behavior for their games by extending a new class from the existing GameInfo class, overriding its functions and variables where appropriate. Unreal applications typically begin their execution with the instantiation of a GameType object and with the calling of its Init member function as a new level is loaded and initialized. Thus, developers can control what happens on level startup in UnrealScript by extending a class from GameInfo and by overriding its Init member function. The Init member function is akin to the main or winmain

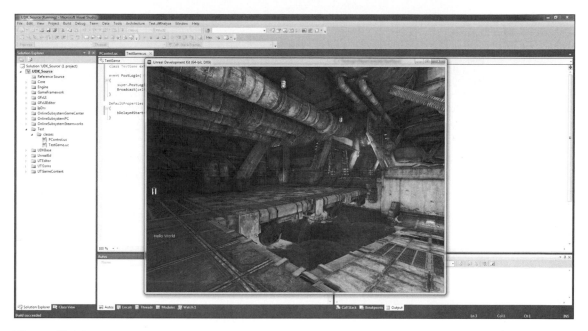

Figure 12.14
Showing a welcome message to the player at level startup using a class extended from `GameInfo`.

function in C++ in that it is called automatically by the Unreal Engine at level startup. This section demonstrates how to create a new extended `GameInfo` class for a sample level that will print a "Hello World" message to the gamer when the level is loaded, as shown in Figure 12.14.

1. Displaying a "Hello World" message on application startup involves changing how the game begins and behaves. This kind of change must be implemented in the `GameInfo` class because this class defines the logic or behavior of a game. More accurately, you must create a new class extended from `GameInfo`. As mentioned, classes in UnrealScript are defined in an UnrealScript source file, one file per class. These files must be added in a subfolder in the Development\Src folder of the UDK installation folder. Thus, to create a new class extended from `GameInfo`, first create a new subfolder in the Development\Src folder named Test to reflect the test nature of your work. Then create a subfolder inside Test named Classes, which will be the folder to house all classes related to the test work. In short, the test work will be housed in the folder Development\Src\Test\Classes. Next, start Visual Studio and open the UnrealScript project. Notice in the Solution Explorer that the Test\Class folder is now listed (see Figure 12.15).

2. Create a new UnrealScript source file in the Test\Classes folder that will be the class file for the class derived from `GameInfo`. To do so, right-click the Test\Classes

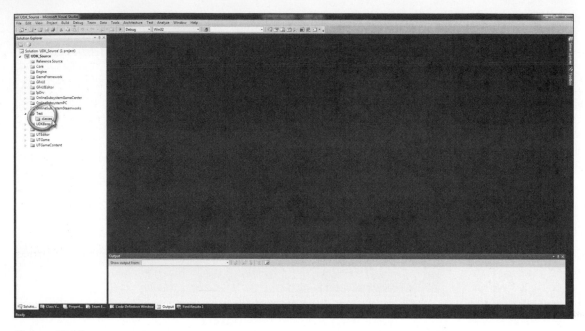

Figure 12.15
Preparing to create a test `GameInfo` extended class in the Development\Src\Test\Classes folder.

folder in the Solution Explorer and choose Add followed by New Item from the menu that appears, as shown in Figure 12.16. The Add New Item dialog box opens.

3. In the Add New Item dialog box (see Figure 12.17), select UnrealScript in the Installed Templates list. Then, in the Name field, type a name for the file you want to add. (I entered `TestGame`.) Finally, click the Add button to add the new UnrealScript source file to the project. The file contains an auto-generated skeleton class in UnrealScript, which you will amend.

Note

The source file added to the project by nFringe contains an auto-generated class whose name matches the filename of the source file, as shown in the following code below. Notice that the `class` keyword marks the beginning of a class definition and that the `extends` keyword prefixes the name of a class from which the current class is derived. Further, note that UnrealScript differs from both C++ and Java in that the first class declaration line is not followed by opening and closing braces (`{}`) to contain the body or implementation of the class. Such symbols would be unnecessary in UnrealScript because a source file contains one and only one class. The `DefaultProperties` code block is similar to (though distinct from) the class constructor function as found in C++ and Java.

```
class TestGame extends Object;

DefaultProperties
{
}
```

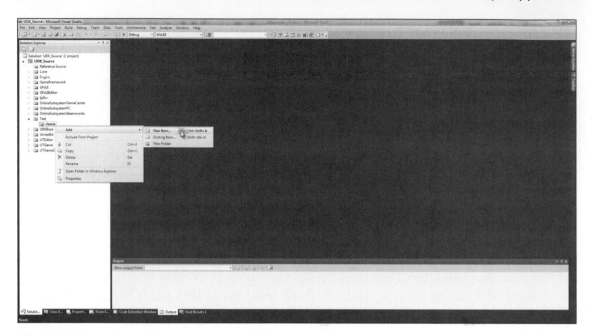

Figure 12.16
Adding a new file via the Solution Explorer.

Figure 12.17
Creating a new UnrealScript class.

4. The generated `TestGame` class is currently extended from the `Object` class, but must be extended from the `GameInfo` class if it is to act as a `GameType` object. For this reason, the declaration line must be changed to reflect this. The complete class definition should read as follows. (Changes are highlighted in bold.)

```
class TestGame extends GameInfo;


DefaultProperties
{
}
```

5. The purpose of these steps is to display a "Hello World" message at level startup using the `GameType` object. The first member function to be called by the Unreal Engine on the `GameInfo` class is the `Init` method, which called as the level is first initialized, before a player (any player) is spawned into the level. It would be futile to print a "Hello World" message at this point because no player would exist in the level to witness its effects. The "Hello World" message should instead be shown when all players are added to the level and are ready to play. One of the `GameInfo` member functions called on this event is the `PostLogin` function, called as a player is spawned into the level (regardless of whether the player has any physical representation in the form of a pawn). The prototype for this function can be found in the GameInfo.uc source file, and is `event PostLogin( PlayerController NewPlayer )`. The event keyword is used here to designate that the function is to act as an event. This function can be overridden in our extended `TestGame` class as follows. (Changes are highlighted in bold.)

```
class TestGame extends GameInfo;

event PostLogin( PlayerController NewPlayer )
{
}

DefaultProperties
{
}
```

6. You override the `PostLogin` function of the `GameInfo` class by declaring and implementing it in a descendent class—in this case, in the `TestGame` class. This function will be used as the entry point for the UnrealScript application and will be where the "Hello World" message is printed to the screen to greet players as

they are spawned into the level. The `PostLogin` function defined in the `GameInfo` class, however, performs many valuable tasks and operations that should also be performed for the descendent class (see GameInfo.uc). It would be useful to execute that code without having to duplicate it in the overridden function in the descendent class. To do this, the `super` keyword can be used in the `TestGame` class to access and call upon the member function and variable implementations in the `GameInfo` ancestor, as shown here. (Changes are highlighted in bold.)

```
class TestGame extends GameInfo;

event PostLogin( PlayerController NewPlayer )
{
    super.PostLogin(NewPlayer);
}

DefaultProperties
{
}
```

7. The `super` keyword is used to call member functions in ancestor implementations. Therefore, the statement `super.PostLogin` calls the `PostLogin` function implemented in the ancestor when called from the overridden version in the `TestGame` class. The next step is to print the message "Hello World" to the Unreal Engine console. To do this, the `Broadcast` function can be called. This function is implemented in the `GameInfo` class. Consider the following code sample. (Changes are highlighted in bold.)

```
class TestGame extends GameInfo;

event PostLogin( PlayerController NewPlayer )
{
    super.PostLogin(NewPlayer);

    //Print Hello World
    Broadcast(self,"Hello World");
}

DefaultProperties
{
}
```

Note

Similar to C++ and Java, the // symbol marks the beginning of a single-line comment, and the /* */ symbols mark the beginning and end of a multi-line comment.

---

8. By default, a UDK game based on the TestGame class will pause at startup for the player to click to fire his or her weapon before beginning gameplay, just as most death-match games wait for a player to signal his or her readiness to begin play. To remove this pause so that gameplay begins as soon as the level loads, assign the bDelayedStart Boolean member variable of the GameInfo class the value of false in the DefaultProperties block. The complete code for the TestGame class follows.

```
class TestGame extends GameInfo;

event PostLogin( PlayerController NewPlayer )
{
    super.PostLogin(NewPlayer);

    //Print Hello World
    Broadcast(self,"Hello World");
}

DefaultProperties
{
    bDelayedStart=false
}
```

Testing GameInfo

The TestGame class has now been created in UnrealScript as a GameType object. It both extends from the GameInfo class and overrides the PostLogin member function to print a "Hello World" message to the console when the player connects to the level. At this stage, two questions arise: First, how can you compile and test the newly created TestGame class? Second, if it is possible to create multiple GameType objects, how does the Unreal Engine know to use the TestGame type as opposed to another game type for any specified level? Both these questions will now be answered.

Compiling the TestGame Class

As you've seen, compiling UnrealScript code involves opening the Build menu and choosing Rebuild All. The UnrealScript compiler, however, will not necessarily compile all source files in all subfolders of the Development\Src folder of the UDK installation. Instead, the UnrealScript compiler will compile only source files in specified subfolders of the Development\Src folder—that is, only files in subfolders that are explicitly mentioned in a compilation list. This list of compilation-eligible folders is found in the file UDKGame\Config\UDKEngine.ini. If the newly created Test folder under Development\Src (used to contain the TestGame.uc source file) is not added to the list of compilation folders, the TestGame class will be ignored during compilation. The following steps detail how to add the Test folder to the compilation list and to compile the UnrealScript source code, including the TestGame class.

1. Open the file UDKGame\Config\UDKEngine.ini in a text-editor application such as Notepad. This file contains a range of configuration settings for different components of the Unreal Engine and of UDK-based games. Each line of the file is arranged in key-value pairing—that is, in the form [Key]=[Value], where [Key] specifies the name of a property to be assigned a value and [Value] refers to data that is to be assigned to the property (for example, Name=John). The list of folders eligible for compilation is listed in the UnrealEd.EditorEngine section of the file. Adding ModEditPackages=Test to the end of that section (see Figure 12.18) will add the Test folder to the compilation list.

Note

The UDKEngine.ini file can contain none, one, or more ModEditPackages commands. The form of the ModEditPackages command is ModEditPackages=FolderName, where FolderName specifies the name of the folder (without its path) to be included in the compilation list. Every ModEditPackages command should specify a unique subfolder of Development\Src to be included in the compilation list.

2. Close and save the UDKEngine.ini configuration file and return to the UnrealScript project in Visual Studio. Select Save All to save the files in the project; then open the Build menu and choose Rebuild All to compile the UnrealScript source code, including the newly created TestGame class. To confirm that the compilation process is successful, check the Output pane at the bottom of the Visual Studio screen. (See Figure 12.19.)

Note

It can also be useful to set the UDKEngine.ini file to read-only, to protect it from any automatic changes that the engine or other UDK tools might make.

Figure 12.18
Adding the Test\Classes subfolder to the compilation list of folders in the Development\Src folder using the `ModEditPackages` command.

Figure 12.19
Compiling the `TestGame` class.

Note

Errors will likely result if Visual Studio and nFringe are compiling UnrealScript while the UDK Editor is running. Ensure that the UDK Editor is not running during compilation, even if the level that is open in the editor does not pertain to the classes that are being coded or compiled in Visual Studio.

Running a Game with the `TestGame` Class

With UnrealScript, compiling code means translating or converting source code into a different, abbreviated form that can be more easily read and parsed by the Unreal Engine. As mentioned, the results of the compilation process are output to the UDK Game\Script folder. The UnrealScript source code having been compiled, this folder should now contain a file featuring the `TestGame` class, named Test.u. When the code for `TestGame` has been compiled successfully, it remains to test the code—that is, to run it and experience it as a gamer. You can run a UDK level immediately from the command line with the compiled `TestGame` type as the active game type. The command-line instruction to run the `TestGame` type for the level `DM-Deck` is `UDK\Binaries\Win64\UDK.exe DM-Deck?game=Test.TestGame` (or `Win32 for 32-bit operating systems`). To better understand what is happening, also run the level using `TestGame` from both the Visual Studio interface and from the UDK Editor, as outlined in the next sections.

Running a Game with the `TestGame` Class from Visual Studio   Perhaps the most convenient method to run a map with a specified game type during its development is from the Visual Studio interface. This approach saves the developer from having to switch from Visual Studio to other applications simply for test and debug purposes. The following steps describe the properties that must be set for the UnrealScript project to run and test a game from Visual Studio.

1. In Visual Studio, right-click the project name in the Solution Explorer and choose Properties from the menu that appears to open the project's Properties page. Then click the Debug tab to view the debug properties for the project. Ensure that both the Load Map at Startup and Start with Specified Game Type checkboxes are enabled. Then, in the Load Map at Startup field, specify the name of the map that should be loaded and run when the UnrealScript project is executed from Visual Studio (in this example, DM-Deck, which ships with the UDK). Next, in the Start with Specified Game Type field, enter the complete name of the `GameType` class to be used as the game type for the selected level. The complete name should be given in the form `Package Name.Game Type Name`—for this project, `Test.TestGame`. See Figure 12.20.

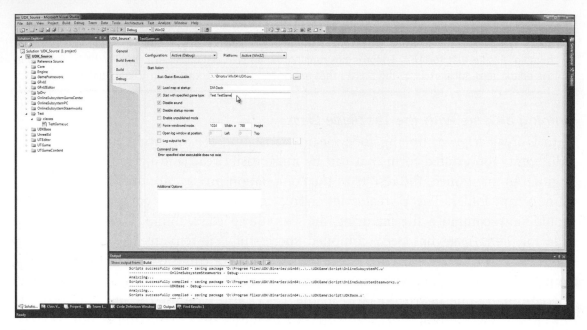

Figure 12.20
Configuring the project properties to run a level using the new `GameType` class.

2. You can now execute the UnrealScript project according to the specified settings. To do so, click the Start Debugging button in the Visual Studio toolbar (see Figure 12.21) or press F5.

Running a Game with the `TestGame` Class from the UDK Editor That is, the UDK Editor can be configured to run its active map using a specified `GameType`. The steps for doing this in the context of the `TestGame` class are as follows.

1. Open the View menu and choose World Properties, as shown in Figure 12.22. A Properties dialog box opens. Most of the properties listed here are member variables of the class `WorldInfo`.

2. In the GameType section of the Properties dialog box, open the Game Type for PIE drop-down list and choose the `GameType` class that will be used for the level whenever it is run from the editor via the Play in Editor button (here, `TestGame`, as shown in Figure 12.23). You can now run the active level from the editor using the newly coded `TestGame` class, either by clicking the Play button in the Visual Studio IDE or by clicking the Play in Editor button in the UDK editor.

Figure 12.21
Running the UnrealScript project from Visual Studio.

Figure 12.22
Accessing the `WorldInfo` properties from the UDK Editor.

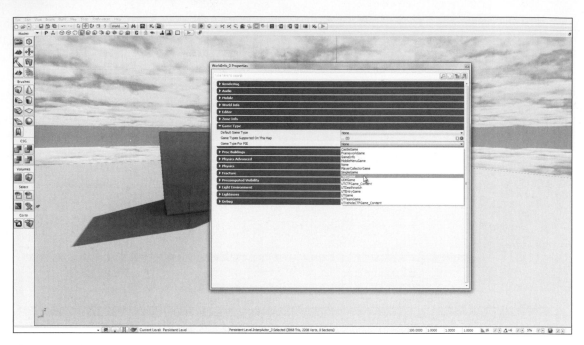

Figure 12.23
Configuring the UDK Editor to run the `TestGame` class.

Closing Thoughts on `GameInfo`

Before proceeding to the next section, it is worth considering three important details about the `GameInfo` class and its descendents:

- **The `GameInfo` class is a singleton class.** Typically, no more than one instance of the class is attached to a single level to act as its game type. The game type for a level is chosen before the level begins and remains the one and only game type for the level throughout its lifetime.

- **`GameInfo` does not persist across levels.** That is, the `GameInfo` class is tied to a specific level and its lifetime and scope can never be longer than or greater than that of the level. The `GameInfo` class is created and terminated at the beginning and end of a level, respectively. That means any instance of a `GameInfo`-derived class cannot persist across levels. It is not possible, therefore, for a `GameInfo` class and its member variables and functions to survive the termination of its associated level. If a game allows the player to change between levels, enabling the player to move from one location to another, then each level will use a separate instance of the `GameInfo` class, neither instance having any connection to the other. This structure for the `GameInfo` class has implications for the design of the game; the `GameInfo` class cannot be relied on to keep game-related information and data (such as player health, score, time limits, and abilities) beyond the termination of a level.

■ **GameInfo delegates its work.** The GameInfo class is intended to act as a manager component or an official representative for the gameplay in a level. That does not mean, however, that it makes sense in terms of software design to have GameInfo perform all gameplay-related work. The default implementation of GameInfo already delegates much of its work to other classes and furthermore inherits a lot of its functionality from ancestor classes. Developers creating classes extended from GameInfo will also likely find that it makes sense to delegate gameplay work to other classes that specialize in performing various tasks—for example, delegating path finding to path-finding classes, line-of-sight calculations to life-of-sight classes, and so on.

Note

The GameInfo class created in this section can be found in the companion files in the file TestGame.uc.

THE ACTOR CLASS

As you learned in Chapter 3, "UDK Fundamentals," an *actor* is any entity, object, or thing—whether visible and tangible or not—that can exist within the coordinate space of a level. Specifically, every actor is an object that shares a common set of essential properties, including position, orientation, scale, and visibility, among others. Examples of actors include static meshes, lights, sounds, volumes, cameras, and practically every entity that can be dragged and dropped into the level from either the Content Browser or the Actor Classes Browser actor—or, more accurately, an Actor class. Every unique actor in the UDK corresponds to a unique Actor class in UnrealScript—that is, to a class that has been derived either directly or indirectly from the Actor class.

The Actor class is intended to define all the essential properties of an actor—those properties that all actors have in common and that they must have in order to be an actor. In line with the UnrealScript class-naming convention, the Actor class can be found in the source file actor.uc. This class is a base class, meaning that developers create new actors not by amending this class directly but by deriving new classes from this class—hence all actor types being extended by some degree of removal from the Actor class.

As you've seen, the UDK ships with a wide range of pre-made Actor classes that can be dragged and dropped into a level as fully functioning actors, such as static meshes.

Figure 12.24
Creating a mobile cube actor with the `Actor` class and UnrealScript.

For this reason, developers will not typically need to create many of their own `Actor` classes. The static mesh actors, the light actors, and the sound actors created already will be comprehensive enough to serve most developmental needs. However, developers who need to create additional functionality in existing actors or completely new and specialized functionality must create their own `Actor` classes in UnrealScript. The kinds of tasks that might involve creating new `Actor` classes in UnrealScript include creating new weapons or enemies, customizing new cameras or lights, or creating new trigger volumes or logic components.

This section of the chapter demonstrates how to code a new `Actor` class for a level—specifically, a cube object that will act as an obstacle to the gamer, blocking his or her path (see Figure 12.24). The actor will also levitate from the ground into the air when shot by a weapon, allowing the player to pass. Once created, this `Actor` class will be available from the Actor Classes Browser in the UDK Editor; you will be able to drag and drop into a level, just like a regular actor.

Declaring the `Actor` Class

The first step in creating the mobile cube obstacle is to create a new UnrealScript source file and declare the `MovingCube` class inside, ensuring that the class both extends from the `Actor` class and is accessible as an actor from the Actor Classes Browser in the UDK Editor. The following steps demonstrate how to do this.

1. Add a new UnrealScript source file to the Visual Studio project named MovingCube.uc, and ensure its class definition starts as follows, extending from the `Actor` class. (Changes are highlighted in bold.)

```
class MovingCube extends Actor;

DefaultProperties
{
}
```

2. The newly added but empty `MovingCube` class extends from the `Actor` class, and thus defines a UDK actor—an object that can exist in a level. Once compiled, however, the `MovingCube` class will not appear as an option in the Actor Classes Browser in the UDK Editor. Its current declaration prohibits this. That means level designers using the editor will have no means of accessing the newly created class in a level via the editor. To rectify this, you must adjust the class declaration using some new keywords and syntax to indicate to the UDK that this class must be added as an actor to the Actor Classes Browser. Specifically, you must use the `placeable` keyword to signal that the object can be dragged and dropped into the level via the UDK Editor. The `ClassGroup` keyword must also be used to indicate where in the tree view of the Actor Classes Browser the class will appear. Add the following code. (Changes are highlighted in bold.)

```
class MovingCube extends Actor
    placeable
    ClassGroup(MyGame,MyCustomActors);

DefaultProperties
{
}
```

3. Compile the code and then view the Actor Classes Browser in the UDK Editor. (See Figure 12.25.)

As it stands, the `MovingCube` class does nothing but replicate the behavior of the base `Actor` class. The `MovingCube` class has no appearance, no mesh representation, and no collision or lighting information, and it exhibits no custom behavior. Therefore, dragging and dropping this actor into the level right now will result in an invisible actor in the scene, whose position and orientation can be determined only by the presence of the transformation gizmo that appears when the actor is

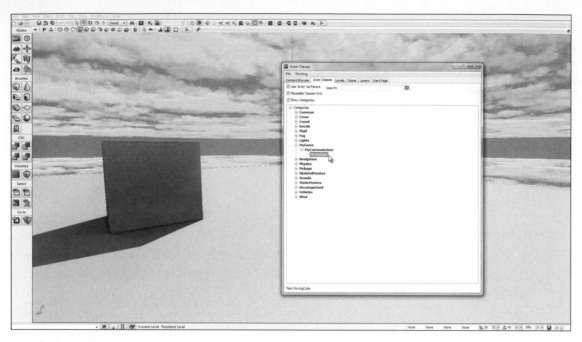

Figure 12.25
Adding an actor to the Actor Classes Browser using the `placeable` and `ClassGroup` keywords for class declarations.

selected in the viewport (see Figure 12.26). This will change as more functionality is added to the class throughout subsequent sections of the chapter.

Defining the Default Actor Properties

As mentioned, the `MovingCube` actor is currently empty. It defines no behavior in addition to that inherited from the base class `Actor`. The upshot of this is that if the actor is added to the level via the Actor Classes Browser, the actor will be completely invisible, having neither substance nor form. This section will address that issue through the `DefaultProperties` block of the class. This block of code will be used to ensure that the actor has a cube mesh body, will act as a collision obstacle (will block the player), and will be illuminated by the scene lighting. The following steps detail how to do this.

1. Close the UDK Editor. Then return to Visual Studio and add the two member variables to the `MovingCube` class shown in bold in the following code. These member variables will be used to ensure that the actor has a static mesh cube body and can be illuminated by scene lighting.

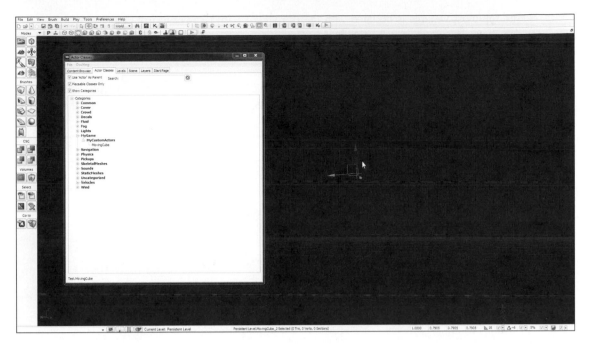

Figure 12.26
The invisible actor in the level.

```
class MovingCube extends Actor
    placeable
    ClassGroup(MyGame,MyCustomActors);

var() const editconst DynamicLightEnvironmentComponent LightEnvironment;
var() const editconst StaticMeshComponent CubeMesh;

DefaultProperties
{
}
```

Source Code Notes

- Both of the variables are declared with the `var()` keyword and the `const` and `editconst` specifiers.

- Variables can be declared using either the `var` or `var()` keyword. Variables declared with `var` are accessible only in UnrealScript. Variables declared with `var()` are published. That is, they can be edited in the actor's Properties panel in the UDK Editor, as shown in Figure 12.27.

- Variables declared with a `const` specifier can be changed in UnrealScript only in the `DefaultProperties` block of code for the class, not in other member functions.

- Variables declared with the `var()` keyword that also feature the `editconst` specifier appear as read-only in the actor's Properties panel in the UDK Editor.

- The top-most variable is declared with the DynamicLightEnvironmentComponent data type. This variable will be assigned default properties in the DefaultProperties code block to ensure the object can be illuminated by static lighting, dynamic lighting, and dynamic-composite lighting.

- The bottom-most variable is declared with the StaticMeshComponent data type, and the DefaultProperties code block for the class will ensure this object represents the static mesh cube body for the actor.

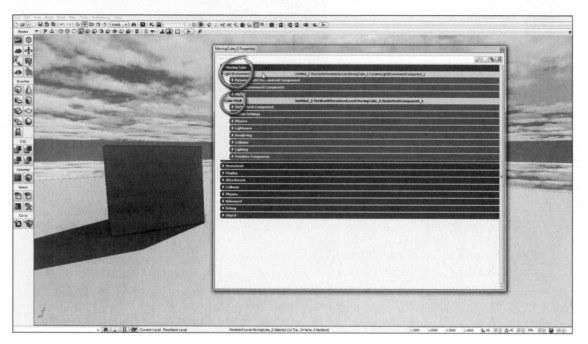

Figure 12.27
Making variables accessible in the actor's Properties panel in the UDK Editor using the var() keyword.

2. Two variables have been defined for the class. These variables will be accessible from the actor's Properties panel in the UDK Editor. It is now time to assign these variables their default, starting, and constant values using the Default-Properties code block for the Actor class. (Changes are in bold.)

```
class MovingCube extends Actor
    placeable
    ClassGroup(MyGame,MyCustomActors);

var() const editconst DynamicLightEnvironmentComponent LightEnvironment;
var() const editconst StaticMeshComponent CubeMesh;

DefaultProperties
{
```

```
begin Object class=DynamicLightEnvironmentComponent Name=MyLightEnvironment
    bEnabled=true
end Object
LightEnvironment = MyLightEnvironment
Components.Add(MyLightEnvironment)

begin Object class=StaticMeshComponent Name=BodyMesh
    LightEnvironment=MyLightEnvironment
    StaticMesh = StaticMesh'EngineMeshes.Cube'
end Object

CubeMesh = BodyMesh
Components.Add(BodyMesh)

CollisionComponent = BodyMesh
bCollideActors=true
bBlockActors=true
}
```

Source Code Notes

- The `DefaultProperties` block begins by defining a new `LightEnvironment` object using the `Begin Object` and `End Object` keywords. The `LightEnviron-ment` object is finally assigned to the `LightEnvironment` member variable and then added as a component of the `Actor` class. Components are external objects that are plugged into the `Actor` class, after which they become a part of the actor. To make a specified `LightEnvironment` object a component of the `Actor` class is to make the `LightEnvironment` object a part of the actor. Thus, the statement `Components.Add(MyLightEnvironment)` ensures that the actor is assigned a `LightEnvironment` object and can be illuminated by scene lighting.

- The `DefaultProperties` block also defines a `StaticMesh` object, which it creates on the basis of the EngineMeshes.Cube mesh—a default cube mesh provided with the UDK and also accessible from the Content Browser. This mesh defines the body of the actor and becomes part of the actor through the `Components.Add(BodyMesh)` state-ment. Additional statements like this could be inserted into the `DefaultProperties` block to add further mesh components to the actor, if required.

- The final section of the `DefaultProperties` block is responsible for creating a colli-sion component for the actor to define its collision information—its extents. This compo-nent is responsible for ensuring that the cube mesh will block the player from traveling through it as a ghost might travel through a wall. Notice that the collision component expects a static mesh, and in this case is assigned the cube mesh used for the body. In most cases, the mesh used for the actor body and the mesh used for the collision com-ponent will be different, because the collision mesh should be a low-poly approximation of the visible mesh. Here, it is not of consequence because both the visible mesh and collision mesh are simple cube primitives.

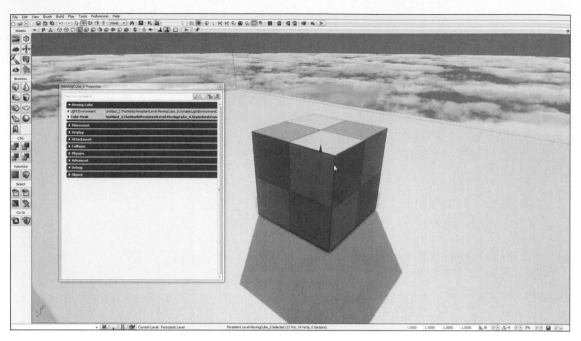

Figure 12.28
A visible and tangible actor created with UnrealScript.

3. Compile the UnrealScript source code in Visual Studio. Then launch the UDK Editor to test the actor in a sample level. As shown in Figure 12.28, the actor now has a visible mesh component that responds to scene lighting and is impassable when collided with at run time.

Making the Cube Move

The final stage in the creation of MovingCube is to create the code that will cause the cube to levitate upward into the air when shot by a weapon. Creating this code will involve using the Tick event. The Tick event is a function of the Actor class that can be overridden in descendent classes to implement custom behavior on a frame-by-frame basis. The Tick event is a function called by the Unreal Engine on every frame of the game (there could be as many as 100 frames per second) for every actor in the scene. MovingCube will have code added to this function to ensure the cube moves (animates) upward over time after being shot. It should be emphasized, however, that developers are recommended to keep Tick event code to a minimum for performance reasons. That is, Tick events should ideally contain only code that cannot be included elsewhere. The method for moving the cube is outlined in the following steps.

1. Close the UDK Editor (if it is not closed already). Then return to Visual Studio, to the `MovingCube` class. To allow the cube to be set in motion, you will need to add three new member variables to the class:

   - **A `CubeSpeed` variable.** This defines the speed (in Unreal world units per second) at which the cube will levitate upward when shot.

   - **A `CubeMove` Boolean variable.** This defines whether the cube should move at all. A value of `false` means the cube is idle and acting as an obstacle to the player, and a value of `true` means the cube is in motion and should levitate upward over time at its specified speed.

   - **A `MaxHeight` variable.** This defines the maximum height (in Unreal world units) at which the cube should stop levitating and remain in a floating state.

   These three variables can be added as follows. (Notice that `CubeSpeed` and `MaxHeight` have been defined using the `var()` keyword to allow them to be changed via the UDK Editor.)

   ```
   var() float CubeSpeed;
   var() float MaxHeight;
   var bool CubeMove;
   ```

2. Assign these three variables default starting values in the `DefaultProperties` block of the class using the following three lines (one line to initialize each variable):

   ```
   CubeSpeed = 10;
   CubeMove = false;
   MaxHeight = 2048;
   ```

3. Add code functionality into the class to identify when the cube mesh has been hit by ammunition and to respond accordingly by initiating the levitation process. The `Actor` class features a `TakeDamage` event, which is called whenever the actor is damaged by a projectile. This function can be overridden in the `MovingCube` class to respond to damage. It should respond by switching the `CubeMove` Boolean variable from `false` to `true` so the `Tick` event (defined soon) can perform its levitation functionality, animating the cube on each frame.

   ```
   event TakeDamage(int DamageAmount, Controller EventInstigator, vector HitLocation, vector Momentum, class<DamageType> DamageType, optional TraceHitInfo HitInfo, optional Actor DamageCauser)
   {
           super.TakeDamage(DamageAmount, EventInstigator, HitLocation, Momentum, DamageType, HitInfo, DamageCauser);
   ```

```
        CubeMove = true;
    }
```

4. The `TakeDamage` event ensures that the actor is notified whenever it is hit by ammunition. The response of the actor to this event is to levitate upward, allowing the player to pass. The levitation animation involves the mesh cube slowly and smoothly rising from the ground into the air until a specified maximum height is reached. This continuous motion can be defined through the `Tick` event, a function called once per actor on each frame of the game. The `Tick` event can be defined as follows:

```
event Tick(float DeltaTime)
{
    local Vector V;

    if(CubeMove)
    {
        V.Z = DeltaTime*CubeSpeed;
        Move(V);

        if(Location.z>=MaxHeight)
            CubeMove = false;
    }
}
```

Source Code Notes

- The `Tick` event is a function prefixed with the word `event`, to indicate that the function is being used as an event.

- The `Tick` event accepts a parameter `DeltaTime`, which is a floating-point value representing the number of seconds that have elapsed since the last `Tick` event. This value will almost always be a fractional number between 0 and 1 because the `Tick` event is typically called many times per second. The value would be 0 if the `Tick` was called more than once on the same frame, and the value would be 1 if exactly one second had elapsed since the last call.

- A local variable of a vector type called `V` is created using the specifier `local`. Local variables in the UDK are variables with function scope, meaning they survive for the duration of the function—no longer, and no shorter. All local variables must be declared at the top of a function. The local variable `V` is a vector (a three-component number) that will be used to calculate the new z-axis position of the cube as it levitates upward.

- If `CubeMove` is set to `true`, then the cube is animated upward over time by multiplying the `DeltaTime` value with the `Speed`, since distance=speed × time.

- If the cube reaches the maximum height, then `CubeMove` is set to `false` to stop levitation.

The completed source for the `MovingCube` class is shown here:

```
class MovingCube extends Actor
    placeable
    ClassGroup(MyGame,MyCustomActors);

var() const editconst DynamicLightEnvironmentComponent LightEnvironment;
var() const editconst StaticMeshComponent CubeMesh;
var() float CubeSpeed;
var() float MaxHeight;
var bool CubeMove;

event TakeDamage(int DamageAmount, Controller EventInstigator, vector HitLoca-
tion, vector Momentum, class<DamageType> DamageType, optional TraceHitInfo
HitInfo, optional Actor DamageCauser)
{
        super.TakeDamage(DamageAmount, EventInstigator, HitLocation, Momentum,
DamageType, HitInfo, DamageCauser);
    CubeMove = true;
}

event Tick(float DeltaTime)
{
    local Vector V;

    if(CubeMove)
    {
        V.Z = DeltaTime*CubeSpeed;
        Move(V);

        if(Location.z>=MaxHeight)
            CubeMove = false;
    }
}
}
DefaultProperties
{
    begin Object class=DynamicLightEnvironmentComponent Name=MyLightEnvironment
        bEnabled=true
    end Object
    LightEnvironment = MyLightEnvironment
    Components.Add(MyLightEnvironment)

    begin Object class=StaticMeshComponent Name=BodyMesh
        LightEnvironment=MyLightEnvironment
        StaticMesh = StaticMesh'EngineMeshes.Cube'
```

```
      end Object

      CubeMesh = BodyMesh
      Components.Add(BodyMesh)

      CollisionComponent = BodyMesh
      bCollideActors=true
      bBlockActors=true
      CubeSpeed = 10;
      CubeMove = false;
      MaxHeight = 2048;
}
```

5. Compile the code and test this actor in the UDK. The actor should be fully functional. Congratulations! Try positioning several different instances of the actor in a row in the level, and shoot each one to raise it upward. Remember to run the game using a game type that supports a weapon to allow shooting, such as UTDeathMatch. You choose the game type from the WorldInfo Properties dialog box (to access it, open the View menu and choose World Properties), as shown in Figure 12.29.

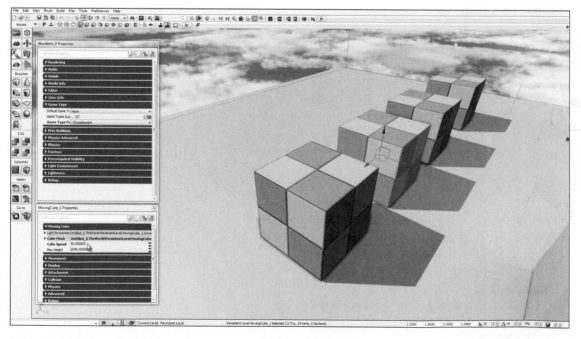

Figure 12.29
Configuring a level with multiple moving cube actors.

Note

The `MovingCube` class created in this section can be found in the companion files in the file MovingCube.uc.

CONCLUSION

This chapter concludes the second part of the book as well as your introduction to UnrealScript—although your work in UnrealScript does not end here. This chapter has considered how to configure third-party tools such as Visual Studio and nFringe; how to write, debug, and compile UnrealScript code; and how create UnrealScript applications with the `GameInfo` and `Actor` classes. Part III, "Building a Project (*The Nexus*)," consists of two chapters and one appendix. The two chapters detail how to make a small, time-critical racing game using most of the tools covered in this book (including UnrealScript). The appendix closes the book by providing answers to some commonly asked questions about the UDK and its toolset, and offering tips, tricks, and guidance for further learning.

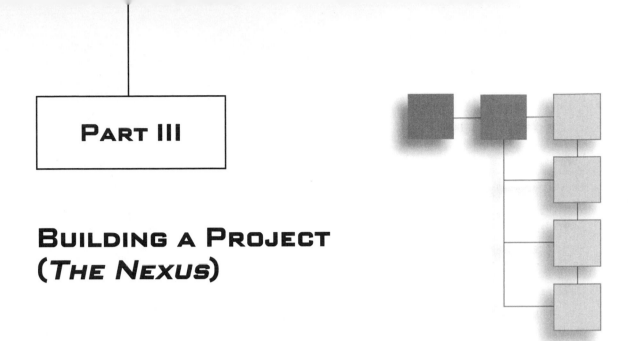

PART III

BUILDING A PROJECT (*THE NEXUS*)

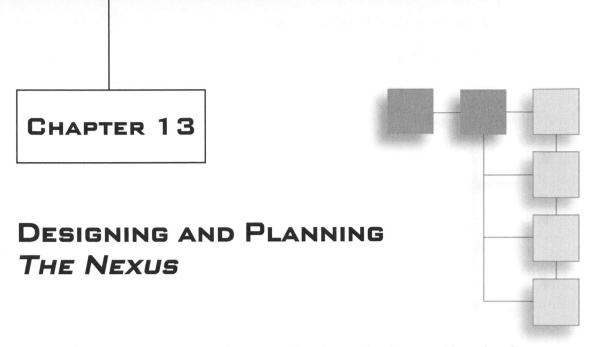

CHAPTER 13

DESIGNING AND PLANNING
THE NEXUS

The most important single aspect of software development is to be clear about what you are trying to build.

—Bjarne Stroustrup

By the end of this chapter, you should:

- Feel more confident about using UDK tools to make games.
- Be able to create a third-person camera in UnrealScript.
- Understand the `Camera`, `Pawn`, and `PlayerController` classes.
- Be able to debug UDK applications with Console Commands.
- Understand a typical game development workflow with the UDK.

This chapter is the first of two that focus on the creation of a functional, yet simple, project in the UDK. Both this chapter and the next aim to apply the skills and knowledge gained from all previous chapters of the book by using the UDK and its associated tools to create a simple game. The focus of the chapters in this part of the book is almost entirely practical. That is, they assume you are already familiar with the theory and concepts discussed in earlier chapters and concentrate on how to apply those theories and concepts to create a working UDK game. Specifically, this chapter relies on the following concepts and tools: Builder Brushes, BSP Brushes, CSG, static meshes, sound waves, sound cues, Unreal Kismet, lighting and Lightmass, and UnrealScript. So let's get started!

Project Overview

The project you will create in this chapter and the next is a UDK game titled *The Nexus*. This game will be a single-player, time-critical racing game played from a third-person chase-view perspective. In this game, the player must traverse an obstacle course within a given period. The player will begin at the starting line and pass through a series of checkpoints toward the finish line, where there will be a nexus, or portal, leading to the next level and obstacle course (The creation of only one level is documented in this book.) The player completes the course successfully by reaching the finish line after having passed through all the checkpoints before the time expires. Passing through a checkpoint will reset the timer. The player fails the course and must replay it if he or she fails to reach the finish line before the timer expires.

Before proceeding further with this chapter, spend five minutes identifying at least five constituent elements of the project that must be implemented in the UDK to create the game—either coded in UnrealScript or created using the UDK Level Editor. Here are a few ideas to get you started:

- **Third-person chase-view camera.** In video games, *third-person perspective* refers to the camera position from which the game world and game events are seen by the player. Third-person perspective is in contrast to first-person perspective, in which the player experiences the game from the point of view of the character he or she is controlling. In first-person games, the player sees the world through the eyes of the main character, as shown in Figure 13.1. Examples of first-person games include *Doom*, *Duke Nukem*, *Oblivion*, *Half-Life*, and *Unreal Tournament*. In contrast, third-person perspective encompasses all camera perspectives in which the game world and events are seen by the player from outside of the main character's body (assuming the game has a main character). Because the term *third-person* is so broad, a number of additional terms are often used with it to narrow its meaning in the context of a particular game. For example, the game created in this chapter will feature a third-person chase-view camera—that is, a third-person camera positioned behind the main character, looking over his shoulder, that follows (chases) him as he moves throughout the level. (See Figure 13.2.)

Note

First-person perspective is the default perspective of all games created using the UDK. All the sample levels created so far have been in first-person perspective.

- **Player character.** Any game that is said to be first person or third person must feature a game character in some form because first- and third-person

Figure 13.1
First-person games show the game world from the eyes of the game character.

Figure 13.2
Chase views are third-person cameras that follow the main character.

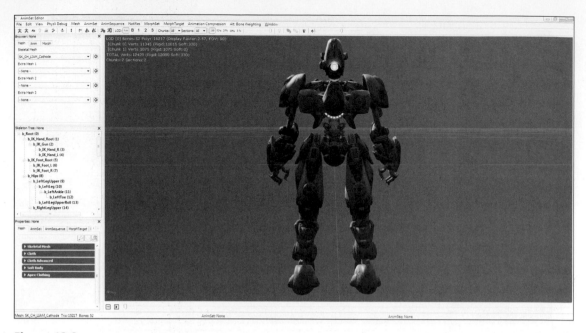

Figure 13.3
The UDK AnimSet Editor, used to view a skeletal mesh to act as a pawn.

perspectives define how the game camera is positioned in relation to the game character. Being third person, *The Nexus* will feature a game character—a mesh representation of the player in the level that will act as the focal point of the camera (see Figure 13.3). The aim of the player will be to navigate this character through the obstacle course to the finish line within a specified time limit. In the UDK, every animated character that is supposed to be a sentient being is known as a *pawn*. Consequently, creating a player character will involve creating a pawn —or more specifically, a `Pawn` UnrealScript class.

■ **Time-limit functionality.** The time limit is instrumental in determining whether the player has succeeded or failed in completing the obstacle course. The time limit is a countdown in seconds that begins at a specified maximum (when the level begins) and decrements second by second to a minimum. The time limit is related to the checkpoints of the obstacle course in that the timer is reset to its maximum whenever the player passes through a checkpoint for the first time. The time limit is also related to the win condition of the level; the level is completed whenever the player reaches the finish line and the time limit has not expired. Conversely, the course is failed if the timer expires before the player reaches the finish line.

■ **Obstacle course checkpoints.** The checkpoint is a physical feature of the obstacle course—a region, mark, or line that occurs between the start and end of the course that must be passed or tagged by the player. A course can contain one or more checkpoints; the player must pass through all of them in sequence before reaching the finish line if he or she is to complete the course successfully. In *The Nexus*, a player can pass through a checkpoint only once, and in so doing will reset the time limit of the course to its maximum. You will implement the checkpoint functionality in the game by extending an UnrealScript class from the `Trigger Volume` class (although static meshes will be used to create a tangible and visible aspect of the checkpoint).

- **Obstacle course.** The obstacle course is the totality of actors that together constitute the course, including the checkpoints and time limit as well as the static meshes, lights, and sounds that can be positioned and arranged in the UDK Level Editor. Creating the obstacle course involves using the UDK Editor to position and arrange a set of actors in a single coordinate space.

CREATING THE THIRD-PERSON CAMERA

The focus of the remainder of this chapter will be the creation of third-person camera class in UnrealScript. First, however, it is worthwhile to explain why it is necessary to create a camera in this way—that is, to create a completely new kind of camera in UnrealScript. There are two main reasons:

- As mentioned, the UDK uses a first-person camera by default on all UDK projects that do not change or override the initial settings, and there is no quick and flexible way in the UDK editor to change this behavior. Although the UDK can be tweaked in UnrealScript or customized through Kismet to use a limited third-person camera, this third-person camera is tailored primarily to death-match shooting games and is not ideally suited to other game types such as this obstacle-course game. Therefore, manually creating a third-person camera is necessary.

- Creating a completely new camera from scratch in UnrealScript is a useful exercise both in learning the UnrealScript language and its class hierarchy and in gaining a stronger understanding of a range of fundamental UnrealScript classes—specifically, the `Pawn`, `PlayerController`, and `Camera` classes. In short, this chapter will demonstrate how to create a functional third-person camera by extending and customizing a set of UnrealScript classes.

In the Unreal Engine 3, the camera and its functionality are encapsulated in the `Camera` class, whose source code can be found in the file camera.uc. This class is a descendent of the `Actor` class (because instances exist in the world coordinate space) and represents the basis on which a camera is made. All instances of cameras

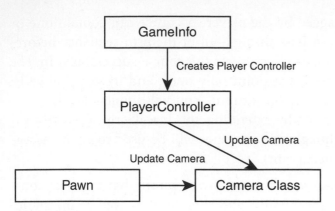

Figure 13.4
Camera work distributed across four classes.

in the Unreal Engine are either directly instantiated from the Camera class or are instantiated from classes that extend from the Camera class in some way.

One might reasonably think that creating a new camera type, such as a third-person camera, simply involves extending a new Camera class and adding third-person functionality where appropriate. Unfortunately, that is not the case because a variety of camera-related tasks are distributed (rather messily, in my view) across several Unreal Engine classes. In short, a specific set of classes can modify the camera, sometimes on a frame-by-frame basis. These modifications frequently override the default camera work coded into the Camera class, even though the names of those classes give you little or no reason to believe they are in any way related to camera functionality. As a result, creating a new camera type via the Camera class involves extending three additional classes: GameInfo, PlayerController, and Pawn. This is to change the way those classes interact with the camera, allowing the Camera class modifications to take precedence. Figure 13.4 illustrates the relationship between these classes, which, except for GameInfo, are considered in further detail in the following sections.

PlayerController

PlayerController is a high-level managerial class that represents the interface between the player and the game. Specifically, PlayerController is the class responsible for accepting input from a player (such as a keyboard or mouse-button press) and converting that input into game-meaningful actions. The GameInfo class, as you saw, was responsible for containing all the player-independent logic or reasoning that governed a game; in contrast, PlayerController is responsible for containing or delegating all logic that is player specific. For example, the work that links a left-mouse-button press to the fire-weapon action in a game is the responsibility of the `PlayerController`. Without `PlayerController`, there would be no connection between the two entities—between input and action. `PlayerController` has a relationship to the game camera because it is a player-specific rather than a game-specific entity. Therefore, `PlayerController` is both the owner of the game camera and the class responsible for instantiating and destroying it. The following member variables and functions of the `PlayerController` class (as seen in the PlayerController.uc source file) are especially relevant when creating custom cameras:

- **PlayerCamera.** This member variable, of type `Camera`, is a reference to the camera object instantiated by `PlayerController` that is associated with the player. This member variable will need to reference a third-person camera class if such a camera is to be associated with the player.

- **CameraClass.** This member variable is of type `class<Camera>`. It is distinct from the `PlayerCamera` variable and the type `Camera`. This variable is not a reference to any active instance of class `Camera`, but is a reference to the camera class itself—to the class to be used by the `PlayerController` when creating a camera for `PlayerCamera`.

- **UpdateRotation.** This function is called once per tick (once per game frame, perhaps many times per second) to update the orientation, if appropriate, of the camera referenced by `PlayerCamera`. This is an example of a function that can override the default camera behavior defined in the camera class. This function will need to be overridden to allow the third-person camera class to take precedence and to have control over how it is positioned and oriented.

Pawn

`PlayerController` represents the abstract, non-tangible unit of logic that defines how a player can interact with the game through input. It is the mother class of both the `Camera` and the `Pawn` classes in that `PlayerController` is responsible for instantiating them. The `Pawn` class defines the physical manifestation of the player in the level. It is the thing (usually a mesh) that represents the player in the level— the ambassador or avatar that the player controls through the `PlayerController` class. In its default and various derivative states (such as `UDKPawn` and `UTPawn`), the `Pawn` class has a set of variables and methods that play a fundamental role in affecting the position and orientation of the camera in the level, typically on a frame-by-frame basis. These include the following:

- **Controller.** This member variable references the owning instance of the `PlayerController` class for this pawn. This variable is not directly related to camera functionality, but can be useful when working with pawns and cameras.

- **CalcCamera.** The `CalcCamera` function, called on the `Pawn` class once per tick, offers the `Pawn` class the opportunity to modify the position and orientation of the camera for the current frame. The `Pawn` class can decline to modify the camera by returning the Boolean value of `false` for the function. This function will therefore be overridden to return `false`, as you shall soon see.

- **BecomeViewTarget.** This member function is called on the `Pawn` class whenever the `Pawn` class is associated with a `Camera` class—that is, whenever the pawn becomes the target of the camera (the thing at which the camera is looking and following).

- **GetDefaultCameraMode.** This member function is called on the `Pawn` class by `PlayerController` whenever `PlayerController` wants to determine the default mode into which the default camera must be set. This function is typically called whenever the player dies and must be respawned in the level. A `Camera` class can be coded to support a range of different modes (first-person mode, third-person mode, and so on); the default mode specifies the mode into which the camera should be set each time the player is spawned.

Camera

The `Camera` class encapsulates a game camera. Although camera work is distributed across multiple classes, those classes nonetheless achieve their work (setting the camera position and orientation) by calling on the member variables and functions of the `Camera` class. The `Camera` class supports three main kinds of properties:

- **Transformation properties.** These properties define what the camera sees through its position and orientation in world space.

- **Lens properties.** These properties—such as field of view (FOV)—determine how a camera sees.

- **Post-processing effect properties.** These properties—such as blur, bloom, and color filtering—operate on the recorded image to change the pixels that are output to the display.

Together, these properties influence how a camera works. That being said, it is mainly the first set of properties—the transformation properties—that pertain to creating a third-person camera.

The Camera class supports fundamental variables and functions, some of which are detailed here:

- **ViewTarget.** The ViewTarget member variable of the Camera class is a data structure that is to some extent misnamed because not all its properties define the object at which the camera is looking (its target). For example, the POV member variable of ViewTarget is used to define the position and orientation of the camera, not the camera target. Similarly, the FOV member variable is used to define the FOV of the camera, not the target. (More on this later in the chapter.)

- **UpdateViewTarget.** This member function is called once per tick on the camera and can be used to update the camera position and orientation.

IMPLEMENTING THE THIRD-PERSON CAMERA

It is now time to start creating the third-person camera in UnrealScript. This chapter assumes that you know how to edit and compile UnrealScript code using either the UnrealScript compiler via the command line or Microsoft Visual Studio with the nFringe add-on installed. (For help with the latter, refer to the section "Getting Started with UnrealScript: PixelMine nFringe and Microsoft Visual Studio" in Chapter 12, "Scripting with UnrealScript.") Creating a third-person camera involves extending four different classes:

- NexusCamera, from the class Camera
- NexusPawn, from the class UTPawn (derived from Pawn)
- NexusPlayerController, from the class PlayerController
- NexusGameInfo, from the class UTGame (derived from GameInfo)

Together, these four classes will work not only to support a third-person camera, but to provide the complete class set for *The Nexus*, which should be complete and playable at the end of the next chapter. The first of the four classes to be implemented for the third-person camera is the NexusCamera class (derived from Camera).

Creating the NexusCamera Class

The Nexus will feature a third-person chase-view camera—a camera outside the main character's body that follows the character as he traverses an obstacle course. The third-person camera will remain locked to the pawn in terms of its position and orientation. That is, the camera will move with the pawn, maintaining the same relative distance between them, and will rotate (yaw) with the pawn to ensure that the back of the pawn is always the central focus of the camera. The class declaration for the NexusCamera class should begin as follows (changes are in bold). Notice that the class derives from the class Camera.

```
class NexusCamera extends camera;

//Vector to store third-person camera offset from player
var Vector CamOffset;

//Fixed pitch of third-person camera
var float FixedPitch;

DefaultProperties
{
}
```

Source Code Notes

- Class NexusCamera extends from class Camera.
- Class NexusCamera contains two member variables: a 3D vector (CamOffset) and a float (FixedPitch).
- Vector CamOffset describes the relative positional offset of the camera from the pawn in Unreal world units. That is, it describes the distance on each axis x,y,z (forward, right, and up) that the camera must be moved from the pawn in order to reach its ideal position. If this vector is (0,0,0), then the camera position will match the pawn position because the vector describes no offset.
- Pitch describes a rotation about the x (horizontal) axis. If a line were drawn through a human head, entering one ear and exiting the other, it would represent the axis around which rotation would be named pitch. To pitch a camera is to make it look up or down. The variable FixedPitch describes the pitch (in Unreal rotation units) that third-person camera will be rotated. (Refer to Figure 13.2; notice that the camera is subtly pitched and offset from the pawn.)

Initializing *NexusCamera*

Initializing a class involves assigning initial values to its member variables at creation time. Initializing the NexusCamera class is therefore a process of assigning starting values to the CamOffset and FixedPitch member variables. These variables can be assigned values as the class is instantiated through the PostBeginPlay event, a function inherited from the Actor class that can be overridden in descendents to perform custom functionality when the class is instantiated. Consider the following code:

```
//Called as object is created
function PostBeginPlay()
{
    super.PostBeginPlay();

    //Define third-person offset
    CamOffset.X=-64;
    CamOffset.Y=0;
    CamOffset.Z=64;

    FixedPitch = -20 * DegToUnrRot;
}
```

Source Code Notes

- The `super` keyword is used in the first line of the function to call the version of this function that exists in the immediate ancestor of this class (i.e., the `Camera` class).

- The `X`, `Y`, and `Z` components of `CamOffset` are set to starting values. Remember that in the UDK, z refers to the up axis. Therefore, the camera will be offset by 64 Unreal world units on both the x axis (forward/backward) and z axis (up/down).

- The `FixedPitch` member variable is a value of -20 degrees multiplied by the UDK-defined constant `DegToUnrRot` order to convert the value of degrees into Unreal rotation units. This pitch rotation will be used to adjust the pitch of the camera.

Tip

Before you proceed, spend five minutes thinking about how you would update the position and orientation for this camera. Scan through the code in Camera.uc and try to locate some of the functions relevant to setting the location and orientation of the camera on a per-tick basis. Read on for answers.

Updating NexusCamera

Camera updates occur once per tick—typically many times per second. The update process happens in the `UpdateViewTarget` function and consists of determining and setting the current position, orientation, and field of view of the camera. Updating the camera once per tick, as opposed to only when required, is what makes it possible for the camera to be animated because animation refers to change over time.

The base `Camera` class already features an implementation of the `UpdateViewTarget` function that should remain unchanged in this derived class except for some amendments that must be made to allow for a custom camera type. For this reason, the original `UpdateViewTarget` function from Camera.uc will be copied and pasted into the `NexusCamera` and then amended as appropriate to override the original. The complete `UpdateViewTarget` function for `NexusCamera`—the longest function in this book—follows. (Changes appear in bold.)

```
//Overrides super class version. Much of this function is identical to the super class
version

function UpdateViewTarget(out TViewTarget OutVT, float DeltaTime)
{
    local vector        Loc, Pos, HitLocation, HitNormal;
    local Vector        XAxis, YAxis, ZAxis;
    local rotator          Rot;
    local Actor            HitActor;
    local CameraActor   CamActor;
    local bool              bDoNotApplyModifiers;
    local TPOV            OrigPOV;
    local Pawn        TPawn;

    // Don't update outgoing viewtarget during an interpolation
     if(   PendingViewTarget.Target   !=   None   &&   OutVT   ==   ViewTarget   &&
BlendParams.bLockOutgoing )
    {
    return;
    }

    // store previous POV, in case we need it later
    OrigPOV = OutVT.POV;

    // Default FOV on viewtarget
    OutVT.POV.FOV = DefaultFOV;

    // Viewing through a camera actor.
    CamActor = CameraActor(OutVT.Target);
    if( CamActor != None )
    {
        CamActor.GetCameraView(DeltaTime, OutVT.POV);

        // Grab aspect ratio from the CameraActor.
        bConstrainAspectRatio= bConstrainAspectRatio ||
CamActor.bConstrainAspectRatio;
        OutVT.AspectRatio= CamActor.AspectRatio;

        // See if the CameraActor wants to override the PostProcess //settings used.

        CamOverridePostProcessAlpha = CamActor.CamOverridePostProcessAlpha;
```

```
            CamPostProcessSettings = CamActor.CamOverridePostProcess;
    }
    else
    {
        TPawn = Pawn(OutVT.Target);
    // Give Pawn Viewtarget a chance to dictate the camera position.
    // If Pawn doesn't override the camera view, then we proceed with our own defaults

        if( TPawn == None || !TPawn.CalcCamera(DeltaTime, OutVT.POV.Location,
OutVT.POV.Rotation, OutVT.POV.FOV) )
            {
        // don't apply modifiers when using these debug camera modes.
        bDoNotApplyModifiers = TRUE;

        switch( CameraStyle )
        {
        case 'CustomCamera' :

        OutVT.Target.GetActorEyesViewPoint(OutVT.POV.Location, OutVT.POV.Rotation);

        GetAxes(OutVT.Target.Rotation, XAxis, YAxis, ZAxis);

         OutVT.POV.Location += XAxis * CamOffset.X + YAxis * CamOffset.Y + ZAxis *
CamOffset.Z;

            OutVT.POV.Rotation.Pitch = FixedPitch;
            break;

        case 'Fixed':
    // do not update, keep previous camera position by restoring
    // saved POV, in case CalcCamera changes it but still returns false
        OutVT.POV = OrigPOV;
        break;

        case 'ThirdPerson':
        case 'FreeCam':
        case 'FreeCam_Default':
            Loc = OutVT.Target.Location;
            Rot = OutVT.Target.Rotation;

    // Take into account Mesh Translation so it takes into account the PostProcessing we
do there.

        if ((TPawn != None) && (TPawn.Mesh != None))
            {
```

```
            Loc  +=  (TPawn.Mesh.Translation  -  TPawn.default.Mesh.Translation)  >>
OutVT.Target.Rotation;
        }

        if( CameraStyle == 'FreeCam' || CameraStyle == 'FreeCam_Default' )
        {
        Rot = PCOwner.Rotation;
        }
        Loc += FreeCamOffset >> Rot;

        Pos = Loc - Vector(Rot) * FreeCamDistance;
        // @fixme, respect BlockingVolume.bBlockCamera=false

        HitActor = Trace(HitLocation, HitNormal, Pos, Loc, FALSE, vect(12,12,12));

        OutVT.POV.Location = (HitActor == None) ? Pos : HitLocation;
        OutVT.POV.Rotation = Rot;
            break;

        case 'FirstPerson'=:
        default:

        OutVT.Target.GetActorEyesViewPoint(OutVT.POV.Location, OutVT.POV.Rotation);

        if ((TPawn != None) && (TPawn.Mesh != None))
        {
        OutVT.POV.Location += (TPawn.Mesh.Translation - TPawn.default.Mesh.Transla-
tion) >> OutVT.Target.Rotation;
        }
        break;
        }
        }
        }

    if( !bDoNotApplyModifiers )
    {
    // Apply camera modifiers at the end (view shakes for example)
    ApplyCameraModifiers(DeltaTime, OutVT.POV);
    }
}
```

Source Code Notes

■ The function begins by declaring a set of required variables. Notice that variables specific
   to a function are declared with the keyword `local`. Local variables are destroyed automatically
   as the function ends.

- The function uses an `if` statement to determine whether it has been called already on this tick. If so, the function exits to avoid repeating its work. Otherwise, it continues.

- The key block of code for this function is the `switch-case` statement, in which the camera determines its type (first-person, free, third-person, and so on) and then calculates its current position and orientation in relation to a pawn through the `OutVT.POV` member variable. `OutVT` is a reference to the camera's `ViewTarget` member variable.

- The position and orientation of the camera can be set through the `OutVT.POV.Location` and `OutVT.POV.Rotation` member variables, respectively. The pawn actor that is the target of the camera can be accessed through `OutVT.Target`. The `OutVT.Target` member is an instance of class `Actor`.

- Notice that the `switch-case` statement is entered only if `TPawn` is `null` or `TPawn.CalcCamera` returns `false`. (`TPawn` is a reference to `OutVT.Target`.) In short, the call to `TPawn.CalcCamera` provides the pawn with the opportunity to override the camera position and orientation. If `true` is returned by this function, the `switch-case` statement of `UpdateViewTarget` is ignored and the camera accepts the position and orientation provided by the pawn. (This is why it will be necessary later in the chapter to extend a new `Pawn` class that will return `false` for this function.)

- The `switch-case` statement is where the original function copied from the `Camera` class has been modified in `NexusCamera` (see the code in bold). Specifically, a new case has been added to the statement to accommodate a new camera type; namely case `CustomCamera`.

- Case `CustomCamera` performs a range of tasks for calculating the position and orientation of a third-person chase-view camera based on the current location and orientation of the view target pawn.

Calculating a Camera: "What's Our Vector, Victor?"

Calculating a third-person chase-view camera involves determining the correct relative position and orientation of the camera based on the world position and orientation of the pawn. The two entities—camera and pawn—are related because the camera must move and rotate in sync with the pawn. The code to calculate the third-person chase-view camera can be found in the `CustomCase` case statement in the previous code sample. This sidebar considers that code further.

The first statement that executed in `CustomCase` is as follows:

```
OutVT.Target.GetActorEyesViewPoint(OutVT.POV.Location, OutVT.POV.Rotation);
```

The function `GetActorEyesViewPoint` is called on the `Pawn` class. This function is inherited by the pawn from the `Actor` class (Actor.uc) and returns the position and orientation not of the actor itself (they can be retrieved through its `location` and `rotation` member variables) but of the eyes of the actor. The position of the pawn and the position of its eyes are different quantities. The position of the pawn typically refers to its center of mass, while the position of its eyes is an offset from that. In addition, the orientation of the pawn is different from the orientation of its eyes, because the body of a pawn can be facing in one direction while its head (and eyes) are turned to face a different direction.

The next statement is as follows:

```
GetAxes(OutVT.Target.Rotation, XAxis, YAxis, ZAxis);
```

The `GetAxes` function is inherited by all classes from the `Object` class (Object.uc). This function accepts four parameters. The first is an input—a `Rotation` object that describes the orientation of an actor or its eyes (as returned in the previous statement). The purpose of the function is to output three perpendicular unit vectors that together describe the local space axes for the actor associated with the rotation. X, Y, and Z will be vectors describing the orientation of axes. That is, they will be vectors that have been rotated from a common point according to the `Rotation` input. It is important to note that the returned vectors are unit vectors, and thus refer only to direction and not to distance. As such, their magnitude will always be 1. Those requiring a refresher on vector mathematics can find more information in the book *Essential Mathematics for Games and Interactive Applications: A Programmer's Guide* by James M. Van Verth (published by Morgan Kaufmann).

The next statement is as follows:

```
OutVT.POV.Location += XAxis * CamOffset.X + YAxis * CamOffset.Y + ZAxis * CamOffset.Z;
```

This statement sets the location of the camera based on the vector axes calculated in the previous statement as well as on the camera offset values initialized in the `PostBeginPlay` event discussed earlier in this chapter. In short, the three vectors representing the local space axes of actor are scaled (multiplied) by the offset values and are then summed (added together) to produce an output vector that specifies a new position for the camera.

The final statement is as follows:

```
OutVT.POV.Rotation.Pitch = FixedPitch;
```

This statement allows for camera yaw and roll rotation but prohibits pitch rotation to ensure that the camera pitch remains constant at `FixedPitch`.

Note

The complete `NexusCamera` class can be found in the companion files in the source file named NexusCamera.uc.

Creating the `NexusPawn` Class

The third-person chase-view camera has now been completely coded in the class `NexusCamera`. Now you need to create the three ancillary `Pawn`, `PlayerController`, and `GameInfo` classes so that the implementation of the `Camera` class is not overridden by their default behavior.

The first of the three classes to be created is the `Pawn` class, which will be named `NexusPawn` and will be overridden from `UTPawn`. The `NexusPawn` class could have been overridden from `Pawn` directly, but I chose `UTPawn` instead to save on workload because it already implements the default game character used in the UDK death-match levels. Specifically, it features an animated mesh character; the ability to hold and use weapons; the ability to run, walk, jump, and crouch; and other behaviors. (See UTPawn.uc for more information.) In short, you'll need to override and redefine a total of four different functions in the NexusPawn class to create a pawn that is compliant with the third-person camera class: BecomeViewTarget, GetDefault-CameraMode, GetBaseAimRotation, and CalcCamera. These will be implemented in sequence.

Becoming the View Target

The BecomeViewTarget function of the Pawn class is called whenever the pawn becomes the focus of a camera, which is often (although not always) when the pawn is first spawned into the level. This function is defined in the UTPawn class and allows the character mesh to be visible to the camera, as though the camera were outside the character's body. It is necessary to call this function because by default the mesh is hidden. This is because the default camera mode is first-person perspective; as such, the gamer would not be able to see his or her body from an outside perspective. The code for this function follows. Notice that the function calls its super class version, and then calls the SetThirdPersonCamera function, passing a value of true.

```
simulated event BecomeViewTarget(PlayerController PC)
{
    super.BecomeViewTarget(PC);
    SetThirdPersonCamera(true);
}
```

Getting the Default Camera Mode

The GetDefaultCameraMode function of the Pawn class returns the human-readable name of the mode into which the active camera will be set whenever the function is called. This function is typically called whenever the pawn is spawned or re-spawned in the level. Therefore, it will be called when the player dies and regenerates at a new location in the level. Thus, the spawning of a pawn is an opportunity for the pawn to affect the mode of the camera. The camera's mode refers to its status, which affects how the camera responds in a range of circumstances. The NexusCamera supports a range of modes, all of which are listed and handled appropriately in the switch-case statement of the function UpdateViewTarget. These modes include CustomCamera, Free, First-Person, Third-Person, and Fixed. The default mode for NexusCamera should be CustomCamera. Therefore, the GetDefaultCameraMode of the Pawn class can be implemented as follows.

```
simulated function name GetDefaultCameraMode( PlayerController RequestedBy )
{
    //Return custom camera as default camera style
    return 'CustomCamera';
}
```

Overriding the Base Aim Rotation

All classes derived from Pawn inherit the function GetBaseAimRotation, which returns a Rotator object describing the orientation of the aim of the pawn (assuming the pawn is the kind of thing that can aim at all). This Rotation object affects both the orientation of the eyes of the pawn and the state of the mesh associated with the pawn. The default implementation of this function in the UTPawn class is not compliant with the custom third-person camera in this project because it affects the rotation of the camera as well as the rotation of the pawn. For this reason, the GetBaseAimRotation function must be overridden in NexusPawn to simply return the current rotation of the pawn, as shown here:

```
simulated singular event Rotator GetBaseAimRotation()
{
    local rotator POVRot;
    POVRot = Rotation;
    return POVRot;
}
```

The *CalcCamera* Function

Pawn-based classes inherit the CalcCamera function, which is called on a per-tick basis from the Camera::UpdateViewTarget function. It gives pawns the opportunity to override the default position and orientation of the camera as specified in the camera class. Pawns that intend to take that opportunity must adjust the camera position and orientation in the CalcCamera function and must also return a value of true for that function. The NexusPawn class will not attempt to override the camera properties and will thus return a value of false for CalcCamera. This function is as follows:

```
simulated function bool CalcCamera( float fDeltaTime, out vector out_CamLoc, out rota-
tor out_CamRot, out float out_FOV )
{
    //Return false so pawn does not set camera position and rotation
    return false;
}
```

Note

The complete NexusPawn class can be found in the companion files in the source file named NexusPawn.uc.

Creating the `NexusPlayerController` Class

Both the `Camera` and `Pawn` classes have been created and are now consistent in the sense that the `Pawn` class will not override the functionality of the `Camera` class. It is still necessary, however, to create `PlayerController` and `GameInfo` classes that are consistent in the same sense with the `Camera` class. As mentioned, the `Player-Controller` class is a managerial component responsible for handling or delegating all player-specific logic in the game. In this section, a new `NexusPlayerController` class will be extended from the standard `PlayerController` class.

The `PlayerController` and its derivatives are relevant to the game camera in two senses:

- The `PlayerController` class is responsible for instantiating and maintaining a reference to the game camera.

- The `PlayerController` class features the `UpdateRotation` function, which affects how the pawn in the level is allowed to rotate based on user input. The rotation of the pawn is significant to the camera because the `Camera::UpdateViewTarget` function sets the rotation of the camera according to the rotation of the pawn.

Your work for the `NexusPlayerController` will consist of overriding the parent class in these two respects.

Setting the `Camera` Class

The `PlayerController` class features two member variables that relate directly to the game camera:

- **`PlayerCamera`.** `PlayerCamera` is a reference to an instance of a `Camera` class that is being used as the active camera for the gamer and that is associated with the `PlayerController` class and the `Pawn` class, if there is one.

- **`CameraClass`.** `CameraClass` is a reference not to a specific instance of a `Camera` class but to a `Camera` class itself—the class that `PlayerController` should use for instantiating its member variable `PlayerCamera`. That is, `PlayerCamera` will be an instance of `CameraClass`.

To configure `PlayerController` to instantiate an instance of `NexusCamera` as the active camera, you must set the `CameraClass` variable to the `NexusCamera` class. This can be achieved using the `DefaultProperties` code block. The complete class declaration so far of the NexusPlayerController along with its Default-Properties block follows:

```
class NexusPlayerController extends PlayerController;

DefaultProperties
{
    CameraClass=class'NexusCamera' //Default camera
}
```

The *UpdateRotation* Function

The PlayerController class inherits a function named UpdateRotation. This function is called once per tick to update the rotation of all actors in the level that PlayerController needs or wants to update. The default implementation of this function in the standard PlayerController class will update the rotation of the pawn based on user input. The problem that currently exists for the third-person camera—and the reason this function must be amended—is that the pawn can aim (and look) both up and down. That is, it can pitch. In contrast, the pitch of the camera remains constant. This mismatch in pitch between Pawn and Camera can make it difficult to control the aim of the pawn. This function must be changed to fix the pitch of the pawn to ensure that the pawn is always looking and aiming ahead in a straight line (at a pitch of 0). The original function from the PlayerController class can be copied and pasted into the NexusPlayerController class and amended to read as follows. (Changes are marked in bold.)

```
function UpdateRotation( float DeltaTime )
{
    local Rotator      DeltaRot, newRotation, ViewRotation;

    ViewRotation = Rotation;
    if (Pawn!=none)
    {
    Pawn.SetDesiredRotation(ViewRotation);
    }

    // Calculate Delta to be applied on ViewRotation
    DeltaRot.Yaw      = PlayerInput.aTurn;
    DeltaRot.Pitch    = 0;

    ProcessViewRotation( DeltaTime, ViewRotation, DeltaRot );
    SetRotation(ViewRotation);

    ViewShake( deltaTime );
```

```
    NewRotation = ViewRotation;
    NewRotation.Roll = Rotation.Roll;

    if ( Pawn != None )
        Pawn.FaceRotation(NewRotation, deltatime);
}
```

Note

The complete `NexusPlayerController` class can be found in the companion files in the source file named NexusPlayerController.uc.

Creating the `NexusGameInfo` Class

The `GameInfo` class requires relatively little amendment to work with `NexusCamera`. The job of the `GameInfo` class will be to instantiate both the default `Pawn` class and the default `PlayerController` class. These classes are instantiated based on the `DefaultPawnClass` and `PlayerControllerClass` member variables, which work in a similar way to the `CameraClass` variable of `PlayerController`. The following code is the complete definition of the `NexusGameInfo` class:

```
class NexusGameInfo extends UTGame;

DefaultProperties
{
    bDelayedStart=false //Start game immediately
    DefaultPawnClass=class'NexusPawn' //Default Pawn
    PlayerControllerClass=class'NexusPlayerController'
}
```

Note

The complete `NexusGameInfo` class can be found in the companion files in the source file named NexusGameInfo.uc.

CONCLUSION

Congratulations! The third-person chase-view camera should now be operational. That is, it should be possible to run a level using the `NexusGameInfo` class and to play that level through a third-person camera. `NexusGameInfo` ensures that all three classes you created—`NexusPlayerController`, `NexusPawn` and `NexusCamera`—are instantiated and used in the application. Figure 13.5 demonstrates the third-person camera in action.

Figure 13.5
Your work so far: the third-person chase-view camera in action.

It is important to remember that the third-person camera created here is but a piece of a larger project that ends in the next chapter: a third-person racing game in which the player must navigate a pawn successfully through an obstacle course under time-critical conditions. The "Project Overview" section of this chapter outlined the five main elements of this game to be implemented: a third-person camera, a pawn, a time limit, a checkpoint system, and a complete obstacle course. These latter three elements are the focus of the next chapter.

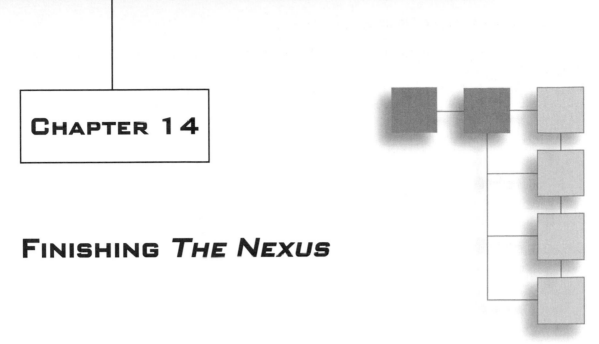

CHAPTER 14

FINISHING *THE NEXUS*

Design should never say, "Look at me." It should always say, "Look at this."

—Attributed to David Craib

By the end of this chapter, you should:

- Be able to create new Trigger Volume classes.
- Appreciate the general practice of extending classes.
- Be able to add timed and time-critical functionality in UnrealScript.
- Understand how to work with custom UnrealScript classes in the UDK Editor.
- Be able to use `exec` functions and Console Commands.

This chapter continues where the last chapter left off, meaning it requires you to have read and completed the previous chapter. That chapter set out the project that would be created, which is the same project that this chapter shall complete. That project is the creation of a game called *The Nexus*. It is a third-person racing game in which the player must navigate a pawn through an obstacle course under time-critical conditions.

The previous chapter detailed the five main constituent pieces of the project to be implemented either in UnrealScript or in the UDK Editor: a third-person chase-view camera, a pawn, a time limit, checkpoints, and an obstacle course. It then went on to detail the implementation of two of those pieces: a functional third-person chase-view camera and a pawn. The functionality for these two pieces is distributed in UnrealScript over four different actor-derived classes: `Camera`, `Pawn`, `PlayerController`, and

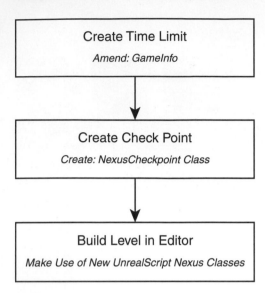

Figure 14.1
The three-step route to completing *The Nexus*.

GameInfo. This chapter focuses on creating the three remaining pieces for the game. The work involved for creating these pieces will require you to amend some existing classes, to create a new class, and to use the UDK Editor.

THE WORK AHEAD

As shown in Figure 14.1, the work ahead consists of amending the existing *Nexus* classes to create a time limit, creating a new class to support checkpoints, and bringing all the pieces together by building an obstacle-course level using the UDK Editor and the Nexus class framework.

AMENDING GameInfo: TIME LIMIT

As mentioned, the objective for the player in *The Nexus* is to safely guide a pawn from the start to the end of an obstacle course under time-critical conditions. *Time critical* in this context means the player is subject to a time limit (measured in seconds). That is, the finish line of the course must be reached before the limit expires. The time limit will begin at a maximum and will count down to a minimum, second by second. There are, however, three important conditions in the game that can cause the timer to stop counting down:

■ The timer will stop when the player reaches the course's finish line because the course will have been completed.

- The timer will restart whenever the level begins, either for the first time or for successive attempts.

- The timer will restart whenever the pawn crosses a checkpoint in the obstacle course for the first time.

Much of this time-limit functionality can be coded into the `GameInfo` class because the time limit applies at a game level and not a player level. That is, the time limit counts down independently of the player and his or her actions. For this reason, the `NexusGameInfo` class must be amended to accommodate the time limit. The full `NexusGameInfo` class is given here; subsequent sections discuss each function further.

```
class NexusGameInfo extends UTGame;

//Limit limit allowed between checkpoints
var int CheckPointTimeLimit;

//Boolean flag determining whether game is won
var bool GameWon;

//----------------------------------------------------------

event PostBeginPlay()
{
    super.PostBeginPlay();

    restartTimer();
}

//----------------------------------------------------------

function exec restartTimer()
{
    ClearTimer(nameOf(timerExpired));
    SetTimer(CheckPointTimeLimit, false, nameOf(timerExpired));
}

//----------------------------------------------------------

function exec timerExpired()
{
    //If game is already won, then return
    if(GameWon)
            return;
```

```
        //If timer expired and game is not won
        PlaySound(SoundCue'KismetGame_Assets.Sounds.Jazz_Death_Cue');
        RestartGame();
}

//---------------------------------------------------------

DefaultProperties
{
        bDelayedStart=false //Start game immediately
        DefaultPawnClass=class'NexusPawn' //Default Pawn
        PlayerControllerClass=class'NexusPlayerController' //Default Player Controller

        CheckPointTimeLimit = 10
        GameWon = false
}
```

Note

The complete `NexusGameInfo` class can be found in the companion files in the source file named NexusGameInfo.uc.

Exec Functions and the Timer

The `NexusGameInfo` class has been amended to include two additional variables that are related to the time limit and to the win condition of the obstacle course generally:

- **CheckPointTimeLimit.** This is an integer variable that specifies the total time in seconds of the time limit. It is also the time at which the time limit will begin.

- **GameWon.** This is a Boolean (true/false) that describes whether the level has been completed successfully. This variable begins as false and will be set to true whenever the player completes the obstacle course before the time limit expires.

The `NexusGameInfo` class also features some additional functions:

- **PostBeginPlay.** The `PostBeginPlay` event will be invoked on the `GameInfo` class as the level begins, and will initiate the time limit by calling the `RestartTimer` function.

- **RestartTimer.** This function calls the `ClearTimer` method to erase or destroy any active timers whose name matches the function argument.

- **SetTimer.** This method is called to initiate a new timer. That is, the `SetTimer` function will create a new timer of a specified duration in seconds

(`CheckPointTimeLimit`) and will call a specified function when the timer expires, that function being `TimerExpired`.

- **`TimerExpired`.** This function will exit immediately on being called if the game is in a win condition, because in that condition timers can have no purpose. Otherwise, it continues. The purpose of this function is to invoke the `fail` condition, in which case a sound is played using the `PlaySound` method and the level is restarted.

Both the `SetTimer` and `TimerExpired` functions are declared using the `exec` function specifier. A function declared as `exec` can be invoked (run) manually and on demand by typing its name into the Unreal Engine Console, a command-line text editor that can be accessed and used in game. The `exec` specifier can be a useful debugging feature for developers, enabling them to quickly call functions by name and to witness their effects in the level.

The timer functionality can now be tested by compiling and running the Unreal-Script code created so far in a sample level. Ensure that the level is associated with the `NexusGameInfo` class. You can test the `exec` console feature through the following steps:

1. Compile the UnrealScript source code and run a sample UDK level with the `NexusGameInfo` class. In Visual Studio, open the Debug menu and choose Start Debugging, as shown in Figure 14.2, or press F5.

2. During gameplay, press the Tab key on the keyboard to open the Unreal Console or the ~ key. The console typically appears at the bottom of the game window as a command line (see Figure 14.3). It will accept a series of text-based commands.

Tip

For a list and explanations of most Unreal Console Commands, visit this page: http://udn.epicgames.com/Three/ConsoleCommands.html.

3. With the Unreal Console open, type the name of any `exec` function to execute that function, as shown in Figure 14.4. When you're finished, press the Tab key again to close the console.

Tip

Before proceeding, use what you've learned about the *Nexus* class framework and about extending classes generally to create a checkpoint actor that a level designer can drag and drop into a level via the Editor to create checkpoint behavior. Keep in mind that checkpoints should reset the level time limit only the first time they are crossed or intersected by the player. Once completed, read on for answers.

Figure 14.2
Running a Visual Studio UnrealScript project.

Figure 14.3
Opening the Unreal Console in game.

Figure 14.4
Running an `exec` function by typing its name into the Unreal Console.

CREATING CHECKPOINTS: EXTENDING TriggerVolume

In *The Nexus*, any level must be able to contain as many checkpoint actors as the level designer requires and the Unreal Engine allows. Further, a level designer must be able to size and position every checkpoint as appropriate for the level, just as designers can size and position any other actor.

The checkpoint is a non-tangible mark, line, or region in the level that, when intersected by the pawn, will perform one of three behaviors (depending on the circumstances):

- If the player has visited the checkpoint previously, then the checkpoint will do nothing, because checkpoints can be touched or crossed only once.

- If the player visits the checkpoint for the first time and the checkpoint is *not* the final checkpoint of the obstacle course (that is, it is not the finish line), then the time limit of the course will be reset back to its maximum.

- If the player visits the checkpoint for the first time and the checkpoint *is* the last in the course (that is, it is the finish line), then the timer is stopped and the win condition is satisfied.

It is time to implement the checkpoint actor as a class in UnrealScript. This actor will be derived from the `TriggerVolume` class, meaning that the checkpoint will be a volume that can be created and added to the level by the designer using the UDK

Editor, the Red Builder Brush, and the Volumes button in the toolbox. The complete class for the `NexusCheckPoint` is given here. Notice that the function overrides the Touch event, which is called for the actor whenever it intersects another actor in the level, whether a pawn or not.

```
class NexusCheckPoint extends TriggerVolume;

//Boolean - has been checked before?
var(Main) bool Checked;
var(Main) bool IsFinal;

event Touch( Actor Other, PrimitiveComponent OtherComp, vector HitLocation, vector
HitNormal )
{
    //If null pawn or not player, then exit
    if(Pawn(Other)==none || !Pawn(Other).Controller.bIsPlayer)
            return;

    //If has been checked previously, then ignore
    if(Checked)
            return;

    //Set checked to true
    Checked = true;

    if(IsFinal)
    {
        //Set game to won
        NexusGameInfo(WorldInfo.Game).GameWon = true;
        WorldInfo.Game.PlaySound(
        SoundCue'KismetGame_Assets.Music.Jazz_Menu_01_Cue');
        return;
    }

    //else
    NexusGameInfo(WorldInfo.Game).restartTimer();
    WorldInfo.Game.PlaySound(
      SoundCue'KismetGame_Assets.Sounds.Jazz_Chatter_Happy_Cue');
}

DefaultProperties
{
    Checked = false
    IsFinal = false
}
```

Note

The complete `NexusCheckPoint` class can be found in the companion files in the source file named
NexusCheckPoint.uc.

BUILDING THE OBSTACLE COURSE

The class framework for *The Nexus* consists of five main classes: `NexusGameInfo`,
`NexusPlayerController`, `NexusPawn`, `NexusCamera`, and `NexusCheckPoint`.
These classes have now been coded completely and should be compiled using either
the UnrealScript Compiler from the command line or the nFringe add-on for Visual
Studio. Once compiled, the classes will become accessible and usable for the level
designer via the UDK Editor and its tools. This section focuses on using the editor
to assemble static meshes, sounds, assets, and classes into a complete, working
obstacle-course level that can be played. The following steps demonstrate the key
stages of developing the level.

1. Open the UDK Editor, open the File menu and choose New, and select the
   Blank Map template map from the dialog box that appears to create a new,
   empty level, as shown in Figure 14.5.

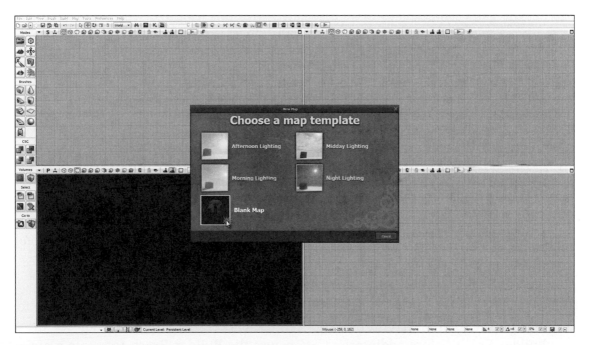

Figure 14.5
Creating a new, empty project in preparation for building the obstacle course.

Figure 14.6
Setting the PIE Game Type parameter to NexusGameInfo enables you to preview and play *The Nexus* from the UDK Editor.

2. Set the game type that is to be associated with this level when run from the editor using either the Play In Editor or Play In Viewport options. To do this, open the View menu and choose World Options to open the WorldInfo Properties dialog box. In the Game Type section, click the Game Type for PIE drop-down list and choose NexusGameInfo, as shown in Figure 14.6. This will enable you to test *The Nexus* in the editor, complete with the time limit and a third-person camera.

3. Create the overall layout for the obstacle course—the walls, floors, and ceilings—using the Red Builder Brush tool in the toolbox. (For more information on the Builder Brush, refer to Chapter 4, "BSP Brushes, the Builder Brush, and CSG.") There is no right or wrong here. I have chosen to create an L-shaped corridor-like environment using the Extrude tools, as shown in Figure 14.7, but feel free to experiment with your own designs if you prefer. Once created, print this Builder Brush into the level as CSG.

4. Hollow out the newly added CSG to ensure that the player will be able to explore the interior. To do this, you can use choose the Hollow option for the Builder Brush before adding the CSG or use the Builder Brush to create a second, smaller, subtractive brush inside the original CSG. (See Figure 14.8.)

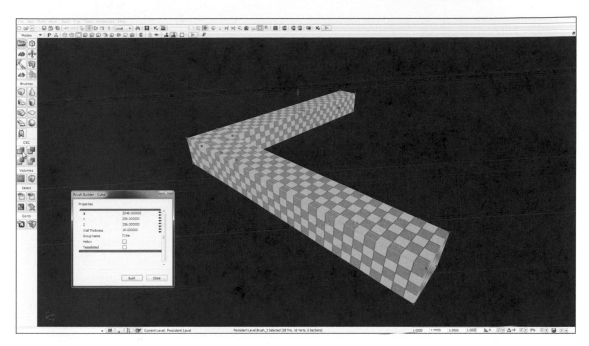

Figure 14.7
Creating the walls, floors, and ceiling of the obstacle course using the Red Builder Brush.

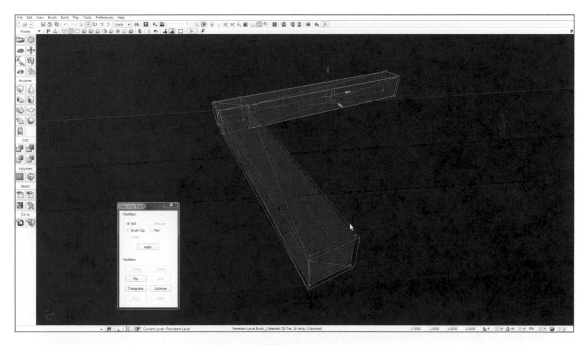

Figure 14.8
Creating a hollowed interior by subtracting a smaller brush from a larger one.

Figure 14.9
Applying architectural materials to the CSG in the level.

5. Use the material, texturing, and mapping techniques discussed in Chapter 5, "Materials, Textures, and UV Mapping," to apply floor, wall, and ceiling materials to all the faces of the CSG surfaces in the level, as shown in Figure 14.9. I used the following materials: M_SupportWall_03 (walls), M_Rockwall_05_Base (ceilings), and M_LT_Floors_BSP_Organic05b (floors).

6. It is now time to add a series of checkpoints equidistantly throughout the level, with one check at the level finish to mark the finish line of the course. The checkpoint actor was derived TriggerVolume, and volumes generally are created using the Red Builder Brush and are added to the level based on the brush as a volume. Use the Red Builder Brush to size a box for a checkpoint and right-click the Volumes button in the toolbar. Notice that the class NexusCheckPoint appears as an option from the Volumes list; select this option to insert the checkpoint into the level. Repeat this process for every checkpoint. (See Figure 14.10.)

7. Select the final checkpoint in the level (the finish line) and press F4 to display its Properties panel. Then ensure that the Is Final checkbox in the Main section is enabled (see Figure 14.11). The checkpoint will now enable the win condition for the level when intersected by the player.

8. Currently, the checkpoints in the level are invisible, non-tangible volumes whose functionality will be activated when the player intersects them. To help the player

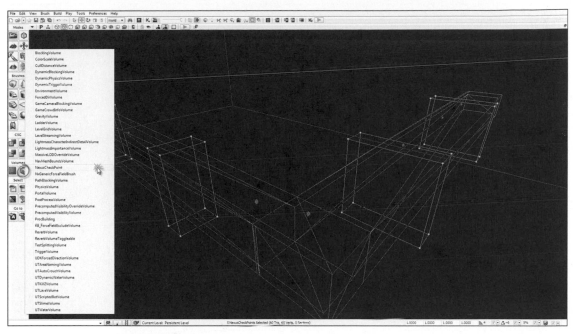

Figure 14.10
Inserting checkpoints throughout the level as volumes created from the Red Builder Brush. Remember, the distance between checkpoints affects the time required for traveling and thus influences the difficulty of the level.

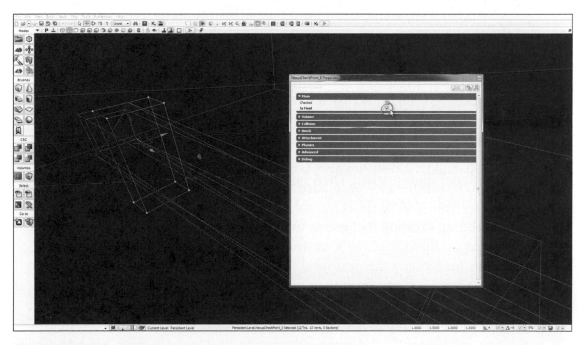

Figure 14.11
Setting the final checkpoint of the level.

Figure 14.12
Marking the checkpoints in the level using static meshes.

identify them, add some static meshes at the location of each checkpoint. Open the Content Browser and drag and drop a suitable mesh for each checkpoint. (I used the S_NEC_Wires_SM_Pipecap01 mesh, as shown in Figure 14.12.

9. The level is complete in terms of layout, materials, and meshes. Now it is suitable to add lighting. For this level, I inserted wall light meshes (S_HU_Mech_SM_Light) across the length of the walls and enabled the Emissive channel of their materials to cast static illumination throughout the level. (Refer to Chapter 8, "Lighting," for more information.) When the lights are added, be sure to surround the level with a LightmassImportance volume to allow for global illumination. Then build production-quality lighting with the Lightmass system. Figure 14.13 shows the results.

10. The final step in creating the level is to add some Kismet work to the final checkpoint to ensure that the player's controls are frozen as the level is complete in preparation for loading the next level. To do this, select the final checkpoint in the Perspective viewport. Then open the Kismet editor. Add a new Touched event for the selected checkpoint node and connect this to a Toggle Cinematic Mode node to disable user input as that event occurs. Figure 14.14 shows the final Kismet graph for the level. (For more information on Unreal Kismet, refer to Chapter 9, "Kismet and Matinee: Beginning with Visual Scripting and Animation."

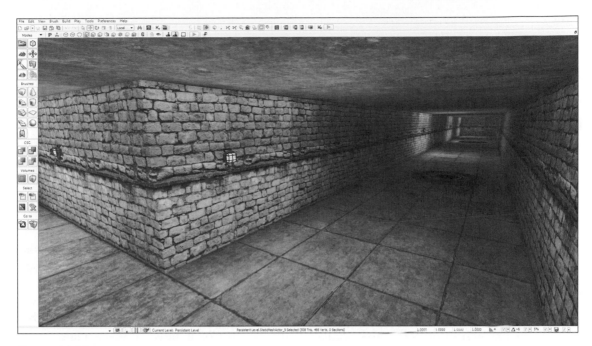

Figure 14.13
Building lighting for the level.

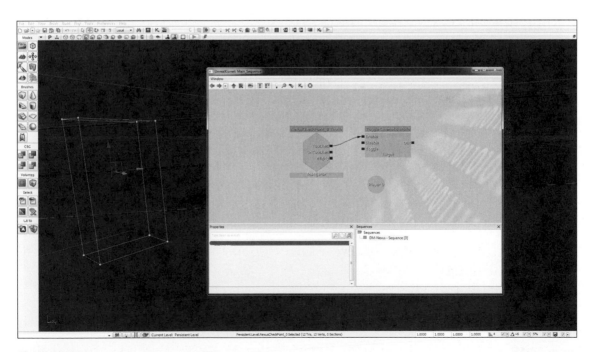

Figure 14.14
Configuring a Kismet graph for the final checkpoint in the level.

Note

The completed *Nexus* game level can be found in the companion files in the file DM-Nexus.udk. Please ensure the Nexus UnrealScript class framework is compiled before opening and running the level.

Conclusion

This chapter and the previous one focused on the development of *The Nexus*, which should now be playable in the UDK Editor (see Figure 14.15). Although the game is basic in the sense that it contains one small, simple level, it nonetheless demonstrates a range of powerful and versatile UDK features. The implementation of the project required you to use most of the UDK development skills and tools covered in previous chapters (such as lighting, materials, meshes, Kismet, modular building, and so on), and introduced new concepts, tools, and techniques (such as the Unreal Console and the Pawn, PlayerController, and Camera classes).

For practice, why not aim to extend *The Nexus* not only by adding more levels, but by adding extra functionality that requires the coding of a new class—a class from which you have not extended before?

Figure 14.15
Finally! The completed *Nexus* game is up and running.

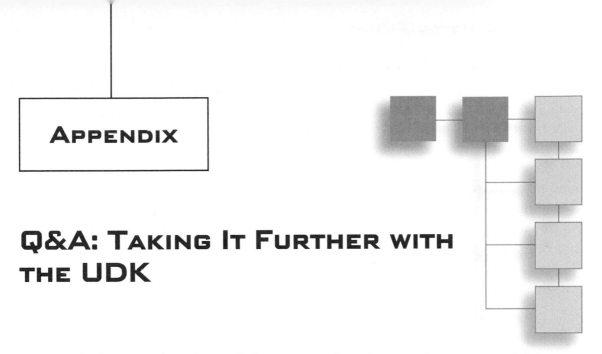

APPENDIX

Q&A: Taking It Further with the UDK

I don't pretend we have all the answers. But the questions are certainly worth thinking about.

—Arthur C. Clarke

This chapter concludes the book by focusing not on a specific topic or feature of the UDK such as lighting or materials, but by trying to briefly consider a range of unrelated UDK topics. These topics are chosen not at random, but are based on questions that I anticipate many readers at this stage will have about the UDK, its tools, and the application of those tools in making games. Assuming you share at least some of them, these questions might trace their origins to different sources. Perhaps some of these questions entered your mind while reading chapters in this book; perhaps others came to you as a result of your own research on the UDK. The purpose of this chapter is to state those questions explicitly and then to provide a brief but instructive answer to them.

The answers provided here are not necessarily the only possible answers that could be given. There are often many routes to the same destination—although some routes may be shorter and smoother than others. In addition, the answers given are not intended to be exhaustive or comprehensive—to detail everything there is to know about the subject. After all, many of the questions and their answers could warrant a complete book of their own. The intention here is more modest: to provide answers that are sufficient to give you a brief overview and a starting point on a road to learning more.

WHAT IS A FRACTURED MESH?

The term *fractured mesh* is a contraction of the more complete term *fractured static mesh*. Fractured meshes are typically used in video games to create destructible scenery such as walls that can be blown apart by explosives (see Figure A.1), wooden boards that can be split in half by punches, and so on. In short, any mesh actor in a level that can be dismantled or pulled apart during gameplay is likely to be a form of fractured mesh. Fractured meshes are so named because a level designer creates them in the Mesh Editor by subdividing a complete mesh into smaller fragments along a set of mathematically defined contours known as *fractures*. Fractured meshes achieve their exploding effect by initially appearing complete and intact as the level begins, but then shattering apart along their predefined fractures whenever affected by an external force.

So how are fractured meshes created? A fractured mesh can be created directly in the UDK Editor from any static mesh that has a collision model. To create a fractured mesh, open the static mesh in the Mesh Editor (for help, refer to Chapter 6, "Building Game Worlds with Static Mesh Actors"), and use the Fracture tool, accessible both from the Tool menu and from the Static Mesh Editor toolbar, as shown in Figure A.2.

Figure A.1
Fractured meshes in action: a hole blown through a wall.

Figure A.2
Accessing the Fracture tool from the Static Mesh Editor.

The Fracture tool can be used to slice a mesh into chunks along a set of auto-generated fractures, and the result of the slicing can be saved as a separate mesh. Use the Num Chunks slider to set the total number of pieces into which the mesh should be subdivided, and then click the Generate button to generate a set of fractures consistent with that number. The result will show in the viewport. Confirm the slicing and save the mesh as a duplicate by clicking the Slice button at the bottom of the Fracture tool. Figure A.3 shows the Fracture tool at work.

WHAT IS SPEEDTREE AND HOW DO I USE IT?

SpeedTree is a third-party application that ships in a lightweight form with the UDK but is separate from the UDK Editor. (The term *lightweight* is used here to indicate that the version of SpeedTree that ships with the UDK is feature limited compared to the complete version, which can be purchased from the SpeedTree Web site.) Speed-Tree is an application for parametrically generating real-time, low-poly foliage models such as trees, bushes, branches, shrubs, plants, and other similar organic models that are often time-consuming to create manually using many modeling applications. (See Figure A.4.) To parametrically generate trees and foliage models is to auto-generate unique models based on a set of numerical and randomized values that the user can type in, such as Number of Branches, Height of Tree, Width of Trunk, and so on.

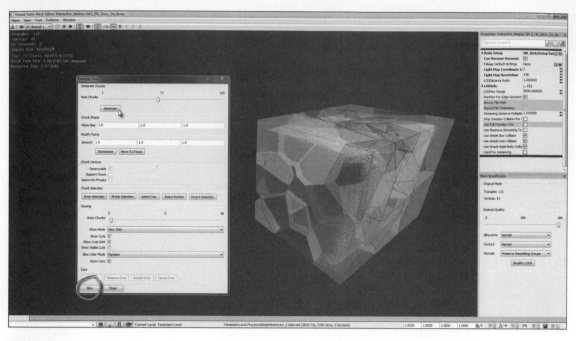

Figure A.3
The Fracture tool being used to slice a static mesh.

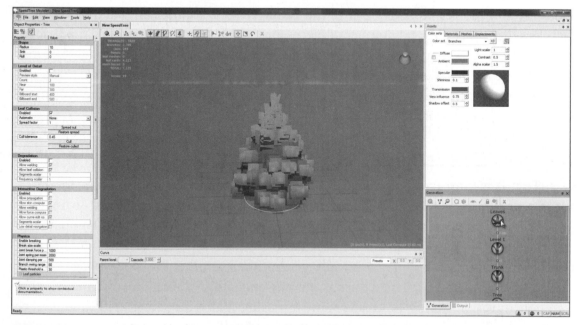

Figure A.4
Creating a tree using SpeedTree.

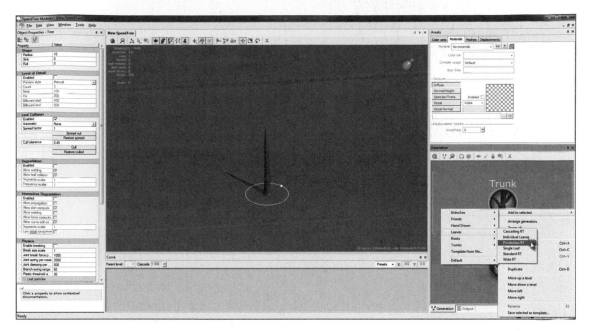

Figure A.5
Creating a simple tree in SpeedTree.

SpeedTree has two components: the SpeedTree Modeler (for generating trees) and the SpeedTree Compiler (for converting trees into a format that can be imported into the UDK). Neither of these two applications is accessible from the UDK Editor interface. Rather, to access them, you must click their respective application icons in the Windows Start menu. (They are found in the Unreal Development Kit > Tools application group.)

To create a tree in Speed Tree, open the SpeedTree Modeler application, open the File menu, and choose New. Then right-click the Tree node in the Generation tab in the bottom-right area of the modeler window to add a new part to the tree—for example, the trunk. The trunk is added as a new node to the graph and can be seen on the tree in the viewport. Additional tree elements can then be added to the trunk via the graph. For example, you can right-click the Trunk node in the graph and add branches. Then, leaves can be added to branches, and so on. (See Figure A.5.)

Note

The Unreal Developer Network features documentation on importing tree models from SpeedTree at the following URL: http://udn.epicgames.com/Three/SpeedTree.html.

Figure A.6
A Bink movie playing as a movie texture on a cube.

What Is Bink?

Bink is a third-party video format and playback technology developed by RAD Game Tools that is integrated into the UDK and the Unreal Engine. In short, using Bink technology and tools, developers can convert standard video files (AVI, MPG, WMV, and so on) into the Bink format (BIK) and play back those videos in the Unreal Engine as animated movie textures that can be applied to the surfaces of geometry via materials. (See Figure A.6.)

Movie files in the BIK format can be imported into the UDK Editor much like other textures: via the Import dialog box, accessible from the Content Browser. (See Chapter 5, "Materials, Textures, and UV Mapping, for more information.) Once imported, Bink movie assets can be dragged and dropped into materials as texture samples and then connected to material channels, such as the Diffuse channel. That material can then be applied to surfaces as usual. (See Figure A.7.)

What Is FaceFX?

FaceFX is a third-party toolset developed by OC3 Entertainment that is distributed with and integrated into the UDK Editor. It is designed primarily to help developers create facial animations for skeletal mesh characters, especially lip-synching animations.

Figure A.7
Configuring a Bink movie.

FaceFX is not limited only to lip-synching character meshes with spoken dialogue, however; it can also be used to create animated facial expressions—angry faces, sad faces, thoughtful faces, etc. In short, FaceFX is used to define a complete set of facial expressions and animations for a specified character at design time so that those expressions can be applied to one or more characters on demand at run-time, as and when required. Figure A.8 illustrates the FaceFX interface being used to edit a skeletal mesh.

The FaceFX toolset is integrated into the UDK in the sense that it can be accessed and used via the Content Browser, and in the sense that facial animations can be played in-game with the Unreal Engine. To create, edit, and apply a set of facial animations for a specified skeletal mesh, right-click that skeletal mesh asset in the Content Browser Asset pane and choose Create FaceFX Asset from the menu that appears. The FaceFX Editor will open, from which a FaceFX animation set can be defined, as shown in Figure A.9.

Note

A guide to the basics of FaceFX can be found at the Unreal Developer Network at the following URL: http://udn.epicgames.com/Three/FaceFX.html.

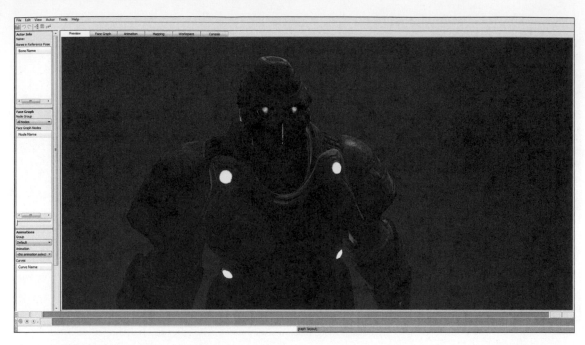

Figure A.8
Defining facial animations for a skeletal mesh using FaceFX.

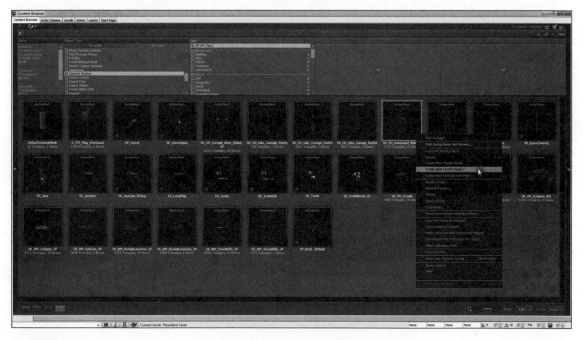

Figure A.9
Creating a FaceFX Asset for a selected skeletal mesh via the Content Browser.

How Can I Work with Persistent Data in UnrealScript?

This question is an abstract form of more practical and context-sensitive questions, such as the following:

- How can I allow gamers to save their games onto a hard drive?
- How can I save the status of a level so that the level will appear as the gamer last left it when the gamer returns to that level?

These questions present the problem of data persistence with the UDK. The UnrealScript classes considered so far, including the GameInfo, Pawn, and PlayerController classes, are all volatile in the technical sense of the word in that they exist in system memory while a level is active in the UDK, but are destroyed when that level ends. The lifetime of an UnrealScript class is no longer or wider than that of the level, meaning that no instance of a class can persist across or between levels. Thus, the question arises as to how it is possible in UnrealScript to save or keep important game data.

There are at least two solutions to the problem of data persistence. Both involve writing data to a file on persistent storage (such as a hard drive). One is to use config classes to save selected properties of a class to an INI file; the second is to use a set of class serialization functions to write and read a complete instance of a class to and from a file respectively. These methods are considered briefly next.

Method 1: config Classes

UnrealScript classes can be declared with the config specifier, which enables them to read and write select member variables to and from a specified INI file in the UDK-Game\Config folder. The following code demonstrates a class that can read a string member variable (FullName) from an INI file named UDKMyConfig.ini. Note that by default the acronym UDK is prefixed to the name of any INI file.

```
class MyActor extends actor
    config(MyConfig); //Declare as config class

var config string FullName; //Declare variable that can be read and saved to file

//Called when object is created
function postbeginplay()
{
FullName="Alan Thorn"; //Assign default value
SaveConfig(); //Save value to ini file.
//Values will automatically be read from file on object creation
}
```

Note

More information on `config` class can be found at the official Unreal Developer Network site, at the following URLs:

- http://udn.epicgames.com/Three/ConfigurationFiles.html
- http://udn.epicgames.com/Three/ConfigSavegameSystem.html
- http://udn.epicgames.com/Two/SaveConfiguration.html

It should be noted that config variables cannot be saved on the iOS platform.

Method 2: Class Serialization Functions

Every class in the UnrealScript hierarchy of classes has access to a set of class serialization functions that are part of the `Engine` class (Engine.uc). These functions allow all compatible member variables of a class to be serialized (written) to a file and read from a file on demand. Specifically, the `Engine::BasicSaveObject` function can be called to write a class to a file, and the `Engine::BasicLoadObject` function can be called to load a class from a file. Consider the following UnrealScript code. See the following URL for more information: http://goo.gl/pnr7m.

```
//Save an object
class'Engine'.static.BasicSaveObject(MyObject,"MySav.bin", true, 1);

//load an object
class'Engine'.static.BasicLoadObject(MyObject, "MySav.bin", true, 1);
```

Note

The `BasicSaveObject` function does not work on the iOS platform.

HOW CAN I VIEW DEBUGGING STATS AT RUN TIME FROM THE CONSOLE?

Debugging stats refers to critical run-time information about a game that is useful to a developer when attempting to diagnose the cause or causes of errors or problems, or attempting to better understand or trace the execution of an application. A selection of informative debug statistics can be shown via the Unreal Console. A complete list can be found at the following URL: http://goo.gl/bVvqq. A selection of them are shown here, with examples.

- **Displaying memory information.** To toggle information about system memory availability, usage, wastage, and allocation (see Figure A.10), use the `STAT MEMORY` command.

Figure A.10
Viewing memory information.

- **Displaying game information.** To toggle information about the game in terms of ticks, performance information, and speed of execution (see Figure A.11), use the `STAT GAME` command.

- **Monitoring variable values.** To monitor the value of a specified variable as it changes over time (see Figure A.12), use the `displayall` command. This command takes the form `displayall <class name> <member variable>`.

How Can I Customize Kismet Using UnrealScript?

Customizing Kismet with UnrealScript involves creating custom nodes that can be inserted into the Kismet graph and connected with other nodes. Each node that can be inserted into the Kismet Graph corresponds to an UnrealScript class. Actions are typically derived from the `SequenceAction` class and events from the `SequenceEvent` class. The following code creates a sample Kismet action (as shown in Figure A.13) that will run the `STAT MEMORY` Console Command when fired. The `STAT MEMORY` command will show a range of memory statistics that are relevant to the run-time performance of the game.

Figure A.11
Viewing game information.

Figure A.12
Monitoring the pawn location with `displayall pawn location`.

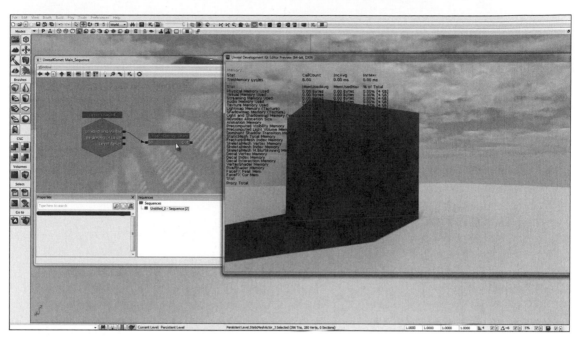

Figure A.13
Examining debug information through the console.

```
class CustomMemoryStat extends SequenceAction;

//Called when node is fired
event Activated()
{
    GetWorldInfo().Game.ConsoleCommand("STAT MEMORY");
}

DefaultProperties
{
    ObjName="Show Memory Stats"
    ObjCategory="My Kismet Actions"
    bCallHandler=false
    VariableLinks.Empty
    InputLinks(0)=(LinkDesc="In")
    OutputLinks(0)=(LinkDesc="Out")
}
```

WHERE DO I GO FROM HERE?

There are many routes that your learning could take at this point with the UDK. The optimal route will likely vary depending on your particular circumstances. There are, however, several Web pages and articles that are likely to prove instructive and useful for a wide range of developers. I recommend that you take at least a brief look through them, if only to determine whether they are relevant for you.

- UnrealScript Reference (http://udn.epicgames.com/Three/UnrealScriptReference.html)
- Unreal FrontEnd (http://udn.epicgames.com/Three/UnrealFrontend.html)
- Gameplay Programming (http://udn.epicgames.com/Three/GameplayProgrammingHome.html)
- Calling DLLs from UnrealScript (http://udn.epicgames.com/Three/DLLBind.html)
- Localized Content (http://udn.epicgames.com/Three/LocalizedTextFiles.html)
- Controlling Input (http://udn.epicgames.com/Three/KeyBinds.html)

INDEX